The art of

Joseph

Conrad

The art of

Joseph
Conrad

a critical symposium

by R. W. STALLMAN

EDITION

Ohio University Press
Athens, Ohio

*For my English 380 graduate students at
the University of Connecticut (1949-1959),
with whom I have enjoyed sharing explorations
of Conrad's works.*

## ACKNOWLEDGEMENTS

To my wife Virginia and to the English Department Secretaries, Mrs. Ebba Hammerberg and Mrs. Edith Lapins, for typing the manuscripts of this volume. To Miss Roberta Smith, Reference Librarian at the University of Connecticut Library, for her constant research-aid. To Mr. John Conrad and Mr. Richard Curle and Dr. Wit Tarnawski for correspondence on various matters, and to Professor Albert J. Guerard, Jr. for his aid in making some decisions about certain selections.

To J. M. Dent & Sons, Ltd. for kind permission to reprint from the Dent Uniform Edition of Conrad's works the biographical and bibliographical notes used in Appendix I of this volume.

To the Thomas Mann Estate and Secker & Warburg, Ltd. and Alfred A. Knopf, Inc. for permission to reprint from *Past Masters and Other Papers,* by Thomas Mann (by permission of Alfred A. Knopf, Inc.). Published 1933 by Alfred A. Knopf, Inc.

To the André Gide Estate and *Mercure de France* (Paris) for the Gide essay first published in *Nouvelle Revue Française* (1924).

To Czeslaw Milosz and *The Atlantic Monthly* for his essay which was first published in the Anniversary Number of *The Atlantic Monthly* (1957).

Also to the Editors of the journals drawn upon for this collection of Conrad criticism, notably Professors Maurice Beebe and William Stafford of *Modern Fiction Studies.*

R. W. S.

November, 1959

# TABLE OF CONTENTS

# PREFACE

In 1980, Joseph Conrad's position as one of the major novelists of the twentieth century is unquestioned. His works are read and taught at all levels and half a dozen different paperback editions of his major short stories and novels are readily available in any urban bookstore. A growing shelf of critical studies—over fifty volumes—, a recent monumental biography, the commitment of Cambridge University Press to a complete scholarly edition of the works and letters, and active Conrad societies in seven countries testify to his appeal. Indeed, Conrad has become ubiquitous in discussions of modern tragedy, of political involvement, of colonial imperialism, of the development of Third World fiction, and of European modernism. *Time* has claimed that "his ominous Slavic intensity and his understated English produced a prose style that generations have found intoxicating. Countless youths acquired their first sense of literary power" from reading works such as "Heart of Darkness." Most recently, the success of *Apocalypse Now*, a free adaptation of Conrad's "Heart of Darkness," shows how clearly Conrad's works have established for us many of the metaphors by which we perceive the human condition in this century.

Such, however, was not always true. In 1936, Elizabeth Bowen, reviewing Edward Crankshaw's *Joseph Conrad: Some Aspects of the Art of the Novel*, noted "Conrad is in abeyance. We are not clear yet how to rank him; there is an uncertain pause." In 1960 when R. W. Stallman's *The Art of Joseph Conrad: A Critical Symposium* first appeared, Conrad's reputation was by no means so secure. Jocelyn Baines' standard biography had not yet been published; the major studies of Albert J. Guerard and Thomas Moser had only recently appeared on the scene; psychological critics were just turning their attention to Conrad; and the "new critics" were finding in Conrad's works even more than the insights of F. R. Leavis had led them to expect. The "uncertain pause" ended not with a brilliant television adaptation attracting a new reading audience as with John Galsworthy and Anthony Trollope, a creative translation as with Leo Tolstoy and Feodor Dostoevski, or loose association with a movement as with Virginia Woolf but rather through the dedication of a number of talented critics and scholars.

A book thus made for the moment, Stallman's collection reflects the state of Conrad studies in the centennial year of Conrad's birth and anticipates, even encourages, a burst of new interest in Conrad's life and works. Stallman intended his collection "to bring Conrad his due recognition" and "to render recognition of the greatness of Conrad as artist, a recognition which is long overdue." To accomplish this, Stallman gathered a number of personal memoirs and provided a sound critical discussion of each major story and novel—an ambitious collective undertaking which required not only the ability to assess at close range what would remain of value in Conrad studies but also the ability to balance and harmonize the various voices. That a reprinting of the collection is deemed appropriate twenty years later suggests Stallman's success on both counts at the very moment when biographical, psychological, and political aproaches were defining their roles in Conrad criticism. The well marked and well thumbed pages of the first edition copies in most libraries demonstrate that the collection has never lacked readers.

A major theme unifies the diverse approaches and voices in the collection. Stallman and the other authors value ambiguity, complexity, irony, multiplicity, and other such features revealed by due care for the close attention to the text. To Stallman, "nothing of Conrad's works at their best is simple"; to Albert J. Guerard "a rich personal novel can hardly be overinterpreted"; to William Moynihan, close reading of "The End of the Tether" "reveals a slight, but clear, thematic relationship . . . and provides a fine example of the use of mythical elements"; to John Howard Wills, "Il Conde" achieves "almost perfect form and complex symbolism"; to Douglas Hewitt, *Chance* marks a decline, "a retreat from the degrees of awareness of the complexities of human emotion found in the early [novels]."

Sophisticated psychological readings, major discoveries in source materials, important insights available from recent biographies, mounting evidence from textual study, and investigations into the cultural and intellectual background of Conrad's works have dated some of the selections, especially the essays on the short stories and "Heart of Darkness," but in general Stallman's collection remains an important reminder of what insightful, thoughtful critics can provide as a starting point for the student, a dialogue for the scholar, and an encore for a particular style of critical thought. In the history of Conrad criticism, *The Art of Joseph Conrad: A Critical Symposium* remains a landmark reminder of what current scholars and critics owe to a few talented, dedicated voices who were committed to seeing Joseph Conrad receive due recognition.

# INTRODUCTION

## R. W. STALLMAN
### The Reputation of Joseph Conrad: 1924-1959*

### (1)

"TODAY IS THE 100TH ANNIVERSARY OF THE BIRTH OF 'THE GREATEST ARTIST WHO EVER WROTE A NOVEL' "—that was November 21, 1957, with H. L. Mencken quoted in the Doubleday advertisement in the New York *Times*. Conrad "transcended all the rules. There have been, perhaps, greater novelists, but I believe that he was incomparable, the greatest artist who ever wrote a novel." But is it not Henry James, Conrad's acknowledged master, who is the greatest artist who ever wrote a novel? Notably in *The Portrait of a Lady* (1881) and again in *The Ambassadors* (1903). James's perfections both in the novel and in the short story far outnumber Conrad's. On James's perfections critical consensus stands mainly in agreement, whereas critical dispute still rages as to which Conrad works constitute his supreme achievements.

No one will dispute that Conrad is the more fascinating personality, at his most interesting because of contradictions in the man and in his works. It's difficult to pin him down. It is, it's not—all's doubleness. Even so for his birthdate: it is *"le 21 novembre/3 decembre,"* as given in G. Jean-Aubry's *Vie de Conrad* (American title: *The Sea Dreamer*). "The first date is according to the Julian (or old style) calendar used by Eastern Orthodox Christianity, then the official religion of Russia; the second refers to the Gregorian (or new style) calendar in use in the Western world, the difference between the two being twelve days in the nineteenth century." (New York *Times:* January 12, 1958: *Letters to the Editor*)

When Conrad died in 1924, the cabled story to the New York *Times* from London "firmly said December 6. Just as firmly, the *Encyclopaedia Britannica,* 1948 and 1954 editions, says the same. On the other hand, *Twentieth Century Authors,* the *New Century Cyclopedia of Names,* the *Dictionary of National Biography,* all cling to Dec. 3. Just to confuse the whole matter, the eleventh edition of *Britannica* puts the year at 1856 rather than 1857 and Gerard Jean-Aubry's *The Sea Dreamer* says Nov. 21, 1857. Just so this matter will never, never come up again, Conrad's son, in London [Borys Conrad], was asked for a decision. The date, for once

* Portions of Parts 2 and 3 of this Introduction are reprinted from the *Kenyon Review* (Spring 1957), "Fiction and Its Critics," and the *Sewanee Review* (Winter 1958-1959): "Conrad Criticism Today."

and all—Dec. 6, 1857." (New York *Times:* December 1, 1957: *In and Out of Books*, p. 8)

Just so this matter will never, never come up again, I inquired of John Conrad, who replied that he did not understand why I should entertain the notion that his father was born on December 6th 1857. "His gravestone bears the date December 3rd; the Centenary Celebrations in Poland were held on December 3rd, and I think this latter fact confirms that December 3rd is the right date." The date, for once and all—Dec. 3rd 1857.

The confusion arose from the mistake of the English translator of the French biography, *Vie de Conrad,* in omitting the second part of Conrad's "double" birthdate (in *The Sea Dreamer,* 1957). In the New York *Times'* correspondences about this much disputed birthdate G. Jean-Aubry's facts in his *Joseph Conrad: Life and Letters* went unnoticed: "Although other dates have been given—even during Conrad's lifetime—as the date of his birth, December 3, 1857, can be taken as certain."[1]

"I never knew to what extent Joseph Conrad was fascinating," but when I first set eyes on him in 1911 (to quote Arthur Symons), "I was fairly startled: there stood before me a Dwarf of Genius; and what further startled me was that he was about the same height as Toulouse Lautrec, whom I had known in Paris—he was a much more formidable Dwarf of Genius, who died tragically young. Conrad expired suddenly, at the age of sixty-seven, in full possession of his powers, and, as he fell dead on the floor from the chair he was seated on, I am told he uttered a great cry. So, I was assured, did Rossetti, who rose up in his bed and cried violently, as if he had seen before him the Vision of Hell." (Symons hints at the Kurtz in Conrad, that side of him which evinces in his fictional works the abnormal.) Ronsard is represented by Pater in *Gaston de Latour* as "A gaunt figure, hook-nosed, like a wizard, who turned you a face all nerves, distressed nerves, and not unkindly." That gives you, says Symons, a certain idea of Conrad's aspect:

> He was exotically cruel; there was a tropical heat in his blood; he vibrated to every sensation, as Verlaine vibrated, as Pachmann vibrates; and, as in the case of Pachmann, there was his indisputable foreign accent, which began by surprising one, but which was really part of his fascination—for he had a fascinating fashion of talking, always, whether in English or in French, with great rapidity and with a wonderful power of evocation which, when it thrilled him most, thrilled me. He had at times the same convulsive chuckle as Verlaine's; his laughter when he was most excited reminded me of Whistler's sharp crackle of laughter, which was as if a rattlesnake had suddenly leapt out; which was in fact a crackling of thorns under the pot, but of flaming thorns, setting the pot in a fury of boiling.
>
> Marlow, being in a sense Conrad's familiar ghost, evokes in this vision of Lord Jim—it might be one of Conrad's less familiar ghosts— a vision of his creator. 'The muscles round his lips contracted into an unconscious grimace that tore through the mask of his usual expres-

sion—something violent, short-lived and illuminating, like a flash of lightning that admits the eye for an instant into the secret convulsions of a cloud.'

*(Notes on Joseph Conrad,* London, Myers & Co., 1925)

Discounting the Pateresque in Symons' portrait, there remains a certain credibility.[2] Conrad protested, in reference to an article Symons wrote about him in 1907: "I did not know that I had 'a heart of darkness' and 'an unlawful soul.' Mr. Kurtz had—and I have not treated him with easy nonchalance. Believe me, no man ever paid more for his lines than I have. But then I possess an inalienable right to the use of all my epithets. The fact is that I am really a much simpler person." (*Notes,* p. 15) I rather believe that Conrad was in fact the complicated person that Symons portrays in his fascinating *Notes.*

If Conrad were a simple person would not his creative products mirror simplicity? But nothing of Conrad's works at their best is simple. "A Simple Tale" is Conrad's deceptive sub-title to *The Secret Agent,* whereas in fact that novel is—by my reading of it—a most complicated novel; as for one thing, in its chronological disarrangements. Deceptive also are those Author's Notes, wherein Conrad professes to be letting us in on his aims as a writer. The prefaces of Conrad (to quote from my 1949 essay on "The Secret Sharer") "stand in striking contrast to the prefaces of Henry James. For whereas Henry James is everywhere telling us what his 'exquisite scheme' is, Conrad is continually telling us that he has no scheme at all." Conrad's accounts of his literary aims and his disclosures of the sources of his tales are highly deceptive, often deliberately misleading. "Conrad's way of affirming a thing is always by affirming its opposite" (Wilson Follett pinpointed this doubleness in Conrad several decades ago). "In Conrad all is ambiguous and contradictory; nothing is absolute; nothing is but what is not." (In *A Critical Symposium,* pp. 285, 288) A telltale phrase occurs in *The Secret Agent:* "in this world of contradictions." Contradictions define the Conradian world. "But should we be troubled by this discrepancy between the two Conrads, the Conrad who praised the simple ideas and sincere emotions and the Conrad of the neurotic illnesses and the dark inwardness?" asks R. P. Warren (p. 216).

Hawthorne, says Arthur Symons, "is haunted by what is obscure, dangerous, and on the confines of good and evil; by what is abnormal, indeed (as in the case of Conrad) if we are to accept human nature as a thing set within responsible limits. . . ." In the same category, although Symons does not name him, is Melville. "Abnormality is the keynote of Conrad's creative genius." (*Notes,* pp. 19-20, 23) "*An Outpost of Progress* contains horrors unspeakable; it is conceived as Swift might have conceived an almost insane satire; it is brought to birth by some primeval sarcasm; . . . One might call it a charnel-house curiosity; the fascination of corruption as in the case of Baudelaire, who was more amorous of corruption than Beddoes; or of Poe, who was more spellbound by the scent of graveyard earth." Beddoes might have made something of Conrad's subject in

*The Secret Agent:* The professor " 'walked frail, insignificant, shabby, miserable—and terrible in the simplicity of his idea calling madness and despair to the regeneration of the world. Nobody looked at him. He passed on unsuspecting and deadly, like a pest in the street full of men.' That is the abnormal end of *The Secret Agent,* a book itself as deadly and as poisonous as some ravaging pestilence. . . ." (*Notes,* pp. 25, 23)[3]

Conrad's polarities are manifested in comparing him with two eminent men who were his contemporaries: Freud (born 1856) and Lord Baden Powell (born 1857): "the first with his claim that all people are ill, the second with his affirmative appeal to activity and his assertion that men may be healthy if they renew in active life their solidarity with their fellow creatures. This comparison may serve to throw some light on Conrad's polarities: on the one hand the breaking off of attachments and a mistrustful probing into the secrets of the human heart, on the other the gospel of fidelity, the search for the ideal and the conception of good service." I am quoting here the English summary of the Polish text of *Conrad Zywy* (*The Living Conrad,* edited by Wit Tarnawski, London, 1957, p. 287). In "Conrad and Polish Culture" Tymon Terlecki writes that Conrad, "like many others of his generation, was emotionally involved in the tragic rising of 1860-63, of which his parents were both victims. It influenced his sensibility and for ever marked his outlook on life; it also directed Conrad's life on to those lines, along which the life and work of other writers of his generation moved. Placed between the vanquished romanticism and the extreme negation of romanticism, they all sided with romanticism, although they also criticised it very strongly." The paradoxical opposition characteristic of the Young Poland writers of Conrad's generation—"the flight from reality and the mastering of reality—has nowhere been so evident as in Conrad." (*The Living Conrad,* p. 285)

There is symbolic significance in Conrad's Christian names Teodor Konrad, as Czeslaw Milosz points out in *A Critical Symposium* (p. 36). "For a Pole the name Konrad symbolizes the anti-Russian fighter and resister." *Konrad* harks back to *Konrad Wallenrod,* the patriotic poem of Adam Mickiewicz, in which the pagan hero converted to Christianity leads the enemy's army into a trap and thus avenges his people's sufferings. "His vengeance is won through monstrous duplicity, the weapon of the oppressed. Thus from his very infancy Joseph Conrad bore a name steeped in Polish tradition. When he signed his first book 'Conrad,' dropping his family name of Korzeniowski as being too difficult for an Anglo-Saxon public, he was well aware of its double meaning."

Double meaning is the mark of the poetic use of language at its best, and Conrad at his best is the novelist as poet executing the same reflexive use of language. He was born with that gift by his very name. He means what he says, but also he means something more.

In *Lord Jim* the youthful hero jumps from the ship—the *Patna.* Milosz speculates (p. 43) that *Patna* hints at "Patria," and Gustav Morf (p. 140) boldly declares that the sinking ship is Poland, doomed to go down. Jim's superiors advise him to jump, and Conrad's uncle and guardian, T. Bobrowski, *"urged him during more than seven years to become a British subject.* And finally, Jim yielded and jumped, *i.e.,* Conrad became a British subject." Etc. Well, that is very interesting. Accused of desertion and betrayal of Poland for having first "jumped" Poland to become a British sailor and next "jumped" Poland to become an English author, Conrad replied to these accusations by writing *Lord Jim,* so Wit Tarnawski suggests.

> It is significant that the main theme of 'An Outcast of the Islands,' written just after Conrad had 'entered' the career of an English writer with 'Almayer's Folly,' is the hero's betrayal of his race and his subsequent punishment—an appalling solitude ending in death. The plot of the novel bears strong resemblance to Conrad's own situation at that particular time and, possibly, we may even see in it such developments as he might have feared for himself. After finishing 'An Outcast,' Conrad wrote 'The Lagoon' and, a year later 'Karain,' both of which are also based on the theme of betrayal—a theme which appears to haunt Conrad's mind in these first creative years. (*The Living Conrad,* p. 294)

The clash between the temperaments and outlook of Conrad's father and Conrad's uncle, who became his guardian after Apollo Korzeniowski's death (1869), may very well account for the split allegiance in Joseph Conrad's personality for simultaneously the romantic outlook *and* the realistic. The clash between these two contradictory personalities—dreamer *and* realist hostile to revolutionary dreams—"may help to elucidate the contradictions to be found in Conrad himself: what may be called his anti-romantic romanticism, his strange blend of Polish patriotism and scepticism toward the 'Polish cause,' his love of adventure and his simultaneous cultivation of order and self-discipline." (Milosz, p. 39)

Conrad fused the literatures of two civilizations, Poland and England, and thereby transcended both. The Polish reader recognizes in Conrad's themes, and even in the rhythm of his phrasings, a kinship or familiar ring. They remind him of "verse lines very close to him, whose sources, upon reflection, can be named. What happened in Conrad was a perfect fusion of two literatures and two civilizations." (Milosz, "Joseph Conrad in Polish Eyes," *A Critical Symposium,* pp. 41-42) While remaining a loyal English citizen, first in the capacity of an English sailor and later in the role of a great English writer, Conrad remained "a 'hundred per cent' Pole in his antecedents, his way of life, his sentiments and mannerisms, yet, at the same time, he was a really good subject of the Queen of England." "When a man assumes a nationality—other than the one to which he was born—he either becomes completely absorbed by the country of his adoption, or else remains what he was at birth, the change of nationality being, in such case, a matter of formality and expediency. But

Conrad had dual nationality." (J. H. Retinger in *The Living Conrad,* p. 288)

"When very ill and feverish, to the despair of Jessie [his wife], he spoke only Polish," Retinger reports in his memoirs *Conrad and His Contemporaries* (New York, 1943). According to John Shand, "Conrad has himself remarked that if he writes in English he still thinks in his native Polish; and it is noticeable that when one is speaking, or trying to speak, in a foreign tongue, one is as apt to use the simile in speech as to use the hands in gesture." Shand thinks that the explanation for Conrad's extravagant use of similes is that Conrad is a foreigner. (*A Critical Symposium,* p. 15) "I know English and French both quite well. I know French well enough to write in that language also—in a very personal style, of course. My English, too, must be personal, I suppose." So R. L. Mégroz reports Conrad in *A Talk with Joseph Conrad* (London, 1926, p. 51). "He denied, in his conversation with me, that he did not habitually think in English, and the suggestion that he thought in French, or Polish, and translated, is proved to be false by the poetic power and unfaltering felicity of his phrase and rhythms in the finest work. . . ." Mégroz (pp. 57-58) is perhaps contradicting John Shand's statement in his *Criterion* article, which appeared two years before Mégroz's book (in *Criterion:* October 1924).

"Although Conrad's style is very idiomatic, yet one comes up against expressions which are wholly foreign, mostly Polish. I pointed a few out to him," Retinger recalls, "and in particular the following two which occur fairly frequently: 'under the angle of eternity' and 'civic valour.' Conrad picked them up bodily from Polish. He agreed with me, and later amused himself by selecting more of such phrases, remarking that he did it unconsciously, but adding the hope that their use might eventually enrich the language." (Retinger in *Conrad and His Contemporaries,* p. 111) As John Wain remarks, Conrad—like Wilde, Shaw, Synge, and Yeats—enriched English literature with much that was not English.

But Wain is mistaken in believing that Conrad made a choice as to writing in English or in French: "In attracting an artist as big as Conrad we, the English, had a stroke of luck. But of course it was more than luck. We had, in those days, the reputation of being a good audience, intelligent and serious enough to deserve the best that a great author could do. Have we still got that reputation? Would a modern Conrad still make that choice?" (In "Joseph Conrad: A Critical Symposium," *London Magazine:* November 1957) Wain here echoes Retinger:

> It is a matter of conjecture what language he would have used had he been given the choice, if he had foreseen that what he wrote in those leisurely hours [boredom at sea turned Conrad to become a writer] would be thought worthy of print, that it would bring him fame in the days to come, that it would have a market value, and that he would be obliged to keep on writing until death. I cannot help thinking it would have been French that he would have chosen as his

medium—because, as he himself not infrequently hinted, he was at first better acquainted with that tongue than with English; secondly, because he was brought up on French literature, which he thought the most versatile, the most universal, and the most cosmopolitan of all.
(Retinger in *Conrad and His Contemporaries*, pp. 105-106)

But Conrad himself answered that question. "The impression of my having exercised a choice between the two languages, French and English, both foreign to me, has got abroad somehow. That impression is erroneous." (Author's Note to *A Personal Record*) Writing Hugh Walpole (June 7th, 1918), he complained:

The only thing that grieves me and makes me dance with rage is the cropping up of the legend set afloat by Hugh Clifford about my hesitation between English and French as a writing language. For it is absurd. When I wrote the first words of *Almayer's Folly,* I had been already for years and years *thinking* in English. I began to think in English long before I mastered, I won't say the style (I haven't done that yet), but the mere uttered speech. Is it thinkable that anybody possessed of some effective inspiration should contemplate for a moment such a frantic thing as translating it into another tongue? And there are also other considerations: such as the sheer appeal of the language, my quickly awakened love for its prose cadences, a subtle and unforeseen accord of my emotional nature with its genius . . . You may take it from me that if I had not known English I wouldn't have written a line for print, in my life. Clifford and I were discussing the nature of the two languages and what I said was: that if I had been offered the alternative I would have been afraid to grapple with French, which is crystallized in the form of its sentence and therefore more exacting and less appealing. But there was never any alternative offered or even dreamed of.
(*Life and Letters,* II, p. 206)

In *A Personal Record* he declares:

The truth of the matter is that my faculty to write in English is as natural as any other aptitude with which I might have been born. I have a strange and overpowering feeling that it had always been an inherent part of myself. English was for me neither a matter of choice nor adoption. The merest idea of choice had never entered my head. And as to adoption—well, yes, there was adoption; but it was I who was adopted by the genius of the language, which directly I came out of the stammering stage made me its own so completely that its very idioms I truly believe had a direct action on my temperament and fashioned my still plastic character.[4]

Conrad told Mégroz that "I picked up my first English by hearing it spoken along the East Coast" (pp. 36-37), and in *A Personal Record* he recalls that his first introduction to English literature was at the age of eight when he read his father's translation of *Two Gentlemen of Verona* and that he read it in English years later when at Falmouth his ship was put up in dry dock, having then purchased a five-shilling one volume edition of Shakespeare's Dramatic Works (pp. 71-72).

It is noteworthy, John Wain reminds us, that Conrad's method is not unlike Shakespeare's. "He has the same technique of working through thematic construction rather than through 'plot' and 'character' in the nineteenth-century fashion." And Retinger observes that technique (the architectural plan of the whole, etc.), all that which the French call *métier,* interested Conrad "more than the plot or the inner meaning of the book—if there was an inner meaning. When I asked him once which of his books he considered the best, he answered without hesitation: '*Nostromo* and *The Secret Agent* because in those I accumulated the most difficult technical obstacles and I overcame them most successfully.'" Again, the "*leit-motif* of his work consisted not in the plot, but in some kind of psychological equation. The finale of the story did not supply the climax of his book, and often its solution was given at the very outset" [as in *Lord Jim,* for example]. (*Conrad and His Contemporaries,* pp. 106-107) The same methods serve for *Nostromo* as for *King Lear,* to quote Wain once more: "The quickest way to the heart of a Shakespeare play when one has laid down the book, or come out of the theatre, is to ask, 'What was that play *about?*' (rather than, e. g., 'What was the hero's character?') and this is certainly the way to understand Conrad." (*London Magazine:* November 1957)

As for Wain's query, "Would a modern Conrad still make that choice? Forgive me if I say that the question seems, at best, very much an open one." Leavis's reply is that "if we, the English, *had* in those days the reputation of being a good audience, intelligent and serious enough to deserve the best that a great author could do, we wholly and lamentably failed to justify it in respect of Conrad." And he adds: "I think it is still true that his greatness as an artist has not had due recognition for what it really is." (*Sewanee Review:* Spring 1958, pp. 182, 200) I agree; as *The Art of Joseph Conrad* testifies, *that* is the purpose of this collection of critical studies—to bring Conrad his due recognition.

## (2)

"I suppose Conrad to be indeed suffering a commercial and fashionable eclipse," Ford Madox Ford wrote in 1937. "I hear that his bric-a-brac and souvenirs fetch almost nothing at auctions. I rang up a dozen booksellers the other day without being able to obtain copies of his work. . . .

"But he will return. Every great man suffers a thirty to sixty years' eclipse after his death—or a longer one if he is immensely great. (In 1663, Samuel Pepys was still talking of *Hamlet* as 'a barbarous and antick piece.')" (*Portraits from Life,* New York, 1937)

At the time Ford noted Conrad's decline (1937), Conrad's achievement had received not more than a half dozen critically significant studies. A pioneer work was Wilson Follett's *Joseph Conrad* (1915) and his essay in the *Bookman* (1928): "Joseph Conrad, 1907." A forgotten study deserving notice today was Donald Davidson's "Joseph Conrad's Directed Indirections," in the *Sewanee Review* for 1925. G. Jean-Aubry's *The Life and Letters of Joseph Conrad* (2 volumes) remains *the* indispensable biographical source-book, but this scholarly tome of 1927 did not spark off any critical revival of Conrad, and during the next decade the only revaluations worth notice—apart from Gustav Morf's fascinating psychological study, *The Polish Heritage of Joseph Conrad* (1930)—were J. W. Beach's chapter on Conrad in his *Twentieth Century Novel* (1932) and Edward Crankshaw's important *Joseph Conrad: Some Aspects of the Art of the Novel* (1936).

In reviewing Crankshaw's illuminating critique of the novel, Elizabeth Bowen remarked that it was well-timed—"Conrad is in abeyance. We are not clear yet how to rank him; there is an uncertain pause. It would be inexact to say that his reputation has declined; his popularity has, at the most, contracted; he is still steadily if not widely read." For the moment, however, his power to command the imagination has lost its grip on us. "The change must be in us," Miss Bowen concludes.

"Conrad is suspect for the very magnificence that had us under its spell: we resist verbal magic now. [But not yet in Faulkner, I might add.] His novels are, in the grand sense, heroic: now we like our heroics better muffled—the terse heroics of the Hemingway school. His dramatic, ironic sense of fate is out of accord with our fatalism. Most vital of all, perhaps, he seems to be over-concerned with the individual: with conscience, with inner drama, with isolated endeavour. Romantic individualism is at a discount now. 'You may take it,' says Conrad, through the mouth of Mills in *The Arrow of Gold*—'You may take it from a man who has lived a rough life, a very rough life, that it is the subtleties of personality, and contacts, and events, that count for interest and memory—and pretty well nothing else.' This we no longer feel—or do not admit." (In the *Spectator*: 1936) But in any literary work, from *Hamlet* to *The Great Gatsby,* what counts for literary interest are "the subtleties of personality," or rather the subtleties of the interrelationships of personalities, the characters of the play or novel, their contacts and events. Complexities toolmark Conrad's art.

All Conrad's heroes and villains are highly simple persons, but the subtlety is in the method of rendering them, and it is the same with Henry James. David Daiches, in *The Novel and the Modern World* (1939), provides one answer to Miss Bowen's criticism:

> He is not drawing-room conscious, because it is not in the drawing-room that the things in experience that interest him most can be clearly seen and presented. And he is not factory conscious, because

the world he understands is less easily revealed through the kinds of group activity and interests that the factory symbolizes; he is concerned rather with a certain kind of intermittent activity that leaves time for leisure and the play of the imagination and the influence of natural—i.e., geographical—environment. Now the most characteristic and important aspects of the civilization of our time lie between the drawing-room and the factory (including both), and the man who does not understand this is bound to be in some sense an exotic (IV).

As M. D. Zabel observed in *Sewanee Review* (1945): "The romantic element is never effaced in his work. It persists as the basis of his popularity and of those excesses of style and treatment which show in his often extravagant phraseology, in his treatment of women, in his sentimentalization of the heroics and the miraculous in human fortunes and character, in his exotic and rhetorical effects, and in the curious naiveté of fatalism which reappears in his last three books." In recasting this passage for his chapters on Conrad in *Craft and Character in Modern Fiction* (1957) Zabel adds: "But if it was not effaced, it was recognized. Conrad himself admitted an inherent romanticism as a component of his imagination and of his ordeal in moral and creative responsibility." In his technique and themes Conrad belongs to our world. His drama of moral isolation, "alienation and spiritual recognition," links him with Mann, Gide, Kafka, Joyce, and Hemingway, with the French existentialists, etc. "But it is doubtful if any of these writers has achieved a more successful *dramatic* version of the problem than Conrad did—a more complete coincidence of the processes of psychic recognition and recovery with the dramatic necessities of the plot; and this for a reason which distinguishes Conrad's contribution to modern fictional method: his imposition of the processes of psychological experience, notably the experience of recognition, on the structure of the plot." (In *A Critical Symposium*, pp. 34, 28)

Zabel's perceptive *Sewanee Review* summary, his *New Republic* articles on Conrad (1941 and 1942), and his important *Portable Conrad* (1947), Albert J. Guerard's *Joseph Conrad* (New Directions, pamphlet, 1947), and E. K. Brown's excellent essay "James and Conrad" (*Yale Review,* 1945) buttressed the trend to Conrad criticism initiated by British critics. First of all by Crankshaw, and then by M. C. Bradbrook's short handbook, *Joseph Conrad: Poland's English Genius* (1941), and by F. R. Leavis's penetrating appraisal of Conrad's works in *Scrutiny* (June and October, 1941). My Conrad *Scrutiny* numbers are at hand as I write this, and I recall my excitement over Leavis's insights when first I read them in 1941. That same year appeared John D. Gordan's *Joseph Conrad: The Making of a Novelist,* which remains today the most important contribution to Conrad scholarship since Jean-Aubry's *Life and Letters* (1927). In 1947 J. M. Dent & Sons Ltd. began issuing the *Collected Edition of the Works of Joseph Conrad,* making available again the Author's Notes which Edward Garnett had collected as *Conrad's Prefaces to His Works* (Dent, 1937).

Shortly after the appearance of R. P. Warren's critical study of *Lord Jim* (in *Sewanee Review:* 1948), I wrote that at the moment there is much that portends a Conrad boom. That it was in the making then seemed possible, but it did not materialize until another decade. Critics in those days concerned themselves almost exclusively with the criticism of poetry. The shift to the criticism of fiction did not begin until the mid-forties, and that accounts for the lag in Conrad criticism. It is only recently, within the present decade, that Conrad's works have begun to be revaluated; subjected to scrutiny *now,* they emerge thus in new light. In Douglas Hewitt's *Joseph Conrad: A Reassessment* (London, 1952) there isn't a single reference to an American Conrad critic, but the fact is that— excepting Crankshaw, Leavis, and Miss Bradbrook—Conrad's critical readers were all American critics. Beginning with J. W. Beach (1932), they included M. D. Zabel (1941, 1942, 1945, 1947), Albert J. Guerard (1947), R. P. Warren (1948), Walter Wright (in *Romance and Tragedy in Joseph Conrad,* 1949); I shall add that I, too, pioneered (1948, 1949). Criticism of Fiction Critics were a decade ago rather scarce; what they were reading *then* was Melville, or Henry James, or Kafka—but Conrad not at all. "Of Conrad little is heard," E. K. Brown complained in 1945. But "I believe that before thirty years have passed, the world of his imagination will fascinate the general reader as surely as it did twenty years ago; and that the close critical examination of his work, which has barely begun, will take a large place in the interpretation of fiction." (In *Yale Review,* 1945) His prophecy is fulfilled (and anticipated) in *The Art of Joseph Conrad.*

Today there's a Conradism in the air—and also in the seminar. Conrad's Centennial (1957) brought forth a Centenary Volume, *The Living Conrad* (issued by the Polish Authors Society of London); Jean-Aubry's *The Sea Dreamer* (Doubleday); a bibliography, Lohf and Sheehy's *Joseph Conrad at Mid-Century: Editions and Studies 1895-1955* (University of Minnesota Press); "A Critical Symposium" (albeit not in fact critical) in *London Magazine;* Czeslaw Milosz's illuminating essay, "Joseph Conrad in Polish Eyes," in *Atlantic Monthly;* and three book-length studies: Richard Curle's *Joseph Conrad and His Characters* (Heinemann); R. F. Haugh's *Joseph Conrad: Discovery in Design* (University of Oklahoma Press); and Thomas Moser's psychological interpretation of Conrad's works, *Joseph Conrad: Achievement and Decline* (Harvard University Press). Other Conradiana for 1957 included five studies of "Heart of Darkness" and reissues of Conrad studies by M. D. Zabel in *Craft and Character in Modern Fiction* (Viking Press), by Irving Howe in *Politics and the Novel* (Horizon), and by Lord David Cecil in *The Fine Art of Reading* (Bobbs-Merrill). This centennial year witnessed also, in addition to reviews of these books, new editions of some of Conrad's works. In 1958 Zabel edited *Lord Jim* with an extensive introduction (Boston: Riverside Editions); F. R. Leavis in *Sewanee Review* (Spring 1958) recast his earlier 1941 reading of *The Shadow Line* (the latter is reprinted in *A Critical Symposium*, pp. 191-198); Ian Watt reinterpreted *The Nigger of the "Narcissus"* in *Nineteenth Century Fiction* (March 1958); and William Moynihan gave "Conrad's 'The End of the Tether': A New Reading" in *Modern Fiction Studies* (Summer 1958; reprinted here, pp. 186-191).[5] In 1958 Conrad was critically scrutinized in Albert J. Guerard's *Conrad the Novelist* (Harvard University Press), and his *Letters to William Blackwood and David S. Meldrum* came to light here and abroad (Duke University and Cambridge University Press). Forthcoming is Jocelyn Baines's biography (Doubleday). At this writing *Modern Fiction Studies* (Summer 1959) offers "The Significance of the Revisions in the Early Versions of 'Nostromo' " by F. R. Karl.

Conrad's rank amongst the greatest authors of fiction, both in the novel and in the short story, is today everywhere acknowledged. (The best short summary of Conrad's achievement that I know of is Guerard's article in *The Reporter* for March 21, 1957.)

A certain critic, however, takes exception to the general acclaim. In the *Hudson Review* six years ago he opined that good fiction is nothing more than "a genuine story." According to his notion, the proper use of language in fiction excludes the poetic. Conrad is at his best at the literal narrative level. This critic does not like symbolism, but then neither does he like Conrad.

"As for myth and symbol," says he, "each has furnished its adherents with a career"; apparently his own career promises to be furnished by literal-minded readings of plots and characters. But even when he finds in Conrad a genuine story (such as "The Secret Sharer") he doesn't like it. He settles on two works as Conrad's best: *Typhoon* and *The Nigger of the "Narcissus."* But I think his choice of *The Nigger* confounds his own platform.

He attacks Conrad for being "the poet in fiction" and claims that Conrad makes symbol and myth business all too clear: "destructively clear, for by the time we have given our energy to relating such coarse, obvious and superabundant clues at the neatly systematic clinical level proper to them—the interest of myth reduced to the interest of murder 'mystery' —we have lost interest and faith in the narrative itself." On the contrary, what's lost I think is interest and faith in this critic as a reader of Conrad. His very phrases give him away: "bargain-basement fatalism," and "popular-priced psychoanalysis."[6] Rather, what's shown here (it seems to me) is how to vulgarize criticism. He accuses Conrad of "catch-all symbolism" and of dishonesty of spirit: "he will without scruple betray his entertaining narrative and his rather unsubtly contrasted characters at the appeal of any portentous image or generalization or symbolic gesture, often wholly impertinent. . . ." As for "The Secret Sharer," it's all too obvious to require any critical scrutiny: "Who could fail to predict every item of the depth psychology paraphernalia that will tidily turn up? And who could possibly miss, on the most inattentive first reading, Conrad's oversimplified, imposed mythical structure, symbol to character in the crudest one-to-one relationship, nailed to the flesh of the narrative in almost every sentence?"

Though the symbolic interpretation of Conrad has Conrad's own sanction,[7] our critic, with his flat-headed insistence that Plot and Character constitute Everything There Is To Say About A Novel, claims that "Conrad might have done better, clinically as well as artistically, if he had been describable by his critical partisans not as a poet in fiction, but as a man who merely tells a tale." Though he doesn't care much for "The Secret Sharer," while admitting it's "a genuine story," he belives it possible to "save" the story by virtue of its being "grounded in the details of life at sea—Conrad's only element, in spite of his angry disclaimers. . . ."

" 'Youth' has been called a fine sea-story. Is it? Well, I won't bore you with a discussion of fundamentals. But surely those stories of mine where the sea enters can be looked at from another angle." Our *Hudson Review* critic sees Conrad straight, not from any angle. He proposes to return us to the simple literal-minded reading that Conrad endured from his contemporary critics, including Richard Curle and William McFee.[8] Wipe out all Conrad criticism since then. Don't mention Conrad's reflexive use of the poetic properties of words. Don't mention symbols; don't mention myths. Don't mention Conrad, except for such Genuine Sea-tales as he produced in *Typhoon* and *The Nigger!* In *The Nigger,* as Conrad declares in *Life and Letters,* II, p. 324), the problem that faces the men on the "Narcissus" "is not a problem of the sea." Barely one-tenth of his work is "sea-stuff," Conrad tried to persuade the literal-minded Richard Curle; "and even of that, the bulk, that is *Nigger* and *Mirror,* has a very special purpose which I emphasize myself in my Prefaces. . . . I do wish that all those ships of mine were given a rest, but I'm afraid that when the Americans get hold of them they will never, never, never get a rest" (II, 316-317).

As Ford Madox Ford (in *Portraits from Life*) said, Conrad "never tired of protesting that he was not a writer about the sea; he detested the sea as a man detests a cast-off mistress, and with the hatred of a small man who has had, on freezing nights of gales, to wrestle immense yards and dripping cordage; his passion became to live out of sight of the sea and all its memories; he never tired of repeating Christina Rossetti's last written words; 'A little while and we shall be/Please God, where there is no more sea.' " "Most of our reviewers," Conrad complained, "seem absolutely unable to understand in a book anything but facts and the most elementary qualities of rendering." Sir Sydney Colvin, for instance, declined to review *The Shadow Line* because he had no first-hand knowledge of the Gulf of Siam.

While admitting the validity of the conception of the artist as conscious craftsman, our *Hudson Review* critic rejects it strategically on the grounds that though "useful" it is also, "in certain constructed over-confident uses that have been made of it, dangerous; and these uses, moreover, seem to possess an irresistible appeal for critics who have uncritically adopted the terminology of modern criticism." (It is dangerous because the faith of the critic that every part of the literary work contributes to the whole leads him to read out of the work more than is warranted by the literal level of plot and character alone.) "Having frequently cheapened the valuable terms they have helped make current, many of our critics, especially in the *literal-minded* second generation of modern criticism, have proceeded to cheapen the crucially valid notion of the artist as craftsman." But who is more literal-minded than the critic who ridicules extra-literal readings of works, and who but himself cheapens the conception of the artist as craftsman by his denigration of Conrad?[9]

After wiping out the entire Conrad canon except for *Typhoon* and *The Nigger of the "Narcissus,"* finally not even *The Nigger* is exempted from his wholesale denigration of Conrad, for on second thought he now finds fault with *The Nigger* (in *Nineteenth Century Fiction*: March 1957). This Conrad detractor remained unidentified in my *Kenyon Review* (Spring 1957) essay, "Fiction and Its Critics," but in a subsequent *Kenyon Review* he identified himself thus: "My article is entitled 'Conrad and the Terms of Modern Criticism.' It appeared in the Autumn 1954 issue of the *Hudson Review*, and I wrote it." The author of this mud-slinging attack on Conrad and his critics is—to identify him, as he wants it that way— M. Mudrick.

M. Mudrick grants Conrad success only in *Typhoon.* He discredits critical readings of Conrad at the symbolic level as unwarranted by the literal level of the text, but he himself misinterprets even the literal level of *The Nigger;* for proof of which I refer you to Ian Watt's "Conrad Criticism and *The Nigger of the 'Narcissus,' "* in *Ninetenth Century Fiction* (March 1958). In a deft demolition of M. Mudrick's notions about *The Nigger,* Ian Watt writes: "But we must not overlook the fact that Mudrick, who cast himself as the spectral Mr. Jones interrupting the feast celebrating Conrad's victory over the critics, is also possessed of a marked cannibalistic trait. . . . In his earlier essay on Conrad, Stallman's reading of 'The Secret Sharer' was his main target; but he now finds *The Nigger of the 'Narcissus'* subject to the same general charge: a heavy overemphasis on 'catch-all' and 'claptrap' symbolism which only a naive predisposition for that sort of thing could possibly render acceptable." "It's a crackerjack," Stephen Crane wrote Hamlin Garland of Conrad's *The Nigger*. It takes a cracker-barrel critic to see it as anything else.

(3)

Whereas Conrad's publishers—Heinemann, Dent, and Doubleday— owe a debt to Conrad, he himself owes, as it were, a debt to Harvard University Press for having published three of the most important studies in the whole field of Conrad criticism: Thomas Moser's *Joseph Conrad: Achievement and Decline* (1957), Albert J. Guerard's *Conrad the Novelist* (1958), John D. Gordan's *Joseph Conrad: The Making of a Novelist*

(1941), a landmark in Conrad scholarship. All three books, it seems fitting to add, would have been rejected by commercial publishing houses as lacking a market because they are too technical.

Moser and Guerard define 1897 to 1912 as the period of Conrad's major achievements, the decline beginning with *Chance* (written 1912). *Chance* was Conrad's first popular success; it paid off almost enough to square his overdrawn account with his benevolent literary agent, James B. Pinker. Its popularity was owed partly to the clever publicity of Alfred A. Knopf, then reader for Doubleday. In marking 1912 as the beginning of Conrad's decline, Moser and Guerard cross no new shadow line. They take the same stand as John Galsworthy in his 1927 summary of his friend's achievement and decline, and most everyone agrees that after *Chance,* "with the exception of 'The Secret Sharer' and some parts of *Victory,* none of his work in that late period was up to his own exalted mark." Only Zabel and Paul L. Wiley profess to find no falling off in Conrad's craftsmanship during his final decade. Hewitt, on the contrary, claims that only the early Conrad works are his best and that his best works belong to the period ending in 1909. Of the later works *The Rover* is salvaged by Miss M. C. Bradbrook, in *Joseph Conrad: Poland's English Genius* (1941), and *The Shadow Line* is ranked with Conrad's best by F. R. Leavis in *The Great Tradition* (1948). I agree with the Guerard and Moser rejection of the later works as inferior craftsmanship; the decline is obvious. As for *The Shadow Line,* while it is all of a piece, it is not a richly textured symbolic work. Guerard makes it the one exception among the later Conrad, seeing it as "Conrad's final important achievement as an artist. It represents his last and largely successful effort to make a minutely rendered material world serve symbolic ends: the real and the symbolic in perilous balance, neither toppling or violating the other." But the first two chapters are seriously defective, he adds; obviously *The Shadow Line* is less perfect than the earlier "Secret Sharer," its companion-piece. Guerard finds *Chance* the only later novel, other than *The Shadow Line,* worth much attention; *Victory* he dismisses altogether, and in agreeing with him now I reverse my viewpoint of a decade ago. Guerard doesn't see any symbolic subtleties in *Victory,* but, as he remarks, "The presence or absence of secret symbolic patterns in *Victory* is a question of little more importance than would be their presence or absence in a good adventure story for boys." While there are many clever devices in it, such as Heyst smoking his cigar before an indolent volcano, etc., I agree with Guerard that "To argue with Leavis about seriousness of theme or with Zabel about parabolic movements or with Stallman and others about secret symbolic intent is to postpone the essential considerations: the quality of the fictional imagination at work, and the quality of the prose. These qualities are such as to make other forms of analysis irrelevant. The time has come to drop *Victory* from the Conrad canon, at least to the degree that *The Trumpet-Major,* once so widely admired, has at last been dropped from Hardy's."

As Hewitt's *Reassessment* (1952) "grew very largely from reflection on the marked inferiority of most of Conrad's later works to his earlier ones," so Moser's study began with the same reflection made during a chronological reading of Conrad's works. Graduate students making a chronological reading of Conrad's works—if they heed Hewitt—would stop with "The Secret Sharer"; if they heed the Galsworthy-Moser-Guerard appraisal, they'd proceed—as they should—into *Under Western Eyes* (1910) and perhaps look into *Chance* (1913).

What brought about the decline and collapse of Conrad's imaginative powers? Fatigue, mental and physical; also Conrad's financial plight—he stood in desperate need of winning over the common reader, "the man who forks out the half crown." To popularize his works he injected into the last six full-length novels the ingredient of love between the sexes. "Love and even passionate love between the sexes now replace the old preoccupation with loyalty to the community, to the brother, to one's self. But Conrad could not, as Moser has abundantly demonstrated, take seriously these new values he professed to believe; his plots and his imagery discredit them." Guerard defines the characteristics of the post-1912 works: narrators who are unequipped to tell their stories effectively, implausible love-scenes, a new cleansed moral universe marked by sentimental optimism, a reconciliation with the normal and the affirmative which damaged his fiction, his technique and his prose. "The last works should be restudied especially by those who admire the early novels, yet regret their pessimism and corrosive analytic bent and austere moralism, and resent their complexity of method. For the qualities were essential rather than incidental to the success. A simple and serene Conrad could not have written *Lord Jim*." True, but if we take the obverse position and prefer the early works because they manifest what Henry James called the imagination of disaster and because they exhibit complexity of method and language, then it becomes a question whether the later works, which lack these complexities and are obviously not works of art, deserve further readings except for the purpose of specialized studies such as Moser's.

His concern is to "demonstrate the weakness of the last period," to account for the decline, and to compare—as Hewitt did before him—the early and late Conrad. "Conrad's decision to finish *Chance* determined his decline. In his early major period, he had . . . either evaded love or subordinated it to other subjects." In the best works of the early period Moser finds three main types of characters—the simple hero, the vulnerable hero, and the perceptive hero—and the pattern of hero, heroine, and rival; in the later period the pattern is the same except that the rival changes to villain. The villain exhibits abnormal attitudes toward love. We are reminded here of Paul L. Wiley's observation that the heroes and villains are doubles, that they have the same basic weaknesses, that the hero is like the villain as essentially an impotent voyeur destined to be destroyed when involved with women. Of the hero-lovers, as Moser observes, only Charles Gould in *Nostromo* is spared a violent death. Hewitt denies that the villains of the love stories are true doubles, on the ground that they lead to no further knowledge of the hero. To quote Moser, "This is just another way of saying that when Conrad writes about love he does not understand his subject." Moser scores a useful pointer: "The extent to which villains dominate the later novels provides us with a good indication of the depth of Conrad's decline."

"*The Arrow of Gold* constantly overwhelms the reader with its pretentiousness. . . . This pretentiousness appears most frequently in those passages proposing the infinity and eternity of the love between George and Rita." We don't need Moser's thesis, however, to recognize the pretentious prose; we know *that* much through scrutiny of Conrad's use of language here. Moser opines of *Lord Jim* that it is probably the best written of the full-length novels, "despite certain obvious flaws," but I contend that the best written Conrad novel is *The Secret Agent;* it is the only one devoid of typical Conradese.

Moser, like Hewitt before him, counterpoints throughout his book the contrasted characteristics of the early and late Conrad. In the play of chance and love the later novels strike a new moral attitude toward the world: "he now considers evil to be external to his heroes and heroines and sees man's greatest good as complete repose, usually achieved through love." His characters are rendered as figures of purity afflicted by an external evil (for example Heyst and Lena in *Victory*), whereas in the early Conrad they were sharers of the dark powers that lurk within us all (as in "The Secret Sharer"). In the later novels the chance event that reveals an evil external to the characters blurs their sense of moral responsibility; as in *The Shadow Line,* failure of luck is confused with failure of conscience. Hewitt made a similar demarcation between internal and external evil as characterizing the difference between the early and the late Conrad. His *Reassessment*—an excellent short critical survey, the best in its kind—received almost no notice in this country on its publication in England in 1952. (I wrote two reviews, neither of which saw print.) Hewitt's thesis deserves recognition: the later Conrad no longer emphasizes the characteristic Conradian sense of guilt. The later Conrad is still preoccupied with the problem of evil, but he now restricts evil to one set of characters—the bad ones pitted against the good. This sharp division of mankind into two camps marks the difference between the early and late Conrad; it is manifested in *Chance* (1913), but not in *The Secret Agent* (1907). Irony in the late Conrad period is "normally defensive," whereas in *The Secret Agent* and other works of the early Conrad the irony is "offensive; it is a weapon to undermine comfortable assumptions and to make us scrutinize more deeply our beliefs and values." Hewitt here scores a very useful insight.

Guerard's declared intention in his comprehensive survey of Conrad's works "is to talk as rigorously and fully about these novels as certain critics talk about poems." His strong desire is not to be superficial. "I have been urged in the past to be more minute and more directly concerned with technique . . . I accede to these urgings ruthlessly." He begins with the question of the revelation of the real Conrad in his writings and concludes that he reveals himself more in his fiction than in his two frankly auto-biographical accounts, *A Personal Record* ("one of Conrad's most subtly and most deliberately constructed books") and *The Mirror of the Sea*. Linked with these is the important series of subjective short novels writ-ten in the first person, ending with *The Shadow Line* (1917). I agree with his dismissal of "Youth" (1898) as the least interesting of the autobio-graphical short novels. His reading of "The Secret Sharer" as symbolizing the classic night journey into selfhood and the unconscious and his similar reading of "Heart of Darkness" are likely to become the classic readings. (In his Introduction to the Signet edition of *Heart of Darkness and The Secret Sharer* [New American Library, 1950]).

Conrad's best works derived from conflicts within himself; he was a divided man. His affirmations are linked with denials. Guerard deduces a series of major inward conflicts: a declared belief that ethical matters are simple, *doubled by* an extraordinary awareness of ethical complexities; a declared distrust of idealism, *doubled by* a strong idealism (his double in this, I'd add, is Stephen Crane); a declared fear "of the corrosive and faith-destroying intellect—*doubled by* a profound and ironic skepticism"; a declared distrust of the unconscious, *doubled by* "a powerful introspec-tive drive that took the dreamer deeper into the unconscious than any earlier English novelist (except possibly Dickens)"; a declared fidelity to law, *doubled by* fidelity to the individual—"with betrayal of the individual the most deeply felt of all crimes." The corollary of this last item in Guerard's catalogue of Conradian contradictions is the conflict between external code and internal conscience. Stephen Crane patented that theme in his *Red Badge of Courage;* Conrad utilized it in his *Nigger of the "Narcissus,"* and from there on it radiates to the core of *The Great Gatsby, Farewell to Arms, The Sun Also Rises,* and Warren's *Night Rider.*

Guerard's *Conrad the Novelist* is the best and most comprehensive critical survey in the whole field of Conrad criticism.[10] Like Moser, Guerard gives Conrad his full due as psychological novelist, but Guerard has no special thesis to trap him and also he has the advantage of being himself a novelist as well as critic.

As for the "striking if uncautious essays" of Stallman and Vernon Young having "undoubtedly brought Conrad new readers," the early Guerard was sometimes uncautious too (so were we all!): he generously admits that Gustav Morf, whose *The Polish Heritage of Joseph Conrad* he "treated rather severely in 1947, was often closer to the truth than I." Guerard in reviewing Zabel's *The Portable Conrad* in the *Nation* of Janu-ary 3, 1948 asked: "Does Mr. Zabel really place 'The Secret Agent' and 'Victory' so high? These are splendid books, but books in the same class as 'Tono Bungay' and 'The Old Wives' Tale.' " The later Guerard, how-ever, now sees *The Secret Agent* as "a small and symmetrical triumph of controlled form." What its form *is* he does not specify; actually the structure of that novel is a very complicated one. Nor has any critic recognized what that marvelous novel is really all about. Even the literal situation is misread by Moser. He reads the story solely for its "love trio": Winnie as heroine, Stevie as hero, and Winnie's husband as rival, which strikes me as forcing things to fit a thesis. "Unlike most rivals, Stevie adores his sister's husband and would do anything for him"—doesn't that contradict the notion of the half-wit as rival? And the affection is all a one-way traffic, from Winnie to Stevie, rather than the obverse. After she plants the knife in Verloc's breast, at this point Moser opines: "Thus ends the love story of *The Secret Agent.*" But isn't that precisely where the only love story in the novel begins, namely the desperate affair between Winnie and Comrade Ossipon?

Guerard concedes that the book "does have its genuine seriousness of theme," but he fails to define it. What Conrad's critics have failed to notice is that the attempt to bomb Greenwich Observatory is in fact an attempt to demolish what Greenwich Observatory stands for—time itself, as all time emanates from there. The theme of the book is time—time *is* "the Secret Agent," the unpredictable exploding man's fixed ideas and theories. The purest criticism, as Guerard says, attends to the text. For my part, it is the method of the G. Wilson Knight of *The Wheel of Fire* which exemplifies that ideal—apply *his* method to modern fiction!

Every complex novel, Guerard reminds us, becomes a different one on later readings. *Lord Jim* is "an art novel, a novelist's novel, a critic's novel—perhaps the first important one in England after *Tristram Shandy,* This means that it becomes a different novel if read very attentively; or, becomes a different novel when read a second or third time." A cryptographic novel, I would add, asks for and rewards the cryptographic reader; his interpretation, the result of years of familiarity with the given work, frequently strikes the casual reader as "irresponsible," whereas what's irresponsible is in fact the casual reader. (As Guerard remarks, many professional critics are casual readers.)

What should we read of Conrad? "Everything," said Paul Claudel, whereupon André Gide studied the English language in order to read Conrad's works. "He was the only one of my elders," Gide wrote, "that I loved and knew." Pointing the way to present-day innovations in the techniques of fiction, Conrad was (as J. W. Beach observed) "the most restless and ingenious experimenter of his time, the one who brought the greatest variety of technical procedures to bear upon the problem of the novelist."

The purpose of *The Art of Joseph Conrad* is to render recognition of the greatness of Conrad as artist, a recognition which is long overdue, by collecting in one volume—and here for the first time—the most critically rewarding analyses of his works together with some of the most interesting personal reminiscences and biographical studies by French, Polish, German, British, and American critics. They include André Gide and Ramon Fernandez; Czeslaw Milosz and Gustaf Morf; Thomas Mann; M. C. Bradbrook, F. R. Leavis, Douglas Hewitt, and Edward Crankshaw; Albert J. Guerard, Dorothy Van Ghent, Paul L. Wiley,

Vernon Young, M. D. Zabel, Thomas Moser, John D. Gordan, and Robert Penn Warren.

*The Art of Joseph Conrad*: *A Critical Symposium* presents in Part I appraisals of Conrad, reminiscences of the man and assessments of his works in general, his artistry and his themes. Part II scrutinizes Conrad's works, individually and chronologically; the critical studies are grouped according to the Conrad work they explicate. The variant readings of "Heart of Darkness" (six essays are here juxtaposed) conflict and will likely elicit further controversy. *The Nigger of the "Narcissus," Lord Jim*, "Heart of Darkness," *Nostromo, The Secret Agent*, and *Under Western Eyes* receive here rather exhaustive close-scrutiny readings. Multiple literary approaches are represented: the biographical, the psychological, the mythological, and the aesthetic or analytical. Here is the best of Conrad criticism since 1924.

*University of Connecticut*
*September 13, 1959*

# NOTES

1. "It was confirmed on two occasions by Thaddeus Bobrowski [Conrad's uncle]: 'You were born at Berdiczew on November 21st' (Bobrowski document); 'You came into the world in 1857, at Berdiczew, on November 21st (Information which may be useful to you).' Which, with the twelve days between the Gregorian and the Russian calendars, makes December 3, 1857. This date, December 3, 1857, is also carried on the Standard Life Insurance Society's certificate in Joseph Conrad's policy of January 21, 1901. Finally, Conrad himself writes in 1897, 'Thanks many times for the book. I see you put the date 3rd of Dec. Did you know that on that day I went over the rise of forty to travel downwards, and a little more lonely than before?' (Letter to Edward Garnett, December 7, 1897.)" *Life and Letters* (New York: Doubleday, Page & Co., 1927), Vol. I, page 4.

2. Other portraits include those by Ford Madox Ford and by R. B. Cunninghame Graham (in *Thirty Tales & Sketches*, New York, 1939, pp. 351-354); here is Ford's portrait of Conrad in *Joseph Conrad: A Personal Remembrance* (Boston, 1924, p. 3):

He was small rather than large in height; very broad in the shoulder and long in the arm; dark in complexion with black hair and a clipped black beard. He had the gestures of a Frenchman who shrugs his shoulders frequently. When you had really secured his attention he would insert a monocle into his right eye and scrutinise your face from very near as a watchmaker looks into the works of a watch. He entered a room with his head held high, rather stiffly and with a haughty manner, moving his head once semicircularly. In this one movement he had expressed to himself the room and its contents; his haughtiness was due to his determination to master that room, not to dominate its occupants, his chief passion being the realisation of aspects to himself.

3. Symons quotes an anonymous critic (p. 27): "Conrad's characters are subject to *idées fixes* springing from contact with an essentially mad world," which as an insight provides the clue to any number of Conrad's works including *Lord Jim, Nostromo, The Secret Agent*, and *Under Western Eyes*.

A fixed idea possessed me in my reading of *The Secret Agent* during the past decade of seminars on that novel, namely that the lady patroness of Michaelis, who is in fact not named in the novel, bore the name Lady Mabel. In proofreading "Time and The Secret Agent" for *A Critical Symposium* (pp. 275-288) I discovered that I had bestowed upon that nameless creature the title Lady Mabel; I append this note here to correct my error. Where did I get that fixed idea? Well, she is named Lady Mabel in the dramatized version of the novel: "The Secret Agent: A Drama in Four Acts" (in *Three Plays,* by Joseph Conrad, London: Methuen & Co., 1934).

4. This passage is quoted, but not accurately, in F. R. Leavis's Conrad article taking issue with John Wain (*Sewanee Review:* Spring 1958). *The Sewanee Review* for Winter 1959, under Correspondence (p. 176), published the Conrad-to-Walpole letter with a note by the correspondent who aimed to set things straight, but what the correspondent failed to notice was that Leavis had already quoted the Conrad-to-Walpole letter in his *Sewanee Review* article (p. 181)!

5. In *A Mencken Chrestomathy* (New York, 1949) Mencken judges "The End of the Tether" to be "one of the most magnificent narratives, long or short, old or new, in the English language, and with 'Youth' and 'Heart of Darkness' it makes up what is probably the best book of imaginative writing that the English literature of the Twentieth Century can yet show" (from *The Smart Set:* December 1922).

6. There exists no proof that Conrad knew Freud's works. He returned Freud's books to André Gide without having opened them. *Lord Jim,* as Gustav Morf points out (in *A Critical Symposium,* p. 141), "is more than a psychological novel, it is a psychoanalytical novel *written before psychoanalysis was founded."* (Italics mine)

7. The nearer a work approaches art, Conrad declared, "the more it acquires a symbolic character. . . . All the great creations of literature have been symbolic, and in that way have gained in complexity, in power, in depth and in beauty." (In *Life and Letters,* II, 205.) Mere realism Conrad scoffed at. "You just stop short of being absolutely real," he wrote Arnold Bennett, "because you are faithful to your dogmas of realism. Now realism in art will never approach reality." And he goes on to say: "And your art, your gift, should be put to the service of a larger and freer faith" (I, 303). "It is in my scheming for effects," he told Richard Curle, "wherein all my 'art' consists. This, I suspect, has been the difficulty the critics felt in classifying it as romantic or realistic" (II, 317).

8. As Thomas Mann asserts, it is "a limitation of Conrad's fame to speak of him only as a writer of sea-tales." (In *A Critical Symposium,* p. 228) Conrad "disliked being labeled a novelist of the sea. He wrote of the sea, as perhaps no one, not even Herman Melville, has written; but dominant in all his writing of the sea is the note of struggle and escape. His hero is not the sea, but man in conflict with that cruel and treacherous element. Ships he loved, but the sea —no." John Galsworthy in *Two Essays on Conrad* (Privately Printed, Freelands, 1930, pp. 46-47).

9. What Conrad "most despised in life was ill-educated theory, and what he most hated blatancy and pretence. He smelled it coming round the corner and at once his bristles would rise." (Galsworthy in *Two Essays on Conrad,* p. 54.)

10. David Daiches's review stands at several points in essential agreement; namely that Guerard's *Conrad the Novelist* is the best critical book on Conrad yet written, that the essays on *Nigger* and *Lord Jim* "can stand as easily the best and fullest critical accounts of these novels," and that *Victory* deserves to be expunged from the list of Conrad's best works. (In New York *Times Book Review:* August 17, 1958, pp. 4, 18.) The connection both Guerard and Moser make between *Lord Jim* and Scott Fitzgerald's *The Great Gatsby,* that Nick Carraway derives from the evasive and moralizing Marlow (see page 34 of *Lord Jim*), was first made in my "Conrad and *The Great Gatsby,*" *Twentieth Century Literature,* I, No. 1 (April 1955).

*PART ONE*

# ANDRÉ GIDE

## Joseph Conrad*

### *(Translated from the French by Charles Owen)*

"I WONDER IF IT'S THE END," I was reading in a letter dated May 30, the last that I received from him; cordial as usual, and like the others penetrated by that sort of bitter liveliness, that slightly unwilling charm, which gave a sea-tang to his friendly impulses; but marked already with a mysterious solemnity, with the presentiment of death.

That letter touched me to the quick like a farewell. I felt myself in arrears with him. I had gone a long time without seeing him again, without writing him. Had I ever been able to tell him—what I wrote him immediately—all the affection, admiration, veneration, which despite so much absence, so much silence, I had never ceased to feel for him? He was the only one of my elders that I loved and knew.

"Here it is almost four years that I've produced nothing of value. Instead I've developed asthma. It's maddening enough. What consoles me is the success (modest, I agree) of the French translations."

Conrad loved France far too much not to attach the greatest importance to French opinion of his work. He was still known only to a small group of admirers. Not till the announcement of his death did the press show any concern. Then they seemed to understand abruptly who it was we had lost.

Claudel was the one who made me aware of Conrad. I am still grateful to him. After a lunch together, as some other companion was speaking enthusiastically about Kipling, Claudel with a slightly disdainful smile threw out the name of Conrad. Not a one of us had yet heard of him.

"What should we read of his?" some one asked.

"Everything," said Claudel. And he cited *The Nigger of the "Narcissus"*, *Youth, Typhoon, Lord Jim. . . .*" None of these books had been translated as yet. I immediately took note of their titles and at my first contact with them was completely won over.

Shortly after, on a trip to England, I had the opportunity of meeting the author in person. Valery Larbaud (if my recollection is correct) went with me. Miss Tobin, a charming young English woman whom Larbaud knew, was to introduce us. Conrad was living then in Kent at Capel House, a small country place near Ashford; it was there that he received us. I lingered several days in the vicinity; returned to Capel House the next year, and we were soon the warmest and best of friends.

* *La Nouvelle Revue française*, Nouvelle série, CXXXV (Paris, December 1, 1924), 649-806, published "Hommage à Joseph Conrad," of which the essays by André Gide, H. R. Lenormand, and Ramon Fernandez are selections here translated anew.

3

Conrad did not like to talk about his life; a sort of modesty, a lack of regard for himself restrained him and kept him silent on his past. His memories of the sea seemed to him now only the raw material for his art, and, because the requirements of his art, as they became involved, constrained him to transpose, to depersonalize and distance from himself by fiction everything he had experienced personally, he was singularly awkward, both in his books and in his conversation, as a raconteur; only in fiction did he feel at his ease.

The sea to him was like an old abandoned mistress whom only an engraving, the picture of a superb sailing vessel in the hall of Capel House, recalled nostalgically to memory.

"Don't look at that," he said as he drew me into the parlor while I was studying that symbol of his first love. "Let's talk books."

Conrad had married, "settled down"; lived with his wife and children, but by and for books. How well he knew our authors. He admired Flaubert and Maupassant and enjoyed talking about them. He especially liked our critics and Lemaître most of all. He didn't care much for Barrès; it's not hard to imagine what this perfect example of man uprooted thought of theories of *déracinement*. As he pronounced opinions only on what he knew, his judgments were very firm; but as they accorded with mine, our conversations went smoothly. On one point only we could not agree: the name even of Dostoievsky made him shudder. I think some journalists, by awkward comparisons, had intensified his exasperation, as a good Pole, against the great Russian; with whom nonetheless he had some subtle points of resemblance, but whom he detested cordially and whom one could not mention without calling up anew his vehement indignation. I should have liked to know what it was he disliked in Dostoievsky's books, but could get from him only vague imprecations.

The first evening I spent at Capel House the discussion just missed being stormy. But this time I was in the same camp with him. Wasn't Miss Tobin taking the liberty of praising Georges Ohnet to the skies? We objected. She held her ground, kept defending her man with arguments that seemed to us absurd, monstrous, speaking of the "restrained brilliance," the "quiet richness" of his art. Conrad got more and more upset, until, Miss Tobin calling Walter Pater to the rescue, we realized suddenly that she was talking not about the author of the too famous *Maître de Forges*, but instead about Giorgione, whose name she was pronouncing in the Italian manner in such a way as to permit the mistake in identity. It had gone on almost an hour. Conrad was at once like a child in his delight over the incident.

Nothing was more cordial, purer, or more virile, than his laughter, than his appearance, than his voice. But like the sea in its moments of calm you felt him capable of violent passion, of tempests. Great as was his curiosity for the dark places in man's soul, he detested any exhibition of the underhanded, the equivocal, or the vile. And I think what I liked best in him was a sort of inherent nobility, rugged, disdainful, and a little despairing, the same quality that he gave Lord Jim and that makes that book one of the most beautiful I know, one of the saddest too, and at the same time one of the most uplifting.[1]

Somebody else will have to speak of the instruction to be drawn from his works, especially since it is the fashion now to search out the lessons in everything. I think the works of Conrad are as profitable as it is possible for art to be today, when on the one hand the study of man tends to turn novelists away from life, and on the other hand the love of life tends to discredit letters. Nobody had lived more savagely than Conrad; nobody had then submitted life to so patient, sensitive, and knowing a transmutation into art.                                                   (1924)

### NOTES

1. In his *Journal 1889-1939,* 23 Fevrier, 1930, p. 971, André Gide writes: "Much interested by the relationship I discover between *Under Western Eyes* and *Lord Jim.* (I regret not having spoken of this with Conrad.) That *irresponsible* act of the hero, to redeem which his whole life is subsequently engaged. For the thing that leads to the heaviest responsibility is just the *irresponsibilities* in a life. How can one efface that act? There is no more pathetic subject for a novel, nor one that has been more stifled in our literature by belief in Boileau's rule: that the hero must remain, from one end to the other of a drama or a novel, 'such as he was first seen to be.' " *The Journals of André Gide,* translated by Justin O'Brien, Vol. III (1949), pp. 94-95. Quoted in M. D. Zabel's Introduction to *Lord Jim* (Houghton Mifflin, 1958), p. xxx. [Editor's note]

## H. R. LENORMAND

## Note on a Sojourn of Conrad in Corsica*
### *(Excerpt, translated from the French by Charles Owen)*

FROM OUR FIRST MEETINGS he had made no secret of the difficulties he was having with his work. We were walking one evening in Ajaccio. The gas had failed in the street lights, and the pitch black of the sky came right down to the surface of the sidewalks. While passing a brushfire some street urchins had lit under a palm tree, he told me he was putting his papers in order. He spoke to me of his will, of his heirs. He was thinking about death and no longer hoped to write the novel which had motivated the trip to Corsica. I knew that the spectres of fatigue and of creative inertia were haunting him. The only really tragic cry that a writer may utter: "I can no longer work!" sounded almost daily in his conversation. Spasms

* From *La Nouvelle Revue française,* Nouvelle série, CXXXV (Paris, December 1, 1924).

of anxiety shook his composure. The difficulties which hobbled progress in the realization of his present artistic aims served as pretext for him to question once again the success of all the other works. I have not forgotten the feeling of astonishment and pity combined, the sort of fraternal terror which came over me, the day I heard him tell me: "I can't find the words to match my thought. I'm never sure what it is I'm affirming. I am out of my mind." The man whose scruples led him to make such a sickly estimate of himself had written the ten novels and the twenty short stories which live on in our minds. Never had doubt more clearly appeared to me as one of the signs of greatness.

This anguish, which in moments of despair made him question even his power to write, did not leave him in the more lucid intervals when he tried to judge his work, to figure out the place it would occupy in literature, to define the relationships between the artist and his art. Each time we began to strip bare the psychological truths which concentrate behind the figures of Lord Jim or Almayer, he would break off as if frightened and murmur: "I'm nothing but a storyteller." But an instant later he would say, "I find myself too sensitive; I've lost all innocence." And I realized that the unmasked faces of his characters had just appeared to him. He alternated between the fear of having made the clouds around them too opaque, and that of having destroyed their mystery in accounting for their motives.

I dared sometimes to wonder if he hadn't managed to deceive himself, voluntarily or not, on the true motives of his heroes. He blamed himself for too much insight, and yet perhaps the angel who lives blind and deaf and with wings folded in the innermost part of artists' souls and presides over the real meaning of their work had practised on him more than one benevolent deception.

One day while we were watching the daughter of his friend P pass by, a girl eighteen years old, whose distracted eyes and wild appearance made me think of the ostracized recluse Alice in "A Smile of Fortune," he said to me, "My whole life, I've been obsessed by the relationship of father to daughter." We talked about *Almayer's Folly*. "It's a book I wrote when I was thirty-six, without any aim. I had no idea I would become a man of letters. I wrote it in a single burst of inspiration and as if in spite of myself." I asked him if he had not had some intention of suggesting that Almayer's eclipse and fall were to be attributed to an unconscious feeling of the exile for his daughter, an incestuous passion hidden behind a paternal affection. He protested against the existence of such an emotion in his hero. When I pointed out to him the passages which had led me to that interpretation—the dreams of futile grandeur which Almayer fondly entertains for Nina, the alternating anger and exaltation which he feels in his child's presence, the murderous impulse which carries him violently against the man she loves, the scene which follows, punctuated throughout with flashes of jealousy,—Conrad was silent, obviously annoyed; then he changed the subject.

Several days later, with respect to *Lord Jim,* I realized that again I had awkwardly touched the point of estrangement between the author and his character. I had ventured into that zone where the fictive being enfolds himself in veils of hypocrisy and dupes his creator on the real nature of his deepest tendencies. We were talking of the incidents which impelled Jim to disappear, each time he met up with a witness of his past failure. "Sense of honor," maintained Conrad. And when I claimed that it would not have been difficult to give more accurate names to the phantoms that prevented the former officer of the Patna from experiencing peace of mind, when I tried to define from the evidence that kind of neurosis of conscience, that frenzy of responsibility from which he suffered, Conrad showed the same uneasiness as on the subject of Almayer. —"I don't want to get to the bottom," he told me. "I want to look on reality as something rough and coarse over which I pass my fingers. Nothing more."

Nothing more. But it was not only from indulgence that he allowed me to try out, on characters about whom I had passionately dreamed, hypotheses which classed them outside the range of feelings in which he intended to enclose them: I saw him question with anguish these beings in whom his genius, enamored of order and restraint, had none the less breathed a life of immense complexity. The children of his imagination stood before him, enlarged, disquieting, and posing enigmas which he didn't always dare to fathom. I was reading at the time *The Interpretation of Dreams and Wit and its Relation to the Unconscious,* the fine translations which Brill published of the two works of Freud. Conrad, who spoke of Freud with scornful irony, carried the books off to his room. He returned them to me on the eve of his departure without having opened them. Thus there was revealed to me the reserve of the artist toward his work and the wisdom of the creator who resolves finally not to force from his creatures their secrets.

I noted some of his preferences and some of his aversions. He praised highly Kipling, Hardy, and Bennett, but he detested Meredith, whose reputation seemed to him to be founded on the conscious bluff of one group of English critics. The false colors, the insipid exoticism of Hichens drew from him a hearty sarcasm. Severe toward Bret Harte, O'Henry, Frank T. Bullen, and even Hawthorne, he spoke of the French writers with a filial affection. Flaubert and Gide were well known to him. He admitted that he knew little of Strindberg. We said nothing about Dostoievsky, whose work seemed to him to exude "a bad and unbearable odor." He admired Turgeniev, "who had subjected all human activities to the test of love."

He urged me to write a novel, for which he had even found me a subject: the decline of men who had arrived at certainty. Our morning talks by the steps of the hotel, or in the evening, in the small living room which he had them fix up for him, did not always leave me with an easy conscience. I knew that it would have been better not to awaken in his presence the dreaming host of his characters, to express by silence the respect and love which his genius inspired in me. But his generosity impelled him to enlighten me, to enrich me constantly, even at the expense of his own peace of mind. I should have liked to exorcise the demons of anguish and doubt which tormented his old age; I fear I only succeeded in exacerbating them.                                                                (1924)


RAMON FERNANDEZ


The Art of Conrad*

*(Translated from the French by Charles Owen)*


IN ALL THE WORKS of Conrad a great silence of the reason, a bold and solemn scorn of logical or rhetorical persuasion, holds sway. With what a fine perception of his medium did he assert that in a novel, as in all works of art, the appeal of one temperament to other temperaments "must be an impression conveyed through the senses," since the problem is one of fixing "passing events" by recreating "the moral, the emotional atmosphere of the place and time."[1] He kept his promise. Few writers have so faithfully, so continually allowed the tangible reality to speak for them, interpreting it but rarely, and then with infinite prudence, and remaining under the immediate influence of its mystery. From beginning to end of his patiently executed works, he persists, not without effort but almost always with success, in overwhelming us with sensations, in saturating us in colors, in sounds, in human voices, in contacts, in visions, in atmospheres, in leaving us vibrant with the thousand emanations from a world which rather understands us than which we understand. And few writers have more knowingly hidden their universe from the grasp of the intelligence. By this very skill in projecting the mystery (which has nothing in common with the somewhat scenic effects of Stevenson) Conrad sets himself off from his fellow Slavs. For them the world is in fact incomprehensible and sometimes, yes sometimes, in spite of themselves; with Conrad on the other hand the precise intelligence of man as observer comes to terms with the emotion of man as actor, but the intelligence instead of interpreting the experience, calls up through creation of an atmospheric picture, the obscure coming into being of the event. A thoughtful mastery of things beyond the grasp of thought, such is the impression which his best books leave on us.

* From *La Nouvelle Revue française,* Nouvelle série, CXXXV (Paris, December 1, 1924). In *Messages,* translated by Montgomery Belgion (Harcourt, 1927), pp. 137-151.

This elaborate impressionism Conrad carries to a point of perfection the more remarkable in that he most often conjures up frenetic actions or indefinable sensations. He takes advantage neither of the withdrawal of a Pater nor of the slow pace of a Proust; for all the impressions communicated there is the added impression of rapidity, of suddenness, of the startling,—the disconnected and confused vision of the dream. From a reading or rereading of his storm scenes comes the presentiment that the one who could not simply recall but develop and bring out by imagery the subtlest shadings of these catastrophic experiences must have made one with him who created them to begin with, and in fact this creative passivity does have something of the divine in it. An impressionism moreover totally subjective. The vision of Conrad concentrates in all its elaboration on the point in our emotional life when the perceptions come to focus and form a moment in our inner consciousness. ". . . in the still streak of very bright pale orange light I saw the land profiled flatly as if cut out of black paper and seeming to float on the water as light as cork."[2] All the physical details are recalled in these pictures, but at the moment of their arrival at and of their fusion into the impression. "The smiling greatness of the sea dwarfed the extent of time. The days raced after one another, brilliant and quick like the flashes of a lighthouse, and the nights, eventful and short, resembled fleeting dreams." (*Nigger of the "Narcissus"*, p. 30) Here the impression extends to a period; it is not a narrative, but rather a *personal memory* that we are given in these pages. Such an art could be compared to a graphic projection, a map. Just as this little gray hatching must represent a mountain, so such pictures of Conrad, inevitable, contain in their immaterial substance a whole ship toiling under the wind in a night without stars. There is an exact equivalence, the projection on the emotional plane corresponding to the precise interrelationships of reality.

The art of Conrad is then the opposite of a descriptive art like Balzac's; it does not trace the reality before man but the man in face of reality; it evokes subjectively integrated experiences because the impression is equivalent to the totality of the perception and because the man suffers it in its entirety and with all his might. His great originality is in having applied this impressionism to the awareness of human beings. "You know," says Marlow, "that I saw him only on that one occasion I told you of. But it may be that a glimpse and no more is the proper way of seeing an individuality." (*Chance*, p. 85) Marlow no doubt deals habitually in irony, but set his sally beside this judgment of Sir Hugh Clifford: "Sir Frank Swettenham and I were agreed that its author's pictures of Malays (in *Almayer's Folly*) were the result, as it were, of a series of flash-light impressions absorbed by a mind of strangely sensitive and imaginative quality, rather than of any deep understanding of the people we both knew so well." ("Joseph Conrad: Some Scattered Memories," by Sir Hugh Clifford, *Bookman's Journal*, XI, p. 3) All of which does not prevent Sir Hugh from exclaiming at the miracle, and us with him, when we see these "flash-light impressions" succeed in sculpting the dark and vibrant figure of Lord Jim. We are surely here on a natural gradient of Conrad's genius: catching a glimpse is the best way of seeing because it is the best way of preserving the human element as if embalmed in our impression and at the same time respecting its living impenetrability. Human emanations are gathered by Conrad in the same way and in the same spirit as the emanations of concrete reality, beneath the level of concepts, and in a state of emotional grace.

In the same spirit of fidelity and abandonment to life Conrad fashions his sumptuous emotive web. He is not content merely to replace narrative by an immediate evocation of the reality of the senses: he devotes himself to seizing things as they come into being, in their formative stages, and so to speak on the hither side of their definition. What I mean is that we experience them before it's possible to define them, to give them a name. ". . . I became bothered by curious, irregular sounds of faint tapping on the deck. They could be heard single, in pairs, in groups. While I wondered at this mysterious devilry, I received a slight blow under the left eye and felt an enormous tear run down my cheek. Raindrops. Enormous. Forerunners of something. Tap. Tap. Tap. . . ." (*The Shadow Line*, p. 113). It is a co-nascence, conforming to the definition Claudel gave of the word. There is transmitted to us a picture of the event possessing the qualities of recollection, of a selective, emotional, and personal recollection, since the recall to memory has as its unique vehicle the shadings of the impression *before* its elucidation by comparison and ratiocination. Conrad applies the same procedure to men. One can say that his characters become palpable, project themselves on our senses, react on our souls; then go moving, enigmatic and alive, in our imaginations. Their mystery is not at all artificial, being simply the result of the incommensurability by thought of what is immediately apprehended by the senses. There are two kinds of mystery: that of things skillfully hidden from us, and that of things we are made to feel completely. The first proceeds from an intellectual construct; the second from a shift in the natural trend of the mind, from our immersion in the life we were before skimming over. That great silence which surrounds Conrad's characters is no less than the complement of the reality of their being.

Those who have read nothing by him but *Chance*, or *Nostromo*, or even *Lord Jim* will hardly approve of these remarks. There is to be sure a great deal of talk in certain of Conrad's books where Marlow makes agitated comment on the actions of his fellows. Conrad has in fact two very different manners, related however by characteristics common to both. Most of his sea stories (*The Nigger of the "Narcissus"*, *The Shadow Line*, "Typhoon," etc.) evoke directly the collective adventure of a ship by a series of perceptions which combine to create an authentic drama, an oppressive present full of hallucinations. These adventures, by the pace and rush of the action, by the pressure of the atmosphere and the violence of nervous discharge, recall the Greek tragedies. They have as their dominant note an extremely painful physical tension around which moral reactions find definition. Tests of human resistance to its very limits, they are remarkable for total absence of breathing space, of play: the men are overwhelmed by the brutal mass of the event. The best stories at their best moments are like maelstroms of feeling which whirl the human mechanism around at abnormal speed. It is at these moments when it actually seems that the man may be obliterated by his very resistance that what there is of the purely human in him reveals itself most startlingly. But each man exists only as a function of his companions; all the existences are as you might say imbricated one on the other and the dramatic present is made up of their conjoined presences. The second manner which *Lord Jim* and *Chance* represent each in its own genre, corresponds to periods of holiday and relaxation. There everything is rest, meditation, nonchalance. The narrator, fully self-possessed, recalls less his own experience than that of others. The evocation is at second hand, it transforms slowly and minutely the past into the present. Chronology is so little regarded that frequently we start in on the future of the story. The word finally, the word as expression of intelligence, recovers its power, replaces the interjections and the curt commands. To be particularly noted in these stories is the combination of recollections and the peculiar nature of the psychological commentary.

Conrad gives several witnesses the chance to speak, and they pass the narrative back and forth to one another. Of the same story he gives us different colorations, the shadings, the observations, the profundity of psychological insight varying with the witness. In addition each of the testimonies is discussed critically by the narrator in chief, Marlow. Hence reality seems composed of pieces brought back and sewn together haphazardly by the author, but what a magnificent art lies hidden in this apparent disorder! Conrad in fact arranges the different views of the same experience in such a way as to produce an effect of transparent superposition. By presenting a series of ordered reflections of life, he obtains a stereoscopic depth. In conformity with the procedure which we've indicated, the smallest episode, indeed, the slightest occurrence, calls up a recollection which becomes actual, substituting a new present for the preceding one. All these presents, which summon, succeed, intersect one another, give an impression of fluttering brilliance which may tire or perplex the reader. The artistic result is none the less remarkable: by about the middle of the book, that personal memory of which we were speaking earlier has been built up, the reader has experienced the characters through a series of unexpected impacts, just as in life.

As for the psychological commentary, it is presented to us merely as *probable*. That is, it never intervenes in the determination of the character. Simply a series of suppositions, hypotheses, it remains tangential to reality; it follows that the opacity of the individual, of the scene is never completely dissipated—directly at least—since, to the fullest extent, the analysis sustains instead of dissolving that breadth of mystery which is the refuge of life. The slight uncertainty makes it constantly glance off, the event is at the same time realized and impenetrable.[3] From another angle the completely tentative quality of the commentary throws the weight of the narrative on to the acuteness of the reader's intuition. We await from the scene, from the impressions which it will bring to life in us, the illumination of the story, the verification of the hypotheses, all of which results in concentrating our attention to the utmost.[4]

Conrad's world presupposes a presence, a subject on whose body that world comes breaking and reflected like a wave. His personalities themselves are outlined in hollows by their reflection on the witnesses. This co-nascence implies an absolute passiveness, to some extent metaphysical. However—and it is here, in my opinion, that Conrad distinguishes himself from the other impressionists and far surpasses them—this observer brings and defends something preciously personal in his confrontation with the inhuman forces of the universe. This precious possession includes the man's aspirations as he faces his ordeal and his desire to retain his integrity and his trustworthiness throughout its course. To doubt "his own fitness to conduct his existence." ("The Duel" from *A Set of Six,* p. 247) is for Conrad the most dismal of weaknesses. "Wherever he stands," he writes elsewhere, "at the beginning or the end of things, a man has to sacrifice his gods to his passions or his passions to his gods. That is the problem, great enough, in all truth, if approached in the spirit of sincerity and knowledge." (*Notes on Life and Letters:* "Henry James," p. 16). But the nature of Conrad's experience gave a singularly striking form to this eternal struggle. The will of the sailor, frequently incommensurable with events, manifests itself by a concentration of its force rather than by an expansion. The captain, Conrad's admirable master, imposes himself less than he hangs on, and he hangs on beyond feeling, and his resistance modifies the world of the elements and the world of men. He hangs on, he is *present,* and after the typhoon his *"J'ai vécu"*[5] would mean "I've been a man." Resistance which has its counterpart in the ease with which the strong man in Conrad reveals himself to other men, suffers infection from them in that virtuous complicity which is palpable throughout in *Lord Jim* and of which the "Secret Sharer" provides the finest expression. We will perhaps never find again in the novel and in the drama the marvelous concurrence of this double loyalty, loyalty towards life as it is, loyalty towards man as he wills to be—the product of a genius, of a character, of an experience equally exceptional. No supreme art, however, without this concurrence.[6] Reading Conrad, I often think of a famous saying by Henri Poincaré, which the former invites us to mitigate, to enrich and fully humanize: man is only a feeble gleam in the tempest, but that gleam resists and that gleam is everything.                                                                  (1924)

NOTES

1. *Nigger of the "Narcissus"*, preface, p. XIII. Page references to Conrad are to the Kent edition, Garden City, N. Y., 1926. [Editor's note: The Kent edition of Conrad's collected works, published by Doubleday, has the same pagination as the Uniform Edition (1923) and the Present Collected Edition (1946) published by J. M. Dent and Sons Ltd.]

2. *Shadow Line* p. 77. This quotation and the following ones give but a very insufficient insight into Conrad's style. These pictures, far from being exceptional, are the very tissue of the text.

3. Equally to be noted is the procedure which consists in imagining scenes which the narrator did not witness. By this placing in the foreground of technical resources which the novelist ordinarily leaves out of sight, Conrad gives to his narratives an exquisite flavor of dream and of probity.

4. See especially the admirable scene of the attempted poisoning in *Chance.*

5. For Conrad's own *"J'ai vécu,"* see *A Personal Record,* p. 94. [Translator's Note]

6. In this brief analysis of Conrad's art, I thought it appropriate to pass over in silence the criticisms one could apply to him. Flaubert didn't always have the best influence on him. His sentences are sometimes overwritten, and the inevitable *and* which precedes the final proposition makes them somewhat monotonous. Occasionally too this magnificent evoker of emotions falls into a purely descriptive art. But the vision called up is ordinarily independent of the wording which only becomes obtrusive when the inspiration slackens. Finally, however beautiful a novel like *Nostromo*, it seems to me to have an artificial air, a little laboured. I would say as much of the first part of *Chance,* so beautiful and so successful in other respects. I would subscribe wholeheartedly to this judgment of the *Times Literary Supplement*: "He never believed in his later and more highly sophisticated characters as he had believed in his early sea men."

JOHN SHAND

Some Notes on Joseph Conrad*

JOSEPH CONRAD was a fine writer, and, I believe, some of his books will be regarded by posterity as part of the heritage in English literature. But he had many faults, and, in the later novels, his vices began to exceed his virtues. In *The Arrow of Gold* and in *The Rescue,* we find him ignoring and even adding to his literary sins. His prose, never very simple, became more and more ornate, and his trick of talking about his characters, instead of showing them to us directly, grew to the point of absurdity. Indeed it is noticeable that his style is most simple and direct in his epic tales of men's struggles with the sea, which are the stories most likely to last; and most clumsy and deliberately picturesque in his "psychological"

* From *The Criterion,* III (October 1924—July 1925), 6-14.

novels, which will the soonest be forgotten. Yet, surprisingly, in the last volume published before Conrad's death, *The Rover,* though it cannot really be called a sea-tale, we find him throwing overboard his long, heavily-adjectived descriptions, his obscurities, his involved construction, all, in fact, that cargo of faults which was sinking him. But strictly speaking this sudden change is not surprising, for it has happened once before— in *The Shadow Line;* which, in point of time, is quite a late book, but, in point of style, belongs to an earlier period. *The Shadow Line,* in simplicity of narration and directness of construction, belongs to *The Nigger of the "Narcissus",* and *The Mirror of the Sea.* Of *The Rover* this can be said also. It is tragic that we shall not be able to see now whether this time the conversion was to be lasting.

Conrad's style is very characteristic. It is slow, heavy, and rather involved, especially in descriptive passages. For Conrad, always a serious artist, is most serious in his descriptions, and seems so anxious to make his readers see all the details of a setting that he often obscures the picture instead of revealing it. He is always inclined to squeeze the last possible word into a sentence, the last possible sentence into a paragraph, and when he sometimes desires to be brief he goes to the other extreme, and writes short, staccato sentences. His extreme use of the simile I shall note later, and his continual use of three adjectives to qualify one object has become obvious even to parodists.

Certainly Conrad's rather "heavy" vocabulary and, in the later psychological novels, his methods of telling the story and presenting the characters are partly due to Henry James. And if his paragraphs are not so tortuous and top-heavy as those of the later Henry James, he is often too obviously under his influence; than whom he could not have chosen a worse model. When I say this, I hope it does not read as if I despised Henry James, for, indeed, I have a great respect for him. What I am objecting to is that Conrad has copied his faults rather than improved on his virtues. For Conrad, as I have said, seems naturally inclined to verbosity; and, as verbosity is as much a vice in literature as it is in conversation, I think I am right in saying that Henry James was the last person he should have studied; and when I say that Conrad has, to a large extent, taken him as a model, I have not only the evidence of my eyes, but also Conrad's word that James is the novelist he most admires and most desires to imitate.[1]

I sometimes imagine that I can see Conrad at his desk leaning over his blank sheets of paper, and for a long while rolling the words of a sentence, the sentences of a paragraph, round his tongue. Remembering perhaps that certain adjectives such as "sombre," or "tropical," must not be used too often; that certain phrases such as "impenetrable forests," or "the illimitable horizon of the sea," must not be worn to death. Then slowly, lovingly, he begins to write what he has so very carefully thought out; using sometimes two pages to a paragraph in his endeavour to make the reader understand, with as vivid an apprehension as his own, the emotions of his characters or the unfeeling beauty of the surrounding world. For instance, the emotional state of Lord Jim after his disgrace; or the gorgeous sunset that fades over the calm sea as Almayer, full of sorrow and despair, watches the daughter whom he loved so much being taken from him. But it is not only because he wishes the reader to feel and to understand so well that Conrad so often overloads his nouns with adjectives, and his sentences with similes: it is also because he is too much in love with the sound of words and the rhythms of his sentences. In so far as the heaviness of his prose is due to his desire to make his readers realise the tragedy, or the ironic comedy, of a situation, I can forgive it, although I do not believe his method to be the best one to obtain the effect desired; but so far as it is merely a striving for opulent word-painting and beautifully cadenced sentences, I must, and do, dislike it.

In the preceding paragraph I remarked that Conrad overloads his descriptions with similes. Now, though nothing is more expressive than an apt simile, nothing is so annoying when unsuitable or out of place; and as Conrad uses this device so frequently the occasional infelicity of his choice is more unpleasing then it would be if he were to use it less often. For using the simile as much as he does begins to make a reader annoyed at the appearance even of a good one; and when the simile is unsuitable or unnecessary, annoyance becomes disgust. I do not think I exaggerate when I say that hardly a page, and never a description of any length, but will contain at least one simile more or less apt; but that sometimes his similes are so far-fetched and unnecessary that they serve more to irritate than to illuminate; and a good explanation of this extravagant usage is, I think, that Conrad is a foreigner; a fact that can never be forgotten, although he writes better English than most modern novelists. Conrad has himself remarked that if he writes in English he still thinks in his native Polish; and it is noticeable that when one is speaking, or trying to speak, in a foreign tongue, one is as apt to use the simile in speech as to use the hands in gesture.

It once occurred to me while reading one of Conrad's books, and I have since confirmed my suspicion beyond all doubt, that the idea behind all his description of backgrounds is this: he tries to make us feel that Nature is watching the behaviour, and observing the thoughts, of his characters, even while she remains entirely indifferent to their joys and sufferings. By giving Nature a mind to reflect on the ephemeral lives of his men and women, he gives the impression that the gods themselves are watching the human comedy with ironic eyes; and by impressing on us at the same time Nature's absolute indifference, he throws into higher relief the passions and sorrows of his characters. This method also vaguely impresses us with the idea that the author himself is something of a god; but that is a minor effect. The great effect is, of course, that the reader is made to feel that, however important his characters may think themselves, Nature, to say nothing of Humanity as a whole, cares nothing for them or for their feelings; and this impression induces in us that resignation to the decrees of Fate which is the essence of Conrad's philosophy; that mood of thought in which most of his characters live, and in which most of his books are written. As we read on we begin to feel, as Conrad apparently does, that Fate is ineluctable: that that which is to be is as unalterable as that which is past, and we begin to feel that, do what we may, Death is the end of all that lives; the sole absolution; and the last consolation for those who find, in Captain Lingard's phrase, that "life is very long."

The following piece of prose, which I swear I have selected at random, and which is therefore perhaps not the best example that could be found to illustrate my idea, is taken from one of the earliest of his novels:

"The big sombre tree . . . condemned to look for ever at the incomprehensible afflictions or joys of mankind, assent in their aspect of cool unconcern the high dignity of lifeless matter that surrounds, incurious and removed, the restless mysteries of the ever-changing, of the never-ending life . . ."

I think this example serves as sufficient illustration of the idea which I believe lies behind all his descriptions of backgrounds, and it shows, as well, Conrad's incorrigible love of adjectives. It is simply packed with words, for he wants to get too much in. I believe he must be able to visualise quite perfectly the scene he is describing, and in his desire to make it as real to us he forgets that minute detail makes it more difficult for us to see what he intends. For instance, look at this sentence taken from "The End of the Tether:"

". . . Captain Whalley stopped short on the apex of a small bridge spanning steeply the bed of a canalised creek with granite shores."

But of that the less said the better. He writes like that too often, however, not to irritate me sometimes into remonstrance.

Someone once told me that Conrad tried his patience too often to balance the pleasure that much of his writing gave him; he further remarked that Conrad was too laboured, did not get on with his story fast enough, and, occasionally, elaborated the obvious beyond endurance. I agree that these charges are not unjust; but I cannot help saying that, although Conrad is deliberately leisured in his prose and in the unfolding of his plot, there is nothing intrinsically wrong in being slow; it is the reader's impatience that had something to do with that criticism. It is true that he digresses too much: that is a fault; but his digressions are a necessary complement to his method of telling a story—an intensely realistic method. Conrad is very conscientious. He tries to make every situation, every chance happening, every action of his characters, seem absolutely inevitable. Another reason for his digressions and sometimes confusing involutions is that he really tells the history of a character from the "outside." He learns everything by hearsay, or by observing the movements and listening to the conversation of his characters; and the natural result of this method of telling a story is the appearance of "Marlow," who tells several of the stories in the first person singular to an invisible but appreciative audience of which, it is supposed, Conrad is a member. This method, though difficult is a perfectly legitimate one; and when well done gives a great sensation of reality. Telling a story from "inside," as if, I mean, the author were constantly popping in and out each person's head as occasion requires, is certainly simpler but often less convincing. There is something to be said for and against both methods, but certainly Conrad's is the most boring when not well done; it therefore demands that care which he so obviously bestows on his work. It may be said, then, that it is this digressional method which gives an air of reality to his stories, though it may be added that it sometimes gives reality to what would otherwise be a bald and unconvincing narrative.

As an example of this digressional method being used to advantage, I refer to the arrival of Gentleman Jones and his gang of ruffians towards the end of *Lord Jim*.[2] Their appearance at the very out-of-the-way Malay village where Lord Jim has fled to hide himself from the world is necessary in order to bring about his tragic end; and Conrad, in a digression showing us exactly the kind of person Gentleman Jones was, and something of what he had been doing before his arrival at Jim's refuge,[3] makes his appearance with his set of ruffians so natural, so inevitable, that you are not in the slightest degree disturbed by it; nor do you feel that the author is loading the dice against his character. That this appearance of reality should be produced is a tribute to Conrad's art and a justification of his digression; for it is absolutely necessary that we should feel this inevitability if the whole tragedy of Jim's failure and death is to be realised.

But a method becomes a monomania when it is carried too far, and Conrad has committed the error of exalting the part above the whole and has turned his method into a madness; and his method being what it is, it has naturally increased that prolixity and vagueness which have always been his worst faults. But to say this is to say that he can no longer write a novel; for the duty of a novelist is to please, and Conrad, though he used to make his reader feel the reality of his story, now makes him feel bored and mystified. Conrad was at first, I expect, unconscious in his choice of a method, but naturally becoming conscious of its value he deliberately cultivated it until, in his latest novels, he has carried it to such a point that it serves more to hide his story than to reveal it, and obscures his wonderful observation of character with lengthy digressions and unnecessary interpolations. His innate seriousness has also helped to bring this about, and his irony is, of course, only the other side of his seriousness. Like James, his humour is elephantine; and he only looks awkward when he tries to be funny; and when we remember, too, that Conrad has always felt so strongly the mystery of life and the incomprehensibility of men's behaviour, we have, I think, part of the secret of his degeneration as a writer. From an artistic point of view Conrad has come to puzzle too much about the profound complexities that lie behind the superficial actions and sayings of mankind, the thousand and one turns of fate that bring about a given situation. He has become too fond of gazing at the Sphinx in all its forms. In man and in matter he is always finding inscrutable intentions; impenetrable men and impenetrable forests and impenetrable the Destiny that causes both to live and die; and Conrad seems not so much to like puzzling about the Sphinx as being puzzled by it: he is, in fact, inclined to sentimentalise about the Infinite. The only thing he seems quite certain about is the meaning of life. It has none, but is only "a mysterious arrangement of merciless logic for a futile purpose."

Now, though this attitude of stoical hopelessness is consistent throughout his books, it is no more than an attitude, though it may be a sincere one. I do not believe that at bottom Conrad thinks that life is futile and unmeaning, for I do not believe that any artist could have created such fine tales as *The Nigger of the "Narcissus,"* "Typhoon," or, best of all, *The Shadow Line,* if he honestly and consistently considered that life was not worth living. And the explanation of this pessimistic pose is, I think, that Conrad is romantic. His pessimism is the intellectual reaction of a disillusioned romanticist to the realities of existence. Owing to the fact that he had to "rough it" for twenty years in that most arduous and disillusioning profession for "romantics"—a sailor's—he had to triumph over the loss of his illusions by adopting a pessimistic attitude. And he was helped to this triumph by the fact that, like everyone else, however sordid and unpleasant any particular incidents might have been, he was able to see them in retrospect behind a veil of romance; and being an artist as well as an ordinary human being, he had the consolation of being able to project in his imagination a world and people of his own creation, which by force of will he was able to translate into the comparative reality of a written story.

That Conrad is essentially romantic we have only to read his stories to see at once. Take *Lord Jim,* for example, or *Victory,* or, better still, *The Mirror of the Sea,* which is not a novel, but a collection of personal experiences and recollections. Observe how romantic is his vision of the Thames as he is towed up from the estuary to the docks for the first time! How very romantic, even while he remains a practical seaman at the same time. For you cannot stand star-gazing while your ship is being towed up a crowded river! So do not think that I mean to imply that Conrad was a romantic fool; for it is certain that he was as efficient in the discharge of his duties as he was romantic in his outlook on life, or he would not have risen to be chief mate in the British Mercantile Marine. *The Mirror of the Sea* is, by the way, Conrad's valediction to his ocean life. It is obvious that he loves the sea and the white-sailed ships which used to go from London docks to all the ports of the world; and he will always be wishing them back again; though to-day those ships have vanished. "Money and men's greed have conquered the sea; the romantic but slow and uncertain, therefore unprofitable, sailing-ship has become almost extinct, and the sea, once a proud, cruel, but wonderful mistress to those who loved her, has become a worn-out drudge, bespattered with the oil, soot, and refuse of steamers that care neither for the tide, the wind, nor the waves." Which simile is surely the exaggeration of a disillusioned romanticist.

But Conrad is a poet as well as a pessimist. No one but a poet could have written some of his passages of descriptive prose; being emotionally felt by the writer the scene is vividly realised by the reader. Some of the scenes he has described in this manner I shall not easily forget. Some of the incidents, for instance, in *The Shadow Line,* which I consider the best of all his stories. It is a prose epic of two men's struggles with a becalmed ship and a crew all stricken with malaria. The story is based on an adventure of the author's and, he says, is practically autobiography. This may or may not account for the simplicity of the diction and the directness of the narrative; the fact remains that *The Shadow Line* is the least marred by the faults which I have noted above. Most of his other stories are more or less spoilt by his digressional methods and too deliberately elaborate prose.                                              (1924)

## NOTES

1. The best essay on this subject is E. K. Brown's "James and Conrad," *Yale Review,* XXXV (1945), 265-285. [Editor's note]
2. Shand has confused *Lord Jim* with *Victory.* Gentleman Jones does not belong to *Lord Jim;* he appears only in *Victory.* It is Brown who makes his appearance at Patusan, where Jim as Tuan Jim rules. [Editor's note]
3. Gentleman Jones arrives at Heyst's refuge on Round Island. (Jim's refuge is Patusan in *Lord Jim.*) [Editor's note]

# M. D. ZABEL

## Chance and Recognition*

CONRAD'S TITLE PAGES always taxed his scruples as severely as any part of his manuscripts, not always to his own satisfaction or to ours in the titles he arrived at, but with notable success in the epigraphs he placed below them. These he used consistently. Mrs. Conrad has said that they were always chosen with extreme care, Conrad taking pains that these "quotations had always a close and direct relation to the contents of the book itself" and that they should express "the mood in which the work was written." Sometimes it is the mood whether of memory, pathos, irony,

* From *The Sewanee Review,* LIII (Winter 1945), pp. 1-23. Reprinted in *Critiques and Essays on Modern Fiction,* edited by John Aldridge (Ronald Press, 1952), pp. 270-285. Reprinted in M. D. Zabel's *Craft and Character in Modern Fiction* (Viking Press, 1957), pp. 147-167.

or tragic conviction, that is emphasized. More often the epigraph hints of the motive or attitude that directed Conrad's shaping of his material and the conception of experience it dramatizes.

The quotation he fixed below the title of *Lord Jim* is a clue not only to the narrative method which, in his long recitatives, monologues, and self-inquisitions, Conrad made his special instrument for the achieving of realism and form but to the psychological compulsion under which his characters, caught in the moral or circumstantial prisons of their lives, are forced to speak, and by which Conrad himself, if we trace his nature in his tales and personal writings, was compelled toward his special kind of art and revelation. "It is certain my conviction gains infinitely, the moment another soul will believe in it": Novalis's aphorism is a key to the necessity that is a source both of Conrad's imaginative method and of his appeal to psychological realists.

Sometimes the complex of fate requires solution by something more violent than an ordeal of personal exoneration. Shakespeare's "So foul a sky clears not without a storm" at the head of *Nostromo* suggests a prevailing symbol. When the novel is of a more exotic or melodramatic tendency, it sustains a sense of the marvelous or miraculous, of a thrilled response to the incredible turns and hazards of fate, of "marvels and mysteries acting upon our emotions and intelligence in ways so inexplicable that it would almost justify the conception of life as an enchanted state"—so reflecting the romantic tendency in Conrad's temperament that involved him in the fortunes of his career and that took a lifetime of discipline to bring to terms with the critical force of his moral intelligence. A French nursery rhyme sets the tone for *A Set of Six:* "Les petites marionnettes / Font, font, font, / Trois petits tours / Et puis s'en vont." A phrase from Boethius— ". . . for this miracle or this wonder troubleth me right gretly"—stands at the head of the autobiographical *Mirror of the Sea. Victory* begins under the spell of three lines from Milton's "Comus":

> Calling shapes and beckoning shadows dire
> And airy tongues that syllable men's names
> On sands and shores and desert wildernesses.

But there is another series of these quotations that indicates even more clearly the idea that possessed Conrad in his reading of experience. It was an idea that doubtless originated in a profoundly significant root-experience of his own temperament and history. He was to employ it as the incentive of his greatest tales. It is suggested repeatedly in his epigraphs from his first book to his last. The quotation on *Almayer's Folly* in 1895 is from Amiel: "Qui de nous n'a eu sa terre promise, son jour d'extase, et sa fin en exil?" Baudelaire's "D'autres fois, calme plat, grand miroir / De mon désespoir" serves as heading to *The Shadow Line* in 1917. An aphorism from La Bruyère acts as a clue to *The Arrow of Gold* in 1918: "Celui qui n'a connu que des hommes polie et raisonnables, ou ne connait pas l'homme, ou ne le connait qu'à demi." The motto for *The Rescue* in 1920 is from Chaucer's "Frankeleyn's Tale":

> "Alas!" quod she, "that ever this sholde happe!
> For wende I never, by possibilitee,
> That swich a monstre or merveille mighte be!"

Most specific of all, the quotation below the title of *Chance*, in 1913, is from Sir Thomas Browne: "Those that hold that all things are governed by Fortune had not erred, had they not persisted there."

The meaning and consistency of these passages is clear. They permit us to summarize briefly, if too simply, the basic theme of Conrad's fiction. His work dramatizes a hostility of forces that exists both in the conditions of practical life and in the moral constitution of man himself. Men who show any fundamental vitality of nature, will, or imagination are not initially men of caution, tact, or prudence, "polis et raisonnables," and they are certainly unlikely to remain so. They are possessed by an enthusiasm that makes them approach life as an adventure. They attack the struggle with all the impulsive force of their illusion, their pride, their idealism, their desire for fame and power, their confidence that Chance is a friend and Fortune a guide who will lead them to a promised goal of happiness or success, wealth or authority. Chance, under this aspect of youthful illusion, is the ideal of expectation and generosity. She is the goddess of the ignorance we prize as sincerity before we learn that sincerity is a virtue which, like James's cipher in arithmetic, depends for its value on the number to which it is attached. She takes the color of her benevolence from youth's impetuosity and ardor, before those qualities have revealed their full cost in experience and disillusionment. It sometimes happens that the illusion we impose on our lives at their outset is not enthusiastic but cynical or pessimistic. The cost then proves all the greater. The hero of "Youth," *The Arrow of Gold,* and *The Shadow Line* is at times supplanted by a man like Heyst in *Victory* or Razumov in *Under Western Eyes,* whose untested misanthropy is as fatally romantic a presumption on the conditions of the responsible life or the obligations of character as an untested optimism. ("Woe to the man whose heart has not learned while young to hope, to love—and to put its trust in life!") An equal enemy lies in wait for both. That enemy— "our common enemy"—leaps from unknown coverts: sometimes from the hiding-places that fate or accident has prepared, but more often and seriously, like the beast in the jungle, from the unfathomed depths of our secret natures, our ignorance, our subconscious or unconscious selves.

When the moment comes the victim is forced to commit himself to it. It is the signal of his destiny, and there is no escape for the one who meets it unprepared. The terms of life are reversed by it. It is the stroke by which fate compels recognition—of one's self, of reality, of illusion, error, mistaken expectation, and defeat. At that moment, if a man can measure up to it, his conscious moral existence begins, an existence for which previous intellectual or theoretical anticipation can never fully prepare. "We begin to love when we have conceived life as tragedy." Chance is no longer beneficent. She is a setter of traps and snares. Her opportunities have become the measure of risk and peril, and her favorites are no longer adventurers or idealists but those who can say, in another sentence of Yeats's that is an explicit phrasing of Conrad's idea: "When I think of life as a struggle with the Daemon who would ever set us to the hardest work among those not impossible, I understand why there is a deep enmity between a man and his destiny, and why a man loves nothing but his destiny."

The crisis in almost every one of Conrad's novels—many of which form a prolonged and exhaustive analysis or sublimation of crisis—arrives when, by a stroke of accident, or by an act of decision or error rising from the secret necessities of temperament, a man finds himself abruptly committed to his destiny. It is a commitment to which all men of morally significant quality are bound. It is the test and opportunity of fundamental selfhood, and there is no escape from it. Its necessity is variously stated in Conrad's books—most memorably perhaps in "Typhoon":

> The sea. . . had never put itself out to startle the silent man, who seldom looked up, and wandered innocently over the waters with the only visible purpose of getting food, raiment, and house-room for three people ashore. Dirty weather he had known, of course. He had been made wet, uncomfortable, tired in the usual way, felt at the time and presently forgotten. So that upon the whole he had been justified in reporting fine weather at home. But he had never been given a glimpse of immeasurable strength and of immoderate wrath, the wrath that passes exhausted but never appeased—the wrath and fury of the passionate sea. He knew it existed, as we know that crime and abominations exist; he had heard of it as a peaceable citizen in a town hears of battles, famines, and floods, and yet knows nothing of what these things mean—though, indeed, he may have been mixed up in a street row, have gone without his dinner once, or been soaked to the skin in a shower. Captain MacWhirr had sailed over the surface of the oceans as some men go skimming over the years of existence to sink gently into a placid grave, ignorant of life to the last, without ever having been made to see all it may contain of perfidy, of violence, and of terror. There are on sea and land such men thus fortunate—or thus disdained by destiny or by the sea.

The full implications of this final sentence extend beyond Conrad's tales and even his life; they give us his judgment on a world lapsed into the anarchy that results from a morality of casuistry and opportunism. It was not only in political and commercial society that he saw that violence at work, with the ramifying evil he depicted in *The Secret Agent* and *Under Western Eyes*—novels whose wholly European or English settings give little occasion for an occluding exoticism, and so bring out the full force of Conrad's critical powers. He saw it in the crisis of civilization which he witnessed in Europe, and he saw it there in terms of a question whose import he felt with personal intensity and even with guilt —the question of the fate of Poland. A few of his essays suggest his long scrutiny of this problem, but explicitly he rarely, if ever, elucidated it. It remains involved in the complex of his tales, which is what makes it memorable and dynamic. To grasp the larger significance of Conrad's vision of the violence in his age requires a special attention to what the tales contain and convey.

Conrad's temperament, like that of his characteristic heroes, was rooted in an impulse, an impetuosity, that involves the poet, as much as the man of action, in a presumption on the laws of moral responsibility. He was initially, by his emotional disposition—and perhaps inevitably, by the dramatic circumstances of his Polish youth and revolutionary heritage— an idealist whose passions were early set at a pitch of heroic resolution, committed to a struggle that called on the fullest indomitability of will and spirit. The stoic sentiment of contemporary romantics—"Nothing ever happens to the brave"—could never be the principle of such a tradition. The fiery hopes of Polish nationalism and the cause of Poland's freedom had already exacted the fullest share of bravery, suffering, and ignominy from Conrad's people, and from his own family. Yet even here the illusion of Providence was not missing. Conrad's father was a nationalist of Shelleyan tendencies, translator of Vigny's *Chatterton* and Hugo's *Hernani* and *La Légende des Siècles*. In his note to *A Personal Record* Conrad protested that his father should not be called revolutionist since "no epithet could be more inapplicable to a man with such a strong sense of responsibility in the region of ideas and action and so indifferent to the promptings of personal ambition," and that he was "simply a patriot in the sense of a man who, believing in the spirituality of a national existence, could not bear to see that spirit enslaved." But Danilowsky, the Polish historian, describes this father as "an honorable but too ardent patriot," who was known to the Tzarist police as an "agitator," author of the seditious mandate that brought about his arrest in October 1861, his imprisonment in Warsaw, and his subsequent deportation to the Government Vologda for a four-year exile which brought on the death of his wife and eventually his own death as well. Apollo Korzeniowski's verse is passionate in its defiance of misfortune:

> Ready is your boat, and in the outspread sails
> Blows the wind, lighthearted,
> Some of us life may deceive,
> You will choose the right way.

> May cowards tremble at lofty waves,
> To you they bring good fortune!
> You know the hidden reefs,
> And are familiar with the tempest!

> Your eager boat, with eagle's wings,
> Will make a rapid passage,

And, steered by reason, governed with strength,
Will reach the shores of fame!

But, resting from your journey,
In the golden lands of fortune,
Remember, O remember with a sigh
Those who perished in the tempest!

This "Korzeniowski strain,"[1] as his wife's relatives called it, with its devotion to Utopian ideals and revolutionary hazards—impulsive, sarcastic, impatient—seems to have served as a warning to the members of the Bobrowski family, whose daughter he courted and who considered him "an undesirable pretender." The Bobrowskis, who were, like the Korzeniowskis, of the land-owning gentry and had a brilliant record as soldiers and patriots, were of more conservative, reformist leanings. They were agricultural, closely devoted as a family, apparently more realistic and cautious in their view of the nationalist cause than the young poet whom they knew as a "red" and who, despite his sensitive character and human sympathies, was famed for his recklessness and scurrilous impatience with temporizers. The hazardous conditions of Conrad's youth (he was only five when his father was arrested and deported), the unsettled fortunes of the family, and his knowledge of his father's courage, must have fostered his early ambitions about his own career. When he turned from the East of Europe which he always feared and disliked, since it represented the national enemy Russia as well as those unfathomed conflicts that reflected his own severe doubt of himself, he looked toward the countries that promised a career of greater certainty. He looked toward France, with her marine service and political opportunities, and more particularly, in these earliest years of his travels, toward Spain of the Carlist cause, in whose service he was to take his first great chance, as a gun-runner and agitator. Conrad's celebrations of the hope and illusion of youth, of innocence, of courage and the bravery it supports in the untested nature of the immature man, of the sincerity which blesses this primitive kind of emotion—these are too evident in his work to be doubted as revivals, in his later memory, of the excitement with which he launched himself on life when he left Poland behind in 1874, at the age of seventeen, and boarded the west-bound Vienna express for Venice and Marseilles, "as a man might get into a dream."

Once Conrad had embarked on that adventure, however, a rival strain of his inheritance asserted itself. How early we cannot tell, for the documents on this part of his life, from 1873 until the middle eighties, are few. Apparently it did not appear during his first years in Marseilles, when he frequented the conservative *légitimiste* circle of the banker Delestang and his wife, or during his first two sea-voyages that ensued from this acquaintance—that in 1875 on the *Mont-Blanc* to Martinique and Le Havre, and that in 1876 on the *Saint-Antoine* to St. Pierre, Port-au-Prince, and the Gulf of Mexico. It apparently did not deter him during the romantic episode among the Spanish legitimists of Don Carlos's cause which involved him between October 1877, and February 1878, in the exploits of the gun-running tartane *Tremolino,* his love affair with the prototype of Rita de Lastaola, his duel with the American J.M.K. Blunt,* and the other escapades (later to be recorded in *The Arrow of Gold*) that caused so much alarm among his relatives in Poland that his guardian uncle, Tadeusz Bobrowski, threatened to stop his allowance and compel him to come home. These experiences terminated in fiasco. Wounded in the duel, Conrad was barely on his legs when his alarmed uncle arrived in Marseilles from Kiev to find his nephew deserted by his Carlist friends, embittered by humiliation, and ready to throw up all adventurous political schemes in favor of a job on an English coaster, the *Mavis,* carrying coal and linseed-oil cargoes between Lowestoft and Constantinople.

When Conrad arrived in Lowestoft on June 18, 1878, he stepped for the first time on English soil, knowing only as much English as he had picked up on the voyage, practically without money, without acquaintances in England, and, as his biographer tells us, "alone in the world." This is the first of two decisive dates in Conrad's life. (The other was to come in 1895.) Poland, Marseilles, Carlism, and youth were behind him. Poverty and the rigorous routine of a merchant vessel descended on him and fixed his life for the next seventeen years.

What now rose in Conrad's personality was a force more familiar to us in his books than the ecstatic emotion of youth which he often celebrates but which he was able to recapture only in moments of lyrical memory and which, as a consequence, never rings as authentically as the darker emotions which now announced themselves and persisted in his nature to the end of his life. His benevolent uncle Tadeusz began to write him in response to the letters which Conrad was sending back to Poland. Conrad's shift from youth, Poland, and France to the unsparing exactions of sea-life was one great transition in his fortunes. He was to submit another, of even severer conditions, in 1895, when he threw up the sea and ventured on a career in literature. He did this not with convinced determination, for he tried repeatedly to get a new command even as late as 1900, when his first five books had been published. These breaks or changes have, as we now observe them, the appearance of having been undertaken with a kind of compulsion of inherent vocation, to test his strength and fortitude in the face of a long-delayed creative necessity; but conscious intention as yet played little part in his actions. Troubled, in the early eighties, by the growing melancholy and passionate introspection induced by long sea-watches, by solitary duties, and by the racking boredom which in later life he confessed to be the one sensation he remembered from his sailing days, he found welling up within him symptoms of the tragic inheritance of his race and family.

His life began in disturbance, danger, and a great ascendant hope. It

* [Editor's note: This legend of the duel is exploded in the article by Jocelyn Baines—Appendix II; see pp. 347-350.]

had become vividly adventurous in France, Spain, and the West Indies. Now, abruptly, it became confined, ruthlessly vigilant, curtailed to the most tyrannous necessities, calculated to the hour and moment by the charts on the captain's table, the needle in the binnacle, the movements of the stars. His voyages to African coasts, the Americas, and the Malay and China seas brought contrast of novelty and exotic discovery, but by the time Conrad took his journey to the Congo in 1890, reality had become unconditional. The continent of Africa and his voyage up its coiled, snake-like river figured as his descent into Hell.[2] His journal of the trip still conveys the agony of that palpable damnation.[3] He returned ravaged by the illness and mental disruption which undermined his health for the remaining thirty years of his life.

Between 1891 and 1895 his voyages were broken by intervals spent alone and homeless in London, with only his uncle remaining of his immediate family (and he was to die in 1894) and a distant cousin by marriage, the Polish-Belgian novelist Marguerite Poradowska, of Brussels, to serve as his confidante in Western Europe. When Conrad lay ill in London in 1891 he received a letter from his uncle Tadeusz which we may take as an account of his predicament written from the point of view of a privileged observer:

My dear boy:
    I begin as I always do, but I ought to address you as "my dear pessimist"; for judging from your letters that description would fit you best. I cannot say that I am pleased by your state of mind, or that I am without apprehension about your future . . . Thinking over the causes of your melancholy most carefully I cannot attribute it either to youth or to age. In the case of one who is thirty-four and has had as full a life as you have had, I am forced to attribute it to ill-health, to your wretched sufferings on the African adventure, to your illness which resulted from them, and to the fact that you have had lately plenty of time to give yourself up to the habit of reverie which I have observed to be part of your character. It is inherited; it has always been there, in spite of your active life.
    I may be mistaken, but I think this tendency to pessimism was already in you as long ago as the days when you were at Marseilles, but it was then part of youth. I am sure that with your melancholy temperament you ought to avoid all meditations which lead to pessimistic conclusions. I advise you to lead a more active life than ever and to cultivate cheerful habits.
    Our country, as Slowack well says (although he himself was not free from the reproach), is the "pan" of the nations, which in plain prose means that we are a nation who consider ourselves great and misunderstood, the possessors of a greatness which others do not recognize and will never recognize. If individuals and nations would set duty before themselves as an aim, instead of grandiose ideals, the world would be a happier place. . . . Perhaps you will reply that these are the sentiments of one who has always had "a place in the sun." Not at all. I have endured many ups and downs; I have suffered in my private life,

in my family life, and as a Pole; and it is thanks to these mortifications that I have arrived at a calm and modest estimate of life and its duties, and that I have taken as my motto *"usque ad finem"*; as my guide, the love of the duty which circumstances define.

It is not to be argued that Conrad's life explains his art in its fullest dimensions, any more than his "ideas" explain his novels, or that we can use his personal documents and letters as a substitute for that explanation. Indeed, his defensive nature made it unlikely that he should write these as such an explanation. The reproofs he expressed to several students of his career indicate that he would have endorsed Eliot's sentence which his own preface to *The Nigger of the "Narcissus"* to some degree anticipated: "The more perfect the artist, the more completely separate in him will be the man who suffers and the mind which creates." Conrad was a dramatic genius and an artist in character; his creations are always more than the sum of his conscious motives and critical intelligence. Any comparison of his personal writings with his novels shows that he found his full voice only when writing imaginatively. Only then does he resist the charge made against him by E. M. Forster when he said that "the secret casket of his genius contains a vapor rather than a jewel." At the same time it is impossible to neglect the value which the events of Conrad's life and the testimony of his intimate correspondence contribute toward the interpretation of his fiction. At the least, these provide us with a comment on the problem he  dramatized in a language which almost perfectly coincides with the spirit of his plots and situations. We know, in addition, how strongly he protested against the purely impersonal order of art advocated by the naturalists; how he considered their novels a perpetuation of the worst vices of the old convention of arbitrary omniscience in fiction; how lifeless he found the critical objectivity of his friend Galsworthy; how he disagreed as vigorously as Yeats did with Stendhal's conception of art as "un miroir qui se promène sur la grande route." Five of his narratives were never denied as autobiographies. He said that all his characters were "at one time or the other known by me." And although it is inevitable that we can never prove the personal basis of his greater novels, we cannot read them without sensing the existence of such a basis, or observing that Conrad's repeated hints of such relevance were expanded and explored from one end of his production to the other.

The letters he wrote Mme. Poradowska between 1890 and 1900 reveal that almost every fundamental problem of his later fiction was sketched or suggested in that correspondence and applied there with remorseless intimacy not to fictitious characters but to his own plight and state of mind. They also reveal that during those critical years of his life, when he was making a harassed transition from maritime service to the profession of novelist, he was already groping for the means and courage to translate these experiences into fictional form, to objectify them dramatically, and thus to come into an intelligent realization of their meaning: to save himself, as he once expressed it, "from the madness which, after a certain point in life is reached, awaits those who refuse to master their sensations and bring into coherent form the mysteries of their lives."

Conrad's sense of the crisis of moral isolation and responsibility in which the individual meets his first full test of character is repeatedly emphasized in his tales, to a degree which has put a special stamp on his heroes. These are men marked by a number of conditions which have become much more familiar during the past half-century than they were when Conrad began to write. Even then however, they had been established by serious novelists and dramatists. James and Ibsen, to name only two, had dramatized the plight of the man or woman on whom life closes down. By divesting him or her of the familiar supports and illusory protection of friendship, social privilege, or love; by throwing the individual violently out of an accepted relationship with family or society, this crisis suddenly makes him aware of a hostile or unknown world which must be learned anew, conquered or mastered, before survival is possible. Obviously this order of drama has a classic ancestry. It is the oldest mode of tragedy. But the social and psychological emphasis of modern times had given it a substance, a basis of practical moral conditions, not always apparent even in Shakespeare. It is this drama of alienation and spiritual recognition which appears in the characteristic novels of Mann, Gide, and Kafka, in Robinson's poems, in Joyce and Hemingway. It is carried to lengths of symbolic extension in *Death in Venice, The Trial, Nightwood,* and ultimately in *Finnegans Wake.* One of its latest appearances is in the novels of the French existentialists, who have given tragedy a new dimension in the irrationality or absurdity of the universe. But it is doubtful if any of these writers has achieved a more successful *dramatic* version of the problem than Conrad did—a more complete coincidence of the processes of psychic recognition and recovery with the dramatic necessities of the plot; and this for a reason which distinguishes Conrad's contribution to modern fictional method: his imposition of the processes of psychological experience, notably the experience of recognition, on the structure of the plot. Even in James, as later in Thomas Mann and André Gide, whose moral drama also took this direction, the ratiocinative element and structural manipulation of the action did not permit an equal immersion in the "destructive element" of psychic reality, an equal coincidence of moral sensibility with form.

The conditions that mark the plight of a Conrad character who is caught in the grip of circumstances that enforce self-discovery and its cognate, the discovery of reality or truth, are remarkably consistent in his books. The condition of moral solitude is the first of them—the isolation of Razumov in *Under Western Eyes,* of Heyst in *Victory,* of Flora de Barral in *Chance,* of Jim himself in *Lord Jim,* and of a large number of other outcasts, exiles, or estranged souls—Willems, Lingard, Mrs. Travers, Mrs. Verloc, Peyrol; even men whom age or accident has suddenly bereft of the solid ground of security or confidence—Captain Whalley, Captain MacWhirr, the young captain on his first command in *The Shadow Line,* or Kurtz of "Heart of Darkness" in his last abandonment of soul. The isolation varies in its nature. Willems is alone because he is a banished wastrel who has made life a law to himself; Mr. George is alone because he is young and irresponsible; Lingard and Captain Whalley have accepted stoically their estrangement from the ties of normal life; Jim and Flora feel themselves excommunicated from society by disgrace and by the false confidence or idealism that has betrayed them; Razumov is isolated by an impenetrable mystery of birth and social alienation; Heyst by the disgust, induced by a fatal vein of skepticism in his nature and so tending toward a nihilism of all values, which follows a misplaced trust in his fellow men. In all these more serious cases, isolation tends to become so absolute that it can be bridged again only by some irresistible compulsion that rises out of the psychic and ethical necessities of character. Life demands justfication by love or honor, as with Flora and Razumov; it exacts justice from the disillusioned, as with Mrs. Verloc; it demands, in the case of Heyst, the last and absolute testimony of honor which only suicide can give. Conrad leaves no doubt of the extreme to which he pushed this condition. Of Heyst we hear that "Not a single soul belonging to him lived anywhere on earth . . . he was alone on the bank of the stream. In his pride he determined not to enter it." And of Razumov: "He was as lonely in the world as a man swimming in the deep sea. . . . He had nothing. He had not even a moral refuge—the refuge of confidence."

But if isolation is the first condition of these lives, it is never an isolation that brings independence or liberty. Freed by choice from normal human ties and obligations, Conrad's men find themselves in the inescapable presence of conscience. "I am being crushed—and I can't even run away," cries Razumov. The solitary may take to debauchery and self-law like Willems: even that does not permit him to escape. He may rise to power and fame like Kurtz: that permits escape least of all. He may believe he has formed a world of his own like Heyst:

> Heyst was not conscious of either friends or enemies. It was the very essence of his life to be a solitary achievement, accomplished not by hermit-like withdrawal with its silence and immobility, but by a system of restless wandering, by the detachment of an impermanent dweller amongst changing scenes. In this scheme he had perceived the means of passing through life without suffering and almost without a care in the world—invulnerable because elusive.

But the world allows no such independence. "No decent feeling was ever scorned by Heyst," and that fact proves his undoing and finally his moral salvation. These men are all brought to discover what the oldest religious systems of the world have advocated: that the more liberty we have, the less we can use. The man who is alone in the world can never escape, for he is always with himself. Unless he is morally abandoned beyond the point of significance through profligacy or irresponsibility, he lives in the company of a ruthless inquisitor, a watcher who never sleeps, a perpetually vigilant judge: with his intinct of identity, the moral imperative of his existence. A novelist who proposes to explore the full experience of the justice imposed on our faculties by conscience will be impelled, like Conrad, to penetrate a world that lies below the appearances of conduct. The explorations made by Conrad in that dimension have advanced, in our time, to the farthest reaches of the unconscious self. If Conrad did not reach those depths he pointed the way to them. *Lord Jim, Chance,* and *Under Western Eyes* join the experiments of Melville, Dostoevsky, James, and Joyce in charting the experience of the unconscious, and the means by which it is to be explored.

It is here that Conrad's work enters a dimension which is ostensibly psychological and which, for purposes of drama and characterization, must appear validly so. But it goes farther. It encounters the problem of appearance and reality, of bringing into single focus the processes of subjective intuition and the conditions of social and moral necessity—the values of egotism and those of ethical fact. It may treat these in terms of the relativity of appearances and sentiments as Proust defined it, but it will also insist on relating the psychic and moral ambiguity of human nature to the ambivalence of reality as art embodies and struggles with it, and finally to the metaphysical condition of value itself. When Conrad enters that dimension fully he leaves his sentimental limitations and prejudices behind him and takes his place as one of the authentic creative imaginations of our time—one who certainly outdistances the other English novelists of his generation.

The order of art to which Conrad addresses himself, less apparently by conscious intention than by instinct and personal necessity, is one that has become paramount in the literature of the Twentieth Century. The ambiguity of truth, the conflict of appearance and reality, the rival claims of the secret and the social self—these are now integral to modern fiction in its major manifestations, whether in Proust or Mann, James or Kafka, Gide or Sartre. They arrive at something like the condition of paradigm in Pirandello's *Six Characters in Search of an Author.*

The six characters emerge from their half-created, unrealized lives and make their claim for the reality of their existence. The play they see being devised on the stage shocks and appals them by its failure to do justice to the truth of their experience. They plead that their agony be given the truth it had in life itself; that their passions and motives be understood; that reality be brought to terms not only with art but with moral insight and compassion. The actors and director who grapple with their pleas can make nothing but a travesty of the tragedy they attempt to enact. Their struggle to render it justice produces, in Pirandello's hands, a metaphysical dilemma. It is not only art that is at odds with life; it is human comprehension itself. But the question insists: can life ever do justice to its own reality? Are suffering, agony, tragedy comprehensible in their own condition? Is it possible for them to achieve comprehension until consciousness, moral sympathy, or art intervene to interpret and define them? Can man, or life, be said to exist in terms of significance until these modes of definition and justice succeed in embodying them? The dilemma, driven to the extreme lengths of suspense and contradiction, ends finally in enigma and fiasco. The question remains unresolved. It collapses under the test of resolution. Conrad's problem in *Lord Jim* was this same problem. There too, in spite of driving Jim's fate to the logic of catastrophe, the question of the reality of his moral identity ends in enigma. But the problem of resolving it had become an obsession with Conrad. It taxed him continuously to the end of his life. At times he resorted to desperate measures of heroism, suicide, or moral compromise to resolve it; sometimes he fell back on the arbitrary formulas of ethical duplicity or stoicism. But it remained to the end the essential theme and animus of his drama.

It is instructive to turn again to Conrad's letters for confirmation of his sense of the crisis which induces the test of selfhood to which he subjects his heroes. When Conrad passed, around 1895, out of the perfectly controlled and adjusted mechanism of sea-life, with its accurate regimen of human relations and balances, he entered into a freedom which he soon discovered to be no liberation but a prison. For him, in those middle years of the nineties, the self was doubly trapped. He found himself alone not only with his poverty and rigorous self discipline but with his creative conscience, now struggling to express itself.

His dramatizations of the trapped sensibility were preceded by that harrowing period in London in which he decided to face a kind of labor that meant daily and yearly solitude, with no give-and-take of human approval or disagreement, with no one to judge his principles or results but himself, and with a brutal aesthetic judgment—soon divested of the amateur excitement with which he wrote *Almayer's Folly*—ruling his waking and sleeping life. It is small wonder that Conrad, who was to make the trapped man the object of his special study, should have always remembered this period of his life, for it marked the beginning of an anxiety and a discipline that were not to end until his death. We find him recurring to the idea of the convict with an insistence, with none of the defiance, that marks Himbaud's salutations to that form of fate in the *Saison en Enfer*. Tormented all his life by the "stérilités des écrivains nerveux" which he shared with Baudelaire, Conrad began the grinding labor of his books. Years later, in 1909, he wrote to Norman Douglas that "there's neither inspiration nor hope in my work. It's mere hard labor for life—with this difference, that the life convict is at any rate out of harm's way—and may consider the account with his conscience closed: and this is not the case with me. I envy the serene fate and the comparative honesty of the gentlemen in gray who live in Dartmoor. I do really. I am not half as decent or half as useful." But earlier, in the nineties, he was already acknowledging that fate to his "cousin" in Brussels, Mme. Poradowska:

> I am not so happy to be working as you seem to think.
> There is nothing very exhilarating in doing disagreeable

work. It is too much like penal servitude, with the difference that while rolling the stone of Sisyphus you lack the consolation of thinking of what pleasure you had in committing the crime. It is here that convicts have the advantage over your humble servant.

Again:

I astonish and perhaps scandalize you by my joking about criminals, while you think me capable of accepting or even admitting the doctrine (or theory) of expiation through suffering . . . there is no expiation. Each act of life is final and inevitably produces its consequences in spite of all the weeping and gnashing of teeth and the sorrow of weak souls who suffer as fright grips them when confronted with the results of their own actions. As for myself, I shall never need to be consoled for any act of my life, and this because I am strong enough to judge my conscience rather than be its slave, as the orthodox would like to persuade us to be.

And again:

Remember, though, that one is never entirely alone. Why are you afraid? And of what? Is it of solitude or of death? O strange fear! The only two things that make life bearable! But cast fear aside. Solitude never comes— and death must often be waited for during long years of bitterness and anger. Do you prefer that?

But you are afraid of yourself; of the inseparable being forever at your side—master and slave, victim and executioner—who suffers and causes suffering. That's how it is! One must drag the ball and chain of one's selfhood to the end. It is the price one pays for the devilish and divine privilege of thought; so that in this life it is only the elect who are convicts—a glorious band which comprehends and groans but which treads the earth amidst a multitude of phantoms with maniacal gestures, with idiotic grimaces. Which would you be: idiot or convict?

The alter ego of the conscience was an inevitable corollary—as Conrad here indicates—of his conception of inescapable selfhood. The *Doppelgänger* becomes part of the drama of character and self-determination. When Jim delivers his long monologues to Marlow; when Flora bares her soul to Marlow, Mrs. Fyne, or Captain Anthony; when Razumov writes his passionate entries in his diary and disburdens his soul to the old language-teacher and finally to Natalie Haldin herself; when Decoud or Gould ruminate their secret histories, these people are really carrying out the drama of their divided natures, objectifying under the compulsion which psychoanalysts have seized upon as therapeutic necessity their souls' dilemmas and thus trying to save themselves from madness. But the divided man—the face and its mask, the soul and its shadow—

figures even more concretely than this in Conrad's dramatic method (though rumination and monologue were usually his own means of giving genuine substance to his realism). The rival character—sometimes a villain, sometimes a friend or lover, sometimes a fellow-fugitive like the "secret sharer" in the story of that name—serves the hero as a transferred embodiment of his other self.

Thus love, or the sense of honor, or the obligation of duty, or even the social instinct itself, enters the novels as a means by which the individual is lifted out of his isolation and morbid surrender. The inward-driving, center-fathoming obsession of the tale becomes reversed and takes a centrifugal direction toward external standards of value. It is finally the world which saves us—the world of human necessities and duty. It may be the world of a ship and its crew, as in *The Shadow Line;* it may be the world of an island and a single fellow-soul, as in *Victory;* it may be that wider world of social and political relationships which Conrad seldom explored fully but which he did build in solid form in *Nostromo* and *Chance.* In one of the most perfect of Conrad's tales, "The Secret Sharer," the allegory of the alter ego is achieved within the narrowest possible limits. In one of the finest of his novels, *Under Western Eyes,* the conception is made to embody the whole complex of Russian history. "The Secret Sharer," as Miss M. C. Bradbrook has pointed out, in the microcosm of the basic concept in Conrad's fiction. Leggatt, the swimmer, had committed murder and so, by a moment's blind action, has ruined his life. He escapes, but finds refuge, naked, under cover of night on a strange ship—"a fugitive and a vagabond on the earth, with no brand of the curse on his sane forehead to stay a slaying hand." The captain hides him in his cabin, learns his guilt, and thus becomes allied to that guilt, the refugee's secret becoming an embodiment of the captain's own secret life. The hidden self of the captain is "exactly the same" as that of the fugitive, who is of necessity concealed from the world, is dressed in a sleeping suit, the garb of the unconscious life, and appears out of and again disappears into the sea, naked again, under cover of darkness. But before he disappears at last, "a free man, a proud swimmer striking out for a new destiny," the captain has come to know the secret self he lives with. His life is changed. He too must address himself to a "new destiny." A new vision of humanity has broken in upon the impersonal regimen of his days—upon the "ideal conception of one's own personality," abstract, illusory, and therefore insecure and perilous, which "every man sets up for himself secretly." The "sharing" has recreated him, stirred him to a sense of his latent moral insecurity, and so enforced in him the necessity of human community—that "unavoidable solidarity" which Conrad persistently invokes as the inescapable commitment of men: "the solidarity in mysterious origin, in toil, in joy, in uncertain fate, which binds men to each other and all mankind to the visible earth."

For Conrad, however existential he may have been by inclination, the commitment could never remain arbitrary. It is a necessity which defines man as human, his moral consciousness as imperative, and his persistence in that consciousness as the fundamental law of life. From this germinal presentation of the case Conrad's drama of the self widens until, in his most ambitious books, it comes to include the larger workings of that law in society and politics, even in the destiny of nations and of races. The growth in his thought from an idealistic conception of life to a critical one, from his temperamental romanticism to his later realism of values, is the drama of his genius in its difficult emergence, its strenuous self-discipline, and its eventual successes. That growth appears most typically in the three novels that show his dramatic method most explicitly— *Lord Jim, Under Western Eyes,* and *Chance,* but it is extended to more sheerly creative feats of dramatization in three other books—*Nostromo,* his most complex historical and political drama, a comprehensive matrix of his moral and ethical sensibility, resonant of a profoundly riddled debate of moralities and creeds of conduct; *The Secret Agent,* his highest achievement in tragic irony; and *Victory,* his most concentrated symbolic narrative.

The romantic element in his work, like the romantic impulse in his nature, was never effaced. It persisted as the basis of his popularity and of the excesses of style and treatment which appear in his evocative tendency in language, in his treatment of the sea, of woman, and of fortune as inscrutable entities, in his exotic and rhetorical effects, in his sentimental emphasis on the heroic and the miraculous in human fate and character, in the fatigued naïveté of fatalism that reasserts itself in his last three novels. But if it was not effaced, it was recognized. Conrad himself admitted an inherent romanticism as a component of his imagination and of his ordeal in moral and creative responsibility. He referred to it late in life in a passage of apology:

> The romantic feeling of reality was in me an inborn faculty. This in itself may be a curse, but when disciplines by a sense of personal responsibility and a recognition of the hard facts of existence shared with the rest of mankind becomes but a point of view from which the very shadows of life appear endowed with an internal glow. And such romanticism is not a sin. It is none the worse for the knowledge of truth. It only tries to make the best of it, hard as it may be; and in this hardness discovers a certain aspect of beauty.

His success came when responsibility and discipline opposed the self-indulgence which a romantic impulse had encouraged in his early emotions and sensibility. When these correctives assert themselves in his pages, they produce the rigor of style and feeling which stiffens and gives structure to the natural extravagance of his emotions, his impulsiveness in sentiment, the untested enthusiasm of his responses to scene, character, and experience. Conrad's development as an artist—with due allowance made for the weakening powers of his later novels—reproduces the ordeal of self-mastery and moral exoneration which he repeatedly dramatized in the lives of his characteristic heroes. "All a man can betray is his conscience," his Razumov says in *Under Western Eyes*. The measure of Conrad's character and his artistry may be taken from the fact that neither his sense of honor nor his sense of realism permitted him to betray the conscience which it took him half his life to discover in himself, and the other half to test and dramatize in his books.          (1945, 1957)

## NOTES

1. On Conrad's Polish inheritance and early life see also Milosz's essay, "Joseph Conrad in Polish Eyes," see below. [Editor's note]
2. On "Heart of Darkness" as a Virgilian descent into Hell see Lillian Feder's essay, "Marlow's Descent into Hell," pp. 162-170. [Editor's note]
3. Cf. Richard Curle's "Conrad's Diary," in *Last Essays* (1926), reprinted from *Yale Review*, XV (1926), pp. 254-266. See also *Life and Letters of Joseph Conrad*, edited by G. Jean-Aubry Vol. I (1927). [Editor's note]


# CZESLAW MILOSZ

## Joseph Conrad in Polish Eyes*

THE WORK OF A WRITER may be said to resemble an iceberg. That part of it which is visible tempts us to explore the larger portion which remains obscure and hidden beneath the surface of the written word. For the literary historian this temptation is an obligation, for he must search for those events and complications in the personal life of an author that influenced his sensibility and determined his choice of aims in life. Such a search is not easy when a writer comes from a country the knowledge of which is only vague or incomplete. This is the case with Joseph Conrad, who was born in the Polish Ukraine one hundred years ago. Elements in his personality that may appear exotic or mysterious to an Anglo-Saxon reader look rather different when viewed by a compatriot, more familiar with the history of his youthful years, before he exchanged the life of his land-locked country for life on the open sea.

Conrad's biographies usually begin by asserting that he came from a noble family. This conjures up the vision of a country mansion, of horses, dogs, and a certain aristocratic style. The reality was different, even though his grandfather, an officer in Napoleon's army and an old-fashioned patriarch, did fit into the traditional pattern of the nobility. What is more pertinent, however, to Conrad's personal history is the fact that his father, Apollo Korzeniowski, was an impoverished poet. He has a place in Polish

* From *Atlantic Monthly*, CC, 5 (Anniversary Issue, 1957), pp. 29-220, 222, 224, 226, 228.

literary history, and some of his verse plays are still performed in Poland, even finding favor with Marxist critics because of their violent diatribes against the propertied classes. Furthermore, Conrad's maternal uncle, Tadeusz Bobrowski, was also a man of letters, being the author of one of the most interesting memoirs of the nineteenth century. The milieu in which the future English novelist grew up was thus a literary one.

When, in 1857, a son was born to Apollo Korzeniowski, he gave him the Christian names Józef Teodor Konrad. The symbolic meaning of the last of these names is clear to any Pole. For a Pole the name Konrad symbolizes the anti-Russian fighter and resister. To understand how it acquired such a meaning it is necessary to go back to the poems of Adam Mickiewicz (the great Polish poet and contemporary of Pushkin) whose verses are known by heart in Poland. One of the most famous of his poems was called *Konrad Wallenrod*. Here the poet's Polish patriotism and his anti-Russian feelings (he was deported to Russia in 1824, being suspected of "revolutionary activities") were thinly masked to circumvent the Czarist censorship, beneath the guise of a historical epic harking back to the days of the medieval wars between the German Teutonic Order and the pagan Lithuanians. Konrad, a pagan converted to Christianity and risen to become Chief of the Order, deliberately leads its army into a trap in order to avenge his people's sufferings. His vengeance is won through monstrous duplicity, the weapon of the oppressed.

Thus from his very infancy Joseph Conrad bore a name steeped in Polish tradition. When he signed his first book "Conrad," dropping his family name of Korzeniowski as being too difficult for an Anglo-Saxon public, he was well aware of its double meaning.

Conrad was born just one year after the conclusion of the Crimean War, that war which shook the Russian Empire to its foundation and gave rise to Polish hopes that liberation from the Czarist yoke was nigh. Not content with poetry, his father became a conspirator, and by 1861 he had become a full-fledged member of a clandestine revolutionary committee in Warsaw.

The father's arrest in that year was a dramatic event which had a decisive impact on the development of the youthful Konrad. Between the sensitive ages of five and ten, those years when one's individuality crystallizes, he found himself the child of political prisoners. The father was first confined for several months in the Warsaw Citadel, where the Czarist police tried to extract from him the names of his fellow conspirators. Failing in this endeavor, they sentenced him to deportation to the north of Russia. He was accompanied in his exile by his wife and the little Konrad. The journey to the east in a horse-drawn carriage and under armed guard was long and painful, and the boy fell seriously ill as they approached Moscow.

A child, as is well known, is peculiarly sensitive to adult dramas, the full meaning of which he is unable to grasp. Here in the frozen north it was more than usually difficult to conceal the drama of the family situation. The great love that father and mother felt for each other acquired as the months went by a desperate character as the severe climate of Vologda, the town to which they had been banished, progressively destroyed Evelina Korzeniowski's health. "Vologda," her husband wrote to a friend in one letter, "is a big swamp, three kilometers long, laid out with criss-crossing wooden passages. The year is divided into two seasons: white winter and green winter. White winter lasts nine and a half months, green winter, two and a half." As the seasons came and went, mother, father, and son wavered between a hopeless despair and a despairing hope that the Czarist authorities might answer their appeal to be moved to a less inclement place of exile. The appeal was eventually heard, and they were allowed to move south to the town of Chernigov, in the Russian Ukraine. But the move came too late to save the ailing Evelina, and her illness ended in her death in 1865, when the young Konrad was just eight years old.

More shut up within himself than ever, the widower now wore a double mourning. For prior to the loss of his beloved wife, he had witnessed the deathblow dealt to the cause he had tried to serve. In 1863 the long-simmering rebellion had finally broken out in Poland and had been ruthlessly crushed by the Russians. Struck down by these two blows, Apollo Korzeniowski tried to will himself to calm, a state of mind that did not come easily to his impassioned nature. Nor in such conditions could his son have experienced much of that youthful joy which is so vital to a child. The boy's only moments of escape were during the summer months, when he could go off on trips with relatives to the Ukrainian countryside, since he himself was not a prisoner. But the winters were long and bleak, and in the evenings Konrad's sole companion was his father, who sat by the light of an oil lamp covering page after page with his cramped angular handwriting. For even now, with all his hopes destroyed, the unsubmissive captive continued to fight a lonely battle against the Czarist system.

One of the products of these long wintry nights by the light of the oil lamp was a treatise entitled "Poland and Russia." Apollo Korzeniowski managed to smuggle it abroad and it appeared unsigned in a Polish émigré paper called *The Homeland,* which was published in Leipzig. It was, as might be expected, a bitter indictment of Russian "barbarity," which "spreads its body from the Frozen Sea to the Black Sea and from the Vistula to the Pacific," and it was full of dark forebodings. "Such as Muscovy is," ran a characteristic passage, "from fear of her own annihilation she is forced to fight outside her borders. Although Europe may avoid the struggle for a long time yet, the moment will come when it will be no longer possible to escape it; but then the time will have been chosen by Muscovy. Thus will Europe be robbed of half its strength."

Throughout these years Konrad's father was his principal teacher, and the cramped conditions of their exile amid foreign surroundings inevitably tightened the bond between them. From his father's correspondence we get a sketchy idea of what his early education consisted of. ("I teach him what I can. Unfortunately it is not much. I protect him against the atmosphere of this place and the kid grows up as in a monastery cell.") But we may safely surmise that it was from his father, as much as from the unhappy conditions of his youthful life, that Conrad derived both his deep-seated antipathy for Russia and that tragic outlook on life which is so evident in his later books.

Joseph Conrad's anti-Russian feelings are too well known to need to be emphasized here. Years later he got very angry when Henry L. Mencken claimed in an article to have discovered typically Slavonic features in his novels. In Conrad's opinion, the Poles were separated from the Slavonic world "not so much by hatred, as by an incompatibility of character." He pointed out that he had read only a few Russian novels—in translation—and he added: "Their mentality and emotionality have always repelled me for reasons of hereditary tendency and personal disposition."

Apollo Korzeniowski's influence on his son, however, was not limited to the political field. The father's writings are marked by a basic skepticism about human nature. He was in particular obsessed by a somber vision of threatening forces which he saw rising up from a state of primeval chaos to overshadow and overthrow civilized man. His fear of Russia was a fear of shapeless elemental powers unsubjected to the rigors and restraints of moral conventions. Here we can perceive a clear continuity of theme between the political tracts of the father and the novels of the son. In Conrad's novels *The Secret Agent* and *Under Western Eyes* neither the Czarist officials nor the anarchists and nihilists recognize the simple rule "One does not do that sort of thing."

In "Heart of Darkness" Kurtz, a dealer in ivory, surrenders to the chaos of Africa, suffers a moral rupture, and while declaiming about the civilizing mission of the white man, takes part in massacres of the natives. This feeling that man, beneath a thin veneer of civilization, is undermined by his instincts was shared by Thomas Mann, and it caused him to consider Conrad as one of the truly avant-garde authors of the twentieth century.

Following his wife's death Apollo Korzeniowski realized that he too would not have long to live, for he was riddled with tuberculosis. His letters betray a growing anxiety about his only child, who, he knew, would soon be left alone in the world. "My health is gravely affected and my beloved boy takes care of me. We are but two on this earth," he wrote to one of his friends. "If only I could set Konrad on his native soil and among good men, link this living body and awakening soul to the body of our society, I would not wish for much more than that. As for myself, I want only to set foot on my own land, to breathe its air, to look upon those I love and to cry: 'Lord, now lettest thou thy servant depart in peace.'"

Liberation came at last, thanks to the efforts of his relatives and to his tuberculosis. In 1867 he obtained a passport for a journey from Russia to Madeira. Taking his son with him, he crossed over into Austro-Hungary. There, however, he abandoned the idea of the voyage, mainly because he lacked the financial means to make it, but also because he was deeply interested in the Polish literary movement in Galicia (the Polish-speaking province which had been incorporated into the Hapsburg Empire). Father and son thus settled down first in Lwów (Lemberg) and then in Cracow. Just two years after crossing the borders of the Russian Empire, Apollo Korzeniowski died. All Cracow went into mourning. The old revolutionary was given a hero's funeral, and it was turned by the populace into a great patriotic demonstration.

His father's death left Konrad an orphan at the age of twelve. His guardian from then on was his uncle Bobrowski, and the adolescent now found himself torn between two contrary influences. His uncle was the complete opposite of his father and he made repeated efforts, and sometimes unpleasant ones, to stifle everything in Konrad that he considered the atavistic inheritance of the "worse" side of the family. No biographer of Conrad can afford to underestimate this spiritual conflict, since the uncle's influence in his nephew's life was a lasting one, giving rise to a correspondence which continued during Conrad's long sea voyages on British ships.

Bobrowski's memoirs show him to have been a wise, educated man of strong convictions. This liberal conservative was a realist with a marked sense of irony. He was hostile to revolutionary "dreams" and he condemned his countrymen's attempts to combat Czarism openly, urging them to pursue a path of gradual reform in the hope of achieving some kind of autonomy within the framework of the Russian Empire. He considered all members of the Korzeniowski family as adventurers and financial failures. Apollo, in his opinion, was as marked with the family stigma as his two brothers (who had shown too great a fondness for alcohol and cards), simply because Apollo was a poet. What was worse, all three Korzeniowskis joined the revolutionary movement and had ended as its victims. One of them had died on the battlefield, another in Siberia, and the third of tuberculosis contracted in exile. Such, Bobrowski thought, is the recompense of dreamers. It was necessary, therefore, to uproot this pernicious heritage from the boy's spirit.

For several years this partisan of sobriety and restraint worked steadily at a sort of memorandum entitled "To the knowledge of my beloved nephew, Konrad Korzeniowski." This document consisted mostly of financial figures, drawn from the family records—figures intended to inculcate in the last flower of the Korzeniowski line a feeling of family culpability, to warn him against prodigality, and to provide him with sane counsels.

This clash between the two powerful personalities of uncle and father may help to elucidate the contradictions to be found in Conrad himself: what may be called his anti-romantic romanticism, his strange blend of Polish patriotism and skepticism toward the "Polish cause," his love of adventure and his simultaneous cultivation of order and self-discipline.

The anxieties of the uncle were not without foundation. His early studies under his father, without companions of his own age, as well as his tragic family situation, had bred habits of solitude which did not bode well for a "useful member of society." The boy had been permitted to read all the books at hand, so he devoured the Polish romantic poets, the novels of Victor Hugo, and volumes of Shakespeare in translation. It is said that at the age of eleven he had already written plays which he staged with the aid of grown-up persons. But he was extremely reluctant to submit to school programs or rules of any kind. His relatives called the young man a "shirker."

The precocity of the young egotist offended those around him from whom he did not attempt to conceal his scorn. Some of his biographers claim that he finished eight years of secondary school in Cracow. Other data support the view that he did not get this amount of schooling, then considered the necessary minimum for a member of the intelligentsia. One of his girl cousins transmitted the following impression of him: "Very developed intellectually; he hated school regulations which tortured and bored him. He used to say he had a great talent and would be a great writer. This, together with the sarcastic ironic expression on his face and his frequent critical remarks, provoked surprise in professors and the mockery of his colleagues. He did not like to restrain himself in anything. At home, at school, on visits, he used to lie back in a half-reclining position." If he received some foundation of knowledge, it was mainly thanks to the books he chose following his own tastes, and to his private tutor, a medical student of Cracow named Adam Pulman. With him, at the age of sixteen, he made his first trip to Western Europe, a three-month ramble through Switzerland.

Not only the fame of Conrad but the severe tone of his books—the tone, after all, of a moralist—must have come as a complete surprise to those who had known him in Cracow. The transformations through which certain individuals pass are never easy to understand for those who live close to them, for they are inclined to see traits of character as a sort of fixed chemical composition. But the same personality factors are able to regroup themselves into continually new combinations. What is necessary for this transformation is experiences that will destroy a pattern, thus preparing a new synthesis. Such an experience for Conrad was his long service in the British Navy.

When the nonchalant youth proclaimed that he would be a great writer, his relatives saw in this only another proof of his vanity. When he announced that he had decided to become a sailor, they received it as one does a child's wish to be a fireman or a locomotive engineer. In a continental country, the thing seemed fantastic, and his obstinacy worried them.

Conrad's devotion to the sea has been the object of many quarrels among literary historians. They have pondered over whether the first stimulus may have been Victor Hugo's *Travailleurs de la Mer,* read in childhood, or the impression made upon him by the Russian port of

Odessa which he visited with his uncle on a vacation from Chernigov. One may wonder whether his dream of such a career was not simply a secret wish for escape from the unresolvable net of Poland. All these are only conjectures. Conrad was a discreet man who placed a filter between his personal feelings and his published works that had little to do with "sincerity." Only indirectly can we distinguish in him a sort of obsession. More than one character in his books seems to be an incarnation of continental conspirators—those fearless and pure-hearted knights—disguised as Malayan chieftains or sea captains, as if to illustrate the maxim: "What is to live in art must die in life."

Why did his relatives, hostile to a career at sea, finally submit before the lad's persistence? Probably they lost hope of doing anything reasonable with him. Yet they looked for a compromise solution: there was talk of placing him in the Hapsburg Naval Academy in Pula. This proved impossible because he was not an Austrian citizen. Though living in Cracow, the boy was registered as a citizen of the Russian Empire. A biographical detail unknown until now (I take it from materials published in Poland in 1956) may also have contributed to the uncle's change of heart. The student, who was giving him trouble enough, had a quite scandalous love affair with a cousin called Tekla Soroczynska. It was deemed advisable to send him as far away as possible. It was hoped that he would thus sow his wild oats and return repentant. His uncle set up an allowance for him of 2000 francs a year, a decent sum at that time, and the adventurer left for Marseilles on October 26, 1874.

Conrad is an English writer and the Poles have never tried to assimilate him into their literature, as they have likewise made no claims to the French poet, Guillaume Apollinaire, whose true name was Kostrowicki. Great Britain, in the form of her ships, gave to the sailor what he had lacked: an understanding of the struggle for life and an awareness of human fraternity in the face of a cruel and indifferent Nature. She gave him also her language. He always spoke it badly, with a strong foreign accent, while his power over it in his writing made him one of the rare phenomena of cultural transplantation in a mature individual.

The matter would be simpler to understand if the exotic seas and continents of his voyages had impressed a primitive imagination—if Conrad had become acquainted with the larger world starting from scratch. Such would have been the case, for example, if he had come from a peasant background, so that all the new notions and impressions he received would have been immediately inscribed on a blank slate in a newly acquired language. But Conrad was a literary type. He had grown up among books and was well acquainted with Polish poetry, devoting himself to it more ardently than to his studies. The Polish reader, then, has a strange feeling as he trips constantly over things that have a familiar ring. Certain themes, and even the rhythms of certain passages in his novels, are reminiscent of verse lines very close to him, whose sources, upon reflection, can be named. What happened in Conrad was a perfect fusing of two literatures and two civilizations.

Conrad was deeply attached to the English language, and from his utterances we may surmise that he found it a vehicle exceptionally well suited to his temperament. His correspondence with his uncle in Polish was undoubtedly full of interesting descriptions of Asian and African ports where he went ashore. Yet Bobrowski's efforts to get him to write for the periodicals of his native country failed. Curiously enough, the uncle, seeking to counteract his nephew's estrangement from Poland, exploited the figure of his father in his arguments. So in a letter of 1881 he says: "Since you have not forgotten Polish (may God bless you; you have my blessing already) and since you even write very well, I must repeat what I have already remarked: it would be wonderful if you would contribute to the magazine *Wedrowiec* in Warsaw. I am sure everyone will be extremely interested in what you have to say. You would in this way tighten your links with your own country, and furthermore it would be a pious act toward the memory of your father, who desired to serve and did serve his nation with his pen."

An immigrant will often, for motives of self-defense, cut himself off completely from his land of origin or show toward it a friendly condescension, thereby contrasting his own success to the miseries of those left behind in the old country. The Irish, the Italians, and the Poles in America furnish many examples of this. Were it possible to find such a tendency in Conrad, it would mean that the problem had lost its acuteness for him and that it could be set aside in an analysis of his work. But, in fact, this matter does not lend itself to simplification. And as we go more deeply into the biographical materials we come to the conclusion that a carefully hidden complex of treason is discernible in some of his writings—a feeling that he had betrayed the cause so fanatically embraced by his compatriots and, above all, by his father.

Literature in Poland and Russia—and this is one of the rare features of similarity between these two dissimilar countries—has traditionally been viewed in a way differing from that of Western Europe. There it is conceived of as an arm in the struggle for the community good. Conrad did not believe in the future of his country and this provided him with a self-justification. But no amount of self-justification can insulate us from doubts about the rightness of our choice.

When his first books brought him fame abroad, his relatives sent him clippings from Polish papers showing the response they had evoked in Warsaw literary circles. But the local press was not always favorable. Conrad was particularly affected by a violent attack made on him by Eliza Orzeszko. This woman, of the suffragette type, was an admired humanitarian novelist in the tradition of Auguste Comte (who was then considered a prophet in Europe). She openly accused Conrad of treason for having offered his talents to a foreign literature.

The process of investigating layers of meaning in a novel is a pretty thankless task. Yet Conrad's enigmatic *Lord Jim* certainly acquires an additional dimension if, as some critics have suggested, we see in it a drama of national loyalties.[1] A sailor leaves his disabled vessel, feeling that it is not possible to save it, and the consequences of that act continue to pursue him to the end of his days. By slightly changing the ship's name, *Patna,* and substituting the word *Patria,* we may touch upon a multiplicity of meaning which sometimes gives the prose its mysterious charm. Yet even if we make full allowances for a strong attachment to one's homeland met to such a degree only in Central and Eastern Europe, the speculation is risky, and the secretive writer that Conrad was does not encourage it.

Nevertheless his adaptation to England, despite his marriage to an Englishwoman, was incomplete. In the recollections of Jessie Conrad we can note the amusing horror provoked in her by periodic visits of "Eastern people," and perhaps a regret that a great sphere of her husband's life remained, for her, inaccessible. Conrad must have applied certain tactics in his relations with her and his English friends. He kept silent on questions bearing upon things foreign to them. This was all the easier for him since he chose to live in England as a matter of personal preference. He was furthermore a patriotic supporter of the British Empire as it confronted the two continental powers he disliked, Russia and Germany. But though an Englishman by choice, he periodically re-emphasized his double loyalty, making it clear that he did not intend to dispense with that duality. When his friend Robert Cunninghame Graham invited him to take part in a pacifist meeting in London in 1899, he answered with a letter containing the following words, sharply underlined: *"There will be Russians at this meeting. Impossible!"* He added that he could not accept the idea of fraternity, not because he considered it unrealizable but because its propagation might weaken "the national sentiment whose conservation is the precise object of my preoccupations."

If we restore its proper meaning to the term "cosmopolitanism"— ignoring the use made of it by Stalinists—and recognize that it covers bad as well as good qualities, then we may say that Conrad, though he traveled to distant parts of the world and wrote about different peoples speaking many different languages, was not really a cosmopolitan. It was impossible for him to be one because of his need for roots. But he knew how to maintain a certain equilibrium between the demands of his double fidelity. "If you will take my word for it," he wrote in a letter to a Polish acquaintance in 1903, "say that in the course of my navigations around the globe, I have never separated myself, either in my thoughts or in my heart, from my native country and that I hope to be received there as a compatriot, in spite of my Anglicization."

The "Heart of Darkness," which appeared at the very beginning of our century, was a Cassandra cry announcing the end of Victorian Europe, on the verge of transforming itself into the Europe of violence. The First World War, which ushered in the new epoch, destroyed many illusions.

In this respect Conrad's fear of anarchy found its somber confirmation. At the same time the war aroused new hopes for the independence of those nations which had been subjected, from the time of the Congress of Vienna, to the control of powerful monarchies. Not doubting of the final victory of the Western Allies, Conrad submitted a memorandum to the British Foreign Office in 1916 entitled "Note on the Polish Problem." It contained a detailed plan for re-creating an independent Poland with access to the sea, under an Allied protectorate. The unforeseen turn of events, and principally the weakening of Russia through the revolution of 1917, brought about the realization of his projects to an extent surpassing his hopes.

Conrad died in 1924, but in the upheavals which later touched the corner of Europe he came from, he had a not unimportant role to play. In the last years of his life, Conrad made his own corrections to Polish translations of his writings. The translators, the best of whom was his cousin, Aniela Zagórska, were conscientious in their task, and his novels became necessary additions to every self-respecting private library in Poland. But as happens to all eminent authors, interest in them rose and fell in waves. Never, though, did his popularity reach such a peak as during the Second World War. The reasons for this were mainly political. Poland's defeat and occupation by the Nazis gave rise to an underground movement—or, rather, to an underground state. Liberation was expected to come from the West. But as the international fronts settled down, it was more and more apparent that Poland had a choice only between a Nazi and a Soviet victory. This meant that the Poles could either be baked or boiled.

The Poles sought support in Conrad for a desperate and gratuitous heroism, and they tried to imitate those of his characters who embodied a fateful loyalty to a lost cause. We shall not judge whether the conclusions they drew from his works were the right ones. In any case, when the Red Army entered Poland and the new Communist government undertook the liquidation of the "underground state," Party journalists proclaimed Conrad an immoral writer and a corrupter of youth. They even went so far as to condemn Conrad's ethical ideas as only useful to capitalists. Thus when he depicted a crew's loyalty toward its captain and its ship, he was in reality serving the purpose of shipowners.

Furthermore, Conrad belonged irremediably to Western civilization, and its prestige had to be deflated. The bureaucrats, gifted with a sound Party instinct, realized that the aristocratic scale of values, dear to Conrad's sailors, pirates, and soldiers, was not compatible with the creation of individuals completely subservient to the state. That is why, after the Stalinists gained control of the literary market through the nationalization of publishing houses and the installation of censorship, they placed Conrad on the black list. Even in the first years after the war, when considerable freedom of expression still existed, new editions of his novels were forbidden, a situation which was naturally perpetuated during the period of insane witch-hunting that followed. Strangely enough, during this same period (1945-1955) theaters performed some of his father's plays, emphasizing their attacks on the nobility and toning down those against the Czarist regime.

When Conrad was "defrosted" in 1955 and Polish publishers began preparing new editions of his works, a careful observer might have seen in this a sign that the "thaw" in Poland was a serious affair. Thus, by a strange detour, his father's wishes in giving him the name of Konrad were finally fulfilled. The son who did not want to assume a burden that had crushed his father had nevertheless become the defender of freedom against the blights of autocracy. (1957)

## NOTES

1. This is Gustav Morf's thesis in his *Polish Heritage of Joseph Conrad* (1930). [Editor's note]

## THOMAS MOSER

## Conrad's Voycur-Villains*

THE INEFFECTIVE, melodramatic conclusions to some of the later novels suggest misunderstanding of material as well as willingness to pander to a popular audience. We can see from Conrad's failure to dramatize the relationship between lovers that his creative imagination is not cooperating with the intended theme that "pairing off is the fate of mankind." Thus we are faced with the question of whether or not a second meaning lies beneath the surface of the later works. Is there an implicit pattern different from the imposed pattern of Conrad's conscious intention? If so, how does this inner meaning relate to the early Conrad's attitude toward love?

One way to approach the problem is through the character of the villain. Although we cannot, as Mr. Hewitt says, take him seriously as a character,[1] we may find him a useful key to the real meaning of the love stories. The villain is interesting because he represents something new and unusual in Conrad. The early Conrad, we recall, is concerned primarily with normal human beings. But the villain of the later period is a grotesque, both in the literary sense of being a caricature, and in the psychological sense of exhibiting abnormal attitudes toward love.

* From Thomas Moser's *Joseph Conrad: Achievement and Decline* (Harvard University Press, 1957), pp. 111-130, a selection from Chapter II ("The Uncongenial Subject"), pp. 51-130. The above title is taken from the text, p. 123.

All the villains show symptoms of marked distaste for physical love. Mr. Jones of *Victory* loathes women; as his lieutenant says, "He can't stand them at all." Old Jörgenson, although he has a wife back home, seems in the second half of *The Rescue*, to feel almost as much antipathy for women as Mr. Jones. Although some of the other villains are married and one even has a child, they clearly do not love their wives, tend to mistreat them, and show, in fact, a surprising taste for celibacy. We recall the suffering of Mrs. de Barral, who finally dies "from neglect, absolutely from neglect" by her husband. The cruelty of Schomberg, Scevola, and de Montevesso toward their wives needs no documentation. What is a little less obvious is the evidence that de Montevesso, for example, may never have slept with his wife at all. The reader of *Suspense* will recall that de Montevesso, after a year of marriage, sends Adéle back to her parents because living with her is "too much of a torture for him." Later, friends offer to have the marriage annulled. Finally, de Montevesso and Adéle come to an agreement whereby she lives with him one month out of the year "to save appearances." In *The Rover*, Conrad states explicitly that Scevola and Arlette have never slept together. Critics have tended to take at face value Conrad's explanation to Garnett that he made Scevola so sexually diffident in order to keep Arlette "untouched"[2] for Réal, suggesting that he is pandering to his reader's sentimentality.[3] But, seen in the larger context of Conrad's villains, Scevola's remarkable ability to curb for ten years his "growing impatience" (as Mr. Wiley sympathetically describes it),[4] seems to result from something more than a desire to please the public.

Although the villain shows distaste for woman as a sexual partner, he is nevertheless capable of exhibiting abnormally possessive feelings over some woman to whom he relates, literally or figuratively, as father to daughter.[5] The best example here is, of course, de Barral. When he gets out of prison, he tells Flora of his love for her in terms that go far beyond the usual expressions of parental affection: "I lived only for you . . . There were only you and me . . . I did nothing but think of you! . . . You haunted me, I tell you." When he learns of his daughter's marriage to Anthony, he chokes until he collapses, and then a "jealous rage" affects his brain like "fumes of wine." When father and daughter go aboard the *Ferndale*, de Barral talks to her as if she were a prostitute (recalling Alvan Hervey's tirade); he tells her that she has "sold" herself, watches her go into her cabin "as if into a house of disgrace." and "gnash[es] his teeth at her" when she goes to speak to her husband. Closest to de Barral as the insanely jealous blood relation is José Ortega, the impotent lover of Rita, his cousin.[6] The other villains whom we have mentioned—Mr. Jones, Schomberg, Jörgenson, Scevola, and de Montevesso—would seem not to fit into de Barral's category since they have no daughters, nor even any nieces (except de Montevesso, who shows considerable dismay over his niece's admiration of Cosmo). Without straying too far from reason, however, we can see that Scevola and de Montevesso stand in relation to their wives as fathers rather than husbands. Of course, they show little fatherly regard, but they perform the father's function of affording shelter and protection for their weak, young wives. Arlette obviously could not have returned to her anti-revolutionist parents' home at Escampobar without the protection of the Jacobin, Scevola. Nor could the anti-revolutionist Adéle Armand and her family have survived without the financial aid and political power of de Montevesso. Even Schomberg (a less likely father one could never expect to meet!) bases his hopes of winning Lena chiefly on the fact that she is "worse than friendless" and he is a "man of substance."

Although the married villains show little active interest in sleeping with their wives, they guard their wives' virtue with the devotion of a father protecting his only daughter. Scevola tries to kill Réal. De Montevesso seems to be planning Cosmo's death. Of course, one reason for the extreme jealousy of these villains where their wives are concerned is that fear of ridicule which so besets Alvan Hervey. De Montevesso, especially, worries about what people will say about his qualifications as a husband.

Fear of sexual inadequacy suggests another characteristic of the villain. Just as he disdains sexual relations with his woman, so is he disdained by her. Moreover, although the villain may come close to triumphing over his male rival, he endangers the woman but little, even though Conrad asserts that she is weak. Instead, the woman triumphs over him. We see that this is true even in the case of de Barral. While he ultimately destroys his wife by neglect, his wife dominates him in the most important step of his life, taking a job in a bank. Even little, unhappy Flora does not consider her father a serious obstacle to the consummation of her marriage with Anthony. De Barral's statements of extreme devotion do not move her. She meets his anger with "absolute candour." When he becomes hysterical, Flora proves to be physically stronger, pulling him back into the cab with ease. Flora returns to her father and ceases quarreling with him only after Anthony rejects her.

The chief villains in *Victory* prove to be no match for their women either. Schomberg plays the bully and his wife the terrified automaton, but she shows more courage than he in searching Mr. Jones' room. She twice interferes with his evil designs, first by helping Lena to escape with Heyst, later by telling Davidson about the Schomberg-Jones plot against the lovers. Ricardo, whom we have not yet discussed, seems at first not to fit any of our categories of villains. After all, Mr. Jones calls him a "woman-lover—[a] prevaricating, sly, low-class, amorous cuss!" As "instinctive savagery," Ricardo seems intended to be an almost allegorical figure of lust. Yet his actions do not match the characteristics attributed to him. We recall his much-heralded charge into Lena's bedroom. ("The instinct for the feral spring could no longer be denied. Ravish or kill—it was all one to him. . .") What an anti-climax the battle proves to be! Despite Conrad's long, solemn account of Lena's strong motivation to resist, the reader knows that her victory over Ricardo results simply from her powerful grip on his windpipe.

Ortega and Blunt, Jörgenson, Scevola, de Montevesso, are all helpless against female opposition. Rita twice frustrates Ortega's efforts to conquer her and laughs at him both times. She, moreover, refuses Blunt's proposal of marriage, tells George the whole story, and then laughs "her deep contralto laugh." When Jörgenson tries to use Mrs. Travers as a messenger to Lingard, she pretends to agree in order to be with Lingard but then betrays Jörgenson by not delivering the message, and precipitates the disaster that costs Jörgenson his life. Scevola is simply another Ortega, "the butt of all the girls," chased by a "mob of angry women," easily managed by old Aunt Catharine, and circumvented even by the timid Arlette, who woos Réal right under her husband's nose. De Montevesso has already been rejected by one woman when he meets Adéle, and he marries her chiefly to spite the first one. Although de Montevesso treats Adéle brutally, he often behaves like a supplicant rather than a master.

Detesting the woman with whom he is coupled, desperately desiring a woman whom he must not have, rejected and dominated by both women, the villain remains an outsider, an onlooker at love's feast. He is, in short, a voyeur, and his most characteristic action is to rage obscenely outside the door of a room where a woman he cannot touch lies waiting for his rival to make love to her. In such a scene, the villain often holds in his hand a deadly weapon which he intends to use against his rival. But the woman or her agent (*not* her lover, the villain's rival) usually frustrates the villain, and the weapon proves adequate only for the self-destruction of its holder. This scene, incidentally, almost evokes from Conrad his flabbiest prose and his most melodramatic action.

The reader will know which scene in *Chance* best fits the pattern: de Barral's attempt to murder his son-in-law. "His fixed idea was to save his girl from the man who has possessed himself of her." Conrad describes the scene in close detail, from the point of view of Powell, and the prose emphasized the "weird and nauseous" look of de Barral's hand as it appears, "short, puffy, old freckled" from behind the curtain, carrying the poison. Powell warns Anthony; Flora and Anthony clear up their misunderstanding; and the foiled de Barral watches their embrace, "puckering his eyes." Anthony carries Flora into the stern cabin to consummate their marriage while de Barral and Powell carry on a strange conversation immediately outside the door. De Barral asks Powell three times, "Did you see it?" Powell thinks that "it" means the poison, but de Barral is really referring to the awful sight of the couple embracing. De Barral, knowing that he has been defeated, begins to compare himself with his rival; then, after a few remarks on the baseness of his "wicked little fool" of a daughter, swallows his own poison.

Schomberg's earlier appearance in "Falk," in *Typhoon and Other Stories,* 1903, revealed the traits of the voyeur—gossiping, eavesdropping, "embracing every human being within range of the tongue"—which he displays in *Victory.* Schomberg's actions are even more clearly prefigured by Cornelius in *Lord Jim.* Cornelius resembles Schomberg in hating his wife, in desiring a girl young enough to be his daughter, and in wishing revenge on the man the girl loves. Too timid to accomplish the revenge himself, Cornelius enlists the aid of a piratical figure with an anonymous name (Brown-Jones) who does succeed, helped by a villainous crew. The scene of Brown's final capture, with his two parched companions in the longboat, Conrad used again in *Victory* for the arrival of Mr. Jones and his two companions on Samburan. In *Lord Jim,* however, Cornelius dies and Jewel persists, whereas in *Victory* Schomberg survives and Lena dies.

But it is Ricardo, in that novel, to whom we must turn for the fullest development of the voyeur in all Conrad. Although Conrad asserts that for Ricardo, unlike Heyst, "life was not a matter of passive renunciation but of particularly active warfare," Ricardo's actions prove that all he wants to do is watch. As soon as he arrives at the island, he takes on the role of "an observer with his faculties greedy for signs." "For what he was watching for was a sight of the girl—that girl! Just a glimpse across the burnt patch to see what she was like. He had excellent eyes." Upon reaching the curtained doorway of Lena's room, Ricardo, like Hervey outside his wife's bedroom door, pauses to finger the texture of the cloth. Then he peeks in and sees Lena doing up her hair, her bare arms raised, silhouetted "against the unshuttered, uncurtained square window-hole."

At last he plunges through the door, and in the ensuing struggle, Lena quickly defeats him and the two act out a scene with sexual implications of the most childish sort. Lena, sitting on the edge of her bed, readjusts her sarong, "which had come undone during the fight." The supposedly "feral" Ricardo, perhaps out of a sense of fair play, decides to expose himself too, thus making another characteristic voyeur gesture. His exhibition is purely symbolic and without doubt unconscious on Conrad's part, but it is nonetheless obvious.

> "All right. I never meant to hurt you—though I am no joker when it comes to it."
> He pulled up the leg of his pyjamas to exhibit the strapped knife.

Remembering that Ricardo meant to "ravish or kill" we are surely justified in seeing the knife as a phallic symbol. Certainly Lena reacts to it in this way, for she glances at the knife with scorn and murmurs, "Ah, yes —with that thing stuck in my side. In no other way." After a short but friendly chat, Ricardo leaves, first asserting, symbolically, that he is still potent: " 'I carry a pretty deadly thing about me . . .' He tapped his leg." Lena and Ricardo complete their symbolic battle for his masculinity in a struggle over the dagger at the climax of the novel. On the realistic level, Lena has two purposes in trying to acquire the dagger: to disarm Ricardo and to rearm Heyst, who has been deprived of his revolver. At the same time, the reader cannot miss the fact that Ricardo himself has virtually no potency left, once he comes into Lena's presence. He tells her that during the day every time he thought about her he thought that his heart would burst one of his ribs. "It has knocked itself dead tired, waiting for this evening, for this very minute. And now it can do no more. Feel how quiet it is!" Ricardo's vigor has been expended upon himself, while he was away from the woman whom he thought he wished to ravish.

Ricardo is clearly doomed. "Dog-tired," he drops to the floor (Lena occupies the only chair). Lena looks down on him thoughtfully: "Woman-like, all her faculties remained concentrated on her heart's desire—on the knife." Ricardo again makes his exhibitionist gesture, tapping his leg; he is "surprised, flattered, by the lighting up of her face." Lena bends over him and asks for the knife; Ricardo obediently hands it to her, claiming now no powers for it, saying only that it is a "good friend." Ricardo has been completely destroyed: "The very sting of death was in her hands; the venom of the viper in her paradise, extracted, safe in her possession—and the viper's head all but lying underneath her heel." We notice here, besides the sexual connotations, Conrad's painful borrowing from Shakespeare: Lena, the Cleopatra of Samburan conquers her Roman, receives a wound under her "swelling breast"—and when she dies, it is without ever having had real Anthony. Ricardo finds himself defeated by Lena and ambushed by Mr. Jones and Heyst. Like Hervey with the fan and Willems with the kriss, he looks "all over the floor" for the dagger and then runs out into the darkness.

*Victory's* melodramatic voyeur scene departs from the pattern we have outlined in one striking particular, the death of Lena. Were Conrad following his usual train of events Ricardo rather than Lena would have died by Mr. Jones' bullet; Heyst would still have died by fire; but Lena would have persisted, eliminating unsatisfactory males until the end of time . . . Although the voyeur scenes as a group are badly written, Lena's death seems to one critic at least, Conrad's "later writing at its worst."[7] Perhaps Conrad wrote thus because he simply did not believe in Lena's death.

*The Arrow of Gold, The Rescue,* and *The Rover* all fit the pattern. Rita and Ortega, in *The Arrow of Gold,* perform the ritual twice, the first time in early childhood. Rita tells George about the occasion, remarking that Ortega "wasn't much bigger than myself but he was older." (The villains are rarely much bigger than the heroines. We recall that Flora easily subdues her father and that Lena is actually bigger than Ricardo and even boosts him out of a window when Heyst approaches.) Like Ricardo, Ortega is an exhibitionist. He dresses well to impress Rita, and he lets her "look at him for half an hour." Rita feels that he, in turn, is staring at her: "I remember trying to hide my bare feet under the edge of my skirt as I sat below him on the ground." Later, Ortega approaches with the inevitable weapon, a switch, in hand. Rita obediently lies down, stiff with fright, but Ortega simply bends over and kisses her neck. This seems both to satisfy and to frighten him: "by that time I was gone dead all over and he could have done what he liked with the corpse but he left off suddenly." For the next two months they enact the same scene daily with Ortega sometimes throwing stones at the entrance to a cavelike shelter where Rita hides.

Years later, Rita and Ortega reënact the scene, this time with George as spectator. Once again it is an interior scene, a room where the woman lies in a negligee, ready for bed (we recall Flora in her robe, Lena first in a sarong, then in a fetching black gown), waiting for George, not Ortega. But the voyeur rages outside the door. Like Alvan Hervey, Ortega fears the ridicule of public opinion: "This story will be all over the world . . . Deceived, decoyed, inveigled, in order to be made a laughingstock before the most debased of all mankind, that woman and her associates." Ortega carries his weapon, although it is antique and inadequate for the intended purpose: "It was an Abyssinian or Nubian production of a bizarre shape; the clumsiest thing imaginable . . . a mere cruel-looking curio of inconceivable clumsiness to European eyes." It serves, however, to save the lovers by wounding Ortega himself when he trips on the stairs.

In *The Rescue*, Jörgenson and Mrs. Travers go through their scene aboard the *Emma* with little emotion. Jörgenson, in fact, shows virtually no interest in Mrs. Travers' charm. He does, however, hold a prolonged colloquy with her at her bedroom door about Lingard's watch, now in Mrs. Travers' possession—and stopped, of course. Jörgenson is surprised that Mrs. Travers opens her door wide, and while he disapproves of her sarong, he nevertheless looks at her. They speak of Lingard, Mrs. Travers casts down her eyes "in intolerable desire," and Jörgenson hastens away. She comes on deck in pursuit and discovers him with a deadly weapon of an unconventional sort. It is a time-fuse which he is making with "several bits of rather thin and dirty-looking rope."

> He tried to wave her away with the stump of the pencil. He did not want to be interrupted in his strange occupation. He was playing very gravely indeed with those bits of string.

Jörgenson intends to set off the powder magazine should his and Lingard's plans fail, because Mrs. Travers does not give Lingard Jörgenson's message, the plans do fail, and one more voyeur dies. Jörgenson, it is true, does not die by his original weapon, the fuse; still, he has a lighted cigar clamped between his teeth when he jumps to his death through the inevitable doorway, the hatch of the powder magazine.

In *The Rover*, the voyeur scene is developed only slightly, and in *Suspense* there is just a hint of it. Throughout *The Rover*, Scevola slouches about spying spitefully upon Arlette and Peyrol. Arlette and Réal. When Arlette lies down on Réal's bed, Scevola tries the handle of the locked door. Later that night he seizes his awkward weapon, the stable fork, and sets out after Réal whom he believes to be hiding in the cabin of Peyrol's boat. Like Ortega, he shouts imprecations outside the door, but then finds himself thrust into the cabin, made a prisoner, and later shot by the British. In *Suspense*, the two voyeur scenes are extremely shadowed and are viewed exclusively from within the heroine's boudoir. Adéle appears first in a dressing gown, then décolleté, each time accompanied by Cosmo. On both occasions there is some evidence that the lovers are being observed: a door moves slightly; footsteps are heard. It is interest-

52   JOSEPH CONRAD: *A Critical Symposium*

ing to notice, incidentally, that the watcher in the first scene is not Cosmo's male rival, de Montevesso, but the latter's sixteen-year-old niece, Clelia. This reminds us that there are minor feminine versions of the voyeur in several of the late love stories. These women object to hero and heroine coupling, often on moral grounds (Mrs. Fyne, Therese, Catharine), but there are sometimes strong hints that, like Clelia, they have designs upon the hero. This does not apply perhaps to Mrs. Fyne, but clearly Therese is interested in George, who detests her, and Catharine has longings, if not for Réal, then surely for his old colleague in love, Peyrol.

It is hardly necessary to note, here, that the voyeur scenes which recur with painful regularity in the later novels are clearly prefigured in the early love stories. Dain, Nina, and Almayer; Willems, Aissa, and her father; Nostromo, Giselle, and Viola, all act in such scenes. But the scenes represent relatively minor flaws in their works, and the rivals are far from stock villains. Only in the triangle of Jasper, Freya, and Heemskirk, at the very end of Conrad's major period, do we see the full-blown villain appear. The extent to which villains dominate the later novels provides us with a good indication of the depth of Conrad's decline.

If we put together all the characteristics of the villain, what is the composite picture? We see a short, dark man, moustached, unhealthy, violent, cowardly, a foreigner and political extremist (of either party, but tending to be a Leftist or, simply, an "anarchist"). Can we discover the source of the Conrad villain? Douglas Hewitt suggests the "schoolboy's adventure story";[8] we might add the stage melodrama and the ballad. The Conrad villain has further, more ominous, analogues. He is the liberal's image of the fascist, and the conservative's image of a communist. He is the stereotyped scapegoat of every generation; he is, at times, that eternal scapegoat, the Jew. We reject the Conrad who makes Cornelius "The Nazarene." Heemskirk, a Dutchman, does not look like a Dutchman, being dark, swarthy, with a "hooked nose." Conrad's intentions about de Barral are fairly clear:

> "Was he a foreigner?" [The narrator asks Marlow.] "It's clearly a French name. I suppose it *was* his name?"
> "Oh, he didn't invent it. He was born to it, in Bethnal Green, as it came out during the proceedings. He was in the habit of alluding to his Scotch connections. But every great man has done that. The mother, I believe, was Scotch, right enough. The father, de Barral, whatever his origins, retired from the Customs Service (tide-waiter I think), and started lending money in a very, very small way . . ."

A survey of the villains reveals also that Conrad intends them to represent something beyond themselves. To virtually every one of them he attaches the adjective "fatal" at least once, and the later ones he explicitly calls the Devil or Satan (Heemskirk, Mr. Jones, Ortega). Critics have tended to defend the overly explicit characterizations of the later villains as part of Conrad's new, allegorical method.[9] Yet we wonder how one can defend their appalling lack of vitality. We must nevertheless admit that Conrad does succeed with these villains to the extent of making their actions relate to their function of symbolizing evil. He accomplishes this partly by an emphasis on their interest in accumulating wealth. A number of the voyeur-villains share a longing for quick and easy money. We think, in particular, of the Great de Barral, the gambler Mr. Jones, and Scevola, who gained a prosperous farm by marrying Arlette. Although interested in money, the villains care nothing for work, for production, for converting money into usable goods. Their characteristic place of business is a dingy, dilapidated office, often in or near a warehouse full of merchandise too old and dusty to be sold. Marlow refers to de Barral's headquarters as "an old enormous rat-infested brick house." Ironically, although de Barral has chosen such a place by instinct rather than design, his customers immediately see it as symbolic of de Barral's devotion to his motto, "Thrift, Thrift, Thrift." In their hunger for money, Conrad's villains have more important antecedents than the bad men of the boy's adventure story: Conrad is in the tradition of writers like the Dickens of *Bleak House* who see evil as *keeping*.

When we turn to examine the role of the heroine in the later love story, we remember the hallmark of the early heroine—garden imagery. We saw the male's fear of the predatory female expressed in those images of rich foliage, of creepers especially, strangling the masculine trees. In the later novels, when Conrad's style is in general much barer of images, the gardens virtually disappear. We do notice traces in Conrad's explicit and rather clumsy application of the Garden of Eden myth in *Victory*. The myth is of course quite convenient—Heyst as Adam, Mr. Jones as Satan, and Lena as Eve—but it serves only to label and not to give meaning to the characters.

While the heroine of the later novels has been taken from her garden, she is still surrounded by heat and light. In our *locus classicus* for the Conrad love story, "The Return," we saw glowing fire and dazzlingly brilliant light associated with Mrs. Hervey and opposed to Mr. Hervey. In virtually every rejection scene throughout Conrad, one or both of these images appears. Nina rejects her father by the light of a campfire. Aissa rejects Willems once by firelight, once in extremely bright sunlight. When Jewel throws her arms around Jim, just before his suicide, the sky over Patusan is "blood-red," but when she pronounces her judgment against Jim to Marlow, the imagery is reversed:

> Her figure seemed shaped in snow; the pendent crystals of a great chandelier clicked above her head like glittering icicles . . . I was chilled as if these vast apartments had been the cold abode of despair.

At the end of *Nostromo*, after the hero's death, Linda climbs up to the top of the lighthouse and looks "like a black speck upon the shining panes." Freya waves good-by to Jasper on his last voyage with the rosy glow of the rising sun on her face. When Flora enters the cabin to choose

Anthony over her father (thus to destroy both), "the light fell strongly on her." She appears to the watching Powell "whiter than the lilies." The most flamboyant of these scenes is, of course, Lena's conquest of Ricardo. But we also notice the emphasis given to firelight, gaslight, and candlelight in the Rita-Ortega-George scene at the end of *The Arrow of Gold*. In *The Rescue*, Mrs. Travers approaches Lingard, bearing his destruction and a lighted torch. Conquered, he lies with his head on her knee in the glow of dying embers.

We have already seen how Conrad defines some of these images within the contexts of their particular stories. In "The Return," the fire is equated with Mrs. Hervey's evil, female, sexual passion. Whiteness has unpleasant connotations throughout "Heart of Darkness." It is associated with Brussels (the sepulchral city) and the inhuman ivory traders; it is associated with falsehood and death, whereas darkness seems to mean truth and vitality. In *Lord Jim*, whiteness, the East, and Patusan form a group of images which express Jim's romantic dreams, his unconscious longings for peace and death. We must be cautious, however, in generalizing about whiteness. In *The Nigger of the "Narcissus,"* whiteness has only good connotations, so it is possible, too, that the later Conrad's use of whiteness with reference to his heroines has meanings which differ from earlier ones. After all, is not Flora "whiter than the lilies"? Conrad's intentions about whiteness are even clearer in *Victory*: Lena dies with "divine radiance on her lips"; while she is dying, Heyst and Davidson look "mournfully at the little black hole made by Mr. Jones's bullet under the swelling breast of a dazzling and as it were sacred whiteness." Again a religious implication—but the awkwardness of "as it were" makes us a little suspicious, makes us want to scrutinize the imagery of the Lena-Ricardo scene.

The scene takes place in a room brilliantly lighted by that somewhat implausible and quasi-religious prop, the eight-branched candelabra. The cool and the meaning of the light change dramatically when Lena seizes Ricardo's weapon:

> At the moment when she bent forward to receive it from him, there was a flash of fire in her mysterious eyes—a red gleam in the white mist which wrapped the promptings and longings of her soul. She had done it.

Although Conrad may assert divine purity for Lena, he has not really departed from his attitude toward Mrs. Hervey in "The Return," where a red gleam meant destructive female passion. In the final crisis between man and woman, Conrad sees woman this way. It is perfectly fitting, symbolically, that Heyst should die in flames in the hut which he shared with Lena.

Conrad rarely accepts this deep-seated terror of the heroines who are always destroying villains and heroes alike. Except in the cases of Amy Foster and Alice Jacobus, he vitiates his female characterizations by sentimentalizing over them. Thus he attributes purity to Flora, sacred divinity to Lena. Even over Aissa, whom Conrad intends to be purely savage, he must wring more than one false tear. In this respect, Conrad differs from Hemingway, who suffers some of Conrad's difficulty in creating women. Except for the mannish Brett Ashley of *The Sun Also Rises,* the heroines of Hemingway novels tend, it is true, to be sentimentalized, particularly Catherine in *A Farewell to Arms* and Maria in *For Whom the Bell Tolls.* In the short stories, however, Hemingway successfully exploits his misogynous feelings in a way that Conrad could not. The classic example is the bitter account of the woman who murders her husband in "The Short Happy Life of Francis Macomber."[10]

There remains to be considered of our love trio only the hero. A survey of the lover-heroes shows that a triangle does not always obtain, that Willems and Yanko, for example, are destroyed without the presence of a villainous rival. This reminds us of Mr. Wiley's perception that the heroes and villains are doubles.[11] The hero and the villain have the same basic weaknesses which the villain acts out explicitly in socially unacceptable behavior. Like the villain, the hero is, essentially, an impotent voyeur, destined to be destroyed when he becomes involved with a woman. In *Lord Jim* and *Nostromo,* Conrad scrutinizes the motives of the defeated lovers's suicides, but in the later novels he does not. The reader may nevertheless wonder whether it is loss of love which motivates Peyrol's and Heyst's suicides or whether it is hurt pride at having proved inadequate lovers. An astonishing number of the major Conradian heroes who become involved with women die violent, melodramatic deaths: Willems, Jim, Decoud, Nostromo, Anthony, Heyst, and Peyrol. Razumov is deafened and George seriously wounded. It is perhaps symbolic of Conrad's career that we leave the hero of the unfinished last novel headed away from his beloved, out to sea . . . Of the lover-heroes only Charles Gould is spared a violent death. As far as the quality of the style is concerned, Jim's death, alone, is told in first-rate, Conradian prose.

We must guard against being surprised, shocked or horrified at Conrad's negative attitude toward love. How could it be otherwise? Conrad sees man as lonely and morally isolated, harried by egoistic longings for power and peace, stumbling along a perilous path, his only hope benumbing labor or, in rare cases, a little self-knowledge. Conrad could not possibly reconcile so dark a view with a belief in the panacea of love, wife, home, and family. In "Amy Foster," Conrad expresses this clearly. Yanko's true state is symbolized by the wretchedness of his arrival in Colebrook; his marriage to Amy is a futile, uncritical, romantic gesture doomed to destroy him. Conrad makes it clear that Yanko's son will have to follow the same journey.

More unusual than his pessimism is the inhibiting effect of sexual subject matter on Conrad's creative processes. The failure of imagination in the love stories can be seen in the woodenness of the actors and their lack of perception. Let us take Conrad's villains as an example. Insofar as they participate in love stories, they fail as caricatures. Although the short account of de Barral's adventure into finance is one of the most interesting passages in *Chance,* de Barral as a jealous father is an utter fraud. These love villains do not fail because Conrad is an inept caricaturist. Conrad at his best creates many successful caricatures although they are never his major interest. All of Jim's doubles are memorable not only for shedding light on Jim's moral problem but also for their vigor as personalities. We think of the fat skipper of the *Patna* and his friend, the "old stager," with delirium tremens. We think, too, of the French lieutenant and of Stein, who come to life, partly at least, because Conrad insists upon their external, national traits. Only Cornelius fails. He infects Jewel, Jim and the prose, which becomes pretentious and verbose. But when Gentleman Brown, ironic reminder of Jim's guilt in the white world, supplants Cornelius, the prose tightens, the action is again absorbing. Douglas Hewitt denies that the villains of the love stories are true doubles for the very good reason that they "lead . . . to no further knowledge"[12] of the hero. This is just another way of saying that when Conrad writes about love he does not understand his subject. Conrad is very honest in his preface to *The Arrow of Gold*: "what is lacking in the facts is simply what I did not know, and what is not explained is what I did not understand myself, and what seems inadequate is the fault of my imperfect insight."

Conrad differs radically from other great modern novelists in his lack of understanding, in his almost belligerent lack of genuine, dramatic interest in sexual problems. Although the Conradian villains could be labeled neurotic, exhibitionist, and unconsciously homosexual, they are really just cardboard figures plucked from nowhere and thrown up as obstacles to sexual consummation. Yet such characters would inspire a Dostoevski to his most intense efforts. Ford Madox Ford claims that Conrad was fascinated by the subject of incestuous love, and we have seen some suggestions of incest. But once again, incestuous love exists in Conrad's novels only as a barrier to sexual consummation, not as a deeply felt human emotion. We must turn to William Faulkner to find a writer who has truly creative interest in the question of incest.

If Conrad, unlike other modern writers, cannot attack the subject of sexual feelings directly, he seems nevertheless able to give meaning to these feelings when his principal subject is a more congenial one. In "Youth," Conrad puts into the older Marlow's account of his first view of the East almost all the images of his stereotyped, lifeless scenes of the rejected voyeur. Conrad calls particular attention to the phallicshaped object in Marlow's hand, mentions the mist, the red light, the perfume of female passion, and the ice of death. But this is not a love story at all— the woman is safely metaphorical—and the prose is Conrad at his richest and most meaningful.

> And this is how I see the East. I have seen its secret places and have looked into its very soul; but now I see it always from a small boat, a

high outline of mountains, blue and afar in the morning; like faint mist at noon; a jagged wall of purple at sun-set. I have the feel of the oar in my hand, the vision of a scorching blue sea in my eyes. And I see a bay, a wide bay, smooth as glass and polished like ice, shimmering in the dark. A red light burns far off upon the gloom of the land, and the night is soft and warm. We drag at the oars with aching arms, and suddenly a puff of wind, a puff faint and tepid and laden with strange odours of blossoms, of aromatic wood, comes out of the still night— the first sight of the East on my face. That I can never forget. It was impalpable and enslaving, like a charm, like a whispered promise of mysterious delight.

The failure of the lover's masculinity, which we have seen to be the implicit subject of the later novels, resembles, of course, the early Conrad's central concern with the test of a man's moral fitness. How often the various early heroes see their test, like the later lovers and voyeurs, through an open door! Young Marlow looks into the burning hold of the *Judea*, then leaps recklessly through the hatchway; an older Marlow peers at Africa's dark heart through the shutters of his cabin; Jim looks into the *Patna's* hold by lantern-light and sees a bulging bulkhead ready to give way; Jukes flinches at the spectacle of coolies rioting in the *Nan-Shan's* hold; the young captain cannot forget his double, sometimes asleep behind the bed-curtains, sometimes bolt upright behind the bathroom door. "The Secret Sharer" reminds us of the love stories in another way: it has two scenes in which at a critical moment a character drops an object in another's presence. The untested captain's lighted cigar, symbolic of his ignorant complacency, plops into the sea when he discovers Leggatt, like a headless corpse, at the bottom of the ladder. When they separate forever at the end of the story, Leggatt drops the captain's hat while swimming and thus provides him with a mark by which to save the ship. In none of these fine scenes does sex intervene, and the images become richly symbolic, bringing added life to Conrad's dramatization of the moral test of manhood.

We might seem to have solved the riddle of Conrad's decline: he tried to write about a subject which he did not understand. Fortunately, we are saved from such an oversimplification by the existence of *The Shadow Line*, a later novel that has nothing to do with women and love. Since *The Shadow Line* does, however, share with the rest of the late work certain serious faults, it suggests that Conrad's decline must stem from something more general than his choice of subject matter. Even without *The Shadow Line* we would be wise not to oversimplify. We should scrutinize our statement that Conrad *chose* to write about love. The fact that Conrad could relax his critical judgment enough to choose love for the subject of a major novel suggests a shift in fundamental attitude. While Conrad's critical comments about himself are not very revealing, he was in practice a fairly good judge of his own work. He was right in abandoning *The Sisters*, "The Rescuer," and *Chance*. He abandoned them because the subject was painful, but also because he knew he was writing badly. But by 1910 Conrad could decide to finish *Chance,* a long novel on a subject that he did not understand. He was looking at things in a new way; he was turning his back on moral judgment.                    (1957)

## NOTES

1. Douglas Hewitt, *Conrad: A Reassessment* (1952), p. 109.
2. *Conrad to a Friend: Letters from Joseph Conrad to Richard Curle,* ed. Richard Curle (1928), p. 299.
3. Albert J. Guerard, *Joseph Conrad* (pamphlet, 1947), p. 23.
4. Paul L. Wiley, *Conrad's Measure of Man* (1954), p. 187.
5. On this topic of Conrad's concern about the relation of father to daughter see Lenormand, pp. 5-9. [Editor's note]
6. José Ortega and Rita appear in *The Sisters* and again in *The Arrow of Gold.* Captain Anthony is from *Chance;* Alvan Hervey is from "The Return," and Mr. Jones and Schomberg are in *Victory.* On *The Arrow of Gold* see Wiley's essay, pp. 317-322. [Editor's note]
7. Hewitt, p. 111.
8. Hewitt, p. 109.
9. See Wiley, p. 135.
10. See Edmund Wilson, *The Wound and the Bow* (1947), pp. 237-240.
11. Wiley, pp. 135-136.
12. Hewitt, p. 96.

# PART TWO

# JOHN D. GORDAN

## The Four Sources*

CONRAD was seldom at a loss for material. In the Preface to *The Nigger of the "Narcissus"* he asserted his absolute moral freedom to select any subject. He felt free to send "a passing glance of wonder and pity" into the dark and the splendid experiences of life.[1] He was not afraid of the pathological, though he did not dwell upon it.[2] "Morbid psychology, be it always understood," he wrote Galsworthy about the character of Hilary Dallison in *Fraternity,* "is a perfectly legitimate subject for an artist's genius."[3] Conrad's first eight books contain unshirking studies of human disintegration. Unfalteringly he traced the decay of Almayer and Willems, the more subtle deterioration of Lingard and Mrs. Travers in *The Rescue,* the sinister corruption of the Belgian agents in "An Outpost of Progress" and "Heart of Darkness." In "The Idiots" he treated actual mental disease. Yet he could also show men rising above the influences that might have led to degeneration. The seamen on the *Narcissus* kept their integrity despite the Nigger and Donkin. Karain emerged from the shadow of madness. Lord Jim established his ideal of himself on the ruins of his past life and died to defend it.

Conrad depended upon instinct to guide him toward the right sort of subject. He tenaciously believed in "that mysterious, extraneous thing which has nothing to do with the theories of art," inspiration.[4] In describing the evolution of *The Secret Agent,*[5] he revealed his instinctive recognition of what Henry James called the germ:

> There must have been, however, some sort of atmosphere in the whole incident because all of a sudden I felt myself stimulated. And then ensued in my mind what a student of chemistry would best understand from the analogy of the addition of the tiniest little drop of the right kind, precipitating the process of crystallization in a test tube containing some colourless solution.

Once inspiration presented a subject, his judgment made strict demands. "The necessary preliminary assumption," as he said of *Lord Jim,*[6] was that the subject should be "interesting." He always stressed this vital characteristic which some writers have found so easy to forget. Interest was to him "the quality without which neither beauty nor, I am afraid, truth are effective. . . ."[7] A story had to contain "the telling, representative facts, helpful to carry on the idea, and, at the same time, of such a nature as not to demand an elaborate creation of the atmosphere to the detriment of the action." A story could not become "wearisome in the presentation of detail and in the pursuit of clearness."[8] After more than a decade of

* From John D. Gordan's *Joseph Conrad: The Making of a Novelist* (Harvard University Press, 1941), Chapter II, pp. 28-74. Some passages have been deleted, and the footnotes renumbered accordingly.

practice as a professional writer, he summed up his experience for Norman Douglas, who was then a beginner. "Try and make it a novel of *analysis* on the basis of some strong situation,"[9] he advised. The circumstances of Conrad's life provide a quick explanation of the formula. Analysis came naturally to the Slav who from boyhood had brooded over a family tragedy. The strong situation appealed to the man who had adventured in Marseilles and sailed the seven seas.

The subjects of the stories were not the product of an energetic inventive faculty, such as Jules Verne or Poe possessed. Time after time Conrad confessed: "I am not a facile inventor. I have some imagination, —but that's another thing."[10] When in "The Informer" and "An Anarchist" he exercised his inventive faculty,[11] the result left much to be desired. His power lay not in invention but in recollection. "One's literary life," he declared, "must turn frequently for sustenance to memories and seek discourse with the shades. . . ."[12] Creation came to him easily—at times came only—when he had some personal experience or some observation to elaborate. He gave a defense of his practice in a comment on "Gaspar Ruiz," which he called

> truly fiction, by which I do not mean that it is merely invented, but that it is truly imagined from hints of things that really happened and of people that really existed. . . . That sort of work is of course of a creative (not reminiscent) nature. . . . I need not say that such knowledge as I had was used throughout with a scrupulous regard to the truth of it. No incident was introduced arbitrarily but only as a necessary touch in the general picture. In this arrangement consists the art of story telling as distinguished from the style.[13]

Dependence upon memory added to his difficulties. Sometimes his personal knowledge of a subject prevented his altering fact to fit the purposes of fiction. In the early days of *An Outcast of the Islands* he grumbled: "Ce qui m'ennuie le plus ce que mes personnages sont si vrais. Je les connais si bien qu'ils m'entravent l'imagination."[14] More often his memory was slow to supply him with suitable material. During his first attempt at *The Rescue,* a novel not stemming from memory, he envied the propagandist whom he usually despised.[15] "Other writers," he complained to Edward Garnett in June, 1896,

> have some starting point. Something to catch hold of. They start from an anecdote—from a newspaper paragraph (book may be suggested by a casual sentence in an old almanack). They lean on dialect—or on tradition—or on history—or on the prejudice or fad of the hour; they trade upon some tie or some conviction of their time—or upon the absence of these things—which they can abuse or praise. But at any rate they know something to begin with—while I don't. I have had some impressions, some sensations—in my time:—impressions and sensations of common things. And it's all faded. . . .[16]

The impressions did not remain faded forever, and Conrad soon discovered that, without becoming a theorist, he could use some of the theorist's sources. Yet the disadvantages of recollection lasted into later years. In 1905 he confessed to Gosse: "Acutely conscious of being neither the interpreter in any profound sense of my own epoch nor a magician evoker of the past either in its spirit or its form, I have often suffered . . . with my work from a sense of unreality, from intellectual doubt of the ground I stood upon . . . especially in the periods of difficult production."[17] But difficulty or no, he depended for his subjects preponderantly upon memory.

Conrad felt a certain delicacy about the exploitation of the past. The repugance showed clearly when, after writing *The Mirror of the Sea* and *A Personal Record,* he was "remonstrated with for bad economy; as if such writing were a form of self-indulgence wasting the substance of future volumes." The advice distressed him. He could not "bring himself to look upon his existence and his experience, upon the sum of his thoughts, sensations, and emotions, upon his memories and his regrets, and the whole possession of his past, as only so much material for his hands."[18] Sometimes he felt almost dishonorable. "It's an odious thing," he said, "to have to write in 'descriptive' fashion of men with whom one talked like a friend and had found acceptance as one of themselves."[19] Yet this memory was responsible for his being a writer.[20] He turned to the past, not to exploit, but "to snatch in a moment of courage, from the remorseless rush of time, a passing phase of life. . . ."[21] *Almayer's Folly* was a commemoration, *The Nigger* and "Youth" were valedictions.[22]

At times Conrad fought the charge of specialization. Vainly he emphasized the general appeal of his "subjects, which are not too specialized as to the class of people or kind of events. . . ."[23] He was niched as a writer of exotic adventure stories and tales of the sea. Though he himself admitted that from "the Eastern Seas . . . I have carried away into my writing life the greatest number of suggestions,"[24] he maintained that other aspects of his work were ignored.[25] Reviewers and readers unfortunately insisted, as William McFee complained, that Conrad was "a two-fisted shipmaster who wrote nothing but tales of adventure in the Orient, tales of brave men rescuing beautiful white girls, or equally brave men falling in love with island princesses."[26] On his visit to America in 1923 the press played him up as a " 'Spinner of sea yarns—master mariner—seaman writer,' and so forth. . . ."[27] His efforts to correct the misunderstanding were futile.[28] At the very end of his life he suggested to Curle an article pointing out that "his stories expand far beyond their frame and appeal to no special public—looking for exotism, or adventure, or the sea. . . ."[29] The labeling has endured so constantly that the manuscript of *Nostromo* was catalogued in 1938 as "Conrad's Great Sea Story."[30] The persistent classification hurt his sales all his life.[31]

In handling actual past experience, his own or another's, Conrad felt unconstrained. A few preliminary conditions had to be fulfilled. The subject—one of the many "subjects of which a writer of tales is more or less conscious within himself. . . ."[32]—had to be ready for treatment. He had to await "the right moment . . . the positive feeling of it, which is a thing that cannot be discussed."[33] The right moment was unpredictable. He once explained, "*The Arrow of Gold* is a subject which I had in my mind for some eighteen years, but which I hesitated to take up till now. . . . I won't attempt to apologize for my opinion that work is not to be rushed at simply because it can be done or because one suffers from mere impatience to do it. A piece of work of any sort is only fully justified when it is done at the right time. . . ."[34] When the material matured through the chemistry of the imagination, he was seldom hampered by its connection with the actual past. "I do not write history, but fiction," he told Jean-Aubry shortly before his death, "and I am therefore entitled to choose as I please what is most suitable in regard to characters and particulars to help me in the general impression I wish to produce."[35]

The general impression often necessitated deviations from fact. Conrad commented on his adaptations of autobiographical material. "Heart of Darkness," he declared, was "experience pushed a little (and only very little) beyond the actual facts of the case for the perfectly legitimate . . . purpose of bringing it home to the minds and bosoms of the readers."[36] *The Shadow Line,* too, was "a piece of as strict autobiography as the form allowed,—I mean, the need of slight dramatization to make the thing actual. Very slight."[37] If Conrad was so unrestricted in dealing with his own experience, he must have felt even freer with the experience of others.

His freedom can be gauged from his reminiscences. "Initiation" in *The Mirror of the Sea,* written in 1905, described a rescue which took place a quarter of a century earlier.[38] The boat on which Conrad was serving "in mid-Atlantic . . . took off the crew of a Danish brig homeward bound from the West Indies."[39] The captain, a Dane, gave a long account of the wreck and a funeral oration upon his ship in the most idiomatic English.[40] In all literalness, the captain would not have spoken English, and Conrad would not have understood or remembered what he said. If the incident took place in 1875 or 1876, Conrad was on a French boat and did not yet know a word of English.[41] Since he felt so unconstrained when writing unofficial history, he could adapt his material at will to the purposes of fiction. It is consequently idle, in a study of the origins of his subjects, to look for exact correspondence. The value of such a study lies not in identification but in an understanding of Conrad's use of his raw materials.

All the ingredients which crystallized in any one story can never be reduced to a formula.[42] Yet some distinctions must be drawn between the various sources of Conrad's material. He himself believed that in the broadest sense "every novel contains an element of autobiography—and this can hardly be denied, since the creator can only express himself in his creation. . . ."[43] At once the danger of oversimplification is apparent; probably Conrad saw it more clearly than anyone. His own statement prevents misinterpretation: "The nature of the knowledge, suggestions or hints used in my imaginative work has depended directly on the conditions of my active life. It depended more on contacts, and very slight contacts at that, than on actual experience. . . ."[44] Here he made a fundamental distinction. His material was derived generally from situations and people with whom he had had no intimate connection and sometimes from personal experiences and realtionships. As he himself put it, some stories, like "The Secret Sharer," grew from "facts gleaned from hearsay or experience in the various parts of the globe"; others, like "Youth," were "a record of experience in the absolute sense of the word."[45] Conrad was but affirming his own practice when he told Norman Douglas: "A man like you, who has seen things and known many people, has got only to descend within himself for material."[46] He might find subjects in another man's life or in his own, but each was capable of imaginative transformation into fiction. If memory yielded nothing, Conrad drew upon another source: the printed page.[47] He was to mine all lodes as instinct moved him.

He began with subjects that he had found in observation of other people's lives. Soon afterwards he made use of his own experience— "experience in the absolute sense of the word."[48] Before the end of the century he turned to hearsay and books for inspiration. The three novels emphasized in this study may not be derived exclusively from one source. Yet predominantly *Almayer's Folly* was based upon observation, *The Nigger of the "Narcissus"* upon more personal experience, and *Lord Jim* upon hearsay and reading.

The indelible impression made by one personality was responsible for Conrad's career as a writer. "But if I had not got to know Almayer pretty well," he insisted, "it is almost certain there would never have been a line of mine in print."[49] He met Almayer in Borneo during his voyages out of Singapore on the *Vidar* in 1887-88.[50] The supposed facts about Almayer were set forth in *Joseph Conrad: Life and Letters* by Jean-Aubry, who apparently obtained them from Captain Craig of the *Vidar*, under whom Conrad had served as first mate.[51] Almayer—for such his name was believed to be in real life also—was a Eurasian, a Dutch half-caste, living in Bulungan up the Bulungan River in East Borneo. Married to a full-blooded Malay, he had one son. He died of a wound received on a python hunt.[52] When Captain Craig talked to Jean-Aubry in 1924, he was seventy and had been a seaman for half a century.[53] He was naturally somewhat confused in his recollections. His memory failed him on many of the facts about Almayer, and unintentionally Jean-Aubry preserved the mistakes in print.

In the summer of 1939 I visited Bulungan to inquire about the people whom, according to Captain Craig, Conrad met there and later introduced into many of his Malayan stories. I discovered that the originals of the characters had lived not in Bulungan but in Berouw (sometimes called Tandjong Redeb) on the Berouw River. The manuscript of *Almayer's Folly* contains a clue for this discovery. Though Conrad called the river in the novel the Pantai, he referred to it twice in the manuscript as the

Brow, a mistake which he corrected before the typescript was made.[54] And Sambir, the name of the village in the novel, was once called Brow in the manuscript, a slip allowed to stand in the typescript and the published text.[55] The differences in the spelling of Berouw are of no account, for Western phonetic renderings of Malay differ greatly.

In Bulungan I learned that one of Almayer's surviving children was Mrs. Andrew Gray of Malang, Java. I obtained an interview with her and Mr. Gray. What she and her husband could remember about Conrad's acquaintances in Borneo I was able to supplement with the records of the Peneleh Cemetery in Sourabaya, Java, with a letter from Mr. V. A. Cools, a resident in Berouw since 1904, and with the recollections of Mr. Pangemanan, now of Bulungan, a resident of Berouw from 1919 to 1925.

Kaspar Almayer of *Almayer's Folly* was drawn from William Charles Olmeijer of Berouw, where Conrad knew him in 1887-88. It is impossible to tell why Conrad altered the name when he kept so many real names in the same novel. Usually he found it hard to call a character drawn from life by any but his actual name. Writing to Mme. Poradowska in 1894 about one of her stories, he confessed: "Du moment que Vous *voyez* le personnage comme Wojtek il est impossible de changer le nom. Je comprends cela très bien."[56] In "Heart of Darkness" when the sinister Mr. Kurtz was first introduced, Conrad called him Klein, the real name of the Belgian agent at Stanley Falls,[57] and corrected it immediately:

meet           Kurtz
In the interior you will no doubt *Monsieur* Mr. Klein. . . .[58]

Twice more on the same page he corrected Klein to Kurtz, which he then followed throughout. In *The Shadow Line* he gave the first mate, drawn from life, the name Burns, but the man's real name, Born, slipped once into the manuscript:

sensations           urns
. . . my own *thoughts* which were not those of Mr. *Born*.[59]

Though the change of Olmeijer to Almayer was almost as slight, Conrad did not betray the name in the manuscript.

. . . . . . . . . . .

In *Almayer's Folly* Conrad used what facts he wanted from Olmeijer's life and altered or discarded the rest. He made Almayer a native of Buitenzorg and of pure Dutch parentage, which increased the humiliation of his marriage and that of his daughter with Malays. Here Conrad completely disregarded the normal Dutch tolerance for Eurasians and laid himself open to Sir Hugh Clifford's charges that he did not understand Malayan life. Almayer came to Borneo as a young man to be Lingard's agent in the handling of forest products which the English Captain exported on his brig. In later life Almayer got into trouble with the Dutch authorities for his intimacy with the natives, to whom he was suspected of selling gunpowder. Though Olmeijer had a large family, Conrad allowed Almayer only a daughter, the focal point of her father's affection, ambition, and final disappointment. The change was fundamental to the conception of the story, which in its melodramatic development illustrated the drastic changes wrought by Conrad's imagination on the facts of Olmeijer's life. Olmeijer did not die until the novel had been out five years, and his death was very different from Almayer's fatal degeneration.[60]

Clearly *Almayer's Folly* was not a record of the life of William Charles Olmeijer but an expansion of the impression made upon the novelist by the man's personality. In *A Personal Record* he left a non-fictional account of the psychological and physical impression Olmeijer made upon him at their first encounter in Berouw. He still called the man Almayer, and *A Personal Record,* it must be remembered, was written long after *Almayer's Folly.* Almayer the character may well have colored Conrad's supposedly untouched recollections of Olmeijer the man. Yet to compare the two Almayers casts light on the novelist's imaginative use of his recollections. Captain Craig of the *Vidar,* who knew Olmeijer much longer than Conrad and who became an enthusiastic reader of the work of his old first mate, called Almayer "an exact moral and physical portrait."[61] The moral impression made by Olmeijer Conrad stressed in fiction and the physical in *A Personal Record.* The comparison brings out Conrad's selection of the morbid side of Olmeijer's character, which, though apparent to the novelist and the officers of the *Vidar,* was naturally not the side emphasized by the Grays and Mr. Cools.

In *A Personal Record*[62] Almayer's face was "round and flat"; his hair was long and black "and a curly wisp of it strayed across his forehead." The years added to his age in *Almayer's Folly* brought with them gray hair, and the forehead lock was shorn. Perhaps its place was taken by "the long white beard" of his old age.[63] The "flapping pyjamas of cretonne pattern (enormous flowers with yellow petals on a disagreeable blue ground) and a thin cotton singlet with short sleeves," which Olmeijer wore when Conrad first saw him on a misty Bornean morning, were transformed in the novel into something more native, "a white jacket and flowered sarong."[64]

Though most of the details of Olmeijer's life were altered the morose aspects of his disposition seem to have been elaborated for the novel. Even the physical characteristics which suggested his sullenness were emphasized. Conrad was so impressed by the actual man's "heavy, painted glance" that he made his creation "sulky-looking."[65] Olmeijer's suspicion, elaborated in the novel, was noted in *A Personal Record.*[66] His "deep-seated mistrust" grew from his desire for success. He appeared "ambitious, aiming at the grandiose," full "of some deep scheme, of some diplomatic plan, of some hopeful intrigue."[67] Almayer revealed just such a personality.

His "dream of wealth and power"[68] was ambitious and grandiose, built on a fantastic desire to discover an inexhaustible El Dorado. Olmeijer hinted to Conrad about his " 'very large interests . . . very important interests . . . up the river.' "[69] These vague references to vast wealth were defined in *Almayer's Folly* as a gold mine in the interior.

Olmeijer's pretensions were treated as a joke by the officers of the *Vidar,* where Conrad heard his name frequently and derisively mentioned.[70] General laughter at Olmeijer's expense was perhaps echoed in the amusement which Almayer inspired in the Dutch officers visiting Sambir.[71] Conrad minimized Olmeijer's claims to distinction. He ridiculed his flock of white geese, " 'the only geese on the East Coast' " of Borneo. Olmeijer sent a goose to the officers of the *Vidar* "as if it were a sort of Court decoration."[72] Perhaps the disparity between the man's conception of his greatness and the means whereby he showed it impressed the incident on Conrad. In the novel when the officers from the Dutch gunboat come to Almayer's house, he said to them, " 'I can give you a goose. Look at my geese—the only geese on the east coast—perhaps on the whole island.' " The phrase, " 'the only geese on the east coast,' " must have been used by the actual man: Conrad employed it again towards the end of the novel.[73]

Olmeijer's house was described by Mr. Gray as unusually large for Berouw and as old-fashioned, with numerous guns in the wall racks. It must have been pretentious because it was nicknamed Olmeijer's Folly by the captain of the *Vidar.*[74] In the novel much was made of the ruinous conditions of the mansion which Almayer built to house his future splendor and where he hid his destitute old age. Indeed Almayer's Folly, "his new but already decaying house—that last failure of his life," was symbolic of the futility of his dreams. The nickname in the novel was bestowed upon the house by the officers of the Dutch gunboat, whom Conrad patterned upon the officers of the *Vidar.*[75]

Olmeijer hated his surroundings and was "always complaining of being lost to the world. . . ."[76] Similarly Almayer was always dreaming of escaping from Sambir to the Europe he had never seen.[77] Conrad twice described the attitude of the actual man as "aggrieved." " 'Nothing was ever quite worthy of you,' " he explained to him in an imagined conversation in *A Personal Record.*[78] " 'What made you so real to me was that you held this lofty theory with some force of conviction and with an admirable consistency.' " Conrad's imagination expanded Olmeijer's self-pity for the latter part of the novel. A sense of grievance caused Almayer's final repudiation of Nina and drove him to burn his old house, to segregate himself in Almayer's Folly from the rest of Sambir, and to drug himself to death.[79] On the lack of "faith, hope or pride," the "absence of any sort of sustaining spirit,"[80] which Conrad noticed in Olmeijer, he based Almayer's psychological and moral degeneration. Obviously Conrad selected the aspect of Olmeijer which appealed to his imagination and developed it as if it were the whole man. It is indeed necessary to distinguish not so much between the Almayers in *A Personal Record* and *Almayer's Folly* as between Olmeijer and Conrad's Almayer.

Of the other figures in *Almayer's Folly* Conrad had little to say, and that little was somewhat ambiguous. *A Personal Record*[81] implied that each character was suggested in some measure by a personality he encountered in Berouw. Yet a study of "the rest of that Pantai band" shows that their origin was complex.

Mrs. Almayer of Sambir, a full-blooded Malay, bore slight resemblance to Mrs. Olmeijer of Berouw, who was a Malay or a Eurasian. Both women were married young, but Mrs. Almayer lived to old age,[82] whereas Mrs. Olmeijer died at thirty-five, according to Mrs. Gray. Conrad provided Mrs. Almayer with a background of violence for which no similarity in fact can be discovered, and the manuscript of the novel reveals changes in details made as he worked out the characterization. He referred first to "the romantic story of some child—a girl—rescued from a piratical prau." Probably the implication that the girl was held against her will prompted him to correct it in the manuscript to "the romantic tale of some child—a girl—found in a piratical prau."[83] She was called the granddaughter of the Sultan of Sulu, and in the manuscript had originally been the daughter of the captain of a Sulu piratical prau, though in the final reading her exact paternity was cancelled.[84] As a young girl she sailed with Sulu pirates on their raids, until Lingard exterminated them. He adopted her, had her educated in a convent in Java, and then married her to Almayer.[85] The convent moved elusively around the island to Java. First it was mentioned unspecifically as "some convent in Java"; next it was declared to be in Sourabaya and then in Samarang.[86] Mrs. Almayer's conventual education was perhaps derived from the experience of five of Olmeijer's daughters, who were sent to a convent in Sourabaya, according to Mrs. Gray, herself brought up as a protestant in Macassar. No closer connection between fact and fiction can be traced.

The origin of Nina Almayer is even more obscure. Mrs. Gray never heard of a Nina in her family. The Olmeijers had six daughters, of whom the eldest could not have been more than twelve in 1887-88; it is unlikely that Conrad had one of them in mind as his heroine. Nina Almayer was sent away from Borneo to be educated, and this possibly reflected the education of Olmeijer's daughters. By allowing Almayer one child and that a girl Conrad increased the isolation of his hero. Nina's love affair with Dain Maroola gave an extra pang to " 'the very anguish of paternity' "[87] stressed in the characterization of Almayer. Nina's crossed strains of Malayan and European provided a heroine of a type that attracted Conrad during his experiences in the East. Years after he completed the novel he confessed, "A dash of Orientalism on white is very fascinating, at least for me; though I must say that the genuine Eastern had never the power to lead me away from the path of rectitude; to any serious extent—that is."[88] The temptation to see in Nina the reflection of a particular personal experience must be firmly repressed.

Lingard played an increasingly important role in the three novels in which he appeared. The Tom Lingard of *Almayer's Folly* and *An Outcast* was apparently founded upon a Captain Tom Lingard whom Conrad met at Berouw. The actual Lingard was a Scotchman, according to Mr. Cools, a trader of considerable consequence. He paid the Sultan of Sambaliung, who ruled Berouw, a relatively large yearly tax of seven hundred florins. He had business connections with the Getle Company of Singapore, and Captain Craig remembered him as "the captain of a schooner which traded between Singapore, Benjarmassim, Cottu, Bulungan, and other Dutch places to the north."[89] Lingard and Olmeijer shared many commercial interests. Mrs. Gray recalled that her father shipped his goods by Lingard's schooner when there was no direct line between Borneo and Java and all shipments had to go via Singapore. Mr. Cools added that before coming to live at Berouw Lingard represented Olmeijer in Bulungan. Lingard's voyages brought him high renown. He was called Rajah Laut by the Malays, and he discovered a channel for ships in the Berouw River still called on the official chart "Baak van Lingard."

It is easy to see what Conrad was inspired to borrow for the Tom Lingard of *Almayer's Folly*. An English trader called Rajah Laut by the Malays, he sailed everywhere in the Dutch East Indies. In Borneo he discovered the channel of the dangerous Pantai River. He guarded the secret jealously, became rich on the trade monopoly, and was a power in the little native state, Sambir. He took Almayer on his schooner as supercargo and then established him as land agent in Sambir to collect goods for shipment. Marrying Almayer to his adopted daughter, Lingard treated him like a son.

The connection between Lingard and Almayer suggests a relationship Conrad observed in Berouw. The actual Captain Lingard, according to Mrs. Gray and Mr. Pangemanan, married a sister of Olmeijer's, but the couple was childless. Lingard had a nephew, Jim Lingard, whom he took as an associate on his ship and later helped to set up as a trader in Berouw. Another nephew, Joshua Lingard, brother of Jim, suspected that Conrad was the author of the stories in which the inhabitants of Berouw appeared as characters. "I had a visit from a man out of the Malay Seas," Conrad wrote Pinker in 1909. "It was like the raising of a lot of dead—dead to me, because most of them live out there and even read my books and wonder who [the] devil has been around taking notes. My visitor told me that Joshua Lingard made the guess: 'It must have been the fellow who was mate in the *Vidar* with Craig.' . . . And the best of it is that all these men of 22 years ago feel kindly to the Chronicler of their lives and adventures."[90]

Jean-Aubry suggested that another inspiration from Conrad's past experience went into Lingard, "traits . . . borrowed from Dominic Cervoni, who, from Conrad's first seafaring days to the end of his literary life, was a sort of familiar demon of his imagination."[91] Perhaps to some extent Cervoni directed Conrad's imagination when he was creating any intensely masculine figure. Yet the characters admittedly modeled on

Cervoni[92] all exhibit a grave, ironic experienced personality in direct contrast with the violent sentimental and naive Lingard. Another influence can also be traced. The conception of Lingard in *The Rescue* apparently owed much to the diaries and letters of the Rajah James Brooke of Sarawak,[93] of whom more will be said in connection with *Lord Jim.*

Conrad modeled some of the minor white characters upon his acquaintances. He gave old Hudig, the great merchant of Macassar who at one time employed both Almayer and Willems, the name and possibly the personality of a Dutch merchant whom he knew in Amsterdam during the winter of 1887 just before he went to Borneo.[94] The account of the actual man can be found in *The Mirror of the Sea.*[95] "Mr. Hudig . . . was a big, swarthy Netherlander, with black moustaches and a bold glance. He always began by shoving me into a chair before I had time to open my mouth, gave me cordially a large cigar, and in excellent English would start to talk everlastingly about the phenomenal severity of the weather." Though Conrad nowhere described the appearance of the fictional Hudig, he seems to have borrowed mannerisms from the actual man. The cordiality was heightened for the merchant's boisterous way with visiting captains, whom he pushed into his inner office and plied with liquor and tobacco.[96] Though in *Almayer's Folly* Hudig spoke in broken English, in the first draft his English was far less foreign than it was after Conrad worked on it.[97] The broken English was completely abandoned in *An Outcast.*[98] Probably Conrad always thought of the character as speaking "excellent English," like the original. In outline, the Hudig of Macassar seems to have sprung directly from the Hudig of Amsterdam.

Another figure who apparently stood for a thumbnail sketch in *Almayer's Folly* was the captain of the *Vidar,* who appeared as Captain Ford. The *Vidar* was a steamer, owned by an Arab, like Ford's boat in the novel.[99] Both Conrad and Jean-Aubry were reticent about the captain's true name: in *A Personal Record*[100] Conrad called him Captain C— and Jean-Aubry followed the disguise even after an interview with him. From an inadvertent reference in one of Conrad's letters he can be identified as Captain Craig.[101]

Conrad's connection with the *Vidar* provided him with many of the arresting natives in *Almayer's Folly* and *An Outcast.* The *Vidar* "belonged to an Arab called Syed Mosin Bin S. Ali Jaffree,"[102] a descendant of Mohammed, as the designation Syed shows. His actual son Abdulla[103] appeared in *Almayer's Folly* as "the great trader of Sambir." Conrad supplied the fictional Abdulla with a nephew, "Syed Reshid, returned from his pilgrimage to Mecca, rejoicing in . . . the proud title of Hadji."[104] He created his fictional Arabs by moving the actual Arabs forward one generation.

·   ·   ·   ·   ·   ·   ·   ·   ·   ·   ·   ·   ·

Conrad's free use of past associations extended even to the geography of *Almayer's Folly.* His four months on the *Vidar* gave him first-hand

knowledge of many places in the East Indies that provided a setting for
his stories. The trading steamer, according to Jean-Aubry, traveled from
Singapore through Carimata Strait to Banjarmassim on the south coast of
Borneo; then through Pulo Laut Strait, with a stop at the island of Pulo
Laut for coal, and across the Strait of Macassar to Dongala on the west
coast of Celebes; back across the Strait to Berouw and Bulungan on the
east coast of Borneo.[105] To these ports of call Richard Curle, who must
have been informed by Conrad himself, added "Palawan in the Sulu Sea
and Palambang in Sumatra,"[106] and Mr. Cools added Samarinda.

In *Almayer's Folly* Conrad gave a general geographic setting but
avoided specific identification of places. In all his later stories he followed
the same principle. He wished to stimulate, not limit the reader's imagination. The names of countries and large cities were sufficiently general, he
believed, to be given without danger from the reader's associations. Yet
exactness in the names of small villages and districts might be dangerous
because of discrepancies between the description and the actual spot. He
made his point of view plain in rebuking Richard Curle:

> Didn't it ever occur to you . . . that I knew what I was doing in
> leaving the facts of my life and even of my tales in the background?
> Explicitness . . . is fatal to the glamour of all artistic work, robbing it
> of all suggestiveness, destroying all illusions. . . . In "Youth," in
> which East or West are of no importance whatever, I kept the name
> of the Port of landing out of the record of "poeticized" sensations. The
> paragraphs you quote of the East meeting the narrator is all right in
> itself; whereas directly it's connected with . . . it becomes nothing at
> all . . . is a dammed hole without any beach and without any glamour,
> and in relation to the parag. is not in tone. Therefore the par., when
> pinned to a particular spot, must appear diminished—a fake. And yet
> it is true![107]

Of the islands Conrad visited on the *Vidar* Borneo was the most important for *Almayer's Folly,* and it is revealed as the general setting of
the story in the eighth paragraph.[108] Though Almayer lived on the east
coast, the identification is not too exact, since Borneo is the second largest
island in the world and the east coast some eight hundred miles long.
The reader is able to associate with such a broad background all he may
have imagined about the East Indies.

In treating the specific scene of the novel Conrad was more cautious.
Since he met Almayer and many of the other characters up the Berouw
River in the little settlement of Berouw, the actual place-names might be
expected. Yet he never mentioned them in *A Personal Record* or the
Author's Note of *An Outcast of the Islands,* in which he discussed the
origins of the characters. For the river in the novel he borrowed the name
Pantai from the southern mouth of the Berouw, a disguise that half re-
veals. In the manuscript he twice referred to the fictional Pantai as the
Brow, inconsistencies corrected by the time the typescript was made.[109]
He took greater precautions to prevent the identification of Berouw with

Sambir, the name of the settlement in the novel. Yet he slipped once into calling the place Brow, a blunder that stood in the manuscript, typescript, and printed text.[110] In the manuscript the settlement was sixty miles from the sea, but in the typescript the distance was only thirty miles.[111] Perhaps he remembered that Berouw lay up river "forty miles . . . more or less."[112] Though no Sambir can be found on the map of Borneo he may have adopted the name from Tandjong (or Point) Sambar, which the *Vidar* passed just east of Carimata Strait, or from an abbreviation of Sambaliung, a name for Berouw on some maps. At Berouw the Berouw River forks; the northern branch is called the Sega and the southern, the Kelai. In the novel the division was mentioned as "the two branches of the Pantai"—"the main stream of the Pantai" and "the Sambir reach."[113] The settlement of Berouw itself is composed of two main villages, Gunung Tabur and Tandjong Redeb, sometimes called Sambaliung. Sambir itself was divided into two settlements: Almayer lived on one side of the river and Lakamba on the other.[114]

Conrad first used and later discarded material that he must have picked up by direct contact. The young man whose indecorous attentions produced Nina's rift with Mrs. Vinck was described in the manuscript as " 'that young fellow from Katz's Brothers' " and "the employé of Messers: Katz Bthers";[115] in the printed text he was called " 'that young fellow from the bank' " and "the young man from the bank."[116] Possibly Katz Brothers was then so well known in the East that Conrad decided to avoid the name. Of the Vincks he made an inconsistent double use. Mr. Vinck was first a clerk of old Hudig's in Macassar.[117] Later the Vincks were reintroduced as "good friends" of Lingard's in Singapore with whom Nina went to live.[118] At some time Conrad must have been strongly impressed by people named Vinck.

Somewhere in Celebes and Borneo he probably came upon a political assassination. Sketching the background of *An Outcast of the Islands,* he describes Sambir as "un petit état malais, dont le dernier mot est: empoisonnement."[119] There is no poisoning in *An Outcast,* and it has been removed from *Almayer's Folly,* although at first the old Rajah of Sambir was murdered. The manuscript, typescript, and first edition differ from the final version:

> Lakamba's visits had ceased when, by a convenient decree of providence and the help of a little scentific manipulation, the old ruler of Sambir departed this life.[120]

> Lakamba's visits had ceased when, by a convenient decree of Providence the old ruler of Sambir departed this life.[121]

Much talk of poisoning remains in the definitive edition.[122]

In his first novel Conrad was trying his imagination upon characters and situations with which he had not been intimately connected. He took actual people and added to their experiences and personalities. He felt free to borrow names, traits of character, events, and backgrounds from his own observation and to shape them as his creative instinct dictated. Such selection was natural to his method of building up a story. Since he never planned his work as a whole, there was every opportunity to add to his original conception. Consequently in any analysis of the sources of his work many of the stories must appear under two classifications and a few under three.

Some stories were so fundamentally the product of observation that minor contributions from other sources must not be exaggerated. *An Outcast of the Islands,* like *Almayer's Folly,* arose primarily from Conrad's acquaintance in Borneo.[123] The Grays recalled that a Dutchman named De Veer lived with Olmeijer in Berouw and that no one else was a regular dependent. De Veer had a broken wrist and a weakness for alcohol. Whether or not De Veer suggested Willems, Conrad had first-hand knowledge of Willem's passion for Aissa—"L'esclavage physique de l'homme par une femme absolument sauvage j'ai vu ca!"[124] It has been briefly noticed in print that the material of the immediate action of *The Sisters* provided the antecedent action of *The Arrow of Gold*.[125] In the later and professedly autobiographical[126] *Arrow of Gold* Conrad recounted his love affair with the Rita who was the heroine of both stories. He must have based *The Sisters* upon observation of Rita and upon the account of her past, in which he played no part but which he probably had directly from her. "The Idiots" was inspired by a glimpse of the unfortunate children themselves.[127] Amy Foster was a servant in the Conrad household for years and impressed the writer with "her animal-like capacity for sheer uncomplaining endurance."[128] Some of the personages in *The Secret Agent*[129] and "The Partner"[130] were drawn from real people and possibly also in "Falk"[131] and "Because of the Dollars."[132] The Author's Note of *Victory*[133] emphasized the importance of observation for Heyst, Lena, Pedro, Ricardo, and Mr. Jones. And glimpses as brief as snap-shots lay behind parts of *Lord Jim*[134] and "Prince Roman."[135]

In *The Nigger of the "Narcissus"* Conrad first used a subject from his own experience. Unlike many authors, who unburden themselves in an autobiographical novel, he left to his sixth story events in which he had played an active part. Even so, he himself was not the center of interest in *The Nigger,* as he was later in "Youth" and "Heart of Darkness." In contrast to his earlier work, *The Nigger* must be considered "a record of experience in the absolute sense of the word." Conrad, as an officer of the *Narcissus,* lived through the storm and the sickness and death of the Nigger, whereas he had no share in the lives of Almayer, Willems, and the others.

A curious inconsistency makes it apparent that Conrad was writing about personal experience. At the beginning he did not appear as a character but told the story omnisciently. On the thirty-third page he entered the story in describing how incidents happened to *us*.[136] Though he was included in this collective *we,* he was not second officer of the *Narcissus,* as he was in actuality,[137] but one of the crew. He took part in the rescue of Wait during the storm: five men went to look for the Nigger, and since four of them were mentioned by name as the boatswain, Belfast, Wamido, and Archie,[138] Conrad himself must have been the fifth, who told what occurred. At the very end of the novel, he emerged from the collective *we* into his own person as *I.*[139] Whatever may explain the inconsistencies in point of view, they bring Conrad into the novel as an actor and confirm the autobiographical quality of *The Nigger.*

Conrad left information about *The Nigger* which shows how his imagination turned personal experience into fiction. In 1914 he implied that the novel was founded on an actual voyage,[140] and in 1923 he allowed Richard Curle to state in an article that "the story of 'The Nigger of the Narcissus' is founded on an actual voyage from Bombay to England made by the author in a ship of that name."[141] Conrad signed on the sailing ship *Narcissus* as second officer at Bombay late in April, 1884, after giving up a berth on a steamer of the British India Line because he was charmed by the beauty of the *Narcissus.*[142] On the voyage he was "acting mate of her (the proper mate crazy—melancholia). . . ."[143] His instantaneous affection for the ship was also felt by the characters in *The Nigger.*[144] The actual *Narcissus* left Bombay on April 28 and reached Dunkirk on October 16.[145] The voyage of more than five months was reflected in the comments on the "long passage" of the *Narcissus* of fiction, though Conrad cut it by a month.[146] The principal events of the real voyage— "an awful gale in the vicinity of the Needles, south of the cape," and the death of a Negro member of the crew[147]—were incorporated into the novel. Conrad altered the sequence of events, for the death of the Negro of the actual *Narcissus* took place "just" after the storm south of the Cape. Conrad said nothing of a near mutiny over the illness of the Negro such as occurred in the story. He remembered that a sailor brought some coffee to the Negro's berth shortly before he died, and in the novel the cook brought Wait " 'a pot of cold tea for your night's drinking' " on the evening of the mutiny.[148] The real Negro died between five and six o'clock in the morning, and James Wait just at dawn.[149]

Into his experiences on the *Narcissus* Conrad wove memories of other passages. The actual ship docked at Dunkirk in Northern France, but "from other voyages . . . made under similar circumstances" he introduced into the novel a superb description of the progress of the *Narcissus* down the Channel, up the Thames, to her pier in London, and also a last glimpse of her crew as they were paid off in the Board of Trade Office on Tower Hill.[150] Sailing up the Thames so stirred him that he amplified the description in *The Mirror of the Sea.*[151] Into the crew of the *Narcissus* he introduced "the two Scandinavians from associations with another ship."[152]

"Most of the personages . . . ," Conrad told Jean-Aubry, "actually belonged to the crew of the real *Narcissus,* including the admirable Singleton (whose real name was Sullivan), Archie, Belfast, and Donkin."[153] All through the manuscript he called "the admirable Singleton" by his real name, Sullivan, though in the serial the pseudonym Singleton was given him, perhaps because of the presence of another Irishman, Belfast, in the novel.[154] Of the officers Conrad made no mention.[155] The character of the Nigger in the novel was modeled closely upon the Negro in the crew of the *Narcissus*.[156] "I had much to do with him," Conrad declared in the preface entitled "To My Readers in America." "He was in my watch. A Negro in a British forecastle is a lonely being. He has no chums. Yet James Wait, afraid of death and making her his accomplice was an impostor of some character—mastering our compassion, scornful of our sentimentalism, triumphing over our suspicions."[157] He visited the Negro in the sick-bay a little before he died, just as Donkin did, though certainly not with the same intent.[158] The Negro's name Conrad had forgotten, and he took the name James Wait from "another nigger we had on board the *Duke of Sutherland*."[159] From the arrival of the actual James Wait aboard the *Duke of Sutherland* he contrived the dramatic opening scene of the novel.[160] *The Nigger of the "Narcissus"* shows how his imagination worked on his "experience in the absolute sense of the word," how he adapted and added until he had produced those pages by which he was willing to " 'stand or fall.' "

In later years Conrad took other subjects from his personal experience. "Youth" and "Heart of Darkness" were far more intimate than *The Nigger* in their revelation of autobiography.[161] They dealt with incidents of great importance in the development of his character. Yet in neither of these stories did he speak in his own person. He invented Marlow, to whom he attributed his own experiences and who tells them to the reader. So pleased was Conrad with Marlow that he used him in stories that were not created from his own "experience in the absolute sense of the word." In "The End of the Tether," which he said was "also the product of experience . . . [belonging] to the time before I ever thought of putting pen to paper,"[162] he sank himself in Captain Whalley. In "Falk," which contained a great deal of personal history,[163] he wrote in the first person, as he did in the autobiographical "Smile of Fortune"[164] and *Shadow Line*.[165] Though *The Arrow of Gold*[166] was also autobiographical, he disguised himself this time, not as Marlow, but as Monsieur George, of undermined nationality. The alterations were part of what Conrad called "the need of slight dramatization"[167] of personal experience.

*Lord Jim* is the best example of the complex sources of Conrad's material. Its origin was fourfold, in observation, personal experience, hearsay, and reading. Though the first two influences were incidental, the last two were of great and equal importance. Hearsay and reading were aspects of Conrad's inspiration scarcely present in *Almayer's Folly* and *The Nigger of the "Narcissus."* Once more the observations can be traced back to *Vidar* days. At Berouw he met Jim Lingard, who acted as a trader in Captain Lingard's interest.[168] Perhaps the connection was carried over into the novel for Stein's friendly interest in Jim and Jim's becoming the representative of Stein and Company in Patusan.[169] According to Mr. Cools, Jim Lingard was called Tuan Jim and, according to Captain Craig, Lord Jim by the officers of the *Vidar* " 'thanks to the swaggering manner he assumed.' " He made several voyages to Singapore in the *Vidar* while Conrad was mate.[170] Here the novelist found the title of his story and his hero's somewhat aggressive carriage, emphasized in the manuscript and toned down in print. Perhaps he also found Lord Jim's romance with Jewel, the beautiful half-caste, in Jim Lingard's marriage with a Malay who, Mr. Cools stated, was half-Chinese. Mr. Cools and Mr. Pangemanan supplied considerable information about the Lingards' numerous children. Two boys and a girl were educated in Singapore. The sons entered the English army and disappeared in the first World War; the daughter became a shop assistant. Another son, Tambi Lingard, was born completely "black face," as Mr. Pangemanan expressed it, and, never recognized by his father, lives like a native in Berouw at present. Jim Lingard himself became well-to-do by lending money to Po Eng Sing, a Chinese trader of Berouw, and lived on the interest. He died about 1923, and his widow married a Malay. His children and career were not to the novelist's purpose. Jean-Aubry and possibly Captain Craig, too, felt that "of course, the real Jim Lingard and the Lord Jim of Conrad's novel have nothing in common except their name and physique."[171]

The picture of Lord Jim was rounded out by a brief glimpse of another man. "One sunny morning in the commonplace surroundings of an Eastern roadstead," Conrad remarked in the Author's Note, "I saw his form pass by—appealing—significant—under a cloud—perfectly silent. Which is as it should be. It was for me, with all the sympathy of which I was capable, to seek fit words for his meaning. He was 'one of us.' "[172] The impression apparently found its way into the story through the eyes of Marlow:

> The third was an upstanding, broad-shouldered youth, with his hands in his pockets. . . . The young chap, making no movement, not even stirring his head, just stared into the sunshine. This was my first view of Jim. He looked as unconcerned and unapproachable as only the young can look. There he stood, clean-limbed, clean-faced, firm on his feet, as promising a boy as the sun ever shone on. . . . He had no business to look so sound.[173]

Conrad added a few touches to the novel from his own experience. When his back was injured by a loose spar on the *Highland Forest* in 1887, he had to stay for weeks in the hospital in Singapore. Instead of sailing home on the *Highland Forest,* he remained in the East and took a berth on the *Vidar* trading to Borneo.[174] Jim also was "disabled by a falling spar" and forced "at an Eastern port . . . to go to the hospital." His "recovery was slow," and, instead of returning to his ship, he stayed in the East and took a berth on a local steamer.[175] Another detail throws light on Conrad's literary preferences. When he was second mate on the unfortunate *Palestine* in 1881, he had with him "a five shilling one-volume edition of the dramatic works of William Shakespeare."[176] Conrad might be said to give the book—in a slightly cheaper edition—to Jim. Jim carried to Patusan "a thick green-and-gold volume—a half-crown complete Shakespeare."[177] Another incident was taken from Conrad's African experiences. In the Congo he was once nearly sucked under by river mud and fainted from his efforts to extricate himself.[178] Jim was stuck in the mud of the Patusan River during his escape from Rajah Allang and fell asleep exhausted after he pulled himself free.[179]

"Facts gleaned from hearsay" shaped the first twenty chapters of *Lord Jim.* In the Author's Note Conrad outlined the growth of the novel and admitted that his "first thought was of a short story, concerned only with the pilgrim ship episode; nothing more."[180] He did not reveal the source of the episode, but in 1923 two letters to the London *Times Literary Supplement,* occasioned by Curle's "History of Mr. Conrad's Books," disclosed it while Conrad was still alive. He never publicly denied his debt. The pilgrim ship incident took place in the Gulf of Aden in August, 1880, and "created a good deal of interest at the time."[181] From October, 1878, to October, 1893,[182] Conrad was continually making voyages to Australian and Eastern ports where he would surely have been told the details of such a notorious event. The letters from Sir Frank Swettenham and from Alfred Holt and Company are full enough to show what Conrad took over entire and what he altered.

In the summer of 1880 an old steamer called the *Jeddah,* carrying about nine hundred pilgrims from the Dutch islands, left Singapore for Jeddah, the port of Mecca.[183] The novel made here no fundamental change. The name of the ship was altered to *Patna,* but she was still a steamer "as old as the hills."[184] In the manuscript of *Lord Jim*[185] the number of pilgrims, which never reached nine hundred, was raised from six hundred to eight hundred. The fictional pilgrims also came "from the outskirts of the East, . . . crossing in small canoes from island to island . . ." until they reached the port of embarkation. Although Conrad did not name the port, the evidence points to Singapore. The place was "a thoroughfare to the East," and in this "Eastern port" Jim was laid up in hospital and joined the *Patna,* a reflection of Conrad's own experience in Singapore. The identification is strengthened by the course of the *Patna:* "She cleared the Strait, crossed the bay, continued on her way through the 'one-degree' passage. She held on straight for the Red Sea. . . ."[186] To this account should be added a canceled sentence from the manuscript:[187] "She went on heading westward across the Bay of Bengal." This identifies the Strait as the Strait of Malacca, the route between Singapore and the West.

Now Conrad began to deviate from the original episode. On August 7, 1880, near Cape Gardafui, the *Jeddah* was abandoned at night during heavy weather by all her officers except one. The old boat was heavily insured, and her owners, the captain himself and Seyyid Muhammad Alsagoff, a Singapore Arab, wished to collect on her.[188] Conrad made the management of the *Patna* more polyglot. She was "owned by a Chinaman, chartered by an Arab, and commanded by a sort of renegade New South Wales German." The disaster took place some six hundred miles beyond Cape Gardafui, past the island of Perim at the mouth of the Red Sea. Though the *Patna* was deserted at night, there was no rough weather: the mysterious accident occurred in the midst of great calm, and the rain squall did not arise until afterwards. The motive for desertion was not a fraudulent insurance scheme, but animal fear that possessed the white men after the accident.[189]

The *Jeddah* was towed to Aden by a ship of the Ocean Steam Navigation Company, "commonly called the Blue Funnel Line," and the deserters reached Aden in a lifeboat.[190] In the novel the *Patna* was towed into Aden by a " 'French gunboat homeward bound from Réunion.' "[191] Conrad seems to have transformed the Blue Funnel Line into the "Blue Star Line" for which Brierly worked,[192] and the Ocean Steam Navigation Company emerged years later as the Oceanic Steam Navigation Company of *Nostromo*.[193] In *Lord Jim* the deserters from the *Patna* were picked up by another ship, the *Avondale*,[194] and taken into a port which Conrad never identified.

This "Eastern port" was the scene of the official inquiry about the *Patna*.[195] In the original incident after the deserters from the *Jeddah* reached Aden, a brief inquiry was carried on there and later a detailed investigation in Singapore.[196] Conrad telescoped the trials into one. The investigation in the novel was certainly not held in Aden, for the officers of the *Patna* were informed that she had been " 'towed successfully to Aden' ":[197] there would be no reason for telling them the name of the port if they too were at Aden. The deserters were also on the *Avondale* several days,[198] too long for the short trip from the island of Perim to Aden. The details given about the "Eastern port" do not fit Singapore so well as Bombay, which Conrad himself visited in 1884.[199]

The "Eastern port," like Bombay, was " 'over six thousand miles' "[200] from Australia, the town had an Esplanade, with decorative grass-plots and a band-stand, just back from the water, and behind the Esplanade was the Harbour Office and the Malabar Hotel.[201] Bombay has a similar plan: the Esplanade has grass-plots and a band-stand, faces the water, and is backed by various government offices and hotels. Though no record of an actual Malabar Hotel can be found, the most distinctive landmark of Bombay is Malabar Hill. Along the Esplanade in the "Eastern port" were gharries and their Tamil drivers.[202] Webster defines a gharry as a wheeled cart or carriage native to India and comments that Tamils are "numerous throughout southern India."[203] In Conrad's port there were Parsee shipping firms and bazaars: rupees were the currency, and the natives had caste-marks; the attendants in the court of inquiry wore Indian dress.[204] Beyond doubt Conrad transferred the scene of the inquiry from Singapore to Bombay, perhaps to give Jim's retreat "towards the rising sun"[205] a more dramatic extent.

Conrad made a striking change in the character and adventures of the one officer of the *Jeddah* who did not leave the ship. He was a junior engineer and remained behind "because he was not quick enough to get into the boat or boats with the other deserters."[206] When the *Jeddah* was picked up, he was made a hero and "taken to Singapore where he found work in a ship chandler's store, grew fat and prospered. That was how he really 'worked out his salvation'."[207] From a tale of undeserved success Conrad created the early chapters of his hero's disillusionment. Jim, who was chief mate in the novel, jumped with the other deserters. He was with them outside the Harbour Office when the Captain made his false report of the *Patna*. There Marlow first saw them after the falsehood had been exposed.[208] in the *Jeddah* anecdote Captain Bragg, who salved the *Jeddah*, "entered the Consulate to report the salving, just as the master of the *Jeddah* was leaving after reporting his vessel lost with all hands."[209] In both cases the Captain got away.[210] Jim faced the inquiry alone. Afterwards he too became a ship-chandler's clerk[211] but not to grow fat and prosper. The way he finally worked out his salvation in a remote Malay state was not inspired by the incident of the *Jeddah*. The Patusan sequence introduced the fourth of the sources of *Lord Jim*.

The first part of *Lord Jim* was not the only story in which Conrad drew upon "facts gleaned from hearsay." He had already used them in "An Outpost of Progress."[212] Later he found in anecdote the source of part of "Typhoon,"[213] "Falk,"[214] "Amy Foster,"[215] *Nostromo*,[216] *The Secret Agent*,[217] "The Brute,"[218] *Under Western Eyes*,[219] "Il Conde,"[220] "The Secret Sharer"[221] "Freya of the Seven Isles,"[222] "Prince Roman,"[223] "The Planter of Malata,"[224] and "The Tale."[225] No other suggestions crystallized in Conrad's imagination more readily than anecdotes.[226]

Jim's adventures in Patusan were apparently influenced by Conrad's reading. The fourth inspiration came late in the development of the story. Conrad recorded that his "first thought was of . . . the pilgrim ship episode; nothing more." After writing "a few pages" and putting them aside in discontent, he "perceived that the pilgrim ship episode was a good starting-point for a free and wandering tale. . . ."[227] At this time he may have taken from certain books the material for Jim's destiny in Patusan. Two hundred and fifteen pages were based on the *Jeddah* incident; the remaining two hundred were devoted to Patusan. The book seems halved with a knife. Conrad was himself well aware of the break. In November, 1900, he admitted to Garnett: "You've put your finger on the plague spot. The division of the book into two parts. . . ."[228] The latter half recalls the two earlier Malayan novels. The Lord Jim of Patusan is the reverse of the Jim of the *Patna*: he is now the romantic in the triumph of fulfiling his dreams instead of the romantic in the despair of disproving them. Countless details confirm the probability that the Patusan episode derived from Conrad's reading about the Rajah James Brooke of Sarawak.

Apparently he had read widely about Brooke, in whom he must have become interested in Borneo, though he never visited Sarawak. No direct mention of the Englishman can be found in any of Conrad's published work or correspondence, but there are indirect references to him in *Almayer's Folly, An Outcast of the Islands,* and *The Rescue.* When Conrad began *Almayer's Folly* in September, 1889, several important volumes dealing with Brooke were available. In 1846 appeared Captain the Hon. Henry Keppel's *Expedition to Borneo of H.M.S. Dido for the Suppression of Piracy: with Extracts from the Journal of James Brooke, Esq., of Sarawak (Now Agent for the British Government in Borneo),* and in 1853 his *Visit to the Indian Archipelago, in H.M. Ship Maeander: with Portions of the Private Journal of Sir James Brooke, K.C.B.* In 1848 was issued Captain Rodney Mundy's *Narrative of Events in Borneo and Celebes down to the Occupation of Labuan: from the Journals of James Brooke, Esq. Rajah of Sarawak, and Governor of Labuan; together with a Narrative of the Operations of H.M.S. Iris.* In 1853 John C. Templer edited *The Private Letters of Sir James Brooke, K.C.B. Rajah of Sarawak, Narrating the Events of his Life, from 1838 to the Present Time.* And in 1876 the first long biography was published, Gertrude L. Jacob's *Raja of Sarawak: An Account of Sir James Brooke, K.C.B., LL.D., Given Chiefly through Letters and Journals.* The titles of these volumes indicate that they are largely composed of extracts from the unofficial writings of Brooke himself. The books repeat one another in parts, and as Conrad made no reference to them anywhere, it is impossible to tell exactly which he knew. He may have known them all equally well.[229]

After an unsuccessful career in India and England, in 1839 Brooke came to Kuching, the capital of the province of Sarawak on the west coast of Borneo, and helped the governor, Muda Hassim, uncle of the Sultan of Borneo, to put down a local rebellion. In 1841 he was officially created Rajah of Sarawak. The rest of his life he devoted to his new people. He fought the pirates; he mastered the treachery of the Bornean princes; he overcame the suspicions of the English government. He gave Sarawak security, justice, and prosperity, and won the confidence and love of the natives. When he died in 1868, he left his nephew to carry on the traditions and the dynasty, still extant, of the only white rajahs in the world.[230]

Such an achievement would have made an incalculable impression on Conrad. His imagination would have turned to good account any knowledge of the English Rajah. The evidence that Conrad supplemented current gossip about Brooke by careful reading is strong not so much in any single point as in the aggregation of small details.[231] The probability of this literary influence is nowhere more apparent than in *Lord Jim,* as my article, "The Rajah Brooke and Joseph Conrad," attempts to show.

The Patusan of *Lord Jim* was not given a definite position in the Malay Archipelago, but all implications put it in northern Sumatra.[232] Yet Borneo may have supplied much of the topography. In August, 1844, the English Rajah wiped out a pirates' nest up the Sakarran River at Patusan —the very name Conrad gave his settlement.[233] When Brooke helped Muda Hassim suppress the Sarawak rebellion, he had to blast the rebels from their forts on "Sarambo, a high detached mountain . . . with a notch in the center." Sarambo was apparently transplanted to Conrad's Patusan, where "there can be seen rising above the level of the forests the summits of two steep hills very close together, and separated by what looks like a deep fissure" so that "the appearance . . . is of one irregular conical hill split in two." From the top of Sarambo Brooke had a magnificent view over "mountain, and vale, and hillock, rivers and sea." From the Patusan twin hills Jim could see " 'the grey spots of villages, and . . . far off, along the coast, the empty ocean. . . .' " The visualizing imagination of the creator seems to have turned the bare statements of the original into pictures.

Much of the background and many specific incidents in *Lord Jim* suggest Brooke. When he arrived in Sarawak, he found the country distracted. His letters recounted the extortion of the chiefs: the poor man "labours, but is robbed of his produce, by some chief, who gives him a mere nominal price for the most valuable articles. . . . for the last ten years there has been no government [and] intrigue and plunder form the occupation of all the higher classes. . . ." Affairs in Patusan bore a noticeable resemblance to Sarawak, except that one man, Rajah Allang, was made specifically responsible for them. "Villages were burnt, men were dragged into the Rajah's stockade to be killed or tortured for the crime of trading with anybody else but himself. . . . The penalty for the breach of the monopoly was death; but his idea of trading was indistinguishable from the commonest forms of robbery." It is little wonder that Brooke— and Jim in his turn—found a rebellion in progress.[234]

If general conditions in Sarawak and Patusan have similarities, the particular events of the war in each country form closer parallels. Muda Hassim, who for four years had tried in vain to suppress it, appealed to Brooke for help. The rebels were in forts on Sarambo mountain, and Brooke constructed fortifications nearby, brought up guns, including two six-pounders, and bombarded the rebel strongholds until they were ready to fall apart. But he could not get his cowardly native soldiers to advance. After nearly three months of intermittent fighting, in which the Malays, to the Englishman's disgust, would not follow up their bombardments by attacks, the rebellion was concluded by negotiation. Brooke now became the nominal rajah of Sarawak and in less than a year was formally invested. In the Englishman's difficulties and success Conrad's selective sense apparently recognized the very train of action to carry Jim to triumph. There are differences of detail, which heighten the dramatic values of the novel. The Patusan scene was further complicated by the existence of two rival factions against Rajah Allang: the party of Sherif Ali, the half-caste Arab, who had started the civil war; and the Bugis party headed by old Doramin, whom Jim aided in the attempt to restore peace to a distracted state. Ali had a fort on one of the twin Patusan hills. With difficulty Jim prevailed over the Bugis' fears and planned a surprise attack. Bringing two seven-pounders up to the summit of the other hill, he constructed a battery there, all under cover of night. At dawn he pounded Ali's fort to splinters, led his forces into the breach at once, and was completely victorious. As a result " 'he became the virtual ruler of the land.' " It is almost as if Conrad refought Brooke's campaign, taking advantage of the errors committed before. The guns were a little larger; the natives' courage was screwed to the sticking-point; the bombardment was followed up immediately; and the war was over in a day instead of three months.[235]

Conrad's reading may also have suggested to him the intrusion of the outside world on the adventurer's domain, from which he built up Gentleman Brown's raid on Patusan.[236] Brown blundered into the river while Jim was in the interior, had his eyes opened " 'as to the home affairs of Patusan,' " and determined to share with Jim. But the unscrupulous ruffian was disappointed in his hopes, though Jim did give him safe passage down the river. On the way down, however, Brown destroyed a party of natives under Dain Waris, Doramin's son and Jim's particular friend Tamb' Itam, Jim's loyal retainer, brought his master news of the slaughter of Dain Waris. A number of these details seem traceable to Brooke. The idea of an unexpected raid up the Patusan River was perhaps inspired by the Englishman's accounts of sudden raids of pirates up Borneo rivers. Furthermore one of the charges brought against Brooke by his foes in Parliament was that he did not allow other interests in Sarawak, and he did turn down offers of help from strangers. Once Brooke, who was absent at the time, was much disturbed by a visit to Brunei of the American frigate *Constitution* to obtain trade concessions from the Sultan. In his letters he confessed that the Americans might have been successful if they had been "better versed in native politics." And Jaffer's announcement to Brooke of Budrudeen's death seems to make its familiar appearance in Tamb' Itam's tale.[237]

By far the most suggestive similarities between the Brookiana and *Lord Jim* lie in characterization. Sometimes it is only a name, again it is the basic psychology of a character that carries the resemblance. Keppel's *Indian Archipelago* may have bestowed the name Kassim on the chief counselor of Rajah Allang. Mundy's *Borneo and Celebes* may have provided many: Elliot for the Master Attendant of the Harbour Office; Matheson for Matherson who first owned the *Fire Queen;* McNeil for M'Neil, the Scotch merchant who befriended Stein. Further evidence indicates that Conrad borrowed the last two names and that he was aware of the influence of his reading. In the manuscript in the Rosenbach Collection[238] they were originally spelled Matheson and McNeil as in Mundy and then corrected to Matherson and M'Neil. . . .

Other characters in *Lord Jim* had probable relationships to personages in Brooke. Muda Hassim for instance, the uncle of the Sultan of Borneo, "a remarkably short man, and slightly built," seems to have had a sort of literary practical joke played upon him: he may have been caricatured as the miserable Rajah Allang, " 'the worst of the Sultan's uncles, . . .

little, . . . wizened,' " and with a " 'frail old body'."[239] Conrad apparently appropriated the Sultan of Borneo with few changes. The man Brooke knew was over fifty, an imbecile, with "an extra diminutive thumb" on his right hand. In *Lord Jim,* the Sultan was " 'an imbecile youth with two thumbs' " on his left hand. All the details which can be duplicated in Brooke and Conrad, however, are not freakish. Though Stein, who gave Jim his chance in Patusan, had no definite model, Conrad may have borrowed two picturesque episodes from the Englishman's life for the German's. On his visit to Celebes Brooke had been warmly received by an old rana who wanted to adopt him as her son. And when Brooke was about to leave Sarawak forever, according to the Jacob biography, he summoned the nobles and chiefs and made the country formally over to his nephew, Captain Brooke. Stein, in his turn, had been definitely adopted in Celebes by old M'Neil, the trader, " 'a privileged friend' " of a Wajo rana there. Feeling himself about to die, M'Neil made over his trading privileges to Stein before the rana and her court. In contrast to Stein, Doramin may owe a good deal to a Bugis mentioned in Mundy's *Borneo and Celebes.* During his voyage to Celebes, Brooke was much impressed by "the *nakodah* Pelewo, a man of upright mind and liberal principles. . . . He is, for a Bugis, very rich, and may be considered the head of the middle class which has arisen in Wajo from the wealth acquired in trade." Pelewo had many sons and daughters whom he married to nobles. Now Doramin, too, was a Bugis, an immigrant from Celebes to Patusan, and " 'of the *nakhoda* or merchant class.' " His wealth made him the head of the two hundred Bugis traders and hence the only power for law and order in Patusan. He was the husband of a woman of noble birth and the father of many daughters and one son, his beloved Dain Waris. The two *nakhodas* have enough in common to suggest how Conrad could fashion a figure on the skeleton of a few suggestions.

The clearest example of Brooke's possible influence on Conrad might naturally be expected in the character of Lord Jim: not the Jim of the *Patna* but Tuan Jim of Patusan. The romantic aspiration and energy of the English Rajah were of the sort to fire the novelist's imagination. The great work the Englishman had accomplished in the teeth of danger, far off the map of Western civilization, was material after Conrad's heart. And in Brooke's achievement in Borneo he seems to have found the perfect pattern for Jim's rehabilitation and fulfilment.

Brooke and Jim shared many parallel experiences. The former had four sisters and a brother: the latter four brothers and presumably a sister. That both were named James and both were called Tuan by the natives who worshipped them must not be entirely discounted by the fact that Conrad knew in Bulungan a Jim Lingard who was called Lord Jim on account of his swaggering manner. Perhaps the ring that Budrudeen sent Brooke in farewell suggested the silver ring that Doramin had given Stein and that Jim brought to Patusan as a token of authority.

Each man won his place with the Malays by suppressing civil dissension, and each was rewarded with supreme authority in the state. As might have been expected, Brooke was supposed by the natives to have charmed the dangerous bore in the Serebas River. To Jim also were ascribed supernatural powers: had not the tide in the river " 'turned two hours before its time' " to help him up to Patusan? Another popular superstition in *Lord Jim* seems to have been worked up from a suggestion in Brooke's letters. The Rajah found a large and fine crystal which he hoped was a diamond—"the (is to be) celebrated 'Brooke Diamond.' " From this Conrad may have elaborated the natives' story that Jim possessed a fabulous emerald, a story which grew out of his name for the girl he loved—Jewel. Certainly the subordinate part Jewel played in the novel could have been conditioned by the lack of sentimental interest in Brooke's life. *Lord Jim* is essentially the story of a man in a man's world. Jewel was not introduced until the novel was two-thirds completed. And the love affair was a subsidary, not an indispensable, factor in the action.

It was Brooke's position in Sarawak that seems to have most inspired Conrad. The inspiration, if such it was, was more of the spirit than of the events of the English Rajah's life among his people. After the suppression of the Dyak rebellion Brooke refused "to have the blood of conquered foes shed" and with difficulty restrained Muda Hassim. Similarly Jim would not let the Bugis " 'pay off old scores' " or depose Rajah Allang when the Patusan civil war was brought to a close. Both men were constructive. Brooke set about improving the chaotic condition of Sarawak according to his ideals. In a passage in his letters he summed these up succinctly: "to establish and encourage the good, to punish the evil-doer, to develop the resources of these countries by personal inspection, to inspire confidence in the native mind, to afford security for property, to prevent the oppression of the poorer and productive classes." And he did travel about his country. He established peace and prosperity upon a foundation of justice for all so successfully that the population of Kuching grew in five years from fifteen hundred to twelve thousand. The responsibility and the work he took squarely upon himself: he was accustomed to "dispense justice for four or five hours a day." By similar procedure Conrad had Jim find his own rehabilitation in the rehabilitation of Patusan. Lord Jim went to work. " 'Whole villages, deserted, rotted on their blackened posts' " no longer. Of such conditions he admitted simply to his friend Marlow, " 'I've changed all that.' " He too traveled about his little state and dispensed justice to a grateful people: He " 'could settle the deadliest quarrel in the country by crooking with his little finger' "; " 'his word decided everything.' "[240] In Patusan the new " 'social fabric of orderly, peaceful life, when every man was sure of tomorrow,' " was " 'the edifice raised by Jim's hands.' "

For their efforts both Brooke and Jim were rewarded by the trust and love of their people. Brooke was able to say: "The confidence of the natives in me personally is astonishing." The affection of Sarawak for him was so great that he wrote home: "Though it may appear vain, I must say that the attachment of the people is to my person, as well as to my government." And what could Jim say? He confided to Marlow: " ' "If you ask them who is brave—who is just—who it is they would trust with their lives? they would say, Tuan Jim." ' " As Marlow put it, Jim had taken " 'the leap that landed him into the life of Patusan, into the trust, the love, the confidence of the people.' "[241]

Conrad's habit of drawing inspiration from his reading lasted throughout his life. Before *Lord Jim* he had probably used the Brookiana in *The Rescue*.[242] Into *The Rescue*[243] he also worked the krissing of a Balinese girl by her relations for giving a flower to a foreigner, an incident taken from Alfred Russel Wallace's *Malay Archipelago*,[244] his "favorite bedside book."[245] He returned to books for part of the inspiration of *Nostromo*[246] and *The Secret Agent*.[247] "Falk" owed something to "a short paragraph in a newspaper."[248] Two books and a letter from a friend provided the subject of "Gaspar Ruiz."[249] "The Duel" sprang from a newspaper paragraph.[250] The greatest amount of reading went into preparation for the Napoleonic novel which Conrad left incomplete at his death. He began reading for it during his stay in Capri in 1905; he worked in the public library in Montpellier in 1907; he was still reading during a vacation in Ajaccio, Corsica, in the winter of 1920, and later that year at the British Museum.[251] "The Warrior's Soul" sprang from the same researches.[252] In a letter to the London *Times Literary Supplement*[253] Miss Mildred Atkinson made a brief but revealing comparison of *Suspense* and the *Memoirs of the Countess de Boigne*. Of *The Rover,* which grew out of *Suspense,* Conrad said: "The first notion of this story originated in the reading of Napoleon's dispatch to the Admiral commanding in Toulon in 1804. . . ."[254]

The origins of Conrad's novels and short stories can generally be traced to four main sources of inspiration. There remain stories about which he left no information and of which the origin has not yet been discovered. Some stories belong under more than one heading. Research and Conrad's own disclosures reveal the importance of first-hand contact with life. The contact was sometimes mere observation of other men, sometimes his own "experience in the absolute sense of the word." Curle declared, "His creative imagination can only work at its best when it is attached . . . to a remembered incident. . . . This sense of contact with life . . . gives to his pages the feeling that things happened so and no otherwise."[255] Yet this judgement leaves out the vital inspiration of anecdote and reading. Only abstractions failed to stimulate Conrad: he was unable to clothe a point of dogma in the flesh and blood of fiction. Taking inspiration from one source at a time or merging all four, he was seldom at a loss for material.          (1941)

NOTES

Unless otherwise designated, all references to Conrad's works are to the Canterbury Edition.

1. *Nigger*, p. xii. Also Edward Noble, ed., *Five Letters by Joseph Conrad Written to Edward Noble in 1895* (London: Privately Printed, 1925), p. 11 .

2. *The Shadow Line: A Confession*, p. viii. He called Scevola, in *The Rover*, "to be frank about it, a pathological case" (*Life and Letters*, II, 326).

3. *Life and Letters*, II, 78.

4. *Nostromo*, p. vii.

5. Page xi.

6. Page vii.

7. *Life and Letters*, II, 116. Writing about his work to Doubleday, Page and Company in 1913, he commented somewhat acrimoniously: "Is it interesting? Well, I have been and am being translated into all the European languages, except Spanish and Italian. They would hardly do that for a bore" (*Ibid.*, II, 147).

8. *Rescue*, p. x.

9. *Life and Letters*, II, 68.

10. *Ibid.*, II, 139. Similar statements appear in *Tales of Unrest* (p. ix): "The sustained invention of a really telling lie demands a talent which I do not possess"; and in *The Arrow of Gold: A Story between Two Notes* (p. ix): "In the case of this book I was unable to supplement these deficiencies by the exercise of my inventive faculty. It was never very strong; and on this occasion its use would have seemed exceptionally dishonest."

11. *Set of Six*, pp. ix-x.

12. *Personal Record*, p. xvii. He communicated the same information to Curle (*Last Twelve Years*, p. 36) and Mégroz (*Joseph Conrad's Mind and Method*, p. 41).

13. *Youth and Gaspar Ruiz* (London and Toronto: J. M. Dent and Sons, Ltd. [1920]), p. 167.

14. Letter to Mme. Poradowska dated "Samedi" and assigned by Dr. Gee to Saturday, August 18, 1894 (Yale).

15. *Personal Record*, p. xvii, and *Nigger*, p. xiv.

16. *Letters from Joseph Conrad*, p. 59.

17. *Life and Letters*, II, 14.

18. *Personal Record*, pp. xv-xvi.

19. *Last Essays*, p. 80. Also *Arrow of Gold*, p. ix.

20. "But if I had not got to know Almayer pretty well it is almost certain there would never have been a line of mine in print" (*Personal Record*, p. 87).

21. *Nigger*, p. xiv.

22. *Personal Record*, pp. 87-89, *Nigger*, pp. 172-173, and *Youth*, pp. 41-42.

23. *Life and Letters*, II, 147.

24. *Shadow Line*, p. ix.

25. See Conrad on the relative importance of subject and treatment (*Letters from Joseph Conrad*, pp. 292-293, and *Life and Letters*, II, 54).

26. "Conrad After Fourteen Years," *Yale University Library Gazette*, XIII (July, 1938), 6.

27. *Life and Letters*, II, 316.

28. *Within the Tides: Tales*, p. viii.

29. Richard Curle, ed., *Conrad to a Friend* (Garden City, New York: Doubleday, Doran and Company, Inc., 1928), p. 153. The suggestion was taken: see the almost verbatim use of this sentence and other parts of the letter in Curle's "History of Mr. Conrad's Books" (London *Times Literary Supplement*, no. 1,128 [August 30, 1923], 570).

30. *The Sea: Books and Manuscripts* (Philadelphia and New York City: The Rosenbach Company, 1938), p. 40.

31. *Conrad to a Friend*, p. 153.

32. *Shadow Line*, p. ix.

33. *Arrow of Gold*, p. viii.

34. *Life and Letters*, II, 213.

35. *Ibid.*, I, 77.

36. *Youth*, p. xi.

37. *Life and Letters*, II, 195.

38. *Ibid.*, II, 20 and *Mirror of the Sea*, p. 143.

39. *Mirror of the Sea*, p. 137. The rescue may well have taken place in 1875 or 1876 when Conrad made his only recorded voyage to the West Indies (*Life and Letters*, I, 33-38). It seems unlikely that on any voyage around the Cape Conrad would have been in mid-Atlantic.

40. *Mirror of the Sea*, p. 146. Almayer, who was Dutch, also used English to speak to the hallucination of Nina, who was half Dutch and half Malay (*Almayer's Folly*, p. 202).

41. *Life and Letters*, I, 47.

42. Conrad showed how complex the chemistry of his subjects could be: "Il Conde (misspelt by-the-by) is an almost verbatim transcript of the tale told me by a very charming old gentleman whom I met in Italy. I don't mean to say it is only that. Anybody can see that it is something more than a verbatim report, but where he left off and where I began must be left to the acute discrimination of the reader who may be interested in the problem. I don't mean to say that the problem is worth the trouble. What I am certain of, however, is that it is not to be solved, for I am not at all clear about it myself by this time" (*Set of Six*, p. vii). Conrad also forgot the exact origins of *The Nigger*.

43. *Personal Record*, pp. xvii-xviii. "Writing about them [his subjects], he is only writing about himself" (*ibid.*, p. xv).

44. *Within the Tides*, p. vii. See also *Last Essays* (p. 211) in which Conrad admitted that "my past had, by the very force of my work, become one of the sources of what I may call, for want of a better word, my inspiration— of the inner force which sets the pen in motion."

45. *Last Essays*, p. 216. The quotations are taken from the preface of *The Shorter Tales of Joseph Conrad*, in which the stories mentioned are included.

46. *Life and Letters*, II, 68.

47. For instance, *ibid.*, II, 13, 41, 240, *Set of Six*, p. viii, and *Nostromo*, p. viii.

48. *Typhoon*, p. ix. Cf. *Last Essays*, p. 216.

49. *Personal Record*, p. 87.

50. *Life and Letters*, I, 95.

51. *Ibid.*, I, 93. Jean-Aubry referred to Captain Craig under the disguise of Captain C—, as Conrad did in *A Personal Record*, but a reference in one of Conrad's letters discloses the full name (*ibid.*, II, 103).

52. *Ibid.*, I, 96.

53. *Ibid.*, I, 94.

54. *Almayer's Folly* MS., chap. II, p. 6, and chap. III, p. 1 (Rosenbach), and TS., pp. 27, 41 (Leeds).

55. *Almayer's Folly* MS., chap. III, p. 14 (Rosenbach), and TS., p. 51 (Leeds), and (Canterbury Edition), p. 42.

56. Letter dated May 2, 1894 (Yale).

57. *Life and Letters*, I, 136.

58. "Heart of Darkness" MS., p. 55 numbered in black pencil (Yale).

59. *Shadow Line* MS., p. 145 (Yale). See *Shadow Line*, p. 62. Born was the actual name (holograph letter from Henry Simpson and Sons to Joseph

Conrad, dated April 5, 1888 [Yale]; misquoted as Burns in *Life and Letters,* I, 106).

60. Olmeijer, born in 1848, left Java for Borneo when a young man and arrived in Berouw in 1870; he was a trader in rattan and rubber and shipped his products through Captain Lingard. He died at fifty-two, on September 2, 1900. [Editor's note, drawn from Gordan]

61. *Life and Letters,* I, 96. Jean-Aubry did not make it clear whether Captain Craig was referring to the portrait of Almayer in *A Personal Record* or in *Almayer's Folly* and *An Outcast.* Other Bornean friends of Conrad's also recognized the source of his creations (*ibid.,* II, 103).

62. Pages 75, 76.

63. *Almayer's Folly,* pp. 35, 103, 205. At first the beard was merely "grey" (*Almayer's Folly* MS., chap. XII, p. 31 [Rosenbach]), but the change of color added years to his appearance.

64. *Personal Record,* p. 74, and *Almayer's Folly,* p. 35.

65. *Personal Record,* p. 76, and *Almayer's Folly,* p. 23.

66. Pages 76-77, 84. Almayer was suspicious of the visiting Dutch naval officers (*Almayer's Folly,* pp. 122-126) and even of his friend Dain Maroola (*ibid.,* pp. 14, 73-74). He suspected Willems of trying to supplant him in Lingard's favor (*Outcast,* pp. 62-64).

67. *Personal Record,* p. 76.

68. *Almayer's Folly,* p. 3.

69. *Personal Record,* p. 86.

70. *Ibid.,* pp. 75-76.

71. *Almayer's Folly,* pp. 35, 121.

72. *Personal Record,* pp. 85, 86.

73. *Almayer's Folly,* pp. 122, 203.

74. *Life and Letters,* I, 102, n. 1.

75. *Almayer's Folly,* pp. 4, 36-37.

76. *Personal Record,* p. 88. Also notice Almayer's complaint that even death as a "way of escape from inclement fortune was closed to him" (*ibid.,* p. 78).

77. *Almayer's Folly,* pp. 3, 18.

78. Pages 77, 88.

79. *Almayer's Folly,* pp. 191-192, 196-207.

80. *Personal Record,* p. 85.

81. Page 9.

82. *Almayer's Folly,* p. 206.

83. *Almayer's Folly* MS., chap. I, p. 8 (Rosenbach). See *Almayer's Folly,* p. 7.

84. *Almayer's Folly* MS., chap. III, p. 13, and chap. II, p. 2 (Rosenbach). See *Almayer's Folly,* pp. 22, 41.

85. *Almayer's Folly,* pp. 7, 21-23. In the manuscript (chap. II, p. 2 [Rosenbach]) Conrad gave Mrs. Almayer's age first as fourteen, then as fifteen, once more as fourteen. Finally he removed it altogether from the printed text (Canterbury Edition, p. 21).

86. *Almayer's Folly,* pp. 7, 9, 10, 22, 41. The location was further complicated by the marriage of the Almayers, which did not take place in Samarang (or Sourabaya) as would be expected but in Batavia (*ibid.,* p. 23). In the manuscript (chap. II, p. 4 [Rosenbach]), the marriage was performed in Singapore, but the change to Batavia was made in the typescript (p. 26 [Leeds]), doubtless because Nina, as a child, was sent to Singapore to be educated (*Almayer's Folly,* pp. 26-27).

87. *Personal Record,* p. 88.

88. *Life and Letters,* II, 183.

89. *Ibid.,* I, 97.

90. *Ibid.,* II, 103.

91. *Ibid.,* I, 97.

92. See *Mirror of the Sea,* pp. 162-183, *Arrow of Gold,* p. viii, and *Nostromo,* p. xii.

93. John D. Gordan, "The Rajah Brooke and Joseph Conrad," *Studies in Philology,* XXXV (1938), 619-625.

94. *Life and Letters,* I, 92-93.

95. Page 51.

96. *Almayer's Folly,* p. 6.

97. Conrad had first: "Welcome Capitan! Ver' you come vrom— . . . I want ponies' "; he changed it: " 'Welgome Capitan! Ver' you gome vrom? . . . I vant bonies' " (*Almayer's Folly* MS., chap. I, p. 6 [Rosenbach]). In the typescript (p. 5 [Leeds]) he was still breaking Hudig's English. In *Almayer's Folly* (p. 6) *Capitan* was altered to *Gapitan*: the *w* in *welcome* remained inconsistent.

98. Pages 18-19, for instance.

99. *Life and Letters,* I, 94, and *Almayer's Folly,* p. 29.

100. Pages 75 ff.

101. *Life and Letters,* I, 94 ff., and II, 103. It is to be noted that Lingard referred to a friend of his named Craig (*Outcast,* pp. 189, 190).

102. *Life and Letters,* I, 94. A bill of lading preserved in the Yale University Library shows that the name was also spelled Syed Mohsin Bin S. Al Jaffree. In the records of the Master Attendant at Singapore it was spelled Syed Moshin bin Salley Ali Jeoffree. Conrad mentioned this Arab, though not by name, as being the owner of the ship, flying the British flag, on which he had been before he received his first command (*Shadow Line,* pp. 4-5). The ship was, of course, the *Vidar,* and it is characteristic of Conrad's use of details from his past that, according to Jean-Aubry, she flew not the British but the Dutch flag (*Life and Letters,* I, 95).

103. *Life and Letters,* I, 98.

104. *Almayer's Folly,* pp. 15, 43-44.

105. *Life and Letters,* I, 95. Also *Personal Record,* p. 75. The spelling of Malay place-names varies with each map and commentator.

106. "Conrad in the East," *Yale Review,* New Series, 12, Part II (1923), 500.

107. *Conrad to a Friend,* pp. 113-114. For the paragraph in question see *Youth,* pp. 37-38.

108. *Almayer's Folly,* p. 5. In the manuscript (chap. I, p. 3 [Rosenbach]) Borneo was mentioned in the fifth paragraph and then omitted from the text.

109. *Almayer's Folly* MS., chap. II, p. 6, chap. II, p. 1 (Rosenbach), and TS., pp. 27, 41 (Leeds).

110. *Almayer's Folly* MS., chap. III, p. 14 (Rosenbach), and TS., p. 51 (Leeds), and (Canterbury Edition), p. 42.

111. *Almayer's Folly* MS., chap. II, p. 4 (Rosenbach) and TS., p. 44 (Leeds). In *An Outcast* (p. 277) which dealt with Sambir, too, the settlement was inconsistently put some fifty-five miles from the sea.

112. *Personal Record,* p. 74.

113. *Almayer's Folly,* pp. 14, 91.

114. *Ibid.,* p. 93.

115. *Almayer's Folly* MS., chap. II, p. 16, and chap. III, p. 15 (Rosenbach).

116. *Almayer's Folly: A Story of An Eastern River* (London: T. Fisher Unwin, 1895), pp. 43, 58, and (Canterbury Edition), p. 30. The second phrase was omitted from the Canterbury Edition (p. 42).

117. *Almayer's Folly,* p. 6. Conrad gave him a wife at this time in *An Outcast* (p. 10).

118. *Almayer's Folly,* pp. 26, 27.

119. Letter to Mme. Poradowska dated "Lundi matin" and assigned by Dr. Gee to Monday, October 29 or November 5, 1894 (Yale).

120. *Almayer's Folly* MS., chap. II, p. 12 (Rosenbach), and TS., p. 32 (Leeds), and (1895), p. 39.

121. *Almayer's Folly* (Canterbury Edition), p. 27.

122. *Ibid.*, pp. 27, 88.

123. *Outcast*, pp. ix-x, and *Life and Letters*, I, 97.

124. Letter to Mme. Poradowska dated "Lundi matin" and assigned by Dr. Gee to Monday, October 29 or November 5, 1894 (Yale).

125. In his preface to *The Sisters* ([New York: Crosby Gaige, 1928], pp. 1-16) Ford Madox Ford failed to notice the similarity, and his omission was pointed out in the *Bookman* (LXVIII [1928], 216-217) by Homer S. Shannon, who made a partial comparison of the two stories. A fuller comparison reveals many similarities. The heroine was named Rita (*Sisters*, p. 55; *Arrow of Gold*, p. 5) and came from the Basque country (*Sisters*, pp. 50-52; *Arrow of Gold*, p. 36). She had a sister who was devoutly religious (*Sisters*, p. 55; *Arrow of Gold*, pp. 141, 335). In the Pyrenees she had been brought up by her uncle, a priest (*Sisters*, p. 52; *Arrow of Gold*, p. 36). Then she was sent to Paris to live with another uncle and his wife, orange merchants (*Sisters*, pp. 50-56; *Arrow of Gold*, pp. 35-36). The family was Carlist (*Sisters*, pp. 51-52; *Arrow of Gold* pp. 47-48, 57). In a pavilion behind the uncle's house in Passy (*Sisters*, pp. 46-50; *Arrow of Gold*, p. 22) lived an enormously rich painter (*Sisters*, pp. 19, 24; *Arrow of Gold*, p. 22) of humble origin (*Sisters*, p. 24; *Arrow of Gold*, p. 47). Other less important details also connect the two stories. Some of the material Conrad used a third time in *The Mirror of the Sea* (pp. 160-161).

126. *Life and Letters*, II, 224, and Richard Curle, ed., *Notes by Joseph Conrad: Written in a Set of His First Editions* (London: Privately Printed, 1925), p. 33.

127. *Joseph Conrad and His Circle*, pp. 37, 40.

128. *Joseph Conrad as I Knew Him*, p. 118.

129. Page xiv. Also Ford Madox Ford, *Return to Yesterday* (London: Victor Gollancz Ltd., 1931), p. 111, and *Joseph Conrad and His Circle*, p. 196.

130. *Joseph Conrad as I Knew Him*, p. 142.

131. *Life and Letters*, I, 108.

132. *Ibid.*, I, 54, n.1, II, 171.

133. Pages x-xvii.

134. Page ix.

135. *Tales of Hearsay* (Concord Edition; Garden City, New York: Doubleday, Page and Company, 1926), pp. 33-35. All further references are to the Concord Edition. Conrad declared the whole story to be true (*Life and Letters*, I, 17, II, 181).

136. *Nigger*, p. 36. There is a reference to "our nigger" (*ibid.*, p. 34); but this *our* could be understood as a sort of general possessive that included the reader.

137. *Life and Letters*, I, 77. The fictional *Narcissus* had a first mate, Mr. Baker, and a second, Mr. Creighton, neither of whom bore Conrad any resemblance.

138. *Nigger*, pp. 64, 65.

139. *Ibid.*, pp. 170-173.

140. *Ibid.*, pp. ix-x.

141. "The History of Mr. Conrad's Books," London *Times Literary Supplement*, no. 1,128 (August 30, 1923), 570. The comments and corrections Conrad made on the manuscript (Beyer) show that the article was semi-official. It appeared in pamphlet form on *Joseph Conrad: The History of His Books* (London: J. M. Dent and Sons, Ltd., n.d.).

142. *Life and Letters*, I, 76-77.

143. Unpublished letter to an unknown correspondent dated February 25, 1912 (Yale).

144. Page 50, for instance.

145. See the photograph of Conrad's certificate of dismissal (*Life and Let-*

*ters*, I, facing p. 82). Jean-Aubry put the day of arrival on October 17 (*ibid.*, I, 77).

146. *Nigger*, pp. 103, 145. The ship was four months out when Jimmy died; his funeral was the day after Flores was sighted, and a week later the *Narcissus* entered the Channel (*ibid.*, pp. 156, 161). Time must be allowed for the ship to get to London.

147. *Life and Letters*, I, 78.

148. *Ibid.*, I, 77, and *Nigger*, p. 113.

149. *Life and Letters*, I, 77-78, and *Nigger*, p. 155.

150. *Life and Letters*, I, 77, 78, and *Nigger*, pp. 167-173.

151. Pages 102-108.

152. *Life and Letters*, I, 77.

153. *Loc. cit.* Also *Joseph Conrad as I Knew Him*, p. xvi.

No real connection can be traced between *The Nigger* and Herman Melville's *Redburn*, in which appeared a religious Negro cook and a malingering white sailor, Jackson. Jackson had some unnamed malady (perhaps tuberculosis, perhaps syphilis) on account of which he shirked his work; he bullied the crew; and he died of a hemorrhage while aloft and fell into the sea. The similarities seem to be only coincidental.

154. It is not altogether impossible that the impression made upon Conrad by the actual Sullivan was strengthened by his memories of an old pilot at Marseilles, him of the incredible age, the extensive recollections, and the respected position among the younger men (*Personal Record*, pp. 131-133).

155. Though a Captain John Anderson has recently been suggested as "the original captain" of the *Narcissus* and "the original of the captain" (*Sea*, p. 41), Arch. Duncan was beyond question the captain of the *Narcissus* (*Life and Letters*, I, facing p. 82).

156. *Life and Letters*, I, 77.

157. *Nigger*, p. ix.

158. *Life and Letters*, I, 77, and *Nigger*, pp. 147-154.

159. *Life and Letters*, I, 77.

160. *Nigger*, pp. 17-18. Conrad at times seems to have confused the events of the *Sutherland* voyage and of the *Narcissus* voyage: in "To My Readers in America" he spoke of "that evening when James Wait joined the ship—late for the muster of the crew . . ." (*ibid.*, p. ix).

161. *Life and Letters*, I, 65-73, 117-143. Also G. Jean-Aubrey, *Joseph Conrad in the Congo* (London: "The Bookman's Journal" Office, 1826).

162. *Youth*, p. xii. During his days on the *Vidar* Conrad was afraid of losing his eyesight (*Life and Letters*, I, 100).

163. *Life and Letters*, I, 104-109. Also *Notes by Joseph Conrad*, p. 23.

164. London *Times Literary Supplement*, no. 1,128 (August 30, 1923), 570. Also *Life and Letters*, I, 113, and *Joseph Conrad as I Knew Him*, p. 139.

165. London *Times Literary Supplement*, no. 1,128 (August 30, 1923), 570. Also *Shadow Line*, p. ix.

166. Pages viii, ix.

167. *Life and Letters*, II, 195.

168. *Ibid.*, I, 97.

169. *Lord Jim*, pp. 202 ff.

170. *Life and Letters*, I, 97.

171. *Loc. cit.*

172. *Lord Jim*, p. ix.

173. *Ibid.*, p. 40.

174. *Life and Letters*, I, 91-95.

175. *Lord Jim*, pp. 11-13.

176. *Life and Letters*, I, 65-73, and *Personal Record*, p. 72.

177. *Lord Jim*, p. 237.

178. *Saturday Review of Literature*, II (1925-26), 700.

179. *Lord Jim,* pp. 251, 253-254.

180. *Ibid.,* p. viii. See a letter to Garnett in May, 1898, in which he referred to a proposed story "*Jim* (20,000)" (*Letters from Joseph Conrad,* p. 138).

181. London *Times Literary Supplement,* no. 1,134 (October 11, 1923), 670.

182. *Life and Letters,* I, 52, 154.

183. London *Times Literary Supplement,* no. 1,129 (September 6, 1923), 588, and no. 1,134 (October 11, 1923), 670.

184. *Lord Jim,* p. 13. Perhaps the name was taken from some ship Conrad encountered during his life at sea. Patna seems to have derived from "a city, district, and division of British India, in the Behar province of Bengal" (*Encyclopaedia Britannica* [11th ed.], XX, 929).

185. Pages 17 (Harvard) and 154 (Rosenbach). [Editor's note: For a description of the divided condition of the manuscript of *Lord Jim,* see pp. 150-152 of Gordan's *Joseph Conrad.*]

186. *Lord Jim,* pp. 11-15.

187. Page 22 (Harvard).

188. London *Times Literary Supplement,* no. 1,129 (September 6, 1923), 588, and no. 1,134 (October 11, 1923), 670.

189. *Lord Jim,* pp. 14, 20, 97, 101.
Perhaps the insurance scheme influenced "The End of the Tether."

190. London *Times Literary Supplement,* no. 1,129 (September 6, 1923), 588, and no. 1,134 (October 11, 1923), 670.

191. *Lord Jim,* pp. 134, 136-137. Clearly Conrad did not know one of the most dramatic details of the rescue, recounted by Sir Frank Swettenham: "When the pilgrims found they had been abandoned . . . , and when they realized their desperate situation, they all left the decks for a while and then reappeared clothed in their winding sheets" (London *Times Literary Supplement,* no. 1,129 [September 6, 1923], 588).

192. *Lord Jim,* p. 57.

193. Page 9.

194. *Lord Jim,* p. 133.

195. Marlow attended the inquiry, after seeing the deserters when they first arrived (*ibid.,* pp. 28, 34, 36). There was no indication of Marlow's or the deserters' going to another city for the inquiry.

196. London *Times Literary Supplement,* no. 1,129 (September 6, 1923), 588.

197. *Lord Jim,* p. 134.

198. Jim had been imagining the voices of the drowning pilgrims " 'day after day' " before he reached the Eastern port (*loc. cit.*).

199. *Life and Letters,* I, 76-77.

200. *Lord Jim,* p. 163. In the port of investigation Marlow met Chester, a native of western Australia, who had come " 'over six thousand miles' " to get capital for his guano island scheme because his attempts to raise money in Auckland and Brisbane had failed (*ibid.,* pp. 164-165).

201. *Ibid.,* pp. 37-39, 42.

202. *Ibid.,* pp. 40, 47.

203. *Webster's Collegiate Dictionary* (5th ed.) pp. 420, 1019.

204. *Lord Jim,* pp. 32, 68, 87, 158, 161. Conrad included what seems to have been a personal reminiscence: during the investigation Jim stayed in the Sailors' Home (*ibid.,* p. 134), where Conrad himself stayed during his visit to Bombay (*Life and Letters,* I, 76).

205. *Lord Jim,* p. 5. Following the statement about the retreat "towards the rising sun," Conrad declared: "Thus in the course of years he was known successively in Bombay, in Calcutta, in Rangoon, in Penang, in Batavia—and in each of these halting-places was just Jim the water-clerk." Though the list of places might cast some doubt on Bombay as the scene of the inquiry, Conrad

clearly was not following the sequence. Jim's first job after the inquiry was in a rice mill in Rangoon (*ibid.,* pp. 152, 187).

206. London *Times Literary Supplement,* no. 1,134 (October 11, 1923), 670, and no. 1,129 (September 6, 1923), 588.

207. *Ibid.,* no. 1,129 (September 6, 1923), 588.

208. *Lord Jim,* pp. 13, 36-48.

209. London *Times Literary Supplement,* no. 1,134 (October 11, 1923), 670.

210. *Ibid.,* no. 1,129 (September 6, 1923), 588, and *Lord Jim,* p. 47.

211. *Lord Jim,* pp. 5, 79.

212. "As for the story itself it is true enough in its essentials. The sustained invention of a really telling lie demands a talent which I do not possess" (*Tales of Unrest,* p. ix). Jean-Aubry believed that Conrad was told the story in Africa: the names of the protagonist, Kayerts and Carlier, he took from two actual men, "an agent and a captain, whom he met in the Congo" (*Life and Letters,* i, 128, n. 2; also *ibid.,* I, 140, n. 1).

213. *Typhoon,* p. vii.

214. *Conrad Memorial Library,* p. 115. Also *Mirror of the Sea,* pp. 63-66.

215. *Joseph Conrad as I Knew Him,* p. 118.

216. Page vii.

217. Page ix.

218. *Set of Six,* p. ix.

219. *Notes by Joseph Conrad,* p. 28.

220. *Set of Six,* p. vii. Also *Life and Letters,* II, 2.

221. *'Twixt Land and Sea,* p. viii.

222. *Life and Letters,* II, 133. Conrad apparently forgot that he had worked the same incident into *The Rescue* (p. 101) as a passing allusion in dialogue.

223. *Tales of Hearsay,* p. xii. Also *Conrad Memorial Library,* p. 365.

224. *Last Essays,* pp. 167, 172.

225. *Tales of Hearsay,* p. xiii.

226. Because of the acknowledged similarity in theme (*Tales of Unrest,* p. ix), "The Lagoon" and "Karain" probably grew from one anecdote which Conrad heard while he was in Borneo.

227. *Lord Jim,* p. viii.

228. *Letters from Joseph Conrad,* p. 171.

229. See my article, "The Rajah Brooke and Joseph Conrad," *Studies in Philology,* XXXV (1938), 615-618.

230. *Ibid.,* pp. 613-615.

231. The aggregation of details, based on internal evidence, in my first article (*ibid.,* pp. 618-633) is reinforced by a piece of external evidence, advanced in a recent article (*ibid.,* XXXVII [1940], 130-132).

232. Speaking with Conrad's authority in "The History of Mr. Conrad's Books," Curle put Patusan "on the south coast of north-west Sumatra . . ." (London *Times Literary Supplement,* no. 1,128 [August 30, 1923], 570).

233. The actual Patusan was "nearly seventy miles" upstream (Henry Keppel, *Expedition to Borneo,* etc. [New York: Harper and Brothers, 1846], p. 269), and the fictional thirty or "about forty" (*Lord Jim,* pp. 200, 226). Here Conrad apparently tempered his reading with his recollection of Berouw, which was "forty miles up, more or less, a Bornean river" (*Personal Record,* p. 74).

234. Another incident in Brooke's career seems to have been refurbished for the novel. There was a tale in Sarawak that even the gentle Muda Hassim had had a young man "chained without covering, and exposed to sun and rain at the entrance of the Balei or Hall" (Henry Keppel, *A Visit to the Indian Archipelago,* etc. [London: Richard Bentley, 1853], II, 104). In the novel one of Stein's captains on a visit to Patusan had been " 'tied up by the neck with a rattan halter to a post planted in the middle of a mud-hole before the Rajah's house' " (*Lord Jim,* p. 240).

235. The fortifications of Brooke's house, from which he dominated his capital, seem to have supplied Conrad with the plans for Jim's. Brooke's was

"surrounded by palisades and a ditch," forming a square, and it contained a mess-room "with every description of firearms . . . ready for use (Keppel, *Expedition to Borneo*, p. 222). Jim's had " 'a deep ditch, an earth wall topped by a palisade, and at the angles guns mounted on platforms to sweep each side of the square' " (*Lord Jim*, p. 340). Both houses were really forts.

236. Conrad did not rely, apparently, upon any of the obvious sources for the character of Gentleman Brown. He compared the character to "his contemporary brother ruffians, like Bully Hayes or the mellifluous Pease, or that perfumed, Dundreary-whiskered, dandified scoundrel known as Dirty Dick . . .' " (*Lord Jim*, p. 352). Though Dirty Dick could not be identified, a search for parallels in the careers of Gentleman Brown and Bully Hays or Ben Pease produced nothing really convincing (see Basil Lubbock, *Bully Hayes: South Sea Pirate* [Boston: Charles E. Lauriat Company, 1931] and Rolf Boldrewood, *A Modern Buccaneer* [New York and London: Macmillan and Company, 1894]). The closest resemblance was the theft of a schooner from the Spanish by Brown (*Lord Jim*, pp. 354-355) and Pease's "seizing a Spanish revenue vessel under the very guns of a fort" (*Modern Buccaneer*, p. 73). Conrad may have picked up the facts he gave in the story of Gentleman Brown from anecdotes never recorded in print.

237. When Brooke's friend Budrudeen was driven to suicide by the enemies of British interests in Brunei, he sent the Englishman his ring and a message of farewell by his faithful retainer, Jaffer (Mundy, *Borneo and Celebes*, II, 129-134).

238. Pages 98, 473.

239. The portrait of Rajah Allang in *Lord Jim* may have been rounded off with a few touches borrowed from the Sultan of Sulu. The latter was accustomed to "the too free use of opium" (Keppel, *Indian Archipelago*, I, 66), like Rajah Allang (*Lord Jim*, p. 228). The Sultan of Sulu also had a suite "dressed with . . . gaudiness, in bright silks" (Keppel, *Indian Archipelago*, I, 67), just like Rajah Allang's " 'youth's in gay silks' " (*Lord Jim*, p. 228).

The character of Rajah Allang seems to contain details taken from reading other than in the Brookiana. In *Last Essays* (pp. 131-132) Conrad mentioned "the Sultan of Perak, or perhaps his brother-ruler next door in Selangor, [who] having listened attentively to a lecture from a British admiral on the heinousness of a certain notable case of piracy, turned round quickly to his attending chiefs and to the silent throng of his Malay subjects, exclaiming, 'Hear now, my people! Don't let us have any more of this little game.' " The anecdote apparently reappeared in *Lord Jim* (p. 250) in the scene in which Jim upbraided Rajah Allang before his court for some of his thefts: "When Jim had done there was a great stillness. Nobody seemed to breathe even; no one made a sound till the old Rajah sighed faintly, and looking up, with a toss of his head, said quickly, 'You hear, my people! No more of these little games.' "

240. It is to be noted that divorce played a prominent part in the legal operations of both Brooke (Keppel, *Indian Archipelago*, II, 19-21) and Jim (*Lord Jim*, p. 269).

241. "The Rajah Brooke and Joseph Conrad," *Studies in Phililogy*, XXXV (1938), 626-633. Footnotes 232-241, above, are supplementary to the footnotes to be found with the article in *Studies in Phililogy*. Slight verbal emendations have been made.

242. *Ibid.*, pp. 619-625.

243. Pages 20-22.

244. (Macmillan's Colonial Library; London and New York: Macmillan and Company, 1890), pp. 133-134.

In an interesting article, "Conrad's Favorite Bedside Book," in the *South Atlantic Quarterly*, XXXVII (1939), pp. 305-315, Miss Florence Clemens collected further evidence, tangible and intangible, of Wallace's influence on Conrad.

Though we did not know each other's conclusions until after they had been reached, Miss Clemens and I, working entirely separately, both noticed the importance of Brooke and Wallace as sources of Conrad's material.

245. Richard Curle, "Joseph Conrad: Ten Years Later," *Virginia Quarterly Review*, X (1934), 431.

246. Page viii.

247. Page xi.

248. *Joseph Conrad as I Knew Him*, p. 118.

249. *Set of Six*, pp. viii-ix. Also *Life and Letters*, II, 299. See also Conrad's preface to *Youth and Gaspar Ruiz*, pp. 167-168.

250. *Set of Six*, p. x. Also J. DeLancey Ferguson, "The Plot of Conrad's *The Duel*," *Modern Language Notes*, L (1935), 385-390.

251. *Life and Letters*, II, 13, 41, 240, and *Conrad Memorial Library*, p. 327.

252. *Letters to the Colvins* (New York: The Anderson Galleries, 1928), p. 31.

253. No. 1,258 (February 25, 1926), 142. Also Miriam Hatheway Wood, "A Source of Conrad's *Suspense*," *Modern Language Notes*, L (1935), 390-394.

254. *Conrad Memorial Library*, p. 340.

255. London *Times Literary Supplement*, no. 1,128 (August 30, 1923), 570.

## VERNON YOUNG

## Lingard's Folly: The Lost Subject*

THREE NOVELS by Joseph Conrad—*Almayer's Folly* (1895), *An Outcast of the Islands* (1896) and *The Rescue* (1920)—comprise what might have been a purposeful trilogy, a tragedy in three acts, centered in the character of Tom Lingard, of misplaced good intentions. Written in reverse chronological order, they record first the consequences and later the inceptions of Tom Lingard's benevolent despotism. The unity of purpose in this novel-in-reverse is more potential than real, yet Albert Guerard, Jr., accepts the trilogy as an essay in moral continuity and finds "the full measure of Conrad's skepticism" reflected in the career of Tom Lingard, "the central figure of his work."[1] Here is a case of the anxious synthesizer completing the author's design for him; to discover in the separate novels consistent mutations of Lingard's tragic flaw is a compliment unjustified by the insecurity of the original conception. The interest of the three novels lies in their collective clue to Conrad's shifts of intention, to his uncertain psychological orientation and to his aesthetic polarities. The two Almayer novels were the first he wrote; *The Rescue*, one of the last. They reveal, studied together, the initiation of a novelist and his anticlimax, the promise and the loss, the beginning of mastery and the collapse of it.

Sequentially, then, in terms of Lingard's folly as subject—which at least

* From *The Kenyon Review*, XV (Autumn 1953), 522-539.

provides us with a convenient narrative chronology—we have, in *The Rescue,* Tom Lingard, freebooter of the East Indian seas who, honoring an obligation to Hassim and Immada, a royal pair of Malayan exiles, becomes involved with a European yachting party, stranded on "his river." His allegiance is divided between the intrigue for reinstating Hassim and the necessity for extricating the whites—for their own safety as well as for the smoother operation of his own plan—among whom the beautiful Mrs. Travers is the determining complication. The issue is frustration and death: frustration of Lingard's aid to Hassim and his sister who, with their followers, are killed. Lingard's self-esteem temporarily collapses; his latent infatuation with Mrs. Travers is paralyzed. The rescued Europeans go one way, Lingard another, "to satisfy," as Guerard pertinently observes, "his humanitarian egotism elsewhere."

Many years later, as recorded in *An Outcast of the Islands,* Lingard, established as an influential trader on his river, salvages Willems (a runaway from a Dutch ship whom he had adopted years before) from the consequences of embezzlement in Macassar, takes him up-river to his trading post to keep him out of trouble. There, at Sambir, he had already established as his agent Almayer, married to his adopted daughter, a captive Malay.[2] The faithless Willems, under the spell of Aissa, a Malay beauty, betrays Lingard and Almayer by guiding Abdulla, an Arab chieftain and rival in trade, into Lingard's river. Lingard abandons Willems to isolation with Aissa, but Almayer, to fat his revenge, sends Willems' Portuguese wife down-river to him, thus creating the circumstances of Willems' death. Lingard leaves to recoup his fortunes in Europe, planning to return for gold, up-river, that will enrich both himself and Almayer.

*Almayer's Folly* enacts the ruinous end of Lingard's folly. Almayer lives in sufferance on the river because Abdulla's party believes he may disclose the location of Lingard's gold. Lingard is off on another of his desperate sorties for capital abroad. Supported by the hope of salvation and renewed identity in Amsterdam with his half-caste daughter, Almayer is irrevocably crushed when Nina falls in love and flees with Dain Maroola, a Malay nobleman. No daughter, no gold, no Lingard: Almayer takes to opium and dies.

Synopsized in this fashion, the story does indeed sound like Lingard's, with Hassim, Willems and the rest simply the victims of his benevolent folly. A further implication of the trilogy, which earlier readers were quick to suggest, is its moral criticism of the British Empire (or of Imperialism generally, since the Dutch come in for the stronger criticism) —a devastating error of the White Man's Burden—meddling in alien politics, killing natives, stranding the lives of its lower-class whites, defending the lives of the higher-class ones, all from the mandates of arrogant philanthropy. Unfortunately for such reconstructions, there is little evidence, either for the controlling subject or its implied corollary, in any of Conrad's published statements. In point of fact, we know that after finishing his first novel, *Almayer's Folly,* he had no intention of writing another. When he was persuaded to do so, he returned to the biographical circumstances that inspired the Almayer tragedy, in which Lingard had played only a retrospective part and Willems hadn't been mentioned, and resuscitated these characters for prominent roles in *An Outcast of the Islands.* Here Lingard fully assumed his part of blundering *deus ex machina.* But the story is centrally Willems'; if he appears, at the climax, as Lingard's fate, Lingard is also *his* fate, and only by having read *The Rescue* first, and then with little justice, could one assert this novel to be primarily a chapter in the history of Lingard's folly.

Following *An Outcast of the Islands,* Conrad had every intention of resuming his action backwards, so to speak, and possibly the difficulty of overtaking a subject which was now unquestionably becoming Lingard's inhibited his resumption of it. Whatever the real cause, *The Rescue* was largely abandoned until 1916 and not finished until May, 1919, over twenty-three years from its commencement. By this time, whatever vital connection with the Lingard complex of events Conrad had once had was no longer available. That he had lost the large sense of what his trilogy could mean should be evident to any reader of *The Rescue.* All Conrad was able to revive of Lingard was the obsessive motivation: misguided chivalry. Clearly, the character is not otherwise recognizable as the youthful version of Almayer's Lingard. The temperamental portrait is radically different. In *An Outcast,* Lingard was bluff, hearty, extraverted, unglamorous, an executed example of Conrad's critique therein of the unconditioned men of purpose whose identity exists only through the opinion of others, "generally honest, invariably stupid, . . . proud of never losing their way"—

> The man of purpose knows where he is going and what he wants. Travelling on, he achieves great length without any breadth, and battered, besmirched, and weary, he touches the goal at last; he grasps the reward of his perseverance, of his virtue, of his healthy optimism: an untruthful tombstone over a dark and soon forgotten grave.

(The young Lingard is simply not so obtuse). The old Lingard has fiercely curled mustaches and "little red eyes" which glare at Almayer "from behind the lowered eyebrows like a pair of frightened wild beasts crouching in a bush." His diction is forthright and nautical. Commenting to Almayer on Willems' treachery, he mutters, "I am jammed on a lee shore this time," and again, "By God! . . . Life is foul! Foul like a lee forbrace on a dirty night. And yet. And yet. One must see it clear for running before going below—for good."

In *The Rescue,* however, he is preparing no such seagoing locutions and his physical appearance, described not only through Edith Travers' seduced vision but by Conrad as author, is extravagantly romantic. He is "erect and supple," has "light chestnut hair curled close about his well-shaped head"; his clipped beard glints vividly in the sunlight, his dark eyebrows pencil a straight line below an unwrinkled brow and his grey eyes glow with the light of a hidden fire. He wears a grey flannel shirt and his white trousers are held at the waist by a blue silk scarf. He is, in short, a candidate for illustration in *Cosmopolitan Magazine*.[3] None the less, he seems alert to shades of conduct, in himself and others, and if we are to believe that after his catastrophic adventure in the Carimata Straits he could persist in the compulsive altruisms attributed to him in the earlier books, we must set him down as a greater fool than Conrad had done.

The sum of the Lingard trilogy, then, is seen to be rather less than its parts and it is in the parts that one may isolate the values, and the disappointments, of Conrad's specific literary art.

The two Almayer novels, among others, derived their existence from Conrad's voyages as mate of the *Vidar* between Singapore and Bulangan in Borneo during the year 1887. According to M. Jean-Aubry, "it was during these voyages that [Conrad] made the acquaintance of Almayer, also of Willems, Abdulla, Babalatchi, Lakamba, and Tom and Jim Lingard." Conrad himself has given us, in *A Personal Record,* an arresting vignette of his first meeting with the disconsolate Almayer, in addition to the reference in his preface to *An Outcast.* His curiosity aroused by the seemingly permanent and hopeless gloom in which the derelict, awaiting his donkey on the misty shore of Borneo, was immersed, he constructed his first literary edifice on the foundations of Almayer's despair. The actual Almayer died, not from the ingratitude of a daughter (he had a son) but from a wound incurred in a python hunt. "But you were always an unlucky man, Almayer"—Conrad was to apostrophize—"Nothing was ever quite worthy of you. What made you so real to me was that you held this lofty theory with some force of conviction and with an admirable consistency."

The key to Conrad's interest in character lies in this reflective address. From the raw material of such cultural castaways as Almayer and Willems, he shaped his principal contribution to the novel: the *predicament* of the isolated man, never a great man, holding with "some force of conviction" to a theory, usually of his own unassailability, until confronted with its repudiation. The type is as old as Shakespeare and can be found, with a self-conscious consistency approaching Conrad's, in the work of Victor Hugo and Herman Melville (and on a lower level of involvement in Robert Louis Stevenson) but Conrad consummated the analysis at a monomaniacal pitch which such talents as Kafka's could assimilate and further abstract.

One understands how, in 1894, an alert publisher's reader (in this case Edward Garnett) must have been impressed by the phenomenon of a first novel submitted by a sea captain, a novel curiously absorbed in details of tropical death, bearing a lugubrious freight of decaying hope and festooned with an unusually luxurious prose. In the light of Conrad's subsequent victories, however, it is difficult to read *Almayer's Folly* as more than a curiosity, an unsure prelude to his mature achievement. Ford Madox Ford used never to tire of reporting that this novel was commenced on the end-pages of a copy of *Madame Bovary*. Any influence of Flaubert's dramatically austere diction and of his acrid detachment is hard to find in the serpentine sentences and adjectival urgency of the Conrad world. The originality of *Almayer's Folly* consists in its *atmosphere:* the subjective apprehension of futility against the amorphous background of the Bornean jungle, the tenebrous *moral* atmosphere that matches the ineluctability of the action. (Speaking by the card, it may be said that the atmosphere is in excess of the action.)

Formally, the novel is insecure. It does open with the "strong impression," one of Conrad's cardinal aesthetic principles: the swift sketching-in of Almayer on Lingard's river, wistfully dreaming of the gold that will take him and Nina to Europe. But after this effective beginning, the second chapter is dense with biographical exposition that checks the narrative flow too soon and does nothing for our sense of Lingard, the prime mover in Almayer's destiny, save to make us curious. The recurrent underlining of parasitical death in the surrounding jungle is gratuitous throughout, not attributed to the projections of a character as it is in *An Outcast* (or in "Heart of Darkness"). In the manner thoroughly exhausted by Thomas Hardy, Conrad, in this novel, tends to set up his backdrop and then move his characters against it, instructing the reader, by a panoply of edited detail, what mood to educe. (Chapter 11 is an especially prolonged example). Drama is not so much summoned as summarized. Also, the lack of a consistent narrative point of view is not, in this experiment, an advantage. The shift of concentration from Almayer to Dain or Nina or Babalatchi is ineffectual, partly because we never know them as well as we do Almayer, partly because Conrad had not yet mastered the portrayal of Malay psychology, mainly because the novel is really too short to justify such a technique. Almayer, despite the credit to be given Conrad in heightening his original, seems to me to be written down in violation of his "effective principle." His circumstances are, indeed, solemn ones, but without having given him the extension of his appearance in *An Outcast,* one surely feels that Conrad is forcing the rhetoric of his tragedy—in the final pages most painfully—turning him into a Lear of the Pantai.

Whatever imperfections this extraordinary first novel suffers from, it does bring into play hints, at least, of the ruling gifts and obsessions of the novelist. With it, Conrad stepped into his magnetic field—life as the steadfast maintenance of a necessary illusion—spun that webbed prose so essentially the medium of the romantic vision, which was to undergo modulations of the exotic up to the controlled illumination of *The Shadow Line* and then return, in *The Rescue* and accompanying terminations, to a strained encore of its earlier floridity. All of Conrad's ruling motifs are adumbrated in *Almayer's Folly*: the terror of isolation, the idiocy of trust in ownership, the uncalculated effects of altruism, the irrepealable alienation of racial opposites, and the destructive elusiveness of Woman. In the latter direction, perhaps quite the silliest of Conrad's deprecations of *la femme fatale* appears in this novel—markedly impertinent, as it is supposed to be discerned by Dain Maroola.

> She drew back her head and fastened her eyes on his in one of those long looks that are a woman's most terrible weapon; a look that is more stirring than the closest touch, and more dangerous than the thrust of a dagger, because it also whips the soul out of the body, but leaves the body alive and helpless, to be swayed here and there by the capricious tempests of passion and desire. . . . It has the same meaning for the man of the forests and the sea as for the man threading the paths of the more dangerous wilderness of houses and streets. Men that have felt in their breasts the awful exultation such a look awakens become mere things of today—which is paradise; forget yesterday—which was suffering; care not for tomorrow—which may be perdition. They wish to live under that look for ever. It is the look of woman's surrender.

The stubborn and overdressed misogyny that devitalizes much of Conrad's writing is here couched in diction that reaches across the intervening masterpieces to the indiscriminate palette of his final novels.

*An Outcast of the Islands* consolidates features merely traced in *Almayer's Folly*. It is, by contrast, an achieved novel and better, I think, than most critics (and Conrad, himself) have given it credit for being. It is dramatic in structure, cyclical in form: this is to say that it proceeds, narrative-wise, by *progression d'effet* and its linear divisions are subsumed under a permeating motif. All the characters are logically disposed, developed and accounted for, while Willems is never superseded as the novel's leading character.

Willems is the striking creation of a complex, common man, a figure of appallingly ignorant vanity, sensitive enough to suffer from want of prestige, not sensitive enough to be honest, and consumed by an overwhelming compulsion to inflict his miserable portion of egotism on anyone whom he considers lower in the moral scale than himself. So long as there is a half-caste wife or a "savage" inamorata to feed his self-aggrandizement, he counts himself, bounded in his nut-shell, king of infinite space. He is the next corrective version, after Dickens, of a democratic stereotype; to borrow John Peale Bishop's distinction (apropos of Moll Flanders), he belongs to the predatory rather than to the exploited poor.

The novel's impulsion is the progressive deterioration of Willems from his first petty crime to his furthest corruption. Here is the opening sentence:

> When he stepped off the straight and narrow path of his peculiar honesty, it was with an inward assertion of unflinching resolve to fall back again into the monotonous but safe stride of virtue as soon as his little excursion into the wayside quagmires had produced the desired effect.

Willems' fatal illusion has been instantly announced and the paragraph proceeds, inexorably, to introduce, in less than a page, the spiritual and social status of the pathetic hero.

> It was going to be a short episode—a sentence in brackets, so to speak —in the flowing tale of his life: a thing of no moment, to be done unwillingly, yet neatly, and to be quickly forgotten. He imagined that he could go on afterwards looking at the sunshine, breathing in the perfume of flowers in the small garden before his house. He fancied that nothing would be changed, that he would be able as heretofore to tyrannize good-humoredly over his half-caste wife, to notice with tender contempt his pale yellow child, to patronize loftily his dark-skinned brother-in-law, who loved pink neckties and wore patent-leather boots on his little feet, and was so humble before the white husband of the lucky sister. Those were the delights of his life, and he was unable to conceive that the moral significance of any act of his could interfere with the very nature of things, could dim the light of the sun, could destroy the perfume of the flowers, the submission of his wife, the smile of his child, the awe-struck respect of Leonard da Souza and of all the da Souza family.

The immediacy and totality of the guiding conception are distinctly Shakespearian, and in the particular sense that recalls A. C. Bradley's interpretation of Shakespeare's feeling for

> the incalculability of evil—that in meddling with it human beings do they know not what. The soul, he seems to feel, is a thing of such inconceivable depth, complexity, and delicacy, that when you intro-duce into it, or suffer to develop in it, any change, and particularly the change called evil, you can form only the vaguest idea of the reaction you will provoke.

Of course, Willems is not a *tragic* hero but he has tragic pretensions, and he has consciousness sufficiently articulate with which to solicit one's wry sympathy. Conrad defines his burden as that of the ignorant who "must feel and suffer from their complexity as well as the wisest; but to them the pain of struggle and defeat appears strange, mysterious, remediable and unjust."

The initial chapter rounds out Willems' small prophetic vision of self-pride and avarice, sounding in its final phrase the *doom-motif* which is one of the unifying themes.

> Before going up the steps of his house he stood for a while, his feet well apart, chin in hand, contemplating mentally Hudig's future part-ner. A glorious occupation. He saw him quite safe; solid as the hills; deep—deep as an abyss; discreet as the grave.

Part I completes his first encirclement, up-river at Sambir—his helpless infatuation for the Malay girl, Aissa, and the "grave" note is sounded again in its last sentence:

With a faint cry and an upward throw of his arms he gave up as a tired swimmer gives up: because the swamped craft is gone from under his feet; because the night is dark and the shore is far—because death is better than strife.

The next section extracts his cupidity completely, for his possession of Aissa is contingent upon his betrayal of Lingard, and another notation of his inextricable moral position has the last word:

He fought without a sound, striking futile blows, dashing from side to side; obstinate, hopeless, and always beaten back; like a man bewitched within the invisible sweep of a magic circle.

The third division shows Conrad's first successful use of the timeshift. Focus of interest moves to old Lingard and Almayer, opening with Almayer's enraged accusations against Lingard's "infernal charity."

Yes! Cat, dog, anything that can scratch or bite; as long as it is harmful enough and mangy enough. A sick tiger would make you happy. . . . A half-dead tiger that you could weep over and palm upon some poor devil in your power, to tend and nurse for you. Never mind the consequences—to the poor devil. Let him be mangled or eaten up, of course! You haven't any pity to spare for the victims of your infernal charity.[4]

The incentive for the outburst is Willems' and Abdulla's raid on the settlement, which we learn now only in the retrospect of Almayer's choleric recital. The episode is terminated by Lingard's leaving to punish Willems, rejecting Abdulla's written offer to deliver Willems, for a concession. Almayer throws the letter into the river where the current bears it away "down-stream towards the sea," the direction of freedom, now closed to Willems, one anticipates, by Lingard's resolution. The remainder of the book brings Willems abandonment and death. Aissa, unloved by the embittered outcast, is shown at the end of Part IV, "thinking of all that had been their love—and she sat in the abandoned posture of those who sit weeping by the dead, of those who watch and mourn over a corpse." The corpse, unmourned, fittingly receives the concluding sentences. Almayer, drunk and uncomprehending, shouts into the jungle at "that far-off and invisible slab of imported granite," Willems' tombstone:

"Where are you, Willems? Hey? . . . Hey? . . . Where there is no mercy for you—I hope!"
"Hope," repeated in a whispering echo the startled forests, the river and the hills; and Almayer, who stood waiting, with a smile of tipsy attention on his lips, heard no other answer.

(Conrad orchestrated this connection with *Almayer's Folly* adroitly. The earlier novel opened with Almayer still hearing "no other answer" but that of hope.)

Besides this thematic punctuation, there are other effective congruences which rehearse the more sustained engagements with action-and-symbol that Conrad was to undertake. In the middle of Almayer's exasperated capitulation of Willems' outrages, he and Lingard break the conversation to concentrate furiously on catching a blue-bottle fly.

> But suddenly the buzz died out in a thin shrill away in the open space of the courtyard, leaving Lingard and Almayer standing face to face in the fresh silence of the young day, looking very puzzled and idle, their arms hanging uselessly by their sides—like men disheartened by some portentous failure.

Two chapters later, the irrepressible Lingard, reassuring Almayer and Nina of his certain discovery of gold in the near future, erects a house of cards for the child and the structure collapses suddenly "before the child's light breath." (A backward anticipation of Nina's desertion of Almayer and his hopes.) And when Lingard leaves Willems in the jungle clearing, his departure is accompanied by a cloudburst—the heavens literally fall on Willems. The river, itself, Lingard's river, is, more evidently than in *Almayer's Folly,* symbol of the natural flow of life which Lingard thinks to control—for humanitarian purposes, he tells himself. The river brings death, finally, to all its beneficiaries except Nina Almayer who returns, by way of it, to the resources of her own race.

Taking Ford Madox Ford at his word, when he claimed that there were only four of Conrad's novels with which he had "absolutely no, however subordinate, a connection," we can agree that the following definition of his and Conrad's literary aim was indeed relevant to *An Outcast of the Islands:*

> . . . a novel was the rendering of an affair: of one embroilment, one set of embarrassments, one human coil, one psychological progression. From this the novel got its unity. No doubt it might have its caesura— or even several; but these must be brought about by temperamental pauses, markings of time when the treatment called for them. But the whole novel was to be an exhaustion of aspects, was to proceed to one culmination, to reveal once and for all, in the last sentence—or the penultimate—in the last phrase, or the one before it, the psychological significance of the whole. (Of course you might have what is called in music the coda).[5]

Strictly speaking, *An Outcast* is not so single a rendering "of one embroilment" as *Almayer's Folly,* since the corollary defeat of Almayer and the intricacies of Sambir politics get their full share of expression, but the "exhaustion of aspects," the unity derived from a central "set of embarrassments" and the musical analogy are all present.

Conrad was desperately unsatisfied with this book, although favorable reviews mollified his remorse. He felt he had failed with the Willems-Aissa relationship and in the execution of chapters renumbered on publication and now unidentifiable—most likely those in Part IV which does contain the weakest writing. His dissatisfaction is best appreciated as a confident anticipation of achieving the more subtle constructions of *The Nigger of* the *"Narcissus,"* "Heart of Darkness" or "The Secret Sharer." What he perennially strove for and more than once perfected was a novel in which the entire action was symbol and in which contingent plot was minimized, a form better suited to his feeling for organic unity than the order of checks and balances which he tried in *An Outcast,* and again, with grave disloca- tions, in *Nostromo.* (So far as the Willems-Aissa passages are concerned, he was rarely at his best when deploying sexual complications; I think these are as persuasive as any he was to write.)

The attentive reader of Conrad's work will find much to treasure in this early novel. Not simply the themes but the very constructs, in terms of character, are forecasts of Conrad's later fictional conflicts. In the rival advantages of Patololo and Omar, with the contrapuntal movement of Abdulla and his councillors ranged against Lingard, there is the pattern of "material interests" to be used in *Nostromo.* Aissa's enslavement of Willems is a concrete rehearsal of all those Conradian times when the conscious man surrenders to, or fearfully glimpses, the heart of darkness.[6] And, in the final confrontation of Willems by Lingard—"You are not a human being that may be destroyed or forgiven. You are a bitter thought, a something without a body and that must be hidden. . . . You are my shame."—one sees a trial edition of the meaning of James Wait to the crew of the "Narcissus," Lord Jim's meeting with Gentleman Brown, the betrayal of Haldin (*Under Western Eyes*), the arrival of Mr. Jones at Heyst's island (*Victory*)—and the secret sharer.

To have properly resolved the direction and meaning of this triology in terms of Lingard's folly, Conrad might have written a third novel in which the *post*-Almayer experience of Lingard would have been the sub- ject: Lingard harrying the marts of Europe in vain effort to return glori- ously to Malaysia and redress—too late—the issues of his benevolence. A conscious engagement by Lingard with the evidence of his unforeseen ruinations would have dignified him as the tragic monitor of Conrad's skepticism that Guerard thinks of his being. But what Conrad wrote in- stead was *The Rescue,* in which the profound and potentially fruitful senti- ment, "When you save people from death you take a share in their life," is no more than a sentence.

As we have seen, *The Rescue* was neither a recovery nor an amplifica- tion; it was a moral retrenchment, a concession to criticism of the heroic ideal while maintaining the aura of the ideal. When Conrad wrote the larger part of this novel, he was beyond the force of its germinal re- quirements; mind stubbornly recreated what the senses had forgotten. Ford has told us how often and anxiously, in the years between, he and Conrad reworked the opening of the book. To its final detriment, evi- dently, since anxiety over exposition failed to save the subject lost, the irony relinquished, the soundings of the brave years between *Nostromo* and "The Secret Sharer" no longer readable. True, the hundred-odd intro- ductory pages of *The Rescue* could as well be scrapped and the novel begin with almost the very words which now open Part III—with Lingard's pre-history to be resumed in Chapter Seven, following the hyperbole of the chapter before, where Lingard liberates "the vision of two years into the night where Mrs. Travers could follow them as if outlined in words of fire." But since plotting is inseparable from total presentation, economy in itself would save nothing but the reader's time. The whole tone is a dying reverberation; the structure is altogether regressive, a reworking of the super-cyclical method which had served Conrad too long since and conclusively strangled itself in the structural labyrinths of *Chance*.

Among the characters, Mr. Travers, who loves only property and prestige and whose conceit never permits him to acknowledge his peril and his indebtedness to Lingard for his very life, is alone thoroughly well conceived and executed. Mrs. Travers, with nothing to hope for after realizing that "the sincerity of a great passion" is, in her husband's case, restricted to his career, is a less heroic and much vaguer simulacrum of Mrs. Gould in *Nostromo*. D'Alcacer, who loved once and lost, is a Heyst (*Victory*) kept alive by decorum. His presence, except as an added instance of the unloved and unloving, seems principally contrived to serve as passive confidant to Ethel Travers, giving the reader an occasionally more intimate view of her. Jörgenson, whose dynamite blows up Lingard's hope of rescue-fulfillment, is a sentimental reversion to the figure of Dr. Monygham in *Nostromo*. None of the Malay characters in this novel has any dimension whatever if measured by the scale of Babalatchi, Lakamba, Abdulla and Aissa—perhaps because, for this book, they were invented outright rather than remembered.

The prose is of a piece with the unchecked illusionism of approach; it recovers the will to the mysterious which Conrad, between 1911 and 1917, had brought under control.[7] Although there are many affectionately accurate descriptions of light on moving water and the qualities of jungle shoreline, there are far too many unauthorized similes expressed in rhetoric to which not even Mrs. Travers or the educated yacht's mate, Carter, could be susceptible. They flow from Conrad's singular opulence of expression and they consistently lead the mind away from the object:

> All was unmoving as if the dawn would never come, the stars would never fade, the sun would never rise any more; all was mute, still, dead —as if the shadow of the outer darkness, the shadow of the uninterrupted, of the everlasting night that fills the universe, the shadow of the night so profound and so vast that the blazing suns lost in it are only sparks, like pin-points of fire, the restless shadow that like a suspicion of an evil truth darkens everything upon the earth in its passage, had enveloped her, had stood arrested as if to remain with her forever.
> . . . a suprisingly heavy puff came in a free rush as if, far away there to the northward, the last defence of the calm had been victoriously carried. The flames borne down streamed bluishly . . . and behold, the shadows on the deck went mad and jostled each other as if trying to escape from a doomed craft, the darkness, held up dome-like by the brilliant glare, seemed to tumble headlong upon the brig in an overwhelming downfall, the men stood swaying as if ready to fall under the ruins of a black and noiseless disaster.

In these, and many other passages, quite apart from the "as if" monotony, the symbolic chiaroscuro which Conrad had used so deliberately in *The Nigger of the "Narcissus"* has become a formula which confuses thought and observation alike.

Among the chances for a controlling principle which Conrad scotched, the most valuable irony in this novel is precisely Lingard's accidental sacrifice of an aristocracy of blood (Hassim and Immada) to a loveless aristocracy of property. Conrad's failure of nerve prevented his clinching the actualities of the Lingard-Travers fiasco. The novel has an "unhappy ending" but this is detonated, not derived. In 1919, Conrad was further away than ever from any closely critical regard of cultural and class relationships, as he was from any commitment to sexual psychology. The scenes between Lingard and Mrs. Travers are disastrous on all but the conversational level, by reason of Conrad's abiding incomprehension of the modalities of physical desire—and of his hindsight necessity here for keeping Lingard celibate. His delineation of Travers' frigid values and of D'Alcacer's courteous impotence is nearer the worldly mark, but insufficient to cancel the puerility of the "romantic interest." And it needs only his use of Lingard's brig as Anima to suggest that the conception was priggish from the start:

> To him she [the brig] was always precious—like old love; always desirable—like a strange woman; always tender—like a mother; always faithful—like the favourite daughter of a man's heart.

If one relates *The Rescue* only to the lost subject of Lingard's folly, one is faced with the most egregious of Conrad's failures. On other grounds, however, it seems inconceivable that a writer who had assisted in the development of one of this century's primary concerns in fiction— the modification of the romantic stance—could have reinstated, during First World War years when shibboleths of Love and Renunciation were severely tested, the unproved glamor of his Victorian youth. By an irony Conrad would not then have perceived, since he expressed no such violent dissatisfaction with *The Rescue* as he had with *An Outcast of the Islands,* he had identified himself with his subject. For in rescuing the "shade" of Lingard from restful oblivion, he was recapitulating the folly of old Lingard, himself, in restoring the fortunes of Willems. As with Lingard, his creation betrayed him because of its innate lack of viability and—to push the simile to its conclusion—he then found it necessary to abandon the creation, characteristically to isolation—and to the unsympathetic mercies of womankind. (1953)

### NOTES

1. *Joseph Conrad,* by Albert Guerard, Jr., *New Directions,* 1947.
2. It can be seen how profusely Conrad implemented Lingard's romantic altruism. In the first two published novels, Lingard has already *rescued* a Malay girl, Almayer and Willems. He also *rescues* Nina Almayer to have her educated in Singapore (recounted in A.F.). In *The Rescue,* Conrad triples the device

by having Lingard *rescue* Jörgenson and, as a result, fail in *rescuing* Hassim and Immada, actually—Mrs. Travers, symbolically. This overloading surely submerges Conrad's freight of pardonable duplications far above the Plimsoll line!

3. Which is where Conrad expected *The Rescue* to be published though it was serialized in a magazine appropriately entitled, *Romance, 1919-1920.* In connection with this publication, Conrad confessed to the "romantic presentation" but believed that its interest was "all in the shades of the psychology of the people engaged." *Joseph Conrad, Life and Letters,* by G. Jean-Aubry, Doubleday, 1927. See Volume I, pp. 94ff.

4. The interpretation is interestingly harsher than Mrs. Travers' view of Lingard's quixotism in *The Rescue.* "It struck her that there was a great passion in all this, the beauty of an implanted faculty of affection that had found itself, its immediate need of an object and the way of expansion; a tenderness expressed violently; a tenderness that could only be satisfied by backing human beings against their own destiny."

5. *Return to Yesterday,* by Ford M. Ford. Horace Liveright, N.Y. 1932.

6. Compare, for instance, the wording of Willems' last attempt to resist Aissa with the climax of Lord Jim's recollection of his jump from the *Patna.* Willems: "He looked drearily above her head down into the deeper gloom of the courtyard. And, all at once, it seemed to him that he was peering into a sombre hollow, into a deep black hole. . . ." Jim: " 'I wished I could die,' he cried. 'There was no going back. It was as if I had jumped into a well—into an everlasting deep hole.' "

7. [Editor's note: For Moser's comment on Young's opinion here, see fnt. 3, p. 331.

# VERNON YOUNG

## Trial by Water: Joseph Conrad's
### *The Nigger of the "Narcissus"**

"Both men and ships live in an unstable element, are subject to subtle and powerful influences, and want to have their merits understood rather than their faults found out."
—Conrad: *The Mirror of the Sea*

"I have no doubt that star-gazing is a fine occupation, for it leads you within the borders of the unattainable. But map-gazing, to which I became addicted so early, brings the problems of the great spaces of the earth into stimulating and direct contact with sane curiosity and gives an honest precision to one's imaginative faculty."
—Conrad: "Geography and Some Explorers" in *Last Essays*

*The Nigger of the "Narcissus"* is the account of a sailing-ship's voyage from Bombay to London by the way of the Cape, during which the ship nearly founders with all hands and the crew is temporarily demoralized

* From *Accent,* XII (Spring 1952), pp. 67-81.

by the presence of a Negro seaman named James Wait. The Negro dies
and is buried at sea; the *Narcissus* arrives in London with no further
incident. *The Nigger of the "Narcissus"* is a study of character on trial,
a memorial to seafarers under sail, together with disclaimers of those who
would have undermined the innocence and pertinacity of their toil. *The
Nigger of the "Narcissus"* is an allegory of temptation and endurance, a
microcosm of the moral world of relationships and responsibilities. And
since, as in all myth, principles as well as patterns of action are reiterated
across space and time, the social motif of *The Nigger of the "Narcissus"*
is referable to the individual psyche, and the novel, under this aspect, is
an adventure of the soul.

It is the third aspect, the mythic, never openly acknowledged by Conrad himself, which gives to the novel its vibratory temper and its perennial
interest. Conrad's fraternal loyalty to the nautical facts of the case is
finally subordinate to his transcendental theme, fortified throughout the
novel by its equivalence in symbolic action. Geography and meteorology
combine with crises of human conduct and with analogues of the
metaphysical cycle to produce a rich complex of correspondences.

The *Narcissus,* then, sails from Bombay to London—which is to say,
from the East (source, for Conrad, of the exotic and the ominous) to
the capital of the mercantile West. The voyage, a routine "homeward
passage," necessitates the traversal of 60° southward to attain 20° north-
ward; to reach home port, the *Narcissus* must sail away from it, so to
speak, down miles of longitude against the West Wind Drift and around
the cape of storms called Good Hope, before she can straighten north
and sail directly home with assisting trade winds. The crucial calamity—
the deadly plunge of the ship on to her *port* side (the left, or sinister,
side)—and the termination of the power which may be said to have
effected it, the death of the Nigger, occur equidistantly from the Zero
Line (the equator of day and night), approximately 40° south and 40°
north, respectively. Mercator's Projection thus becomes a corollary
graph of the crew's spiritual ordeal.

Leaving one continent for another, the *Narcissus* sails *out* of darkness
*into* darkness, since Conrad's moral geography was opposite in value
to Herman Melville's, for example. The sea, "the unstable element,"
was, to Conrad, the amniotic ocean of life, itself: like life uncertain, incalculable but enchanting and worthier of men's challenge than the land.
In all Conrad's novels, the land is the home of the enemy. The jungle,
the forest, the city: these are his symbols of treachery. The sea, however
disastrous or inclement it may become, is as neutral and as irrefutable
as the life-cycle; it is the given, if "destructive element,"[1] and in the face
of it man's duty is, like Singleton's in this novel, to "steer with care."

Conrad's earliest fictional commitments to the antipodal character of
land and sea are underlined in this novel. The land lies "within the
frontier of infamy and filth, within that border of dirt and hunger, of
misery and dissipation, that comes down on all sides to the water's edge

of the incorruptible ocean . . ." The *Narcissus,* a creature of light, was born in darkness, "in black eddies of smoke, under a grey sky, on the banks of the Clyde. The clamorous and sombre stream gives birth to things of beauty that float away into the sunshine of the world to be loved by men." When she leaves Bombay with her yards hoisted she becomes "a high and lonely pyramid, gliding all shining and white, through the sunlit mist. The tug turned short round and went away towards the land [resembling] an enormous and aquatic black beetle, surprised by the light, overwhelmed by the sunshine, trying to escape with ineffectual effort into the distant gloom of the land . . ."[2] Upon arrival in the Thames at the end of the voyage, the *Narcissus* re-enters the cloud: "the shadows of soulless walls fell upon her, the dust of all the continents leaped upon her deck, and a swarm of strange men, clambering up her sides, took possession of her in the name of the sordid earth. She had ceased to live."

Wait, the Negro, originally a product of the jungle, one supposes—he is specifically alluded to as a West Indian, enforcing the equation of West and Death—is, with Donkin, "the independent offspring of the ignoble freedom of the slums full of disdain and hate for the austere servitude of the sea," set off against the Able Seaman, Singleton, who, in forty-five years, has lived no more than forty months ashore. The narrator's final reflection on the crew recapitulates this sheep-and-goats distinction. "I never saw them again . . . Singleton has no doubt taken with him the long record of his faithful work in to the peaceful depths of an hospitable sea. And Donkin, who never did a decent day's work in his life, no doubt earns his living by discoursing with filthy eloquence upon the right of labor to live. So be it! Let the earth and the sea each have its own."

By not accepting the moral dichotomy of land and sea as a highly charged metaphor, the reader of *The Nigger of the "Narcissus"* might well accuse Conrad of sentimental sophistry; accepting it, he will be in a position to appreciate how effectively it is co-featured with the other symbolic properties—particularly with the permeating use of color contrasts. White and black, pink or blue and black, light and shade, sun and cloud, gold and darkness—within the total form, these oppostions are vitally operative, usually accompanied by relative variations of weather. So much is this tonality the index to Conrad's alignment of moods and forces that its most pertinent appearances are well worth isolating before taking up considerations less purely visual.

Among other possible reasons for preferring the finally established title to earlier ones (among which were *The Forecastle: A Tale of Ships and Men* and *Children of the Sea: A Tale of the Forecastle*), Conrad surely felt the force of the black and white dualism, while taking advantage, perhaps, of the British association of narcissus with death, thereby giving a paradoxical twist to the pairing of skull and blossom, root and flower.³ In any case, the title indubitably sets the key which is sounded in the very first sentence:

> Mr. Baker, chief mate of the ship *Narcissus,* stepped in one stride out of his lighted cabin into the darkness of the quarterdeck.

When the Negro, Wait, joins the ship,

> He held his head up in the glare of the lamp—a head vigorously modelled into deep shadows and shining lights . . .

After he retires, groaning, to his bunk in the forecastle,

> Singleton stood at the door with his face to the light and his back to the darkness.

(This vignette, sharpening here the presence of Wait, reverberates long after in one of the most remarkable sentences in the book when, at the end of the voyage, the older man steps up to the shipping-office pay table:

> Singleton came up, venerable—and uncertain as to daylight; . . . his hands, that never hesitated in the great light of the open sea, could hardly find the small pile of gold in the profound darkness of the shore.)

During the voyage, every climax of weather as well as every dramatic position in which Wait figures is similarly balanced. Emerging from the forecastle, Wait

> Seemed to hasten the retreat of departing light by his very presence; the setting sun dipped sharply, as though fleeing before our nigger . . .

As the men struggle to extricate Wait from behind the bulkhead while the ship is capsizing,

> in the sunshiny blue square of the door, the boatswain's face, bearded and dark, Wamibo's face, wild and pale, hung over—watching . . .

As they are crossing the equator, when the influence of Wait has settled into its most oppressive effects,

> The invisible sun, sweeping above the upright masts, made on the clouds a blurred stain of rayless light, and a similar patch of faded radiance kept pace with it from east to west over the unglittering level of the waters. At night, through the impenetrable darkness of earth and heaven, broad sheets of flame noiselessly; and for half a second the becalmed craft stood out with its mast and rigging, with every sail and every rope distinct and black in the centre of a fiery outburst, like a charred ship enclosed in a globe of fire.

(The ship on the line of the equator and the square-rigging against the sky form a monogram of a fiery cross.) Concurrent with the dead calm after land is first sighted, Wait, attended by Donkin, lies dying in the deckhouse. His last words are

> "Light . . . the lamp . . . and . . . go."

Donkin, after stealing Wait's money is

> . . . just in time to see Wait's eyes blaze up and go out at once, like
> two lamps overturned together by a sweeping blow . . . [Outside]
> sleeping men, huddled under jackets, made on the lighted deck
> shapeless dark mounds that had the appearance of neglected graves
> . . . The ship slept. And the immortal sea stretched away, immense
> and hazy, like the image of life, with a glittering surface and lightless
> depths.

The coda that follows the marine burial of Wait is brisk and lambent;
the prose throws off saltatory images of light which conquer those of
darkness (and which, incidentally, involve an energetic sequence of
"pathetic fallacy") :

> . . . the clouds swifter than the ship, more free, but without a home.
> The coast to welcome her stepped out of space into the sunshine.
> The lofty headlands trod masterfully into the sea; the wide bays
> smiled in the light . . . At night the headlands retreated, the bays
> advanced into one unbroken line of gloom. The lights of earth mingled
> with the lights of heaven; and above the tossing lanterns of a trawling
> fleet a great lighthouse shone steadily, like an enormous riding light
> burning above a vessel of fabulous dimensions.

The *Narcissus* is berthed and her men are "scattered by the dissolving
contact with land." The narrator last sees them, their pockets full of
money,

> swaying irresolute and noisy on the broad flagstones before the Mint.
> They were bound for the Black Horse, where men, in fur caps with
> brutal faces and in shirt sleeves, dispense out of varnished barrels
> the illusions of strength . . .

A concluding ambience balances the earliest view of the men as they
had mustered on deck in Bombay:

> The dark knot of seamen drifted in sunshine . . . The sunshine of
> heaven fell like a gift of grace on the mud of the earth, on the re-
> membering and mute stones, on greed, selfishness . . . And to the
> right of the dark group the stained front of the Mint, cleansed by the
> flood of light, stood out for a moment dazzling and white like a
> marble palace in a fairy tale. The crew of the *Narcissus* drifted out of
> sight.

The reader will discover for himself many more such images than
I have thought necessary to display here: these are perhaps sufficient
to verify Conrad's purposive employment of them. It will have been
seen that although these dark-and-light oppositions mainly express
conventional connotations of death and life, evil and good (land and
sea, left and right), there are moments when they represent no such
clear antinomy. White hail streaming from a black cloud, the dark
boatswain against the bright blue door, a "withered" moon, and others,

are clearly not intended to be consistent with the moral polarities conveyed by the general thematic continuity; they are simply part of an absorption in tonal antithesis. In the superb sentence of the gold in the darkness of the shore, gold and darkness are not opposed but correlated, morally speaking—as they are again in that extraordinary touch of the men going from the light-flooded Mint to the Black Horse. This oblique manipulation of symbols may be better appreciated in the light of a statement on cinematic art, which, as Edward Crankshaw was first among critics to point out, Conrad's art so often resembled.[4] Writing on the subject of cinematic color values, Sergei Eisenstein declared, in *The Film Sense*:

> In art it is not the *absolute* relationships that are decisive, but those *arbitrary* relationships within a system of images dictated by the particular work of art. . . . the *emotional intelligibility* and function of color will rise from the natural order of establishing *the color imagery of the work, coincidental with the process of shaping the living movement of the whole work.*

In *The Nigger of the "Narcissus,"* what Conrad's imagery substantiates above all is the apocalyptic nature of the novel's outline. The four Empedoclean elements, the polar variants of night and day, hell and heaven, West and East, encompass the cosmological pyramid which is the subject. In "the living movement of the whole," Conrad's symbolism subscribes to no single order of religious values; it synthesizes universally recurring emblems in man's expression of his destiny and places them at the service of the novel's contingent subject, the moral effects of illusion.

> The true peace of God begins at any spot a thousand miles from the nearest land; and when he sends there the messengers of his might it is not in terrible wrath against crime, presumption and folly, but paternally, to chasten simple hearts—ignorant hearts that know nothing of life, and beat undisturbed by envy or greed.

An exaggerated reassertion of oceanic felicity, this paragraph is also the nuclear designation of the *Narcissus'* voyage as a trial by water, not so much to initiate as to chasten, to test the illusion of invulnerability which each man wears in varying proportion. The primary agent of this trial is the Nigger, James Wait. "I belong to the ship," is his calm announcement to the chief mate as he stands muster. In the occult vocabulary he would be described as an *elemental,* a servant of the general law of nature; from the psychological bias, he is an embodiment of the subconscious, instinctual but regressive quality in man. Twentieth-century anthropology, to say nothing of sociology, has perhaps diminished, if not discredited, for most of us, the spell of the lurid, the mysterious or the evil in the person of the Negro, but it would be a mistake to see in James Wait only an exercise of Conradian chauvinism. Conrad's experience with African backcountry savages certainly justified his using the type as illustrative of the black-magical and the unevolved. When describing Wait's face as "pathetic and brutal: the tragic, the mysterious, the repulsive mask of a nigger's soul," he was enjoying the privilege, apparently inevitable to their psychology, which the white races have taken upon themselves, of seeing the dark races as either exotic or sinister, but in any case inferior.

Metaphysically, Wait serves a purpose comparable to that of El Negro in Melville's "Benito Cereno": he is the *spirit* of blackness, archetype of the unknown forces from the depths. With this important difference, however: he is not sensationally demonic but, rather, insidious and emanating. His role is a rehearsal, in Conrad's literature, of that "barbarous and superb woman" in "Heart of Darkness" who, as the steamboat leaves with the damned and moribund remains of Kurtz, stretches "tragically her bare arms after [them] over the sombre and glittering river." Wait, by a form of adjuration less explicit, more accessible to the gullibility of simple men, all but deprives the crew of their will to live. Consentient with the natural perils that haunt its progress, he accompanies the *Narcissus* across the waters of strife, casting his spell on the probity of the crew's endeavors.

A symbol of postponement, his name is cardinal token: Wait. Conrad plays upon it when the Nigger belatedly joins the ship, shouting "Wait" to the astonished officer who takes the word as an insolent injunction rather than as a name. Wait's burial at sea re-emphasizes the tenacity of his inertia, for when the plank is first raised to slide his body overboard, he holds fast until one of the sailors, after screaming "Jimmy, be a man! . . . Go, Jimmy . . . ," gives the corpse needed impetus with a light push.[5] But *Wait* has also, by virtue of the Nigger's retarding and oppressive action, the force of the other spelling, *weight*. (Immediately following his plummet from the deck, "The ship rolled as if relieved of an unfair burden.") From his bed-ridden vantage point, supine and seemingly helpless, he drags on the inital resistance of the men like an anchor, beguiles their sympathy, gradually vitiates their resolution by the pathos of his induced condition. (Naturalistically, his eventual death may be construed as psychogenic.) His appeal is to the slacker in each man's heart, awakening the desire to rebel, abandonment of duty and luxury of irresponsible rest.

The near undoing of the crew is the result of their returning good for evil, a practice which, in extremity, was to Conrad a sin of pride. As he wrote in a letter to Marguerite Poradowska,

> . . . to return good for evil is not only profundly immoral but dangerous, in that it sharpens the appetite for evil in the malevolent and develops (perhaps unconsciously) that latent tendency towards hypocrisy in the . . . let us say, benevolent.

Similarly to Lingard in Conrad's Almayer novels, the crew of the *Narcissus* become victims of benevolent egotisms, and their sponsorship, like Lingard's, is betrayed. Wait meets their compassion with abuse; he flaunts his death-urge before their living eyes.

> He fascinated us. He would never let doubt die. He overshadowed the ship. Invulnerable in his promise of speedy corruption he trampled on our self-respect, he demonstrated to us daily our want of moral courage; he tainted our lives.

The determining incident of their slavery occurs when they rescue Wait from the deck-house in which he is trapped by the storm; though he insults them for their pains, they are more than ever in his power. They come to exemplify the negative hazard involved in the young Lingard's Oriental sentiment that "When you save people from death you take a share in their life."

In the oblique hours of rescue, they have been on a very long journey toward oblivion.

> The return on the poop was like the return of wanderers after many years amongst people marked by the desolation of time.[6]

They have undergone the first trial, entered the dominion of death and been reborn; the salvage of Wait effects a respite, a temporary release from danger, in the manner of the old tales in which an ogre was freed from a cave, a witch from an oak-tree or an imp from a bottle. Freedom is gained only by entering into closer bondage with the genie.[7] The weather clears, the sea is calmed.

> . . . from that time our life seemed to start afresh as though we had died and had been resuscitated. All the first part of the voyage, the Indian Ocean on the other side of the Cape, all that was lost in a haze, like an ineradicable suspicion of some previous existence.

The more extreme test is to follow. Their solidarity with the defecting Negro established by their plucking him to safety, the crew members arise to articulate discontent when Wait finally offers to turn to with the men and his services are refused by Captain Allistoun, who is privately convinced that the Nigger is indeed going to die. The fatally deluded allegiance of the men will not let them believe this. No longer able to distinguish the smell of mortality, they offer their disbelief to Wait as a propitiation, as if he were the totem, the cult-object of a primitive clan. "The desolation of time" has obliterated their etiological powers and returned them to the rudimentary form of communal belief through contagion (for which Emil Durkheim has provided the term *surexcitation*).

As it becomes unmistakably evident that Wait will die and his "fleshless head" resembles "a distinterred black skull," disbelief changes to anxiety. And, as Singleton has predicted, Wait dies after land is sighted; the reaction is one of sullen surprise.

> We did not know till then how much faith we had put in his delusions. We had taken his chances of life so much at his own valuation that

his death, like the death of an old belief, shook the foundations of our society. A common bond was gone; the strong, effective and respectable bond of a sentimental lie.

Wait is stitched into a canvas and dropped overboard into the "lightless depths"—to starboard, toward the East, the night, the land, and the direction of rebirth.

The men of the *Narcissus* are modified by James Wait in accord with the drift of their respective temperaments. The trial by water corroborates either the virtue or the ignoble fallacy of their necessary illusions. Captain Allistoun is never for a moment intimidated by Jimmy's malingering. He it is who keeps his head when the *Narcissus* heels and the carpenter, in a panic, grabs an ax with which to cut the masts free. Allistoun forbids the action, thereby saving all hands. While the half-drowned men cling to the canted deck, waiting for death, he remains on the poop, eyes ahead for the first opportunity to shout "wear ship." (On the analogy of the psychic organism, Allistoun is the *super-ego,* dominating consciously the subterranean murmurs of defeat. His insistence that Wait remain in his cabin is a further act of will over the emerging death-wish; he refuses it the light of day.) The last order he gives to the officer on leaving the ship summarizes his supreme rationality: "Don't forget to wind up the chronometers tomorrow morning."

Singleton, in less authoritative measure, is the Captain's moral counterpart in the forecastle. A singleton is an independent card in a suit; whether or not Conrad chose this association, the name is, in any case, a reflection of the sailor's forthright characteristic: single tone.

Singleton lived untouched by human emotions. Taciturn and unsmiling, he breathed among us—in that alone resembling the rest of the crowd.

He is heavily tattooed and is first introduced as "the incarnation of barbarian wisdom serene in the blasphemous turmoil of the world." The simplicity of Singleton's candor is the exact countercheck to the simplicity of the Nigger's deceit: the sea and the jungle. Less than a week after leaving Bombay, Singleton meets the Negro's foul misanthropy with the disconcertingly direct question, "Are you dying?" During the Cape disaster he remains braced at the wheel and, in common with the others, derives from the experience its lesson for his own identity. Charley, the youngest of the crew, is "subdued by the sudden disclosure of the insignificance of his youth"; "Singleton was possessed of sinister truth . . . the cook of fame—."

The "sinister truth" is Singleton's recognition of his mortality.

Old! . . . like a man bound treacherously while he sleeps, he woke up fettered by the long chain of disregarded years.

His indifference to Wait's corruption is born not of rational understanding but of fearlessness bred from experience and from a simple
set of convictions little different from belief in magic (white magic—
he signs his name with a cross). Singleton and the cook, together,
represent the veracity that sometimes lurks in inherited superstition.
Singleton's naive science of cause and effect is certainly not refuted by the
circumstance that Jimmy *does* die in sight of land and that wind *does*
rise after his submersion.

Podmore, the religious fanatic, is scorned by the Captain and the
embarrassed men alike, but he is, nonetheless, the cook—their nourisher.
While they sprawl helplessly on the toppling ship, only Podmore has
the imagination to sense their position in relation to eternity. After
serving the men from the water-cask, he sits to leeward and shouts back
to the men's congratulations,

> . . . but the seas were breaking in thunder just then, and we only
> caught snatches that sounded like: "Providence" and "born again."

Podmore braves the diluvial decks to reach the galley and incredibly
makes coffee for the crew.

> Afterwards Archie declared that the thing was "meeraculous" . . .
> and we did our best to conceal our admiration under the wit of fine
> irony. The cook rebuked our levity, declaring himself, with solemn
> animation, to have been the object of a special mercy for the saving
> of our unholy lives . . .

While Wait slips toward death, the men's unbelief is reproved by
Podmore's fatuous exaltation at the hope of saving the Negro's soul. He
is momentarily inspired:

> He saw flowing garments, clean-shaved faces, a sea of light,—a lake
> of pitch . . . He had prayerfully divested himself of the last vestige
> of his humanity. He was a voice—a fleshless and sublime thing,
> as on that memorable night—the night when he went walking over the
> sea to make coffee for perishing sinners.

Enraptured and preposterous Podmore may be, but his certainty that
the Nigger's soul is possessed by the Devil is closer to the spiritual nexus
of experience than the callous nescience of men like Donkin. The crew
members in general never do understand the moral meaning of James
Wait. But the cool rationality of Allistoun, the intuitive wisdom of
Singleton, and the overheated zeal of Podmore discover, behind the
mask of a dying shirker, the infra-human visage of the Satanic.

Donkin, the Cockney, is the lowest common denominator, the eternal
and omnipresent grumbler, a thing of rags and patches with no soul of
his own. He feeds on other men's identities as he wears their cast-off
clothes. At the beginning of the voyage, he appears in the forecastle,
truculent, half-naked, squealing of his "rights."

He knew how to conquer the naive instincts of that crowd. In a moment they gave him their compassion, jocularly, contemptuously, or surlily; and at first it took the shape of a blanket thrown at him as he stood there with the white skin of his limbs showing his human kinship through the black fantasy of his rags. Then a pair of old shoes fell at his muddy feet . . . The gust of their benevolence sent a wave of sentimental pity through their doubting hearts.

Donkin is a moral cadger, a robber of sentiment, an advance edition of the more subtle dereliction practiced by Wait, and he becomes the transmitter of Wait's metaphysical loafing. A fair-weather sailor, he is always the first to scream, to complain, to curse. "Venomous and thin-faced, he glared from the ample misfit of borrowed clothing as if looking for something he could smash." Alternately deriding and defending the Nigger, he is, appropriately enough, the only one present at his death, for it is fitting that Wait should vanish into darkness attended by his familiar spirit. Donkin discharges his futile hatred at the dying man, hurls a biscuit at him (the bread—the common bond) and steals his money (a subtle reversal of Singleton at the pay table: Donkin finds *his* "small pile of gold in the profound darkness of" the deckhouse). In this death watch, Donkin suffers the terror of absolute moral isolation. And the animus of Wait inhabits the unholy frame of Donkin to the last. In his final appearance, at the Board of Trade pay-office, *dressed in another suit of clothes,* he pronounces maledictions on the assembled crew who have declined to drink with him:

> "You won't drink? . . . No! . . . Then may ye die of thirst, every mother's son of yer! Not one of yer 'as the sperrit of a bug. Ye're the scum of the world. Work and starve!"

The mercurial Belfast suffers most, perhaps, from the burden of Wait's travesty of humility. Belfast is the man who steals the pie for Jimmy, who pulls him head-first from the deckhouse, who persuades the poised corpse to leave the ship. His over-sentient imagination springs from love unconditioned by clear discrimination of its object and he remains in hysterical subjection to a Beelzebub whom he has mistaken for a divinity. On shore he begs pitously for a relic of Wait's belongings which have been sealed up and delivered to the Board of Trade. Through his inconsolable affection for the departed he articulates, incompletely, the character of Wait as scapegoat:

> "You were his chum, too . . . but I pulled him out . . . didn't I? Short wool he had . . . He wouldn't go . . . He wouldn't go for nobody!" He burst into tears. "I never touched him—never—never!" he sobbed. "He went, for me like . . . like . . . a lamb."

The iconography of *The Nigger of the "Narcissus"* was not accomplished without a dangerous compromise between the naturalistic, biographical material and its symbolic transmutation, as I have footnoted above. Fearful of overstressing the subaqueous world of the under-consciousness, the symbol-producing level of the psyche which, in fact, was the most dependable source of his inspiration, Conrad overloaded his mundane treatment of the crew. As separate units of consciousness they are beautifully deployed for angels of relationship, but no one can deny that their professional virtues are overwritten, almost to the detriment of the narrative's aesthetic integrity. It is clear, in this direction, that Conrad had difficulty in serving myth and memory with equal justice. His narrator-perspective is awkwardly handled. The novel gets under way in the third person; in the middle of the second chapter it switches abruptly to the viewpoint of first person plural and remains there until the coda section, when it becomes first person singular. Presumably an unspecified member of the deck crew has carried the narration; in this case the contents of the thoughts of Mr. Creighton and of the cook, and many of the conversations, between Allistoun and his officer or between Donkin and Wait, for example, are impossibly come by. And, with this handicap, the gilded sermonizings on the crew's high endeavor are doubly hard to accept. If Conrad was solicitous for the phenomenal level of his narrative, he might at least have supplied a recorder to whose endowments his own opulent prose would have been more apt. However, this novel was an early trial in the marriage of subject with its coordinating agencies; Conrad's craft was not yet wholly adequate to sustain an unfailing integrity of means.

Most curiously, quite apart from stylistic considerations, the novel prefigures the inhibition that Conrad thereafter suffered from in developing or acknowledging his more clairvoyant perceptions. Neither in the famous preface, appended to the 1914 edition, and the foreword that accompanied it, nor in his private communications on the subject, will one find any admission of cabalistic intent. The aesthetic of the preface, with its eloquent impressionism, is far too general to have any more bearing on this novel than on any other. The foreword guards the secret skillfully, while teasing suspicion that there is a secret: ". . . in the book he [Wait] is nothing; he is merely the center of the ship's collective psychology and the pivot of the action." Merely! Overt suggestions that he had enlisted transpersonal powers always launched Conrad into protests of respectability and of allegiance to the terrestrial, into panicky and often absurd interpretations of his own work (witness his fantastic explanations of "The Secret Sharer" and of *The Shadow Line*), into willful distortion of some of his finest literary efforts. But D. H. Lawrence has warned us: "Never trust the artist. Trust the tale."

*The Nigger of the "Narcissus"* is a fable with many layers of interconnection. "A work that aspires, however humbly, to the condition of art, should carry its justification in every line." So begins the preface to this work and in so far as the novel, itself, seeks to establish "the power of occult forces which," Conrad concedes elsewhere, "rule the fascinating aspects of the visible world," it does carry its justification. Without the other dimensions, it would be merely a tale of ships and men burdened by an irridescent futility of expression. As it is, the metaphors which significantly cluster at every magnetic point in the narrative illuminate the infernal core of its theme as, on the equator, the *Narcissus* floats in the aurora of the lightning, "like a charred ship enclosed in a globe of fire."

(1952)

## NOTES

1. This phrase from *Lord Jim* was radically misemployed by Stephen Spender (in *The Destructive Element,* 1935), following the lead of I. A. Richards, and criticism since has largely accepted the misinterpretation. To reread the passage closely in the knowledge of Conrad's Neptunian bias is to discover, with Crankshaw, that "the destructive element" equals, not the chaos of experience, and a "state of complete unbelief" (Spender), but rather the normative and traditional element of being. "The way is to the destructive element submit yourself . . . If [a man] tries to climb out into the air . . . he drowns." In this figure, the *air* should be the destructive element by Spender's interpretation! [Editor's note: On the Destructive Element see also interpretations by Dorothy Van Ghent (pp. 143-144) and R. P. Warren (pp. 218-219)].

2. The antithesis here is unquestionably a sidelong glance at the Egyptian figure of the pyramid, prime-symbol of direction and sun-worship, and of the scarab, symbol of creative energy.

3. The fact of there having been an actual ship, *Narcissus,* and an actual Wait in Conrad's seafaring experience is of course less important than his retention of the facts he could artistically transmute. The possible bearing of the old *Narcissus* legend I but hesitantly advance. The sea certainly *reflects* the collective moral features of the crew: ". . . the sea knew all, and would in time infallibly unveil to each the wisdom hidden in all the errors, the certitude that lurks in doubts." This mirror tests the vanity of all aboard, but I have no wish to urge the image beyond reasonable evidence for its fitness; notoriously, symbols have a life of their own.

4. In *Some Aspects of the Art of the Novel* (1936). [Editor's Note].

5. Conrad later discloses that the boatswain had forgotten to grease the plank and that the carpenter had left a protruding nail—a somewhat vulgar irony, one must admit, to safeguard his fear of wholesale commitment to the irrational.

6. Note the similarity of Donkin's return from his nocturnal vigil with the dying Nigger: ". . . as though he had expected to find the men dead, familiar things gone for ever: as though, like a wanderer returning after many years, he had expected to see bewildering changes."

7. In *The Hero with a Thousand Faces* (Pantheon-Bollingen, 1949, pp. 69 ff.), Joseph Campbell discusses the role of the supernatural helper in the monomyth. This helper, often a guide or supporter, may be dangerous, "the lurer of the innocent soul into realms of trial," sometimes signifying "the inscrutability of the guide that we are following, to the peril of all our rational ends."

# ALBERT J. GUERARD

## The Nigger of the "Narcissus"*

THE COMPLEXITIES of *Almayer's Folly* are those of a man learning—and with what a perverse instinct for the hardest way!—the language of the novelist. *The Nigger of the "Narcissus"* is the first of the books to carry deliberately and with care the burden of several major interests and various minor ones. The one interest which existed for most readers in 1897 remains a real one today: the faithful document of life and adventure at sea. The story is indeed the tribute to the "children of the sea" that Conrad wanted it to be: a memorial to a masculine society and the successful seizing of a "passing phase of life from the remorseless rush of time."[1] It is certainly a tribute to this particular ship on which (for her beauty) Conrad chose to sail in 1884. But is also a study in collective psychology; and also, frankly, a symbolic comment on man's nature and destiny; and also, less openly, a prose-poem carrying overtones of myth. No small burden, and one which Conrad carried with more care than usual: one passage exists in as many as seven versions.[2] "It is the book by which, not as a novelist perhaps, but as an artist striving for the utmost sincerity of expression, I am willing to stand or fall."[3]

A rich personal novel can hardly be overinterpreted, but it can be misinterpreted easily enough. The dangers of imbalance are suggested by three other masculine narratives which similarly combine faithful reporting and large symbolic suggestion. *The Red Badge of Courage* may well present a sacramental vision and still another of the ubiquitous Christ figures which bemuse criticism; the patterns of imagery are challenging. But it is also, importantly, a record of military life.[4] So too I would allow that "The Bear" contains primitive pageant-rites, initiation ritual, the Jungian descent into the unconscious, perhaps even the Jungian mandala. These matters put the critic on his mettle. But he should acknowledge that some of the story's best pages concern hunting in the big woods and the vanishing of these woods before commercial encroachment. The dangers of imbalance are even more serious when provoked by a slighter work, such as *The Old Man and the Sea*. To say that the novel is about growing old, or about the aging artist's need to substitute skill for strength, is plausible. But can a critic be satisfied with so little? One has gone so far as to find a parable of the decline of the British Empire. This, I submit, takes us too far from the boat and the marlin attached to its side; from the small greatness of a story whose first strength lies in its faithful recording of sensations, of fishing and the sea.

* From *The Kenyon Review*, XIX (Spring 1957), pp. 205-232. Reprinted in Albert J. Guerard's *Conrad the Novelist* (Harvard University Press, 1958), pp. 67-81.

*The Nigger of the "Narcissus"* (sixty years after the event) is peculiarly beset with dangers for the critic. For Conrad has become fashionable rather suddenly, and comment on this story has passed almost without pause from naïve recapitulation to highly sophisticated analysis of "cabalistic intent." The older innocence is suggested by Arthur Symons' complaint that the story had no idea behind it, or by a journeyman reviewer's remark that James Wait had no place in this record of life at sea.[5] An example of recent sophistication is Vernon Young's important essay "Trial by Water," in the Spring 1952 issue of *Accent*.[6] A single sentence will suggest its bias: "Fearful of overstressing the subaqueous world of the underconsciousness, the symbol-producing level of the psyche which, in fact, was the most dependable source of his inspiration, Conrad overloaded his mundane treatment of the crew." The comment is provocative; it leads us to wonder whether the crew isn't for this fiction, too numerous. Yet we must rejoin that the crew is very important, and that many of the book's greatest pages have little to do with this subaqueous world. There remains the vulgar charge yet real menace that the critic may oversimplify a novel by oversubtilizing and overintellectualizing it—not merely by intruding beyond the author's conscious intention (which he is fully privileged to do) but by suggesting patterns of unconscious combination which do not *and cannot operate* for the reasonably alert common reader. Much of any serious story works on the fringes of the reader's consciousness: a darkness to be illumined by the critic's insight. But that insight remains irrelevant which can never become aesthetic enjoyment, or which takes a story too far out of its own area of discourse. I say this with the uneasy conviction that criticism should expose itself to as many as possible of a novel's suasions, and that it is only too easy (above all with a Conrad or a Faulkner) to stress the abstract and symbolic at the expense of everything else. One might begin by saying that *The Nigger of the "Narcissus"* recasts the story of Jonah and anticipates "The Secret Sharer" 's drama of identification. This is a truth but a partial truth. And how many partial truths would be needed to render or even evoke such a mobile as this one. Touch one wire, merely breathe on the lovely thing and it wavers to a new form! In the pursuit of structured meaning—of obvious purpose and overtone of conviction and "cabalistic intent" and unconscious content; of stark symbol and subtle cluster of metaphor—one is tempted to ignore the obvious essentials of technique and style. One may even never get around to mentioning what are, irrespective of structure or concealed meaning, the best-written pages in the book. They are these: the arrival of James Wait on board, the onset of the storm, the overturning of the ship, the righting of the ship, old Singleton at the wheel, the quelling of the mutiny, the death of Wait and his burial, the docking of the ship, the dispersal of the crew.

It seems proper for once to begin with the end: with that large personal impression which an embarrassed criticism often omits altogether. *The*

*Nigger of the "Narcissus"* is the most generalized of Conrad's novels in its cutting of a cross-section, though one of the least comprehensive. It is a version of our dark human pilgrimage, a vision of disaster illumined by grace. The microcosmic ship is defined early in the second chapter with an almost Victorian obviousness: "On her lived truth and audacious lies; and, like the earth, she was unconscious, fair to see—and condemned by men to an ignoble fate. The august loneliness of her path lent dignity to the sordid inspiration of her pilgrimage. She drove foaming to the south as if guided by the courage of a high endeavour." Or we can narrow the vision to a single sentence near the end: "The dark knot of seamen drifted in sunshine." The interplay of light and dark images throughout conveys the sense of a destiny both good and evil, heroic and foolish, blundered out under a soulless sky. If I were further to reduce the novel to a single key-word, as some critics like to do, I should choose the word *grace*. In thematic terms not the sea but life at sea is pure and life on earth sordid. Yet the pessimism of *The Nigger of the "Narcissus"* is (unlike that of *The Secret Agent*) a modified pessimism, and the gift of grace can circumvent thematic terms. Thus England herself is once imaged as a great ship. The convention of the novel is that the gift of grace may fall anywhere, or anywhere except on the Donkins. The story really ends with the men clinging for a last moment to their solidarity and standing near the Mint, that most representative object of the sordid earth:

> The sunshine of heaven fell like a gift of grace on the mud of the earth, on the remembering and mute stones, on greed, selfishness; on the anxious faces of forgetful men. And to the right of the dark group the stained front of the Mint, cleansed by the flood of light, stood out for a moment dazzling and white like a marble palace in a fairy tale. The crew of the *Narcissus* drifted out of sight.[7]

So the novel's vision is one of man's dignity but also of his "irremediable littleness"—a conclusion reached, to be sure, by most great works in the Christian tradition. In "Heart of Darkness," *Lord Jim,* and "The Secret Sharer" we have the initiatory or expiatory descents within the self of individual and almost lost souls; in *Nostromo* we shall see the vast proliferation of good and evil in history and political institution. But *The Nigger of the "Narcissus"* presents the classic human contradiction (and the archetypal descent into self) in collective terms, reduced to the simplicities of shipboard life. The storm tests and brings out the solidarity, courage, and endurance of men banded together in a desperate cause. And the Negro James Wait tests and brings out their egoism, solitude, laziness, anarchy, fear. The structural obligation of the story is to see to it that the two tests do not, for the reader, cancel out.

Presented so schematically, Conrad's vision may seem truly Christian. But this is indeed a soulless sky. In the restless life of symbols sunlight is converted, at one point, to that inhuman Nature which Man must oppose. The Norwegian sailor who chatters at the sun has lost his saving separateness from Nature, and when the sun sets his voice goes out "together with the light." The "completed wisdom" of old Singleton (one of the first Conrad extroverts to achieve some of his own skepticism) sees "an immensity tormented and blind, moaning and furious . . ." And in one of the novel's central intellectual statements (the first paragraph of the fourth chapter) the indifferent sea is metaphorically equated with God, and the gift of grace is defined as labor, which prevents man from meditating "at ease upon the complicated and acrid savour of existence." The dignity of man lies in his vast silence and endurance: a dignity tainted by those who clamor for the reward of another life. The message is rather like Faulkner's, and these good seamen are like "good Negroes." But here too, as in other novels of Conrad, man's works and institutions must prepare him to profit from even such grace as this. From our human weakness and from the eternal indifference of things we may yet be saved . . . by authority, tradition, obedience. Thus the only true grace is purely human and even traditional. There are certain men (specifically Donkin) who remain untouched. But such men exist outside: outside our moral universe which is both dark and light but not inextricably both. And James Wait, as sailor and person rather than symbol? I am not sure. He seems to suffer from that "emptiness" which would be Kurtz's ruin: "only a cold black skin loosely stuffed with soft cotton wool . . . a doll that had lost half its sawdust."

This, speaking neither in terms of gross obvious intentions and themes nor of unconscious symbolic content but of generalized human meaning and ethical bias, is what *The Nigger of the "Narcissus"* says. This is its reading of life.

"My task which I am trying to achieve is, by the power of the written word to make you hear, to make you feel—it is, before all, to make you *see*."[8] The sea story is beyond praise; there is no need to defend the amount of space and emphasis Conrad gives it. The long third chapter on the storm is one of the summits of Conrad, and the pages on the righting of the ship one of the summits of English prose. This is, as few others, a real ship. At the start the solidarity of the forecastle is built up gradually, presumably as on any ship, then disrupted by the foul Donkin and the lazy, narcissistic Wait. A sham fellowship first occurs when the seamen give clothing to Donkin, and is increased by their lazy sympathy for the malingering Negro. The true solidarity is created by the exigencies of the storm, and during the worst hours of crisis the good seamen are significantly separated from Wait, who is trapped in his cabin, buried. With the storm over the individuals again become Individuals, and by the same token capable of mutiny. In the Conrad universe we often have this sense of a few men banded together in desperate opposition to a cosmic indifference and to human nature itself. For this voyage ordinary men have come together, been isolated by their weaknesses, and have come together again. On land they separate once more; for one last poignant moment they are the dark knot of seamen drifting in sunshine. "Good-bye brothers! You were a good crowd. As good a crowd as ever fisted with wild cries the beating canvas of a heavy foresail; or tossing aloft, invisible in the night, gave back yell for yell to a westerly gale." The novel is also about that solidarity Conrad admired but rarely dramatized.

In these last sentences of the novel Conrad himself is speaking, rather than the anonymous narrator. And this is perhaps the best place to consider the often-noted waywardness in point of view. The novel opens with objective reporting, and the first narrative voice we hear is stiff, impersonal, detached, a voice reading stage directions. But Conrad's natural impulse is to write in the first person, if possible retrospectively; to suggest action and summarize large segments of time. His natural impulse is to meditative and often ironic withdrawal. (It is author not narrator who pauses to comment on the popularity of Bulwer-Lytton among seamen: an extreme withdrawal.) On the seventh page the narrator momentarily becomes a member of the crew, but we must wait until the second chapter for this identification to be made frankly. Meanwhile we may detect in Conrad a restless impatience with the nominal objectivity adopted—a coolness of manner sharply broken through as he speaks out his admiration for Singleton, his contempt for Donkin. Passionate conviction energized Conrad's visualizing power as nothing else in the chapter did; and we have immortally the Donkin of white eyelashes and red eyelids, with "rare hairs" about the jaws, and shoulders "peaked and drooped like the broken wings of a bird . . ."

With the second chapter, and the sailing of the ship, the prose takes on poetic qualities. A meditative observer outside and above the *Narcissus* sees her as "a high and lonely pyramid, gliding, all shining and white, through the sunlit mist." We return briefly to the deck for a paragraph of flat reporting, then have the developed and Victorian analogy of the ship and the earth with its human freight. The paragraph has the kind of obviousness an intentionalist would welcome, but I suspect its real purpose was tactical. By generalizing his ship in this gross fashion, Conrad freed himself from the present moment and from the obligation to report consecutively. "The days raced after one another, brilliant and quick like the flashes of a lighthouse, and the nights, eventful and short, resembled fleeting dreams." And now he can pursue his natural mode: to hover selectively over a large segment of time, dipping down for a closer view only when he chooses. On the next page (as though to achieve still further retrospective freedom) the narrator identifies himself as a member of the crew. Suddenly we are told that Mr. Baker "kept all our noses to the grindstone."

The subsequent waverings of point of view are the ones that have disturbed logicians. Vernon Young puts their case clearly: "Presumably an unspecified member of the deck crew has carried the narration; in this case the contents of the thoughts of Mr. Creighton and of the cook, and many of the conversations, between Allistoun and his officer or between Donkin and Wait, for example, are impossibly come by."[9] The classic answer to such logic is that all eggs come from the same basket. It may be given more lucidly thus: the best narrative technique is the one which, however imperfect logically, enlists the author's creative energies and fully explores his subject. We need only demand that the changes in point of view not violate the reader's larger sustained vision of the dramatized experience. Creighton's thoughts (since he is no more nor less than a deck officer) can violate nothing except logic. But serious violation does occur twice: when we are given Wait's broken interior monologues (pages 113, 149). For we are approaching the mysterious Negro's death, and it has been the very convention of the novel that Wait must remain shadowy, vast, provocative of large speculation; in a word, symbolic. The very fact that he comes in some sense to represent our human "blackness" should exempt him from the banalities of everyday interior monologue. It would be as shocking to overhear such interior monologue of Melville's Babo or of Leggatt in "The Secret Sharer."

For the rest, the changes in point of view are made unobtrusively and with pleasing insouciance. What is more deadly than the ratiocinations of a narrator trying to explain his "authority," as the Marlow of *Chance* does? The movement of point of view through this novel admirably reflects the general movement from isolation to solidarity to poignant separation. So the detached observer of the first pages becomes an anonymous member of the crew using the word "we." He works with the others during the storm and joins them in the rescue of Wait; and he too, both actor and moralizing spectator, becomes prey to sentimentalism, laziness, fear. Then in the final pages the "we" becomes an "I," still a nameless member of the crew but about to become the historical Joseph Conrad who speaks in the last paragraph. "I disengaged myself gently." The act of meditative withdrawal at last becomes complete. Approach and withdrawal, the ebb and flow of a generalizing imagination which cannot leave mere primary experience alone—these are, in any event, the incorrigible necessities of the early Conrad, and they account for some of his loveliest effects.

So we have first of all, reported and meditated, the sea story and memorial realism suggested by the early American title, *The Children of the Sea*. But there is also (and almost from the beginning) the insufferable Negro James Wait. In his own right he is mildly interesting: as a lonely and proud man who is about to die, as an habitual malingerer whose canny deception becomes at last desperate self-deception. But his role in the novel is to provide the second test; or, as Conrad puts it in his American preface, "he is merely the centre of the ship's collective psychology and the pivot of the action." Merely! His role is to provoke that sympathetic identification which is the central chapter of Conrad's psychology, and through it to demonstrate Conrad's conviction that sentimental pity is a form of egoism. In their hidden laziness the members of the crew sympathize with Wait's malingering; later, seeing him die before their eyes, they identify their own chances of survival with his. The process of identification (dramatized with little explanation in *Lord Jim*) is defined explicitly here:

> Falsehood triumphed. It triumphed through doubt, through stupidity, through pity, through sentimentalism . . . *The latent egoism of tenderness to suffering appeared in the developing anxiety not to see him die* . . . He was demoralising. Through him we were becoming highly humanised, tender, complex, excessively decadent: we understood the subtlety of his fear, sympathized with all his repulsions, shrinkings, evasions, delusions—as though we had been over-civilised, and rotten, and without any knowledge of the meaning of life.[10]

It could be argued that Conrad recapitulates too obviously, and reiterates rather too often, Wait's demoralizing influence. But the process of irrational identification was little understood by readers in 1897, or in fact by many readers since. It required explication. Thus the sentence I have italicized, almost the central statement of the novel, was omitted in Robert d'Humières' translation.[11] The "egoism of tenderness to suffering" must have struck him as meaningless.

Such, on the "mundane" or naturalistic level of psychology, is the function of Wait; and even the captain is finally corrupted by pity. He pretends to share in Wait's self-deception: "Sorry for him—like you would be for a sick brute . . . I thought I would let him go out in his own way. Kind of impulse." And this moment of pity causes the incipient mutiny. As for the crew, they cared nothing for Wait as a human being, hated him in fact, but had accepted him as a precious token. "We wanted to keep him alive till home—to the end of the voyage." But this is, of course, impossible. James Wait must die in sight of land, as Singleton said, and the *Narcissus* cannot finish her voyage until the body of Wait (like the living bodies of Leggatt and of Jonah) has been deposited into the sea. Then but only then the "ship rolled as if relieved of an unfair burden; the sails flapped." And the ship rushes north before a freshening gale. To the personal and psychological-naturalistic burden of Wait is added—almost "unfairly" for a story of little more than 50,-000 words—the burden of an audacious symbolic pattern. In certain early pages Wait is A Death, and a test of responses to death. But ultimately he is written in larger terms: *as something the ship and the men must be rid of before they can complete their voyage.* What this something is— more specific than a "blackness"—is likely to vary with each new reader. But its presence as part of the wavering mobile, as a force the story must allow for, raises crucial questions of technique.

Conrad's task, briefly, was to respect both flesh ("A negro in a British forecastle is a lonely being")[12] and symbol; to convey a vivid black human presence which could yet take on the largest meanings; which could become, as in Melville, "the Negro." Conrad faces the double challenge with the moment Wait steps on board, calling out that name which is mistaken for an impertinent command, "Wait!" Whether or not Vernon Young is right in detecting a play on the word (Wait: weight, burden), symbolic potentialities exist from the start. As we shall first see of Leggatt only a headless corpse floating in the water, so here we see only a body. "His head was away up in the shadows." And—cool, towering, superb—the Nigger speaks the words which, in a true morality, a symbolic force might speak: "I belong to the ship." But what saves the scene (what prevents the reader from detecting larger meanings too soon) is its concrete reality. The ambiguous arrival at once provokes action and talk, a dramatic interchange. And when it is over the magnitude of the Nigger is firmly established. We are able to accept that first "cough metallic, hollow, and tremendously loud," resounding "like two explosions in a vault."

I would insist, in other words, that Old Ben is also a real bear,[13] and Babo a fleshly slave, and Moby Dick a real whale, and James Wait (though his name was "all a smudge" on the ship's list) a proud consumptive Negro. It is truly the critic's function to suggest potentialities and even whole areas of discourse that a hasty reading might overlook. But the natural impulse to find single meanings, and so convert symbolism into allegory, must be resisted. James's classic comment on "The Turn of the Screw" is relevant here: "Only make the reader's general vision of evil intense enough, I said to myself—and that already is a charming job—and his own experience, his own imagination, his own sympathy (with the children) and horror (of their false friends) will supply him quite sufficiently with all the particulars. Make him *think* the evil, make him think it for himself, and you are released from weak specifications."[14] Or, as Robert Penn Warren remarks, every man has shot his own special albatross. I am willing with Vernon Young to accept that Wait suggests the subconscious, the instinctual, the regressive; or, with Morton D. Zabel, to see him as the secret sharer and "man all men must finally know"; or, with Belfast more curtly, to know that Satan is abroad. This is neither evasion nor a defense of solipsism, I trust, but mere insistence that no rich work of art and no complex human experience has a single meaning. Wait is, let us say, a force; an $X$. But it is his role to elicit certain responses from the crew, and, through them, from the reader.

Thus our task is not to discover what Wait precisely "means" but to observe a human relationship. And the clue to any larger meanings must be found, I think, in the pattern of Wait's presences and absences. He is virtually forgotten (after that first dramatic appearance) while the men get to know each other and the voyage begins; he is something they are too busy to be concerned with. We return to him only when they have little work to do; when "the cleared decks had a reposeful aspect, resembling the autumn of the earth" and the soft breeze is "like an indulgent caress." And he is literally forgotten (by crew as well as reader) during the worst of the storm. After he is rescued, he is again neglected for

some thirty pages, and returns only with the sinister calm of a hot night
and beshrouded ocean. In the two major instances, the lazy Donkin is
the agent who takes us back to him, the Mephistopheles for this Satan.
The menace of Wait is greatest when men have time to meditate. Thus
Conrad's practical ethic of a master-mariner (seamen must be kept busy)
may not be so very different from the ethic of the stoic pessimist who
wrote psychological novels. The soul left to its own devices scarcely bears
examination, though examine it we must.

The pages of Wait's rescue (63-73) are central, and manage brilliantly
their double allegiance to the real and to the symbolic. Here more than
anywhere else, even on a quite naturalistic level, the two sides of the seamen coexist, the heroic and the loathsome. "Indignation and doubt grap-
pled within us in a scuffle that trampled upon our finest feelings." They
risk their lives unquestioningly to rescue a trapped "chum." Yet these
men scrambling in the carpenter's shop, tearing at the planks of the
bulkhead "with the eagerness of men trying to get at a mortal enemy,"
are compulsive, crazed, and full of hatred for the man they are trying to
save. "A rage to fling things overboard possessed us." The entire scene is
written with vividness and intensity: the hazardous progress over the
half-submerged deck, the descent into the shop with its layer of nails
"more inabordable than a hedgehog," the smashing of the bulkhead
and tearing out of Wait, the slow return to a relative safety. Everything
is as real and as substantial as that sharp adze sticking up with a shining
edge from the clutter of saws, chisels, wire rods, axes, crowbars. At a
first experiencing the scene may seem merely to dramatize the novel's
stated psychology: these men have irrationally identified their own survival with Wait's and are therefore compelled to rescue him. Ironically,
they risk their lives to save a man who has already damaged their fellowship, and who will damage it again.

But the exciting real scene seems to say more than this. And in fact it
is doing an important preparatory work, in those fringes of the reader's
consciousness, for Wait's burial and for the immediate responding wind
which at last defines him as "symbol." On later readings (and we must
never forget that every complex novel becomes a different one on later
readings) the resonance of these pages is deeper, more puzzling, more
sinister. We observe that the men remember the trapped Wait only when
the gale is ending, and they are free at last to return to their normal desires. Thereupon they rush to extricate what has been locked away. The
actual rescue is presented as a difficult childbirth: the exploratory tappings
and faint response; Wait crouched behind the bulkhead and beating with
his fists, the head thrust at a tiny hole, then stuck between splitting
planks; the "blooming short wool" that eludes Belfast's grasp, and at last
the stuffed black doll emerging, "mute as a fish" before emitting its first
reproach. At least we can say, roughly, that the men have assisted at the
rebirth of evil on the ship.

It may well be that Conrad intended only this (and conceivably less), or to insist again that men are accomplices in their own ruin. But the larger terms and very geography of the scene suggest rather a compulsive effort to descend beneath full consciousness to something "lower." The men let themselves fall heavily and sprawl in a corridor where all doors have become trap doors; they look down into the carpenter's shop devastated as by an earthquake. And beyond its chaos (beneath all the tools, nails, and other instruments of human reason they *must* fling overboard) lies the solid bulkhead dividing them from Wait.* The imagery of this solid barrier between the conscious and the unconscious may seem rather Victorian. But the Jungians too tell us that the unconscious is not easily accessible. In such terms the carpenter's shop would suggest the messy preconscious, with Wait trapped in the deeper lying unconscious.

This is plausible enough, but does not account for the curious primitive figure of Wamibo glaring above them: "all shining eyes, gleaming fangs, tumbled hair; resembling an amazed and half-witted fiend gloating over the extraordinary agitation of the damned." Wamibo could, if we wished, take his obvious place in the Freudian triad (as savage super ego)—which would convert Wait into the id and the whole area (carpenter's shop and cabin) into all that lies below full consciousness. But such literalism of reading, of psychic geography, is not very rewarding. It could as usefully be argued that Wamibo is the primitive figure who must be present and involved in any attempt to reach a figure still more primitive, as the half-savage Sam Fathers and half-savage Lion must be present at the death of Old Ben. Is it not more profitable to say, very generally, that the scene powerfully dramatizes the compulsive psychic descent of "Heart of Darkness" and "The Secret Sharer"? In any event the men emerge as from such an experience. "The return on the poop was like the return of wanderers after many years amongst people marked by the desolation of time." (As for the rescued Wait, he presents the same contradictions as the rescued Kurtz. Wait locked in his cabin and the Kurtz of unspeakable lusts and rites suggest evil as savage energy. But the rescued Wait and the rescued Kurtz are "hollow men," closer to the Thomist conception of evil as vacancy.)†

* "Then the mariners were afraid, and cried every man unto his god, and cast forth the wares that were in the ship into the sea, to lighten it of them. But Jonah was gone down into the sides of the ship; and he lay, and was fast asleep" (Jonah 1:5). It is *Jonah* who must be cast out. But he has *already* had an experience of descent: "The waters compassed me about, even to the soul: the depth closed me round about, the weeds were wrapped about my head. I went down to the bottom of the mountains; the earth was about me for ever: yet hast thou brought my life from corruption, O Lord my God" (2: 5, 6).

† One is reminded of the surrealist disorder of the cuddy on the *San Domenick,* where Babo shaves Don Benito: the room an effective image of the unconscious, whatever Melville intended. And, more distantly, of Isaac McCaslin's discarding of gun, watch, compass (comparable to the tools thrown overboard) as he moves toward his archetypal confrontation of the unconscious and primitive. To the few intentionalists who may have consented

So the night journey into self is, I think, one of the experiences this scene is likely to evoke, even for readers who do not recognize it conceptually as such. But it may evoke further and different responses. It is so with any true rendering of any large human situation, be it outward or inward; life never means one thing. What I want to emphasize is not the scene's structuring of abstract or psychic meaning only, but its masterful interpenetration of the realistic and symbolist modes. Its strangeness and audacity (together with its actuality) prepare us for the symbolic burial which is the climax of the novel.

"We fastened up James Wait in a safe place." It is time to return to technical matters, and specifically to the art of modulation that was one of Conrad's strengths.

The ambiguous episode of a suspect heroism is over, Wait is again forgotten, and the chapter returns to its record of a genuine not specious courage. The impression left by the storm test must finally be affirmative, and we move toward that impression at once. Podmore madly offers to make hot coffee; and succeeds. "As long as she swims I will cook." And already the *Narcissus* herself has shown a tendency to stand up a little more. In the final pages of the third chapter the white virginal ship with her one known weakness is the human protagonist exerting a puny stubborn will; old Singleton is the indestructible machine. But the ship's heroism rubs off on the men. Captain Allistoun gives the command to "wear ship," the men do their work, but their eyes and ours are fixed on the wounded, still-living *Narcissus.* "Suddenly a small white piece of canvas fluttered amongst them, grew larger, beating." The ship makes several distinct attempts to stand up, goes off as though "weary and disheartened," but at last with an unexpected jerk and violent swing to windward throws off her immense load of water. And now she runs "disheveled" and "as if fleeing for her life," spouting streams of water through her wounds, her torn canvas and broken gear streaming "like wisps of hair." The chapter ends with old Singleton still at the wheel after thirty hours, his white beard tucked under his coat. "In front of his erect figure only the two arms moved crosswise with a swift and sudden readiness, to check or urge again the rapid stir of circling spokes. He steered with care."

This is the end of the first great test. But this is also and only, and almost exactly, the middle of the novel. These men united by crisis must return again to the egoism of their several lives, and hence face again that other test of their selfish allegiance to Wait. The return to Wait (i.e., to

---

to read this far: a great intuitive novelist is by definition capable of dramatizing the descent into the unconscious with some "geographical" accuracy, and even without realizing precisely what he is doing. If he is capable of dreaming powerfully he will dream what exists (the "furniture" of the mind) as he will dream archetypal stories. The more he realizes what he is doing in fact, the greater becomes the temptation to mechanical explanation and rigid consistency to received theory.

the Wait theme) posed one of the sharpest of the novel's many tactical problems: how to modulate downward from the heroic to the everyday, then upward again to the symbolic death and burial. Such "modulations" (for they are much more than transitions) take us close to Conrad's technical art at its best; they show an exceptional sense of how language can manipulate the reader's sensibility.

The end of the storm was grand enough to break such a novel in two. What sentence, to be precise, what particular level of language could succeed such a stroke as "He steered with care"? In *Typhoon* Conrad solves, with one laconic sentence, the whole problem of transition: "He was spared that annoyance." In *Lord Jim* we are told, a little more evasively, "These sleeping pilgrims were destined to accomplish their whole pilgrimage to the bitterness of some other end." The one fact to be communicated is that the ships did not sink; that these men were reprieved. But in *The Nigger of the "Narcissus"* the reader's feelings and beyond them his attitude toward the crew must be handled with extreme care.

Here is the way it is done. I submit the paragraph not as an example of supreme prose but rather to suggest that Conrad's evasiveness and diffiulty, his grandiloquence even, may serve at times a dramatic end and solve a tactical problem:

> On men reprieved by its disdainful mercy, the immortal sea confers in its justice the full privilege of desired unrest. Through the perfect wisdom of its grace they are not permitted to meditate at ease upon the complicated and acrid savour of existence, *lest they should remember and, perchance, regret the reward of a cup of inspiriting bitterness tasted so often, and so often withdrawn from before their stiffening but reluctant lips.* They must without pause justify their life to the eternal pity that commands toil to be hard and unceasing, from sunrise to sunset, from sunset to sunrise; till the weary succession of nights and days tainted by the obstinate clamour of sages, demanding bliss and an empty heaven, is redeemed at last by the vast silence of pain and labour, by the dumb fear and dumb courage of men obscure, forgetful, and enduring.[15]

The paragraph does tell us something: these men were reprieved, and had no chance to rest from their labors. Everything else might seem to belong to that rhythmed and global moralizing that enrages certain lovers of the plain style. And in fact the lines I have italicized do border on double talk. Is the "cup of inspiriting bitterness" life itself? And if so, how can it be withdrawn "so often"? We seem to have a passage as suspect, logically, as the famous one on the "destructive element." And even Conrad must have come to wonder what these lines meant, for he removed them from the definitive edition.

The rest of the paragraph offers, most obviously, its dignity of tone. We move from the elevation of Singleton steering with care to the austere elevation of a narrator's statement on man and destiny, before returning to the drenched decks and exhausted swearing crew. But the language is more highly charged than it might seem at a first glance. The double metaphor (*sea—indifference justice—God*) is obvious enough, underlined as it is by so much irony: *reprieved, disdainful mercy, immortal, in its justice, the perfect wisdom, grace, justify, the eternal pity, commands toil to be hard, redeemed.* The paragraph expresses an ultimate skepticism; or, a conviction that man's dignity lies in his courage, labor and endurance. But the particular Conradian difficulty (or "tension") comes from the suddenness of the narrator's subversive intrusions. Thus the men desire life; it is the narrator who reminds us that life is unrest. And the sages who tarnish man's dignity by their references to an afterlife demand only the bliss of heaven. It is the narrator who remarks (a parenthesis within a parenthesis) that this heaven is empty. There is much more to say about the passage, and it would be interesting to know whether such flowing rhythms do not carry most readers, unnoticing, past these ironies. In general, however: not merely the austerity of tone and dignity of rhythm but the very difficulty of the language help to manipulate the reader's feelings, chill them even, in a way quite necessary at this point in the story.

This fine management of the reader through tone, style, and structure is the largest achievement, in 1897, of Conrad's technique. It would require a comment as long as Conrad's fourth chapter to describe and analyze the tact with which it leads us through the hard work of the storm's aftermath, through the desolation of the forecastle, through Singleton's physical collapse and also his collapse into skepticism, through Donkin's mutinous talk—back to Wait's cabin as the source of contagion. "The little place, repainted white, had, in the night, the brilliance of a silver shrine where a black idol, reclining stiffly under a blanket, blinked its weary eyes and received our homage. Donkin officiated." Only through many careful modulations (the gray human mixture a little darker after each) can we be made to accept the fact that such a brave crew would be capable of mutiny. The chapter is certainly more flawed than any of the others. But the transitional task it had to accomplish, and modulative task, was much the most difficult.

"A heavy atmosphere of oppressive quietude pervaded the ship." Thus begins the fifth and last chapter. The threat of mutiny has been broken; we are nearing the end of the voyage; ultimate meanings must be achieved now or not at all; and James Wait must die. Like Melville in *Benito Cereno* Conrad had prepared us early in the story for the themes of ambiguity and death by mortuary images:

Over the white rims of berths stuck out heads with blinking eyes; but the bodies were lost in the gloom of those places, that resembled narrow niches for coffins in a whitewashed and lighted mortuary.

The double row of berths yawned black, like graves tenanted by uneasy corpses.

> And alone in the dim emptiness of the sleeping forecastle he appeared
> bigger, colossal, very old; old as Father Time himself, who should have
> come there into this place as quiet as a sepulchre to contemplate with
> patient eyes the short victory of sleep, the consoler.[16]

Beyond this Conrad has more than once asked us to regard the ship as a
microcosm, and (in the rescue scene) has appealed darkly to the fringes
of consciousness. But the hardest task remains, and this is to bring the
symbolic possibilities of the ship and of Wait into full awareness. To put
matters crudely: we must be directly prepared for the occult circumstance
of a wind rising the moment Wait's body reaches the sea.

Singleton's prediction—his Ancient Mariner's knowledge that "Jimmy
was the cause of the head winds" and must die in the first sight of land
—accomplishes something. But the somber rhythms and Coleridgean distracted movement of the ship accomplish more. And there is at last the
critical moment itself, a moment requiring audacity. How convince the
reader that *anything* can happen on this more than ordinary ship? One
way would be to use such words as "illusive," or frankly to say that nothing in the ship is "real." But more than flat statement is required to make
us accept Coleridge's phantom ship. One could further suggest death
through allusions to the moon, or *evoke a magic ship and transnatural
night by imposing images of snow and cold and ice upon a hot night.*
One could, indeed, appeal to the reader's recollection of *The Ancient
Mariner.* And all this occurs, is done, in the last modulative paragraph:

> On clear evenings the silent ship, under the cold sheen of the dead
> moon, took on a false aspect of passionless repose resembling the
> winter of the earth. Under her a long band of gold barred the black
> disc of the sea. Footsteps echoed on her quiet decks. The moonlight
> clung to her like a frosted mist, and the white sails stood out in daz-
> zling cones as of stainless snow. In the magnificence of the phantom
> rays the ship appeared pure like a vision of ideal beauty, illusive like
> a tender dream of serene peace. And nothing in her was real, nothing
> was distinct and solid but the heavy shadows that filled her decks with
> their unceasing and noiseless stir: the shadows darker than the night
> and more restless than the thoughts of men.
>
> Donkin prowled spiteful and alone amongst the shadows, thinking
> that Jimmy too long delayed to die. That evening land had been re-
> ported from aloft . . .[17]

These are matters of style: style as temperament, style as meaning,
style as suasion and manipulation of the reader. And in *The Nigger of the
"Narcissus"* we are watching the formation of a great style in which
meditation becomes dramatic. We are dealing with a temperament chroni-
cally addicted to approach and withdrawal, and which can make the very
ebb and flow of generalizing intellect an element of suspense. Thus a scene
of action may be suddenly broken off and the reader alienated, *removed,*
by the act of meditative withdrawal. And this removal intensifies the
drama:

He shrieked in the deepening gloom, he blubbered and sobbed, screaming: " 'It 'im! 'It 'im!" *The rage and fear of his disregarded right to live tried the steadfastness of hearts more than the menacing shadows of the night that advanced through the unceasing clamour of the gale.* From aft Mr. Baker was heard:—"Is one of you men going to stop him—must I come along?" "Shut up!" . . . "Keep quiet!" cried various voices, exasperated, trembling with cold.[18]

This sudden deliberate distancing of narrator and reader will give *Lord Jim* and *Nostromo* some of their richest effects.

The writing of *The Nigger of the "Narcissus"* remains uneven, though vastly superior to that of the earlier stories. But the Conradian richness, it must be admitted again, is built out of initial excess. "The Lagoon" and its parody* have shown us what Conradese could be, with its pervasive melodrama of language and landscape and its monotonies of sentence structure. The most monotonous paragraph in *The Nigger of the "Narcissus"* occurs in the first chapter, before the narrator has begun to speak in his own right and voice. We have instead a writer methodically blocking out and methodically enriching a static scene and mood. The passage suggests some of the indulgences which could, chastened, become strengths:

> Outside the glare of the steaming forecastle the serene purity of the night enveloped the seamen with its soothing breath, with its tepid breath flowing under the stars that hung countless above the mastheads in a thin cloud of luminous dust. On the town side the blackness of the water was streaked with trails of light which undulated gently on slight ripples, *similar to* filaments that float rooted to the shore. Rows of other lights stood away in straight lines *as if* drawn up on parade between towering buildings; but on the other side of the harbour sombre hills arched high their black spines, on which, here and there, the point of a star *resembled* a spark fallen from the sky. Far off, Byculla way, the electric lamps at the dock gates shone on the end of lofty standards with a glow blinding and frigid *like* captive ghosts of some evil moons. Scattered all over the dark polish of the roadstead, the ships at anchor floated in perfect stillness under the feeble gleam of their riding-lights, looming up, opaque and bulky, *like* strange and monumental structures abandoned by men to an everlasting repose.[19]

The paragraph is unmistakably Conradian, and has its genuine felicities; the rhythm of any one of the overextended periods is lovely. But the passage fails by attempting too many felicities; analogy becomes a weary obligation, to be met once or twice each sentence. And yet, the captive ghosts and monumental abandoned structures operate in a characteristic manner: taking the reader on far meditative journeys from their banal tenors, to "evil moons" and "everlasting repose." We are invited to dream and are being imposed upon by a temperament. A doubtful procedure, if the object is to clarify the tenor. But that is not Conrad's object, which is

*[Editor's note: Max Beerbohm's parody of "The Lagoon" in *A Christmas Garland,* 1913, pp. 123-30.]

to create a tone and bemusing impression. Far more conducive to monotony are certain repetitions: the regular assignment of one adjective and one only to approximately half the nouns (the French "glow blinding and frigid" comes as a relief); the almost identical length of the first three flowing periods and of the second, fourth, and fifth sentences; and the predictable positioning of the subject in four sentences out of the five. This is, one detects, the prose of a writer even more devoted to cadence than to evil moons; who must (for the moment) externalize rhythms rather than visions; who enjoys expending to its fullest each long drawn-in breath. The first sentence is in fact the most Conradian of all, since it pushes past no less than five natural stopping-places. The style (as in certain other novels the plot and over-all structure) refuses the reader's reasonable expectations, and hence—if it does not merely lull—excites a certain strain. This impulse to frustrate the reader's ear will presently, and even in this novel, produce great prose.

Another reader, less conscious of rhythms, would be irritated by the fact that the night's purity is "serene" and repose "everlasting." Let us acknowledge at once that Conrad, early or late, could stock a sizable dictionary of bromidic clichés. Another way to put it is that some of his best pages are built with exceedingly obvious blocks. Most readers would agree (unless they are compiling dictionaries) that the first five pages of the second chapter, the sailing of the *Narcissus* and its first days at sea, are successful. But if one is compiling a dictionary! The water sparkles *like* a floor of jewels, and is as empty *as* the sky; the upper canvas *resembles* small white clouds; the tug *resembles* a black beetle (this analogy extended for twelve lines), a ship on the horizon lingers and hovers *like* an illusion; stars people the emptiness of the sky, are *as if* alive, are *more intense than* the eyes of a staring crowd, and *as inscrutable as* the souls of men; the ship is a microcosm of the earth (extended for a full paragraph) and is a high and lonely pyramid; the days are *like* flashes of a lighthouse and the nights *resemble* fleeting dreams; the Captain is "such *as* a phantom above a grave," his nightshirt flutters *like* a flag; and his gray eyes are still and cold *like* the loom of ice. He seldom descends from the Olympian heights of his poop.

How does Conrad get away with so much obviousness, as by and large he does? For one thing, the elaborate rhythms are both more varied and more "spoken" than in the first chapter, and this emerging meditative voice gives us, along the way, a good deal of authenticating nautical detail. Further, some of these analogies work visually and morally at the same time. The high and lonely pyramid is also lovely: "gliding, all shining and white, through the sunlit mist." But the tug, stained by land and steam, leaves a memorable round black patch of soot on the water, "an unclean mark of the creature's rest." The analogies taken together have begun to establish two of the novel's secondary meanings: its contrast between life at sea and life on land, its contrast between sail and steam. And even the captain as a phantom above a grave has its place in a novel depending upon much mortuary imagery to prepare us for the occult death of Wait. As for the studied and Victorian analogy of the ship and the earth, it can well be argued that Conrad should have permitted the reader so to generalize his ship. But we would be the poorer if we censored all Conrad's deeply meant skeptic's comments on our human lot. "The august loneliness of her path lent dignity to the sordid inspiration of her pilgrimage." We would be the poorer without that sentence and its several considered judgments.

In the best pages of *The Nigger of the "Narcissus,"* the storm action in Chapter III, the elaborate prose conveys action, motion, as well as a trembling and menaced beauty of sound.* But some of the striking Conradian effects are based on insistences which turn out to be obvious, and on a certain lack of inhibition. In context the docking of the *Narcissus* is very moving. It sums up the differences of sea and land, high endeavor and commerce, the beautiful and the sordid; it is the violation of the virgin by the soiled and practical; it brings the great adventure to an end. Only by underlining our text do we discover how obvious the insistences have been, in this devaluation of the land: "the steaming brows of millions of men," "drifts of smoky vapours," "an immense and lamentable murmur," "the anxious earth," "the shadows deepened," "barges drifted stealthily on the murky stream," "begrimed walls," "a vision of disaster," "a mysterious and unholy spell," and—horror of horrors in this story of masculine integrity and weakness—"two bareheaded women." "The *Narcissus* came gently into her berth; the shadows of soulless walls fell upon her, the dust of all the continents leaped upon her deck, and a swarm of strange men, clambering up her sides, took possession of her in the name of the sordid earth. She had ceased to live."

"My Lord in his discourse discovered a great deal of love to this ship." Conrad began with the ship, and it is with the *Narcissus* that the critic is well advised to end. And not only because the sea story as sea story is one of the greatest in English fiction. For the ship reminds us of the novel's overall structural problem, which I have neglected to discuss. This structural problem, and even Conrad's solution of it, can be simply stated. It is only in the doing, only in the demands for sensitive modulation made by every paragraph, that such matters become truly difficult! The problem was simply to avoid writing two distinct short novels, one optimistic and the other pessimistic. The two tests and two impressions of human

---

* Consider the imitative rhythms of these lines, and the dramatic change of the sentence from passive to active force, ending in a dying close: "The hard gust of wind came brutal like the blow of a fist. The ship relieved of her canvas in time received it pluckily: she yielded reluctantly to the violent onset; then, coming up with a stately and irresistible motion, brought her spars to windward in the teeth of a screeching squall. Out of the abysmal darkness of the black cloud overhead white hail streamed on her, rattled on the rigging, leaped in handfuls off the yards, rebounded on the deck—round and gleaming in the murky turmoil like a shower of pearls. It passed away" (p. 53).

nature must not be allowed to cancel out; we must forget neither the men's sentimentality and egoism nor their heroic endurance; at the last, the dark knot of seamen must drift in sunshine.

Conrad's tact becomes evident once we conceive any other structure than the one he actually presents. Had the near-mutiny and Wait's death occurred before the storm, we would have had the two short novels, and been left with a more affirmative statement than Conrad wanted to make. Had Wait's demoralizing effect begun only after the storm, we would have been left with no affirmation at all. The first necessity, then, was to introduce the Wait-story (tentatively, on the whole realistically) before the storm, return to it briefly during the storm, but give it major symbolic import only afterward. We are introduced to dim potentialities of anarchy and fear before knowing, through much of the third chapter, a magnificent courage and endurance. So much is simple indeed, in the describing. But having the near-mutiny and symbolic death occur after the storm still threatened, of course, to leave an impression essentially negative and, it may be, excessively symbolic. What is to remind us, after Wait's burial, that these men were also, had also been, true extrovert children of the sea? How could the story redress its balance? The obvious answer would be to show them reacting heroically to another great storm. But this too would have left an imbalance, and invited further circular movements.

What Conrad does, instead, is to give up any close view of the men; to focus attention on the ship rather than on them; to make *her* swift homeward progress heroic; to distance the reader from human perils either outward or inward and so confer on the crew, by association, some of the ship's glamour. The individuals on board give way to the ship as microcosm and finally to the ship as ship. Thus the object that unifies the two stories is not really an object at all, but the white female ship, which had left the stained land and now returns to it. What connects nearly every page is the *Narcissus* herself. At the very end the seamen are revalued by our distaste for the children of commerce, who can dismiss Singleton as a disgusting old brute; and the *Narcissus* is consecrated by the land that stains her. Crew and ship become part of history:

> The dark knot of seamen drifted in sunshine. To the left of them, the trees in Tower Gardens sighed, the stones of the Tower gleaming, seemed to stir in the play of light, as if remembering suddenly all the great joys and sorrows of the past, the fighting prototypes of these men; press-gangs; mutinous cries; the wailing of women by the riverside, and the shouts of men welcoming victories. The sunshine of heaven fell like a gift of grace on the mud of the earth, on the remembering and mute stones, on greed, selfishness; on the anxious faces of forgetful men. And to the right of the dark group the stained front of the Mint, cleansed by the flood of light, stood out for a moment dazzling and white like a marble palace in a fairy tale. The crew of the *Narcissus* drifted out of sight.[20]

"I disengaged myself gently." And by the same token the reader disengages himself from an adventure both extraordinary and intimate.

There are novels whose endings suggest a continuation of the lives we have watched. But *The Nigger of the "Narcissus"* is a completed experience, recorded of a dead time; the voyage becomes at last the book we have just read.

In mere outline the matter is as simple as that. But there are novelists who in all their calculating careers never achieve such a triumphant simplicity and rightness of structure. [21]          (1957)

## NOTES

1. Preface, *The Nigger of the "Narcissus."*
2. John D. Gordan, *Joseph Conrad: The Making of a Novelist* (Cambridge, Mass., 1941), pp. 141-144.
3. "To My Readers in America" (Preface of 1914), *The Nigger of the "Narcissus."*
4. See the Modern Library edition of *The Badge of Courage,* Introduction by R. W. Stallman (1951), and the Harper Classics edition, Introduction by Daniel G. Hoffman (1957). The former is reprinted in *Stephen Crane: An Omnibus* (Knopf 1952, Heinemann 1954). [Editor's note]
5. Gordan, *Joseph Conrad,* pp. 286, 289.
6. See pp. 108-120. [Editor's note]
7. *The Nigger of the "Narcissus,"* (Kent ed., 1926), p. 172.
8. Preface, *The Nigger of the "Narcissus."*
9. Vernon Young, "Trial by Water," *Accent* (Spring 1952), pp. 80-81. [Editor's note: See pp. 108-120 of the present text]
10. *The Nigger of the "Narcissus,"* pp. 138, 139.
11. This was called to my attention by Mrs. Elizabeth Von Klemperer, who is preparing a dissertation on James and Conrad in France.
12. "To My Readers in America."
13. The reference here is of course to Faulkner's "The Bear." [Editor's note]
14. Henry James, Preface to *The Aspern Papers.*
15. *The Nigger of the "Narcissus,"* p. 90. My italics.
16. *Ibid.,* pp. 8, 22, 24.
17. *Ibid.,* p. 145.
18. *Ibid.,* p. 76. My italics.
19. *Ibid.,* pp. 14-15. My italics.
20. *Ibid.,* p. 172.
21. Ian Watt's "Conrad Criticism and *The Nigger of the 'Narcissus,' Nineteenth Century Fiction,* XII (March 1958), pp. 257-283, which is mainly a critique of the denigration of Conrad's *Nigger* by M. Mudrick in the March 1957 *Nineteenth Century Fiction,* makes critical appraisal of several studies of the *Nigger,* including the essays by Guerard and Young. Among these studies is James E. Miller's re-examination of the *Nigger* in *P.M.L.A.* for December 1951. It is his discussion of the critical issues Conrad's use of language raises that gives Watt's essay an importance. M. D. Zabel, in his Introduction to the Harper & Brothers edition of the *Nigger* (1951), makes some points of comparison between the *Nigger* and "The Secret Sharer." [Editor's note]

# GUSTAV MORF

## On *Lord Jim\**
## *(an excerpt)*

IN SPITE OF his origin and of his careful education, Jim "jumps." In all probability, he would not have done it, had not his very superiors urged him to go, and had not the ship been sure to sink the next moment. This is exactly what happened to Joseph Conrad. *The sinking ship is Poland.* The very names are similar. *Patna* is the name of the ship, and *Polska* the (Polish) name of Poland.[1] *Poland (i.e.,* polonity) is doomed to disappear in a short time. There is, rationally speaking, no hope whatever for her. Such was at least the opinion of Jim's superiors, *i.e.,* of Conrad's uncle and guardian, T. Bobrowski. The machines have been stopped, *i.e.,* the independent Polish Government has ceased to exist. At this moment, Jim's superiors advise him to "jump," but Jim did not want to for a long moment. As a matter of fact, Conrad's uncle *urged him during more than seven years* to become a British subject. And finally, Jim yielded and jumped, *i.e.,* Conrad became a British subject.

But then, the ship is successfully towed to Aden by a French gunboat. This is the expression of the repressed hope that every genuine Pole ever cherished at the bottom of his heart (Nicholas B., for instance, who prophesied that Conrad would see "better times"), the hope that the day would come when Poland would be saved. That is why of all things it is a *French gunboat* that rescues the *Patna.* Ever since the rise of Napoleon, the Poles have expected their help to come from France. The Polish national anthem "Poland is not yet lost" is a song which originated in the Polish legions serving under Napoleon.

These are the facts of Conrad's life, and his wishes and fears which underlie the first part of *Lord Jim.* The second part of the book (from chapter 19 onwards) is not less symbolic than the first. But while the first part is the representation of a real state of affairs, the second part is the expression of Conrad's fear that the desertion of his native country might ultimately prove a fault by which he had forfeited his honour. The final destruction of Jim consecrates the author's triumph over the guilt-complex. Tuan Jim's defeat is Joseph Conrad's victory. A man who, like Jim has suffered so much, and who has paid off his debt with his death, is no longer guilty. His death adds much to the poignancy of his fate; it really makes him *a hero.* If we did not regret Jim's fate (though feeling its inevitability), the novel would have missed the mark. This is the reason why *Lord Jim* must of necessity have what is called "an unhappy ending." In fact, Jim's death is the only satisfactory closing note. Now we can absolve Jim entirely. His memory will be that of a man of unstained

* From Gustav Morf's *The Polish Heritage of Joseph Conrad* (Sampson Low, Marston & Co., 1930), pp. 163-166.

honour. This ending is also logical, since Conrad assumes from the very beginning that the conflict is insoluble.

R. Curle made (in his *Joseph Conrad* 1914) a remark which is strangely inadequate, when he wrote that Jim is "not an Englishman at all, but a passionate and melancholy Pole." Jim, like Hamlet, is the personification of that brooding part which every introvert possesses, and which will govern him if he does not govern it. All the difference between a normal person and a neurotic is that the former can keep that part in its proper place, that, unlike Jim (but very much like Conrad), he masters his fate. That is why Jim is not a Pole, but simply a neurotic and, as such, a perfectly true and convincing character. There are thousands of English men and women like him, thousands whose lives are obscured and sometimes destroyed by guilt-complexes. They do not, as a rule, die in such romantic circumstances as Jim or Hamlet, but end by suicide or in a lunatic asylum. Their fate may be less pathetic because it is not grasped and expressed by the mind of an artist, but it is just as real.

*Lord Jim* is unique amongst Conrad's books. It is perhaps not his best, but his most intimate. It is a book in which he tells us more about the darker sides of his personality than in *A Personal Record* and the *Mirror of the Sea* put together, for in these two books Conrad has taken great care that no "Conrad en pantouflies" (to use his own expression) should appear before the public. In *Lord Jim,* Joseph Conrad exteriorized, in a symbolic form, the deepest conflicts that arose from the dualism Polish-English within himself.

*Lord Jim* is more than a psychological novel, it is a psychoanalytical novel writen before psychoanalysis was founded. It appeared in 1900, the very year when Freud published his first book *Interpretation of Dreams,* which indirectly helps us to explain the novel. Both books, one in a subjective, the other in an objective form, threw light upon "that side of us which, like the other hemisphere of the moon, exists stealthily in perpetual darkness, with only a fearful ashy light falling at times on the edge." (*Lord Jim,* p. 93).

It was only in the nature of things that Conrad should dislike Freud intensely, as he disliked Dostoievski. Freud was in possession of the same truths as himself, but he appeared to him as a too crude, a too explicit double of himself. (1930)

## NOTES

1. [Editor's note: Milosz speculates that *Patna* hints at "Patria," See p. 43.]

# DOROTHY VAN GHENT

## On *Lord Jim* *

MARLOW's last view of Jim, on the coast of Patusan, is of a white figure "at the heart of a vast enigma." Jim himself is not enigmatic. The wonder and doubt that he stirs, both in Marlow and in us, are not wonder and doubt as to what *he* is: he is as recognizable as we are to ourselves; he is "one of us." Furthermore, he is not a very complex character, and he is examined by his creator with the most exhaustive conscientiousness; he is placed in every possible perspective that might help to define him. The enigma, then, is not what Jim is but what we are, and not only what we are, but "how to be" what we are.

Jim's shocking encounter with himself at the moment of his jump from the *Patna* is a model of those moments when the destiny each person carries within him, the destiny fully molded in the unconscious will, lifts its blind head from the dark, drinks blood, and speaks. There is no unclarity in the shape that Jim saw at that moment: he had jumped—it is as simple as that. But because the event is a paradigm of the encounters of the conscious personality with the stranger within, the stranger who is the very self of the self, the significance of Jim's story is *our own* significance, contained in the enigmatic relationship between the conscious will and the fatality of our acts. Jim's discovery of himself was a frightful one, and his solution of the problem of "how to be" was to exorcise the stranger in a fierce, long, concentrated effort to be his opposite. The oracle spoke early to Oedipus, too, in his youth in Corinth, telling him who he was— the man destined to transgress most horribly the saving code of kinship relations—and Oedipus's solution of the problem of "how to be" was the same as Jim's: he fled in the opposite direction from his destiny and ran straight into it.

Jim is one of the most living characters in fiction, although his presentation is by indirection, through Marlow's narrative; that indirection is itself uniquely humanizing, for we see him only as people can see each other, ambivalently and speculatively. He is nevertheless an extraordinarily simplified *type,* obsessed with a single idea, divested of all psychological attributes but the very few that concretize his relationship with his idea. The simplification is classical; it is a simplification like that of Aeschylus' Orestes, possessed by the divine command, and like that of Sophocles' Oedipus, possessed by his responsibility for finding out the truth. Conrad is able thus to imply a clear-cut formal distinction between the man and his destiny (his acts), even though he conceives destiny as immanent in the man's nature and in this sense identical with him. Here is Jim, "clean-limbed, clean-faced, firm on his feet, as promising a boy as the sun ever shone on," and there are his acts—the destruction of his best friend, the

* From Dorothy Van Ghent's *The English Novel* (Rinehart, 1953), pp. 229-244. See also Notes and Questions pp. 440-454.

destruction of himself, the abandonment of the Patusan village to leader-lessness and depredation. Similarly Orestes and Oedipus, human agents simplified to a commanding ethical idea, are analytically separable from their destinies, the *anankē* or compelling principle fatally inherent in their acts. This subtle but tangible distinction between the human agent and his destiny allows the classical dramatists to orient clearly what we may call the metaphysical significance of the hero's career, the universal prob-lem and the law of life which that career illustrates. We see the hero as an ideal human type (literally "idealized" through his devotion to an idea of ethical action); but his fate is pitiful and terrible—a fate that, if a man's deserts were to be suited to his conscious intentions, should fall only on malicious, unjust, and treasonable men; and the problem, the "enigma," thus raised is the religious problem of the awful incongruity between human intention and its consequences in action, between ethical effort and the guilt acquired through such effort; and the law—if a law appears—will be the law that justifies, to man's reason and feeling, that appearance of awful incongruity. Conrad's treatment of Jim's story is classical in this sense, in that he sees in it the same problem and orients the problem in the same manner.

"In the destructive element immerse," Stein says, voicing his own solu-tion of the problem of "how to be." There is no way "to be," according to Stein, but through the ideal, the truth as it appears, what he calls "the dream," although it is itself "the destructive element." "Very funny this terrible thing is," Stein says,

> "A man that is born falls into a dream like a man who falls into the sea. If he tries to climb out into the air as inexperienced people en-deavour to do, he drowns—*nicht wahr?* . . . No! I tell you! The way is to the destructive element submit yourself, and with the exertions of your hands and feet in the water make the deep, deep sea keep you up. So if you ask me—how to be? . . . I will tell you! . . . In the de-structive element immerse."

Stein's words are but one outlook on the universal problem that is Jim's, but it is the outlook dramatized in Jim's own actions. It is that dramatized by Sophocles also. Oedipus "submitted" himself to his ideal of the respon-sible king and citizen, self-sworn to the discovery of the truth. It was the "destructive element," bringing about the terrible revelation of his guilt. So also Jim submits himself to his dream of heroic responsibility and truth to men, fleeing from port to port, and finally to Patusan, to realize it. And, again, the ideal is the "destructive element," bringing about the compact with Brown (a compact made in the profoundest spirit of the dream) and inevitably, along with the compact, destruction. The irony is that Jim, in his destructiveness, was "true." This is the classical tragic irony: the incongruity and yet the effective identity between the construc-tive will and the destructive act.

Whether Conrad goes beyond that particular tragic incongruity to the other ancient tragic perception, of ennoblement through suffering, is doubtful. The "enigma" that Marlow finds in Jim's career has this other dark and doubtful aspect. When, at the end, after receiving Doramin's bullet, "the white man sent right and left at all those faces a proud and unflinching glance," is he really fulfilled in nobility in our sight? Has his suffering, entailed in his long and strenuous exile and his guilt and his final great loss, given him the knowledge, and with the knowledge the nobility, which is the mysterious and sublime gift of suffering? The answer is doubtful. We need to bring to bear on it the fairly inescapable impression that the only character in the book in whom we can read the stamp of the author's own practical "approval" is the French lieutenant who remained on board the *Patna* while it was being towed into port. The French lieutenant would not have acted as Jim did in the last events on Patusan—indeed [it] is inconceivable in the Patusan circumstances. If, in Conrad's implicit evaluation of his material, the French lieutenant represents the ethically "approved" manner of action and the only one, Jim can scarcely support the complete role of the tragic hero of the classical type, the hero who achieves unique greatness through suffering. (The French lieutenant suffers only for lack of wine.) For our notion of what constitutes a "hero" is thus surely divided: if the French lieutenant's heroism is the true heroism, Jim's is not, and conversely. No doubt the division—and it seems to be real in our response to the book—is associated with a division of allegiance on Conrad's part,[1] between emotional allegiance to Jim's suffering and struggling humanity, in all its hybristic aspiration, and intellectual allegiance to the code represented by the lieutenant, in all its severe limitation and calm obscurity. With this division in mind, it is impossible to identify the "view of life" in the book as a whole with Stein's view of life, impressive as Stein is in his broad and enlightened sensitivity: for the French lieutenant knows nothing of a "destructive element," and if he did—which he could not—would doubtless think that to talk of "submitting" oneself to it was sheer twaddle.

What intervenes between Conrad's ambivalent attitude toward Jim's story and the attitudes of Aeschylus and Sophocles toward their subjects is modern man's spiritual isolation from his fellows. Jim's isolation is profound, most profound and complete at that last moment when he "sent right and left at all those faces a proud and unflinching glance": here his aloneness in his dream—his illusion—of faith to men is unqualified, for the material fact is that he has allowed a brigand to slaughter Dain Waris and his party, and that he has left the village open to ravage. Moral isolation provides a new inflection of tragedy. Orestes freed Argos from a tyranny, and Oedipus freed Thebes from a plague. Their guilt and suffering had a constructive social meaning; they had acted for the positive welfare of the citizens; and that social version of their heroism, internal to the dramas in which they appear, is the immediate, literal basis of our (because it is the citizen-chorus's) appraisal of their heroism. But Jim— to use parallel terms—destroys his city. Thus there is nothing structurally internal to Jim's story that matches the positive moral relationship, in the

ancient dramas, between the social destiny and the hero's destiny, the relationship that is presented concretely in the fact that the hero's agony
is a saving social measure. There is nothing to mediate, practically and
concretely, between Jim's "truth" and real social life, as a benefit to and
confirmation of the social context. Jim is alone.

And yet one asks, is his last act, when he "takes upon his head" the
blood-guilt, an atonement? If it were so, it would be atonement not in
quite the same sense that the madness and exile of Orestes and the blinding and banishment of Oedipus were atonements, for these involved the
restoration of community health, whereas Jim's final act brings about
(projectively) the destruction of the community—but in the necessary
modern sense, necessitated by the fact of the disintegration of moral
bonds between men: an atonement for that social sterility, a sacrifice
offered in the name of moral community. If it were so, Jim would still be,
metaphorically speaking, the savior of the city. No doubt Sophocles, civic-
minded gentleman, did not "approve" of Oedipus: when parricide and
incest occur in the leading families, what are the rest of us to do? how
is the world's business to be kept up decently? what model shall we look
to? But the Greek cities were said to have carried on quarrels over the
burial place of Oedipus, for his presence brought fertility to the land. So
also the story of Lord Jim is a spiritually fertilizing experience, enlightening the soul as to its own meaning in a time of disorganization and
drought; and Conrad's imagination of Jim's story has the seminal virtue of
the ancient classic.

In James's *The Portrait of a Lady* we watched the creation of a self.
In Conrad's austerely pessimistic work, the self stands already created,
the possibilities are closed. Again and again, and finally on Patusan, a
"clean slate" is what Jim thinks he has found, a chance to "climb out," to
begin over, to perform the deed which will be congruent with his ideal
of himself. "A clean slate, did he say?" Marlow comments; "as if the
initial word of each our destiny were not graven in imperishable characters
upon the face of a rock." The tension, the spiritual drama in Conrad, lie
in a person's relation with his destiny. The captain in "The Secret
Sharer" acknowledges his profound kinship with a man who has violently
transgressed the captain's professional code (the man has murdered another seaman during a voyage, and murder at sea is, in Conrad, something worse than murder; whatever its excuses, it is an inexcusable breach
of faith with a community bound together by common hazard); but by the
acknowledgment he masters his own identity, integrates, as it were, his
unconscious impulses within consciousness, and thereby realizes self-
command and command of his ship. In contrast with the captain of "The
Secret Sharer," Jim repudiates the other-self that has been revealed to
him; at no time does he consciously acknowledge that it *was* himself who
jumped from the *Patna*—it was only his body that had jumped; and his
career thenceforth is an attempt to prove before men that the gross fact
of the jump belied his identity.

James works through recognitions; the self-creating character in James develops by taking into consciousness more and more subtle relations—"seeing" more in a world of virtually infinite possibilities for recognition, and thus molding consciousness, molding himself. Conrad works through epiphanies, that is, through dramatic manifestations of elements hidden or implicit in the already constructed character. The difference of method is suggestive of the difference of world view: in James, the world ("reality" as a whole) being, as it were, an open and fluid system, essentially creative; in Conrad, a closed and static system, incapable of origination though intensely dramatic in its revelations. (Paradoxically, the environments in James's open world are the closed environments of city and house, while those in Conrad's closed world are those of the open, the mobile sea.) The word "epiphany" implies manifestation of divinity, and this meaning of the term can serve us also in analyzing Conrad's method and his vision, if we think of the "dark powers" of the psyche as having the mysterious absoluteness that we associate with the daemonic, and if we think mythologically of a man's destiny both as being carried within him, and, *in effect*—since his acts externalize his destiny—as confronting him from without.

The sunken wreck that strikes the *Patna* is one such epiphany in *Lord Jim,* and this manifestation of "dark power" is coincident with and symbolically identifiable with the impulse that makes Jim jump, an impulse submerged like the wreck, riding in wait, striking from under. Outer nature seems, here, to act in collusion with the hidden portion of the soul. But Conrad's supreme mastery is his ability to make the circumstance of "plot" the inevitable point of discharge of the potentiality of "character."[2] The accident that happens to the *Patna* is not merely a parallel and a metaphor of what happens to Jim at that time, but it is the objective circumstance that discovers Jim to himself. The apparent "collusion" between external nature and the soul, that gives to Conrad's work its quality of the marvelous and its religious temper, is thus, really, only the inevitable working out of character through circumstance.

Another major epiphany is the appearance of Brown on Patusan. The appearance of Brown is, in effect, an externalization of the complex of Jim's guilt and his excuses for his guilt, for he judges Brown as he judged himself, as a *victim of circumstances* (the distinction is radical) rather than as a character exposed by circumstances, at least to be given that benefit of doubt which would discriminate intention from deed, ethos from the objective ethical traits to be seen in a man's actions. Therefore he gives Brown a "clean slate," a chance to "climb out"—from himself! But Jim's compact with Brown is more than a compact with his own unacknowledged guilt; it is at the same time, and paradoxically, a lonely act of faith with the white men "out there," the men of Jim's race and traditions, the men upon the sea whose code he had once betrayed, the "home" from which a single impulse of nerves had forever exiled him. Brown is the only white man who has appeared on Patusan to put to test Jim's ethical community with his race and his profession, and in "taking upon his head" responsibility for Brown's honor, he is superbly "true" to that community. But his truth is, effectively, betrayal; it is "the destructive element." Since only a chance in thousands brings Brown to Patusan, again outer nature seems to have acted in collusion with the "dark power" within Jim's own psyche, in order to face him once more with his unacknowledged identity when he is in the full hybris of his truth and his courage. But again the apparent collusion is only the working out of character through circumstance.

The impossibility of escape from the dark companion within leaves a man more perfectly alone in this world because he has that companion—who is always and only himself. The physical settings of Jim's career concretize his isolation. In constant flight from the self that he reads on men's lips but that he refuses to acknowledge except as a freakish injustice of circumstances, and, as he flees, pursuing the heroic ideal which would reconstitute him in the ranks of men where his salvation lies (for, as Conrad says, "in our own hearts we trust for our salvation in the men that surround us"), he comes finally to Patusan, ascends the river to the heart of the island, unarmed (why carry a loaded revolver when it is only oneself that one must face?)—ascends, that is, the dark paths of his own being back to its source:[3] "thirty miles of forest shut it off."

The first description that Marlow gives of the interior of the island is of a conical hill that is "split in two, and with the two halves leaning slightly apart," and in his reminiscences he returns frequently to the image of the hill (it is, indeed, the hill up which Jim hauled the cannon, in his first great exploit when he won the faith of the natives and became their protector), particularly to a scene of moonlight when the moon is rising behind the fissured mass.

> On the third day after the full, the moon, as seen from the open space in front of Jim's house . . . rose exactly behind these hills, its diffused light at first throwing the two masses into intensely black relief, and then the nearly perfect disc, glowing ruddily, appeared, gliding upwards between the sides of the chasm, till it floated away above the summits, as if escaping from a yawning grave in gentle triumph. "Wonderful effect," said Jim by my side. "Worth seeing. Is it not?"
>
> And this question was put with a note of personal pride that made me smile, as though he had had a hand in regulating that unique spectacle. He had regulated so many things in Patusan! Things that would have appeared as much beyond his control as the motions of the moon and the stars.

On Marlow's last night on the island he sees the same spectacle again, but the mood is different, oppressive.

> I saw part of the moon glittering through the bushes at the bottom of the chasm. For a moment it looked as though the smooth disc, falling from its place in the sky upon the earth, had rolled to the bottom of that precipice: its ascending movement was like a leisurely rebound; it disengaged itself from the tangle of twigs; the bare contorted limb of

some tree, growing on the slope, made a black crack right across its face. It threw its level rays afar as if from a cavern, and in this mournful eclipse-like light the stumps of felled trees uprose very dark, the heavy shadows fell at my feet on all sides . . .

Together Jim and Marlow watch "the moon float away above the chasm between the hills like an ascending spirit out of a grave; its sheen descended, cold and pale, like the ghost of dead sunlight." Carried to the mind by the image of the fissured hill, with the suspiciously ghostlike moon floating out of the chasm, is the relentless solitude of Jim's fate. He is not only an outcast from his kind but he is also an outcast from himself, cloven spiritually, unable to recognize his own identity, separated from himself as the two halves of the hill are separated. And the rebounding moon, in which he has so much pride, "as though he had had a hand in regulating that unique spectacle," remains in the mind as a figure of the ego-ideal, even that ideal of truth by which, Marlow says, Jim approached "greatness as genuine as any man ever achieved": its illusionariness, and the solitude implied by illusion. At the end, after all —when the silver ring that is the token of moral community falls to the floor, and through Jim's "truth" his best friend has been killed and the village under his protection betrayed—Jim is only what he has been; he is of the measure of his acts. To be only what one has been is the sentence of solitary confinement that is passed on everyman. It is in this sense, finally, that Jim is "one of us."

Since Jim is "one of us," the truth about Jim will be—within the scope of the expressiveness of Jim's story—a truth about life; and in view of this responsibility, Conrad's task of evaluation demands that *all* the accessible evidence be presented and that it be submitted to mutually corrective hypotheses of its meaning. There are Jim's actions, which are concrete enough and simple as the concrete is simple. But the significance of action is significance in the judgments of men, which are various; and as soon as judgment is brought to the act, the act becomes not simple but protean. *What,* then, *is* the act? The question defines Conrad's method in this book, his use of reflector within reflector, point of view within point of view, cross-chronological juxtapositions of events and impressions. Conrad's technical "devices," in this case, represent much more than the word "device" suggests: they represent extreme ethical scrupulosity, even anxiety; for the truth about a man is at once too immense and too delicate to sustain any failure of carefulness in the examiner.

The omniscient early chapters give briefly the conditions of Jim's upbringing, his heroic dreams, two incidents in his sea training, the *Patna* voyage up to the moment when the submerged wreck strikes, and the courtroom scene with Jim in the dock: that is, the first chapters take us up to the point where the accused is placed before us and the processes of judgment have to begin. From here, Marlow takes over. Marlow is unofficial attorney both for the defense and the prosecution. He selects, objectifies, and humanizes the evidence on both sides, but he lets it—

intensified and set in perspective through his intelligent, freely roaming curiosity—speak for itself. Marlow is the most familiar narrative mechanism in Conrad's work; and in this particular book *Marlow has to exist.* For Jim's "case" is not an absolute but a relative; it has a being only in relation to what men's minds can make of it. And Marlow provides the necessary medium of an intelligent consciousness, at once a symbol of that relativity, a concretization of the processes by which just judgment may be evoked, and—through his doubt and reverence—an acknowledgment of the irony of judgment of the relative.

The few particulars that are given of Jim's home environment are all we need to give the word "home" potency for this chronicle: there is the parsonage, its decency, its naïveté, its faith, its sterling morality, its representativeness of "the sheltering conception of light and order which is our refuge." In the thirty-fifth chapter, where Marlow takes final farewell of Jim, and Jim says,

> "I must stick to their belief in me to feel safe and to—to" . . . He cast about for a word, seemed to look for it on the sea . . . "to keep in touch with" . . . His voice sank suddenly to a murmur . . . "with those whom, perhaps, I shall never see any more. With—with—you, for instance."

The parsonage home, as well as the community of men upon the sea, contains the "those" with whom Jim must keep in touch through faithfulness in word and act. "Home" is the ethical code which enables men to live together through trust of each other, and which, in so binding them, gives them self-respect. The exclusiveness and naïveté of the parsonage background interpret the symbol of "home" in all its own relativity, its merely provisional status in the jungle of the universe. When we close the book, the symbol of "home" is as ghostlike as the moon over Patusan. But it is the only provision for salvation, in the sense in which Conrad uses the word salvation when he says, "In our own hearts we trust for our salvation in the men that surround us."

The two incidents in Jim's early sea training, the storm in Chapter 1, when he was "too late," and, in Chapter 2, his disablement at the beginning of a hurricane week, when he "felt secretly glad he had not to go on deck," counterpoint his belief in himself with actualities of frustration. A certain distinct polarity is already established, between his dreams and the "facts"; and when, in Chapter 2, Jim suddenly decides to ship as mate on the *Patna,* it is as if we saw a bar magnet curved into a horseshoe and bent until its poles closed, sealing personal will and the fatality of circumstances in a mysterious identity that is the man himself; for his unexplained choice of the *Patna* is in more than one sense a choice of exile. He could have gone back to the home service, after his convalescence; but he throws in his lot with the men he has seen in that Eastern port (and disdained) who "appeared to live in a crazy maze of plans, hopes, dangers, enterprises . . . in the dark places of the sea," and with those others who had been seduced by "the eternal peace of Eastern sky and sea," who talked "everlastingly of turns of luck . . . and in all they said—in their actions, in their looks, in their persons—could be detected the soft spot, the place of decay . . ." Moreover, on the *Patna* he is in a special sense a man alone, alone with a dream that is unsharable because he is among inferiors: the third chapter presents "the *Patna* gang" from Jim's point of view—"those men did not belong to the world of heroic adventure . . . he rubbed shoulders with them, but they could not touch him; he shared the air they breathed, but he was different . . ." Is his choice of the *Patna* a measure taken to protect his dream from reality? Is it thus significant of his "soft spot"? There is no choice but reality, and actually none but the single, circumscribed, only possible choice that is one's own reality—witnessed by Jim's jump from the *Patna,* as by his shipping on the *Patna* in the first place.

When Sophocles, in his old age, wrote of Oedipus again, he had Oedipus assert his innocence and curse those who had banished him; for Oedipus had acted in ignorance of the circumstances, and therefore could not be held guilty for them. Jim puts up a fight as Oedipus did, and the causes involved are the same: is the self deducible from circumstances? is one guilty for circumstances? is one guilty for oneself when one has no choice but to be oneself? is one guilty for oneself when one is in ignorance of what oneself is? if, with lifelong strife, one refuses to acquiesce in the self, is one guilty for the self? who has a right to pronounce this judgment?

Obviously from this point another device of presentation must be used, other than either objective presentation by the author or subjective presentation through Jim, for Jim is too youthful, idealistic, and ingenuous to throw light on himself, and "objectivity"—the objectivity of the camera and the sound recorder—is hopelessly inadequate to the solution of these questions. Marlow has to take up the case, and Marlow—intelligent professional man of the sea, and insatiably curious psychological observer—brings to bear on it not only Jim's own evidence (and his friendship with Jim draws from Jim much more than he could ever say for himself—brings out gestures and tones, situations and impulses, that only sympathy could bring out), and not only the reactions of the judges (and the judges are more in number than those in the courtroom), but also a marvelously sensitive registration of the concrete detail of life, bits of color and form and movement, a chin, a hand, a shuffle, a vase of dry flowers, a striped pajama suit, that could not be admitted as "evidence" in a formal inquiry, but that are nevertheless essential psychological evidence to the sensitive investigator.

The *Patna* gang has to be presented over again, not now from Jim's point of view but from Marlow's. So far as the *Patna* gang is concerned, the question is, is Jim one of them or "one of us"? Marlowe has only to see the group on a street corner to know that Jim is not one of them; but he pushes further—he is around when the fat captain, in his night-suit, squeezes into the ramshackle gharry and disappears, "departed, disappeared, vanished, absconded; and absurdly enough it looked as though he had taken that gharry with him." It is Marlow's impression of the obscenely ridiculous captain that conveys to us the captain's sur-reality: he is, through Marlow's view, not simply stupid and inferior as he appeared to Jim, but a frightful manifestation of underground evil, as mysterious and unaccountable in its apparition as the captain's vanishing with the gharry is complete; that the captain wears a sleeping suit (like the murderer in "The Secret Sharer") emphasizes the psychological, that is to say spiritual, symbolism of his evil; he is another epiphany, a "showing" from the daemonic underground of the psyche—but he is only that, and the psyche, Jim's psyche, is more than the obscene man in the sleeping suit.

Then Marlow interviews the chief engineer in the hospital, the man with the noble head and the pink toads under his bed. The effort is an effort again to test his perception that Jim is not one of them, but "one of us"; for the initial perception alone is scarcely to be trusted, since Jim, whatever his excuses, had identified himself with the *Patna* gang by jumping from the ship. The pink toads under the chief engineer's bed are a fearful inversion of Jim's own dream: they too are a dream—and the dreamer has a noble head. The pink toads are a horrible degeneration of the dream. They serve as a commentary on the dream that cannot be evaded (no more than can the captain in the sleeping suit). But Jim had stayed for the trial, while the captain had disappeared, the chief engineer had cultivated the d.t.'s, and the second engineer wasn't around (the little man will reappear later, for the act is immortal). It is Jim's dream that makes him stay for the trial, and therefore Jim's dream cannot be identified with the chief engineer's, however identifiable they are in illusionary quality and spiritual potency. Marlow's visit with the chief engineer fixes this judgment of a difference, as well as of a similarity.

These two observations of Marlow's project the question of identity (the question "Who am I?" that is Oedipus's as well as Jim's), that can only be decided by comparison of like things and different things, discrimination of congruences and incongruences. Two identifications of Jim with other persons have been rejected—although even the impulse to distinguish suggests subtle similarities between the objects compared, and we can never forget that Jim was in the lifeboat with the *Patna* gang, though at the other end. The rest of the narrative moves through a devious course of identifications and distinctions. Brierly, the unimpeachable professional seaman, in some astounding way identifies himself with the accused man, Jim, and commits suicide. Is this another version of Jim's "jump"? If so, in avoiding by suicide the possibility of being Jim, Brierly succeeds merely in being what he was trying to avoid; this is Jim's "case" all over again. The loathsome Chester also identifies himself with Jim; Chester instantly spots him as the man for his job—fantastic exile on a guano island; "He is no earthly good for anything," Chester says,—"he

would just have done for me"; the man has a "soft spot," and for men
with a soft spot, as Jim himself had observed, "death was the only event
of their fantastic existence that seemed to have a reasonable certitude of
achievement"; for Chester, Jim is "one of us" in a sense that disgusts
Marlow, and Marlow's disgust with Chester and therefore with Chester's
appraisal of the man helps us to measure Jim: but the fact that Marlow,
during those grueling hours in the hotel room when he is writing factitious
letters in order to give Jim a chance for privacy with his ordeal, can
hesitate between recommending Jim for a decent job and turning him
over to Chester still suggests a doubt as to what "one of us" means,
whether it has Chester's meaning or Marlow's.

The French lieutenant whom Marlow encounters, though he is a
sympathetic man, does *not* identify himself with Jim; and curiously, while
the French lieutenant represents the approved ethos of the profession
(and not only of the profession of the sea, but of the profession of being
human, as the author evaluates his material; for, in that evaluation, being
human, as humans ought to be, *is* a profession, with an austere Spartan-
like discipline[4]), he is the only person in the book who does not, in some
way, identify himself with Jim except for Cornelius and Brown, who hate
him as an opposite and as an indictment of their evil (perhaps the captain
of the *Patna* and the chief engineer could be included here, but their
presentation is more objective and their attitudes less determinable; although the same point would hold): that is to say that the only cases in
which subjective identification with Jim does not take place are those of
a man—the French lieutenant—who is above Jim's failings by virtue
of his mediocrity, and of men who are below Jim's problem by virtue of
their psychotic maliciousness. The portrait of the French lieutenant is
extremely careful, as all the portraits in the book are done with extreme
care, for on the nature of the man who judges depends the validity of the
judgment.

> He clasped his hands on his stomach again. "I remained on board
> that—that—my memory is going (*s'en va*). Ah! *Patt-nà. C'est bien ça.
> Patt-nà. Merci.* It is droll how one forgets. I stayed on that ship thirty
> hours . . ."

And just a moment before, we have learned that "all the time of towing
we had two quartermasters stationed with axes by the hawsers, to cut us
clear of our tow in case she . . ." The French lieutenant's failure to remember even the name of the ship, on which he had stayed for thirty
hours *after* Jim had jumped, and the laconic tone of the information
about the quartermasters' assignment, are a judgment of Jim in terms
of Jim's own dream. The French lieutenant's unconscious heroism is the
heroism that Jim had made a conscious ideal; and his witness measures
Jim's failure by the painful difference of fact. And yet this damning commentary appears as inconclusive as that of the pink toads under the chief
engineer's bed; it is as far from and as near to "the case."

The distinguished naturalist Stein offers another approach. Stein has been a hero of action like the French lieutenant, but he is also a hero of the intellect, and, in his way, a psychologist, a philosopher, and an artist. Stein is able to identify himself with Jim through his own profound idealism (as Marlow does through doubt). But Stein's idealism, so far as we know, has never differentiated itself from his actions; he has the gift of nature which is itself ideal; he had known, Marlow says, how "to follow his destiny with unfaltering footsteps." Stein "diagnoses the case" of Jim, making it quite simple "and altogether hopeless" by framing it in the question: "how to be." "I tell you, my friend," he says,

> "it is not good for you to find you cannot make your dream come true, for the reason that you not strong enough are, or not clever enough. *Ja!* . . . And all the time you are such a fine fellow, too! *Wie?* . . . How can that be? . . ."
> The shadow prowling amongst the graves of butterflies laughed boisterously.

Stein gives Jim his great chance to make his dream come true, by sending him to Patusan. This journey is ambiguous: "once before Patusan had been used as a grave," Marlow reflects; while Stein prowls "amongst the graves of butterflies," Brierly's remark about Jim recurs to Marlow's mind: "Let him creep twenty feet underground and stay there"; and there is the fissured hill at the heart of Patusan, whose chasm is like a "yawning grave," from which the moon (the dream) rises "like an ascending spirit out of a grave . . . like the ghost of dead sunlight." The ancient mythical heroes, Odysseus and Aeneas, made the "journey underground" to Hades in search of wisdom, and brought it back to daylight —the wisdom which was knowledge of their own destinies. And shadowily behind them is the barbarous ritual that made a king by burying him and disinterring him, a surrogate perhaps, or a "story" (mythos), to stand for the killing of an old king and his "resurrection" in a new one. In the grave of Patusan—"the secular gloom and the old mankind"—Jim's dream does come true. But the doubt remains as to whether, like the ancient heroes, he brought back to daylight the wisdom of his destiny— or, in other terms, whether in that grave an old self was really buried and from it a new one congruent with his dream was resurrected.

The test of daylight, of the bright sea beyond the dark island, offers itself only through Brown. Jim identifies himself with Brown in two ways, through his guilt, and through his honor: Brown is at once the "dark power" in Jim's psyche and his only effective bond with the brightness outside himself, the community of tradition to which "we trust for our salvation." Brown's ambivalence for Jim is Jim's own ambivalence, and it is, in its most extensive sense, the ambivalence that exists in all historical and personal stages of experience where law (the "code") and the self question each other—as well in the Athens of Thucydides and Euripides as in our own time, and as well, we must surmise, in Conrad as in Jim. The tale Conrad prepared to narrate was a tale in the manner of the older classical dramatists, wherein law—whether divine, as with Aeschylus, or natural, as with Sophocles—is justified to the self, whatever its agonies of discovery. But he managed to do a tale that put both the law and the self to question, and left them there. At the end (dated July 1900), Stein does not help:

> Stein has aged greatly of late. He feels it himself, and says often that he is "preparing to leave all this; preparing to leave . . ." while he waves his hand sadly at his butterflies. (1953)

## NOTES

1. Albert Guerard discusses this division of allegiance in his *Joseph Conrad* (New York: New Directions, 1947).
2. Morton Dauwen Zabel points this out in his Introduction to *The Portable Conrad* (New York: The Viking Press, Inc., 1947).
3. The observation is made by Mr. Guerard in *Joseph Conrad,* cited above.
4. In his *Joseph Conrad,* Mr. Guerard thoroughly clarifies this issue.

## JEROME THALE

## Marlow's Quest*

CONRAD'S "Heart of Darkness" has all the trappings of the conventional adventure tale—mystery, exotic setting, escape, suspense, unexpected attack. These, of course, are only the vehicle of something more fundamental, and one way of getting at what they symbolize is to see the story as a grail quest. Though Conrad is sparing in his explicit use of the metaphor ("a weary pilgrimage amongst hints for nightmares"), it is implicit in the structure of the action. As in the grail quest there is the search for some object, and those who find and can see the grail receive an illumination. Marlow, the central figure, is like a knight seeking the grail, and his journey even to the end follows the archetype. His grandiose references to the dark places of the earth, his talk of the secret of a continent, the farthest point of navigation, his sudden and unwonted sense that he is off not to the centre of a continent but to the centre of the earth— these, occurring before he starts his journey, give it the atmosphere of a quest.

And in the journey itself there are the usual tests and obstacles of a quest. After Marlow passes through the bizarre company headquarters in Brussels and the inanity surrounding his voyage to the African coast,

* From *University of Toronto Quarterly,* XXIV (July 1955), 351-358.

he makes a difficult and painful journey inland. At the central station he begins a seemingly routine task—going up the river to bring back a sick company agent—which will become his quest. Gradually he learns a little about Kurtz, at first a name; disgust with the manager and reports about the remarkable agent in the jungle make him increasingly eager to see the man. As Marlow's interest in Kurtz mounts, so do the trials and obstacles that are part of Marlow's test. The journey creeps on painfully in the patched ship. Near the end, just before the attack, Marlow realizes that Kurtz is the one thing he has been seeking, the "enchanted princess" in a "fabulous castle," whose approaches are fraught with danger.

The grail motif is of course connected with the profuse—and somewhat heavy-handed—light-darkness symbolism.[1] The grail is an effulgence of light, and it gives an illumination to those who can see it. This is the light which Marlow seeks in the heart of darkness. The grail that he finds appears an abomination and the light even deeper darkness, yet paradoxically Marlow does have an illumination: "it threw a kind of light on everything about me." The manager and the others travelling with Marlow are constantly called pilgrims, "faithless pilgrims," and for the faithless there can be no illumination. At the end of his quest Marlow does not find what he had expected all along, a good man in the midst of darkness and corruption. Instead he receives a terrible illumination. Such experiences are as ineffable as they are profound, and this is why the meaning of Marlow's tale must be expressed so obliquely, like the "glow that brings out the haze."

The nature of Marlow's illumination is determined by the remarkable man who is its occasion. And to comprehend Kurtz we must look into the reasons for Marlow's attitude towards him. Marlow is listening to the manager condemning Kurtz's methods as "unsound." "It seemed to me I had never breathed an atmosphere so vile, and I turned mentally to Kurtz for relief . . . it was something to have at least a choice of nightmares." Why must Marlow choose a nightmare at all? Because what he sees in one of the nightmares is so compelling that he cannot remain neutral before it.

Marlow's choice is made easier for the reader to accept by the fact that even before meeting Kurtz Marlow finds himself on Kurtz's side. Marlow has been disgusted by everything connected with the company; he learns that the manager schemes against Kurtz, because Kurtz, like Marlow, is one of the new gang, "the gang of virtue." The unseen apostle of light becomes the alternative to the cowardly plunderers. But Marlow is not trapped into an incredible allegiance; he knows what he is choosing when he later makes his real choice. Nor is it an unconsidered gesture of escape from the moral decay of the hollow men. His choice is a deliberate one.

Given Marlow's nature and his function in the story his choice must be based on something positive in Kurtz. There are strong hints in the story that Kurtz is a good man gone wrong in the jungle. But if he is merely a victim of unusual circumstances, a man to be pitied, then Marlow's choice is as sentimental as that of Kurtz's fiancée. The causes of Kurtz's tragedy are within—in his towering ambition, and his rootless idealism. Yet the jungle is important, for what happens to Kurtz can happen only under some such conditions. And what Marlow values in Kurtz is so paradoxical that it can be seen only against a dark and mysterious jungle and the corruption of colonial exploitation.

What is it in Kurtz that compels a choice and that produces such a profound change in the imperturbable Marlow? Simply that Kurtz has discovered himself, has become fully human; and Marlow's illumination, the light that is his grail, is a similar discovery about himself and all men.[2]

Marlow tells us in "Youth" that the wreck of the *Judea* was "the endeavor, the test, the trial of life . . . a chance to find out what one can do." "Heart of Darkness," in spite of its stagey background, treats this theme of self-discovery in a much less romantic, and, I think, more profound way than "Youth." Here self-discovery is not just the thrill of finding out what one can do, but the deeper task of finding out what one is, of coming to grips with the existence of the self.

The discovery of what it means to be is not easy. "There's no initiation into such mysteries"; there can only be a confrontation. Only Kurtz, and in a lesser degree Marlow, make the breakthrough. The experience gives a man knowledge that leaves him uneasy with himself and contemptuous of those who do not have it. Hence Marlow's caustic tone to his hearers, safely insulated against such knowledge, "each moored with two good addresses, like a hulk with two anchors, a butcher round one corner, a policeman round another, excellent appetites, and temperature normal." Marlow emphasizes that Kurtz is wasted and feverish from this knowledge; "it was not disease"—only the outward manifestation of what went on in Kurtz. Marlow with his own awareness is disgusted with the people he sees on the streets in Brussels: "Their bearing, which was simply the bearing of commonplace individuals, going about their business in the assurance of perfect safety, was offensive to me like the outrageous flauntings of folly in the face of a danger it is unable to comprehend."

Existence is dangerous, menacing; too dangerous for most of us to discover. Illusion and ignorance, which Conrad treats with a mixture of indulgence and scorn, are what save most of us. "The inner truth is hidden,—luckily, luckily." Women are fortunate to be out of it, living in a beautiful world that does not admit and cannot stand the light. What Marlow has learned through Kurtz he feels he must withhold from Kurtz's fiancée, for it is perilous to "the salvation of another soul." "I could not tell her," Marlow says; "It would have been too dark—too dark altogether."

For such a discovery the context of Africa is important and necessary. From the first pages this is impressed upon us. Marlow opens his tale suddenly and mysteriously, "And this too has been one of the dark places of the earth." The Romans who came to Britain, says Marlow with some irony, were men enough to face the darkness. In some inland post one of them felt the savagery that had closed round him, "that mysterious life of the wilderness that stirs in the forest, in the jungles, in the hearts of wild men." He has to live "in the midst of the incomprehensible, which is also detestable. And it has a fascination, too, that goes to work upon him. . . . Imagine the growing regrets, the longing to escape, the powerless disgust, the surrender, the hate!"

The importance of this kind of *milieu* is developed through both symbol and statement, and Marlow seems at times to suggest that Africa had been the cause of Kurtz's destruction. "It had caressed him . . . got into his veins, consumed his flesh, and sealed his soul to its own." But there can be no mistake: Kurtz is not a passive victim of Africa. Africa is like  existence, is truth. In contrast to the muddle and haze of the company's operations, Africa is real. The blacks have a vitality "that is as natural and true as the surf along the coast." And Marlow altogether prefers his crew of cannibals to his passengers. Ironically, what is dark in "darkest Africa" is not the land or the people, but the world introduced by the bringers of light and civilization.

In another sense, however, Africa seems dark. The jungle is "a rioting invasion of soundless life, a rolling wave of plants, piled up, crested, ready to topple over the creek, to sweep every little man of us out of his little existence." Africa seems dark because it is the test, the condition under which one can come into contact with the self. The journey to the heart of Africa is the journey into the depths of the self: Kurtz and Marlow travel into the heart of Africa and into the heart of man. The knowledge that is there is so terrifying that its occasion must seem sinister too.

In the depth of the jungle, Marlow tells us repeatedly, one is on one's own; there is no external restraint. "Anything can be done in this country." One feels, and Marlow says that one ought to feel, atavistic impulses, a "kinship with that wild passionate uproar." "If you were man enough you would admit to yourself that there was in you just the faintest trace of a response to the terrible frankness of that noise, a dim suspicion of there being a meaning which you so remote from the night of first ages could comprehend." Africa awakens "forgotten and brutal instincts . . . the memory of gratified and monstrous passions." It "whispered to him things about himself which he did not know, things of which he had no conception till he took counsel with this great solitude—and the whisper proved irresistibly fascinating." Outside some such context existence in its simplicity cannot be met. Too many things keep us from travelling into the interior of the self in which we exist.

> You can't understand. How could you?—with solid pavement under your feet, surrounded by kind neighbors ready to cheer you or to fall on you, stepping delicately between the butcher and the policeman, in the holy terror of scandal and gallows and lunatic asylums—how can

you imagine what particular region of the first ages a man's untrammelled feet may take him into by the way of solitude—utter solitude without a policeman—by the way of silence—utter silence, where no warning voice of a kind neighbor can be heard whispering of public opinion.

Kurtz's experience of the way of silence, the way of solitude, is like that of the mystics: the withdrawal from the world into silence and solitude to come into contact with the self. The solitude of the heart of Africa is symbolically appropriate for such an operation. Here Kurtz is free externally and internally. In the depths of Africa Kurtz is not hampered by outside restraint. Paralleling this he has journeyed into the depths of the primal self where there are no internal checks on his freedom. The setting of the discovery is aboriginal in the anthropological sense, and, more than this, it is aboriginal in a metaphysical sense. Kurtz's soul "being alone in the wilderness . . . had looked within itself, and by heavens! I tell you it had gone mad." For in the mind of man, which "contains all things," there are terrifying possibilities.

And the discovery of the self is the discovery of one's freedom. Away from the grooves that society provides for keeping us safely in a state of subsisting, we can discover that we are free to be, to do anything, good or evil. For the mystic it means the freedom to love God. For Kurtz it means the freedom to become his own diabolical god. This radical freedom as it exists in Kurtz seems to Marlow both exalting and revolting. Exalting because it makes man human, revolting because in Kurtz it is so perverted and so absolute as to exceed all human limits and become inhuman. By distinguishing these two aspects of Marlow's response, we can make meaningful his commitment to Kurtz. To put it another way, we can sum up the two aspects of Kurtz's freedom in the phrase "I am." On the one hand, to say "I am," is to say that I exist, to say that I am free and have immense possibilities in my grasp. On the other, "I am" is the phrase which only God can utter, because only God exists simply and completely. For Kurtz to say "I am" is the ultimate and complete assertion of himself to the exclusion of all else, the assertion that he is a god.

Before Kurtz's discovery of his existence can become Marlow's illumination it has to be realized by both of them. The revelation proceeds through Kurtz to Marlow, and Marlow's full illumination, his full realization of what it means to be, must wait upon a realization in Kurtz that brings out and confirms what Marlow has already seen in him. A final awareness in Kurtz is needed to make meaningful and universalize Kurtz's experience. For Kurtz has accepted his freedom, has become human, but he has not evaluated what being human means. He must assent to the knowledge he has been trying to keep off. This realization, which must be distinguished from the agonizing discovery of his existence, can come only as its fruit. Authentic self-knowledge demands a real existent as its object. Having discovered that he can exist,

Kurtz must now evaluate existence. "The horror! the horror" is this evaluation.

The most we can hope for in life, Marlow tells us, is "some knowledge of yourself—that comes too late." Marlow comes close to death and finds that he has nothing to say. Kurtz "had something to say. He said it. Since I had peeped over the edge myself, I understand better the meaning of his stare, that could not see the flame of the candle, but it was wide enough to embrace the whole universe, piercing enough to penetrate all the hearts that beat in the darkness."

Only after Marlow passes his final test, his brush with death, does the full significance of Kurtz come to him. Kurtz's last cry takes us to the meaning of the whole African venture for Marlow, the illumination he receives. For Marlow sees that Kurtz's cry is more than self-knowledge, more than an insight into the depths of his own evil. It is an insight into the potentialities in all men, it gives the perspective in which we must see Kurtz's discovery of himself. Kurtz's cry is no deathbed repentance which makes him a hero to whom Marlow can be loyal. It is for Marlow a terrible illumination, for in Kurtz Marlow discovers not simply one man become evil, but a universal possibility. Deprived of the insulation of society, the protecting surface, faced with the terrible challenge, we discover that we are free; the very fact is terrifying, for in that choice lies the unpredictable, even the Kurtzian.

Marlow's illumination comes only after Kurtz's last words and after Marlow's encounter with death; his choice of nightmares is not based on this evaluation. Marlow has chosen before Kurtz utters his cry, and the cry only enables Marlow to see more fully what he has already seen at the time of his choice. At the time he chooses Kurtz, Marlow declares that Kurtz is "remarkable," and to the end of the story he uses no stronger—indeed no other—epithet than this. Its occasional ironic uses only point up to its understatement. And "remarkable" is Marlow's comment on Kurtz's acceptance of his freedom.

And this is so remarkable that Marlow chooses it even in a man like Kurtz, a man who actualizes his existence only in the evil fulfilment of a monstrous megalomania. What Marlow values in Kurtz is both moral and non-moral. Moral because whether a man exists, has the capacity to act as a human being, is the most important moral fact about him. Non-moral because existence is prior to morality considered as a set of norms for acting and judging conduct. Kurtz's triumph is ontological. He existed as a human being capable of good and evil. His tragedy is moral, for he existed subject to no law or standard.

Marlow finds it hard to explain Kurtz and justify his own stand. He keeps telling his hearers, "You couldn't understand." His evaluation of Kurtz is presented through a series of contrasts and antitheses. The manager is a "flabby, pretending, weak-eyed devil," the brickmaker a "papier mâché Mephistopheles." Marlow prefers to these the devils of violence, greed, desire, for they are "strong, lusty, red-eyed devils, that sway and drive men," real devils that at least demand some commitment of the self. Kurtz is a genuine devil, a god in his Satanic rites. He can inspire horror and revulsion in Marlow, whereas the manager, neither feared nor loved, inspires only "uneasiness." Kurtz commits himself totally to evil, the manager keeps up appearances. Kurtz throws himself into action, though evil; the manager, ruled by caution, murmurs, and does evil by omission.

What is evil in the manager and his men is not their conniving, their opportunism, their neglect of Kurtz, but their moral impotence. In Kurtz evil is incarnate. In the company-men evil is a privation, not of goodness but of existence. Marlow condemns them on ontological as much as moral grounds. Too self-loving, too much the victims of their own life-killing prudence for a surrender even to evil, they are, like Leon Bloy's middle class, incapable of mortal sin. They are not evil, for they are not even alive, not capable of the humanity involved in making a choice for good or evil. Kurtz has made the journey to the depths of the self, he has responded to the fascinating and terrible appeal of existence. His choice is for evil, but it is a human choice—and it is to this humanity that Marlow turns with positive relief, even though it is a nightmare.

And it is a nightmare of enormous proportions. Kurtz fails so horribly because he has no "inborn strength," no capacity for faithfulness, no code. Marlow's usual term for this is "restraint." The more one has realized himself, and become capable of all things, the more restraint is needed. And Marlow makes a great deal of restraint. He is amazed at the restraint in the cannibals that keeps them from eating the pilgrims. The manager's restraint, keeping up appearances, is but a parody that excites Marlow's scorn and makes the manager worse than Kurtz. The accountant immaculately dressed amidst moral and physical disintegration, keeping his books in apple pie order though a dying man lies on the floor, is admirable because he has some order, some code, some commitment outside the self. This is why the seamanship manual, with its "simple-hearted devotion to the right way of doing things," seems so precious to Marlow; it is a symbol of the restraint, the devotion, that both Kurtz and the manager lack.

Neither Kurtz with his abandon, nor the manager with his getting on in the world, has this restraint, this "devotion to the backbreaking business" rather than to the self. The self unharnessed must be used in terms of something outside itself. Better live by an absurd code, like the accountant, than by none at all. As Marlow says, "What redeems it is the idea only . . . an unselfish belief in the idea—something you can set up, and bow down before, and offer a sacrifice to." Marlow is ironic when he applies the phrase to the Romans, but the irony is lifted as the story progresses. And in Kurtz's final cry the "idea" becomes part of Marlow's illumination. Kurtz, living outside all norms, yet knows that they exist and condemn him. Implicit in his cry is an admission of what he has evaded, a realization of the insufficiency of his total commitment to himself and of the validity of the standards which condemn him. And through Kurtz, Marlow, the seaman who has always lived by a code, grasps its necessity and its validity.[3]

This is the last stage of Marlow's initiation, of his confrontation with what it means to be human. Kurtz is the grail at the end of Marlow's quest, and of all those who come into contact with Kurtz only Marlow—the faithful pilgrim—experiences an illumination. The manager reduces Kurtz to his own terms and cannot see him. The Russian sailor, who admires Kurtz, is too much a fool—perhaps a wise fool—to recognize the challenge that Kurtz has met. The two women each see and love Kurtz, but a false Kurtz, a lie, which Marlow must meet with another lie.

Most people are not capable of understanding Kurtz; the policeman and the two good addresses shelter them from the terror of being. But Marlow has had his illumination, and like Gulliver come back to England, he cannot stand the smug faces of the people walking down the streets, unaware of the challenge and the danger. Their knowledge of life seems "an irritating pretense." They do not know that they are and therefore they are not. Marlow scorns them because in the quest for Kurtz he has discovered the dreadful burden of human freedom. His full illumination, his grail, is not transcendent being but the heart of man. Yet it demands the same tests in the journey of purification and produces an illumination equally awful. (1955)

### NOTES

1. Cf. Wilfred S. Dowden, "The Light and the Dark Imagery and Thematic Development in Conrad's 'Heart of Darkness,'" *Rice Institute Pamphlet,* XLIV (April 1957), 33-51. [Editor's note]

2. In "Tragic Pattern in Conrad's 'Heart of Darkness,'" *College English,* VI (1944), Leonard Dean sees Marlow as a static character: "In fact, Marlow's moral insight appears to be nearly as penetrating at the beginning of his journey as at the end. It was perhaps inevitable, given his artistic function, that he should be a static character." With this interpretation Stewart C. Wilcox, in an essay on "Heart of Darkness" forthcoming (at this writing) in *Philosophical Quarterly,* takes issue. "It is not true, however, that Marlow has merely been an observer of Kurtz or that his character is static. . . . Kurtz is his double whom he must face in order to know himself, and he has been tainted by the evil which he must learn before he can transcend it, for circumstances tempt him into becoming a Pharisaical Pilgrim." [Editor's note]

3. That it can be interpreted as a Freudian allegory testifies to the richness and validity of Conrad's story. Kurtz is like the id, the unharnessed primal forces. The manager represents a crushing amount of super-ego that destroys life by its timid and fearful unwillingess to release and use those forces. Marlow, at least at the end of the story, stands for ego, an awareness of the forces within him and a conscious use and control of them. His journey is a symbol of the process through which we discover the deepest recesses of the self and make use of its power. Whether the whole story could be adequately described in terms of some such allegory I do not know; certainly, much of the imagery of darkness and the jungle makes sense in those terms.

LILLIAN FEDER

# Marlow's Descent Into Hell*

MARLOW'S JOURNEY in Conrad's "Heart of Darkness" is usually interpreted as a study of a descent into the unconscious self.[1] Of course, the
voyage into the heart of darkness is, on one level, a symbolic representation of an exploration of the hidden self and therefore of man's capacity
for evil. However, Conrad is not merely narrating a psychological experience; he is dealing with a significant moral conflict. If this were
simply a story concerned with the two aspects of the mind of man, the
conscious and the unconscious, what would be Conrad's point in treating
so extensively the condition of the natives in the Congo? Moreover, without studying some of Conrad's most powerful and most consistent
imagery, it is impossible to explain the role of Kurtz's "Intended," which is
important in the development of the theme. In "Heart of Darkness,"
Conrad is depicting Marlow's discovery of evil and the responsibilities
to himself and to others which this knowledge places upon him. In telling
the story of Marlow's attainment of self-knowledge, Conrad does not
use the language of psychology. Instead, he employs the imagery and
symbolism of the traditional voyage into Hades.

By associating Marlow's journey with the descent into hell, Conrad
concretizes the hidden world of the inner self. Through image and
symbol, he evokes the well-known voyage of the hero who, in ancient
epic, explores the lower world and, in so doing, probes the depths of his
own and his nation's conscience. A study of "Heart of Darkness" from
this point of view discloses some interesting parallels, but, more important,
by setting Conrad's story in relief against a background rich in associations, it reveals the essential unity of his political and personal themes.
Moreover, such a reading shows how Conrad, by combining the traditional imagery of the epic descent with realistic details from his own
experience in the Congo, created an image of hell credible to modern
man.

Though Marlow's journey recalls the epic descent in general, it is
most specifically related to the visit to Hades in the sixth book of the
*Aeneid*. In Vergil's poem, Aeneas' descent is part of his initiation for the
role of leader of the Roman people. Vergil emphasizes the fact that
truth is to be found in the heart of darkness; thus, the Sibyl who, in
Vergil's words, "obscuris vera involvens" (hides truth in darkness),
guides Aeneas. Moreover, just as Aeneas is about to enter Hades, Vergil
interrupts his narrative to ask the very elements of hell, Chaos and
Phlegethon, to allow him to reveal the secrets buried in the darkness
and depths of the earth. Aeneas' voyage to Hades is one means by which
he learns of the tragedy implicit in the affairs of men; this is the price
he pays for fulfilling his duty as founder of Rome. In the lower world

* From *Nineteenth-Century Fiction*, IX (March 1955), 280-292.

he looks both into past and the future and, having observed the penalties for personal crimes, he is told of the bloodshed and cruelty which are to weigh on the conscience of his nation—the cost of Rome's imperial power. Aeneas, the pious and worthy man, learns truth through a descent into darkness.

The basic similarity between Marlow's journey and that of the epic hero, the descent to find light, is obvious. There are many close parallels between the two voyages, however, which must be demonstrated.

At the beginning of the sixth book of the *Aeneid,* just before Aeneas descends to Hades, Vergil creates an atmosphere of pervading gloom. He speaks of the "gloomy woods" (VI, 238), and repeats the phrase "per umbram" (through the gloom) (VI, 257, 268), in setting the scene for Aeneas' entrance to Hades. Conrad too establishes this somber mood. Even before Marlow begins his story, Conrad repeats the word "gloom" continuously in his description of the friends gathered together to hear the tale. Thus, in the second papagraph of the story he mentions a "mournful gloom" (p. 490);[2] in the third, "the brooding gloom" (p. 490); in the fourth, "the gloom to the west" (p. 491); in the fifth, "the gloom brooding" (p. 491); and in the seventh, once more "a brooding gloom" (p. 493). Marlow, sitting there like an idol, seems to have brought with him the atmosphere of the world he is about to recreate for his friends.

Just before he begins his story, Marlow, looking out at the Thames, mentions the Romans and their conquest of England. "They were men enough to face the darkness," he says. "They were conquerors." He then goes on to speak of the brutality of the Romans: "It was just robbery with violence, aggravated murder on a great scale. . . ." Conquest, he says, "is not a pretty thing. . . . What redeems is the ideal only. An idea at the back of it; not a sentimental pretence but an idea; and an unselfish belief in the idea—something you can set up, and bow down before, and offer a sacrifice to" (pp. 494-496).

Implicit in Marlow's remarks is the theme of the *Aeneid,* for Vergil is concerned with this "idea," the heroic goal as justification for Rome's plunder and cruelty; moreover, Conrad, like Vergil, sees the tragic limitations of those dedicated to the heroic ideal. Thus, at the very beginning of "Heart of Darkness," the Roman legend, prophesied and justified in Hades, provides an archetypal background for Kurtz's deeds and for Marlow's discovery of himself in a hell perhaps more terrible than Vergil's, but no less enlightening.

Before Marlow may descend into the heart of darkness, he must, like the epic hero, perform certain duties. His visit to the company office suggests a necessary rite performed before the fateful journey. The city itself "makes [him] think of a whited sepulcher"; the office is in "a narrow and deserted street in deep shadow," and there is "a dead silence" (p. 500). The house itself is "as still as a house in the city of the dead" (p. 502). Thus, Conrad creates the deathly gloom of the world Marlow is about to enter.

In the company office, two women are knitting black wool. Conrad plainly uses these women to symbolize the fates, who, like Aeneas' guide, the Sibyl of Cumae, know the secrets of the heart of darkness. Marlow feels uneasy during these "ceremonies" (p. 501). He describes one of the two knitting women:

> . . . a cat reposed on her lap. She wore a starched white affair on her head, had a wart on one cheek, and silver-rimmed spectacles hung on the tip of her nose. She glanced at me above the glasses. The swift and indifferent placidity of that look troubled me.

She seems to know everything. Marlow goes on to say, "An eerie feeling came over me. She seemed uncanny and fateful" (p. 501). Like the Cumaean Sibyl, the two women guard the way to hell.

> Often far away there I thought of these two, guarding the door of darkness, knitting black wool as for a warm pall, one introducing, introducing continuously to the unknown, the other scrutinizing the cheery and foolish faces with unconcerned old eyes (pp. 501–502).

Then Marlow uses the Latin farewell, evoking its literary and legendary associations: "Ave! old knitter of black wool. *Morituri te salutant*" (p. 502). Conrad uses images of death, but they do not suggest actual death so much as they do the legendary world of the dead, where, paradoxically, the affairs of the living are interpreted and understood. When he is finally ready to leave, Marlow says that he feels as though "instead of going to the center of a continent," he is "about to set off for the center of the earth" (p. 504).

But before he may descend into the heart of darkness, Marlow has another duty to perform. Like Aeneas, he must attend to the remains of someone who has died. Aeneas has buried Misenus, a former comrade (VI, 149–182), and Marlow tries to recover the remains of Fresleven, his predecessor. Marlow feels compelled to perform this rite. "Nobody seemed to trouble much about Fresleven's remains, till I got out and stepped into his shoes," he says. "I couldn't let it rest though. . . ." (p. 499).

In Marlow's first observations about the Congo, he uses the imagery of hell. Thus, the members of the "chain gang" seem to him to have a "deathlike indifference" (p. 509); strolling into the shade, he says, "It seemed to me that I had stepped into the gloomy circle of some inferno" (p. 510). "Inferno," of course, suggests the Christian hell as well as the Latin "Inferna," but Conrad's development of the image is so like Vergil's description of Hades in the *Aeneid* that it seems to evoke the classical hell more readily than the Christian one. His depiction of the natives in the jungle is like Vergil's description of the tormented shades in Hades: "Black shapes crouched, lay, sat between the trees leaning against the trunks," and, like the figures at the entrance to Vergil's Hades, their very attitudes express "pain, abandonment, and despair." Like Vergil's "Diseases . . . Famine . . . and Poverty (terrible shapes to see)" (VI, 275–277), Conrad's figures are "nothing earthly now, nothing but black shadows of disease and starvation, lying confusedly in the greenish gloom." "They are moribund shapes," like suffering shades in hell, "free as air—and nearly as thin." Upset by the sight of one of these men and "his brother phantom," Marlow says, "I don't want any more lingering in the shade," and he returns to the station, but even there, surrounded by the symbols of civilization, the well-dressed agents and their well-kept books, he is aware of "the grove of death" (pp. 510–514).

Up to this point, Conrad has employed the associations of Hades to build up suspense, to tell the reader indirectly that this is no ordinary voyage. He had exploited the strangeness, the mystery, and the pathos of the ancient symbol of hell. Now he uses it with a new brilliance to suggest not only mystery but evil as well. Moreover, through this symbol, he suggests the tragic proportions of his theme and his characters. While he waits at the station, the wilderness surrounding it seems to Marlow "great and invincible, like evil or truth," and when one night a grass shed containing calico and beads bursts into flames, Marlow says that it seemed as if "the earth had opened to let an avenging fire consume all that trash" (p. 520).

As Marlow goes deeper and deeper into the jungle, the image of hell is intensified, until finally hell and the Congo are equated. Once again there are interesting comparisons between Vergil and Conrad. The ambiguous sign "Approach cautiously" (p. 542), which, Marlow explains, has little practical use since it could only be found after one had reached the place where it is inscribed, is reminiscent of the Sibyl's warning: "facilis descensus Averno . . . Sed revocare gradum superasque evadere ad auras,/Hoc opus, hic labor est" (VI, 126–129). The descent into Avernus is easy, but to return into the upper air, this is the task, this the struggle.

When Aeneas first enters Hades, Vergil compares the underworld with a forest (VI, 270–271). To reach the lowest depths of Erebus, Aeneas must take a journey down the river Styx, which is surrounded by marshes. The boat seems unfit for the journey, but finally Aeneas steps out on the mud and sedge of the shore (VI, 411–416). Vergil's description of this journey is brief, but he creates an atmosphere of gloom and ugliness very like that which Conrad suggests in his extended account of Marlow's voyage into the heart of darkness. Marlow too has a difficult voyage on a boat that is unsuited to the journey. He and his companions seem like "phantoms," and the earth seems "unearthly." The "black and incomprehensible frenzy" he approaches is at once the jungle, the region of "pre-historic man," and the depths of hell which Kurtz has created and in which he has been destroyed (pp. 537–540). When Marlow has penetrated the jungle, even the natural world seems unearthly. The trees seem to be "changed into stone." He describes his feelings: "It was not sleep—it seemed unnatural, like a state of trance." The mournful cries of the natives are reminiscent of the groans of the shades in hell. To

Marlow, "the rest of the world was nowhere. . . . Gone, disappeared; swept off without leaving a whisper or a shadow behind" (pp. 544–546).

When he has almost reached the heart of darkness, Marlow loses his helmsman. Here again Conrad seems to be following Vergil, for Aeneas too loses his helmsman, Palinurus, just as his ship is approaching the shore of Cumae. Palinurus loses his balance and falls overboard; when he has swum to safety, "barbarous people attack [him] with swords," and he is killed, his body floating into the sea (VI, 349–362). Marlow's helmsman is killed by a native's spear, and he is buried in the sea. Both die "insontes" (guiltless), loyal to their leaders. Aeneas, meeting the shade of Palinurus in Hades, learns of the tragic sacrifice for his mission, and Marlow feels in the dying look of his helmsman a profound intimacy which he cannot forget, for it is a personal tie with one of the victims sacrificed to the "emissaries of light." Even more than the groans of the natives, the dying helmsman's last insight, innocent and profound, suggests the tragic consequences of Kurtz's betrayal.

In dealing with Kurtz, Conrad constantly repeats the imagery of hell. Marlow speaks of how the jungle has "sealed his soul to its own by the inconceivable ceremonies of some devilish initiation," and wonders "how many powers of darkness claimed him for their own." Marlow says of Kurtz, "He had taken a high seat amongst the devils of the land—" and insists "I mean literally" (p. 559), thus using Kurtz as a symbol for the triumphant evil powers of hell. Yet Kurtz, at the same time that he symbolizes the spirit of evil, must keep his identity as a man. It is significant that at this point Conrad shifts his image from one associated with the Christian view of hell to one out of the classical Hades. Thus, he goes on to refer to Kurtz not as a devil but as a shade, and, by using the Homeric and Vergilian word for the soul in Hades, he suggests that Kurtz has had a previous existence. Marlow says, "I am trying to account to myself for—for—Mr. Kurtz—" But even his name seems the wrong title for him, and Marlow ends his sentence with "for the shade of Mr. Kurtz." He continues, "This initiated wraith from the back of Nowhere honored me with its amazing confidence before it vanished altogether." He refers to Kurtz or Kurtz's shade as "it" (pp. 560–561).

In Marlow's refusal to hear the details of Kurtz's atrocious ceremonies, Conrad emphasizes again his image of hell. Marlow says that these details would be more "intolerable" than even the heads on the stakes, for "that was only a savage sight," a sight not untypical of a real jungle. However, what Marlow fears is his feeling of being "transported into some lightless region of subtle horrors, where pure, uncomplicated savagery was a positive relief, being something that had a right to exist— obviously—in the sunshine" (p. 574). Thus, Conrad contrasts the real jungle with the habitat of Kurtz, and the savagery of reality is a relief from the horrors of Kurtz's hell.

Not only Kurtz, but everyone around him, seems to have both an actual existence in the Congo and a symbolic one in Hades. The natives are described as "dark human shapes" not moving but "flitting indistinctly against the gloomy border of the forest"; the native woman is a "wild and gorgeous apparition of a woman" (p. 577). And Kurtz becomes, as the climax of his career approaches, more and more the creature of hell.

Marlow is eager to deal with Kurtz, or as he refers to him, with "this shadow," and he follows him into the depths of the jungle where he is participating in his fiendish rites. In the description of their meeting, Conrad evokes again and again the associations of Hades. As Marlow approaches, Kurtz rises "unsteady, long, pale, indistinct, like a vapor exhaled by the earth, and swayed slightly, misty and silent." The setting is hell itself, with fires looming between the trees and a constant murmur of voices. "A fiend-like" figure appears. At this point Conrad refers to Kurtz as "that Shadow," this time capitalizing the initial letter, as one does in a name, for Kurtz here is a shade of hell, "this wandering and tormented thing."

Moreover, Marlow has one means of controlling Kurtz: the threat, "you will be lost, . . . utterly lost," doomed to hell entirely. These words draw Kurtz back, but even so Marlow, regarding him, says, "I before him did not know whether I stood on the ground or floated in the air," for they have not left hell (pp. 583–586). Indeed, the journey next day merely reiterates the image. The crowd "flowed out of the woods again," and, like the wretched shades of Vergil's Hades watching Aeneas' boat, they stood on the shore murmuring and gesturing (p. 587). And the native woman, like Vergil's shades who "tendebant [que] manus" (stretched out their hands), pleading to be taken aboard (VI, 314), "stretched tragically her bare arms after us over the somber and glittering river" (p. 588).

When Kurtz speaks, Marlow feels that some "supernatural power" has forced the words from him, for even on shipboard Kurtz is described as a "shade"; Marlow says that the "shade" of the original Kurtz "frequented the bedside of the hollow sham" he had become. Thus he implies that the original Kurtz, with all his lofty "ideas," his "station," his "career," and his "Intended," was but a "shade," impotent even at the height of his career. Now he is reduced to a "hollow sham" of his once noble ideal of himself. Marlow too even as he leaves the Congo is still under its influence. He accepts "the choice of nightmares forced upon [him] in the tenebrous land invaded by these mean and greedy phantoms" (pp. 588–589).

Kurtz's last cry, "The horror," does not indicate that he has had a last-minute conversion. Instead, it is another means by which Conrad implies that this lost soul, this dark shade, is also a man. If Kurtz did not retain at least enough humanity to be horrified by a last glimpse at his own life, then what meaning could his disintegration have? As Conrad distinguishes between the actual jungle and Kurtz's jungle which has become a hell, so he distinguishes between the man Kurtz once was and the creature he has become, who retains just enough humanity to cry out in horror.

Even Marlow's memory of Kurtz after his death is different from "the other memories of the dead that accumulate in every man's life." Kurtz returns to Marlow as a remembrance of a shade in hell and as a suggestion of eternal torment and gloom, "a shadow darker than the shadow of the night. . . ." (p. 597). Entering the home of Kurtz's "Intended," Marlow feels that he carries with him the gloom and terror of the heart of darkness.

> The vision seemed to enter the house with me—the stretcher, the phantom bearers, the wild crowd of obedient worshippers, the gloom of the forests, the glitter of the reach between the murky bends, the beat of the drum, regular and muffled like the beating of a heart—the heart of a conquering darkness (p. 597).

Moreover, Kurtz's "Intended" is portrayed as no ordinary young woman; she too seems part of the lower world. She lives not in the jungle of Kurtz's hell, but in "a street as still and decorous as a well-kept alley in a cemetery," in a room whose windows are "like three luminous and bedraped columns," and whose piano is "like a somber and polished sarcophogus." This lady with her "pale head," who comes "floating" toward Marlow "in the dusk," her brow "surrounded by an ashy halo" has withdrawn from life to guard the memory of Kurtz (pp. 597–598). She is given no name except the abstraction, "the Intended," for she has no existence apart from Kurtz. Through his imagery Conrad suggests that she inhabits her own section of Hades, the section devoted to the patient and disappointed shades who carry on their own "mysteries" (p. 599).

Marlow's visit to this lady is the last lap of his journey to Hades. She recalls for him the "eternal darkness" despite the fact that hers is a faith with an "unearthly glow." Speaking to her, Marlow is certain that he will remember the "eloquent phantom," Kurtz, as long as he lives, and he will remember her too, a "tragic and familiar Shade, resembling," in her last traditional gesture of the longing shade, her arms stretched out, "another one, tragic also, and bedecked with powerless charms, stretching bare brown arms over the glitter of the infernal stream, the stream of darkness" (p. 602). Through the image of the "infernal stream," Conrad unites these two shades. On each side of the stream of hell, without understanding, they devote themselves to the darkness Kurtz has created.

I have demonstrated the extent and consistency of Conrad's use of the imagery of hell to suggest Kurtz's world and his influence. My reading offers no new interpretation of the story as a whole, but rather an extension of a long accepted view. It is fairly obvious that "Heart of Darkness" has three levels of meaning: on one level it is the story of a man's adventures; on another, of his discovery of certain political and social injustices; and on a third, it is a study of his initiation into the mysteries of his own mind. The same three levels of meaning can be found in the sixth book of Vergil's *Aeneid*. Like Aeneas, Marlow comes to understand himself, his obligations, and the tragic limitations involved in any choice through this three-fold experience. Kurtz, like Aeneas, starts out as an "emissary of light," but, unlike Vergil's hero, he cannot conquer himself. Through Kurtz's experience, Marlow learns that a man is defined by his work: Kurtz's work has created a hell in the jungle, which destroys him. The symbol of the lower world suggests not only an imaginative union between the ancient world and the modern one, but a judgment on the morality of modern society.

From its beginning, Marlow's journey seems fated. He is destined by the needs of his own spirit, which Conrad concretizes in his response to the knitting "fates," to understand himself through a study of the world he lives in. By viewing that world indirectly, through an image, Marlow comes to closer grips with it than he has ever before been able to.

The epic descent is always a journey to find someone who knows the truth. Marlow realizes long before he has penetrated the Congo that the real purpose of his journey is to meet Kurtz and talk with him. When he discovers Kurtz, he finds, on one level, a man who has committed unspeakable crimes against his fellows. But on another and more important level, he finds a man who has allowed himself to sink to the lowest possible depths of evil, and, by observing Kurtz, Marlow realizes that in all men there is this possibility. In other words, he discovers the potential hell in the heart of every man.

In the Congo, there are no supernatural beings; all is credible on a purely realistic level. However, the imagery of hell, with its suggestion of the supernatural, implies the terror and violent suffering which Kurtz, the betrayer of light, must face. And, through the imagery of hell, Conrad makes Kurtz's struggle in the Congo symbolic of an inner defeat. Kurtz, on the one hand, has betrayed the natives and reduced them to poverty and subservience, but he has also betrayed the humanity in himself. He has reduced the natives to tormented shades, for he has robbed them of a living will and dignity and, in so doing, he has himself become a shade; his will is the victim and servant of his own hellish whims.

Marlow too has faced the terrors of hell, and, though he escapes, he learns wisdom at a price. He owes a debt to Kurtz, for Kurtz has been man enough to face the hell within him. Unlike the agents who turn away from the challenge of hell, Kurtz has gone all too far in his weird exploration. Through Kurtz's failure, Marlow learns about his own capacity for evil and his capacity to resist it. He realizes that without involvement, there is no restraint, and he makes his choice of "nightmares." He is even willing to experience a kind of spiritual death in the sacrifice of lying for Kurtz. Ironically, the reward of his victory over the elements of hell is his knowledge of human limitation; thus, while he repudiates Kurtz, he remains loyal to him. In this loyalty there is an acknowledgement of the eternal existence of the hell within, to be met and conquered again and again by every man; moreover, there is the tragic acceptance of the eternal possibility of defeat.

I have said that Kurtz's "Intended" is as much a shade as Kurtz is. Indeed, Conrad calls her by that name and identifies her, through his imagery, with the world of the dead. She, like the natives, has sacrificed all that is living in order to believe in Kurtz. Marlow refers to her at one point ironically as such a "thunderingly exalted creature as to be altogether deaf and blind to anything but heavenly sights and sounds." For such a person, the "earth . . . is only a standing place." By contrast, he says, for most people, the earth "is a place to *live* in, where we must put up with sights, with sounds, with smells, too, by Jove!—breathe dead hippo, so to speak, and not be contaminated" (p. 560). Kurtz's "Intended" sacrifices life to a dead ideal. She has not breathed "dead hippo"; she has not faced the darkness. Like Kurtz, she has chosen death. He has been conquered by his inhuman guilt; she by her inhuman innocence, by her unwillingness to pay the price of life, the acceptance of a knowledge of ugliness and evil. Marlow does not disillusion her, in part because of his loyalty to Kurtz, and in part because of the futility of telling the truth, brutal and ugly, like the "dead hippo" or the sights, sounds, and smells of the world, to a woman who, because of her unwillingness to face life, has become a shade. Thus, when she asks Marlow for Kurtz's last word, instead of repeating Kurtz's remark, "The horror," Marlow says that the last word he pronounced was her name. This is his final tribute to the world of the dead, his last "ceremony." For this reason the lie has a taint of mortality for him.

Speaking of the artist, Conrad says that "he must descend within himself, and in that lonely region of stress and strife, if he be deserving and fortunate, he finds the terms of his appeal."[3] And in *Victory,* he says, "It is not poets alone who dare descend into the abyss of infernal regions, or even who dream of such a descent."[4] In "Heart of Darkness" Conrad used the imagery and symbolism of Hades to create that otherwise formless region into which not only the artist but every man must descend if he wishes to understand himself. Moreover, through the imagery of hell, with its timeless associations, the private struggle is united with man's public deeds, his responsibilities, and his history.          (1955)

## NOTES

1. Notably by Albert J. Guerard in *Joseph Conrad* (New Directions, 1947) and in his Introduction to the Signet Edition of "Heart of Darkness" and "The Secret Sharer" (1950). [Editor's note]

2. All quotations from "Heart of Darkness" are taken from *The Portable Conrad,* ed. Morton Dauwen Zabel (New York, 1947), pp. 490-603.

3. *The Portable Conrad,* p. 706.

4. *Victory,* The Modern Library ed. (New York, n.d.), p. 207.

ROBERT O. EVANS

# Conrad's Underworld*

WHEN T. S. Eliot prefaced "The Hollow Men" with the memorable, if
brief, quotation from Conrad's "Heart of Darkness," "Mistah Kurtz—he
dead," he was commenting, for his own reasons, on the finality of Kurtz's
descent into the underworld, much as preachers have been known to
indicate Hell as the reward for sinful life. But the poem does not really
deal much with "lost, violent souls," but rather with the "stuffed men,"
a category to which Conrad's Marlow perhaps belonged before he made
his journey up the great river in Hades. It is not entirely clear from the
story whether Kurtz also began as one of the "hollow men" or not, but
that point is not important, for Conrad's hero is Marlow, and the story
deals with change in his character. Kurtz enters the picture, as it were,
only incidentally at the end as an agent in Marlow's acquisition of knowledge. The "Heart of Darkness," like Eliot's poem, is written for the futile
ones "gathered on this beach of the tumid river"; it is not much concerned
with eternal damnation in the sense that the inhabitants of Dante's
*Inferno* are dead and have gathered their deserts. The story is developed
in terms of symbols, and it is, of course, not always possible to distinguish
a clear separation between the symbolic and literal levels of meaning.
For instance, Kurtz is plainly alive when Marlow begins his journey
and still alive when Marlow reaches him, but symbolically there is no
doubt that he is the arch-inhabitant of Hell or that Marlow, too, has been
journeying through Hell, much as Dante did in the *Inferno.* Superficially
there are differences; for example, Marlow travels alone while Dante had
Virgil for his guide. But that Africa represents Hell and the great river,
Acheron, Phlegethon, Styx, or all the rivers of Hell together is a traditional interpretation of the story.

Recently Miss Lillian Feder has pointed out a number of significant
parallels with Virgil's descent in the sixth book of the *Aeneid,* but the
"Heart of Darkness" is more than a reworking of an old theme in modern
guise.[1] There is no question that Conrad employed epic machinery borrowed from Virgil. Essentially the story is neither a recitation of Kurtz's
awful degradation nor the simple history of Marlow's enlightenment. It
is a journey through the underworld, for purposes of instruction as well
as entertainment, calculated to bring into focus Conrad's moral vision,
as it affects the mass of humanity struggling on the brink of the "tumid
river." The story is really concerned with modern ethical and spiritual
values and has far more significance for the reader than any transmutation
of Virgil's descent could have. Clearly it was not possible for Conrad,
writing in the twentieth century, to view the world with a disregard for
Christian ethics, as Virgil had to do. Accordingly one would expect Conrad

* From *Modern Fiction Studies,* II (May 1956), pp. 56-62.

to have a deeper significance than Virgil. Moreover, as one of his main themes, the descent into Hell, was not Virgil's exclusive property, it would not seem likely that Conrad should owe Virgil more than Dante, or even Milton. I shall attempt to show that he did in fact make extensive use of the *Inferno* in the general structure of the story, and by his adoption of epic techniques and epic themes he accomplished something almost unique in the short story, or novelette. The "Heart of Darkness" is not the apex of a genre but rather a special use of form towards which Conrad had been painfully working in order to express his particular, ethical view of the universe.

It is not necessary to review the broad parallels with the *Aeneid* here. Much of the Virgilian machinery is commonplace anyhow. Perhaps it is an overstatement of the case to point out, as Miss Feder does, that when "Aeneas first enters Hades, Virgil compares the underworld with a forest" (VI, 270–271), for Dante, too, woke to find himself "lost in a dark wood." The rivers of Hell belong to every myth. The knitters of black wool in the company offices may resemble the Cumaean Sibyl, but they are not entirely unlike Milton's guardians, Sin and Death, and the difference in their ages suggests such a relationship. Nevertheless, Conrad does appear to draw on Virgil as well as other sources. He may use a Latin farewell, "Ave! old knitter of black wool," but he also makes statements like Marlow's, that he felt as if he "were about to set off for the center of the earth," a direction that seems more closely related to Dante's cosmology than to Virgil's.

From the beginning of the story there is little question where Marlow's journey will lead him, but, as Miss Feder says, the Hell into which Marlow descends is legendary rather than an actual place. This problem of how to give Hell being without the same sense of existence that Dante experienced is one of the most difficult a modern artist can face. One knows it is there, but where exactly is it? As Graham Greene recognized, "there are a thousand names for it, King Solomon's mines, the 'heart of darkness' if one is romantically inclined . . . [etc.]" (*Journey Without Maps,* p. 8). Conrad solves his enigma by deft manipulation of symbols and imagery. Marlow, looking at a map of his projected journey, remarks that he is "going into the yellow—dead in the center." But as the symbolic level of meaning shifts slightly, most of the other references to Hell are described as properly black. Marlow's appointment is to replace a man who was killed in an argument over two "black hens," an image carefully related to the two females that surround Kurtz. The knitters are working "black wool." Marlow's first contact with the natives is with black men, whose loins are bound in "black rags." The single, outstanding descriptive detail about the European traders is their "black mustaches." The background of Kurtz's mysterious painting was "almost black—somber." The river is black; "there were shiny patches on the black creek." Even the natives' confidence is a "black display." Thoughts are black. And again, later, the men themselves are no more than grains of sand in a "black Sahara." Conrad colors Hell rightly but only after making it clear, partly through imagery, that it is not a literal place.

Perhaps the author's use of the *Inferno* is not quite so explicit as that of the *Aeneid*, but it is probably more important to the development of the story. In the first place, besides being shorter, Virgil's journey is ideologically simpler than Dante's, and the progression into the underworld in the sixth book of the *Aeneid* is accomplished at a fairly steady rate, while Dante's journey is interrupted; that is, he travels and then stops and comments, continues, and so on. In these respects "Heart of Darkness" is more closely modelled on the Italian epic than on the Latin original. But it is the epic nature of the story that is important; throughout Conrad makes considerable use of epic machinery. For example, the story begins *in media res,* but the scene on shipboard in the estuary of the Thames, in sharp contrast to the opening scene of, say, Galsworthy's "The Apple Tree," is no mere enveloping action; it is as much an integral portion of the story as the initial scene of the *Odyssey*. Moreover, as Conrad's vision is ethical, he takes pains to connect the Thames with the great river in Africa, thus implying that Marlow's experience is meaningful for the modern world. But Conrad does not allow his meaning to rest on a subtle implication; he troubles to explain that this is no simple sea-yarn. It lacks, he says, the "direct simplicity, the whole meaning of which lies within the shell of a cracker nut . . . Marlow was not typical [i. e. of the spinners of sea stories]." This is also a clear statement that the story must not be read literally. Despite the complex symbolism almost everything is in the foreground; Conrad takes a few chances on the readers' imaginations. He once said that it was the duty of the artist to make the reader "see." An early example of his foreground technique occurs when he has Marlow inform the assembled company that the Thames, too, "has been one of the dark places of the earth." A veneer of civilization has perhaps brought some light to England, but I am inclined to believe that Conrad's choice of tense, *has been,* is at least partly ironical, for later, though he specifically avoids attacking British civilization in this story, it becomes clear that his opinion of western culture is not high. Readers of *Victory* may recall how stinging he could be when he wished. But the artistic technique of placing nearly everything in the foreground may, in some fashion, be responsible for the shallow interpretation of the story that has arisen, that it is little more than an attack on British imperialism. I have no doubt that Conrad lacked enthusiasm for colonial policy, as his Congo Diary[2] reveals, but in this work he specifically avoids attacking it.

Instead he uses epic machinery to elucidate his ethical purpose. He goes to what might have been, in the hands of a lesser artist, absurd lengths to incorporate epic qualities. For example, near the beginning of the story there is the familiar list of ships, starting with the *Golden Hind* but ending, significantly I think, with *Erebus* and *Terror*. These men-of-war are appropriate for "Heart of Darkness." Still, it is interesting to compare the passage with Masefield's realistic poem. Conrad has nothing to say here about the "dirty British coaster . . . laden with pig iron and cheap tin trays." As with colonial policy, he is concerned with the shabbiness of modern life only where it cuts across his moral vision.

It is not easy to determine exactly how closely Conrad relied on Dante. I do not mean to imply that he has slavishly enlisted under any master, but the structure of the "Heart of Darkness," at least from the moment of Marlow's arrival at the first station on the African coast, closely resembles a skeletalized version of the *Inferno*. And even prior to Marlow's landing the characters in the story would appear to fit nicely into Dante's threshold to Hell. Perhaps the knitters of black wool are slightly misplaced; Dante might have introduced them earlier. The directors themselves, though they do not realize it, belong in the Vestibule, as men whose lives have warranted neither great infamy nor great praise. Seamen who have abandoned the sea, they are now businessmen. They seem to fit, as Miss Sayers says, into "the Vestibule . . . the abode of the weathercock mind, the vague tolerance which will neither approve nor condemn, the cautious cowardice for which no decision is ever final." Conrad does not openly lay these charges on the directors, for the initial scene is one of the few places in the story where everything is not in the foreground. But of the whole group only Marlow is shown to have adhered to the true purpose of life, the development of ethical insight, and he is the only one who still follows the sea, a distinction of symbolic importance. Actually Marlow has little space to devote to the directors; they serve as Marlow's audience, but they are not the audience the author is trying to convince. "Heart of Darkness" is not their story. They are really incapable of understanding it, as Conrad suggests when he puts in the narrator's mouth the insipid remark, "we knew we were fated . . . to hear about one of Marlow's *inconclusive* experiences" (italics mine). But at least they are capable of sensing something special about Marlow, for the same speaker relates that Marlow "had the pose of a Buddha preaching in European clothes and without a lotus flower." This is plain description of Marlow's mission.

The continentals, too, are "hollow men" living in or near the Vestibule, except perhaps for the guardians. Some, of course, are better than others. The doctor, like the narrator on the *Nellie,* has some realization of the importance of Marlow's journey, shown by his farewell, "Du calme, du calme. Adieu." The women in the story, beginning with Marlow's aunt, are not really damned but live in an unreal world of their own, incapable of understanding. Miss Feder has suggested that Kurtz's fiancee may occupy a special corner of Hades because she is related, through imagery, to Kurtz and, she says, has no separate existence apart from him. It is quite true that when the reader meets her she appears dressed in black, but I do not think the color alone enough to consign her to Hell. She is mourning for Kurtz in a mistaken, over-sentimental but not abnormal fashion. And her existence does not entirely depend on him. Conrad uses her primarily for an agent in Marlow's eventual discovery of the ethical nature of life. Structurally she is bound to Marlow. Symbolically Conrad simplified Marlow's problems until they are mostly bound in the experience of falsehood. The most distasteful action Marlow is capable of is a lie, but twice he is brought to tell one. On the first occasion he lies for practical reasons in order to obtain rivets to repair the steamer, symbolizing dishonesty in the course of the normal business of life. Of course, the lie is successful. But later, when he visits Kurtz's "Intended," Marlow tells another lie, this time with no ulterior motive, and this selfless though intrinsically sinful action, a sort of parable, completes his moral vision. Conrad needs the fiancee for Marlow far more than he does to explain Kurtz's presence in Africa. She, like Marlow's aunt, simply does not understand the real world. The women of this story live in a special, mythical realm of their own.

The close structural parallel between the "Heart of Darkness" and the *Inferno* is not explicit at the Vestibule stage. Moreover, Dante borrowed the Vestibule from Virgil, though Conrad's tenants resemble Dante's far more than the Latin poet's. But from the landing in Africa and Marlow's descent into Limbo the relationship becomes unmistakable. Immediately preceding the real descent, Conrad devotes several paragraphs to explanation, in symbolic terms, of his special Hades. He carefully separates Africa from modern civilization by describing machinery rusting uselessly on a hillside. Graham Greene, faced with a similar need himself when he wrote *Journey Without Maps,* showed acute sympathy for Conrad's problem. Describing his own feelings he wrote, "A quality of darkness is needed, of the inexplicable . . . one sees . . . to what peril of extinction centuries of cerebration have brought us." Conrad, too, gives Marlow a preconception of what he would have to face: "I foresaw that in the blinding sunshine of that land I would become acquainted with a flabby, pretending, weak-eyed devil of a rapacious and pitiless folly." The "blinding sunshine," related to the "yellow" of the map, stresses the reality that supplies vitality to the myth.

Next Conrad turns to Marlow's meeting with the Chief Accountant, noteworthy for his gentle annoyance at having his work disturbed by a dying man on a litter placed in the office with him. The accountant is beyond the violence and the brutality. He keeps up appearances. He does not really suffer. Accordingly, he resembles Dante's tenants who have "sinned not; yet their merit lacked its chiefest // Fulfillment, lacking baptism, which is // The gateway to the faith which thou believest." The accountant belongs in Limbo.

From the coast up the river to the second station the characters in the story closely resemble the inhabitants of Upper Hell. Conrad does not follow Dante's eschatology strictly, but certainly the ivory traders belong with the lustful, gluttonous, wrathful. The second station is the abode of the fraudulent, through which blows, appropriately, "a taint of imbecile rapacity . . . like a whiff from some corpse." The idea is Dante's;

the passage actually may have been drawn from a notation in the Congo Diary, "saw at a camp place the dead body of a Backongo. Shot? Horrid smell."[3] He describes the station at length, its "air of plotting, [where the inhabitants] intrigued and slandered and hated each other," in terms that would be appropriate for Dante's City of Dis, that domain in the *Inferno* of those whose sins of violence and fraud involve exercise of the will.

From the second station on, up the river to Kurtz's outpost, Conrad carefully draws his characters as if they now inhabited Nether Hell. Nevertheless there is a fundamental difference between the "Heart of Darkness" and the *Inferno* at this stage. The inhabitants of Conrad's City of Dis actually travel further into the underworld; Dante's damned are fixed. I think this is an essential part of Conrad's solution to the problem of making Hell real though not actual. Moreover, the geography of Hell is, naturally, somewhat altered. As Marlow travels up the river on the steam launch, the natives are literally downtrodden blacks, but they resemble those who are violent against their neighbors. In fact, violence is one of their few distinguishing characteristics. The traders, now called Pilgrims primarily because they move about in Hell, take on the attributes of the circles they have entered. They too become violent, firing wickedly if ineffectually into the underbrush. The Russian trader that Marlow and his company encounter does seem slightly out of place in terms of Dante's scheme, for he appears to be a heretic. Conrad actually calls him a "harlequin," a verbal resemblance that is perhaps more than coincidental. He is not himself one of the violent; his real sin is accepting Kurtz as a false god. Their relationship is also in the foreground, though Conrad does not enlarge upon it. The trader merely remarks of Kurtz, "This man has enlarged my mind," suggesting intellectual sin, which heresy is. Conrad leaves little doubt about their relations in the readers' minds. The trader has not meditated about his connection with Kurtz; "it came to him, and he accepted it with a sort of eager fatalism." Marlow explains, "I must say that to me it appeared about the most dangerous thing in every way he had come upon so far." A writer could scarcely leave less to the imagination. Then, at the center of the underworld, Conrad presents Kurtz, perhaps something of a disappointment, because he does nothing but talk and die, to a reader schooled on the modern short story. But Kurtz fits Dante's scheme perfectly, as traitor to kindred, having put behind him all relations with Europe, to country, having abandoned even the platitudinous lip-service to the civilizing ideal upheld by the others, to guests, having turned upon the trader who nursed him, to God, having set himself up as a "graven image" in the center of Hades. In short Kurtz is the living Lucifer even without the unspeakable rites mentioned by Marlow.

His native queen, on the other hand, is an emendation to the complicated Dante-like system, though she completes Kurtz's degradation. In a sense she is not materially different from the aunt and the fiancee. In her ambitious dreams, which differ from theirs only because she is more primitive, she is out of touch with the real world. Another structural difference between the two works seems to lie in the fact that Conrad neglected the final circle of Dante's Hell, the frozen Lake of Cocytus. But Conrad's Hell is mythical. Literally Kurtz was alive when Marlow reached him. Death was still his immediate future, and perhaps he is not symbolically fixed in ice, like the Alberti brothers, because Conrad wished to suggest that evil as he was, a still worse fate awaited him. His final words, "the horror, the horror," may not only refer back to his Satanic service but may also look ahead to an everlasting horror.

I have devoted some time to showing that the structural basis of the "Heart of Darkness" resembles that of the *Inferno*. As Marlow descends deeper into Hades, he meets characters whose sins loosely correspond with those in the Italian epic. But Conrad by no means runs through the list of the seven deadly sins with their numerous subdivisions. In fact he does not conceive evil dialectically, but he roughly follows a tripartite division of sin of his own making, materially different from but not certainly related to the commonplace medieval conception. At the first station is the accountant, doomed but not suffering, in Limbo; at the next, the City of Dis, the ivory traders much as Dante would have treated them; finally, Kurtz, Lucifer himself, taking on the attributes of all the sins in which he has participated. Such a conception would be familiar to Dante, for superimposed on the complicated structure of his Hell is the threefold machinery of Vestibule, Upper Hell, Nether Hell. Conrad's structure is epic; he was not writing the usual sort of short story. As Miss Feder recognizes, he was heroically depicting "Marlow's discovery of evil and the responsibilities to himself and to others which this knowledge places upon him."

On the other hand, Miss Feder contends that Conrad employed the descent into Hell theme, at least to some extent, in order to "build up suspense, to tell the reader indirectly that this is no ordinary voyage." The voyage is certainly extraordinary, but, as I have pointed out, Conrad does not impart this information through implication. He states it so plainly and so often that the reader can scarcely mistake his meaning. Nor can I agree that the epic theme is employed to develop suspense. As I have shown, Conrad takes pains to adhere to epic structure, patterned after that of the *Inferno*. Suspense is a very slight element in both the classical epic and in Dante and of minor importance in the "Heart of Darkness." Conrad's goal, as Schiller said of Homer, is "already present in every point of his progress." From the first scene on the deck of the cruising yawl, *Nellie,* the reader is aware—even before the descent into Hell theme commences—that he is not listening to an ordinary sea-yarn. Marlow is no common sailor, any more than Christ's disciples were. He is described as sitting "cross-legged right aft . . . resembling an idol." The initial action is connected chronologically, through the epic list of ships, with heroic actions of the past. The Thames is geographically connected with all the other waters of the world and mythologically with the underworld. The preliminary scene, no mere enveloping action calculated to add versimilitude, tends to do away with suspense.

In a geographical sense as well, the story progresses from incident through journey to further incident, avoiding climax by diversions of great intrinsic value, much as Dante progresses through the various circles of Hell. And because of this technique few experienced readers are likely to find themselves breathless as they journey with Conrad into the dark continent. The strength of the story lies not in the suspense it develops but in the power of its clear moral insight and in the readers' realization that they, too, could perhaps under trial follow in Marlow's footsteps. As Graham Greene has remarked, "Here you could measure what civilization was worth."

Conrad does not always employ this technique. *Victory,* for example, develops suspense much as most modern novels do and even hinges in the final analysis on a gunshot. But "Heart of Darkness" never leaves the reader in much doubt about the outcome. There is really no question that Marlow might follow the fate of Kurtz, because of the initial action, nor that Kurtz might conceivably be saved. Conrad's reader moves through the episodes much as Homer's does. Far more important than suspense is what Goethe and Schiller called the "retarding element." Erich Auerbach claims, in *Mimesis,* that suspense in the modern sense tends to rob the audience of emotional freedom; whereas the opposite technique in the epic creates it. For the development of Conrad's purpose, the promotion of ethical insight, the reader must be left emotionally free so that he can judge not only Kurtz's action but Marlow's as well, and draw the right conclusions from them. I contend that Conrad was fully aware of this problem and realized that a solution in modern prose form was extremely difficult. Throughout his career he struggled towards an answer. *The Shadow Line* and "The Secret Sharer" are attempts in the same direction, but it was only with the happy adoption of epic technique in "Heart of Darkness," based largely on the descent into Hell theme which Conrad borrowed from Dante and Virgil, that he achieved complete success.                                                          (1956)

## NOTES

1. "Marlow's Descent into Hell," *Nineteenth-Century Fiction,* IX (March, 1955), pp. 280-293. [Editor's note: Reprinted here, pp. 162-170]

2. "Conrad's Diary," edited by Richard Curle, *Yale Review,* XV (January 1926), pp. 254-266, and in *Last Essays* (1926). [Editor's note]

3. In *Yale Review,* XV (January 1926), p. 261. [Editor's note]

# THREE NOTES ON
# "HEART OF DARKNESS"

## WILLIAM BYSSHE STEIN

## (1) The Lotus Posture and the "Heart of Darkness"*

ALTHOUGH Robert O. Evans' "Conrad's Underground" offers some interesting "epic" parallels to the "Heart of Darkness," it fails, I think, to cope with the moral experience in terms of the structure of the story. While I will not deny that there is a rough development of the myth of the descent into the underworld, this pattern of action cannot be viewed by itself and in itself. It must, rather, be seen in the Jamesian frame Conrad provides. Mr. Evans, to be sure, takes note of this important element of structure, but unfortunately he does not consider it to have a function. I refer, of course, to the Buddha tableaux, the positioning of which cannot be ignored, the two at the beginning, the one near the middle, and the other in the final paragraph of the work.

Mr. Evans even goes so far as to introduce his fragmentary citations from the tableaux into the context of Marlow's recital; actually they belong to the perspective of the first person narrator who acquaints us with the adventurer. Conrad deliberately restricts them to the vision of the latter because, as Mr. Evans is aware, he is one of the four auditors who cannot possibly understand the significance of a subtle spiritual voyage. All four are blinded by their infatuation with the material aspects of the world. Yet, as I shall show, the tableaux of the lotus postures instruct the reader how to interpret Marlow's descent into the underworld—his own, not Virgil's or Dante's.

Most of us, I am sure, are familiar with the stylized postures and gestures of Indian art, that is, with their appearance, not their meaning. Conrad, if we can claim Marlow as his "altar" [sic] ego, not only understood them; he believed in them. The first tableau, for instance, catches the hero in the physical position prerequisite to Yoga meditation, contemplation, and absorption. On the brink of the spiritual fulfillment that comes with self-recollection (a mode of personal salvation diametrically opposed to the Occidental belief that perfection is acquired from without, for in the Indian view the process is one of bringing into consciousness what lies in a dormant and quiescent state, the timeless reality of one's being), Marlow's lotus posture shows he is ready to engage in an exercise of intense introspection; he is ready to contemplate the chaos out of which order or cosmos comes: "Marlow sat *cross-legged* right aft. . . . He had *sunken cheeks, a yellow complexion, a straight back,* an *ascetic aspect,* and *with his arms dropped, the palms of hands outward,* resembled an idol (italics are mine)." This description gives evidence of the self-mortification, the denial of the tyranny of physical matter, which precedes the introversion of consciousness. And surely the combination of gestures by the

* From *Modern Fiction Studies*, II, 4 (Winter 1956-57), pp. 235-237.

limbs is enough to command alert attention; or is Conrad, like Marlow, addressing himself to the inadvertent curiosity of a reader as dull as the observer? In effect, it seems to me that Conrad in setting up this tableau is ridiculing the moral complacency which, confronted by a form of religious discipline older by far than Christianity, is so incapable of expanding its understanding.

A similar irony asserts itself in the next tableau, for again Marlow's posture is the occasion for deprecation: "he had the pose of a Buddha preaching in European clothes and without a lotus-flower." But while we are engaged in a consideration of these blind impeachments, let us not forget that the springboard for Mr. Evans' treatment of the story as epic is this same narrative voice. It is he who invokes the romance of the sea: the *Golden Hind, the Erebus,* and the *Terror.* If he is also a representative of the class Conrad is mocking, then Mr. Evans is not justified in citing these images in proof of his thesis.

Indeed, the basic irony of the "Heart of Darkness" resides in the preoccupation of Marlow's auditors with the external aspects of the descent into the African underworld. Conrad's repetition of the word "meditation" is a rubric here. He wishes to stress that Marlow's journey is only important to the degree that he can vicariously relive Kurtz's lapse into primitive degradation. This emphasis is likewise affirmed in Marlow's virtual obsession with Kurtz, the passionate interest in the man that grew as he proceeded towards the inner station. It is also manifest in Marlow's meticulous recreation of every facet of his trip, beginning with the interview on the continent. This recapitulation is necessary if he is to follow Kurtz's soul to the brink of utter damnation.  After all, the latter's enlightenment consists of the sudden insight into his appalling inhumanity: " 'the horror' " and the "depths of his meanness." And Marlow leaves no doubt that he himself is party to the experience: "But his soul was mad. Being alone in the wilderness, it had looked within itself, and, by heavens! it had gone mad. I had—for my sins, I suppose—*to go through the ordeal of looking into it myself* (italics mine)." But, of course, the nature of his enlightenment is different from Kurtz's, and at this point his lotus posture defines itself.

In an exercise of arduous spiritual discipline, symbolized in his physical bearing and studied introversion, "worn, hollow, with downward folds and drooped eyelids, with an aspect of concentrated attention," he lives through, to the very limit, a particular role in life. And in suffering its consequences, he fathoms and exhausts its contents. He descends into his own hell of fear, desire, and fleshly limitations, bearing all the suffering of his attachment to matter. At the last moment, he resists the attraction which Kurtz acknowledges. He breaks free from the forces of the flesh. With the story of his spiritual journey told, he sits in the inturned lotus posture, detached from the conditions, the victories, and the vicissitudes of time: "Marlow ceased, sat apart, indistinct and silent, in the pose of the meditating Buddha." And, as before, the narrator-observer is beguiled by outward appearance. Marlow has voyaged alone among the temptations which entangle man in time. He has not communicated with his auditors. He stands apart from them, the anonymous ascetic, cleansed and purged by his introspective ordeal.

This is all that Conrad tells the reader. The symbolic consecration to the ideal of Buddhahood constitutes the refinement of the experience in the heart of darkness. Whatever spiritual implications one finds in the story must be based on the tableaux. In effect, we have journeyed along "the way of the Bodhisattva." We have stood on the brink of time and eternity with Kurtz and Marlow, and we have seen the latter transcend this pair of opposites. We have also witnessed his triumph over inward suffering and toil. Although qualified to enter nirvana, like the true Bodhisattva, Marlow remains in the world to work for the salvation of all people. In his stage of enlightenment he teaches what his descent into the imperfections of the human soul has taught him— egoless compassion. Cancelling out all personal desire and fear, he has made available to humanity the gift of complete renunciation. To every suffering, striving creature, trapped in the karmic processes (enslavement to matter), he offers the inexhaustible wisdom of selflessness.

This interpretation, without the slightest exaggeration, emerges out of scrupulous focus on the structure of the story. A vision of spiritual reality is framed in the Buddha tableaux. Its meaning is not dependent upon any "epic" technique. If anything, consistent with Marlow's ironical attitude towards his audience, whatever parallels to the pagan and Christian underworlds that he broaches must be looked upon ironically. And here again I feel that Mr. Evans in his concern with a pattern of symbolism has slighted another of Conrad's conscious artistic practices. I refer in this instance to tone. Mr. Evans is quite aware of this device but never in the perspective of its effects upon thematic meaning. The self-mockery that pervades the Marlow recital, it seems to me, must operate to temper the ego climate of epic endeavor. Outward heroics are hardly a reflection of the compassionate Buddha.[1]

(1956-57)

NOTES

1. Cf. Stein's companion-piece to the present essay, "Buddhism and the 'Heart of Darkness'," *Western Humanities Review,* IX (Summer 1957), pp. 281-285 [Editor's note.]

SEYMOUR GROSS

(2) A Further Note on the Function of the Frame in "Heart of Darkness"*

DESPITE the frequency with which Conrad's "Heart of Darkness" has been discussed, the function of the frame in the novelette—the four men who sit on the deck of the *Nellie* and listen to Marlow's tale—

* From *Modern Fiction Studies,* III, 2 (Summer 1957), pp. 167-170.

has either been ignored or somewhat misconstrued. For example, Robert O. Evans in his "Conrad's Underworld"[1] asserts that "actually Marlow [Conrad] has little space to devote to the directors. They serve as Marlow's audience, but they are not the audience the author is trying to convince. The "Heart of Darkness" is not their story. They are really incapable of understanding it, as Conrad suggests when he puts in the narrator's mouth the insipid remark, "We knew we were fated . . . to hear about one of Marlow's inconclusive experiences.'"

Similarly, William Bysshe Stein, in his "The Lotus Posture and 'The Heart of Darkness,'"[2] recognizes the moral importance of the structure of the story and interestingly explicates the Buddha imagery in the frame, but nevertheless agrees with Mr. Evans that Marlow's story falls upon the spiritually deaf ears "of the four auditors who cannot possibly understand the significance of a subtle spiritual voyage."

I believe it is a mistake, however, to lump the four auditors together indiscriminately. As a matter of fact, Conrad subtly but emphatically differentiates one of the listeners—the first narrator—from the other three. What Evans and Stein say is true for the other three men, who, it turns out, are indeed incapable of comprehending the staggering implications of Marlow's tale. These three, in the frame, reflect all those in the actual experience—the corrupt pilgrims, the fantastic Russian, the company officials—who are unable to grasp the "hidden truth" of the moral abysm into which they have descended. For these three men, Marlow's tale (as Kurtz himself had been to the others in the story) is at worst ridiculous, at best an adventure story to listen to and forget. The only comment one of the three makes during the telling of Marlow's tale is "absurd," which understandably evokes from the experientially wiser Marlow the angry exclamation, "Absurd! . . . This is the worst of trying to tell. . . . Here you all are, each moored with two good addresses, like a hulk with two anchors, a butcher round one corner, a policeman round another, excellent appetites, and temperature normal—you hear—normal from year's end to year's end. And you say, Absurd! Absurd be—exploded! Absurd!" And when the terrifying saga of human degradation and triumph is concluded, the only thing the Director can find to say is the practical but, in the context, morally obtuse comment, "We have lost the first of the ebb." This group in the frame reflects all those in the actual adventure, and by extension in life, who are "too much of a fool to go wrong—too dull even to know [they] are being assaulted by the powers of darkness."

The first narrator is something else again. He is hardly, as Mr. Stein asserts, "dull" and incorrigibly "beguiled by outward appearance," "a representative of the class Conrad is mocking." He, in the frame, stands in the same relationship to Marlow as Marlow stood to Kurtz in the actual experience. He is precisely "the audience the author is trying to convince," for he is a man, as becomes increasingly apparent, who is capable of "facing the darkness" and of accepting its black message. It is true, as Mr. Evans asserts, that his comment about Marlow's inconclusive tales is insipid; but it must be noted that this is the kind of superficiality he is capable of only *before* he has lived through Marlow's tale, just as Marlow considers his own judgment before he has lived through Kurtz as being that of "a silly little bird." Both Marlow and the first narrator, metaphorically speaking, start at the same place, take the same trip, and arrive at the same destination.

When we first meet the narrator, he is a potentially sensitive but essentially optimistic man—a man who sees and evaluates experience from a *"lightened"* (though hardly enlightened) point of view. Although we are told nothing directly about him, the manner in which Conrad has him describe things serves to reveal the delusion of his moral innocence, a delusion which Marlow's tale is to shatter in precisely the same way as the reality of Kurtz's degradation shattered Marlow's own "mournful and senseless delusion."

The imagery of light with which the first two pages of the story are studded serves both as an index to the narrator's innocence and as an ironic prologue to Marlow's opening comment—"And this also . . . has been one of the dark places on the earth." For the first narrator, the Thames is a "benign immensity of unstained light," enveloped in a mist of "gauzy and radiant fabric"; on her "luminous" waters the sails of the barges "seemed to stand still in red clusters of canvas sharply peaked, with gleams of varnished sprits." After the day ends "in a serenity of still and exquisite brilliance," "Lights of ships moved in the fairway—a great stir of lights going up and going down." Moreover, his conception of the history of the river—which Conrad ironically comments upon in Marlow's harrowing tale of the first Romans struggle with "the fascination of the abomination"—is the epitome of bright, shadowless naiveté. For him, the history of the Thames is only "ships whose names are like Jewels flashing in the night of time," carrying "bearers of a spark from the sacred fire" to glorious conquests. "What greatness had not floated on the ebb of that river. . . . The dreams of men, the seed of commonwealths, the germs of empires." Marlow is soon to give him another kind of vision of the men who go into the heart of darkness: "the growing regrets, the longing to escape, the powerless disgust, the surrender, the hate."

Although the narrator, with the others, at first merely sits back patiently to listen to Marlow's yarn, by the time Marlow has threaded his way through about a third of his experience, he suffers a severe shock to his moral equilibrium. In the symbolic darkness which has enveloped the group, Marlow becomes for the narrator "no more . . . than a voice," just as Kurtz, to Marlow, had also "presented himself as a voice." And it is a disturbing voice. "The others might have been asleep, but I was awake. I listened, I listened on the watch for the sentence, for the word, that would give me the clew to the faint uneasiness inspired by this narrative that seemed to shape itself without human lips in the heavy night air of the river." At this point, Marlow's tale seems to hold out for the narrator the promise of some moral revelation, which is exactly what Kurtz had come to represent for Marlow at an analogous point in his experience. (For example, when Marlow thinks that Kurtz is dead, he says, "I couldn't have felt more lonely desolation somehow, had I been robbed of a belief or had missed my destiny in life.")

The narrator's moral progress is completed in the final paragraph of the story. Marlow's tale of "diabolic love and unearthly hate" has literally bowed the narrator with the sheer immensity of its implications. Immediately after the Director's banal comment, he says, "I raised my head. The offing was barred by a black bank of clouds, and the tranquil waterway leading to the uttermost ends of the earth flowed somber under an overcast sky—seemed to lead into the heart of an immense darkness." The transformation has been complete: "the benign immensity of unstained light" has become "the heart of an immense darkness." Now he, like Marlow, will be set apart from all those who do not know the truth.

The recognition of the reflective function of the frame in "Heart of Darkness" not only serves to reinforce the thematic implications of the story in much the same way as, for example, Gloucester's tragedy reinforces Lear's, but adds a new aspect to the work as well. That the narrator is able to arrive at his moral insight through "literature," as Marlow had arrived at his through experience, demonstrates Conrad's faith in the moral efficacy of experience through literature. Louis Armstrong once remarked that there are people who if they don't know, you can't tell them. What Conrad seems to be saying is that these people can't be told either by life or literature. It seems to me, then, that the "Heart of Darkness" is not only an enduring comment on the nature of man, but a parable on the possibilities of moral knowledge as well.                                         (1957)

### NOTES

1. See pp. 171-178. [Editor's note]
2. See pp. 179-181. [Editor's note]

## ROBERT O. EVANS

## (3) Further Comment on "Heart of Darkness"*

TWO NOTES in MFS by Mr. Stein and Mr. Gross, both of which take issue with certain details in my article, "Conrad's Underworld," though not my thesis, deserve cautious amplification. No one would argue with Mr. Gross' conclusion that the 'Heart of Darkness' is not only an enduring comment on the nature of man, but a parable on the possibilities of moral knoweldge as well." I am not so sure this conclusion inevitably proceeds from the argument that the first narrator on the deck of the *Nellie* passes through a moral experience analogous to Marlow's own—with the same sort of beneficial results. If the speaker in the frame secures any moral knowledge whatsoever, it is purely

* From *Modern Fiction Studies,* III, 4 (Winter 1957-58), 358-360.

vicarious and not the direct result of experience. I am willing to concede that Conrad's treatment of him is slightly different from that of the other directors; after all, he has a voice. But I do not think Mr. Stein misconstrues the story in lumping the directors together and considering the speaker, too, as "beguiled by outward appearance." Perhaps this narrator is sufficiently aware of the moral realm to recognize that they have "lost the first of the ebb," but he is not sufficiently aware to want to do anything about it or realize a prerogative has been presented to him. Conrad's vision is moral; thus I cannot believe, though he may wish to suggest parallels between the two narrators, that he intends for us to believe the speaker in the frame vicariously and almost idly profited from Marlow's yarn almost as much as Marlow himself. The tale, it still seems to me, is clearly directed at the reader, who may somehow apply the moral knowledge gleaned from it to his own experience.

There are other aspects in which the story in the frame parallels that in the center. Marlow's vision of the Roman commander ordered north from relative security to the Thames frontier, it seems to me, is a historical miniature of the main story, one in which, Conrad says, the Roman does his unpleasant duty because he was man "enough to face the darkness." Perhaps Mr. Stein, by concentrating on the "lotus posture" tableaux of Marlow as a cross-legged Buddha "preaching in western clothes," misplaces the emphasis Conrad desired when he concludes that "outward heroics are hardly a reflection of the compassionate Buddha." In the first place, there is really no doubt about the fact that Marlow was capable of outward heroics; the journey into darkness, itself, was one of the most heroic in literature. The moral courage required to lie to Kurtz's Intended at the end of the story, despite the moral lessons Marlow has learned from Kurtz and despite his opinion of a lie as the epitome of evil, is not inconsiderable. Conrad seems to wish the reader to think of Marlow at the time he is telling the story as one making a recollection in tranquillity. Marlow has earned his godlike detachment by actively journeying up the Congo and into the depths of Hell; at the moment he is presented in "lotus posture" this aspect of his life is done, though Conrad deliberately suggests the role of prophet may not be an easy one.

There is a further difficulty in making Marlow a spokesman for Yoga. I find nothing in the description of Marlow's posture which makes it necessary to identify him with anything more than the commonplace image of Buddha. Such a statue carved in ivory and set on a black base can be purchased anywhere in the Orient for a few shillings. It seems unlikely that Conrad knew a great deal about eastern religion or that he intended to suggest that the end of life is contemplative self-abnegation, the anti-karmic way. But if he did intend to suggest anything beyond the fact of identification of Marlow with the god, there is no reason to believe that he meant for Marlow to advocate, as Mr. Stein implies, an end of life similar to that upheld by Krishna when he said: "The man who casts off all desires and walks without desire, with no thought of a *Mine* or an *I*, comes unto peace." So far as I can ascertain from the *Bhagavadgita,* Krishna was not obligated to alter his position to address the Arjuna, or fighting caste: "To a knight there is no thing more blessed than lawful strife" or "Make thyself ready for the fight; thus shalt thou get no sin." There are certainly no external reasons to assume that Conrad ever read deeply in the documents of eastern religion, but if he did he must certainly have known that there is more than one way to salvation. The one that best fits Marlow, not in "lotus posture" but throughout the action of the story, is the way of Karma, which leads to the end, as perhaps Marlow has been led, to contemplation—but comtemplation of the ethical consequences of actions in terms of future existence. The way of the warrior, like the way of the Roman commander, resembles the way of the sailor who journeyed into Hell. Stated differently, it seems to me that Conrad would perforce sub-scribe to Milton's doctrine: "I cannot praise a fugitive and cloistered virtue."

Mr. Stein's suggestion that Marlow serves as Conrad's "altar" ego is also most interesting, aside from the play on words. It was once thought Conrad's Congo journey was the turning point of his career, after which he seriously took up writing, but it now seems that he took with him on that trip the MS of *Almayer's Folly*. Nevertheless, as M. Jean-Aubry, Conrad's biographer, points out, the journey may have shaken his confidence in the sea, as it robbed him of health. Marlow, however, has stuck with the sea, the real word of action; whereas the others on the deck of the *Nellie,* including Mr. Gross' candidate, have all deserted it. Thus while both explications are inter-esting and present valuable supplementary information about a story which now seems far more profound than readers have hitherto recognized, both, I think, deserve some qualification. Both depend too heavily on relatively minor matters of incident or image, at the ex-pense of the primary image, the pervasive darkness. With Conrad there is no easy, Jamesian clue, as it were, to the pattern in the carpet.

(1957-58)

## WILLIAM MOYNIHAN

## Conrad's "The End of the Tether": A New Reading*

IN A PREFATORY NOTE to *Youth,* Conrad says, "The three stories in this volume lay no claim to unity of artistic purpose."[1] Seven years later, in a letter to F. N. Doubleday, Conrad wrote, "In my view every volume of my short stories has a unity of artistic purpose. . . . the volume of *Youth* . . . in its component parts presents the three ages of man (for that is what it really is, and I knew very well what I was doing when I wrote "The End of the Tether" to be the last of that trio)."[2] Although

* From *Modern Fiction Studies,* IV (Summer 1958), 173-177.

Conrad's later view on the composition of the volume is obviously the more accurate, critics seem to have considered "The End of the Tether" only in the light of his prefatory remarks. A close-reading of the "Tether" reveals a slight, but clear, thematic relationship with the two previous stories, and provides a fine example of the use of mythical elements in creating an ironic-tragic Conradian hero.

Running throughout the volume *Youth* is a thematic pattern of struggle. The boy faces physical difficulties. Kurtz and Whalley contend not only with physical difficulties, but also with the forces of evil. The differences between Kurtz's struggle and Whalley's are profound, but, in many respects, Whalley's tragedy is a refinement and a detailed depiction of a spiritual disintegration such as befell Kurtz. The use of darkness in each story reflects the shifting emphasis. In "Youth" it is the darkness of night and storm. In the second story it is a land of darkness, of misery, literally the "heart of darkness." The "Tether" opens with a mixture of images of dazzling light and darkness. The "smudge of darkness" on the horizon reveals Whalley's physical blindness as well as his approaching "dark night of the soul," and at the story's close the whole world is engulfed in blackness.

Captain Whalley, like Kurtz, is considered a "remarkable man." Far from being a sentimental figure, he deserves a place with other notable ironic-tragic Conradian heroes. He is a simple, one-dimensional man unexpectedly exposed in his old age to the ravages of the three-dimensional forces of reality. But Whalley is not, as a first reading of the story might tend to indicate, simply an old and just man trapped by his love for his daughter into a cruel death. He does not blunder as majestically as Lear, but he blunders as fatally, and with equal finality. A wilderness finds out Whalley just as it found out Kurtz. Although the captain is not found out early, he is found out as surely, and he is found to be just as "hollow."

Conrad frequently describes Whalley an ironic terms. Whalley is referred to as a kind of patriarch whose physical strength (like Kurtz's voice) is a phenomenon. When he is described in terms of a tree: "With age he had put on flesh a little, had increased his girth like an old tree . . ." (187), the idea echoes Ben Johnson's "It is not growing like a tree/In bulk doth make man better be." And when Conrad calls Whalley a "lonely figure walking purposefully, with a great white beard like a pilgrim, and with a thick stick that resembled a weapon" (181), it is reminiscent of the exploiters of "Heart of Darkness"—'pilgrims" who went about "with staves in their hands" (80). This patriarchal figure is further described as "defenceless before the insidious work of adversity, to whose more open assaults he could present a firm front, like a cliff that stands unmoved the open battering of the sea, with a lofty ignorance of the treacherous backwash undermining its base" (183). That Whalley, the peerless sea captain and man of deep religious faith, is a tree, a cliff, rather than a great spiritual force is the ironic kernel of the story. His best friend, Mr. Van Wyk "wondered sometimes how much of it [Whalley's serenity] was due to the splendid vitality of the man, to the bodily vigour which seems to impart something of its force to the soul" (293). Whalley is a man of physical strength, not spirtual. When his physical strength is impaired, he is destroyed. The "horror" which overcame Kurtz, idealistically adventuring in Africa, overcomes the placid and serene Victorian seaman, and both men die with guilt on their souls.

Van Wyk provides another focus for the character of the captain. The two men support opposing views of life. Van Wyk, a cynic, says the older man will eventually come around to his way of thinking and that by the time he is a hundred he "will probably consent to die from sheer disgust." Whalley answers, "God forbid." But these are the precise feelings of the old man at the time of his death.

Similar devices of dramatic irony are used throughout the story in a pattern of prophecy, myth, and fate—a framework almost Grecian—against which Whalley's personal failure, his tragedy, is revealed.

There are two persons, Whalley's daughter and his son-in-law, who are in a sense immediate causes for his predicament and who mirror ironic aspects of the story. His daughter had married her own unwise choice, and Whalley recognizes that her husband would "go under with the sheer weight of bad luck" (175) which foreshadows his own bad luck. As the pale young man finally "gave up his unprofitable game, and sat down—in an invalid's bath-chair at that" (176), so the captain shortly is forced to sit in his "roomy cane arm-chair" (165) on the deck of the *Sofala*.

The chance-luck motif which Captain Whalley keynotes is expanded by his mate Sterne, an inferior Iago, who calls his discovery of Whalley's blindness "a stroke of luck," and it reaches its climax in Massy, the ship's owner-engineer. It was through lottery that Massy won the money to buy the ship. While the blind captain takes his chances on sailing his ship by the compass, below deck Massy sits madly trying to concoct a magic number, a winning number. And the end comes when Massy becomes "tired of waiting for some chance . . ." (314).

Conrad consistently employs the "mystical numbers." The *Sofala* has been ploughing its course for seven years. Whalley is sixty-seven years old. It is his third year on the *Sofala*. Van Wyk remembers a dozen captains. Three palms are the landmark which signals their shift in course. The river is three parts water. It was a thirty-day trip with a three-day layover.

Massy's wheel of fortune is not the only thing which hints of the story's concentric design and the omnipresence of a fate which rules men's lives. The old captain comes to the *Sofala's* port of registry to look for freight for the *Fair Maid,* "and her letter met him there." This comes half-way through the story. After selling his ship, "it struck him that it was to this port, where he had just sold his last ship, that he had come with the very first he had ever owned" (193). While plying his trade route, he thinks about going "back again in reverse order, seeing the same shores from another bearing, hearing the same voices in the same places, back again to the *Sofala's* port of registry" (167).

Captain Whalley's last ship, the *Sofala,* provides the clearest example of the symbolic and mythical background Conrad created for the testing of the conventionally holy seaman. When Whalley first hears of the ship, he plays with its name, calling it a "queer name," a "bizarre sound" (212). The ship is obviously intended to be a symbol of death. Whalley thinks of it as "a dead thing and no mistake." It lay there "as cold and still and pulseless as a corpse." "In the solitude of the avenue, all black above and lighted below, Captain Whalley, considering the discretion of his course, met, as it were incidentally, the thought of death" (214).

A less apparent point about the *Sofala* is its relationship to the king-killing custom practiced in Sofala, a region in Africa. Kingship is imaged in Whalley's physical splendor, his captaincy, and his fatherhood. In becoming captain of the *Sofala,* he assumes a role parallel to that of the kings of Sofala, and his last days resemble their last days. Sterne says the life of a ship's pilot is "made as weighty as the lives of kings" (250). It is the financial need of his daughter that forces the captain to invest his meager capital in the steamer *Sofala.* For, just as the "kings of Sofala were regarded as gods by their people" and were expected "to give rain or sunshine" as was necessary,[3] so was Captain Whalley regarded by his daughter. He feels he is "reaping the true reward of his life by being thus able to produce on demand whatever was needed" (175).

The Sofala kings were expected to die for "a slight bodily blemish, such as the loss of a tooth. . . . To put an end to such defects they killed themselves, saying that the king should be free from any blemish, and if not it was better for his honor that he should die and seek another life where he would be made whole. . . ."[4] Whalley kills himself. The cause of his destruction is a bodily defect—blindness. And the reason he kills himself is similar, though obviously not identical. He dies because his blindness prevented him from being perfect, from being a "king" to his daughter.

Whalley had bought a splendid cruising ship, the *Fair Maid,* as his "last command." He planned to die on this ship, and on the day of his funeral he wanted the *Fair Maid* scuttled at sea. One of the ways the legendary Sofala kings might die was to be enclosed in an air-tight room with a nubile virgin, in other words, a *fair maid.*

Aboard Whalley's death-barque are three other white men, each imaging aspects of the human wilderness which "finds out" Whalley. Massy is vicious, malevolent. Sterne is a plotter, "always . . . on the lookout for an opening to get on" (239). Jack, unthinking, unconcerned, vegetative life, further counterpoints the "majestic and benign" captain. It is Jack who, in his drunken ravings, sounds the final Cassandra-like prophecy—Massy will win.

The tragedy of Captain Whalley is sealed by neither faith nor love, but by pride. His pride convinced him that God wanted what he wanted. God was somebody in the home office; so long as he understood and appreciated what the Captain intended, all was well. "His Creator knew what use he was making of his health—how much he wanted it . . . (271).

Whalley admits, "I began to tamper with it [his conscience] in my pride" (300). "Not even the sign of God's anger" could make him forget his daughter (or what he thought was love of his daughter). But unlike Abraham, who had faith in God regarding Isaac, Whalley feels "like the blinded Samson, I would find the strength to shake a temple upon my head" (301). This is precisely what he does.

The vain emphasis on *his* doing something, the inability to trust God, the "whole life . . . conditioned by action," all worked together to make him ignore the "act of God"—his blindness. Sterne says he "pretended to struggle against the very decree of Providence." He classifies himself as a man who "stood up against God Almighty Himself." "He had lived on without any help, human or divine. The very prayers stuck in his throat. What was there to pray for? and death seemed as far as ever. . . . The hand of God was upon him, but it could not tear him away from his child. And, as if in a nightmare of humiliation, every featureless man seemed an enemy" (303).

The growth of evil from the imperceptible flaw of his dealings with the grotesque Massy reaches satanic proportions. To Mr. Van Wyk he seemed a man who "would accept no help from men, after having been cast out, like a presumptuous Titan, from his heaven" (305). His pride made it impossible for Whalley to believe that "they also serve, who only stand and wait."

What haunted him was the prospect that he could not save his daughter, that his power was at an end. He thought "the punishment was too great for a little presumption, for a little pride" (324). And this undercuts the sentimental aspects of the story.[5] Because Whalley, despite his fault, is still the most worthy and sympathetic character in the ironic and fallen world in which he lives, the reader does feel that his punishment is too great.

Whalley reaches "the end of the tether" when Massy deflects the compass with pieces of iron. For him "the light had finished ebbing out of the world" (333). Repeating the treachery by which Massy destroyed the ship, Whalley takes the iron from Massy's coat and stuffs it into his pockets. He, "who had made up his mind to die, should [not] be beguiled by chance into a struggle." His hands, like Massy's, must necessarily be reddened by the rust-blood of the iron. Blackness blinds the world. "They, looking from the boat, saw the *Sofala*, a black mass upon a black sea. . . ." (333).                                                    (1958)

NOTES

1. Joseph Conrad, *Youth* (New York, 1903), p. ix. All page references are from this volume.

2. G. Jean-Aubry, *Joseph Conrad, Life and Letters,* II (New York, 1927), p. 338. Also see Conrad's letter to Alfred A. Knopf (Aubry, p. 150), where, regarding the *Falk* volume, Conrad said, "I don't shovel together my stories in haphazard fashion. 'Typhoon' belonged to that volume; on artistic and literary

grounds; and its absence ruined the chances of the other stories. The reading of that first story attuned the mind for the reception of the others." R. W. Stallman, in "Conrad and 'The Secret Sharer,' " *Accent*, IX (Spring 1949), 131-143, discusses contradictions between prefaces and letters and concludes that Conrad employed strategic feints and "cunning strategy by which he everywhere conceals what his books are really about."

3. J. G. Frazer, *The Golden Bough* (New York, 1922), p. 317.

4. Frazer, p. 317.

5. In *Joseph Conrad: Achievement and Decline* (1957) Thomas Moser remarks on distinctly inferior works about love: "Tomorrow" (in *Typhoon and Other Stories*, 1903), "Gaspar Ruiz" (in *A Set of Six*, 1908), disasters equal to those of *The Sisters*, "The Rescuer," and "The Return." "Almost as bad results obtain in two stories more ambitious in intention than these potboilers, 'Falk' (in *Typhoon and Other Stories*, 1903) and 'Freya and the Seven Isles' (in *'Twixt Land and Sea*, 1912)." "Love does not, perhaps, explain Conrad's other long, ambitious failure of this period, the uneconomical, sentimental 'End of the Tether' (published in *Youth and Two Other Stories*, 1902). Nevertheless, hints of Captain Whalley's incestuous love for his daughter and of Massy's and Van Wyk's homosexual attraction to the old captain indicate that confusion about sexual material may have contributed to Conrad's difficulty with the story." (Pages 99, 218). [Editor's note]

# F. R. LEAVIS

## On "Typhoon" and *The Shadow Line**

Woman and the sea revealed themselves to me together, as it were: two mistresses of life's values. The illimitable greatness of the one, the unfathomable seduction of the other, working their immemorial spells from generation to generation fell upon my heart at last: a common fortune, an unforgettable memory of the sea's formless might and of the sovereign charm in that woman's form wherein there seemed to beat the pulse of divinity rather than blood.

THIS COMES FROM a bad novel, one of Conrad's worst things, *The Arrow of Gold*. It is a sophisticated piece of work, with a sophistication that elaborates and aggravates the deplorable kind of naïvety illustrated in the quotation. Not that the author's talent doesn't appear, but the central theme—and the pervasive atmosphere—is the "unfathomable seduction" of the "enigmatic" Rita; a glamorous mystery, the evocation of which (though more prolonged and elaborated) is of the same order as the evocation of sinister significance, the "inconceivable" mystery of Kurtz, at the close of "Heart of Darkness." If any reader of that tale had felt that the irony permitted a doubt regarding Conrad's attitude towards the Intended, the presentment of Rita should settle it.

* From F. R. Leavis's *The Great Tradition* (Chatto & Windus, 1948), pp. 182-191.

"Woman" figures in *The Rescue,* the book that in publication preceded *The Arrow of Gold* (both came out just after the 1914 war, though *The Rescue* belongs essentially to Conrad's early period). The glamour here is a simpler affair—less sophisticated and more innocent. But if *The Rescue* lacks the positive badness of *The Arrow of Gold,* it is, on a grand scale, boring in its innocence. The seduction of Woman as represented by Mrs. Travers is less insistently and melodramatically "unfathomable" than in the later book, but cannot sustain the interest Conrad demands for it; so to say that it is, in the formal design, adequate to balancing Heroic Action as represented by Lingard—King Tom, idealized seaman-adventurer—is not to say anything very favourable about the whole. *The Rescue,* in short, is an Academy piece—"sombre, colourful, undeniably a classic" the reviewers may have said, and its Grand Style staging of the conflict between Love and Honour (a kingdom at stake) against a sumptuously rendered *décor* of tropical sea, sunset, and jungle is, in its slow and conscientious magnificence, calculated to engender more deference than thrill, and so can't even be recommended as good boy's reading—though it offers little to adults. The book, in fact, is not altogether a surprising kind of thing to have come from a sailor of pertinacious literary talent and French literary education. The reason for bringing it in just here is to enforce the point that Conrad, for all his sophistication, exhibits a certain simplicity of outlook and attitude. About his attitude towards women there is perceptible, all the way through his literary career, something of the gallant simple sailor.

The sailor in him, of course, is rightly held to be a main part of his strength. It is not for nothing that "Heart of Darkness," a predominantly successful tale, is told by the captain of the steamboat—told from that specific and concretely realized point of view: appraisal of the success of the tale is bound up with this consideration. But the stress up till now has fallen upon Conrad's weaknesses. It is time to ask where the strength may be found in its purest form. There will, I think, be general approval of the choice of "Typhoon" as a good example. But I am not sure that there is as general a recognition of just where the strength of "Typhoon" lies. The point may be made by saying that it lies not so much in the famous description of the elemental frenzy as in the presentment of Captain Mac-Whirr, the chief mate Jukes and the chief engineer Solomon Rout at the opening of the tale. Of course, it is a commonplace that Conrad's distinctive genius comprises a gift for rendering the British seaman. But is it a commonplace that the gift is the specific gift of a novelist, and (though the subtler artist doesn't run to caricature and the fantastic) relates Conrad to Dickens? Consider, for instance, this:

> He was rather below the medium height, a bit round-shouldered, and so sturdy of limb that his clothes always looked a shade too tight for his arms and legs. As if unable to grasp what is due to the difference of latitudes, he wore a brown bowler hat, a complete suit of a brownish hue, and clumsy black boots. These harbour togs gave to his thick

figure an air of stiff and uncouth smartness. A thin silver watch-chain looped his waistcoat, and he never left his ship for the shore without clutching in his powerful, hairy fist an elegant umbrella of the very best quality, but generally unrolled. Young Jukes, the chief mate, attending his commander to the gangway, would sometimes venture to say, with the greatest gentleness, "Allow me, sir,"—and, possessing himself of the umbrella deferentially, would elevate the ferrule, shake the folds, twirl a neat furl in a jiffy, and hand it back; going through the performance with a face of such portentous gravity, that Mr. Solomon Rout, the chief engineer, smoking his morning cigar over the skylight, would turn away his head in order to hide a smile. "Oh! aye! The blessed gamp. . . . Thank 'ee, Jukes, thank 'ee," would mutter Captain MacWhirr heartily, without looking up.

Consider the exchanges between Captain MacWhirr and Jukes over the Siamese flag, deplorably, poor Jukes feels ("Fancy having a ridiculous Noah's ark elephant in the ensign of one's ship"), substituted for the Red Ensign. Consider the accounts of the home backgrounds of MacWhirr and the chief engineer.

It is to be noted further that these backgrounds in their contrast with the main theme of the tale afford a far more satisfactory irony (it is, in fact, supremely effective) than that, in "Heart of Darkness," of the scenes at Brussels. At the same time it is to be noted that there is in "Typhoon" no sardonic Marlow, commenting on an action that he is made to project; whereas, though "Heart of Darkness" *is* given from the point of view of the captain of the steamboat, that captain *is* Marlow—Marlow, for whom Conrad has more than one kind of use, and who is both more and less than a character and always something other than just a master-mariner. For comment in "Typhoon" we have the letters home of Solomon Rout, the chief engineer, and the letter of Jukes to his chum. In short, nothing in the story is forced or injected; the significance is not adjectival, but resides in the presented particulars—the actors, the incidents and the total action: we are given the ship, her cargo and her crew of ordinary British seamen, and the impact on them of the storm.

The ordinariness is, with a novelist's art, kept present to us the whole time; the particular effect of heroic sublimity depends on that.

> And again he heard that voice, forced and ringing feeble, but with a penetrating effect of quietness in the enormous discord of noises, as if sent out from some remote spot of peace beyond the black wastes of the gale; again he heard a man's voice—the frail and indomitable sound that can be made to carry an infinity of thought, resolution and purpose, that shall be pronouncing confident words on the last day, when heavens fall, and justice is done—again he heard it, and it was crying to him, as if from very, very far—"All right."

—Conrad can permit himself this, because the voice is that of the unheroically matter-of-fact Captain MacWhirr, whose solid specific presence, along with that of particularized ordinary sailors and engineers, we are never allowed to forget:

A lull had come, a menacing lull of the wind, the holding of a stormy breath—and he felt himself pawed all over. It was the boatswain. Jukes recognized these hands, so thick and enormous that they seemed to belong to some new species of man.

The boatswain had arrived on the bridge, crawling on all fours against the wind, and had found the chief mate's legs with the top of his head. Immediately he crouched and began to explore Juke's person upwards, with prudent, apologetic touches, as became an inferior.

Or take this:

The boatswain by his side kept on yelling. "What? What is it?" Jukes cried distressfully; and the other repeated, "What would my old woman say if she saw me now?"

In the alleyway, where a lot of water had got in and splashed in the dark, the men were still as death, till Jukes stumbled against one of them and cursed him savagely for being in the way. Two or three voices then asked, eager and weak, "Any chance for us, sir?"

"What's the matter with you fools?" he said brutally. He felt as though he could throw himself down amongst them and never move any more. But they seemed cheered; and in the midst of obsequious warning. "Look out! Mind that manhole lid, sir," they lowered him into the bunker. The boatswain tumbled down after him, and as soon as he had picked himself up he remarked "She would say, 'Serve you right, you old fool, for going to sea.'"

The boatswain had some means, and made a point of alluding to them frequently. His wife—a fat woman—and two grown-up daughters kept a greengrocer's shop in the East-end of London.

The seamen are their ordinary selves, the routine goes forward in the engine-room, and the heroic triumphs of the *Nan-Shan* emerge as matters-of-fact out of the ordinariness:

"Can't have . . . fighting . . . board ship,"

says Captain MacWhirr through the typhoon, and down into the 'tween-deck, into the human hurricane of fighting coolies, go Jukes and his men as a routine matter-of-fact course, to restore order and decency:

"We have done it, sir," he gasped.
"Thought you would," said Captain MacWhirr.
"Did you?" murmured Jukes to himself.
"Wind fell all at once," went on the Captain.
Jukes burst out: "If you think it was an easy job—"
But his captain, clinging to the rail, paid no attention.
"According to the books the worse is not over yet."

And the qualities which, in a triumph of discipline—a triumph of the spirit—have enabled a handful of ordinary men to impose sanity on a frantic mob are seen unquestionably to be those which took Captain MacWhirr, in contempt of "Storm-strategy," into the centre of the typhoon. Without any symbolic portentousness the Captain stands there the embodiment of a tradition. The crowning triumph of the spirit, in the guise of a matter-of-fact and practical sense of decency, is the redistribution—ship devastated, men dropping with fatigue—of the gathered-up and counted dollars among the assembled Chinese.

In *The Shadow-Line,* also in common recognition one of Conrad's masterpieces (it is, I think, superior to "Heart of Darkness" and even to "Typhoon"), we have the same art. It has been acclaimed as a kind of prose *Ancient Mariner,* and it is certainly a supremely sinister and beautiful evocation of enchantment in tropic seas. But the art of the evocation is of the kind that has been described; it is not a matter of engendering "atmosphere" adjectivally, by explicitly "significant" vaguenesses, insistent unutterablenesses, or the thrilled tone of an expository commentator, but of presenting concretely a succession of particulars from the point of view of the master of the ship, who, though notably sensitive, is not a Marlow, but just a ship's master; an actor among the other actors, though burdened with responsibilities towards the crew, owners and ship. The distinctive art of a novelist, and the art upon which the success of the prose *Ancient Mariner* essentially depends, is apparent in the rendering of personality, its reactions and vibrations; the pervasive presence of the crew, delicately particularized, will turn out on analysis to account for the major part of the atmosphere. The young captain, entering the saloon for the first time and sitting in the captain's chair, finds he is looking into a mirror:

> Deep within the tarnished ormolu frame, in the hot half-light sifted through the awning, I saw my own face propped between my hands. And I stared back at myself with the perfect detachment of distance, rather with curiosity than with any other feeling, except of some sympathy for this latest representative of what for all intents and purposes was a dynasty; continuous not in blood, indeed, but in its experience, in its training, in its conception of duty, and in the blessed simplicity of its traditional point of view on life. . . .
> Suddenly I perceived that there was another man in the saloon, standing a little on one side and looking intently at me. The chief mate. His long, red moustache determined the character of his physiognomy, which struck me as pugnacious in (strange to say) a ghastly sort of way.

The disobliging and disturbing oddity of the mate turns out to be due to the sinister vagaries and unseemly end of the late captain:

> That man had been in all essentials but his age just such another man as myself. Yet the end of his life was a complete act of treason, the betrayal of a tradition which seemed to me as imperative as any guide on earth could be. It appeared that even at sea a man could become the victim of evil spirits. I felt on my face the breath of unknown powers that shape our destinies.

The sinister spell that holds the ship is characteristically felt in terms of contrast with the tradition and its spiritual values, these being embodied in the crew, a good one, who carry on staunchly against bad luck and disease. The visiting doctor himself is "good" in the same way. The story ends, it will be noted, on the unexpected parting with the faithful Ransome, the exquisitely rendered seaman with a voice that is "extremely pleasant to hear" and a weak heart:

> "But, Ransome," I said, "I hate the idea of parting with you."
>
> "I must go," he broke in. "I have a right!" He gasped and a look of almost savage determination passed over his face. For an instant he was another being. And I saw under the worth and the comeliness of the man the humble reality of things. Life was a boon to him—this precarious, hard life—and he was thoroughly alarmed about himself.
>
> "Of course I shall pay you off if you wish it."
>
> I approached him with extended hand. His eyes, not looking at me, had a strained expression. He was like a man listening for a warning call.
>
> "Won't you shake hands, Ransome?" I said gently. He exclaimed, flushed up dusky red, gave my hand a hard wrench—and next moment, left alone in the cabin, I listened to him going up the companion stairs cautiously, step by step, in mortal fear of starting into sudden anger our common enemy. It was his hard fate to carry consciously within his faithful breast.

These things are worth many times those descriptions of sunsets, exotic seas and the last plunge of flaming wrecks which offer themselves to the compilers of prose anthologies.

This is at any rate to confirm the accepted notion of Conrad to this extent: that his genius was a unique and happy union of seaman and writer. If he hadn't actually been himself a British seaman by vocation he couldn't have done the Merchant Service from the inside. The cosmopolitan of French culture and French literary initiation is there in the capacity for detachment that makes the intimate knowledge uniquely conscious and articulate. We are aware of the artist by vocation, the intellectual who doubles the seaman, only when we stop to take stock of the perfection of the rendering and the subtle finish of the art.

But this fine balance, this identity, isn't always sustained. In Marlow, who (as remarked above) has a variety of uses, the detachment is separated off. As a main participant in events though, by his specific rôle as such, a detached one, he gives his technical function a dramatic status in the action, and the author a freedom of presence that, as we have seen, constitutes a temptation. Elsewhere Marlow is frankly a method of projection or presentation—one that we learn to associate with Conrad's characteristic vices and weaknesses. In "Youth," for instance, one of the best-known of the tales, though not one of the best, he goes with the cheap insistence on the glamour, and with that tone which, here and in other places, makes one recall the formula of the early reviewer and reflect that the prose laureate of the British seaman does sometimes degenerate into a "Kipling of the South Seas." (And this is the point at which to note that Conrad can write shockingly bad magazine stuff—see the solemnly dedicated collection called *Within the Tides*.)

In *Lord Jim* Marlow is the means of presenting Jim with the appropriate externality, seen always through the question, the doubt, that is the central theme of the book. Means and effect are unobjectionable; it is a different matter from the use of Marlow elsewhere to pass off a vaguely excited incomprehension as tremendous significance. But *Lord Jim* doesn't deserve the position of pre-eminence among Conrad's works often assigned it: it is hardly one of the most considerable. There is, in fact, much to be said in support of those reviewers who (Conrad tells us) "maintained that the work starting as a short story had got beyond the writer's control," so that what we have is neither a very considerable novel, in spite of its 420 pages, nor one of Conrad's best short stories. The presentment of Lord Jim in the first part of the book, the account of the inquiry and of the desertion of the *Patna*, the talk with the French lieutenant—these are good Conrad. But the romance that follows, though plausibly offered as a continued exhibition of Jim's case, has no inevitability as that; nor does it develop or enrich the central interest, which consequently, eked out to provide the substance of a novel, comes to seem decidedly thin.

The eking out is done mainly from the world of *Almayer's Folly, An Outcast of the Islands*, and *Tales of Unrest*, those excessively adjectival studies in the Malayan exotic of Conrad's earliest vein. Those things, it had better be said here, though they are innocuous, and no doubt deserved for their originality of setting some respectful notice when they came out, will not be urged by judicious admirers of Conrad among his claims to classical rank. In their stylistic eloquence, which suggests a descent from Chateaubriand, their wearying exoticism, and their "picturesque" human interest, they aren't easy to re-read.

No, *Lord Jim* is neither the best of Conrad's novels, nor among the best of his short stories. If, on the other hand, his most considerable work had had due recognition, it would be known as one of the great novels of the language. For *Nostromo* is most certainly that. And it complicates the account of Conrad's genius in that it doesn't answer to the formula arrived at above. He is not here the laureate of the Merchant Service, the British seaman happily doubled with the artist—an artist whose "outsideness" with regard to the Merchant Service is to be constated only in the essential degree of detachment involved in an adequately recording art. In *Nostromo* Conrad is openly and triumphantly the artist by *métier*, conscious of French initiation and of fellowship in craft with Flaubert. The French element so oddly apparent in his diction and idiom throughout his career (he learnt French before English) here reveals its full significance, being associated with so serious and severe a conception of the art of fiction.

The controlling conception of the novelist's art is severe, but the novel is luxuriant in its magnificence: it is Conrad's supreme triumph in the evocation of exotic life and colour. Sulaco, standing beneath snow-clad Higuerota, with its population of Indians, mixed-bloods, Hidalgos, Italians and English engineers, is brought before us in irresistible reality, along with the picturesque and murderous public drama of a South American state. This aspect of Conrad's genius in *Nostromo* has had full recognition; indeed it could hardly be missed. What doesn't seem to be a commonplace is the way in which the whole book forms a rich and subtle but highly organized pattern. Every detail, character and incident has its significant bearing on the themes and motives of this. The magnificence referred to above addresses the senses, or the sensuous imagination; the pattern is one of moral significances.                    (1941, 1948)

## GUSTAV MORF

## On Nostromo*

It seemed to him that every conviction, as soon as it became effective, turned into that form of dementia the gods send upon those they wish to destroy. But he enjoyed the bitter flavour of that example with the zest of a connoisseur in the art of his choice.—(*Nostromo*)

A CURIOUS LEGEND has formed around *Nostromo*, the legend that this novel is based mainly on Conrad's impressions received during a two days' visit to Venezuela, in 1876. The whole legend (for it is nothing else, as we shall see) has arisen from Conrad's own ambiguous statements, and has come to be accepted simply because of the insufficient knowledge of Conrad's Polish past, on which the novel is really built.

When Conrad was working on *Nostromo*, he wrote to R. B. Cunninghame Graham, in a letter dated 8th July, 1903:

I am dying over that cursed *Nostromo* thing. All my memories of Central America seem to slip away. I just had a glimpse twenty-five years ago—a short glance. That is not enough *pour bâtir un roman dessus*. And yet one must live.

The idea has been taken up by John Galsworthy, who wrote in his *Reminiscences of Conrad* [1925] that "in *Nostromo* Conrad made a continent out of just a sailor's glimpse of a South American port, some twenty years before."

This view does not stand a closer examination of the facts. Very few things in that novel can be called typically Central American, and even these Conrad might have got to know through his reading. All the really

* From Gustav Morf's *The Polish Heritage of Joseph Conrad* (Sampson Low, Marston & Co., 1930), pp. 127-148.

important facts, and, what is more, all the characters are taken from Polish or Mediterranean, reminiscences. The revolution theme itself, which might seem to be so characteristic of Latin America, reminds one distinctly of the struggle between Poles and Russians.

The key to the understanding of *Nostromo* can be found in its "Author's Note" where . . . Conrad states distinctly that Antonia Avellanos was modelled on that Polish girl ("my first love") who gave him, on his departure for France, a final hand-squeeze which he was to remember his whole life. If that be so, then Martin Decoud would be Conrad himself as a youth, for Antonia is to Martin Decoud exactly what her Polish model was to young Conrad. This supposition is fully confirmed by a close study of this curious character. Conrad has drawn a parallel between himself and Decoud in his "Author's Note," and a study of Martin Decoud throws a new light on his youth, his relations to Poland, and his patriotic sentiments.

Don Martin Decoud (so Conrad disguises himself), "a dilettante in life," "the adopted child of Western Europe," has been living in Paris for several years. There he had been "an idle boulevardier, in touch with some smart journalists, made free of a few newspaper offices, and welcomed in the pleasure haunts of pressmen." All this is closely modelled on Conrad's own life in Marseilles, as he describes it in *The Arrow of Gold,* and this manner of existence has the effect on Decoud's character it had had on Conrad's:

> This life induced in him a Frenchified—but most unFrench—cosmopolitanism, in reality a mere barren indifferentism posing as intellectual superiority.—(*Nostromo,* p. 152.)[1]

It is true that the young man does not then see himself as he is:

> He imagined himself French to the tips of his fingers. But far from being that *he was in danger of remaining a sort of nondescript dilettante all his life.*—(p. 153.)

Exactly as in Conrad's case, a more active life and a complete change of scene save him. He helps to sell arms to the silver mine in San Tomé and, moved by a curious impulse, decides to accompany the precious consignment to Sulaco himself. The cause of this unexpected zeal is the longing to see Antonia again, whom he "used to know when she wore her hair in two plaits down her back" (p. 155). Eight years had passed since he had seen her for the last time, but he had never forgotten that "girl of sixteen, youthfully austere, and of a character already so formed that she ventured to treat slightingly his pose of disabused wisdom." This is most certainly a personal reminiscence, as a comparison with the "Author's Note" will show, and the same may be said of what follows:

> On one occasion, as though she had lost all patience, she flew out at him about the aimlessness of his life, and the levity of his opinions. He was twenty then, an only son, spoiled by his adoring family. This

attack disconcerted him so greatly that he had faltered in his affection of amused superiority before that insignificant chit of a school-girl. But the impression left was so strong that ever since all the girl friends of his sisters recalled to him Antonia Avellanos by some faint resemblance, or by the great force of contrast.—(p. 155.)

Once back in his native country, to which he had grown a stranger, his cosmopolitan superiority and superficiality soon gives way to patriotic feelings. He is "moved in spite of himself by that note of passion and sorrow unknown on the more refined stage of European politics" (p. 156). *Passion* and *sorrow*, the very words one would be tempted to use when characterizing the Polish risings of 1831 and 1863!

Decoud had only meant to come on a short visit, but once landed, his country claims him irresistibly, and the very embodiment of that claim is the beautiful Antonia:

> But when the tall Antonia, advancing with her light step in the dimness of the big bare Sala of the Avellanos' house, offered him her hand (in her emancipated way), and murmured, "I am glad to see you here, Don Martin," he felt how impossible it would be to tell these two people that he intended to go away by the next month's packet . . .—(p. 156.)

> The pressure of Antonia's hand was so frank, the tone of her voice was so unexpectedly unchanged in its approving warmth, that all he found to say after his low bow was:
> "I am unexpressibly grateful for your welcome; but why need a man be thanked for returning to his native country? I am sure Doña Antonia does not think so."—(p. 157.)

The importance of this passage cannot be overrated. It is, I think, *nothing less than the exact picture of what Conrad thought would happen to him if he returned to his native country,* a picture expressing, as do certain dreams, a definite psychological situation, namely his apprehension that a day would come when his country would claim him in the name of bonds which are stronger than practical resolutions.

So Decoud stays in Sulaco. He puts his talents as a journalist at the service of a patriotic cause by taking the direction of the newspaper *El Porvenir* ("The Future"). When the revolution breaks out, and the troops of the dictator Montero are approaching, he is the only one who urges resistance upon the frightened Sulaco notabilities, and who refuses to submit to the authority of the new ruler. This episode is very significant. With all the recklessness which youth and love can inspire, Decoud-Conrad steps into the middle of these weaklings and opportunists and pours out upon them all his scorn and contempt for their undignified behaviour.

The notabilities are assembled in a big room in Avellanos' house. Decoud comes in, asking bluntly: "What are you deliberating upon, gentlemen?" Several voices reply at once: "On the preservation of life and property," and Don Juste adds: "Till the new officials arrive." And then follows a great scene in which Joseph Conrad "dreams" that he is playing the heroic and patriotic part which it was not given to him to play in reality:

> I walked up to the table blindly, as though I had been drunk. "You are deliberating upon surrender," I said. They all sat still, with their noses over the sheet of paper each had before him, God only knows why. Only Don José hid his face in his hands, muttering, "Never, never!" But as I looked at him, it seemed to me that I could have blown him away with my breath, he looked so frail, so weak, so worn out. . . .
>
> "Do you know," I cried, "what surrender means to you, to your women, to your children, to your property?"
>
> "I declaimed for five minutes without drawing breath, it seems to me. . . . And then for another five minutes or more, I poured *out an impassioned appeal to their courage and manliness,* with all the passion of my love for Antonia. For if ever man spoke well, it would be from a personal feeling, denouncing an enemy, defending himself, or pleading for what really may be dearer than life. . . . I *absolutely thundered at them.* It seemed as if my voice would burst the walls asunder, and when I stopped I saw all their scared eyes looking at me dubiously. And that was all the effect I had produced! Only Don José's head had sunk lower and lower on his breast. I bent my ear to his withered lips and made out a whisper, something like, "*In God's name, then,* Martin, my son!"
> —(pp. 235, 236.)

Decoud-Conrad had insisted on action. He had exclaimed, alluding to a well-known proverb: "There is never any God in a country where men will not help themselves" (p. 237). And now he is challenged by Don José himself to show the way. He is called to lead the people, to organize resistance, to lay the foundations of the new Occidental Republic!

Coming out of the assembly, he perceives Antonia in the gallery:

> As I opened the door, she extended to me her clasped hands.
> "What are they doing in there?" she asked.
> "Talking," I said, with my eyes looking into hers.
> "Yes, yes, but. . . ."
> "Empty speeches," I interrupted her. "Hiding their fears behind imbecile hopes. They are all great Parliamentarians there—on the English model, as you know." I was so furious that I could hardly speak. She made a gesture of despair. . . . "It is a surrender," I said . . . "But it's more than talk. *Your father told me to go on in God's name.*"
> . . . there is that in Antonia which would make me believe in the feasibility of anything. . . .
> "*Your father himself,* Antonia," I repeated, "*your father, do you understand? has told me to go on.*"—(pp. 237-239.)

Martin Decoud *goes on* indeed, but the way he carries out his glorious mission is very Conradesque and very Polish. He is a true Korzeniowski. His real achievement stands in a strange contrast with his exalted plans. It is true that the Occidental Republic is formed in the end (obviously a creation of no stability, but even that little is done without Decoud.

Immediately after having been called upon to organize the resistance against the approaching tyrant, Decoud has a meeting with Mr. and Mrs. Gould and Antonia. As the best means of dealing with the situation, they hit upon the idea of exporting the silver lying in the Custom House near the harbour, in order to get the support of a foreign man of finance. Decoud, assisted by Nostromo, is to accompany the silver himself to the next port beyond the frontier. The two leave Sulaco that very night with their precious cargo. The description of the voyage through the dark night, of the two men without a lamp on board a treasure ship, and always on the look-out for the ship of an enemy, is obviously based on reminiscences of Conrad's Mediterranean voyages on the *Tremolino,* in which the old Dominic (really the original of Nostromo) and the young Conrad were smuggling arms to Spain. In the following passages, for instance, Joseph Conrad most certainly records his personal experience of his early seafaring life:

> It seemed to him that the wharf was floating away into the night; but it was Nostromo, who was already pushing against a pile with one of the heavy sweeps. Decoud did not move; the effect was that of being launched into space . . .
> The two men, unable to see each other, kept silent till the lighter, slipping before the fitful breeze, passed out between almost invisible headlands into the still deeper darkness of the gulf. For a time the lantern on the jetty shone after them. The wind failed, then fanned up again, but so faintly that the big, half-decked boat slipped along with no more noise than if she had been suspended in the air.— (pp. 260, 261.)

> It was a new experience for Decoud, this mysteriousness of the great waters spread out strangely smooth, as if their restlessness had been crushed by the weight of that dense night.—(p. 261.)

And this passage again, describing the effect of the night upon the waters on the novice, is certainly a personal reminiscence dating back to Conrad's first voyages:

> . . . the enormous stillness, without light or sound, seemed to affect Decoud's senses like a powerful drug. He didn't even know at times whether he were asleep or awake. Like a man lost in slumber, he heard nothing, he saw nothing. Even his hand held before his face did not exist for his eyes. The change from the agitation, the passions and the dangers, from the sights and sounds of the shore, was so complete that it would have resembled death had it not been for the survival of his thoughts. In this foretaste of eternal peace they floated vivid and light, like unearthly clear dreams of earthly things that may haunt the souls freed by death from the misty atmosphere of regrets and hopes. Decoud shook himself, shuddered a bit, though the air that drifted past him was warm. He had the strangest sensation of his soul having just returned

into his body from the circumambient darkness in which land, sea, sky, the mountains, and the rocks were as if they had not been.—(p. 262.)

The end of the lighter is very much like the end of the *Tremolino,* related in *The Mirror of the Sea* (p. 179). In the *Mirror,* Dominic and Conrad, chased by a ship of the Customs, wreck their boat on a rock near the coast and escape by swimming ashore. In *Nostromo,* the appearance of Montero's (the usurper's) steamboat which nearly runs the lighter to the bottom, obliges the two men to bring the leaking ship ashore on the near island. Decoud stays with the treasure while Nostromo returns to Sulaco under cover of the night.

And now begins the tragedy of loneliness and despair for poor Decoud. Stranded on an island, unable to get back to Sulaco (where, by the way, he would have been shot by the usurper's mercenaries), he loses more and more the control over his nerves and finally commits suicide. He puts four silver ingots into his pockets, rows out to sea in the dinghy and, leaning overboard so as to fall into the water as soon as his hands would lose their grip on the gunwale, he shoots himself. An empty dinghy with a stain of blood, floating on the waters of the gulf, are the only traces of the incident.

Even this suicide, which at first sight seems wholly invented, is based on reminiscences of Conrad's Mediterranean voyages to Spain, as he relates them in *The Mirror of the Sea* and *The Arrow of Gold.* In the latter, Joseph Conrad speaks of the shipwreck of the *Tremolino* in these words:

> At last came the day when everything slipped out of my grasp. The little vessel, broken and gone like the only toy of a lonely child, the sea itself, which had swallowed it, throwing me on shore after a shipwreck that instead of a fair fight *left in me the memory of a suicide.* —(p. 256.)[2]

Decoud's idea of weighting himself with silver is very probably derived from an episode which happened during the shipwreck of the *Tremolino.* According to what we read in *The Mirror of the Sea* (pp. 176-182), Dominic had decided to *kill* their ship, and Conrad went in consequence down to the cabin in order to fetch ten thousand francs in gold which he kept there in a locker. The money was in a belt (the same belt which we shall meet again in *The Rover*), but when Conrad came down he found that belt and money were gone. He went at once on deck and told Dominic:

> "What did you want to do with it?" he asked me, trembling violently.
> "Put it round my waist, of course," I answered, amazed to hear his teeth chattering.
> "Cursed gold!" he muttered. *"The weight of the money might have cost you your life, perhaps."*—(p. 178.)

The thief was Cesar, who played on the *Tremolino* very much the same part as Hirsch on the lighter in *Nostromo.* But Dominic knew how to deal with Cesar. He knocked the fellow overboard, and "the wretch *went down like a stone with the gold.*"—(p. 181.)

A few other details in the description of Decoud's suicide are such distinct reminiscences that their study actually throws fresh light on the character of Conrad himself and on his romanticism. Decoud cannot bear to be alone:

> The brilliant "Son Decoud," the spoiled darling of the family, the lover of Antonia and journalist of Sulaco, was not fit to grapple with himself single-handed. Solitude from mere outward condition of existence becomes very swiftly a state of soul in which the affectations of irony and scepticism have no place. *It takes possession of the mind, and drives forth the thought into the exile of utter unbelief. . . . In our activity alone do we find the sustaining illusion of an independent existence as against the whole scheme of things of which we form a helpless part.* Decoud lost all belief in the reality of his action past and to come. On the fifth day an immense melancholy descended upon him palpably.—(*Nostromo*, p. 497.)

And now, as would a true romantic, Decoud *absorbs himself in his melancholy.* He derives from the painful analysis of his own state of mind a sort of sensuous pleasure, as certain people experience when ruminating over imaginary wrongs. He sees his mistake as if through a magnifying glass. He had believed in action, in effort, in a future for his country, in his own exalted mission. In the bustle of life, in the midst of persons who inspired him, who told him to go on, he had not seen the monstrosity of his audacity. But now that he was alone with himself, these illusions dispersed and he saw himself as he was, "a victim of the disillusioned weariness which is the retribution meted out to intellectual audacity" (p. 501), and the sense of the "utter uselesseness of all effort" is brought home to him:

> . . . as if to escape from this solitude, he absorbed himself in his melancholy. The vague consciousness of a *misdirected life given up to impulses whose memory left a bitter taste in his mouth was the first moral sentiment of his manhood.* But at the same time he felt no remorse. What should he regret? *He had recognized no other virtue than intelligence, and had erected passions into duties. Both his intelligence and his passion were swallowed up easily in this great unbroken solitude of waiting without faith.* Sleeplessness had robbed his will of all energy, for he had not slept seven hours in the seven days. *His sadness was the sadness of a sceptical mind. He beheld the universe as a succession of incomprehensible images.*—(p. 498.)

Three days afterwards he commits sucide. His last words are "It is done" (the very words in which Conrad had learnt the death of his father), and then the waves cover "the talker, the novio of Doña Antonia."

Decoud and Antonia are not the only familiar figures which we can recognize in *Nostromo*. The striking similarity between a remark of Conrad's on Garibaldi and a remark of Bobrowski's on Apollo Korzeniowski has already been mentioned. Another interesting character is Don José Avellanos whose life-story and portrait bear many traits borrowed from Conrad's father and Conrad's uncle. He is Antonia's father, and therefore (since Antonia is Decoud's *novio* or cousin) Decoud's (i.e. Conrad's) relative, perhaps his uncle. He is described as a "genuine old Roman— *vir Romanus*—eloquent and inflexible", as a "man of good counsel, though rendered timid by his horrible experiences of Guzman Bento's time" (pp. 169-93), as a sincere patriot of the prudent kind. Don Avellanos has a nephew, Moraga, to whom he writes many letters (p. 93). He is a man of great influence in the whole province, and has written a book of memoirs, political and social, which was never published, but whose MS., entitled *Fifty Years of Misrule,* the author of *Nostromo* is supposed to have used. This is most certainly an allusion to Bobrowski's *Memoirs,* which were not published until six years after their author's death, but of whose existence Conrad had known long before through his uncle. Other traits again are borrowed from Apollo Korzeniowski. Don José Avellanos founds a newspaper (*El Porvenir*) just as Conrad's father founded the fortnightly *Slowo.* Don José has been an ardent patriot in his young days, he has "displayed in the service of the endangered Ribiera Government an organizing activity and an eloquence of which the echoes reached even Europe." He has been working for the "establishment of that national self-respect without which—he declared with energy—'we are a reproach and a byword amongst the powers of the world'." (p. 137.) He loved his country with sincerity and uninterest and "had served it lavishly with his fortune during his diplomatic career." Everybody had heard of his subsequent captivity and barbarous ill-usage under Guzman Bento." This savage dictator, who is presented as having overthrown the national Ribiera Government, has all the traits of the "Muscovite" type of Russians as Conrad sees them in *Under Western Eyes*:

> Guzman had ruled the country with the sombre imbecility of political fanaticism. The power of Supreme Government had become in his dull mind an object of strange worship, as if it were some sort of cruel deity. It was incarnated in himself, and his adversaries, the Federalists, were the supreme sinners, objects of hate, abhorrence, and fear, as heretics would be to a convinced Inquisitor.—(*Nostromo,* p. 137.)

It is easy to see how well this applies to the struggle between the Poles ("Federalists") and the Russians. What follows is obviously modelled on Apollo's life-story. Avellanos is made a prisoner by the Army of Pacification (the very word Conrad uses when speaking of the repression of the Polish rising), and is driven about with many others at the rear of this army, in chains and half-naked. So terrible are his sufferings that he seems "only to exist in order to prove how much hunger, pain, degradation, and cruel torture a human body can stand without parting with the last spark of life."—(pp. 137-138.)

There is still another figure in *Nostromo* presenting an unmistakable likeness to Conrad's father: Giorgio Viola, the Garibaldino. Conrad calls him "the Idealist of the old humanitarian revolutions" and characterizes him as a "man of the People as free as possible from his class-conventions and all settled modes of thinking" (p. XI). He is not a leader above the others, not a general or a commander, but simply a man exercising over his equals that irresistible influence which an uncommonly strong belief confers:

> He does not want to raise himself above the mass. He is content to feel himself a power—within the People.—(p. XII.)
> In his firm grip on the earth he inherits, in his improvidence and generosity, in his lavishness with his gifts, in his manly vanity, in the obscure sense of his greatness, and in his faithful devotion with something despairing as well as desperate in its impulses, he is a man of the People, their very own unenvious force, disdaining to lead but ruling from within.—(pp. XII-XIII.)

This curious man considers himself as an exile (the word is used on p. 32), for he had come to Costaguana because he could "not live under a king" (p. 25). He had taken an active part in Garibaldi's struggle for a united and republican Italy. "He had lived amongst men who had declaimed about liberty, died for liberty, with a desperate exaltation, and with their eyes turned towards an oppressed Italy." He had passed the best years of his life in an atmosphere of armed struggle, of sacrifice, of patriotic appeal. The clash of arms and the inflamed language of proclamations had been the most familiar sounds to his ear. And all the time he had been keeping his eye on the great leader Garibaldi (Italy's Kosciuszko), the man who symbolises the Republican liberty:

> He had never parted from the chief of his choice—the fiery apostle of independnce—keeping by his side in America and in Italy till after the fatal day of Aspromonte, *when the treachery of kings, emperors, and ministers had been revealed to the world* in the wounding and imprisonment of his hero—*a catastrophe that had instilled into him a gloomy doubt of ever being able to understand the ways of Divine justice.*—(p. 29.)
> The spirit of self-forgetfulness, the simple devotion to a vast humanitarian idea which inspired the thought and stress of that revolutionary time, had left its mark upon Giorgio in a sort of austere contempt for all personal advantage. This man . . . had all his life despised money. The leaders of his youth had lived poor, had died poor. It had been a habit of his mind to disregard to-morrow. It was engendered partly by an existence of excitement, adventure, and wild warfare. But mostly it was a matter of principle . . . it was a puritanism of conduct . . . This stern devotion to a cause had cast a gloom because the cause seemed lost.—(p. 31.)

Giorgio's exterior also resembles strongly that of Conrad's father. The most striking feature about the Garibaldino is his "shaggy, white leonine head" (p. 16), which is mentioned again and again, on p. 20 ("leonine face"), p. 25 (*id.*), p. 26 (*id.*), p. 32 ("white mane," "old lion"), p. 337 ("white leonine mane") and p. 466 ("leonine white head").

Other Polish traits and reminiscences have gone into the making of *Nostromo*. The General Barrios, for instance, represents that type of soldier-gambler which was not uncommon in the Korzeniowski family:

> All his life he had been an inveterate gambler. He alluded himself quite openly to the current story how once, during some campaign (when in command of a brigade), he had gambled away his horses, pistols, and accoutrements, to the very epaulettes, playing *monte* with his colonels the night before the battle. Finally, he had sent, under escort, his sword (a presentation sword, with a gold hilt) to the town in the rear of his position to be immediately pledged for five hundred pesetas with a sleepy and frightened shopkeeper. By daybreak, he had lost the last of that money, too, when his only remark, as he rose calmly, was, "Now let us go and fight to the death."—(p. 162.)

A few remarks may also be made on the fictitious Central American state that forms the scene of the novel. The word Costaguana is obviously formed on the model of Costarica, but the name is less flattering, since it is derived from guano. (It may be a mere coincidence that *guana* is the Polish genitive of *guano*). That Conrad should have chosen rather a contemptuous expression to design his fictitious state, may seem very questionable, since Costaguana stands for Poland, but the difficulty is more apparent than real. Conrad loved Poland as Antonia and Decoud love Costaguana (the latter actually dies for it), but he hated like poison the usurpers who ruled the country, together with the incapable and weak opportunists or the blind idealists and makers of new eras and new revolutions. And these types obviously formed the majority in Costaguana, as they formed the majority in the Poland of 1870, or, for that matter, of 1903. This character sketch of the Costaguanero, which Conrad puts into the mouth of Decoud, applies very well to the Poles:

> There is a curse of futility upon our character: Don Quixote and Sancho Panza, chivalry and materialism, high-sounding sentiments and a supine morality, violent efforts for an idea and a sullen acquiescence in every form of corruption.—(p. 171.)

Eastern corruption, indeed, is not at all absent from Costaguana. Mr. Gould, on his arrival in the country, finds "circumstances of corruption . . . naïvely brazen" (p. 142). Conrad even tells at length the complicated story of an attempt at bribery. The bribery could not succeed because its object preferred the satisfaction of a personal revenge to a pecuniary advantage. Mr. Gould had had the misfortune of offending the present Minister of Finance and

> it so happened . . . that the Finance Minister . . . was a man to whom, in years gone by, Mr. Gould had, unfortunately, declined to grant some small pecuniary assistance, basing his refusal on the ground that the

applicant was a notorious gambler and cheat, besides being more than half suspected of a robbery with violence on a wealthy ranchero in a remote country district, where he was actually exercising the function of a judge.—(p. 54.)

Once in power, this man revenged himself by burdening Mr. Gould with a silver mine which, to an incompetent man like Mr. Gould, could only bring losses, especially as heavy taxes were immediately levied on it. Mr. Gould naturally tried to bribe the mistress of the Minister, but in vain:

> *"Pas moyen, mon garçon,"* replied that florid person. *"C'est dommage, tout de meme. Ah! zut! Je ne vole pas mon monde. Je ne suis pas ministre, moi! Vous pouvez emporter votre petit sac."*—(p. 55.)

Another Polish reminiscence seems to underlie Mrs. Gould's description of Sulaco:

> . . . we are very proud of it. It used to be historically important. The highest ecclesiastical court, for two vice-royalties, sat here in the olden time.—(p. 35.)

Now, one has only to read the article *Cracow* in the *Encyclopaedia Britannica* to see at once the resemblance with Cracow. Cracow was once the most important town in Poland, the seat of the first bishopric, and the residence of several kings. After the partitions, it became the capital of Galicia, and the rallying point of the Polish patriots.

On p. 479 of *Nostromo* may be found another Polish reminiscence. Every year the owner of a famous coffee plantation sends three sacks of coffee beans to a patriotic society in remembrance "of the third of May," the date of an important battle. Now it so happens that the third of May (the only date mentioned in *Nostromo*) is one of the most important dates in Polish history, so important, indeed, that it is now the National Day. On that day, in 1791, the famous "Constitution of the Third of May" was adopted by the Diet, converting Poland into a hereditary limited monarchy with ministerial responsibility, and abolishing the *liberum veto* and other anomalies.

And finally, the "alien complex" is not absent from *Nostromo*. It is easy to imagine how often Conrad's Polish name must have been not only mispronounced but sneered at during his seafaring life. Conrad never says a word about it (a hint may be found on p. 119 of *A Personal Record*), but this does not mean that he did not resent it. He did certainly mind it, since he adopted the name Conrad long before his first book was published. (John Galsworthy, who met him on board the *Torrens,* knew him as Mr. Conrad.) But if Conrad's resentment was repressed, it expressed itself all the better in an indirect way. The name *Nostromo* is a corruption of the Italian *Nostro uomo,* and it is an Englishman, Captain Mitchell, who is responsible for it. Conrad insists several times upon the fact:

The Italian sailor, *whom all the Europeans in Sulaco, following Cap-*
*tain Mitchell's mispronunciation, were in the habit of calling Nostromo*
(p. 43).
*He whom the English called Nostromo* (p. 29).
"You mean Nostromo?" said Decoud.
*"The English call him so, but that is no name either for man or*
*beast"* (p. 232).
". . . the praise of *people who have given you a silly name*—and
nothing besides—in exchange for your soul and body" (p. 256).
"Who are you?"

Already Nostromo had seemed to recognize Dr. Monygham. He had
no doubt now. He hesitated the space of a second. The idea of bolting
without a word presented itself to his mind. No use! *An inexplicable re-*
*pugnance to pronounce the name by which he was known kept him*
*silent a little longer.* At last he said in a low voice:
"A Cargador" (pp. 424, 425).

*Nostromo* is not only a remarkable achievement from a literary point
of view, but also full of significance for the psychologist. It is one of the
best examples of the compensatory function of artistic creation. All the
repressed Polish reminiscences, sentiments, aspirations and resentments,
lying deep under the surface of the artist's conscious mind, had their day
of rehabilitation when this book was written. Disguised in the robe of
fiction, and speaking a different tongue (though not an unfamiliar language), they rose to the daylight to amuse the onlooker and to tell of
things far off, long gone by, but never forgotten. Without them, there
would be no *Nostromo*.                                                (1930)

### NOTES

1. The pagination is the Dent edition. [Editor's note]
2. On Conrad's attempted suicide, see Appendix II, pp. 347-354. [Editor's
note]

## ROBERT PENN WARREN

## On *Nostromo**

EARLY IN 1903, from Pent Farm, which he had rented from Ford Madox
Ford, Joseph Conrad wrote to John Galsworthy: "Only with my head full
of a story, I have not been able to write a single word—except the title,
which shall be, I think: *Nostromo*." On July 8 of the same year, he
wrote to R. B. Cunninghame Graham: "I am dying over that cursed
*Nostromo* thing. All my memories of Central America seem to slip away.
I just had a glimpse 25 years ago,—a short glance. That is not enough

* First published in the Modern Library edition of *Nostromo* (1951), as
Introduction by R. P. Warren.

*pour batir un roman dessus.*" Then on September 1 of 1904, in a letter to Galsworthy, came the cry of triumph: "Finished! Finished! on the 30th in Hope's house in Stanford in Essex." Three days later, in a letter to William Rothenstein, the note of triumph has faded away:

> What the book is like, I don't know. I don't suppose it'll damage me: but I know that it is open to much intelligent criticism. For the other sort I don't care. Personally, I am not satisfied. It is something —but not *the* thing I tried for. There is no exultation, none of that temporary sense of achievement which is so soothing. Even the mere feeling of relief at having done with it is wanting. The strain has been too great, has lasted too long.

And the same day he wrote to Edward Garnett: "*Nostromo* is finished; a fact upon which my friends may congratulate me as upon a recovery from a dangerous illness."

It was not *the* book that Conrad had tried for. Let us grant that much, for who has ever written *the* book he tried for? But it remains Conrad's supreme effort. He had, as he was to say later in *A Personal Record,* "like the prophet of old 'wrestled with the Lord' for my creation, for the headlands of the coast, for the darkness of the Placid Gulf, the light on the snows, the clouds on the sky, and for the breath of life that had to be blown into the shapes of men and women, of Latin and Saxon, of Jew and Gentile." Here in *A Personal Record,* the tone of fatigue and frustration has gone: the memory of the heroic struggle remains. And in 1920, in the Preface to *The Secret Agent,* which had been composed years before, just after *Nostromo,* Conrad refers to *Nostromo* as "an intense creative effort on what I suppose will remain my largest canvas."

In many ways *Nostromo* is more fully the fruit of a creative effort than is any other of his stories. It is not a story of those parts of the world that he had known best, the Malay Peninsula and the China seas —the part where some critics, bemused by Conrad's exoticism and their own notion of his alienation from the modern world, would locate his best work. Rather it is a story of a part of the world that Conrad had never laid eyes on, the West Coast of South America. In general his fiction had depended, by his own account in the Preface to *Within the Tides,* on the conditions of his active life, even though more on "contacts, and very slight contacts at that, than on actual experiences." In the Author's Note to *Nostromo* we discover what "contact" had suggested Nostromo's story and how different the germ in real life is from the imaginative fulfilment. But the story of the stolen silver, suggested by the thievery of a cynical ruffian, and the figure of the Magnificient Capataz, suggested by old Dominic, padrone of the *Tremolino* in the days of Conrad's youth, and the severe charm of Antonia, suggested by Conrad's first love back in Poland, and even the sceptic Decoud, suggested perhaps by some deep, inner voice of Conrad himself, account for little of the finished novel. And they give us nothing of the land, remote and magisterial and vivid, that Conrad evoked in that supreme effort of his imagination.

For it was imagination and not recollection on which he had now to depend. Long before, in 1875 and 1876, when on the *Saint-Antoine* (running guns for a revolution), Conrad had been ashore for a few hours at ports on the Gulf of Mexico, but of the coast that might have given him a model for his Occidental Province and its people he knew nothing. There were books and hearsay to help, the odds and ends of information. But in the end, the land, its people, and its history had to be dreamed up, evoked out of the primal fecund darkness that always lies below our imagination. The very tempo of the book seems to re-enact for us the process of its creation: the stately vistas and massive involutions of the early chapters while the mists part, as it were, from the land; the nervous concentration of force and complication of event when the individual passions sublimate themselves in historical process; the moment of pause and poise when history has become anecdote and the creative conquest seems to have been complete; then, last, the personal story of Nostromo, before Linda's final, unappeasable cry—"Never! Gian' Battista!"—rings out over the dark Gulf, the part that is really a violent *coda* to the book, the product of the "volcanic overflow" with which, Conrad tells us, he finished his twenty months of agonized concentration. The land and all in it was dreamed up, but it is one of the most solid and significant dreams that we know, more solid and significant than most of our actualities. It is, in my view, the masterwork of that "puissant rêveur," as Gustav Kahn once called Conrad.

*Nostromo* has not, however, been universally acclaimed. Some readers with whom it is dangerous to disagree have not found it to their taste. For example, Joseph Warren Beach harbors serious technical objections, as does Albert Guerard, Jr., who finds the first part an "uncontrolled elaboration of historical detail," and here and elsewhere misses a detached narrator; Morton Zabel speaks of the "dramatic impenetrability"; even F. R. Leavis, who has done a perceptive and laudatory essay on the novel and finds it Conrad's masterpiece, ends his remarks by saying that the "reverberation of *Nostromo* has something hollow about it," and that "with the color and life there is a suggestion of a certain emptiness." My purpose is not to answer these objections, though some answers will be implied if I do manage to carry out my purpose, the purpose of saying what kind of book *Nostromo* is and what it means.

We can begin with the proposition that *Nostromo* is central for Conrad's work. When *Nostromo* appeared in 1904 Conrad had already published eight books, and this work included *The Nigger of the "Narcissus"* and *Lord Jim* and the famous novelettes "Heart of Darkness" and "Amy Foster." Already the world of Conrad's imagination had exhibited its characteristic persons and issues. Already we can find the themes of isolation and alienation, of fidelity and human solidarity, of moral infection and redemption, of the paradox of action and idea, of the "true lie," of the problem of history. The characteristic themes and situations and persons had emerged, but had emerged piecemeal, though in *Lord Jim* and "Heart of Darkness" Conrad had begun to move toward the massive synthesis and complex interfusion which was to engage him in *Nostromo.* As the earlier fiction seems to move toward *Nostromo,* so later fiction seems to represent, by and large, specializations and elaborations of elements that had been in suspension in that work.

To take some examples, Dr. Monygham is an older and more twisted Lord Jim, the man who had failed the test, not like Jim by abandoning his post and breaking the code of the sea, but by betraying friends under the torture of a South American dictator. His personal story, like the story of Jim, is the attempt to restore himself to the human community and to himself, though he, unlike Jim, survives the attempt. Mitchell and Don Pépé belong to the tribe of Captain MacWhirr of "Typhoon," those men who by lack of imagination (and Conrad took imagination to be a great gift and a great curse) never see all that life may contain "of perfidy, of violence, and of terror," and who, perhaps for that very reason, may cling simply and nobly to duty and fidelity.

Gould himself is a kind of cousin of Kurtz of "Heart of Darkness," though Gould is doomed to his isolation, not like Kurtz by avarice, vanity, and violence, by refusing his mission as a light-bringer, by repudiating the idea, but by accepting his mission as light-bringer and bearer of the idea. He accepts his mission, but ironically enough he falls a victim to the impersonal logic of "material interests" and in the end is the slave of his silver, not by avarice, not by vanity, certainly not vanity in any simple sense, but because he has lost love to the enormous abstraction of his historical role. As Kurtz betrayed his Intended to the Heart of Darkness, so Gould betrays his wife to what he takes to be the Heart of Light.

As for Emilia Gould, she is the victim of her husband's mission. Over against the abstractions, she sets up the human community, the sense of human solidarity in understanding and warmth and kindness outside the historical process. It is to her that the dying Nostromo makes his confession. It is she who compels the devotion of the bitter Dr. Monygham. Around her the other characters gather to warm their hands, as it were, at her flame. All but Charles Gould, bemused by his silver and his mission. Her role corresponds, in a way, to the role of Tekla in *Under Western Eyes,* who had been led into revolutionary activity by her sympathy for suffering, had been disillusioned by the character of the revolutionary prophet and tyrannical "feminist" whom she serves and by the abstractions he utters, and finds her fulfilment only when she can devote herself to the broken, dying, guilt-tortured Razumov. As Conrad puts it: "There was nothing in that task to become disillusioned about." But without that flicker of sardonic irony, he says of Mrs. Gould: "It had come into her mind that for life to be large and full, it must contain the care of the past and of the future in every passing moment of the present."

Somehow related to both Charles Gould and Emilia Gould stands the old Garibaldino, Giorgio Viola. He, like Emilia Gould, believes in the human bond, in a brotherhood of liberty, and has risked his life in the hope of bringing the day of liberty nearer to men; but like the idealism of Charles Gould, his idealism is tainted with abstraction. Tainted, but not destroyed, and some warmth remains in his nobility of purpose and his Roman rigor. Viola leans toward Nostromo, would take him as a son, and perhaps we find a symbolic force in this. For Nostromo is the natural man, the son of the people with the pride of the people, contemptuous of the "hombres finos," with their soft hands inexpert on tiller or rifle, half magnificent unconscious animal and half the confused, conscious, tempted man,* who is virtuous merely by vanity, for until the combination of opportunity and rancor strikes him he wants nothing but "reputation," that full awareness of his identity ideally projected in the minds and on the tongues of men. As he says to Charles Gould, who wants to reward him for his heroism: "My name is known. . . . What more can you do for me?" This is the man whom old Viola would draw into his orbit by uniting him with Linda, the daughter who carried something of the Garibaldino's depth and fidelity. But Nostromo, who has lived by his vanity, though his vanity idealized, turns to the other daughter Giselle, the "bad" daughter, and dies by consequence. Nostromo has natural grandeur; but natural grandeur unredeemed by principle, by idea, is not enough.

Without too much wrenching we may take Nostromo's significance as a parallel to that of Captain Brierly in *Lord Jim*. Brierly is the "natural" hero, his achievements all the product of luck and sound nerves and vanity; his suicide results when, seeing Jim on trial for cowardice, he realizes that the natural heroism is not enough and cannot find more in himself to sustain him. We may even say that Nostromo, too, commits a kind of suicide: he has destroyed the self by which he had lived. When, after the theft of the silver, he returns to the port but does not resume his work, he asks Captain Mitchell, "How can I look my Cargadores in the face after losing a lighter?" And Mitchell replies that it had merely been a fatality, that it could not have been helped. *"Si, si!"* Nostromo replies and turns away. It all now seems fated to Nostromo, fated because he had had nothing to depend on to prevent his succumbing and therefore cannot see how things could have been otherwise. But the whole passage bears a

---

* We may take as the key passage about Nostromo the moment at the end of Chapter VII of Part III, when Nostromo, having swum from the Isabels after the burying of the silver, goes to sleep in a "lair" of grass and then wakes: "He stood knee deep amongst the whispering undulations of the green blades with the lost air of a man just born into the world. Handsome, robust, and supple, he threw back his head, flung his arms open, and stretched himself with a slow twist of the waist and a leisurely growling yawn of white teeth, as natural and free from evil in the moment of waking as a magnificent and unconscious wild beast. Then, in the suddenly steadied glance fixed upon nothing from under a thoughtful brow, appeared the man."

kind of double meaning: Nostromo's smile that wrenched Captain Mitchell's heart, and the *"Si, si!"* as he averts his head. He has lost what he had lived by.

Last, we turn to Decoud, the sceptic. He is one of the isolated men, not isolated by foreign blood and speech like the poor gabbling hero of "Amy Foster," nor by a crime like Kurtz or Lord Jim, nor by his conception of his role or mission like Gould or Viola, nor by personal history like Flora de Barral and Captain Anthony of *Chance* with their "mystic wound" that alienates them from each other.

Decoud's isolation is more like the isolation of Heyst of *Victory;* it is intellectual; that is, whatever its origin may be, even though in such a mystic wound as that of Flora, it presents itself to its victim, and to us, in terms of reason and argument, as a philosophy. But Decoud's philosophy is not the philosophy of Heyst. Heyst fancies himself as the absolute observer, who shrinks from all involvement in life except such involvement as his detached kindness permits. Decoud is a connoisseur of sensation, a *boulevardier,* a dilettante of experience, who "recognized no other virtue than intelligence, and had erected passions into duties." He has only tolerant amusement, tinged with scorn, for the Goulds, for "the sentimentalism of people that will never do anything for the sake of their passionate desire, unless it comes to them clothed in the fair robes of an idea." But for Decoud even his own scepticism becomes the subject of scepticism. With self-irony he observes how his passion for Antonia casts him in the role of the father of a revolution and the herald of Progress, and later in the role of heroic adventurer when he finds himself on the dark Gulf in the lighter with Nostromo and the load of silver. And referring to Charles Gould, whose sentimentalism he has just remarked on, he can say that such men "live on illusions which somehow or other help them to get a firm hold of the substance." Where Heyst comes to conversion with the last words, "Ah, Davidson, woe to the man whose heart has not learned while young to hope, to love—and to put its trust in life!" Decoud comes to his end with no vision beyond that which scepticism can achieve by preying upon scepticism, the objective recognition of the pragmatic efficacy of faith despite the fact that faith is an "illusion." What this signifies, however, in the total pattern of the novel we shall come to later.

So much for the main characters of *Nostromo* and their relation to the Conradian family of characters. But we cannot speak of the characters as such, for Conrad, in one sense, had little concern for character independently considered. He is no Dickens or Shakespeare, with relish for the mere variety and richness of personality. Rather, for him a character lives in terms of its typical involvement with situation and theme: the fable, the fable as symbol for exfoliating theme, is his central fact. Therefore in placing the characters of *Nostromo* we have necessarily touched on the situations and themes. But let us linger a moment longer on this topic.

Conrad writes in *A Personal Record:* "Those who read me know my conviction that the world, the temporal world, rests on a few very simple ideas, so simple that they must be as old as the hills. It rests notably, among others, on the idea of Fidelity." Or again in his tribute to the Merchant Service in 1918, an essay called "Well Done": "For the great mass of mankind the only saving grace that is needed is steady fidelity to what is nearest to hand and heart in the short moment of each human effort." Fidelity and the sense of the job, the discipline of occupation which becomes a moral discipline with its own objective laws, this, for example, is what saves Marlow in "Heart of Darkness" as it had saved the Roman legionaries, those "handy men," when they had ventured into the dark heart of Britain.

Fidelity and the job sense make for the human community, the solidarity in which Conrad finds his final values, "the solidarity of all mankind in simple ideas and sincere emotions." It is through the realization of this community that man cures himself of that "feeling of life-emptiness" which had afflicted the young hero of *The Shadow Line* before he came to his great test.

The characteristic story for Conrad becomes, then, the relation of man to the human communion. The story may be one of three types: the story of the MacWhirr or the Don Pépé or the Captain Mitchell, the man who lacks imagination and cannot see the "true horror behind the appalling face of things," and who can cling to fidelity and the job; the story of the Kurtz or Decoud, the sinner against human solidarity and the human mission; the story of the redemption, of Lord Jim, Heyst, Dr. Monygham, Flora de Barral, Captain Anthony, Razumov.

The first type of story scarcely engages Conrad. He admires the men of natural virtue, their simplicity, their dogged extroverted sense of obligation and self-respect. But his attitude toward them is ambivalent: they are men "thus fortunate—or thus disdained by destiny or by the sea." They live in a moral limbo of unawareness. They may not be damned like Kurtz or Decoud and achieve that strange, perverse exultation of horror or grim satisfaction by recognizing their own doom, or be saved like Dr. Monygham or Flora de Barral. We may almost say that their significance is in their being, not in their doing, that they have, properly speaking, no "story"; they are the static image of the condition which men who are real and who have real "stories" may achieve by accepting the logic of experience, but which, when earned, has a dynamic value the innocent never know. The man who has been saved may reach the moment of fulfilment when he can spontaneously meet the demands of fidelity, but his spontaneity must have been earned, and only by the fact of its having been earned is it, at last, significant. Therefore, it is the last type of story that engages Conrad most fully, the effort of the alienated, whatever the cause of his alienation, crime or weakness or accident or the "mystic wound," to enter again the human communion. And the crisis of this story comes when the hero recognizes the terms on which he may be saved, the moment, to take Morton Zabel's phrase, of the "terror of the awakening."

In this general connection some critics have been troubled by, or at least have commented on, the fact that Conrad's prefaces and essays, and even his autobiographical writings and letters, seem ambiguous, contradictory, false, or blandly misleading in relation to the fiction. His comments on Fidelity, such as that above from *A Personal Record,* and his remarks on human solidarity, seem so far away from the dark inwardness of his work, this inwardness taken either as the story of his heroes or as the nature of his creative process. When we read parts of *A Personal Record,* for example, we see the image of the false Conrad conjured up by reviewers long ago, the image that William McFee complained about: "a two-fisted shipmaster" telling us simply how brave men behave. And we realize how far this image is from the Conrad who suffered from gout, malaria, rheumatism, neuralgia, dyspepsia, insomnia, and nerves; who, after the Congo experience and its moral shock, says of himself, "I lay on my back in dismal lodgings and expected to go out like a burnt-out candle any moment. That was nerves . . ."; who suffered "moments of cruel blankness"; who on one occasion, years later, had two doctors attending him, each unaware of the other, and who at the same time emptied all medicine into the slop; who advised an aspiring writer that "you must search the darkest corners of your heart," and told the successful and simple-souled Galsworthy, a sort of MacWhirr of literature, "the fact is you want more scepticism at the very fountain of your work. Scepticism, the tonic of minds, the tonic of life, the agent of truth—the way of art and salvation"; and who said of his own work, "For me, writing —the only possible writing—is just simply the conversion of nervous force into phrases."

But should we be troubled by this discrepancy between the two Conrads, the Conrad who praised the simple ideas and sincere emotions and the Conrad of the neurotic illnesses and the dark inwardness? No, we should not, but in saying that we should not I mean a little more than what has been offered elsewhere as a resolution of the discrepancy, the notion that the introverted and lonely Conrad, with a sizable baggage of guilts and fears, yearned, even as he mixed some contempt with his yearning, for the simplicity and certainty of the extroverted MacWhirrs of the world. I mean, in addition to this, a corollary of what has been said above about the story of awakening and redemption being the story that engaged Conrad most fully.

Perhaps the corollary can be stated in this fashion: If the central process that engaged Conrad is the process of the earned redemption, that process can only be rendered as "story," and any generalization about it would falsify the process. Instinctively or consciously Conrad was willing to give the terms of the process, the poles of the situation as it were, but not an abstract summary. The abstract summary would give no sense of the truth found within, in what, according to the Preface to *The Nigger of the "Narcissus,"* is "that lonely region of stress and strife."

There is another discrepancy, or apparent discrepancy, that we must confront in any serious consideration of Conrad—that between his professions of scepticism and his professions of faith. Already I have quoted his corrosive remark to Galsworthy, but that remark is not as radical as what he says in a letter to R. B. Cunninghame Graham:

> The attitude of cold unconcern is the only reasonable one. Of course, reason is hateful—but why? Because it demonstrates (to those who have courage) that we, living, are out of life—utterly out of it. The mysteries of a universe made of drops of fire and clods of mud do not concern us in the least. The fate of humanity condemned ultimately to perish from cold is not worth troubling about . . .

Here, clearly enough, we see the trauma inflicted by nineteenth-century science, a "mystic wound" that Conrad suffered from in company with Hardy, Tennyson, Housman, Stevenson, and most men since their date.

Cold unconcern, an "attitude of perfect indifference" is, as he says in the letter to Galsworthy, "the part of creative power." But this is the same Conrad who speaks of Fidelity and the human communion, and who makes Kurtz cry out in the last horror and Heyst come to his vision of meaning in life. And this is the same Conrad who makes Marlow of "Heart of Darkness" say that what redeems is the "idea only," and makes the devoted Miss Haldin of *Under Western Eyes* say of her dead heroic brother, "Our dear one once told me to remember that men serve always something greater than themselves—the idea."

It is not some, but all, men who must serve the "idea." The lowest and the most vile creature must, in some way, idealize his existence in order to exist, and must find sanctions outside himself. This notion appears over and over in Conrad's fiction. For instance, there is the villainous Ricardo of *Victory,* one of the three almost allegorical manifestations of evil. "As is often the case with lawless natures, Ricardo's faith in any given individual was of a simple, unquestioning character. For a man must have some support in life." Or when Ricardo thinks of the tale of how Heyst had supposedly betrayed Morrison:

> For Ricardo was sincere in his indignation before the elementary principle of loyalty to a chum violated in cold blood, slowly, in a patient duplicity of years. There are standards in villainy as in virtue, and the act as he pictured it to himself acquired an additional horror from the slow pace of that treachery so atrocious and so tame.

Then there is the villain Brown of *Lord Jim.* When, after Jim has allowed him to escape, he falls upon the unsuspecting men of Dain Waris, the act is not a "vulgar massacre":

> Notice that even in this awful outbreak there is a superiority as of a man who carries right—the abstract thing—within the envelope of his common desires. It was not a vulgar and treacherous massacre; it was a lesson, a retribution . . .

Even bloodthirstiness or villainy must appeal beyond itself to the "idea." The central passage of *Lord Jim,* Stein's speech about the "destructive element," is the basic text for this theme of Conrad:

> A man that is born falls into a dream like a man who falls into the sea. If he tries to climb out into the air as inexperienced people endeavor to do, he drowns—*nicht wahr?* . . . No! I tell you! The way is to the destructive element submit yourself, and with the exertions of your hands and feet in the water make the deep, deep sea keep you up.

I take this, in the context of the action, to read as follows: It is man's fate to be born into the "dream"—the fate of all men. By the dream Conrad here means nothing more or less than man's necessity to justify himself by the "idea," to idealize himself and his actions into moral significance of some order, to find sanctions. But why is the dream like the sea, a "destructive element"? Because man, in one sense, is purely a creature of nature, an animal of black egotism and savage impulses. He should, to follow the metaphor, walk on the dry land of "nature," the real, naturalistic world, and not be dropped into the waters he is so ill-equipped to survive in. Those men who take the purely "natural" view, who try to climb out of the sea, who deny the dream and man's necessity to submit to the idea, to create values that are, quite literally, "super-natural" and therefore human, are destroyed by the dream. They drown in it, and their agony is the agony of their frustrated humanity. Their failure is the failure to understand what is specifically human. They are the Kurtzes, the Browns, in so far as they are villains, but they are also all those isolated ones who are isolated because they have feared to take the full risk of humanity. To conclude the reading of the passage, man, as a natural creature, is not born to swim in the dream, with gills and fins, but if he submits in his own imperfect, "natural" way he can learn to swim and keep himself up, however painfully, in the destructive element. To surrender to the incorrigible and ironical necessity of the "idea," that is man's fate and his only triumph.

Conrad's scepticism is ultimately but a "reasonable" recognition of the fact that man is a natural creature who can rest on no revealed values and can look forward to neither individual immortality nor racial survival. But reason, in this sense, is the denial of life and energy, for against all reason man insists, as man, on creating and trying to live by certain values. These values are, to use Conrad's word, "illusions," but the last wisdom is for man to realize that though his values are illusions, the illusion is necessary, is infinitely precious, is the mark of his human achievement, and is, in the end, his only truth.

From this notion springs the motif of the "true lie," as we may term it, which appears several times in Conrad's fiction. For a first example, we may think of the end of "Heart of Darkness," when Marlow returns from the Congo to his interview with Kurtz's Intended, whose forehead, in the darkening room, "remained illumined by the unextinguishable light of belief and love." She demands to know her beloved's last words, and

Marlow, confronted by her belief and love, manages to say: "The last word he pronounced was—your name." He is not able to tell her the literal truth, the words, "The horror! The horror!" that Kurtz had uttered with his failing breath. If he had done so, "it would have been too dark— too dark altogether . . ." He has, literally, lied, but his lie is a true lie in that it affirms the "idea," the "illusion," belief and love.

Again, in *Under Western Eyes,* Miss Haldin speaks of bringing Razumov, supposedly the friend of her dead brother, to speak to the bereaved mother: "It would be a mercy if mamma could be soothed. You know what she imagines. Some explanation perhaps may be found, or—or even made up, perhaps. It would be no sin."

And even in *Nostromo* the lie that is true, that is no sin, reappears. The incorruptible Capataz, dying, is on the verge of telling Mrs. Gould the secret of the stolen treasure, but she will not hear him. When she issues from the room, Dr. Monygham, with the "light of his temperamental enmity to Nostromo" shining in his eyes, demands to know if his long-nourished suspicion of the "incorruptible" Nostromo is correct. He longs to know, to soothe the old wound of his own corruptibility. "He told me nothing," Mrs. Gould says, steadily, and with her charitable lie affirms forever the ideal image of the dead Capataz.

Scepticism is the reasonable view of the illusion, but scepticism, the attitude of the intelligence that would be self-sufficient, cannot survive, ironically enough, except by the presence of illusion. The fate of the sceptic Decoud, the "imaginative materialist," who had undertaken to be the natural man in that he had erected passions into duties, is the key parable, among many parables in Conrad, of the meaning of scepticism. Decoud had thought himself outside of the human commitments, outside the influence of the "idea," the worshipper of reason, which told him that the only reality is sensation. In so far as his scepticism is "natural," he recognizes the scepticism of Nostromo, the natural man who, "like me, has come casually here to be drawn into the events for which his scepticism as well as mine seems to entertain a sort of passive contempt."

But Decoud's worship of nature and reason are not enough. As soon as he finds himself outside the human orbit, alone with sea and sky, he cannot live. Even scepticism demands belief to feed on; the opposite pole of the essential situation must be present for scepticism to survive.

> Solitude from mere outward condition of existence becomes very swiftly a state of soul in which the affectation of irony and scepticism have no place . . . After three days of waiting for the sight of some human face, Decoud caught himself entertaining a doubt of his own individuality. It had emerged into the world of cloud and water, of natural forces and forms of nature. In our activity alone do we find the sustaining illusion of an independent existence as against the whole scheme of things of which we form a helpless part.

Decoud has reached the ultimate stage of scepticism: his scepticism has dissolved his identity into nature. But even at this moment of his spiritual, and physical, death, he experiences the "first moral sentiment of his manhood," the vague awareness of "a misdirected life." Now both intelligence and passion are "swallowed up easily in this great unbroken solitude of waiting without faith." In this "sadness of a sceptical mind," he beholds "the universe as a succession of incomprehensible images." His act of shooting himself and letting his body fall into the sea is merely the literal repetition of an already accomplished fate: he is "swallowed up in the immense indifference of things."

How are we to reconcile the moral of the story of Decoud, or of Heyst, with Conrad's statements of a radical scepticism, or, even a radical pessimism, the notion of man as a savage animal driven by a black ego? Can we say, as F. R. Leavis says, that "*Nostromo* was written by a Decoud who wasn't a complacent dilettante, but was positively drawn towards those capable of 'investing their activities with spiritual values'—Monygham, Georgio Viola, Señor Avellanos, Charles Gould"? Or can we say, as Albert Guerard, Jr., says, that against man's heart of darkness we can "throw up only the barrier of semi-military ethics; courage, order, tradition and unquestioned discipline; and as a last resort, the stoic's human awareness of his own plight, a pessimism 'plus sombre que la nuit' "? Both these statements are, in one sense, true. They do describe the bias of Conrad's temperament as I read it, but they do not describe, to my satisfaction at least, the work that Conrad produced out of that temperament. We must sometimes force ourselves to remember that the act of creation is not simply a projection of temperament, but a criticism and purging of temperament.

If Conrad repudiates the Decouds of the world, even as they speak with, as Leavis says, his "personal *timbre,*" he also has for the MacWhirrs of the world, the creatures of "semi-military ethics," a very ambivalent attitude, and some of the scorn of a man who knows at least a little of the cost of awareness and the difficulty of virtue. In other words, his work itself is at center dramatic: it is about the cost of awareness and the difficulty of virtue, and his characteristic story is the story of struggle and, sometimes, of redemption. Scepticism, he wrote to Galsworthy, is "the tonic of minds, the tonic of life, the agent of truth,—the way of art and salvation." This is, I suppose, a parallel to Hardy's famous statement: ". . . if way to the Better there be, it exacts a full look at the Worst. . . ." It is a way of saying that truth is not easy, but it is also a way of saying that truth, and even salvation, may be possible. Must we choose between the Decouds and the MacWhirrs? There is also Stein, and Emilia Gould, who thought: "Our daily work must be done to the glory of the dead, and for the good of those who come after."

Let us turn, at long last, to *Nostromo,* the novel. In this book Conrad endeavored to create a great, massive, multiphase symbol that would render his total vision of the world, his sense of individual destiny, his sense of man's place in nature, his sense of history and society.

First, *Nostromo* is a complex of personal stories, intimately interfused, a chromatic scale of attitudes, a study in the definition and necessity of "illusion" as Conrad freighted that word. Each character lives by his necessary idealization, up the scale from the "natural" man Nostromo, whose only idealization is that primitive one of his vanity, to Emilia Gould, who, more than any other, has purged the self and entered the human community.

The personal stories are related not only in the contact of person and person in plot and as carriers of variations of the theme of illusion, but also in reference to the social and historical theme. That is, each character is also a carrier of an attitude toward, a point of view about, society; and each is an actor in a crucial historical moment. This historical moment is presumably intended to embody the main issues of Conrad's time: capitalism, imperialism, revolution, social justice. Many of the personal illusions bear quite directly on these topics: Viola's libertarianism, with its dignity and leonine self-sufficiency and, even, contempt for the mob; Charles Gould's obsession in his mission; Avellanos's liberalism and Antonia's patriotic piety; Holroyd's concern with a "pure form of Christianity" which serves as a mask and justification for his imperialistic thirst for power; even the posturing and strutting "Caesarism" of Pedrito Montero, whose imagination had been inflamed by reading third-rate historical novels.

All readers of Conrad know the classic picture of imperialism at its brutal worst in "Heart of Darkness," the degradation and insanity of the process, and remember the passage spoken by Marlow:

> The conquest of the earth, which mostly means the taking it away from those who have a different complexion or slightly flatter noses than ourselves, is not a pretty thing when you look into it too much. What redeems it is the idea only.

In "Heart of Darkness" we see the process absolutely devoid of "idea," with lust, sadism, and greed rampant. In *Nostromo* we see the imperialistic process in another perspective, as the bringer of order and law to a lawless land, of prosperity to a land of grinding poverty. At least, that is the perspective in which Charles Gould sees himself and his mine:

> What is wanted here is law, good faith, order, security. Anyone can declaim about these things, but I pin my faith to material interests. Only let the material interests once get a firm footing, and they are bound to impose the conditions on which alone they can continue to exist. That's how your money-making is justified here in the face of lawlessness and disorder. It is justified because the security which it demands must be shared with an oppressed people.

This passage and Gould's conception of his own role may be taken as the central fact of the social and historical theme of *Nostromo*. But how does Conrad intend us to regard this passage? Albert Guerard, Jr., in his careful and brilliant study of Conrad, says that the mine "corrupts

Sulaco, bringing civil war rather than progress." That strikes me as far too simple. There has been a civil war, but the forces of "progress"—i.e., the San Tomé mine and the capitalistic order—have won. And we must admit that the society at the end of the book is preferable to that at the beginning.

Charles Gould's statement, and his victory, are, however, hedged about with all sorts of ironies. For one thing—and how cunning is this stroke! —there is Decoud's narrative, the letter written to his sister in the midst of the violence, that appears at the very center of the book; and the voice of the sceptic tells us how history is fulfilled. For another thing—and this stroke is even more cunning—old Captain Mitchell, faithful-hearted and stupid, the courageous dolt, is the narrator of what he pleases to call the "historical events." His is the first human voice we have heard, in Chapter II of Part I, after the mists part to exhibit the great panorama of the mountains, campo, city, and gulf; and in Chapter X of Part III, just after Nostromo has made his decision to ride to Cayta and save the Concession and the new state, the voice of Captain Mitchell resumes. He is speaking long afterwards, to some nameless distinguished visitor, and now all the violence and passion and the great anonymous forces of history come under the unconscious irony of his droning anecdotes. We can say of Captain Mitchell what Conrad says of Pedrito Montero, inflamed by his bad novels read in a Parisian garret: his mind is "wrapped . . . in the futilities of historical anecdote." Captain Mitchell's view is, we may say, the "official view": "Progress" has triumphed, the world has achieved itself, there is nothing left but to enjoy the fruits of the famous victory. Thus the very personalities of the narrators function as commentary (in a triumph of technical virtuosity) as their voices are interpolated into Conrad's high and impersonal discourse.

But we do not have to depend merely on this subtle commentary. Toward the end of the book, at a moment of pause when all seems to be achieved on a sort of Fiddler's Green at the end of history, a party has gathered in the garden of the Casa Gould. They discuss in a desultory way the possibility of a new revolution, and the existence of secret societies in which Nostromo, despite his secret treasure and growing wealth, is a great force. Emilia Gould demands: "Will there never be any peace?" And Dr. Monygham replies:

> There is no peace and no rest in the development of material interests. They have their law, and their justice. But it is founded on expediency, and is inhuman; it is without rectitude, and without the continuity and force that can be found only in a moral principle. Mrs. Gould, the time approaches when all that the Gould Concession stands for shall weigh as heavily upon the people as the barbarism, cruelty, and misrule of a few years back.

The material interests have fulfilled their historical mission, or are in the process of fulfilling it. Even Charles Gould, long before, in defining his mission to bring order through the capitalistic development, had not seen that order as the end, only as a phase. He had said: "A better justice will come afterwards. That's our ray of hope." And in this connection we may recall in *Under Western Eyes* how, after hearing the old teacher of languages give his disillusioned view of revolution, Miss Haldin can still say: "I would take liberty from any hand as a hungry man would snatch at a piece of bread. The true progress must begin after." In other words, the empire-builder and hard-bitten realist Gould and the idealistic girl, join to see beyond the era of material interests and the era of revolution the time of "true progress" and the "better justice." Somewhere, beyond, there will be, according to Miss Haldin's version, the period of concord:

> I believe that the future will be merciful to us all. Revolutionist and reactionary, victim and executioner, betrayer and betrayed, they shall all be pitied together when the light breaks on our black sky at last. Pitied and forgotten; for without that there can be no union and no love.

Emilia Gould, trapped in her "merciless nightmare" in the "Treasure House of the World," leans over the dying Capataz and hears him say, "But there is something accursed in wealth," and then begins to tell her where the treasure is hidden. And she bursts out: "Let it be lost for ever." Symbolically, this is her moment of vision, her repudiation of the logic of material interests.

If in this moment of vision, Emilia Gould and (in a sense that we shall come to) Conrad himself repudiate the material interests as merely a step toward justice, what are we to make of revolution? We may remember that Conrad most anxiously meditated the epigraphs of his various books, and that the epigraph of *Nostromo* is the line from Shakespeare: "So foul a sky clears not without a storm." It is innocent to think that this refers merely to the "storm" which is the action of the novel, the revolution that has established the order of material interests in Sulaco. If the sky has cleared at the end of that episode, even now in the new peace we see, as Dr. Monygham sees, the blacker and more terrible thunderheads piling up on the far horizon.

"Heart of Darkness" and *Nostromo* are, in one sense, an analysis and unmasking of capitalism as it manifested itself in the imperialistic adventure. Necessarily this involves the topic of revolution. The end of *Nostromo* leaves the sky again foul, and in the years immediately after finishing that novel Conrad turns to two studies of revolution, *The Secret Agent*, begun in 1905 and published in 1907, and *Under Western Eyes*, begun in 1908 and published in 1911. These books are in their way an analysis and unmasking of revolution to correspond to the already accomplished analysis and unmasking of capitalism and imperialism. In the world of revolution we find the same complex of egotism, vanity, violence, and even noble illusion. As the old teacher of languages in *Under Western Eyes* puts it:

A violent revolution falls into the hands of the narrow-minded fanatics and of tyrannical hypocrites at first. Afterwards comes the turn of all the pretentious intellectual failures of the time. Such are the chiefs and the leaders. You will notice that I have left out the mere rogues. The scrupulous and the just, the noble, humane, and devoted natures; the unselfish and the intelligent may begin a movement—but it passes away from them. They are not the leaders of a revolution. They are its victims: the victims of disgust, of disenchantment—often of remorse. Hopes grotesquely betrayed, ideals caricatured—that is the definition of revolutionary success. There have been in every revolution hearts broken by such successes.

We could take this, in appropriate paraphrase, as a summary of the situation at the end of *Nostromo*. There is the same irony of success. There has been the same contamination of the vision in the very effort to realize the vision. As Emilia Gould reflects: "There was something inherent in the necessities of successful action which carried with it the moral degradation of the idea."

Man, however, is committed to action. The Heysts, who repudiate action, find their own kind of damnation. Wisdom, then, is the recognition of man's condition, the condition of the creature made without gills or fins but dropped into the sea, the necessity of living with the ever-renewing dilemma of idea as opposed to nature, morality to action, "utopianism" to "secular logic" (to take Razumov's terms from *Under Western Eyes*), justice to material interests. Man must make his life somehow in the dialectical process of these terms, and in so far as he is to achieve redemption he must do so through an awareness of his condition that identifies him with the general human communion, not in abstraction, not in mere doctrine, but immediately. The victory is never won, the redemption must be continually re-earned. And as for history, there is no Fiddler's Green, at least not near and soon. History is a process fraught with risks, and the moral regeneration of society depends not upon shifts in mechanism but upon the moral regeneration of men. But nothing is to be hoped for, even in the most modest way, if men lose the vision of the time of concord, when "the light breaks on our black sky at last." That Platonic vision is what makes life possible in its ruck and confusion, if we are to take Conrad's word from the essay called "Books":

I would require from him [the artist] many acts of faith of which the first would be the cherishing of an undying hope; and hope, it will not be contested, implies all the piety of effort and renunciation. It is the God-sent form of trust in the magic force and inspiration belonging to the life of this earth. We are inclined to forget that the way of excellence is in the intellectual, as distinguished from emotional, humility. What one feels so hopelessly barren in declared pessimism is just its arrogance. It seems as if the discovery made by many men at various times that there is much evil in the world were a source of proud and unholy joy unto some of the modern writers. That frame of mind is not the proper one in which to approach seriously the art of fiction. It gives an author—goodness only knows why—an elated sense of his own superiority. And there is nothing more dangerous than such an elation to that absolute loyalty towards his own feelings and sensations an author should keep hold of in his most exalted moments of creation.

To be hopeful in an artistic sense it is not necessary to think that the world is good. It is enough to believe that there is no impossibility of its being made so.

Nothing, however, is easy or certain. Man is precariously balanced in his humanity between the black inward abyss of himself and the black outward abyss of nature. What Conrad meant by and felt about man's perilous balance must already be clear, if I can make it clear at all. But now I shall speak of *Nostromo* as an image of this.

The setting of the story, the isolation of Sulaco, is in itself significant. The serrated wall of the Cordillera, hieratic and snow-capped, behind the Campo, the Azuera and the Golfo Placido, define a little world that comes to us as complete—as a microcosm, we may say, of the greater world and its history. Man is lost in this overwhelming scene. The story of the two gringos, spectral and live, on the peninsula of Azuera is, of course, a fable of greed and of the terrifying logic of material interests unredeemed. But it is also a fable, here at the threshold of *Nostromo,* of man lost in the blankness of nature. At the center of the book, to resume the same theme, we find the story of Decoud, who loses his identity into the "world of cloud and water, of natural forces and forms of nature." When he commits suicide, he falls into the "immense indifference of things." Then at the very end of the novel, in the last paragraph, Dr. Monygham, in the police-galley, hears the wild, faithful cry uttered by Linda, the name of Nostromo: "Never! Gian' Battista!"

> It was another of Nostromo's triumphs, the greatest, the most enviable, the most sinister of all. In that true cry of undying passion that seemed to ring aloud from Punta Mala to Azuera and away to the bright line of the horizon, overhung by a big white cloud shining like a mass of solid silver, the genius of the magnificent Capataz de Cargadores dominated the dark gulf containing his conquests of treasure and love.

This, too, is a fable: the passionate cry in the night that is a kind of triumph in the face of the immense indifference of things. It is a fable with a moral not unlike that of the second of Yeats's "Two Songs from a Play":

> Whatever flames upon the night Man's own resinous heart has fed.

Or to take another fable, one from Conrad's essay on Henry James:

> When the last aqueduct shall have crumbled to pieces, the last airship fallen to the ground, the last blade of grass have died upon a dying earth, man, indomitable by his training in resistance to misery and pain, shall set this undiminished light of his eyes against the feeble glow of the sun. . . .

For my own part, from a short and cursory acquaintance with my kind, I am inclined to think that the last utterance will formulate, strange as it may appear, some hope now to us utterly inconceivable.

I have tried to define my reading of Conrad's work in general and of *Nostromo* in particular. In these matters there is not, and should not be, an ultimate "reading," a final word and orthodoxy of interpretation. In so far as a work is vital, there will continually be a development, an extrapolation of significance. But at any one moment each of us must take the risk of his sensibility and his logic in making a reading. I have taken this risk, and part of the risk is the repudiation, or at least criticism, of competing interpretations.

There is one view, not uncommonly encountered, that Conrad did not intend his fiction to have "meaning." We encounter, for example, the comment of Edward Crankshaw: "Bothering about what Conrad meant in 'Heart of Darkness' is as irrelevant as bothering about what Mozart meant in the Haffner Symphony." Conrad himself gives some support to this view in his sceptical bias, in his emphasis on the merely spectacular value of life, and in not a few of his remarks on his literary intentions, particularly in the famous one: "My task which I am trying to achieve is, by the power of the written word, to make you hear, to make you feel—it is, before all, to make you *see*."

All of this seems to me, however, to mean nothing more than that Conrad was an artist, that he wanted, in other words, to arrive at his meanings immediately, through the sensuous renderings of passionate experience, and not merely to define meanings in abstraction, as didacticism or moralizing. Conrad made no split between literature and life. If anything, he insisted on the deepest inward relationship. As he put it about the writer in the essay "Books": "It is in the impartial practice of life, if anywhere, that the promise of perfection for his art can be found, rather than in the absurd formulas trying to prescribe this or that particular method of technique or conception." Over and over again, in one way or another, Conrad said what he says in the Author's Note to *Chance:* "But every subject in the region of intellect and emotion must have a morality of its own if it is treated at all sincerely; and even the most artful writer will give himself (and his morality) away in about every third sentence." And even to the famous sentence about his intention being, before all, to make us "*see*," we find an addition: "That—and no more, and it is everything." To seeing in its fullest sense, to "our sympathetic imagination," as Conrad says in "Autocracy and War," we must look "for the ultimate triumph of concord and justice."

If in *A Personal Record* Conrad declares himself an "imperfect Esthete," in the same sentence he admits that he is "no better philosopher." Leavis goes so far as to affirm that Conrad cannot be said to have a philosophy: "He is not one of those writers who clear up their fundamental attitudes for themselves in such a way that we may reasonably, in talking of them, use that portentous term." In discussing this remark, as

I am about to do, I run the risk of making Conrad's work seem too schematic and of implying that he somehow sat down and worked out a philosophy which he then projected, with allegorical precision, into fiction. I mean nothing of the sort, but I do mean to say that in my judgment Leavis takes Conrad's work as too much a casual matter of temperament. For I think that even if Conrad is as "imperfect" philosopher as esthete, he is still, in the fullest sense of the term, a philosophical novelist.

The philosophical novelist, or poet, is one for whom the documentation of the world is constantly striving to rise to the level of generalization about values, for whom the image strives to rise to symbol, for whom images always fall into a dialectical configuration, for whom the urgency of experience, no matter how vividly and strongly experience may enchant, is the urgency to know the meaning of experience. This is not to say that the philosophical novelist is schematic and deductive. It is to say quite the contrary, that he is willing to go naked into the pit, again and again, to make the same old struggle for his truth. But we cannot better Conrad's own statement for the philosophical novelist, the kind of novelist he undertook, quite consciously, to be: "Even before the most seductive reveries I have remained mindful of that sobriety of interior life, that asceticism of sentiment, in which alone the naked form of truth, such as one conceives it, can be rendered without shame."

For him the very act of composition was a way of knowing, a way of exploration. In one sense this is bound to be true of all composition, but the matter of degree and self-consciousness is important in our present distinction, even crucial. We know a little of how *Nostromo* came to be, how it rose out of a feeling of blankness, how its composition was, in sober fact, an exploration and a growth, how the "great mirage," as Edward Garnett called it, took shape until it could float before us, vivid and severe, one of the few mastering visions of our historical moment and our human lot.                                                    (1951)


# THOMAS MANN


## Conrad's *The Secret Agent**
## (*an excerpt*)


WHEN some years ago I visited The Hague, John Galsworthy was lecturing there on "Conrad and Tolstoi." Who it was, whom Galsworthy was

* From Thomas Mann's *Past Masters and Other Papers,* translated by H. T. Lowe-Porter (Martin Secker; Alfred A. Knopf, 1933), pp. 234-247. First published as an Introduction to the German translation of *The Secret Agent* (*Der Geheimagent,* c. 1926) and reprinted in his *Die Forderung des Tages* (1930).

setting beside the Russian colossus, I had no notion; and my amazement increased when I heard that André Gide had learned English in order to read Conrad in the original. Since that time I have read some of the best works by this narrative genius: the daemonic story of a storm, called *The Nigger of the "Narcissus,"* and that of a calm, called *The Shadow Line;* also some of those whose scene is laid partly or wholly on shore, like *Chance,* a performance of great technical intricacy and brilliant virtuosity, and the altogether thrilling "crime story," *The Secret Agent.* I have read enough to feel it laid upon me to give something of him to the German public, whether maritime or not—and perhaps not maritime, perhaps just this very admirable *Secret Agent,* for the reason that it would be a limitation of Conrad's fame to speak of him only as a writer of sea-tales. I agree that this man's very deepest and most personal experience has been the sea, his perilous fellowship with that mighty element; certainly his greatest creative achievements lie in this field. But his virile talent, his Englishness, his free brow, his clear, steady and humorous eye, his narrative verve, power and grave-faced whimsicality, show up as well when the author stops on dry ground and observes what goes on there; sees it, sees through it and gives it form and body, as in the story lying before me, this exciting, yes, thrilling tale, a "crime story," as I said, and a political novel to boot, the history of a foreign embassy intrigue and its tragic human outcome.

It is an anti-Russian story, plainly enough, anti-Russian in a very British sense and spirit. Its background consists in politics on the large scale, in the whole conflict between the British and the Russian political ideology; I think it possible that this conflict has always formed the background—I will not say the motive—of the Pole's passionate love of England. If I were dealing with a German the hypothesis would be a doubtful one. We are metaphysicians; neither consciously nor unconsciously would we ever yield the political that much influence upon our mental life.[1] But we have begun to feel that perhaps other people are different; and that feeling is the source of my guess that Polish Russophobia is here expressing itself in British.

And particularly in the figure of Mr. Vladimir, secretary to the representative of a foreign, all too foreign, power in London. The guilt of the whole affair lies at his door. He is a man of considerable elegance, though the author seems to agree with the verdict of one of the characters who calls him a "hyperborean swine." Of polished manners in general, he betrays in emotion a "somewhat oriental phraseology" and a guttural accent that is not only un-English but un-European, even Central Asiatic. "Descended from generations victimised by the instruments of arbitrary power," it says of him, "he was racially, nationally and individually afraid of the police. He was born to it. But that sentiment, which resembled the unnatural horror some people have of cats, did not stand in the way of his immense contempt for the English police." "The vigilance of the police," says he, or one of his subordinates says it for him, "and the severity of the magistrates! The general leniency of the judicial procedure here, and the utter absence of all repressive measures, are a scandal to Europe. What is wished for just now is the accentuation of the unrest—of the fermentation which undoubtedly exists." An international conference, that is, is to be held in Milan to combat social revolution. "What we want is to administer a tonic to the conference in Milan," he said airily. "Its deliberations upon international action for the suppression of political crime don't seem to get anywhere. England lags. This country is absurd with its sentimental regard for individual liberty. . . . England must be brought into line."

This anti-Sarmatic satire, however light the touch, speaks pride of English freedom and English civilisation in every line. Hated Russia, hated now in British but perhaps originally in Polish, is made to bear the guilt of all the human tragedy which is the matter of the novel: the death of little Stevie, the murder of the pitiable rascal Verloc and the suicide of his wife. Is Conrad more English in any of his shipboard tales than in this political detective story? An upright British Police Commissioner says to Mr. Vladimir: "What pleased me most in this affair, is that it makes such an excellent starting-point for a piece of work which I've felt must be taken in hand—that is, the clearing out of this country of all the foreign political spies, police, and that sort of—of—dogs." "Dogs" is an expression of Mr. Vladimir, an Oriental, Central-Asian sort of expression, to speak in that singular guttural tone which the Soviet agents of to-day probably command quite as well as did persons of Mr. Vladimir's kidney. I mention this only to show that our novel is not out of date because its action takes place under the Czars, and that the conflict of West and East which forms its political background has lost nothing in timeliness by a change of government.

And here another guess: the unequivocal, the even tendentious Western bias of this extraordinary writer, who has for years been famous in England, France and America—might it not perhaps be responsible for the limited scope of his reputation in a country like ours, which must always instinctively shrink from casting a decisive vote on one side or the other? There was a time when it looked as though we had chosen, as though we had voted, politically and culturally, on the side of the East; and that was just the time when Conrad's name was becoming celebrated throughout the Western world. For us the possessor of this narrative gift stands in the shadow of Dostoiewsky—a shadow which, we are free to confess, even to-day—we feel could swallow up three or four Conrads. And yet time changes all things; that epileptic, apoclyptic visionary has to a certain extent lost his power over the German mind; we are groping our way back from the Byzantine-Christian East to the Centre, and so to that in us which is of the humanistic and liberal West. Probably the very fact that a leading publisher is now getting out a German edition of Conrad's chief works is evidence of his better chances of success among us.

No, Conrad is far from being the size of Dostoiewsky. But is it size

alone that conditions our love? If so, then our present epoch, which so
far has produced forms much more slender and inconsiderable than those
of the nineteenth century, would have small claims on our affections—
and we have already pronounced on the latter as great indeed, though
most unhappy. Let us confess that the products of our own century, so
much less heroic than those of the nineteenth, do not even excel them in
refinement. In Wagner, in Dostoiewsky, even in Bismarck, the nineteenth
century combines a giant growth with the extreme of subtlety, with a
refinement of technique which even borders on the morbid and the
barbaric. But perhaps the very abandonment of this characteristic, at once
sickly and savage, an Asiatic element, one might almost say, has actually
conditioned the smaller structure of our own time. At least we do find it
a more congenial and brotherly epoch, by contrast with the paternalistic
spirit of yesterday. Perhaps our more modest scale is due to our aspirations toward a purer, brighter, healthier, almost might one say a more
Greek humanity than the monumental gloom of the nineteenth century
knew. And the Anglomania of Conrad the Slav, his scorn of Central
Asian gutturals, may be rooted in these very aspirations—or this very
task—of ours.

I would not forget the world-revolution, nor the spiritual advantages
that to-day are bound up with good relations with the East. Every open-
eyed Westerner to-day envies the Central European on purely geographical grounds, for advantages which would doubtless have to be surrendered
in going over completely to the bourgeois West. In a sense we should
have to reckon with a penalty—even without conceding that English
against Continental-European means in itself a lowering of the level. More
form, with more limitations—was that the alternative the Slav faced when
he made his choice? No, that puts it badly. What he gave up were the
advantages of barbarism, which he did open-eyed. What he got was
reason, moderation, the open-minded attitude, intellectual freedom, and
a humour that is saved by its Anglo-Saxon robustness from falling into
the sentimental and bourgeois. A crisp, breezy humour it is, animated to
some extent by the sentiment expressed somewhere in *The Secret Agent,*
that "this world of ours is not such a very serious affair after all." He
shows small memory of the reverence for suffering that is a feature of
Eastern Christianity; when he speaks of the hook which a poor old coach-
man has sticking out of his sleeve instead of an arm, he does so with a
dryness that expresses grim enjoyment of life rather than a sense of pity.
Often, in unobtrusive details, this humour is refreshingly comic: as when
he describes the cab drive and the glass of the nearby-house fronts rattling
and jingling as though about to collapse behind the cab; or the mechanical
piano, whose keys seem to be played on by a vulgar and impudent ghost,
who breaks off as though gone grumpy. The author does not, even faintly,
change his key in describing a murdered man: "Mr. Verloc did not seem
so much asleep now as lying down with a bent head and looking intently at
his left breast. And when Comrade Ossipon had made out the handle

of the knife he turned away from the glazed door and retched violently."
Here all ado is lacking. The gaze turned upon the horrible is clear,
lively, dry-eyed, almost gratified; the spirit of the narration is impressively
English, and at the same time it is utra-modern, post-middleclass. For I
feel that, broadly and essentially, the striking feature of modern art
is that it has ceased to recognize the categories of tragic and comic, or
the dramatic classifications, tragedy and comedy. It sees life as tragi-
comedy, with the result that the grotesque is its most genuine style—
to the extent, indeed, that to-day that is the only guise in which the
sublime may appear. For, if I may say so, the grotesque is the genuine
anti-bourgeois style; and however bourgeois Anglo-Saxondom may
otherwise be or appear, it is a fact that in art the comic-grotesque has
always been its strong point.

No, Conrad's leaning to the West is not an indication of artistic or
intellectual surrender to the bourgeois point of view. He puts into Mr.
Vladimir's mouth a question full of social and critical implications when
he makes him ask: "I suppose you agree that the middle-classes are
stupid?" and when Mr. Verloc replies "They are," we have no doubt
that the author shares the opinion of the two men. Conrad is too much
artist and free spirit to be doctrinaire in his socialism—or to be Socialist
at all save in the freest sense and as a child of his time. Marxism is
represented in the book by the monomania of the solitary Michaelis,
the "ticket-of-leave apostle." Conrad's revolutionaries are hardly lovable
types; the psychology of his social rebels is strongly pessimistic in kind;
and his scepticism of social utopias is revealed in the description of one
insurgent of "an immense and nice hospital with a garden of flowers,
in which the strong are to devote themselves to the nursing of the
weak," whereas another, a miserable little terrorist and professor of
dynamiting, dreams of quite another kind, a world like a slaughter-
house, whither the "weak" are carried to be extinguished. But all this
sarcasm is hardly bourgeois in intention. It is very pretty irony to say
of the good Mr. Verloc that his function was to protect society, not to
improve it or pass judgement upon it; the irony becomes great satire
when it deals with the main action of the book, the dynamite outrage
which is to stimulate the Milan conference, and with the object upon
which it would be most profitably directed. "Of course, there is art.
A bomb in the National Gallery would make some noise. But it would
not be serious enough. Art has never been the fetish of the middle-class.
It's like breaking a few back windows in a man's house; whereas if you
want to make him really sit up, you must try at least to raise the roof.
There would be some screaming, of course, but from whom? Artists—
art critics and such like, people of no account. . . . But there is learning—
science. Any imbecile that has got an income believes in that. He does
not know why, but he believes it matters somehow. It is the sacrosanct
fetish. . . . It will alarm every selfishness of the class which should be
impressed. They believe that in some mysterious way science is at the

source of their material prosperity. They do. . . . Murder is always with us. It is almost an institution. The demonstration must be against learning—science. . . . What do you think of having a go at astronomy? . . . There could be nothing better. . . . The whole civilised world has heard of Greenwich. The very bootblacks in the basement of Charing Cross station know something of it. See? . . . Go for the first meridian. You don't know the middle-classes as well as I do. Their sensibilities are jaded. The first meridian. Nothing better, and nothing easier, I should think."

These judicious instructions of Mr. Vladimir to poor Verloc are the satirical height of the book. Its author is not, of course, the kind of creature who despises science. Nor, on the other hand, would he care much for a society based wholly upon it and throbbing to its dicta; and he speaks of "that glance of insufferable, hopelessly dense sufficiency which nothing but the frequentation of science can give to the dullness of common mortals." Disregard for art, for what constitutes the things of the mind, combined with boundless credulity and reverence for utilitarian science—that Conrad feels to be bourgeois. If his attitude toward the proletariat is not quite orthodox, that is obviously because science, on the other side of Marxism, has become the heritage and fetish of the proletariat; nobody will deny that Bolshevism is a sternly scientific conception of the world.

Comrade Ossipon, for instance—nicknamed "Doctor"; sometime medical practitioner without diploma, peripatetic lecturer to labour unions on the social future of hygiene, author of a confiscated pamphlet on "The Corroding Vices of the Middle Classes"—Comrade Ossipon is scientific. "Typical of this form of dengeneracy" is what he says, condescendingly, of little Stevie's circle-drawing, that singular occupation, practised with so much assiduity, a cosmic chaos as it were, or the efforts of an insane art to portray the inconceivable. Of course Comrade Ossipon refers to the ear-lobes and to Lombroso. And "Lombroso is an ass," answers him a still greater enemy of the existing order; and the author characterises this as a "shattering blasphemy." "Did you ever see such an idiot? For him the criminal is the prisoner. Simple, is it not? What about those who shut him up there—forced him in there? . . . And what is crime? Does he know that, this imbecile who has made his way in this world of gorged fools by looking at the ears and teeth of a lot of poor, luckless devils? Teeth and ears mark the criminal? Do they? And what about the law that marks him still better—the pretty branding iron invented by the overfed to protect themselves against the hungry? Red-hot applications on their vile skins, hey? Can't you smell and hear from here the thick hide of the people burn and sizzle? That's how criminals are made for your Lombrosos to write their silly stuff about." With all this "blasphemy" the author probably feels a certain, perhaps considerable, degree of sympathy. But his own way of looking at and describing little Stevie shows that his objections to Lombroso's science—

as a cheapish middle-class product—rest not upon social grounds, but upon profounder, religious ones.

Stevie, as revealed during the cab drive and the ensuing conversation with his sister Winnie, in so far as his "peculiarity" permits one to speak of conversation; this deficient little Stevie, who nevertheless is lovable above and beyond all values in life, and whom Winnie so loves that she avenges his death in the most frightful, self-immolating manner —Stevie is far and away the finest figure in the book, and conceived with the liveliest and most affecting sympathy. Here Russian influence is plain: without Dostoiewsky's Idiot, Stevie is unthinkable; we must admit that Dostoiewsky's attempt to present the purest and holiest in our humanity on a basis of the pathological is incomparably greater in its scope; yet here too we have an effort to cannonise the clinically deficient. Our author's very modern power of seeing both sides is shown in his never belittling the pathological side of the case or romantically closing his eyes to it. He makes a naturalistic concession to science by characterising Stevie's "peculiarity" as a family trait; and gives pathological significance to his sister's deed by mentioning the sudden and striking likeness she shows with her brother at the moment of it. None the less, the dominant psychology here is one with a religious implication which shows Comrade Ossipon's "scientific" opinion of Stevie for what, from the human point of view, it really is: a shabby pseudo-education. Indeed, there is a subtle yet unmistakable suggestion that Comrade Ossipon's remark is what drops into the harassed mind of Verloc the first germ of the idea that he might use Stevie in the political crime he meditates; thus science is once more compromised, once more found guilty from the human point of view.

All which is not bourgeois, but neither is it good orthodox proletarianism. It is evidence of the untrammelled objectivity which is the business of the class-free writer—if perhaps only his; and everywhere in Conrad's books it is displayed at its liberating task. In his judgement of the sexes he is objective: speaks of the sensitivity that can exist in the masculine nature alongside exasperating brutality; and finds that women are naturally more artful than men and much more ruthlessly avid for detail. So also he is aloof and critical in his attitude toward classes and masses, to all the apparent and temporary contradictions in the world. The sarcasm he directs against "hygienic idleness" as a form of existence is quite good socialism; but he also knows how to make repulsive to the soul of the reader the type of the hoarse-voiced agitator —as in *The Nigger of the "Narcissus";* and he says of his terrorists that they are not a hair better than the powers invoked against them. "Like to like. The terrorists and the policemen both come from the same basket. Revolution, legality—counter moves in the same game." That is not the idle indifference of a detached observer. It is the refusal of a very much engaged intelligence to hang miserably in the air between contraries. "You revolutionists," he says, or makes someone say, "are the slaves of the social convention, which is afraid of you; slaves of it as much as the very police that stand up in defence of that convention. Clearly you are, since you want to revolutionise it. It governs your thoughts, of course, and your action too, and thus neither your thought nor your action can ever be conclusive."

Conrad's objectivity may seem cool; but is a passion—a passion for freedom. It is the expression of very same love and passion that drove the young Pole to sea; and that—as once in the case of Ivan Tourgeniev —was doubtless the profoundest motive of his cultural relations with the West. This love of freedom cannot be confused with bourgeois liberalism, for he is an artist; and it is far too robust to be classed as aestheticism. The extent of Conrad's artistic success in Germany will be measured by his talent. His intellectual message will be for those among us who believe—in opposition to the views of the large majority —that the idea of freedom has a role to play in Europe that is not yet played out. (1926, 1933)

### NOTES

1. One speculates on Mann's bitter disillusionment, his theory being exploded by subsequent events. [Editor's note]

# R. W. STALLMAN

## Time and *The Secret Agent*\*

"I suppose you know that the world is selfish, I mean the majority of the people in it, often unconsciously I must admit, and especially people with a mission, with a fixed idea, with some fantastic object in view, or even with only some fantastic illusion."

*The Arrow of Gold,* II, 1.

As *The Secret Agent* is among Conrad's lesser known works, though it is among his greatest, a brief summary may be useful to the reader who has not read it recently. The story, to quote Miss Bradbrook's summary in *Joseph Conrad: Poland's English Genius* (1941), "has for its main event a 'senseless outrage' staged by Verloc the *agent provocateur,* which unexpectedly involves the death of his feeble-minded young brother-

\* Reprinted from *Texas Studies in Literature and Language,* Vol. I, No. 1 (Spring 1959). In shortened form this essay was read on the Critic's Program at the University of Texas; also at the University of Missouri, in October 1957. It was also read at the New England College English Association held at Connecticut College, in April 1958.

in-law. Mrs. Verloc, whose maternal passion for Stevie is the main-spring of her simple existence, and who has never suspected her husband's activities, kills Verloc, and then in blind terror puts herself into the hands of one of the revolutionary party [Comrade Ossipon], who leaves her stranded on the Calais steamer. She throws herself overboard in despair. Such is the story, but its melodramatic events are all told with a deliberate and consistent foreshortening. They are described purely and externally, and always with an ironic overtone" (page 48).

The story had its inception in an incident reported to Conrad by Ford Madox Ford, an attempt to destroy Greenwich Observatory with a bomb. The bomb-thrower, who was half an idiot, succeeded only in blowing himself to pieces. His sister afterwards committed suicide. From this germinal seed Conrad constructed the sordid world of the Verlocs, and it may be noted (to quote Oliver Warner's *Joseph Conrad*, 1951) that such a *milieu* is seldom met with elsewhere in Conrad. The whole book is conceived in an ironical temper, as Conrad defined it in a letter to R. B. Cunninghame Graham (October 7, 1907): "a sustained effort in ironical treatment of a melodramatic subject." While different from the majority of Conrad's works, the difference, as Douglas Hewitt, observes, is on the surface—"it is a difference of presentation rather than of the preoccupations which lie at the back of it. There is no central character in whom the problems of value are worked out, no ·character who is the focal point of the moral issues involved. It is more nearly a comedy than any other novel of Conrad—a comedy which is intensely serious and in which the pity and scorn of which he speaks in the 'Author's Note' are most important." The element of brutal and sordid farce, which appears also in "Heart of Darkness" and in "Falk," is here dominant. (From *Conrad: A Reassessment*, 1952, p. 85.) Recasting the novel, Conrad later succeeded in creating a remarkable play: *The Secret Agent—A Drama in Four Acts.* (1923).

(1)

Though *The Secret Agent* is one of the most cryptographic works in all British fiction, Conrad perversely appended to *The Secret Agent* the sub-title: "A Simple Tale." The only thing simple in it is the simpleton Stevie, and even he is rather a complicated character. Perhaps it's Conrad's bogus sub-title—A Simple Tale!—that has beguiled Conrad's critics and unwary readers into the trap of dismissing *The Secret Agent* —his richest work of art—as having no more claim to merit than as an excellent example of detective fiction (the critic is Ernest Baker), "a good Hitchcock thriller" (W. T. Webster); or as an example of the political fable (Irving Howe). One critic claims that it wouldn't be read at all were it "signed by an unknown name." A splendid book, he concedes, but it's a book "in the same class as *Tono Bungay* and *The Old Wives' Tale*."[1] F. R. Leavis hasn't so much as scratched the surface of this book, but he does recognize it as "indubitably a classic and a mas-

terpiece, and it doesn't answer to the notion at all—which is perhaps why it appears to have had nothing like due recognition." How can
it possibly earn due recognition as long as its hidden meaning passes
unnoticed?

All's chaos and confusion; all's incongruous and irrational, but nevertheless logic designs the structure of *The Secret Agent.* One critic attributes "the horror of the tale" to the notion that ordinary reason cannot
comprehend the dialectic of evil, and he concludes that "the whole
chain of circumstances defies the logic of thought." (Paul L. Wiley in
*Conrad's Measure of Man,* 1954, page 109). No work of art defies
the logic of thought. A cryptographic work of art gets itself read only
by the cryptographic reader. What Marlow says of Jim's plight in *Lord
Jim* applies to *The Secret Agent:* "There is to my mind a sort of profound and terrifying logic to it."

What has eluded Conrad's critics of *The Secret Agent* is the simple
fact that all time—legal time, civil time, astronomical time, and Universal Time—emanates from Greenwich Observatory *and* that Verloc's
mission, in the intended bombing of Greenwich Observatory, is to destroy
Time Now, Universal Time, or life itself. Conrad's cosmic irony is
exemplified in Mr. Vladimir's theory that "the blowing up of the first
meridian is bound to raise a howl of execration" (II). It's no wonder that
Mr. Verloc is unnerved by Mr. Vladimir's orders—"Go for the first
meridian."[2] *His mission is the destruction of space and time,* as the
great circle of Greenwich meridian is the zero from which space is
measured and time is clocked. From Greenwich zero terrestial longitudes
are reckoned, and what are these when mapped but concentric circles?
Stevie, Winnie Verloc's brother, spends his time drawing "circles,
circles, circles; innumerable circles, concentric, eccentric; a corruscating
whirl of circles that by their tangled multitude of repeated curves,
uniformity of form and confusion of intersecting lines suggested a
rendering of cosmic chaos, the symbol of a mad art attempting the inconceivable" (III). It is ironical that Stevie, the only artist in the world
of *The Secret Agent,* is a half-wit.

Stevie's circles diagram the design of the book. First of all, every
person in *The Secret Agent* is rendered as a circle of insularity, each
insulated from another by his own self-love, by self-illusions and fixed
ideas or theories, while like eccentric circles each selfhood impinges upon
another by sharing some portion of its attributes, outlook or theory.
The novel presents an ironic concatenation of theories or illusions shocked
to zero by the impingements of reality, by the impingements of the
unexpected and the unpredictable.

Ex-convict Michaelis—"round like a tub," having been fattened up
during fifteen years in a damp and lightless prison at the expense of an outraged society—expounds in Adolf Verloc's shop certain theories con-
stituting his apostolic credo; but when his tirade is cut short by a
harsh laugh from Comrade Ossipon, Michaelis thereupon falls into

silence—and Stevie into drawing circles. What they all have in common is an abhorrence of ideas which contradict and upset their own. Insularity characterizes everyone in the novel. "There was no young man of his age in London more willing and docile than Stephen, she affirmed; none more affectionate and ready to please, and even useful, as long as people did not upset his poor head." Theories excite the irrational Stevie; they make him mad! Michaelis talks to himself, only to himself, "indifferent to the sympathy or hostility of his hearers, indifferent indeed to their presence, from the habit he had acquired of thinking aloud hopefully in the solitude of the four whitewashed walls of his cell . . . sinister and ugly like a colossal mortuary for the socially drowned" (III). The mere fact of "hearing another voice disconcerted" Michaelis painfully; he was no good at discussion.

It was the theory of violence which Karl Yundt declared in refutation of Michaelis' optimism that excited Stevie into drawing circles, as though to erect order out of chaos. More theorist than terrorist, Yundt is optimistic in his pessimism: " 'I have always dreamed,' he mouthed fiercely, 'of a band of men absolute in their resolve to discard all scruples in the choice of means, strong enough to give themselves frankly the name of destroyers, and free from the taint of that resigned pessimism which rots the world. No pity for anything on earth, including themselves, and death enlisted for good and all in the service of humanity—that is what I would have liked to see' " (III). Ironically, "The famous terrorist had never in his life raised personally as much as his little finger against the social edifice." Each revolutionist accuses the other of being pessimistic about the future, and each outdoes the other in optimistic theories aimed at the destruction of the world as it is. Michaelis' "optimism began to flow from his lips. He saw Capitalism doomed in its cradle, both with the poison of the principle of competition in its system. The great capitalists devouring the little capitalists . . . and in the madness of self-aggrandizement only preparing, organizing, enriching, making ready the lawful inheritance of the suffering proletariat" (III). As the toothless terrorist Yundt puts it, the nature of our present economic conditions is cannibalistic. Cannibalism and gluttony are evoked in the image of Adolf Verloc butchering some meat for his supper on the night of Stevie's slaughter: "The piece of roast beef, laid out in the likeness of funereal baked meats for Stevie's obsequies, offered itself largely to his notice. And Mr. Verloc again partook. He partook ravenously, without restraint and decency. . . ." (XI) Cannibalism is suggested by the butcher knife in the Verloc household—the knife-motif is recurrent throughout the novel and culminates in the murder scene—and again by "the knife of infuriated revolutionists," which is the knife that Verloc fears. After the explosion at Greenwich Park nothing is left of Stevie but a mound of rags "concealing what might have been an accumulation of raw material for a cannibal feast" (V).

Although the theories of the revolutionists amount to cannibalism, they profess confidence in the future of life on this globe. "The human-itarian hopes of the mild Michaelis tended not towards utter destruction, but merely towards the complete economic ruin of the system." Lady Mabel, his patroness, supports Michaelis (in a cottage at Greenwich Park) and believes in his Theory of the Future. She fails to see that his theory has a hole in it. Universal ruin, as prophesied by Michaelis "would leave the social values untouched. The disappearance of the last piece of money could not affect people of position. She could not conceive how it could affect her position, for instance" (VI). Mr. Verloc, who himself has no future, is Vice-President of the Future of the Proletariat—who likewise has no future. Nobody has any future because nobody shares life or time now; nobody enjoys life except the moron Ossipon, who regards himself as quite the lady-killer. Professor X scorns Michaelis, the visionary prophet of the future. " 'Prophecy! What's the good of thinking what will be.' He raised his glass. 'To the destruction of what is,' he said, calmly" (XIII),[3] As Conrad remarks, "perverse unreason has its own logical processes"—a remark which is exemplified in the person of Professor X, who has a built-in bomb secured to his emaciated body, a sane man insanely equipped to blow himself instantaneously into eternity. The great word that Michaelis utters is Patience, and with that word Patience we've epitomized the character of Professor X, for he exercises heroic patience in his lifelong quest to perfect the perfect detonator—one which doesn't go off at the wrong time! Perverse unreason is ex-emplified also by Michaelis, the Apostle, who is—like Stevie—a harmless creature and "a little mad." His ideas are "inaccessible to reasoning."

"You wouldn't deceive an idiot," says Mr. Vladimir (First Secretary of the Russian Embassy) to Secret Agent Verloc, whereupon Verloc proceeds to deceive the idiot Stevie. Stevie is blown to shreds on the road to Greenwich Observatory while carrying a varnish-can containing a bomb prepared by Professor X, and at the sight of what's left of him an idiotic constable opines "with stolid simplicity: 'He's all there. Every bit of him. . . .' " (V) Poor Stevie never was all there, but then neither is Professor X. It is he, rather than the idiot Stevie, who represents madness personified. "Lunatic!" he shouts at Michaelis, and lunatic is Verloc's label for his wife just before she murders him. Perverse un-reason is exemplified by Winnie Verloc, when after the murder she "imagined her incoherence to be clearness itself" (XII). Or again by Mr. Vladimir, whose "wit consisted in discovering droll connections be-tween incongruous ideas. . . ." (II) Like Professor X, Vladimir is obsessed by a theory of bomb-throwing—if only "one could throw a bomb into pure mathematics." Mr. Vladimir's theory is to attack the sacrosanct fetish of our society. It's not religion, not art, not royalty; it's science. Therefore have a go at astronomy! "Such an outrage combines the greatest possible regard for humanity with the most alarming display of ferocious imbecility."

In the final scene at the Silenus beer-hall the "incorruptible Professor" echoes the sham journalistic sentiment of the newspaper reporting the suicide of Winnie Verloc: "Madness and despair! Give me that for a lever, and I'll move the world" (XIII). He'll move it by blowing it up! Madness and despair sum up his plight as well as Winnie Verloc's, and Winnie in turn shares identity with the irrational Stevie. Just before plunging the carving knife into her husband's breast, "As if the homeless soul of Stevie had flown for shelter straight to the breast of his sister, guardian, and protector, the resemblance of her face with that of her brother grew at every step, even to the droop of the lower lip, even to the slight divergence of the eyes" (XI). Every person in *The Secret Agent* shares identity with another; each circled selfhood overlaps.

As the revolutionists depend upon conventions, so Chief Inspector Heat depends on life—whereas Professor X depends on death: "I depend on death, which knows no restraint and cannot be attacked" (IV). "Like to like. The terrorists and the policeman both come from the same basket. Revolution, legality—counter moves in the same game" (IV). Policeman Heat *and* the social rebels against law and order, they are products of the same machine ("one classed as useful and the other as noxious"). They share a common bond. Heat "could understand the mind of a burglar, because, as a matter of fact, the mind and instincts of a burglar are of the same kind as the mind and instincts of a police officer. Both recognize the same conventions, and have a working knowledge of each other's methods and of the routine of their respective trades" (V). Law and Order *versus* Rebellion against Convention, these two worlds coalesce—like Stevie's eccentric circles, "repeated curves of form and confusion." This situation, the ironic center of the narrative, is expressed otherwise in the Professor's contempt: "You revolutionists . . . are the slaves of the social convention, which is afraid of you; slaves of it as much as the very police that stands up in defense of that convention. Clearly you are, since you want to revolutionize it" (IV). Thus identities overlap, one interfusing with another.

Indolence, immobility, and rotundity characterize Winnie's mother, the plump Winnie Verloc, fat and lazy Verloc, Comrade Ossipon, and Michaelis ("Round like a distended balloon"); prison has fattened up Verloc and likewise Michaelis—"pathetic in his grotesque and incurable obesity." The swollen legs of Winnie's mother have rendered her inactive. Inactive also are the revolutionists—Yundt, Ossipon, Michaelis, and Verloc. Chief Inspector Heat has kinship with the fat revolutionists, while the Assistant Commissioner of Police—"tall and thin"—has kinship with the thin terrorists—Yundt, Professor X, and the innocent Stevie. Each is afflicted with a deformity. The Professor's "stunted stature" has its parallel in the stunted mentality of Stevie—he can't remember even his own name and address! "An absurdity," as Razumov in *Under Western Eyes* reminds us, "may be the starting-point of the most dangerous complications" (III, I).

Everybody in *The Secret Agent* is a fragmented and frustrated anonymity. *Nameless* are Professor X, Winnie's former butcher lover, Winnie's unscrupulous and deformed mother, the clever and non-commital Assistant Commissioner, and Secret Agent △ (as the nameless Adolf Verloc is known in the files of the Russian Embassy). Verloc's alias is Prozor; and Alexander Ossipon, among women intimate with him, goes by the name of Tom; Michaelis is known as the Apostle; Lady Mabel—disciple of the Apostle Michaelis—is known as the Patroness; and the Home Secretary, Sir Ethelred, as the Presence, as the Personage, and also as The Chief. Even when Conrad's characters have names, their identity remains fragmented. Heat, Vladimir, Wormdt, Toodles, Lombroso—all of them lack first-names. Without last names are Lady Mabel, Sir Ethelred, and Stevie—named after Saint Stephen, the martyr. Everyone in *The Secret Agent* is a fragmented selfhood, anonymous or deformed. The purpose of these characteristics is to indicate their lack of vitality and their insulation from life. The insularity of Verloc's perverted and deadly existence is signified by the triangle sign designating his nameless selfhood, and again by the triangle of the street in which his box of a house is located, and by that sign Verloc is reduced to an abstraction. "There was no sparkle of any kind on the lazy stream of his life" (XI). A lifeless automaton, Verloc has no more vitality than the poisoned atmosphere of the Russian Embassy, where nothing exists suggesting life or contact with it except a faintly buzzing house-fly. "The useless fussing of that tiny, energetic organism affected unpleasantly this big man threatened in his indolence" (II).

Everything exists in contradiction of itself, and nothing is but what is not. Winnie Verloc, whom we recognize as personifying death, is also described as representing "the mystery of life". The mystery of life is, of course, simply its unpredictableness. As the emblem of life Winnie Verloc is ironically handicapped by a half-wit brother, a crippled and deformed mother, an anonymous and morally perverted husband, and a lover—Comrade Ossipon—by whom she is betrayed. Life is represented in *The Secret Agent* as irrational (for example, Stevie and the Professor), unreal and devoid of vitality (Verloc), routine and dull (the Assistant Commissioner), conventional (Winnie Verloc), deformed and prostituted (Winnie's mother). The life of Winnie's mother has consisted in running what Conrad politely calls "business houses" where "queer gentlemen" boarded. One conjectures that Winnie, being a dutiful daughter to her "impotent" mother, contributed certain accommodations to these queer gentlemen. While the change from her Belgravian house to Adolf's shop affected her legs adversely, the moral sensibility of Winnie's mother presumably was not exactly shocked when she found herself housed in Verloc's shop of shady wares, as by then this Madame of Business Houses was no doubt rather familiar with them. Of all the persons in *The Secret Agent* the only one spared and protected from the author's grotesque and cosmic ironies is Winnie's mother, and what protects her is the fact of her early removel to an almshouse.

Verloc's contact with life is through Winnie, and Stevie's future depends upon her protection. Everyone is supported or protected by a woman: Yundt, nursed by the woman he betrayed; Michaelis, sustained by his patroness, Lady Mabel; and Comrade Ossipon, whose selfish ego finds satisfaction in women who "put some material means into his hands." It is ironical that the Assistant Commissioner of Police is ruled by a domineering wife, a cantankerous woman who has thwarted his prospects of a career in Europe, wherefore he has nothing to look forward to but evening games of whist at the Explorer's Club. At the crisis, after the bombing at Greenwich Observatory, it is Verloc's bond of respectability that traps him—the convention of a virtuous attachment. Verloc would leave the country at once, just as the police have urged him to do, " 'only he felt certain that his wife would not even hear of going abroad. Nothing could be more characteristic of the respectable bond than that,' went on, with a touch of grimness, the Assistant Commissioner, whose own wife, too, had refused to hear of going abroad. . . . 'From a certain point of view we are here in the presence of a domestic drama' " (X). By playing whist at the Club, the Assistant Commissioner is protected from facing into his own domestic drama—he and his cardtable cronies approach the game "in the spirit of co-sufferers, as if it were indeed a drug against the secret ills of existence. . . ." (V) Conradian irony has reduced a story about revolutionists to their domestic drama, a domestic drama which—whether located in the Verloc household or in Lady Mabel's parlors—represents sanctuary from the secret ills of existence, sanctuary from life or time itself. Winnie Verloc's attempt to escape with Comrade Ossipon to the Continent, to find sanctuary there under the illusion that he is her savior and lover, is thwarted at the start— how escape the island? "The insular nature of Great Britain obtruded itself upon his notice in an odious form" (XII). Stevie's sanctuary from reality lies in the fact that his grasp of language is limited, for he knows only the names of things and ideas that are simple enough not to upset him. "Certain simple principles had been instilled into him so anxiously (on account of his 'queerness') that the mere names of certain transgressions filled him with horror" (VIII). Like Stevie, Lady Mabel and Michaelis live outside of time or reality, of which they are as ignorant as is Sir Ethelred—he has no time for details. "Don't go into details. I have no time for that. . . . Spare me the details" (VII). But it is the details, concrete things and facts, that comprise the reality of life; all else is an abstraction.

Ford Madox Ford speculates that the London of *The Secret Agent* is a city "rather of the human soul than any place in topography. Similarly the Anarchists of *The Secret Agent* are Anarchists of Nowhere: the Enemies of any society. . . ." (In *Thus to Revisit,* 1921). On the contrary, Conrad has rooted his characters in a specific city (not just "A City"); London he knew intimately, far more intimately than his friend Ford speculates. And furthermore he has utilized the actualities of London—

its streets and houses—to provide his characters analogies of themselves or their plight. Verloc's house in Soho is located in a triangular well of "blind houses and unfeeling stones" (XII). *That* defines Verloc himself, unfeeling and blind to the realities. "But Mr. Verloc was not in the least conscious of having got rusty" (II). He's as rusty as "the rusty London sunshine struggling clear of the London mist" to shed a lukewarm brightness into the First Secretary's Russian Embassy room, where Conrad deposits Verloc for Chapter II. At the outrageous hour of halfpast ten in the morning—outrageous because Verloc, a night prowler, is as unfamiliar with the sun as he is with life itself—Verloc departs from Soho for the Russian Embassy. He goes westward—not towards the sun. It's "a peculiarly London sun—against which nothing could be said except that it looked bloodshot. . . . It hung at a moderate elevation above Hyde Park Corner with an air of punctual and benign vigilance. The very pavement under Mr. Verloc's feet had an old-gold tinge in that diffused light, in which neither wall, nor tree, nor beast, nor man cast a shadow. Mr. Verloc was going westward through a town without shadows in an atmosphere of powdered old gold" (II). The bloodshot and shadowless sun identifies itself with Verloc. Its coppery gleams fall on the broad back of his blue overcoat and produce "a dull effect of rustiness."

The coppery gleams and old-gold tinged light befit Verloc's present mood of self-satisfaction. He's in a mood of opulence as he broods on his Theory of Protection, surveying "through the park railings the evidences of the town's opulence and luxury with an approving eye. All these people had to be protected. Protection is the first necessity of opulence and luxury." (His theory is upset by the contrary theory of the First Secretary, a theory having to do with destruction rather than protection.) That Verloc, secret agent, casts no shadow befits his anonymity. It signifies also that he has no future.

Verloc casts no shadow, but he's had a shady past. It includes five years' rigorous confinement in a fortress for betraying the design of a new British fieldgun, a woman having betrayed him. Conrad's description of Verloc as the "betrayer of the secret and unlawful proceedings of his fellow-men" applies overtly to his role as revolutionist; but also covertly it applies to his social role as owner of a shop of shady wares (including pornographic literature), as here again he deals in the unlawful proceedings of his fellow-men. Verloc's shop—"a square box of a place"—is located in "a shady street . . . where the sun never shone. . . ." The insularity of Verloc's household is indicated also by the fact that news from the outside world seldom reaches Brett Street: newsboys never invade it—"It was not a street for their business." Verloc's shop, behind which lives the Verloc household masked by a glazed door, is a front masking his activities as *"agent provocateur."* It wasn't out of love for Winnie that he transported her and her impotent mother and imbecile brother from their Belgravian house to Soho, where he set up the shop with money supplied by Winnie. He gathered that trio and their furniture "to his broad, good-natured breast" so as to provide himself thereby a protective mask. It's a shock to Verloc to be told off by Mr. Valdimir that anarchists don't marry and that he has discredited himself in his world by his marriage. "This is your virtuous attachment—eh? What with one sort of attachment and another you are doing away with your usefulness" (II).

The novel begins (in Chapter II) with Verloc, the domesticated *agent provocateur,* wrenched from his habitual routine—"Mr. Verloc, going out in the morning. . . ." Verloc seldom goes out in the daytime, whereas the Professor seldom goes out at night. Like Verloc, Ossipon "slept in the sunlight." Verloc nominally left his half-wit brother-in-law in charge of the shop during the day, and then—as there was practically no business —the shop-door remained closed. At night "it stood discreetly but suspiciously ajar"—for the shady customers of the shady wares, the queer gentlemen who "dodged in sideways, one shoulder first, as if afraid to set the bell going. The bell, hung on the door by means of a curved ribbon of steel, was difficult to circumvent. It was hopelessly cracked; but of an evening, at the slightest provocation, it clattered behind the customer with impudent virulence" (I). The bell signifies life, the sound of life vibrating in the silence of Brett Street, where the sun never shines and "all the sounds of life seemed lost as if in a triangular well of asphalt and brick" (XII). And that is why the door stands ajar for the queer customers of pornographic wares; so that they can enter without ringing the virulent bell—life, hostile to their moral and sexual impotence. When Winnie Verloc tends the shop, customers "get suddenly disconcerted at having to deal with a woman. . . ." (I). The shop-bell rings, and the solitary deadness of the silent place is disturbed, stirred into life. It has an "aggresive clatter"; it disturbs Stevie until it quiets down. It also unnerves Chief Inspector Heat, the clatter of the cracked bell causing him "to spin round on his heel" (IX). Again, its clatter associates with Verloc's mood of restlessness and Stevie's nervous shuffling of his feet (VIII). When its clattering ceases, the tenants of the shop sense a vacancy, a loss (VIII). "And when the cracked bell ceased to tremble on its curved ribbon of steel *nothing stirred* near Mrs. Verloc, as if her attitude had the looking power of a spell" (IX). After murdering Verloc, Winnie is stirred to life by her chance encounter with the unscrupulous Ossipon, whose only saving attribute is his passionate nature. (Winnie's other romance was with a butcher, whom she rejected for a gentleman—whom she, in turn "butchers".) Ossipon sets the bell clattering both on his entrance and exit from the shop, and it frightens him so much that he pins his arms to his side in "a convulsive hug." "Comrade Ossipon had no settled conception now of what was happening to him" (XII). The bell shatters his stability and self-possession. Is it any wonder then that the "queer gentlemen" try to sidle past that symbolic bell?

That cracked bell associates with moods of bewilderment and con-fusion. At the Silenus beer-hall instead of a bell there is a mechanical piano, whose deafening din confounds explosions of theories voiced by Ossipon and his beer-hall companion, the Professor. It's a slightly defective mechanical piano and "lonely"—executing airs *unaccompanied,* "a valse tune with aggressive virtuosity" (IV). Like the cracked bell with its "aggressive clatter," this "semi-grand piano" signifies life. What's life but the companion of death, each competing against the other! Death is represented by the lonely and mechanical Professor X, who is but the ghost of a human being ("I am deadly"), an automaton executing mad theories with agressive virtuosity, eloquent but slightly cracked. The piano plays distant airs in painfully detached notes, or else it clatters "through a muzurka in brazen impetuosity, as though a vulgar and imprudent ghost were showing off. The keys sank and rose mysteriously" (IV).

As Razumov in *Under Western Eyes* remarks: "There is nothing, no one, too insignificant, too absurd to be disregarded. . . ." It is the in-significant *things* in *The Secret Agent,* the minute particulars of life, that manifest reality; and the characteristic of these pieces of reality is their absurdity—the cracked bell, the cracked wedding ring, the lonely mechanical piano, Verloc's round hat rocking on its crown, Stevie's coat-label, the buzzing fly. All "mere trifles," but not one of these pieces of reality is too insignificant, too absurd to be disregarded. *They each signify the unpredictable,* the absurdly incongruous thing which disturbs routine existence by the sudden fact of its uncalled for and unexpected in-trusion. The nature of reality in *The Secret Agent* is irrational, incongru-ous and incalculable. Take for example, that section of London where the Russian Embassy is located—across from Chesham Square at Num-ber 10.

> With a turn to the left Mr. Verloc pursued his way along a narrow street by the side of a yellow wall which, for some inscrutable reason, had No. 1 Chesham Square written on it in black letters. Chesham Square was at least sixty yards away, and Mr. Verloc, cosmopolitan enough not to be deceived by London's topographical mysteries, held on steadily, without a sign of surprise or indignation. At last, with business-like persistency, he reached the Square, and made diagonally for the number 10. This belonged to an opposing carriage gate in a high, clean wall between two houses, of which one *rationally enough* bore the number 9 and the other was numbered 37. . . .

No. 37 is on Chesham Square, but actually it belongs to Porthill Street. Here, as throughout the novel, the expected does not occur. Rather, what occurs is the unexpected, the irrational. There is no logical sequence to these stray and misnumbered edifices: The fact that No. 37 "belonged to Porthill Street . . . was proclaimed by an inscription placed above the ground-floor windows by whatever highly efficient authority is charged with the duty of keeping track of London's strayed houses." Let these houses get up and rearrange themselves in logical order! "Why powers are not asked of Parliament . . . for compelling those edifices to return where they belong is one of the mysteries of municipal adminstration" (II).

(2)

"Conrad's secret theory examined," F. Scott Fitzgcrald wrote in his *Notebooks*; and the secret of Conrad's scheme? Well, he wrote the truth— "adding confusion however to his structure." Adding confusion to his structure, Conrad has dislocated the chronology of narrated events so as to shape his narrative in circular form. The circular design of *The Secret Agent* manifests Conrad's commentary on human progress, and in this Conrad is at one with Hawthorne: Progress is but circular—a spiral of concentric circles.

The event which initiates all subsequent action—namely the explosion at Greenwich—is first made known in Chapter IV. The first three chapters present preliminary matters and serve as Prologue to the drama. The event which concludes the drama—namely Winnie Verloc's death by drowning—is made known by Ossipon's report of it to the Professor in the Silenus Restaurant—through a newspaper now ten days old. Likewise in Chapter IV, Stevie's death by fireworks is rendered as a reported event, reported subsequent to its occurrence, and again it is made known through the newspaper which Ossipon reads to the Professor in the Silenus Restaurant: a "rosy sheet, as if flushed by the warmth of its own convictions, which were optimistic." Its account of the Greenwich affair is incomplete, and the sentimentalized newspaper report of Winnie's suicide is likewise fragmentary. Of the three main events—the explosion, the murder, and the suicide—only the murder scene is presented as a point-present action, whereas the first and the final events are reported piecemeal through multiple points of view. As the drama ends where it began, the final scene duplicating in setting and in method of presentation the scene in Chapter IV which initiates the entire action, *The Secret Agent* is designed in circular form.

Each of the three main events occurs in a single location, without movement or transition to another place; hence each scene is an enclosed unit, boxed in or encircled. Other than these three enclosed actions in IV, XI, and XIII (the action in IV and in XIII is verbal), all the other scenes present an action or movement progressing from place to place, a journey which ends where it began and which therefore figures as circular. Chronologically, the narrative begins with Chapter II: Mr. Verloc leaves his shop and journeys to the Russian Embassy, and then after his inverview with Mr. Vladimir he returns to the shop, where his arc-like journey began. The opening phrase of the novel—"Mr. Verloc, *going out in the morning*"—is misleading inasmuch as Mr. Verloc does not go out of the shop until the scene of Chapter II, all of Chapter I being a cutback taking us *inside* the shop. It's rather like a picturefilm run backwards; in effect time stands still. The scene of Chapter III, Verloc's shop where the revolutionists expound their various theories, is a self-contained unit of verbal action, enclosed as in a circle. This scene occurs the night of Verloc's harrowing interview with Mr. Vladimir, and then a week elapses between III and VIII, which scene is wrenched from the chronology—in time-sequence VIII follows III. Here again the action is in circular form: from the shop Winnie's mother is taken in "The Cab of death" to the almshouse, Winnie and Stevie returning then to the shop where their journey began. At the beginning of IX Verloc has returned from the Continent, and ten days have elapsed since the incident of the cabman and his mistreated horse, for whom Stevie has the bizarre and "symbolic longing" to make them happy by taking them both to bed with him! In IX Verloc takes an afternoon walk with Stevie, and the next morning they again leave the shop, Verloc returning this time alone. As we knew in Chapter IV, which in time-sequence occurs a few hours after the opening parts of IX, Stevie's been blown to bits—a revelation made to Winnie by Chief Inspector Heat through her identification of Stevie's coat-label. Meanwhile Verloc, who has gone out with an unidentified foreigner (the Assistant Commissioner), returns from the Continental Hotel to the shop. In IX thus three journeys take place (each figuring in circular-form, A to B and back to A).

In time-sequence Chapter IV follows IX, Conrad designing the structure of his book to evoke his theme. The theme of *The Secret Agent* has to do with time, the destruction and confusion of time itself, and *the confused chronology of narrated events by their disarrangement from time effects a structure which is at one with the theme.* Relocated chronologically, subsequent to Chapter IX come chapters IV, V, VI, VII, and then X (which begins where VII ends). In each of these scenes a circular action is rendered. Stevie's circles, "repeated curves" suggesting "form and confusion," diagram the design of the whole novel.

The scene of the murder (XI), which is the climax of the whole domestic drama, occurs simultaneously with the scene which concludes Chapter X. Thus as identities overlap from character to character, so likewise scenes overlap in the time-sequence. And actions circle back to their beginnings. In Chapter XII Winnie leaves the shop (having murdered her husband) and, on encountering Ossipon, she persuades him to return to the shop. Everything circles back upon itself. Actions are thus enclosed in circle form. The scenes in IV and XIII, occurring in the Silenus Restaurant, and in III and XI, occurring in the Verloc shop, present verbal actions only, gestures and words without movement from place to place; these four scenes are self-enclosed. All four of these scenes have to do with violence, theories or acts of violence. That Conrad is tinkering with the clock is hinted at in the scene of the Cab of Death: "and time itself seemed to stand still" (VIII). By backtracking the narrative progression, time is rendered as if standing still, and the same effect is created where one scene overlaps another simultaneously. The calendric span of the narrative is one month, precisely 31 days; but while much time elapses on the author's clock the fact is that all the events *enacted* take place within four days.[4] In the murder scene the clock of narrated events slows down, and momentarily time seems to stand still.

In his *Joseph Conrad* (1947) Mr. Albert Guerard says: "We would not begrudge a hundred slow-moving pages devoted to a study of Winnie Verloc's feelings, but twenty pages sacrificed to the largely physical approach to the murder of her husband seems excessive. . . ." But this misses the intent and the significance of the whole thing. There are in fact more than thirty pages devoted to the murder, of which the preliminaries—beginning with Verloc's irony: "You'll want all your wits about you after I am taken away" (page 232 in the Dent Edition)—consume twenty pages. It is 8:25 p.m. when Winnie, prevented by Verloc from leaving the house, feels trapped and entertains the notion of stabbing—"she wanted a knife" (256). It is ten minutes to nine when, just after planting the butcher-knife in her husband's "broad, good-natured breast," Mrs. Verloc "raised her head slowly and looked at the clock with inquiring mistrust" (264). When next she looks up mechanically at the wooden clock, "She thought it must have stopped. She could not believe that only two minutes had passed since she had looked at it last. Of course not. It had stopped all the time. . . . She seemed to have heard or read that clocks and watches always stopped at the moment of murder for the undoing of the murderer" (268-69). It's not only the wooden clock on the wall that has stopped, but also the author's clock—notably at the moment of the murder. What Marlow in *Lord Jim* explains—"All this happened in much less time than it takes to tell, since I am trying to interpret for you into *slow speech* the instantaneous effect of visual impressions"—describes precisely what Conrad creates in the slow prose of the murder scene—a sense of time suspended.[5]

At the signal from her recumbent spouse, "Come here" (a call "intimately known to Mrs. Verloc as the note of wooing"), "she started forward at once, as if she were still a loyal woman bound to that man by an unbroken contract." He has the fixed idea that she is still his devoted wife, and she is possessed by the "fixed idea" that he "had taken the 'poor boy' away from here in order to kill him . . . the man whom she had trusted, took the boy away to kill him!" The shock of Stevie's death has torn her personality "into two pieces, whose mental operations did not adjust themselves very well to each other." "She had become cunning."

> Her right hand skimmed slightly the end of the table, and when she had passed on towards the sofa the carving knife had vanished without the slightest sound from the side of the dish. Mr. Verloc heard the

creaky plank in the floor, and was content. He waited. Mrs. Verloc was coming.

But not to woo him!

> As if the homeless soul of Stevie had flown for shelter straight to the breast of his sister, guardian, and protector, the resemblance of her face with that of her brother grew at every step, even to the droop of the lower lip, even to the slight divergence of the eyes. But Mr. Verloc did not see that. He was lying on his back and staring upwards.

Conrad has shifted his camera from Winnie's to Adolf Verloc's point of view, and the effect of slow speech is created both by this shift in point of view and by the repetition of a motif which impedes the temporal progression. Here is a prose representation of slow time:

> He saw partly on the ceiling and partly on the wall the moving shadow of an arm with a clenched hand holding a carving knife. It flickered up and down. Its movements were leisurely. They were *leisurely enough* for Mr. Verloc to recognize the limb and the weapon.
> *They were leisurely enough* for him to take in the full meaning of the portent, and to taste the flavour of death rising in his gorge. His wife had gone raving mad—murdering mad. *They were leisurely enough* for the first paralyzing effect of this discovery to pass away before a resolute determination to come out victorious from the ghastly struggle with that armed lunatic. *They were leisurely enough* for Mr. Verloc to elaborate a plan of defence involving a dash behind the table, and the felling of the woman to the ground with a heavy wooden chair. *But they were not leisurely enough* to allow Mr. Verloc the time to move either hand or foot. The knife was already planted in his breast. It met no resistance on its way. Hazard has such accuracies (262-63).

Mr. Verloc's time-sense lags, and his theory of the situation is shattered by the incalculable. Theory or Fixed Idea *versus* the Shock of the Unpredictable—*that* patterns everything in the book.

Mrs. Verloc, in turn, is likewise confounded by a fixed idea. It's the fixed idea that a murder stops the clock. Whereas it seems to her that much time has elapsed since the moment of the murder, "As a matter of fact, only three minutes had elapsed from the moment she had drawn the first deep, easy breath after the blow, to this moment when Mrs. Verloc formed the resolution to drown herself in the Thames. But Mrs. Verloc could not believe that" (269). (She cannot believe that it's been only three minutes.) The clock, *that too* has deceived her. A ticking sound breaks the silence of the room, but she cannot believe that it could possibly come from the clock on the wall because it doesn't fit her theory. Nevertheless, "It grew upon her ear, while she remembered clearly that the clock on the wall was silent, had no audible tick. What did it mean by beginning to tick so loudly all of a sudden? . . . Mrs.

Verloc cared nothing for time, and the ticking went on. She concluded it could not be the clock, and her sullen gaze moved along the walls, wavered, and became vague, while she strained her hearing to locate the sound. Tic, tic, tic." Suddenly, what replaces the *ticking* of the seemingly stopped clock is the trickling of blood from Verloc's corpse, the drops falling "fast and furious like the pulse of an insane clock. At its highest speed this *ticking* changed into a continuous sound of trickling" (265). The Conradian pun identifies clocks and blood, time and life.

As "Mr. Verloc was temperamentally no respecter of persons" (XI), neither was he a respecter of conventions nor of time and reality. In his denial of Time Now he shares with Winnie Verloc, who cared nothing for time, and with Professor X, whose lifetime project is the destruction of what *is*. And again, like Professor X, Verloc's resemblance "to a mechanical figure went so far that he had an automaton's absurd air of being aware of the machinery inside him" (IX). Verloc has no ideas, and his wife thinks only in images. So they are pretty much in accord, and especially so once Verloc is dead: "Except for the fact that Mrs. Verloc breathed these two would have been perfectly in accord: that accord of prudent reserve without superfluous words, and sparing of signs, which had been the foundation of their respectable home life" (XI). Their domestic existence for seven years has been "stagnant and deep like a placid pool. . . ." In mourning for Stevie, Mrs. Verloc dresses in black and masks her face with a black veil: "all black—black as commonplace death itself, crowned with a few cheap and pale flowers." She personifies death veiled as life. When Ossipon discovers the bloody truth that Mrs. Verloc is a murderess, he is terrified. "He saw the woman twined round him like a snake, not to be shaken off. She was not deadly. She was death itself—the companion of life." At the end, having drowned herself, all that remains of Winnie is her wedding ring. That "gold circlet of the wedding ring on Mrs. Verloc's left hand [had] glittered exceedingly with the untarnished glory of a piece from some splendid treasure of jewels, dropped in a dust-bin."

When Winnie had fled the shop, what stopped her at the door was this memento of her late husband: "A round hat disclosed in the middle of the floor by the moving of the table rocked slightly on its crown in the wind of her flight" (XI). Unnerved by that hat, she fails to turn out the light and she leaves the door ajar. Bewilderment and confusion occur again when Comrade Ossipon first sees the hat on his returning to the shop to put out the light and close the door. Now "the true sense of the scene he was beholding came to Ossipon through the contemplation of the hat. It seemed an extraordinary thing, an ominous object, a sign. Black, and rim upward, it lay on the floor before the couch as if prepared to receive the contributions of pence from people who would come presently to behold Mr. Verloc in the fulness of his domestic ease reposing on a sofa. . . . Mr. Verloc did not seem so much asleep now as lying down with a bent head and looking insistently at his left breast. And when Comrade Ossipon had made out the handle of the knife he turned away from the glazed door, and retched violently" (XII). Ossipon "was not superstitious but there was too much blood on the floor; a beastly pool of it all round the hat." This blood-encircled hat upsets his theory that Verloc was the person who was blown to bits at Greenwich. Here's the hat, and there's Verloc sound asleep.

Even at dinner Verloc wore his round hat, and—hatted thus—he indicates his disrespect for conventions, social rituals, and the very feast of life. *That hat represents life misused or denied.* Thus Verloc disregarded "as usual the fate of his hat, which, as if accustomed to take care of itself, made for a safe shelter under the table" (XI). Having fished under the sofa for his misplaced hat, Verloc on finding it "held it *as if he did not know the use of a hat*" (IX). To Stevie, on the contrary, Verloc's hat was a sacred object because it belonged to his beloved mentor and savior. Stevie on one occasion pounced on that hat "and bore it off *reverently* into the kitchen." Whereupon Mrs. Verloc remarked: "You could do anything with that boy, Adolf. . . . He would go through fire for you. He—" (IX), And he does just that. He goes through fire for him. From the fireworks of the exploded bomb the only thing left to identify the disintegrated victim is a rag of a velvet collar with an address-label sewn on it—Stevie's sister had sewn it there as a precaution lest poor Stevie forget his home-address. It is this label that traps Verloc.

"That his wife should hit upon the precaution of sewing the boy's address inside his overcoat was the last thing Mr. Verloc would have thought of. One can't think of everything. That was what she meant when she said that he need not worry if he lost Stevie during their walks. She had assured him that the boy would turn up all right. Well, he had turned up with a vengeance!" (XI) Chief Inspector Heat is bewildered by this unaccountable evidence—it confounds his theory. "I don't account for it at all, sir. It's simply unaccountable. It can't be explained by what I know" (VI). What's to be explained about that triangular label is that it is at once the emblem of Verloc's betrayal of humanity *and* the emblem of Winnie's fidelity, her devotion and love for a human being. Verloc has sacrificed an idiot for an idea, a human being for a theory, the concrete thing for the abstraction. Abstractions earned nothing but Conrad's scorn.

The triangle which identifies the anonymous Secret Agent Verloc (triangular sign signifying both anonymity and insularity) links with the triangle of Brett Street where Verloc lives insulated from sunlight and from life itself. Triangles and circles in *The Secret Agent* have multiple significances. Now there is nothing unpredictable about Mr. Verloc, theoretically speaking from Chief Inspector Heat's point-of-view, and yet the triangular sign of Verloc's identity becomes—in the triangle of the coat-label—*the emblem of the unpredictableness of things.* Again, betrayal and fidelity are written there—the whole moral meaning of the novel. Only Winnie would have thought of that label, out of love for her brother. And he alone, that half-wit, believed in *Verloc*—believed in man. How irrational can one get?

(3)

When Stevie is confused he draws circles, and when Winnie is confused she remembers Stevie drawing circles: "Mrs. Verloc was sitting in the place where poor Stevie usually established himself of an evening with paper and pencil for the pastime of drawing these coruscations of innumerable circles suggesting chaos and eternity" (XI). When Stevie drew circles it was while sitting beside a clock. By drawing circles Stevie found sanctuary from time and from the revolutionists' theories of violence against time. He found sanctuary against chaos and confusion in the form manifested by a circle. What Stevie designed, however, was itself chaos and confusion: "a coruscating whirl of circles that by their tangled multitude of repeated curves, uniformity of form and confusion of intersecting lines suggested a rendering of cosmic chaos, the symbolism of a mad art attempting the inconceivable" (III). What is inconceivable is eternity. "But eternity," as Comrade Ossipon envisions it, "is a damned hole" (XIII). A circle, itself the sign of perfection of form, represents thus a hole in time's continuity—time confused and chaotic, disarranged, terminated (as signified by the blood-encircled hat), or suspended (as signified in the murder scene when clock-time seemingly stops.) Circles and their emblematic objects associate with conditions or states of mental confusion *because* they represent the impingement of the unexpected thing, symbolizing Time the Unpredictable. That's what Time, as distinguished from calculable clock-time, *is*. Eternity's a damned hole. What eternity lacks is precisely what characterizes life or time's continuity, namely the unpredictableness of things. As Razumov in *Under Western Eyes* leaves Haldin's rooms he becomes a figure in "eternity"—with his watch broken, time stands still. When Stevie draws circles representing eternity, holes in time, he is "very good and quiet," and when Razumov attempts to define Eternity the Inconceivable he defines it as "something dull and quiet. There would be nothing unexpected—don't you see? The element of time would be wanting" (I). Obsessed with his theories and fixed ideas, Chief Inspector Heat is not very wise since true wisdom "is not certain of anything *in this world of contradictions*. . . . His wisdom was of an official kind, or else he might have reflected upon a matter *not of theory but of experience* that in the close-woven stuff of relations between conspirator and police there occur unexpected solutions of continuity, *sudden holes in space and time*" (V).

The time-bomb—comprised of Chemical X and concocted by Professor X—is unexpectedly exploded by X, the unknown and incalculable factor in Verloc's calculated plot, in Vladimir's theory of bomb-throwing, and in Chief Inspector Heat's fixed idea. "Impossible!" exclaims Heat on first learning of the explosion. What is deadly to fixed ideas is X, the unknown thing. The example is the root of a tree-stump on which Stevie stumbled, blowing himself into eternity. In that unexpected obstacle of a tree-stump Nature asserts its supremacy against man's conspiracy to destroy what *is*. The attack on the first meridian represents anarchy against Time, blasphemy against God and Nature. "The attack must have all the shock-ing senselessness of gratuitous blasphemy" (Vladimir to Verloc, II).

Whereas Vladimir's theory aims at the destruction of science, Professor X's theory aims at the destruction of conventions by which mankind is restrained. Exterminate the multitude—the weak, the flabby, the silly, the cowardly, the faint of heart, and the slavish of mind. "Theirs is the king-dom of the earth. Exterminate! Exterminate! That is the only way of progress. . . . Every taint, every vice, every prejudice, every convention meets its doom" (XIII). "To destroy public faith in legality was *the im-perfect formula* of his pedantic fanaticism. . . . He was a moral agent—that was settled in his mind" (V). In fact, however, *the only true moral agent is Time.* Lady Mabel, on temperamental grounds, "defies time with a scornful disregard, as if it were a rather vulgar convention submitted to by the mass of inferior mankind." Chief Inspector Heat, contemplating the instantaneous death of the victim of the explosion, rises momentarily "above the vulgar conception of time." "Instantaneous! He remembered all he had ever read in popular publications of long and terrifying dreams dreamed in the instant of waking; of the whole of past life lived with frightful intensity by a drowning man as his doomed head bobs up . . . for the last time." Heat experiences an epiphany—he envisions ages of atrocious pain and mental torture as being contained "between two successive winks of an eye" (V). Verloc's eyes, because they are "not well adapted to winking," perceive nothing of life in the Moment Now —Time Now happens between two successive winks. The Privy Council-lor of the Russian Embassy, Wurmt, is literally shortsighted, and in the second sense of the word the Revolutionists of the Future are also short-sighted.

It is not until Mrs. Verloc confronts the clock after the murder that now, for the first occasion in her life, she is made aware of time. It's not until Verloc is dead that he is rendered as though he were alive, for then as he lies murdered on the sofa and Ossipon leaves the shop, the cracked bell clatters "as if trying in vain to warn the reposing Mr. Verloc of the final departure of his wife—accompanied by his friend" (XII). To perfect a detonator adjustable "to all conditions of action, and even to unexpected changes of conditions," Professor X needs more time. Exterminate Universal Time: "what's wanted is a clean sweep and a clear start for a new conception of life." "But the time! the time! Give me time! Ah! that multitude too stupid to feel either pity or fear. Some-times I think they have everything on their side. Everything—even death—my own weapon." Blow-me-to-bits Professor X (he is death "en-listed in the service of humanity") rebukes Chief Inspector Heat, who personifies the convention of life: "I am doing my work better than you're doing yours." Much better, no doubt of that, since Professor X is, to identify him, Death—the human representation of deadly time. Agent of Death, and therefore "I shall never be arrested." He is a parody of Time the Unpredictable. Insofar as he is human he is also imperfect, for no man can convert himself into a perfect automaton no matter how much machinery he carries inside himself. "The worst is that the manner of exploding is always the weak point with us." In the explosion at Maze Hill Station, an unpredicted event confounds the calculated one— Stevie is blown to bits, instead of the first meridian. The imperfect bomb detonates—symbolically—at the wall protecting Greenwich Observatory, and—appropriately at Maze Hill.

Theories—scientific, political, sociological, economic, psychological— all are reduced to zero by Conrad's diabolic irony. What protection against life that we devise consists of superstitions, myths, theories, conventional conceptions of reality, systems and creeds, codes of behavior by which society is manipulated and controlled; in sum, all that the muddling intellect contrives. The nihilism of *The Secret Agent* ends in a covert affirmation of the supremacy of life. Could we but manipulate reality so that what happens happens as predicted, but no! Time Now is the Unpredictable, life in all its irrational particulars; including X the unknown event. Wherefore I conclude that it is Time the Unpredictable—agent of life and death—that Conrad's novel cryptographically intends as *the* Secret Agent. (1957, 1959)

NOTES

1. Albert J. Guerard in his 1947 pamphlet-study, *Joseph Conrad,* considered *The Secret Agent* as "a *tour-de-force,* and a rather unsuccessful one at that." Guerard was trapped by his thesis that "Conrad's failure is fairly conspicuous whenever there is no character with whom he can identify himself, no sympathetic yet skeptical observer" (pp. 65-66). He takes an entirely different position on *The Secret Agent* in his *Conrad the Novelist* (1958). [Editor's note]

2. The world "in *The Secret Agent* appears stricken with moral insanity which breaks out in the incomprehensible attack on the fifth [sic] meridian," Paul L. Wiley writes in *Conrad's Measure of Man,* p. 107. Perhaps it is because he has his meridians mixed that the attack seems to him incomprehensible.

3. In *The Terrorists: The Story of the Forerunners of Stalin,* by Robert Payne (Funk & Wagnalls, 1957), Sergey Nachayev, one of the terrorists who flung bombs and wrote inflammatory pamphlets, who believed in science and little else, was consumed by "a pure thirst for destruction." His self-abnegation and monstrous insolence and arrogance reminds us of Conrad's Professor X. "Our task," said Nachayev, "is total, terrible, universal and merciless destruction."

4. One week elapses between Chapter III and the subsequent scene in VIII, ten days elapse between VIII and IX (Verloc disappears on a trip abroad), and ten days elapse between XI and the final scene in XIII. Chapter IX uses up two days; Chapter VIII one additional day; II and III comprise another additional day. Everything *happens* within these four days, beginning with the events of II-III, then VIII, then IX.

5. In *The House of Seven Gables* Hawthorne, in the famous death-scene of Judge Pyncheon in Chapter XVIII, creates by a shift in the point of view the effect of a halted segment of time, a symbolic representation of a frozen moment. The parallel is Chapter XI of *The Secret Agent.* Judge Pyncheon

holds his watch in his left hand, but clutched in such a manner that you cannot see the dial-plate." Time ticks on, but not for Judge Pyncheon; and, as in *The Secret Agent,* the narrative progression comes to a standstill by the shift in the point of view—Hawthorne addresses the corpse: "Rise up, Judge Pyncheon!" A housefly alights on the dead man's forehead, and then on his chin, "and now, Heaven help us! is creeping over the bridge of his nose, towards the would-be chief-magistrate's wide open eyes! Canst thou not brush the fly away? Art thou too sluggish?"

Hawthorne's house-fly resettles in the Russian Embassy of *The Secret Agent,* where Verloc hears it buzzing against the window-pane (II). Conrad has also lifted from *The House of Seven Gables* the shop-bell, which before and after the death-scene clatters to return us from that halted segment of time to the recognition of the Moment Now—back to time rushing on with life. In *Macbeth* the time-period of Duncan's murder is framed first by the bell that is rung to bring Macbeth his wine and finally by the bell that clatters to alarm the castle, and so perhaps Conrad and Hawthorne both pawned their bell from Shakespeare.

In both *Macbeth* and *The House of Seven Gables* the bell transports us from the framed segment of time terminated, a hole in time's continuity and in the progression of narrated events; transports us back from this segment, of time fixed and dead, to life and time's flux. (Verloc's shop-bell has the same symbolic import, but its symbolic import is not confined solely to this one.) In *The Secret Agent* the shop-bell rings both before and after the murder, but the interim consumes such a time-span that only the chronologist would notice this bell-enclosing device.

As for other points of comparison, both Hawthorne and Conrad render the dead man as alive, *and* render the living as more dead than alive (with the exception of Holgrave and the scissor-grinder and Ned Higgins and Venner, etc.); in *Macbeth* the resurrected Banquo contends against the living Macbeth, and this ghost destroys his enjoyment of point-present nowness. The Pyncheons are similarly haunted by Maul's curse. All three works dramatize the theme of time.

Both Hawthorne and Conrad evince a predilection for circles. Concentric circles diagram the seven generations of Pyncheons, and circular selfhoods—patented by Hawthorne—reappear conspicuously in *The Secret Agent.* Another point of a parallelism is the circular form of both novels. Again, both novels open on a cutback in the time-sequence, the opening action in both novels beginning in Chapter II.

# JOHN HOWARD WILLS

## Adam, Axel, and "Il Conde"*

"IL CONDE," the last and finest story of *A Set of Six* (1908), has been neglected by Conrad's critics. At most, there have been for it a few words of praise or a paragraph or two as to its "meaning." In view of its almost perfect form and complex symbolism, one can only wonder why it has been so neglected. Perhaps because of its tranquillity.

* From *Modern Fiction Studies,* I, No. 1 (1955), 22-25.

Conrad himself subtitled it "A Pathetic Tale." Tranquil or no, however, it is one of Conrad's greatest short stories. Like all but "Typhoon,"
of his other great stories—like "Heart of Darkness," "Youth," "Amy
Foster," and "The Secret Sharer"—"Il Conde" has it Marlovian narrator massing and charging its material. He is as effective as his more
famous cousins. As one listens to "the magic suggestiveness" of his
language, images become symbols, symbols allegories.

There are two allegories in "Il Conde." The more obvious might be
called, in Paul Wiley's words—although not applied to this story—the
Fall or Expulsion from Eden allegory.[1] In less formal language, it
might be called the allegory of Red Riding Hood and the wicked wolf.
At the outset the narrator stresses the order, security, and geniality of
the Count's world. It was, he says, a "kindly existence, with its joys
and sorrows regulated by the course of Nature—marriages, births,
deaths—ruled by the prescribed usages of good society and protected
by the State." The narrator is somewhat amused by the Count's refined
notions and rather glaring naïvité. He cannot imagine the old boy having "an adventure." Like Red Riding Hood, however, he does have his
"adventure"; he does meet his wicked wolf: "And his eyes gleamed. His
white teeth, too. I could see them. He was very ferocious. I thought
to myself: 'If I hit him he will kill me.'" The wolf of Conrad's story—
and my analogy is justified by the narrator's tone—is a young and gang-
sterish South Italian, "a very powerful Camorra." It is he who reveals
to the Count the several evils of the world. In him the old Count sees
his own degradation and death. It is he, also, who opens the paradisal
gates and thrusts the Count into the wilderness beyond.

The narrator's ironic re-creation of that expulsion relies heavily upon
aural symbolism to parallel and enrich the literal account. The Count's
world has ever been haunted by a quiet, melodious music: "Mimes
and flute-players, in fact." He is a frequent visitor of the Naples opera,
and owns a piano before which he sits "to make a little music" for himself. When seeing the narrator off at the train station, he announces
"his intention of going after dinner to listen to the band in the public
garden, the Villa Nazionale." He will amuse himself "by hearing excellent music and looking at the best society." (And this "best society"
later becomes terribly ironic.)

The Villa Nazionale resembles Eden, with its "grass plots, bushes,
and flowerbeds," its "alleys of trees," and its "Mediterranean splashes."
As the Count enters it, he can hear the "harmonious phrases" of "elaborate music" and "great waves of sonority" ebbing "out into the darkness." Then almost immediately a false chord sounds: "sweet sounds
mingled with bursts of brassy roar, sudden clashes of metal, and grave,
vibrating thuds." The "harmonious phrases" come "persuasively
through a great disorderly murmur of voices and shuffling of feet on
the gravel of that open space." (And here, Conrad, through his narrator, renders the "pathetic premonition" strictly in aural terms—fore-

shadowing even the literal premonition of the Camorra's first appearance.) Disregarding these dissonances, however, the Count strolls quietly down the "alleys of trees." "I can imagine him," the narrator wryly remarks, "enjoying to the full, but with his usual tranquillity, the balminess of this southern night and the sounds of music softened delightfully by the distance."

By this time the images have acquired symbolic value, and they effectively parallel and enrich the allegory of expulsion. The Count now tells our narrator of the robbery: "The clarionet . . . was finishing his solo, and I assure you I could hear every note. Then the band crashed *fortissimo,* and that creature rolled its eyes and gnashed its teeth, hissing at me with the greatest ferocity, 'Be silent! No noise or —' " A few paragraphs later, the narrator, understanding the aural irony of this violent scene, delightfully carries it on in aural terms. As the Count, he says, is on the point of "being disembowelled by the push of the long sharp blade resting murderously against the pit of his stomach . . . great waves of harmony [go] on flowing from the band." Moreover, the robbery itself, he says, is accompanied "by the sweet trilling of flutes and clarionets sustained by the emotional drone of the hautboys." Finally, he gives to the expulsion itself, the closing of the gates, its rather grotesque musical parallel: stripped of his joy, his honor, his security, sitting "all in a heap, panting with the shock of the reaction," the old Count hears the band "executing with immense bravura, the complicated finale," ending with "a tremendous crash." Thus, that wilderness in which the Count now finds himself is a world of gross and infernal noises as well as of hair-raising sights. Standing at the very gates, he can hear the cracking of thunderbolts, the snarling of wolves.

The aural symbolism ends with the crashing of the gates behind the Count. The expulsion allegory, however, does not. The poor Count has yet to realize the nature of the world and its creatures beyond those gates; and he realizes this only on the way to and, especially, within the Cafe Umberto. This ultimate revelation is also carefully prepared for. During the expulsion the Count has found his strongest emotions stirred. The animality of the Camorra has somehow awakened a corresponding animality in himself. And "he was disgusted with himself," in that the Camorra treated him as any other brute creature. "He was shocked at being the selected victim, not of robbery so much as of contempt." With the Count outside the gates, Conrad further develops the idea of the Count's increasing animality by both the tenor of his actions and the narrator's re-creation of those actions. Thus, the narrator reports of the Count: "As his agitation calmed down somewhat, he became aware that he was frightfully hungry. Yes, hungry. The sheer emotion had made him simply ravenous." He gets into a tramcar (which will take him both to town and food) "by a sort of instinct." In town, he gets off on "the Piazza San Ferdinando," where he remains "in distress . . . like a lost dog"—precisely the animal epithet he earlier applied to the Camorra, though, I repeat, his gnashing white teeth more nearly suggest Red Riding Hood's wicked wolf. Conrad carries his expulsion allegory to a masterful conclusion. Within the Cafe Umberto the Count receives his ultimate revelation of the world and its inhabitants. Seeing his assailant at another table, the Count inquires his name of the fawning pedlar, Pasquale.

> "That *Signor Conde*," he said, beginning to rearrange his wares busily and without looking up, "that is a young *Cavaliere* of a very good family from Bari. He studies in the University here, and is the chief, *capo,* of an association of young men—of very nice young men."
> He paused, and then with mingled discretion and pride of knowledge, murmured the explanatory word "Camorra" and shut down the lid. "A very powerful Camorra," he breathed out. "The professors themselves respect it greatly . . . *una lire e cinquanti centesimi, Signor Conde.*"

The wilderness now completely engulfs the old Count. "A numbness" comes over him. He finally realizes that the world into which he has so violently been thrust is a world where power alone—the law of fang and claw—is respected. Pedlars and professors alike pay homage to *centesimi.*
But it is the ferocious beasts themselves—the objects of such homage —which trouble the old Count most of all. Who are they? Aristocrats. University men. As Marlow would certainly have said: some of us. Yet, the nature of the beast is not yet completely clear to the old Count. He must look into the mirror of the Umberto (as the captain must look into the mirror of his "secret sharer"). There, venomously confronting him stands the *Cavaliere*: " 'Ah! So you have some gold on you—you old liar—you old *birba*—you *furfante*! But you are not done with me yet.' " Indeed, the young man's words are true: the old Count has not done with him yet. Liar! *Birba! Furfante!* Again his animal emotions are violently stirred. Is this the way others see him? Can he really be those bestial things? Worthy of a stronger beast's contempt? But maybe everyone . . . Suddenly it comes clear! At the concert there were very many of these "leering or scowling" young men. In fact, at the time of the robbery he was far from sure whether the "moody young man" who earlier shared his table was the same one who was robbing him. Also, when he first entered the Umberto, he again recognized the "type." He had thought, "The young officer over there reading a paper was like that, too. Same type. Two young men farther away playing draughts also resembled—" He had "lowered his head with the fear in his heart of being everlastingly haunted by the vision of that young man." The nature of man is now completely clear to the poor Count: all men are beasts, liars, *birbas, furfantes*—even though (and this is what so dreadfully hurts) they masquerade as something better. Perhaps they have always masqueraded as something better. Yes, wait a moment! The expression on the face of the

*Cavaliere* had reflected "that peculiar expression of cruel discontent to be seen only in the busts of some Roman emperors" the Count had observed in the Museo. So! The world has always been the infernal place it is now: a wilderness, ruled alone by the longest fangs, the sharpest claws.

Being a beast in such a wilderness, the Count has no will to exist any longer; thus, soon after his adventure, overriding the arguments of our sympathetic narrator, he leaves "southern Italy for good and all," when "to go home really amounted to suicide for the poor Count": "And now he was going to his grave. He was going to it by the *train de luxe* of the International Sleeping Car Company, *via* Trieste and Vienna. As the four long, sombre coaches pulled out of the station I raised my hat with the solemn feeling of paying the last tribute of respect to a funeral *cortège*. *Il Conde's* profile, much aged already, glided away from me in stony immobility, behind the lighted pane of glass. *Vedi Napoli e poi mori!*"

But there is a second and more subtle allegory in "Il Conde." Essentially, it is the Ivory Tower myth of the *fin de siècle*, embodied most famously perhaps—thanks to the efforts of Edmund Wilson—in the character of Adams Axel.[2] The Count has come to Naples to escape pain: "At my time of life freedom from physical pain is a very important matter." He is certain that the ancient aristocratic Romans "knew very well what they were doing when they built their villas on these shores . . . They came down to this seaside in search of health, bringing with them their trains of mimes and flute players." The Count too has his "mimes and flute players." In the Count's illusion, beyond the Alps is the place of pain. He has gone there briefly each year, and only out of necessity, to see his married daughter. When one year he stayed as late as the middle of September, he was laid up for three months with his "painful and alarming rheumatic affection."

Now, the Count's tendency to avoid physical pain is symbolic of his tendency to avoid pain in general—and, ultimately, reality itself. Thus his "rheumatic affection" (like Ransome's bad heart) symbolizes his own animality, his own mortality; and his "dislike of the busts and statues of Roman emperors in the gallery of marbles" with their "expressions of cruel discontent" ultimately symbolizes his dislike of seeing animality in others. Like Axel in his castle, the old Count carefully barricades himself against the wilderness.

But the wilderness will not be denied. It comes to meet him exactly as it comes to meet Lord Jim in Patusan, D'Hubert at his country retreat, Axel (and this name is certainly symbolic) Heyst upon his island. It follows him over the Alps into Naples. In fact, it has always been in Naples. It follows him to the concert. Even then he desperately attempts to shake it off. At the concert he is pained by the expression of the young man who shares a table with him. He gets up and leaves. Being "tired of the feeling of confinement," he enters an alley of the gardens. Paradoxically, it is precisely there, while running away, within "an atmosphere of solitude and coolness," amid "the sounds of music delightfully softened by the distance" that he meets the reality of himself. It is the Conrad recognition scene: Jim's meeting with Gentleman Brown, D'Hubert's with Feraud, Heyst's with his three infernal shades.

Perhaps, in tracing the two allegories, I have not sufficiently emphasized Conrad's historical comment in "Il Conde." It seems to me that by linking the Count with the aristocratic Romans "who came down to this seaside in search of health," Conrad is really attempting to account for the decay of civilization—anywhere and any time. Counts and other men best qualified for leadership have throughout the ages, Axel-like, run away from the fangs and claws of emperors and Camorras. Barbarism has ultimately invaded and conquered all lands. Rome, thus, became wilderness. So, too, modern society, where counts—and the universality of the poor Count is certainly suggested by the narrator's assigning him neither name nor nationality—instead of (in good wholesome Captain MacWhirr's words) "facing it," glide away "in stony immobility" within "the *train de luxe* of the International Sleeping Car Company." (1955)

### NOTES

1. In Paul L. Wiley's *Conrad's Measure of Man* (University of Wisconsin Press, 1954). His chapter on *The Arrow of Gold* is reprinted pp. 317-322). [Editor's note]
2. Cf. Edmund Wilson's *Axel's Castle* (Scribner's, 1931, 1947). In reference to the symbolism implicit in Axel Heyst's name see "Conrad's *Victory*" in *The Art of Modern Fiction*, by Ray B. West, Jr. and R. W. Stallman (Rinehart, 1949). In *Studies in Philology*, XLVIII (January 1951), 98-106, Katherine Gatch suggests the likely source for Conrad's Heyst: "Conrad's Axel." [Editor's note]

## ALBERT J. GUERARD

### *Under Western Eyes**

*Under Western Eyes* is a great tragic novel. It is Conrad's final and in some ways most moving treatment of his central story of betrayal and self-punishment. The terms of "The Secret Sharer" are now reversed. The Razumov who chooses to protect society and who betrays the outlaw brother and double Victor Haldin has betrayed himself first of all. But it is rather with *Lord Jim* that *Under Western Eyes* demands to be examined, if only because the two novels are more comparable in length and density. Once again we have the story of a not uncommon man whom chance and suffering render extraordinary; who suddenly has to face a

* From Albert J. Guerard's *Conrad the Novelist* (Harvard University Press, 1958), pp. 231-253.

boundary-situation and most difficult choice; whose crime both makes and breaks him. The act of betrayal, carrying him out of one solitude and into another, lends him a somber magnitude and new moral awareness, and compels him to destroy himself at last. Responses will vary among different readers and different generations as to which act of betrayal was the more fundamental, Razumov's or Lord Jim's. (In the early 1950's, in America, neither the informing on Haldin nor the employment as a police spy would have seemed anything but commendable to certain readers.) But the plot of *Under Western Eyes* builds more impressively than *Lord Jim's,* after the betrayal occurs, and offers a less equivocal pattern of redemption. *Under Western Eyes* never threatens to descend into popular adventure and romance, as *Lord Jim* occasionally does.

Why then does it occupy a slightly less commanding position in the Conrad canon? Presumably because it is distinctly the less original novel of the two. The study of Razumov's guilt and of the Russian temperament generally cannot fail to remind us of Dostoevsky, though Conrad's is a different and far more orderly manner. And there is a much less impressive dramatization of certain psychological processes than in *Lord Jim.* The art of *Under Western Eyes,* moreover—its manipulation of the reader through structure and texture, plot and reflexive reference—is more conventional. It does not to the same degree stand between the reader and the material to control that reader's response. *Under Western Eyes* is Conrad's best realistic novel. But it is not an "art novel" of infinite complexity, and it does not, like *Lord Jim,* change and greatly expand on second and subsequent readings.

Razumov in himself (considered, that is, apart from the narrator's musings on him) is psychologically a fuller and more important creation than Lord Jim. Or, at least, he is a more interesting person. The initial betrayal and the half-conscious stages leading to it are dramatized with great subtlety and economy. For the decision to inform on Haldin is no sudden accident of failing will or swift forestalling vision. At the outset Razumov is "as lonely in the world as a man swimming in the deep sea." He has seen his father Prince K——— once. Once too he saw his half-sisters descend from a carriage, and "felt a glow of warm friendliness towards these girls who would never know of his existence." For he has only the "immense parentage" of Russia, and no more intimate conscious longing than for the silver medal offered by the Ministry of Education for a prize essay. He combines, rather curiously for Conrad, the vulnerable solitary and the sane hard worker. "Razumov was one of those men who, living in a period of mental and political unrest, keep an instinctive hold on normal, practical, everyday life. He was aware of the emotional tension of his time; he even responded to it in an indefinite way. But his main concern was with his work, his studies, and with his own future." Some day, perhaps, he will be a "celebrated old professor."

This is the unawakened man. His stable existence is shattered in the worst possible way when Haldin appears in his room to acknowledge the assassination and ask for help. "The sentiment of his life being utterly ruined by this contact with such a crime expressed itself quaintly by a sort of half-derisive mental exclamation. 'There goes my silver medal!' " He is all the more indignant when Haldin tells him one of the reasons why he was chosen for this confidence: he had no family to suffer in the event his complicity came out. "Because I haven't that, must everything else be taken away from me?" Yet he sets out on his errand of mercy to find the driver Ziemianitch, impelled by instinctive loyalty to a fellow student and perhaps even by his "personal longings of liberalism." The account of his approach to political conversion on that night is brief but extremely convincing: his egoism and fear create the doctrinal commitment which alone can rationalize the betrayal. Thus the inert drunken Ziemianitch, whom he beats in frustrated rage, provokes meditations on power and the "stern hand." And Razumov's personal plight ("done for" between "the drunkenness of the peasant incapable of action and the dream-intoxication of the idealist incapable of perceiving the reason of things") is by implication national.

At this point, "conscious now of a tranquil, unquenchable hate," he has his first phantom vision of Haldin lying on his bed as if dead. The half-conscious mind at least is approaching that decision to betray. "Must one kill oneself to escape this visitation?" In rage he stamps his foot on the snow, and under it feels the "hard ground of Russia, inanimate, cold, inert, like a sullen and tragic mother hiding her face under a winding-sheet." He experiences an intuition of Russia's "sacred inertia," which must not be touched, and of absolute power which must be preserved for the great autocrat of the future. Within, some "superior power had inspired him with a flow of masterly argument." The superior power is his ability to rationalize and generalize selfish aims. It interweaves, indeed masterfully, his concern with his possibly ruined career and his awareness of Haldin as a disruptive political force; his selfish rage and his theory of the throne. He is disturbed in his reflections by the yell of one sledge-driver to another, "Oh, thou vile wretch!" But the phrase drives him on rather than deters him. Immediately afterward he experiences his hallucination of Haldin lying in the snow across his path. He forces himself to walk over the breast of the phantom—and decides to give Haldin up. Betray him? "All a man can betray is his conscience. And how is my conscience engaged here; by what bond of common faith, of common conviction, am I obliged to let that fanatical idiot drag me down with him?" His decision, as the narrator remarks, "could hardly be called a decision. He had simply discovered what he had meant to do all along." And when the long evening is ending (after he has informed on Haldin, after Haldin has left his room) he hears himself say "I confess"; and thinks of himself as on a rack. This is, surely, great dramatic writing. But the drama is largely within.

For the remainder of the novel Razumov is always on a rack; or on the two racks of fear and guilt. There are times when it is difficult to distinguish between the two, and if the analysis of guilt is more impressive, the dramatization of fear is more exciting. The greatest actual menace is a Dostoevskian *dédoublement* and consequent reckless volubility and snarling uneasiness. Razumov watches appalled his own indiscretions and temptations to confess. Even before Haldin is arrested, he speaks to General T—— with dangerous violence. The rack turns after the police visit to his room and more swiftly through the interview with Councillor Mikulin. Even as he talks Razumov is appalled by his own flow of hasty words, and during the interview has a frightening vision of "his own brain suffering on the rack—a long, pale figure drawn asunder horizontally with terrific force . . ." And when he becomes a police spy (having found no other answer to Councillor Mikulin's sinister question "Where to?") the real danger is immeasurably increased.

In Geneva he is unwisely talkative with Peter Ivanovitch and with Sophia Antonovna, who had been sent to Geneva to verify an identity. He insists unwisely on the distrust of the exiles, but he had largely invented that distrust; he is aware of his savage curtness and cannot control it. "Even as he spoke he reproached himself for his words, for his tone. All day long he had been saying the wrong things. It was folly, worse than folly. It was weakness; it was this disease of perversity overcoming his will." From the first moment he behaves unwisely in front of the killer Necator, who will presently burst his eardrums. In the grand traditional pattern Razumov, literally menaced by death, is throughout his own worst enemy. When he has finally won outward impunity he must, because of that other rack of guilt, confess what no one would have ever discovered.

The two racks turn in unison. It would be hard to conceive a plot more successfully combining dramatic suspense and psycho-moral significance. Through the second and much of the third part the reader has no certain knowledge that Razumov, welcomed in Geneva as the late Haldin's friend and associate, is actually a police spy. The motives for his presence might as plausibly be inward ones: a self-destructive tempting of fate; a compulsion to confront those most likely to destroy him; even, an unconscious effort to appease guilt through reenactment of the crime. "Ah, Peter Ivanovitch, if you only knew the force which drew—no, which *drove* me towards you! The irresistible force." Razumov is thinking of Councillor Mikulin. But the reader is likely to think of a generalized self-destructiveness, and the reader not Razumov would be right. That *is* the hidden motive, hidden even from him. Thus Razumov, in his "satanic" game of suggesting yet concealing a second and truer meaning from Peter Ivanovitch, stumbles with unconscious irony upon a third and truest one. Only he can do the "work" of redeeming himself through confession; he has indeed been impelled, by the strongest of psychic drives; he does not stand before Ivanovitch confessed, but someday he will. And a "blind tool" he may well be, though at the end he will go as far as possible toward converting compulsion into moral choice. But Razumov, of course, has no idea he is saying all this:

"You have been condescending enough. I quite understood it was to lead me on. You must render me the justice that I have not tried to please. I have been impelled, compelled, or rather sent—let us say sent—towards you for a work that no one but myself can do. You would call it a harmless delusion: a ridiculous delusion at which you don't even smile. It is absurd of me to talk like this, yet some day you will remember these words, I hope. Enough of this. Here I stand before you—confessed! But one thing more I must add to complete it: a mere blind tool I can never consent to be."[1]

By delaying as long as he does the formal revelation that Razumov is Mikulin's agent, Conrad preserves a sympathy that would (with a more abrupt procedure) have been lost. We must see Razumov suffer before we see, nakedly, this second of his crimes. And the "deceptive" impression that Razumov is obeying a psycho-moral compulsion is not deceptive at all. He has been sent to Geneva to write incriminating reports on the exiles. He will write instead his diary and condemning self-analysis.

The novel's anatomy of guilt is Dostoevskian, which means that it is true; the difference is that Conrad's method is infinitely more selective. His dramatization of the phantom, for instance, and its slow attenuation from sharp hallucination to symbolic force and allusion, is remarkably tactful and convincing. The original vision on the snow (coinciding with the decision to give Haldin up) is reported in a cool, matter-of-fact prose. It is a "phenomenon," and Razumov tackles it calmly. But when he reaches his room, and finds Haldin lying on his bed as though already dead, he reflects: "I have walked over his chest." He touches Haldin's shoulder and at once feels "an insane temptation to grip that exposed throat and squeeze the breath out of that body, lest it should escape his custody, leaving only a phantom behind." The vision during the Mikulin interview of his own brain suffering on the rack is also of this Haldin-phantom. And shortly after that interview (as we glance ahead to Part IV) Razumov sees Haldin as a "moral specter infinitely more effective than any visible apparition of the dead." He thinks that the specter cannot haunt his own room, through which the living Haldin had blundered; supposes, glancing at the bed, that he would never actually see anything there. But only two pages later he does.

Through much of the second and even third parts we have little chance to see the phantom, since we long watch Razumov from the outside. But we note his stammering "compelled" remarks to Madame de S—— that he too had had an "experience," had once seen a phantom. The interview with Sophia Antonovna, treated more subjectively, shows that the phantom has become featureless; is becoming, so to speak, a component of mental discourse. "He had argued himself into new beliefs; and he had made for himself a mental atmosphere of gloomy and sardonic reverie, a sort of murky medium through which the event appeared like a featureless shadow having vaguely the shape of a man; a shape extremely familiar, yet utterly inexpressive, except for its air of discreet waiting in the dusk."

Razumov thinks of it as "not alarming." But this quiet prose certainly conveys alarm, and on the next page his allusions to Madame de S——'s spiritualist powers and to the "cold ghost" of a tea seem mildly obsessive. The phantom, which had been "left behind lying powerless and passive on the pavement covered with snow," is perhaps most powerful when embodied in Mrs. Haldin and Nathalie on the long night of confessions. "The fifteen minutes with Mrs. Haldin were like the revenge of the unknown." There is something Razumov cannot understand in her manner; she is as white as a ghost; she falls into an incomprehensible silence. But the terms are naturalistic; Haldin continued to exist, but "in the affection of that mourning old woman." Razumov strides from the room, leaving her behind; it is "frankly a flight." But he comes upon Nathalie. "Her presence in the ante-room was as unforeseen as the appearance of her brother had been." And the time for a full confession has come.

The phantom (whether as hallucination, psychic symbol, or shorthand notation of anxiety) does not have the major part in the story of Razumov's torment. The ferocious ironies of his situation, rather, constitute that major part: to be honored by his fellow-students for a supposed complicity in the assassination; honored by Haldin himself for his "unstained, lofty, and solitary" existence; welcomed by the Geneva exiles with respect and by Nathalie Haldin with a dedicated passion, and who has, thanks to the betrayal, the only real conversation with his father in his whole life. Razumov's immediate response (waking chilled on the morning after Haldin's capture) is not fear or shame but a plausible mental stagnation and inertia. His "conservative convictions . . . had become crystallized by the shock of his contact with Haldin." However, his notes and books have become a "mere litter of blackened paper." He compels himself to go to the library, but an "infinite distress . . . annihilated his energy." The apathetic state passes, after the interview with Councillor Mikulin, into an actual psychosomatic illness, briefly and brilliantly described.[2] He emerges from it to find things "subtly and provokingly" changed. But he continues to suffer from ennui, the fitfulness and dread when outside alternating with a total inertia when at home. One might suppose the room would become "morally uninhabitable." But this does not happen, perhaps because Razumov has now entered into his second and testing solitude:

> On the contrary, he liked his lodgings better than any other shelter he, who had never known a home, had ever hired before. He liked his lodgings so well that often, on that very account, he found a certain difficulty in making up his mind to go out. It resembled a physical seduction such as, for instance, makes a man reluctant to leave the neighborhood of a fire on a cold day.[3]

The portrait is psychologically and dramatically true. But it cannot be conveyed through summary, nor reduced to the shortcuts of psychological discourse. The very great scene of Razumov's confession to Nathalie

Haldin cannot (though we recognize such elements as the phantom) be abstracted at all. The scene is as it were irreducible. Even the furnishings of the little ante-room, with its remorseless light and its hooks recalling the hook on which Ziemianitch was found hanging, seem part of the inward experience. The drama is intensified by the unconscious irony of the teacher of languages, who thinks he is to witness a love scene: "The period of reserve was over; he was coming forward in his own way." Razumov is indeed coming forward; but "watching himself inwardly, as though he were trying to count his own heart-beats, while his eyes never for a moment left the face of the girl." He exists, speaks under the greatest conceivable strain. For this is now a matter of life and death, of moral life or death. The great spectacle is of the mind breaking willfully not compulsively through its long habit of evasion, calculating its moves, pausing long enough to ask about the efficacy of remorse; and circling down to the truth. The denunciation of self does not involve a blind jump from one state of being to another. The final speeches, on the contrary, bring into play and as it were into the open all the essentials of Razumov's being, and all the terms of his conflict. His triumph is a genuine one.

For the crime which had broken Razumov has now fully made him. Thus he has the strength necessary, after leaving Nathalie Haldin, to add certain confessions to his diary and then go before the assembled revolutionists at the house of Julius Laspara, there to put his back against the wall and make his public confession. "He was the puppet of his past," yet also a free agent to some degree. The comment made later by Sophia Antonovna applies well enough to both confessions:

> Well, call it what you like; but tell me, how many of them would deliver themselves up deliberately to perdition (as he himself says in that book) rather than go on living, secretly debased in their own eyes? How many? . . . And please mark this—he was safe when he did it. It was just when he believed himself safe and more—infinitely more— when the possibility of being loved by that admirable girl first dawned upon him, that he discovered that his bitterest railings, the worst wickedness, the devil work of his hate and pride, could never cover up the ignominy of the existence before him. There's character in such a discovery.[4]

The written confession (pages 358-362) raises the one serious question concerning the characterization's over-all authenticity and firmness. For the Razumov of these pages, whose voice and style are fairly convincing, claims to have been a much more cynical person, in his relationship with Nathalie Haldin, than we have had any reason to suspect. A few sentences (which I draw together from two pages of the novel and which therefore falsify their texture and pace) will indicate how very much is claimed:

> I was given up to evil. I exulted in having induced that silly innocent fool to steal his father's money. He was a fool, but not a thief. I made him one. It was necessary. I had to confirm myself in my contempt and

hate for what I betrayed . . . Listen—now comes the true confession. The other was nothing. To save me, your trustful eyes had to entice my thought to the very edge of the blackest treachery . . . And do you know what I said to myself? I shall steal his sister's soul from her. When we met that first morning in the gardens, and you spoke to me confidingly in the generosity of your spirit, I was thinking, "Yes, he himself by talking of her trustful eyes has delivered her into my hands!" If you could have looked then into my heart, you would have cried out aloud with terror and disgust . . . Perhaps no one will believe the baseness of such an intention to be possible . . . every word of that friend of yours was egging me on to the unpardonable sin of stealing a soul . . . I returned to look at you every day, and drink in your presence the poison of my infamous intention.[5]

The conception is a powerful one: Dostoevskian if not Russian, perhaps simply human. Moreover, it is at least logically consonant with a psychology which sees in reënactment one of the spirit's few ways of coping with unappeased guilt. One function of the phantom is to remind us, and Razumov, that Haldin must be killed again and again. And the conception appears plausible enough if we go outside the novel to speculate on the possibilities for evil of a man who has done what Razumov has already done. And yet it seems (coming so late in the story) rhetorical, arbitrary, untrue. One reason may be that symbolic reënactments are rarely as conscious as this. A more important reason is that we have known Razumov only as a man on the two racks of fear and guilt. He has had little time for anything else. But most of all, the claims seem untrue to everything we have seen of his relationship with Nathalie Haldin.

The very first meeting was a brief one. But her first remarks to Razumov—"You are Mr. Razumov" . . . "Can't you guess who I am?" . . . "Victor—Victor Haldin!"—are enough to send him reeling against the wall of the terrace. (Later, Razumov is "tempted to flight at the mere recollection" of that meeting.) His response to the first interview in the narrator's presence is a curious irritability and an "unrefreshed, motionless stare, the stare of a man who lies unwinking in the dark, angrily passive in the toils of disastrous thoughts." There is no reason to believe, here, that the "disastrous thoughts" are other than those prompted by fear and guilt. Furthermore, not all our view of Razumov's relationship with Nathalie Haldin is from the outside. Whatever intentions he had to "steal the soul" would surely have come out on the occasion of Peter Ivanovitch's request that he, *la personne indiquée,* bring Nathalie to the Chateau Borel group. Tekla explains to him, a few minutes later, why such a contact would be ruinously disillusioning for her. The occasion for evil is thus propitious. But Razumov's inward reaction is a vague one of *dédoublement,* loathing, uneasiness.

Was the diabolism confessed in writing then only an after-thought, a new idea discovered this late in the novel and too attractive to expunge? The more probable explanation is that Conrad, writing here in Razumov's

name for the first time, returned imaginitively to his original plan for
the novel. It was to have been entitled *Razumov*, and would have involved much more melodrama. And it would have dramatized a much
greater cynicism:

> 2d in Genève. The student Razumov meeting abroad the mother
> and sister of Haldin falls in love with that last, marries her and, after
> a time, confesses to her the part he played in the arrest of her brother.
>
> The psychological developments leading to Razumov's betrayal of
> Haldin, to the confession of the fact to his wife and to the death of
> these people (brought about mainly by the resemblance of their child
> to the late Haldin), form the real subject of the story.[6]

The temptation to steal the soul may be described as another "lost
subject."

Otherwise, the characterization of Razumov is altogether impressive.
It would be futile to try to define with exactness the creative situation
behind it. There are depths below depths in these matters, and a symbolic
repudiation of self may turn out to be, finally, a secret justification. But
the situation was certainly an intense one, involving no small degree of
intellectual identification with Razumov, informer and police spy. It is
as though an officer sharing far more of Conrad's convictions than Jim
had leaped off the *Patna*. The author recognizes the egoistic sources of
Razumov's conversion, and he does not share the mystical absolutism of
his new faith. But he lends to Razumov the very language of his own
scorn of visionaries, even the favorite and personal *secular:* "Visionaries
work everlasting evil on earth. Their Utopias inspire in the mass of
mediocre minds a disgust of reality and a contempt for the secular logic
of human development." He would agree with Razumov that "twenty
thousand bladders inflated by the noblest sentiments and jostling against
each other in the air are a miserable incumbrance of space, holding no
power, possessing no will, having nothing to give."

Thus the reasoned political credo Razumov writes immediately after
Haldin's arrest could serve as Conrad's own:

> History not Theory.
> Patriotism not Internationalism.
> Evolution not Revolution.
> Direction not Destruction.
> Unity not Disruption.[7]

The student Razumov at the outset shows, moreover (and in the Author's
Note as well as in the text), the supreme maritime virtues of sanity and
steadiness. Even the betrayal of Haldin, seen in the context of Conrad's
respect for law and distrust of revolution, could be said to correspond
with certain authorial convictions.

But only with convictions, and only with certain of these. The energiz-
ing conflict derives from the fact that Razumov, this sane conservative

scorner of visionaries and servant of law and victim of revolutionary
folly, is (when he informs on Haldin) dramatized as committing a crime;
he has violated the deepest human bond. This implication seems to me
unarguable. If it were not present, the rest of the novel would be morally
meaningless. And it is of course the suffering guilty man (rather than
the "ordinary young man" with "sane ambitions" of the Author's Note)
who elicits the prolonged act of novelistic sympathy. "You have either
to rot or to burn," Sophia Antonovna remarks in a different context. The
Razumov of the opening pages (whose "main concern was with his work,
his studies, and with his own future") rots. He has not yet entered the
moral universe, and he enters it by committing the crime. But thereafter
he elicits as much sympathy (not approval) as any of Conrad's protagonists. The achievement of this dramatic sympathy is all the more remarkable, of course, because Razumov is not just any betrayer of the
human bond. He is also a Russian.

"The most terrifying reflection (I am speaking now for myself) is that
all these people are not the product of the exceptional but of the general
—of the normality of their place, and time, and race . . . The oppressors
and the oppressed are all Russians together; and the world is brought once
more face to face with the truth of the saying that the tiger cannot change
his stripes nor the leopard his spots." Thus Conrad wrote of his characters
years afterward, and three years after the Revolution, in his Author's
Note. But the novel itself shows no little ambivalence, and perhaps its
greatest act of imaginative integrity (i.e., fidelity to such truth as the
dream discovers) is its marked creative sympathy with Russia and Russians, a sympathy which extends even to some of the revolutionary exiles.
"I think that I am trying to capture the very soul of things Russian,"
Conrad wrote to Galsworthy. But he was at least briefly captured by that
soul, and on the devil's side without knowing it. The narrator, to be
sure, makes certain negative statements which Conrad would have signed
in an essay or preface: on the spirit of Russia as the spirit of cynicism;
on Russian scorn of the practical forms of political liberty; on her "terrible corroding simplicity in which mystic phrases clothe a naïve and hopeless cynicism"; on her detestation of life, "the irremediable life of the
earth as it is . . ."[8] But the novel's over-all tone is compassionate, and
especially toward the sufferings reported by Tekla and Sophia Antonovna.

"Sometimes I think that it is only in Russia that there are such people
and such a depth of misery can be reached." There runs throughout a
counterpoint of East and West, which is in part a counterpoint of the
suffering and the secure. "It is a very miserable and a very false thing to
belong to the majority," Nathalie Haldin says, and the narrator pleads in
defense of England's "bargain with fate" that she too has had tragic times.
The contrast, if not between those who burn and those who rot, is between those who burn and those who have escaped from the fire. The
teacher-narrator (at times much less sympathetic to Russia than is the
novel as a whole) once seems almost to speak for its own uneasy con-

science: "It is not for us, the staid lovers calmed by the possession of a conquered liberty, to condemn without appeal the fierceness of thwarted desire." Russia exists, to borrow Rathenau's famous phrase, in the soul-saving "abyss of sin and suffering."

The counterpoint becomes necessarily, and a little unluckily for the West, a counterpoint of Russia and Switzerland. And in the area of cool judgment there can be little doubt as to Conrad's preferences. They are for the order and stability of Swiss democratic institutions, as for the stolid decency of the English narrator. But Geneva is the "respectable and passionless abode of democratic liberty," and the narrator himself composes a very tendentious contrast whose sympathies go in an entirely different direction. He considers the Bastions, where Nathalie Haldin and Razumov will meet:

> I saw these two, escaped out of four score of millions of human beings ground between the upper and nether millstone, walking under these trees, their young heads close together. Yes, an excellent place to stroll and talk in. It even occurred to me, while we turned once more away from the wide iron gates, that when tired they would have plenty of accomodation to rest themselves. There was a quantity of tables and chairs displayed between the restaurant chalet and the bandstand, a whole raft of painted deals spread out under the trees. In the very middle of it I observed a solitary Swiss couple, whose fate was made secure from the cradle to the grave by the perfected mechanism of democratic institutions in a republic that could almost be held by the palm of one's hand. The man, colourlessly uncouth, was drinking beer out of a glittering glass; the woman, rustic and placid, leaning back in the rough chair, gazed idly around.[9]

The counterpoint of Swiss and Russian would seem to be, as we consider all the references to Geneva and consider all of the narrator's complacencies, not merely one of the secure and the suffering, but also of the respectable and the anarchic, the decent and the messy, the complacent and the compassionate, the mercenary and the mystical, the "saved" and the tragic, the abstract and the human. The narrator's own obtuseness is one of the great sources of this created sympathy for the damned. His mumbling about "Western readers" and about "a lurid, Russian colouring" at the moment of the Haldins' most intense grief, increases sympathy for the Russians generally. And his astonishment because the revolutionists visit the deafened Razumov throws an unfavorable light on his own automatic moralism, and a final light on their unexpected compassion.

Irving Howe's argument that the novel is weakened because it develops too little sympathy for the revolutionaries strikes me, in fact, as seriously mistaken.[10] It would be unreasonable to demand much for the squeaky-voiced killer Necator (himself a police spy, as it turns out) or for Julius Laspara. But Tekla in her appointed role as nurse and companion of the punished sinners (she herself recruited by a "saintly apple-woman") is a familiar Dostoevskian figure of compassion. Her narrative to Nathalie Haldin (pages 149-155) is a moving account of suffering "inside Russia." It subtly prepares us, moreover, for Razumov's own fate, and on a second reading functions as very striking reflexive reference. (Her humble offer of her services to Razumov reveals an ear for feminine speech and feminine logic—or, it may be, a compassionate imagination rather than ear —not evident in the earlier novels.) And even the "wrong headed" Sophia Antonovna, as Conrad calls her in his Author's Note, wins some of the affection he normally accords durable old soldiers. For this is what she is: the white-haired veteran of revolution who had begun going to the secret societies at sixteen, and who had cut her hair as a "first step towards crushing the social infamy."

A novelistic sympathy for these women is natural enough. But there may also exist, in addition to such sympathy and in addition to a normal unconscious sympathy with the outlaw, a creative sympathy with the exceptional buffoon or exceptional object of contempt. Such may be the truest meaning of Milton's alliance with Satan, or of Shakespeare's with Iago and Richard III. And Dostoevsky's power to dramatize the fool as from within, many fools in fact, is one of the sure tokens of his genius. There is some of this in Conrad. He groups the feminist Peter Ivanovitch and Madame de S—— as "fair game" in his Author's Note. "They are the apes of a sinister jungle and are treated as their grimaces deserve." But the ironic account of Peter Ivanovitch's absurd heroic progress across Siberia, engirdled by his chain ("that simple engine of government") is one of the summits in Conrad's work.

It has a quality of vividness, humor, and phrasing that only imaginative sympathy can achieve. Mere scorn could not conceive the disastrous dropping of the file, or the faint jingling of the chain, or the "naked tawny figure glimpsed vaguely through the bushes with a cloud of mosquitoes and flies hovering about the shaggy head," or the leaves and twigs in his tangled hair that astonish his rescuer. Indeed mere scorn could hardly dramatize so well a fatuousness which describes the events leading up to his obtaining of the file as an "obscure episode . . . in the history of ideas in Russia." The retrospective narrative and image of Ivanovitch and his cloud of mosquitoes notably affects our present view of him riding in a landau with Madame de S—— in Geneva: "the 'heroic fugitive' . . . sitting, portentously bearded and darkly bespectacled, not by her side, but opposite her, with his back to the horses. Thus, facing each other, with no one else in the roomy carriage, their airings suggested a conscious public manifestation." We may borrow the word. It may be that the imaginative sympathy (combined of course with the deepest scorn) is for Ivanovitch as a total, realized manifestation of a type.

*Cosas de Russia* . . . This novel, if we are to believe either the classics of Russian fiction or the enigmatic accounts of current events, does come remarkably close to the "very soul of things Russian." The brief glimpses of life in St. Petersburg are most convincing. So too are Victor Haldin, with his strange speech on the "divine" resignation of the Russian soul; and the long bony student living on the fringe of conspiracy, and the contradictions of "Madcap" Kostia; and the fanatic General T——, and the weary Prince K—— with his aura of Western culture. Nathalie's vision of unity and her contempt for political parties are Russian; so too is her mystical vision of a time of concord. "Listen, Kirylo Sidorovitch. I believe that the future will be merciful to us all. Revolutionist and reactionary, victim and executioner, betrayer and betrayed, they shall all be pitied together when the light breaks on our black sky at last." Will Russians in their "land of spectral ideas and disembodied aspirations" turn always to autocracy and turn "at last from the vain and endless conflict to the one great historical fact of the land"? In any event the trial of Councillor Mikulin reminds us that much that has seemed grotesque in the Soviet system is, simply, Russian:

> Later on the larger world first heard of him in the very hour of his downfall, during one of those State trials which astonish and puzzle the average plain man who reads the newspapers, by a glimpse of unsuspected intrigues. And in the stir of vaguely seen monstrosities, in that momentary, mysterious disturbance of muddy waters, Councillor Mikulin went under, dignified, with only a calm, emphatic protest of his innocence—nothing more. No disclosures damaging to a harassed autocracy, complete fidelity to the secrets of the miserable *arcana imperii* deposited in his patriotic breast, a display of bureaucratic stoicism in a Russian official's ineradicable, almost sublime contempt for truth; stoicism of silence understood only by the very few of the initiated, and not without a certain cynical grandeur of self-sacrifice on the part of a sybarite.[11]

*Under Western Eyes* is not, like *The Secret Agent,* a small and symmetrical triumph of controlled form. It sets itself few technical boundaries, yet occasionally overflows even these to leave momentary impressions of clumsiness. Certain scenes in the second and third parts, carried on the "deluge of dialogue," are much too long. In this middle section of the novel, moreover, Conrad sometimes fails to conceal his embarrassment in the presence of acute problems of point of view. And the elderly teacher of languages and unprofessional narrator (who shows himself such an expert novelist through most of the first part) creates unnecessary obstacles by raising the question of authority. For this naturally leads us to examine and question his. Should he not rather have pretended to that truest authority which has nothing to do with Jamesian logic, and which he phrases very well in the second sentence below?

> Wonder may be expressed at a man in the position of a teacher of languages knowing all this with such definiteness. A novelist says this and that of his personages, and if only he knows how to say it earnestly enough he may not be questioned upon the inventions of his brain in which his own belief is made sufficiently manifest by a telling phrase, a poetic image, the accent of emotion. Art is great! But I have no

art, and not having invented Madame de S——, I feel bound to explain how I came to know so much about her.[12]

The source and breadth of a narrator's information is of little importance as such. An example of looseness will serve, which would doubtless have caused James to groan. The nominal authority for the early St.
Petersburg chapters is Razumov's diary, a diary which for the reader
scarcely exists. This authority is obviously exceeded when the narrator
enters Prince K——'s study, there to discover him "sitting sadly alone."
The one thing of importance here violated, however, is the reader's intimate identification with Razumov. The instance is trivial and serves to
remind us that Conrad too could forget about that diary. (Though it
presumably was a protective, interposed instrument of no little use to
his imagining.) A far more radical clumsiness—a clumsiness almost
amusing in such a great novel—occurs in the first pages of Part III, as
the narrator shuttles back and forth between Razumov's subjective view
and his own eyewitness report. And there is to be sure the classic moment
of awkwardness when (page 317) the narrator walks into his own narrative by coming into Razumov's line of vision.

But these are small flaws in the surface of a major success. The narrative method evidently worked, since it helped or at least permitted
Conrad to dramatize his major scenes, rather than report them; and
helped him to achieve his meaning without recourse to *The Secret Agent's*
heavy verbal irony. The method (in its combination of the meditative
and the dramatic, the personal and the objective) is in part a development of that used in *Lord Jim*. It represents a serious effort to extend
the possibilities of first-person narration without losing most of its generic
advantages.* The teacher of languages is, unlike the Marlow of *Lord Jim,*
the only narrator of the novel. But he manages to function at certain
times as third-person omniscient observer, at other times as first-person
eyewitness-participant. The first part, though based on a "document," is
as forthright and as economical as the opening chapters of *Lord Jim*. It
can evoke the assassination in a few paragraphs (here really relying, of
course, on more than the document) and can present Razumov and his
plight in a few pages.

The relative expertness of *Under Western Eyes* shows itself in the
swiftness with which Conrad escapes nominal limitations, and converts
a narrow point of view to, functionally, an ampler one. Thus the narrator
who begins by disclaiming "the possession of those high gifts of imagination and expression" achieves, by page 12, all the dramatic power of
the traditional observing point of view. Already he has made us forget
that "documentary evidence" and even made us forget himself. So too
Haldin's narrative-within-narrative report (through dialogue) of the as-

* Among the generic advantages: eyewitness credibility and the authority
of spoken voice, ease and naturalness of time-shift and transition, freedom to
select only a few details or incidents. It can be a great relief to have one's
"omniscience" formally limited, as it must be here.

sassination becomes, after only a few lines, a direct dramatizing of the event: intervening voices are silenced. In Part II Conrad again quickly disposes of his nominal authority (that Nathalie Haldin is telling the narrator about her visit to the Chateau Borel) and substitutes a dramatic third-person account of the event. We thus at least escape the weary game of quotation marks within quotation marks that mars *Lord Jim* and especially *Chance*. The particular technical compromise was one designed to satisfy both the reader (with his desire for dramatic immediacy) and the author (with his need for a literal detachment in space or time). Through certain scenes the reader appears to be experiencing life directly in a fictional present. But for the writer these protective screens still secretly existed: that the time is really past, that the imagination is at double or triple remove from the scene, that voices and documents are interposed.

The curious interruption and leap forward to the "later on" of Councillor Mikulin's trial is a clue, if we needed one, that this vivid and violent drama is (for Conrad's imagination) in the past. But it is the narrator's function as obtuse participant and observer to give, from page 100 on, a strong sense that we are in a fictional present time: watching new persons unexpectedly appear and unexpected events unroll, speculating on Razumov's status, and living through the very drama of ambiguity and discovery. The teacher of languages again protests, at the outset of the second part, his lack of professional skill. He "would not even invent a transition," he says—while accomplishing with ease the major transition from Councillor Mikulin's "Where to?" to the society of Nathalie Haldin and her mother.

At this point the narrative contracts to a very slow-moving present. We must wait some thirty-five pages for a further hint that Razumov and Nathalie Haldin may meet, sixty-seven pages for them to come face to face, seventy-two pages for those words that will send Razumov reeling against the wall. The delay is doubtless excessive. But some delay was certainly needed to make acceptable the melodramatic *donnée:* that Razumov will be sought out and admired by the sister of the man he betrayed. The illusion of presentness also permits the narrator's blundering unconscious ironies. For he is reconstructing a time when the first part of his narrative was unwritten. So in his fussy, innocent way he too can send Razumov reeling, as when he bluntly remarks: "There was something peculiar in the circumstances of his arrest. You no doubt know the whole truth . . ." The last interview of Razumov and Nathalie Haldin is, as much as any scene in fiction, happening "now." And for the reader watching that scene the narrator's presence may seem unimportant; may even be forgotten. But his presence, and the fact that this interview nominally occurred in the past, were extremely important to Conrad. They permitted him to keep his saving distance, and so permitted him to write coherently of violence and without embarrassment of passion.

One of the great dangers of an obtuse narrator and Jamesian fool is, of course, the invitation to write imperceptive prose for the sake of accurate characterization. The danger would seem most severe where the general mode is realistic, as it is in *Under Western Eyes*. But this is a problem that James, Gide, Mann, Ford, and others have solved, and Conrad here solves it with little waste of time. A few brief passages suggest in their phrasing the narrator's old-maidish side. It comes out even in his comments on his lack of professional skill. "In the conduct of an invented story there are, no doubt, certain proprieties to be observed for the sake of clearness and effect." But from such a passage the narrator moves very quickly to an efficient, evocative prose not unlike that of James. "Mr. Razumov's record, like the open book of fate, revives for me the memory of that day as something startlingly pitiless in its freedom from all forebodings." Only a few pages after this he attains the major accent and lucid controlled irony of the Peter Ivanovitch portrait. Admittedly such a narrator was incapable of the strange rich connotative effects and subtly disturbing rhythms of *Lord Jim*. And perhaps Conrad too was incapable of them by now. But this self-effacing and more rational prose has the great merit of not interfering with the drama of ideas or with the drama of betrayal and redemption. The narrator's style was natural to Conrad, as the style of *The Secret Agent* was not. And it is probably capable of accomplishing a greater variety of effects. The prose style too points to the remarkable control Conrad kept, in *Under Western Eyes,* over very strong personal feelings. This exciting novel is also a triumph of intelligence.

Conrad himself remarked that the old teacher of languages was useful to him in several ways, and so must be useful to the reader: "in the way of comment and by the part he plays"; as an eyewitness to "produce the effect of actuality"; as a friend and listener for Miss Haldin, "who otherwise would have been too much alone and unsupported to be perfectly credible."[13] Conrad succeeds, we may repeat, in making the narrator's comment nearly always dramatic: a difficult and important achievement. His editorials on the Russian character and on Western rectitude may well reflect Conrad's cool views. But they are so timed and so phrased as to help create sympathy for the despised and the damned. And this too is, to recapitulate, a triumph of art and integrity. For the Russians also are human. "The obligation of absolute fairness was imposed on me historically and hereditarily, by the peculiar experience of race and family, in addition to my primary conviction that truth alone is the justification of any fiction which makes the least claim to the quality of art or may hope to take its place in the culture of men and women of its time."

This slightly graceless sentence from the Author's Note holds for me an accent of high sincerity.[14]                                    (1958)

## NOTES

1. *Under Western Eyes* (the "Kent Edition"), pp. 228-229.
2. *Ibid.,* p. 298.
3. *Ibid.,* p. 299.
4. *Ibid.,* p. 380.
5. *Ibid.,* pp. 359-360.
6. Letter to John Galsworthy, January 6, 1908. *Life and Letters,* II, 65.
7. *Under Western Eyes,* p. 66.
8. *Ibid.,* pp. 67, 104.
9. *Ibid.,* p. 175.
10. "Joseph Conrad: Order and Anarchy: The Political Novels," *Kenyon Review,* XV (Autumn 1953), 505-521.
11. *Under Western Eyes,* pp. 305-306.
12. *Ibid.,* p. 162.
13. Author's Note.
14. [Editor's note: See also M. D. Zabel's study of *Under Western Eyes* in his *Craft and Character in Modern Fiction,* (Viking Press, 1957), pp. 187-207.]

# R. W. STALLMAN

## Conrad and "The Secret Sharer"*

### I

THE NEARER a work approaches art, Conrad declared, "the more it acquires a symbolic character. . . . All the great creations of literature have been symbolic, and in that way have gained in complexity, in power, in depth and in beauty." (*Life and Letters,* by G. Jean-Aubry. II, 205.) It is a mistake to assume that Conrad subscribed to the theory of Realism, the illusion that literature is copyistic of reality. And yet if you take the author at his professed intention, which in his Author's Notes appears to be no more than to render faithfully the facts of the visible world unadorned by conscious invention, you tend to be bound to this misconception. No wonder that his readers failed to see what his books were about, or that his critics persistently pigeon-holed him under that infernal classification—Realist! Privately he protested (as in his letter to Richard Curle, II, 316), but publicly he helped to make that label stick. His conception of the art of the novel must be pieced together from the scattered dicta of his letters and from hints directly or allegorically imbedded in his imaginative works—as in the "Heart of Darkness" where Marlow, that master craftsman, talks in cunning analogies. In the prefaces the professed trade secrets are seldom the key ones, but in the tales Conrad frequently reveals

* From "Conrad and 'The Secret Sharer,'" *Accent,* IX (Spring 1949), 131-143.

them. We know when Marlow says "I am not disclosing any trade secrets" that Conrad in these key words is actually opening up the door. Even if you take his artistic credo from the letters, you are apt to misconstrue his intent as artist. In making the pronouncement that "All the great creations of literature have been symbolic," Conrad was alluding to *Victory*—which is to say that *Victory* is a symbolic work. And yet in this same letter (written to Barrett H. Clark) he goes on to profess that *Victory* is a very simple book: ". . . and indeed I must say that I did not wrap it up in very mysterious processes of art . . . . and I don't think there is a critic in England or France who was in any doubt about it." Now this is nothing less than a strategic feint to conceal the secret intentions of *Victory,* and it is characteristic of that cunning strategy by which he everywhere conceals what his books are really about. His books are never so obvious as he would have his readers believe. Their artistic secrets eluded all his contemporary critics, and these included his closest literary friends. His unwary and imperceptive critics assumed that Conrad in his prefaces was continually striving to make clear the motives by which he was impelled, that here in his public commentaries on his craft he was making intimate disclosures about his literary aims and the bases upon which his books rest—and all this solely in order to help his readers to comprehend them. The claim of his prefaces that his public has understood his books is belied by the complaint of his letters: "I have not been very well understood. I have been called a writer of the sea, of the tropics, a descriptive writer, a romantic writer—and also a realist."

The fact is that Conrad's theory of the novel is no other than the modern canon that every work of art is symbolic. Every great novel has a symbolic meaning, imparts a significance which transcends mere plot or fable. Symbolism, it has been aptly said, does not deny Realism; it extends it. Realism in art has to do with technique. Realism attaches to methods of presenting points of view, methods of psychological insights, devices of chronology, of grouping and perspective. It is in such technical matters of grouping and perspective that the "realism" of Conrad's books consists. "It is in my scheming for effects," he told Richard Curle, "wherein almost all my 'art' consists. This, I suspect, has been the difficulty the critics have felt in classifying it as romantic or realistic." (II, 317.) Of course, a work which is realistic in method, as Robert Louis Stevenson once pointed out, may yet be hollow at its core. But the fact remains that if a work attains an illusion of achieved reality it attains it through technique—or not at all.

Because a novel is a product of language, a novel depends for its very life upon the word. What we term the characters of a novel are nothing more than the author's verbal arrangements. Being composed of words, they function (as Bonamy Dobrée puts it) as the part-symbols out of which the whole symbol is constructed. Conrad's credo—"Give me the right word and the right accent and I will move the world"—transposes into "Give me the right symbol and the right rendering and I will make a world." For Conrad, "the *whole* of the truth lies in the presentation;

therefore the expression should be studied in the interest of veracity. This is the only morality of *art* apart from *subject*." (I, 280.) The criterion of absolute correspondence between the characters, events and effects of art with those of reality constitutes, I think, a critical fallacy. Realism taken as plastic or graphic verisimilitude, critically considered, is plainly irrelevant. Truth in art consists not in the artist's fidelity to the observed facts of the actual world; it consists, rather, in the artist's fidelity to the felt truth of his vision. And it is *there* that the honor of the writer lies— in his fidelity to his image-making conception. Truth in art lies in the faithful formulation of patterned images. On his conscience, the artist must create his vision with the utmost fidelity to what Conrad called "the image of truth abiding in facts . . . ." Images are true and their rendering is true when they create a potential scheme of relationships to the other images, so that the meaning each part elicits and the effect they produce keep scrupulously true to the conceiving purpose of the whole which controls them. Fidelity is the crux of Conrad's artistic code as well as of his moral code. And fidelity is also the theme upon which almost all his imaginative works pivot.

Mere Realism—the exact and lifelike registration of the observed facts of actual experience—Conrad himself scoffed at. "You just stop short of being absolutely real," he wrote Arnold Bennett, "because you are faithful to your dogmas of realism. Now realism in art will never approach reality." And he goes on to say, "And your art, your gift, should be put to the service of a larger and freer faith." Every artist is at bottom a Realist whose aim is to evoke an impression of "life as it actually is," but his work approaches art only insofar as his images of reality take upon themselves the dimension of symbols. Surely every artist is first of all an Impressionist whose aim is to make his readers feel and see as he himself saw and felt, but what distinguishes his work as art is not his achievement in mere pictorial intention. Marlow in "Heart of Darkness" makes us see and feel the overpowering sinister atmosphere of the wilderness as Conrad himself saw and felt it, so that (to quote F. R. Leavis) "the details and circumstances of the voyage to and up the Congo are present to us as if we were making the journey ourselves." True, but we do not make that journey solely for the sake of the evoked atmosphere. That is not everything. There is a great deal more. Some secret intention controls Conrad's realistic and pictorial particulars, by which the atmosphere gets itself engendered; but what Marlow must make us perceive is this controlling subsurface purpose. The river of our journey through that impenetrable jungle of unspeakable secrets ascends significantly and symbolically towards Kurtz—towards the theme.

## ·II

Everything in "The Secret Sharer" is charged with symbolic purpose. It is this symbolic part of the business that eludes the reader, if not the moral and psychological intention, since these meanings which attach to the narrative or surface level are less likely to be missed. On a first reading it appears perhaps as simply a spectacular story about a young, newly appointed sea-captain who risks his ship and his career in order to rescue a refugee who happens to bear a striking resemblance to himself. He is a fugitive from the legal consequences of an act of manslaughter; he has killed a man in a desperate scrape, but he is "no homicidal ruffian." The captain, recognizing their connection in thoughts and impressions, identifies the stranger with himself, guesses his guilt and shares his conscience. He hides him in his cabin and takes extraordinary pains to conceal him from the crew. He risks everything for the sake of this stranger. To help him reach land so that he can begin a new life, the captain takes his ship as close into land as possible, and, while the swimmer makes for shore, he watches in terror the approaching mass of land shadows which threaten to engulf the ship. What saves him is the warning marker left by the swimmer ("the saving mark for my eyes"). It is the captain's own hat, by which he can tell that the ship has gathered sternway. The ship is saved, and the captain at last is fitted for his task. He has established perfect communion with his ship. As he catches a last glimpse of his hat, the captain senses again that mysterious identity with the secret sharer of his cabin and of his thoughts. He describes him as though he were describing himself: "a free man, a proud swimmer striking out for a new destiny."

Conrad's most characteristic works are stories of action: *Nostromo, The Secret Agent, Victory, Suspense.* In "The Secret Sharer" the external action consists almost solely in the drama of the ship in the moment of the captain's crisis. Action and plot are subsidiary to the analysis and exhibition of a psychological process. This psychological or internal action, from which the external drama is projected, prepares for its counterpart and at the climactic moment coincides with it. The whole story may be defined as a prolonged analysis of a series of tensions anticipating one culminating moment, the moment of the captain's crisis and triumph. The story is charged, however, not only with suspense and impending crisis but also with meaning. Like Henry James, his acknowledged master, Conrad is an intensely conscious craftsman. Again like Henry James, Conrad in his prefaces and Author's Notes lets us in on his aims as a writer. With Conrad, however, the accounts of the sources of his tales and the disclosures about his literary aims are highly deceptive, often deliberately misleading.

The prefaces of Conrad stand in striking contrast to the prefaces of Henry James. For whereas Henry James is everywhere telling us what his "exquisite scheme" is, Conrad is continually telling us that he has no scheme at all. "You must realize," he admonished Norman Douglas, "the inconceivable stupidity of the common reader—the man who forks out the half crown." The problem was to win over the common reader, and how could he win over the common reader if, as Conrad put it, he gave him all the bones? "It might destroy their curiosity for the dish." As a matter of fact Conrad felt much the same as Arnold Bennett felt about the public comprehension. The public comprehension, Bennett observed, is limited severely because "Only other creative artists can understand a creative artist." Which is to say that every artist has his secret intentions. Conrad not only concealed his secret intentions but even disguised them by planting his Author's Notes with bogus trade secrets about his literary aims and false clues as to what his books are really about. Conrad's readers need only D. H. Lawrence to tip them off—"Never trust the artist. Trust the tale." As Albert Guerard points out, for the author to describe only the source of "The Secret Sharer," to profess that the story is the account of a real incident which occurred on such and such a ship (the *Cutty Sark,* specifically), is to provide the reader with a false clue. The real fact is that Conrad has contrived his story with a secret intention. We can get at it only through the story itself. We can work it out, to start with, by questioning certain central motives—the facts basic to the why and the wherefore of what happens in the story.

Even the reader who reads only for "the story" is likely to ask some of the questions, the key ones being these: (1) Why does the captain undertake the risk to his ship for this particular stranger, a risk which he would not impose upon her for any other? (2) Why must he take the ship as close into land as possible?

If we, as Conrad's readers, happen to think in the manner of the chief mate ("He was of a painstaking turn of mind. As he used to say, he 'liked to account to himself' for practically everything that came in his way . . ."), we certainly will try to evolve a theory about the captain and his secret sharer. But to do so, in emulation of the chief mate we had better "take all things into earnest consideration." We had better answer our question first of all at the narrative or literal level. It's a fact that what the youthful sea captain does for this fugitive, whose mishap was not entirely of his own making, is what any other young sea captain might do, out of common decency, in order to save a decent young chap. He feels impelled to do this out of a moral necessity, his relationship to the fugitive being that of host to guest. But why does he make this commitment? —why for the sake of this particular stranger? Well, the fact that the captain bears an uncanny resemblance to him—Leggatt's similarity not only in appearance and age but in background and experience and in situation—provides us one answer. (It's this sense of identity that prompts the remark: "I saw it all going on as though I were myself inside that other sleeping-suit.") Besides, the captain recognizes not alone this physical identity but also a psychic one. "He appealed to me as if our experiences had been as identical as our clothes." Each feels that he is "the only stranger on board," and each feels that he has, as it were, "something to swim for." Each stranger is isolated and wholly alone, pitted against the world and being tested by it. What impelled Leggatt to swim out to the ship was his lonesomeness ("I wanted to be seen, to talk with somebody, before I went on"), and the same impulse motivates the captain and prompts him to greet the newcomer so hospitably.

Hospitality, welcome, and self-recognition are stressed from the start. "A mysterious communication was established already between us two —in the face of that silent, darkened tropical sea." Later in thinking back to this moment Leggatt confides: "It's a great satisfaction to have got somebody to understand. You seem to have been there on purpose." The same confession could have come from the captain. Each stranger feels the same urgency to communicate with somebody in order to unburden his plight.

It is this mutual, sympathetic understanding of what the other's plight means to him that bolsters and morally fortifies their spiritual being, Leggatt's no less than the captain's. "And then you speaking to me so quietly—as if you had expected me—made me hold on a little longer." Leggatt's "calm and resolute" voice induces in the captain a corresponding state of self-possession. Through Leggatt that initial mood of calm and resolute self-confidence with which the captain begins and ends his arduous enterprise is gradually reinstated. Leggatt, as we later get to know him, is bold and enterprising, proud and stubborn, determined in moral fiber. While the captain's remark "You must be a good swimmer" has reference to the fact that the nearest land is as far distant as the land at the very bottom of the sea, there is also an implied ethical judgment in these words of encouragement and appraisal. To be "a good swimmer" is to be "a strong soul." What the captain marvels at in his double is "that something unyielding in his character which was carrying him through so finely." The overconfident soul of the swimmer stands in contrast to the self-questioning, Hamletlike soul of the newly appointed captain. He observes about the fugitive that there was nothing sickly in his eyes or in his expression, and, with this telling reflection about himself, he notices that "he was not a bit like me, really; yet, as we stood leaning over my bed-place, whispering side by side, with our dark heads together and our backs to the door, anybody bold enough to open it stealthily would have been treated to the uncanny sight of a double captain busy talking in whispers with his other self." When Leggatt happens to rest a hand "on the end of the skylight to steady himself with, and all that did not stir a limb," the captain simultaneously rests a hand too on the end of the skylight. When on a later occasion the captain made a move "my double moved too." As "the double captain" is about to slip from the ship into the sea, the captain, struck by a sudden thought, snatches his hat and rams it "on my other self." He visualizes Leggatt's plight as his own: "I saw myself," he says, "wandering barefooted, bareheaded, the sun beating on my dark poll." Again and again "[W]e, the two strangers in the ship, faced each other in identical attitudes." And in identical clothes. It is the captain's secret self that is "exactly the same" as the fugitive, who, dressed in "the ghostly gray of my sleeping suit" (the garb of the unconscious life), must always remain concealed from the eyes of the world.

In terms of the ethical allegory, Leggatt is the embodiment of the captain's moral consciousness. His appearance answers the captain's question—"I wondered how far I should turn out faithful to that ideal conception of one's own personality every man sets up for himself secretly." In darkness he first appears, mysteriously "as if he had risen from the bottom of the sea," and "the sea-lightning played about his limbs at every stir; and he appeared in it ghastly, silvery, fish-like." At the first sight of him "a faint flash of phosphorescent light, which seemed to issue suddenly from the naked body of a man, flickered in the sleeping water with the elusive, silent play of summer lightning in a night sky." And at the last sight of him, when the secret sharer is making for the shore of Koh-ring (an unknown island), there issues from the discarded hat the same mysterious light: "White on the black water. A phosphorescent flash passed under it." It's all very mysterious. Leggatt's emerging in a sudden glow from "the sleeping water" seems very much like the flash of an idea emerging from the depths of the subconscious mind. "It was, in the night, as though I had been faced by my own reflection in the depths of a somber and immense mirror." That dark glassy sea mirrors the captain's *alter ego*. In terms of the psychological allegory, Leggatt represents that world which lies below the surface of our conscious lives. Just before he makes his appearance the riding-light in the fore-rigging burns, so the captain imagines, "with a clear, untroubled, as if symbolic, flame, confident and bright in the mysterious shades of the night." These moral qualities, though the captain attributes them to the riding-light, belong with equal and very suggestive appropriateness to the captain's as yet undisclosed second self. The captain's subconscious mind has anticipated, in the fiction of the symbolic flame, the idea of a second self—the appearance, that is, of someone untroubled, unyielding, self-confident. (The captain is just the opposite, being of a mind troubled and filled with self-doubt.) The symbolic flame materializes in human form. Leggatt bodies forth the very commonplace upon which the whole story is built: no man is alone in the world, for he is always with himself. Leggatt, this other self, becomes the psychological embodiment of the reality, the destiny, the ideal of selfhood which the captain must measure up to. He provides him the utmost test.

All this, in sum, answers our first question: Why is it that the captain risks his ship for this particular stranger? The initial matter-of-fact answer prepared us for, or rather teased us into making, the allegorical one. In answering the first question we have anticipated the answer to the second: Why is it that the captain must take his ship as close into shore as possible? To begin with a fact, the ship, as the story opens, is anchored inside the islands at the mouth of the river Meinam and is lying cleared for sea. (Her location and voyage can be traced on a map.) She is in dead calm and waits for "the slightest sign of any sort of wind." "There was not a sound in her—and around us nothing moved, nothing lived, not a canoe on the water, not a bird in the air, not a cloud in the sky." At last there's enough wind to get under way with, and then for four days she works down "the east side of the Gulf of Siam, tack for tack, in light winds and smooth water. . . ." When the wind comes and the ship first moves to his own independent word—precisely at this point it is that the captain begins to come to terms with his ship. At midnight of the fourth day out she is put round on the other tack to stand in for shore, and still at the following noon she has had no change of course. The captain has by now attained enough self-confidence to dare this risky maneuver—"to stand right in. Quite in—as far as I can take her." His excuse for the order to the mate is that the ship isn't doing well in the middle of the gulf, and at the mate's terrified protest he retorts: "Well —if there are any regular land breezes at all on this coast one must get close inshore to find them, mustn't one?" And this is why, *literally* why, he must shave the land as close as possible.

It is not solely in order to shorten Leggatt's stretch to shore. For Leggatt, that expert swimmer, is capable of making it from almost two miles out. (From the islet to the ship, he figured, "That last spell must have been over a mile.") It's not a test of Leggatt. It's a test of the captain. "The youngest man on board (barring the second mate), and untried as yet by a position of the fullest responsibility. . . ." He is "the only stranger on board . . . a stranger to the ship; and if all the truth must be told, I was somewhat of a stranger to myself." For four days the ship has had a captain who has not been "completely and wholly with her. Part of me was absent." Though she has had "two captains to plan her course for her," nevertheless she is still, so to speak, a ship without a captain. The time has come for the irresolute commander to command—to prove to the crew, to the world, and to himself that he is fitted for his task. It is time that he put to trial that secret conception of his ideal self, to reckon, in sum, with that destiny which from the start he has anticipated with such intensity. For four days the ship has had very little wind in her sails. Instead of waiting for the wind to come to him he determines now to go after it. It's *his* conscience that is on trial ("on my conscience, it had to be thus close—no less"). It's not a test of the crew—"They had simply to be equal to their tasks; but I wondered how far I should turn out faithful to that ideal conception of one's own personality every man sets up for himself secretly." "All a man can betray is his conscience," Conrad wrote in *Under Western Eyes*. The captain does not betray, even though the entire world seemed leagued against him. Everything—"the elements, the men were against us—everything was against us in our secret partnership; time itself—for this could not go on forever." And "It was now a matter of conscience to shave the land as close as possible—for now he must go overboard whenever the ship was put in stays. Must! There could be no going back for him." Nor for the captain: "I had to go on." Not to let Leggatt strike out for land would be "a sort of cowardice"; it is cowardice not to face up to one's destiny. Like Leggatt, who has "something unyielding in his character," the captain is tenaciously determined not to compromise his soul. There are limits to self-knowledge, however, and beyond this dividing mark of self-knowledge no man dare go. We are told that "all the time the dual working of my mind distracted me almost to the point of insanity." "On that enormous mass of blackness there was not a gleam to be seen, not a sound to be heard." The black hill of Koh-ring hangs right over the ship "like a towering fragment of the everlasting night," and such a hush falls upon her "that she might have been a bark of the dead floating in slowly under the very gate of Erebus." It is the ship, but it is also the captain's soul, that is almost swallowed up beyond recall. "I think I had come creeping quietly as near insanity as any man who has not actually gone over the border." "My God! Where are we?" cries the terrified mate. "Lost!" The captain has Leggatt to fortify him, whereas the terrified mate hasn't even "the moral support of his whiskers." The transferred moral quality of Leggatt has infused itself into the captain's soul and it is this transaction—symbolized in the spot of white hat—that saves him. (The hat is Conrad's symbol for his theme of fidelity.) It is by virtue of his fidelity to that ideal of selfhood that the captain triumphs, and at that decisive moment of his destiny when he measures up to it a new existence begins for him—a spiritually unified one. It begins for him when the cabin is emptied and Leggatt, the secret sharer of his cabin and of his thoughts, has been deposited into that once dark and mysterious but now sunlit sea.

### III

"We cannot escape from ourselves," Conrad has said, and more than once, both in his novels and in his Author's Notes. We cannot escape from ourselves, from our past, from our memories. It is in this sense that "the creator can only express himself in his creation," wherefore "every novel contains an element of autobiography."—*A Personal Record*. Once, in writing *The Secret Agent*, Conrad "had to fight hard to keep at arm's length the memories . . . lest they should rush in and overwhelm each page of the story. . . ." Memories molded Conrad's art. All his imaginative work is founded on personal reminiscences of actual incidents and people encountered during his twenty years of active sea life. But, though all of his writing draws upon personal contacts with reality, the experience in every one of his stories "is but the canvas of the attempted picture." Of all his narratives less than a half dozen can be claimed as "autobiographies." The "Heart of Darkness" is taken straight from life, but even this, the most directly autobiographical of all his stories, represents experience pushed beyond the actual facts of the event. There is this personal basis for Conrad's art, but his art is nevertheless impersonal. "The more perfect the artist," T. S. Eliot has declared, "the more completely separate in him will be the man who suffers and the mind which creates." Conrad is that artist. "The Secret Sharer" provides us the perfect instance of a work of art which is at once personative and yet a wholly depersonalized and anonymous creation.

It is said that this story was written in order to resolve a personal

crisis; writing it served Conrad as a neurotic safety valve. But whatever
that crisis was which motivated him to the act of creation, it is nevertheless by no means identical with the imagined one confronting the sea
captain. The private plight of the author has been objectified in a dramatic framework of meaning that is impersonal and universalized. The
story is autobiographical only in a spiritual sense. The captain's problem,
however, can be read as an allegory of Conrad's problem, for the situation between the captain and his secret sharer corresponds to the situation
between the artist and his creative act. Read thus, "The Secret Sharer"
is a double allegory. It is an allegory of man's moral conscience and of
man's aesthetic or artistic conscience. "The artist," wrote Flaubert in one
of his letters, "ought to be in his work like God in Creation, invisible
and all powerful; let him be felt everywhere but not seen." Conrad's
story allegorizes the plight of Conrad as artist. His problem is to come
to terms with his story, even as the captain's problem is to get on terms
with his ship. "My strangeness, which had made me sleepless, had
prompted that unconventional arrangement, as if I had expected in those
solitary hours of the night to get on terms with the ship of which I knew
nothing, manned by men of whom I knew very little more."

The artist in his act of creation is of necessity estranged from normal
everyday life. "In this breathless pause at the threshold of a long passage
we seemed to be measuring our fitness for a long and arduous enterprise,
the appointed task of both our existences to be carried out, far from
all human eyes, with only sky and sea for spectators and for judges."
Isolated with his vision, he begins in self-doubt his newly appointed
task. Everything seems to threaten perfect communion with his vision.
Being faced by "the breath of unknown powers that shape our destinies"
(as the young captain in *The Shadow Line* says) he anticipates the possibility of failure. Sky and sea and "all that multitude of celestial bodies
staring down at one"—the entire world seems hostile to the creator in his
creative enterprise. Everything—"the elements, the men were against us
—everything was against us in our secret partnership; time itself—for this
could not go on forever." As the captain must establish communion with
his ship, so the artist must establish perfect communion with the things
created, and command over them. The artist, Conrad admits in his Note
to *The Nigger of the "Narcissus,"* "the artist descends within himself, and
in that lonely region of stress and strife . . . finds the terms of his appeal."[1]

The artist in the act of creation tests his integrity, even as the sea
captain tests his in the dangerous act of maneuvering the ship. The problem of the artist—indeed the problem which every man confronts—is
resolved, no less than the captain's, by the trial he imposes upon his secret
self. It is his creative conscience that he must not betray. No man of
uncommon moral quality can escape this test of selfhood. That "The
Secret Sharer" comes round is by virtue of the creator's fidelity to his
vision. He has measured up to that ideal of artistic integrity, that ideal
conception of one's aesthetic conscience, which every artist sets up for

himself secretly. She weathers the crisis, the crisis which every creator risks. She comes round, she succeeds! Nothing can stand between them after that. "Nothing: no one in the world should stand now between us, throwing a shadow on the way of silent knowledge and mute affection, the perfect communion of a seaman [or of an artist] with his first command." He has mastered "the feel of my ship," and now, like that other invisible stranger, he is at last "a free man, a proud swimmer striking out for a new destiny." (1949)

## NOTE

I have left my reading of "The Secret Sharer" essentially as originally published (1949). Since then another critic argues that Leggatt is not the captain's ideal; he is a failure. "If Leggatt has failed, as he so plainly has, can he stand as 'the psychological embodiment of the reality, the destiny, the ideal selfhood which the captain must measure up to'? Literally, Leggatt is strong and firm because, having failed, he has no expectations." I find no evidence, however, that Leggatt is without expectations, without hope. In what sense is Leggatt a failure?

He is a success in saving the *Sephora,* and he is a success in escaping the law and transcending its hollow forms of authority, dehumanizing and abstract codes personified by Captain Archbold. And Leggatt is a success too in saving the captain-narrator, by serving him as model in being simultaneously his double and his opposite ("he was not a bit like me, really"). At every point in his defeated career Leggatt is courageous, resolute, confident, resourceful, bold and enterprising, proud and unyielding. I call this the condition of success, and so does Conrad. Leggatt has spirit and tenacity, whereas Captain Archbold is characterized solely by his "spiritless tenacity." It is the vexed captain-narrator who doubts success and expects only the worst: "And as to the chapter of accidents which counts for so much in the book of success, I could only hope that it was closed. For what favorable accident could be expected?" The captain-narrator gains certitude through Leggatt, "a strong soul" inspiring him with the undaunted spirit of youth. "Something to swim for" sums up his determination, his expectations amidst black waters and hopeless prospects of being salvaged.

Leggatt makes his appearance immediately after the captain has broken protocol, immediately after notifying the second-mate of "my unheard-of caprice to take a five hours' anchor-watch on myself." The parallel to the captain's breaking of the rules is Leggatt's unlawful deed aboard the *Sephora.* It is an irrational act that the captain commits in taking Leggatt aboard and concealing him in his cabin, an act of immaturity or inexperienced judgment; Leggatt's case again provides the parallel. The *Sephora* affair stands as the metaphor of the captain's plight.

Conrad's way of affirming a thing is always by affirming also its opposite. No Conrad hero attains an unmitigated success. The example is

Lord Jim, or the captain of "The Secret Sharer." It's always success-failure, or failure-success, the one measured by the other. So too for Leggatt: "The same strung-up force which had given twenty-four men a chance, at least, for their lives, had, in a sort of recoil, crushed an unworthy mutinous existence." The only flat failure is Captain Archbold. He epitomizes man's subjugation to legalized conventions; he represents the external law, Leggatt the internal. The storm that threatened the *Sephora* and the lives of her crew—"it was a sea gone mad! I suppose the end of the world will be something like that"—causes the crack-up of fixed authority and of the code he represents. In spite of his having served thirty-seven years at sea (twenty of them spent in "immaculate command"), at the crisis Captain Archbold loses his nerve and whimpers in terror while the helpless ship runs for her life. Leggatt, acting without authority, saves the ship by setting the foresail, but meanwhile he has had to do away with an insolent shipmate who obstructed his rescue of the *Sephora.* Captain Archbold regarded Leggatt as unfit to serve as chief mate of the *Sephora,* yet he himself at the crisis is unfit to command. So the captain-narrator, similarly, doubts whether he is fit to command, whereas Leggatt, having learned through failure, succeeds in remaining confident and in self-control, unnerved by his plight. The captain is instructed by his example, by the example of his other and opposite self. Leggatt murdered a shipmate in a moment of loss of self-control; so the parson's son becomes by circumstances a murderer and thus, as judged by the external law, a failure. But his failure is matched by his success. He restores order to the irrational crew and the uncontrolled ship—at the expense of committing an irrational act in a fit of temper. He had no choice: "Do you think that if I had not been pretty fierce with them I should have got the men to do anything?"

The man he murdered in a fit of temper was one of those "Miserable devils that have no business to live at all. He wouldn't do his duty and wouldn't let anybody else do theirs." He had to silence him in order to save ship and crew. It is at this point in the narrative that the captain, recognizing that "my double there was no homicidal ruffian," remarks: "He appealed to me *as if our experiences* had been as identical as our clothes." What this tells us is that the captain recognizes a kinship between himself and Leggatt not only in physical appearance, in age, in background (they are both Conway graduates), and in situation, but also in what each has experienced. What the young captain has experienced we do not know, but he has experienced enough of life to enable him to recognize the potentiality in himself for committing an irrational and possibly even a criminal act and to sympathise therefore with Leggatt's plight.[2] "I saw it all going on as though I were myself inside that other sleeping-suit." It is the recognition of the capacity for guilt from which no man dares to presume himself exempt. He recognizes in Leggatt, apart from his unlawful act, not his weakness but his strength, physically and spiritually. Unlike the captain, there is "nothing sickly in his eyes or in his expression." He seems "invulnerable." Unlike the captain, Leggatt has the cool-headed capacity for analyzing his past experience, the situation from which he has successfully escaped; the capacity for thinking *as* "a stubborn if not a steadfast operation; something of which I should have been perfectly incapable." The captain's "troubled incertitude" draws strength from Leggatt's invulnerability, his moral courage. Though both are dressed in sleeping-suits, the garb of the unconscious life (as M. C. Bradbrook was first to point out), the difference is that the captain is committed to the outer and conscious life of the ship and crew, whereas his other self, because guilty, must remain concealed from the eyes of the world. Ironically, Leggatt concerns himself with the outer world, as in his asking at the very start of his encounter with the captain what the time is; whereas the captain, reflecting inwardly at the start, dismisses his officers and takes over their deck-duty and thereby prevents "the anchor-watch being formally set and things properly attended to. I asked myself whether it was wise ever to interfere with the established routine of duties even from the kindest of motives." It is through his inadequacy and negligence, his not keeping to the established routine and external code, that he meets the outcast Leggatt. At that moment of their meeting the captain is a failure, and Leggatt (in one sense) a success.

The characteristic of Conrad's works is the opposition or conflict between the inner and outer standards, between the standards of conscience and those of external codes, conventions and laws. Lord Jim, crucified by legalized convention, vindicates himself by creating Patusan, a world of his own making (as it were), Patusan being symbolic of the inner world untouched—until Brown arrives—by the outer world of convention. In *Nostromo* neither the external world nor the internal one is exempt from corruption; Nostromo, representing the romantic self-deluded idealist, betrays his "incorrigible" integrity. In *Victory,* Heyst is destroyed by the external world, by Gentleman Jones, the exponent of its corruption and evil; ironically, he is nevertheless saved by having committed himself to the necessity of participating in life, through Lena. In "Heart of Darkness" the corrupted Kurtz is "incorruptible," and though a moral sham he is nevertheless saved by Marlow because he earned redemption of his inner darkness by disclosing its truth; "It was an affirmation, a moral victory paid for by innumerable defeats, by abominable terrors, by abominable satisfactions. But it was a victory! That is why I have remained loyal to Kurtz to the last." In *The Nigger of the "Narcissus"* the ideal— Jim Wait—is exposed as a sham. In "The Secret Sharer," to the contrary, the values lie in the weighted scale of the inner world, and it is similarly so in *Lord Jim,* "Heart of Darkness," and *Under Western Eyes.*

Leggatt does not consider himself a failure, any more so than Lord Jim. He judges himself (like Lord Jim) by his own internal code: Not Guilty. "What can they know whether I am guilty or not—or of *what* I am guilty, either? That's my affair." To the retributive laws of society he refuses to submit because he considers himself subject only to the laws of conscience. He's no more a murdering brute than the captain. Whereas at the start the captain's ideal of selfhood is a simple and naïve conception, at the end it has undergone a radical change through the captain's experiencing Leggatt's destiny *as if* his own, through his experiencing the reality of his other self, through his recognition of their bond of guilt. That Leggatt has committed a criminal act (that "brand of Cain" business) signified the dark potentialities within us all. It is in this double sense that Leggatt stands as the psychological embodiment of the captain's conscience. His double consciousness embraces predicaments of the internal and the external code. "Do you see me before a judge and jury on that charge?" Leggatt asks him. The captain shares Leggatt's convictions that the inner standard is what man must rightly be judged by, that the final appeal is to that ideal of selfhood which every man secretly sets up for himself. The ideal is conscience, and that is what Leggatt represents. It's the same for Kurtz and Razumov and Nostromo. In Conrad all is ambiguous and contradictory; nothing is absolute; nothing is but what is not. The critic who pigeon-holes Conrad's heroes as "failures" oversimplifies by half-truths.                            (1959)

## NOTES

1. In *A Personal Record* (pp. 98-99), describing the terrible strain put upon him during the formidable period of creating *Nostromo,* Conrad speaks of his plight in the same terms as the sea-captain in "The Secret Sharer". "The Secret Sharer" dramatizes this experience:

"All I know is that, for twenty months, neglecting the common joys of life that fall to the lot of the humblest on this earth, I had, like the prophet of old, 'wrestled with the Lord' for my creation, *for the headlands of the coast, for the darkness of the Placid Gulf* . . . , and for the breath of life that had to be blown into the shapes of men and women. . . . These are, perhaps, strong words, but it is difficult to characterize otherwise the intimacy and the strain of a creative effort in which mind and will and conscience are engaged to the full, hour after hour, day after day, *away from the world,* and to the exclusion of all that makes life really lovable and gentle—*something for which a material parallel can only be found in the everlasting sombre stress of the westward passage round Cape Horn. For that too is the wrestling of men with the might of their Creator, in a great isolation from the world, without the amenities and consolations of life, a lonely struggle under a sense of overmatched littleness, for no reward that could be adequate, but for the mere winning of a longitude. . . .*" (Italics mine.)

Again, in his preface to *The Secret Agent* he speaks of "the mass of oppressive doubts that haunt so persistently every attempt at creative work." *Conrad's Prefaces,* ed. Edward Garnett, p. 110.

2. Guerard makes the same point in his excellent introduction to the Signet edition of "*Heart of Darkness*" and "*The Secret Sharer*" (1950): 'What does this unreflective and immediate sympathy for a 'double' mean but sympathy for one's second, irrational self? The captain hides and protects Leggatt because he vaguely realizes—for the first time in his life—that he too might have stumbled into such a crime." "The two novels alike exploit the ancient myth or archetypal experience of the 'night journey' of a provisional descent into the primitive and unconscious sources of being."

# DOUGLAS HEWITT

## "The Secret Sharer"*

THOUGH IT WAS NOT published until 1912 in the volume *'Twixt Land and Sea,* "The Secret Sharer" was written in November, 1909. Conrad had taken up and set aside *Chance,* finished *The Secret Agent,* just completed *A Personal Record,* and was engaged in writing *Under Western Eyes,* which he finished two months later.

It is a remarkable story and its extraordinary virtues have attracted surprisingly little attention.[1] It belongs very obviously, in the nature of the interests displayed and in some similarities of treatment, to the same phase of his writing as "Heart of Darkness", *Lord Jim* and *Nostromo.* But it marks the end of this period. The previous works show the central character confronted by some realization of the nature of his beliefs or by some "deadly incubus"—the knowledge of the link with Mr. Kurtz or Gentleman Brown, the disturbing awareness of "the foundation of all the emotions" or of the disastrous results of Don Carlos Gould's idealism. From this knowledge or from these relationships there is no escape; in the nature of the case no solution of the problems is possible. The narrator of "The Secret Sharer" is similarly faced by the realization of a bond between him and Leggatt, but he finds a solution; at the end of the story he frees himself from the haunting presence of his "other self".

The setting of the story is typical of Conrad's work in its emphasis on the isolation of the little self-contained world of the ship and on the supremely important position of the narrator-captain. So far as outward power is concerned, he reflects: "I could do what I liked, with no one to say nay to me within the whole circle of the horison".[2] At the end, when he is giving Leggatt, the secret sharer of his cabin, an opportunity to escape, although he seems to his officers and men to be wantonly running the ship aground yet he is still obeyed. The crew know that their safety is in his hands, yet he is still the captain and they leave their fate to him.

The intruder on this isolation is Leggatt, the fugitive who swims out to the ship, and it is made abundantly clear that he is only able to come on board because of the state of mind of the captain, a state in which he feels "somewhat of a stranger" to himself. He decides to set no anchor-watch and to stay on deck alone and explains that:

> My strangeness, which had made me sleepless, had prompted that unconventional arrangement, as if I had expected in those solitary hours of the night to get on terms with the ship of which I knew nothing, manned by men of whom I knew very little more.[3]

It seems at first as though he will achieve his purpose. In a passage whose irony very soon becomes apparent, he says:

* From Douglas Hewitt's *Joseph Conrad: A Reassessment* (Bowes & Bowes, 1952), VI, pp. 70-79.

> . . . as I passed the door of the forecastle I heard a deep, quiet, trustful sigh of some sleeper inside. And suddenly I rejoiced in the great security of the sea as compared with the unrest of the land, in my choice of that untempted life presenting problems, invested with an elementary moral beauty by the absolute straight-forwardness of its appeal and by the singleness of its purpose.
>
> The riding-light in the fore-rigging burned with a clear, untroubled, as if symbolic flame, confident and bright in the mysterious shades of the night.[4]

Immediately after this he notices that the rope-ladder has not been hauled in as it should, but checks his annoyance with the reflection that his own action is responsible for this. The ladder is there because he has decided to dismiss all hands and keep watch himself in the endeavour to overcome his feeling of "strangeness". When he tries to pull the ladder aboard, he finds the man hanging on the bottom of it. Leggatt asserts later, when he is the "secret sharer" of the narrator's thoughts, that it was the ladder alone which saved him.

> I wasn't capable of swimming round as far as your rudder-chains [he says] And, lo and behold! there was a ladder to get hold of.[5]

The captain does not consciously decide to conceal the fugitive, any more than Marlow consciously decides to accept the "unforseen partnership" with Kurtz. As soon as he sees him, he reflects later: "A mysterious communication was established already between us two—in the face of that silent, darkened tropical sea."[6] Leggatt speaks of him as talking to him quietly—"as if you had expected me". The closeness of this mysterious communication is emphasized from the very start of their relationship, first because of the accident of a similarity of clothes:

> In a moment [the captain says] he had concealed his damp body in a sleeping-suit of the same grey-stripe pattern as the one I was wearing and followed me like my double on the poop.[7]

As Leggatt tells his story it is as though the captain were seeing his own reflection "in the depths of a sombre and immense mirror", so that he can say: "I saw it all going on as though I were myself inside that other sleeping-suit".[8] There is a phrase which is strongly reminiscent of those which tell of the link between Lord Jim and Gentleman Brown: "He appealed to me as if our experiences had been as identical as our clothes".[9] This is, above all, what is stressed—the bond between the captain and the intruder with his burden of guilt. The bond is the closest possible; Leggatt is described as his "double" or his "other self" more than twenty times in the course of the story. When the captain of the *Sephora* comes in search of Leggatt and says that he "wasn't exactly the sort for the chief mate of a ship like the *Sephora*," the captain reflects:

> I had become so connected in thoughts and impressions with the secret sharer of my cabin that I felt as if I, personally, were being

given to understand that I, too, was not the sort that would have done for the chief mate of a ship like the *Sephora*.[10]

He feels "utterly incapable of playing the part of ignorance properly",[11] so that, as he says;

> I could not, I think, have met him by a direct lie, also for psychological (not moral) reasons. If he had only known how afraid I was of his putting my feeling of identity with the other to the test! But, strangely enough— (I thought of it only afterward)—I believe that he was not a little disconcerted by the reverse side of that weird situation, by something in me that reminded him of the man he was seeking— suggested a mysterious similitude to the young fellow he had distrusted and disliked from the first.[12]

The link is not, as in "Heart of Darkness" or *Lord Jim*, with someone obviously wicked. The crime of Leggatt is a very modified one in the eyes of the narrator and we remember that when a reviewer described him as a "murderous ruffian" Conrad said that he was "simply knocked over" by such a misunderstanding. But there is, in Leggatt, a feeling of guilt, the knowledge that he has, like Lord Jim, transgressed against the code of society. He can speak of the man he has killed as one of the "miserable devils that have no business to live at all", but he is prepared to accept "the 'brand of Cain' business". "I was ready enough", he says, "to go off wandering on the face of the earth".

We are not, moreover, concerned with the precise nature of Leggatt's offence, for there is no indication that the captain feels any shadow of guilt specifically because the man he is hiding is a murderer. Leggatt is an embodiment of his original feeling of being "a stranger" to himself, of that fear that there are parts of himself which he has not yet brought into the light of day and that these aspects of his personality may interfere with "that ideal conception of one's own personality every man sets up for himself secretly". What disturbs him is that there is a secret sharer at all, for he brings to light his own suspected insecurity.

The captain leads a life of whispers and sudden concealments and, inevitably, his nerves begin to go to pieces. He shouts at men or whispers suddenly, stops men from entering his state-room, feeling all the time that "it would take very little to make me a suspect person in the eyes of the ship's company".[13] They begin to assume that he is either mad or drinking, and his mental state expresses itself for him, too, in the knowledge that it impairs his ability to command.

> This [he says] is not the place to enlarge upon the sensations of a man who feels for the first time a ship move under his feet to his own independent word. In my case they were not unalloyed. I was not wholly alone with my command; for there was that stranger in my cabin. Or rather, I was not completely and wholly with her. Part of me was absent. That mental feeling of being in two places at once

affected me physically as if the mood of secrecy had penetrated my very soul.[14]

As a result the orders which should spring to his lips without thinking or reflection do not come; "all unconscious alertness" deserts him; it requires an effort of will to call his mind back from his "secret double" to the "conditions of the moment".

Every detail of the story is perfectly concrete, perfectly naturalistic, yet this is far more a nightmare story than any other—far more than such obviously "painful" stories as "Freya of the Seven Isles", which appeared in the same volume. The feeling of "duality" is pushed to the point at which the captain fears for his sanity, because this "confused sensation of being in two places at once" is set against his endeavour to retain his grasp on normality—embodied here as the ability to command his ship and deal with his crew. During breakfast, on the morning after Leggatt has come aboard, he says:

> . . . all the time the dual working of my mind distracted me almost to the point of insanity. I was constantly watching myself, my secret self, as dependent on my actions as my own personality, sleeping on that bed, behind that door which faced me as I sat at the head of the table. It was very much like being mad, only it was worse because one was aware of it.[15]

On the fourth day of "miserable juggling with the unavoidable" he reaches the climax of this torment of trying to reconcile the knowledge of the secret sharer with his duty as shipmaster. The steward goes to hang up the captain's coat, opens the door of the bathroom, where Leggatt is concealed, and does not see him hiding in the bath. The captain waits for the inevitable discovery, and, when it does not come, his bewilderment and his mixture of feelings about Leggatt come out in his first reflection:

"Saved", I thought., "But no! Lost! Gone! He was gone!"[16]

At this stage in his experience he actually fears that he may already be insane.

> . . . an irresistible doubt of his bodily existence flitted through my mind [he says]. Can it be, I asked myself, that he is not visible to other eyes than mine? It was like being haunted . . . I think I had come creeping quietly as near insanity as any man who has not actually gone over the border.[17]

But from this position escape is possible, as it is not possible for the central characters of the earlier stories. This is because the situation of the narrator in "The Secret Sharer" is a stage nearer the purely symbolic than that dealt with in the other works. As I have shown, the presence of Leggatt is so nightmarish, not because he makes the captain aware of any inadequacy or wrongness in his ideas and beliefs, but rather because the relationship between them is itself an objective correlative of such knowledge. After the death of Kurtz, Marlow is left with his mind uneasy and with the feeling that the last words of the dying man were "a moral victory", but in "The Secret Sharer" the whole of the narrator's "strangeness" has been so completely embodied in the person of Leggatt that seemingly it can be got rid of.

Leggatt can, in fact, be marooned on one of the islands that fringe the Gulf of Siam. But the captain feels that he cannot do this easily. Although he knows that he may be endangering his ship by taking such a risk, he feels that, as he says, "It was now a matter of conscience to shave the land as close as possible".[18] Clearly it is not physical considerations alone which determine this need: Leggatt can swim too well for that. It seems, rather, that the captain feels that to exorcise his "other self" he must run as close to disaster as possible, knowing all the time, as he says, that

> all my future, the only future for which I was fit, would perhaps go irretrievably to pieces in any mishap to my first command.[19]

Thus, finally, the narrator and Leggatt are separated; even that hat which the captain thrusts on the fugitive's head[20] falls off in the water and acts as a mark by which he can gauge the progress of the ship.

> Now I had what I wanted [the captain says]—the saving mark for my eyes. But I hardly thought of my other self, now gone from the ship, to be hidden forever from all friendly faces . . . I watched the hat —the expression of my sudden pity for his mere flesh. It had been meant to save his homeless head from the dangers of the sun. And now—behold—it was saving the ship, by serving me for a mark to help out the ignorance of my strangeness.[21]

Now at last the captain can feel certain of his ability to command, as he could not when he gave his first order and knew that he was not "wholly alone" with his command. Now he can say:

> Already the ship was drawing ahead. And I was alone with her. Nothing! no one in the world should stand now between us, throwing a shadow on the way of silent knowledge and mute affection, the perfect communion of a seaman with his first command.[22]

"Strangeness"—the knowledge of the "secret double"—has been exorcised and normality restored.

* * *

This story, as I have pointed out, marks the end of one phase of Conrad's work; the preoccupations are fundamentally the same as in the earlier books but the situation is so presented that a solution can be offered. It is noticeable that after this a change comes over his writing, and when we consider the form which it takes we are struck at once by a parallel between it and "The Secret Sharer". The story might almost be an allegory of Conrad's future development.

The Conrad of the group of stories and novels which we have been considering is as obsessed by the consciousness of the "other self" as the narrator of "The Secret Sharer". There is a potentially evil or discreditable side to the natures of all his central characters, a seed of corruption in all their idealisms, a suspicion that all our most elevated feelings derive at bottom from the same root as the hunger of Falk which had to be satisfied by cannibalism.

There can be little of quietness or optimism or security in such a view of human life, and the works are indeed disturbing and, like Marlow's reminiscences, "inconclusive". The price of peace of mind for Conrad seems to be much the same as it is for the narrator of this story. He turns away from these preoccupations. In the later works, as we shall see, there is no longer this emphasis on the sense of guilt and this indefinable compact with the "secret double". The simple virtues of honesty, courage and fidelity to one's comrades, whose insufficiency has been one of the main themes of works like "Heart of Darkness" and *Nostromo*, are in the later books sufficient guides. It would, of course, be too much to say that no doubts of them are ever expressed, but such expressions are rarely more than perfunctory and they never carry the same weight of feeling and criticism as in the early books. One consequence of this removal of tension from the experience of his central figures is that his characters tend more and more to fall into two groups—the good and the bad.

The contrast in outlook is very clearly seen if we compare the significance of the description in this story of the

> great security of the sea . . . that untempted life presenting no disquieting problems, invested with an elementary moral beauty by the absolute straightforwardness of its appeal and by the singleness of its purpose[23]

with similar passages in *Chance,* or with an extract from a letter to Mrs. Sanderson which he wrote in 1917:

> The naval training has a peculiar quality, and forms a very fine type. For one thing it is strictly methodized to a very definite end which is noble in itself and of a very high idealistic nature, while on its technical side it deals with a body of systematized facts which cannot be questioned as to their value. . . .

In "The Secret Sharer" the reflection is profoundly ironic, coming as it does immediately before the appearance of Leggatt, who presents the most "disquieting problems" it is possible to imagine. For the Conrad of the early works the "strictly methodized" and "highly idealistic" sea life is no defence against the recognition of the presence of the secret sharer. The virtues which it fosters are unable to deal with Mr. Kurtz or with the dilemma of Captain Whalley. But there is no irony in such references in *Chance* or the later letters. It is in this context that we must think of Conrad's idealization of naval life after he had become a public figure. It is not enough to see it merely as an ageing man's nostalgia for the life he had led as a young man nor as a romanticization for the newspaper public. Rather is it an inevitable result of this turning away from the preoccupations of the works before "The Secret Sharer".

I prefer to restrict speculation on the significance of this story's coming soon after he had finished the plunge into his own Polish past which took shape—carefully edited, as all Conrad's reminiscences are—in *A Personal Record,* and while he was writing *Under Western Eyes,* in which his feelings about his early life under the Tsarist tyranny are clearly involved. It is possible that by such speculation we could construct plausible and even correct theories about his feelings concerning his childhood and adolescence, but it would help us little in the task of evaluating his work. What we are concerned with is the presence of a crisis within the works, and of the existence of this there can be little doubt.

There seems to have been within him a continual war between the recognition of the "heart of darkness" and the desire to rest securely on unquestioned values. His letters tend to show that the desire for security was the more conscious, but in the best of the early works the "other self" cannot be denied. We have seen something of the struggle emerging in the flaws and insufficiencies of parts of *Lord Jim.* With "The Secret Sharer" Conrad seems to resolve this conflict for his peace of mind, and we must now consider the works which follow it.                    (1952)

## NOTES

1. Hewitt seems not at all cognizant of Conrad criticism in America. His book contains not a single reference to an American critic of Conrad. [Editor's note]

2. *'Twixt Land and Sea: Tales,* 1912, p. 113.

3. *Ibid.,* p. 95.

4. *Ibid.,* p. 96.

5. *Ibid.,* p. 110.

6. *Ibid.,* p. 99.

7. *Ibid.,* p. 100.

8. *Ibid.,* p. 102.

9. *Loc. cit.*

10. *Ibid.,* p. 119.

11. *Ibid.,* p. 120.

12. *Loc. cit.*

13. *Ibid.,* p. 110.

14. *Ibid.,* p. 125.

15. *Ibid.,* pp. 113-14.

16. *Ibid.,* p. 129

17. *Ibid.,* p. 130

18. *Ibid.,* p. 139.

19. *Ibid.,* p. 135.

20. The degree of identification is, perhaps, stronger here than anywhere else in the story. "I saw *myself* wandering barefooted, bareheaded, the sun beating on my dark poll. I snatched off my floppy hat and tried hurriedly in the dark to ram it on my other self" (p. 138, my italics).

21. *'Twixt Land and Sea: Tales,* 1912, p. 142.

22. *Ibid.,* p. 143.

23. *Ibid.,* p. 96.

# EDWARD CRANKSHAW

## Joseph Conrad: *Chance**

WE HAVE by now, I hope, some idea of the extraordinary circumstances governing Conrad's art. His use of the indirect narrative with the aid of Marlow and other devices we are familiar with. On the assumption that there is nothing causeless, if not under the sun then at least in the expression of a responsible mind, we have looked for the reason for Conrad's choice of method and found it to lie in the attempt of an entirely subjective temperament to live up to a self-imposed ideal of objectivity. If Marlow is a bore, which anyone is at liberty to think, Conrad is also a bore; the two are inseparable.

I have already quoted Mr. Garnett's phrase, to be found in his preface to *Letters from Joseph Conrad,* that Marlow came into being simply because he saved Conrad trouble. That is a curious thing to say about a scrupulous artist with an extremely high opinion of his medium; in a sense, nevertheless, it is true, but not in the sense, I imagine, that Mr. Garnett intended. If it can be said that an Englishman speaks English because it saves him trouble, then the phrase about Marlow is true; if it can be said that a man walks on the towpath rather than swims to his destination to save himself trouble, then it is true. But we do not as a rule walk rather than swim to save ourselves trouble, but because it is our natural means of progression. To save ourselves trouble we ride rather than walk, and Conrad never, never rode.

The phrase might possibly be true in another sense, although here we are getting on to dangerous ground. Marlow was not the only device used by Conrad to give a subjective eye an objective focus. In *Nostromo* he took up a standpoint exceedingly difficult to maintain, the standpoint of the objective observer recording physically observed facts with such accuracy that they reveal their inner significance to the reader. The standpoint is not maintained with perfect consistency throughout the book; at times a junior Marlow is successfully introduced in the person of Decoud, and at times a train of thought is rendered or a passage of interior monologue, usually with not the happiest effect; but the main attitude is the recording and selection of observed facts. In *The Secret Agent* we have an all but perfect *tour de force* in another technique which we shall have to glance at later on. And then we have the first person stories. It may be true to say that Conrad found all these methods more trying than the Marlow method, even that method as employed in *Chance,* and he may have taken Marlow as the lesser of two evils. But to jump out of the fire and into the frying-pan is a gesture surely inadequately described as a saving of trouble.

* From Edward Crankshaw's *Joseph Conrad: Some Aspects of the Art of the Novel* (John Lane, 1936), VI, pp. 120-134.

The only book in which the Marlow device is the obvious device is *Youth*, but if Marlow is the line of least resistance here, for once the line of least resistance is the right line. *Youth* is a personal experience of Conrad's which he desired to present neat and untampered with, to relate at first hand; the subject is less a set of facts than a subjective mood haloing a set of facts. And this cannot possibly be done by an external rendering; there must on the part of the hero be a great deal of thought and feeling in it. To Conrad, unable to render thought and feeling in sustained detail objectively, the employment of the first person is imperative. He could have told the tale himself, as he did in *The Shadow Line*, but happily he did not and consequently gained in clarity and vividness. In *Lord Jim* and in "Heart of Darkness" Marlow may have saved him a certain amount of trouble, but he must have caused him a great deal more worry than he saved. And in *Chance* and *Under Western Eyes* the trouble he gives is stupendous. In *Under Western Eyes*, indeed, the obstacles raised by that inoffensive teacher of languages are never fully overcome.

Only in these very limited senses, and then all too dangerously, can it be said that Marlow saved Conrad trouble. The idea in any case is a misleading one, for it carries the implication that if he had gone to sufficient trouble he could have written *Chance* in the manner of, say, Ford Madox Ford's Tietjens novels. And this manner was to him an impossibility for the reasons I have tried to suggest.

In perfect opposition to the more usual view of Marlow and all he stands for we have Henry James prostrating himself in a kind of embarrassed, slightly reproachful awe before the technique of *Chance*. His reproach, the reproach of a fellow novelist unlikely himself to be accused of *ca'canny*, is not that Conrad went about saving himself trouble, but that he simply cried out for it and welcomed it wide-armed, or even that he rushed straight into it, open-eyed, and with a self-immolatory ardour almost indecent:

"It places Mr. Conrad absolutely alone as a votary of the way to do a thing that shall make it undergo most doing. The way to do it that shall make it undergo least is the line on which we are mostly used to see prizes carried off; so that the author of *Chance* gathers up on this showing all sorts of comparative distinction. He gathers up at least two sorts— that of bravery in absolutely reversing the process most accredited, and that, quite separate, we make out, of performing the manoeuvre under salvos of recognition . . . the general effect of *Chance* is arrived at by a pursuance of means to the end in view contrasted with which every other current form of the chase can only affect us as cheap and futile; the carriage of the burden or amount of service required on these lines exceeding surely all other such displayed degrees of energy put together."

But while Mr. James, as he would have to (I quote from the essay on "The New Novel"—1914—in *Notes on Novelists*), fully and most delicately recognizes the extreme subtlety of the method of *Chance*, and while his estimate of Marlow is a thousand times nearer the mark than the usual one, we shall, if we agree on our conclusions as to Conrad's particular psychological limitations, be compelled to dissent, sharply enough, but not at all bluntly, from the implications in that essay that Conrad deliberately went out of his way to make his task as hard as possible. Methods are conditioned by temperament, and the methods Conrad used, or something like them, were the outcome of necessity. It would be more accurate, I think, to say that with the ideal of objectivity before him and ridden by an artist's conscience he had no option but to write *Chance* as he did. The gratuitous element is the ideal of objectivity, which Henry James would have been the first to uphold.

Curiously enough, indeed, in that same article James touches on this matter of objectivity in a way most illuminating for our purpose: "*Chance is* an example of objectivity, most precious of aims, not only menaced but definitely compromised; whereby we are in presence of something really of the strangest, a general and diffused lapse of authenticity which an inordinate number of common readers . . . have not only condoned but have emphatically commended. They can have done this but through the bribe of some authenticity other in kind, no doubt, and seeming to them equally great if not greater, which gives back by the left hand what the right hand has, with however dissimulated a grace, taken away. What Mr. Conrad's left hand gives back then is simply Mr. Conrad himself."

Henry James in those passages is concerned chiefly with the difficulty of succeeding with the method of *Chance* once it is fairly under way, a method "ridden . . . by such a danger of steeping his matter in perfect eventual obscuration as we recall no other artist's consenting to with an equal grace." But the first difficulties, and difficulties in themselves of a kind which make the notion of Conrad employing Marlow to save trouble look silly, arise prolifically on the plane of pure mechanics, in the setting of the method in motion.

In *Youth* Marlow is the central figure and the book is about his experience, or his reception of that experience. But *Chance* is not about Marlow at all. It is about everybody but Marlow, indeed; and this fact is the motive of the first problem of all. Conrad desiring to write about Flora de Barral and Captain Anthony, wanting in his way to unveil his characters completely, yet denied by temperament the direct approach, having to deal in shades of apprehension and perception too delicate and fine to be caught by the straightforward treatment of *Nostromo,* needed in the story a character to talk round it. The qualifications required of such a commentator are neither common nor few. He must *know,* he must be experienced in life, he must perceive, he must understand, he must be sympathetic, and he must be interested in people for their own sakes. The actors in the story, the protagonists that matter, we know: Mr. and Mrs. Fyne, Roderick Anthony and Flora de Barral, the wicked governess, Mr. Powell, Mr. Franklin—not, if one may say so, a very subtle crowd, not one of them sufficiently perceptive and dispassionate to watch a subtly complex situation and interpret it in its finest, most ambiguous shades. And so somebody has to be brought in from the outside, and the obvious man for the job is Marlow, retired from action for the past ten years. Marlow, once he is in, will save Conrad a lot of trouble; oh, indubitably. . . . But how to get him in? And one of the most remarkable things about *Chance* and about Conrad's technical brilliance generally, is the satisfactory way in which this excessively thorny problem is solved.

To the casual glance it may seem to add pages to the length of the book, wanton pages: Marlow has not only to be got in, he has also to be held in so that he does not fall out again. Those pages are certainly so much cover for that situation, precarious, yet never allowed to appear so, being held secure by Conrad's infinitely scrupulous justification of Marlow's every action. But they serve other purposes as well; they must serve other purposes or there can be no valid excuse for their inclusion. With any writer but Conrad there would be no valid excuse.

The thing is managed perfectly. Marlow, who has no business at all in that gallery, is made to have a business. The very first step is hard enough, the initial establishment of his relations with the Fynes. These are not the kind of people one would expect to find in Marlow's circle, and nobody was more aware of that than Conrad. It has to be made clear, Marlow himself makes it clear, that the Fynes are not his friends at all but the merest accidental holiday acquaintances, in a measure amusing to this student of humanity, but even more boring than amusing. So far so good. That in itself is enough to show off the Fynes and even to get Marlow introduced to, or rather into touch with, the mysterious and suicidal "girl friend," with Miss Smith, Flora de Barral. But it is now essential for Marlow to know all about Flora's history up to the all but fatal walk beside the quarry; and the only way, the only reasonable way, in which he can come upon this is through one or other of the Fynes. This argues a state of intimacy with that family which Marlow did not enjoy and in normal circumstances was never likely to enjoy. And it is here that the average novelist, granted that he had survived even thus far (which is improbable), would almost certainly have run his story on the rocks. He would have committed an assault on the integrity of character either on the part of Marlow or of the Fynes by making them all become close friends. But Conrad, knowing Marlow, knowing the Fynes, knew perfectly well that such a consummation could not be hoped for on this side of the grave. It could have been contrived with some plausibility; he could have cooked, so to speak, his characters as politicians cook statistics; he could, out of his infinite resource, easily have thrown dust into the reader's eyes. But Conrad was never a thrower of dust, and with extreme ingenuity (whether conscious or unconscious has no relevance) he contrived to put Marlow into Mrs. Fyne's confidence while keeping the two for all normal purposes as far removed from one another as they ever were, as they for ever must be. This is achieved with such a show of spontaneity and ease that one cannot tell whether a certain turn in the story arose out of that necessity or whether the necessity was miraculously eased by a certain turn in the story. We have in fact, as so often throughout *Chance,* that perfect fusion of content and technique which is the greatest delight that art can offer. The narrative takes on the aspect of a supercharged engine (if so far-fetched a comparison is allowed) with all that is implied therein. All things, so to speak, work together for good in a process which I should like to call super-augmentation of effect, a process which of all novelists Conrad wrought to most perfection.

We begin with Marlow as a superficial acquaintance, a tame chess-player for Fyne. By chance he happens to be walking by the quarry at the precise moment when Flora is having her suicidal intentions undermined by the antics of a ridiculous dog. That same dog introduces him to Flora herself. The next appreciable step forward is Flora's flight to Captain Anthony, or rather, in the first instance, her simple disappearance. Marlow is still in no closer communion with the Fynes, but the chance of his walk by the quarry bears fruit, a second crop indeed, since the first was our introduction to Flora. He remembers her evidently unbalanced state of mind, and this memory throws for him an ominous shadow down into the present. It is because of that walk, and only because of that, and at his suggestion (a suggestion he was made to regret after five minutes' experience of Mr. Fyne's pedestrian faculty), that he joins up with Fyne, turns an aimless search into an extremely pointed one, and, its vainness established, returns with Fyne to his house. And there he encounters Mrs. Fyne, for the first time in her life thrown slightly off her balance, and in the emotional hours of the night at that. For a moment Marlow and the Fynes are on common ground. Without establishing an accord Conrad has accomplished a significant contact, significant enough at least to give perfect plausibility to Mrs. Fyne's coming to him for moral support when, on the reception of Flora's letter, she finds herself, again for the first time in her life, openly at odds with her husband. This little quarrel is of extreme importance too, for besides throwing a light of positively blinding illumination on the Fynes themselves it leaves Mrs. Fyne, an outraged woman, in a state of isolation. She must talk to somebody; she cannot talk to Fyne: and so she turns to the man in whom she imagines herself to have seen a streak of most unmasculine sagacity and against whom she is thrown in her entirely womanly search for support in face of her inoffensive husband. The contact, the intimate contact, is thus established, with Marlow jibbing away all the time and doing his best, as he would, to break it. But it is, so far as Mrs. Fyne is concerned (and it is *her* contact, Marlow remaining passive), an entirely emotional contact, and when that particular emotion has blown itself out the relapse into the *status quo* is inevitable and normal. Marlow never set eyes on her again. But Mrs. Fyne retained her illusion of his sagacity for just long enough to spill enough beans to keep the story running. And from that contact, so hard to establish and so beautifully contrived, Marlow learns about Flora's girlhood all that is necessary for his story. And from that contact, too, directly springs Marlow's opportunity to get from Flora's own lips her own story and her version of that all-important walk by the quarry. During all this time Conrad has been getting Marlow in and at the same time making him work for dear life, like an unsalaried apprentice.

For Flora's own narrative was as difficult to contrive as Mrs. Fyne's. First the meeting has to be contrived (it is made the direct outcome of the false intimacy of Marlow and the Fynes) and then Flora has to reveal her own past, or those aspects of it which she alone knows. And this, obviously, can only be done with a comparative stranger as the second party. People will not reveal themselves to their established friends as Flora revealed herself to Marlow; but wearied by their burden of secret knowledge they are driven to talk to somebody, and there, miraculously at hand, was the perfect listener, perfect in manner and in position, physical position, that is. And so it goes on. It is beautiful.

It may be countered that there is nothing particularly original in this, that all life is strung on a chain of cause and effect, and that all novels, if they are to have any air of inevitability, must also be so contrived. And that is true enough as to kind. What is here significant is the degree, the highly complex contrapuntal pattern that is achieved without a hint of strain. The whole of *Chance,* in this way, is a masterpiece of construction of a kind that can only be called fugal. The small example we have taken, which we took primarily to show Conrad's inspired handling of Marlow, his working of a stubborn element into a rigid narrative without any sense of strain (and it is enough, I should say, to show that Marlow, even physically, caused Conrad far more trouble than he saved him), also serves to illuminate the contrapuntal texture of the book. Here I do not refer to the sort of counterpoint practised by Mr. Huxley, the simple interweaving of lives, but to a suggestive, aesthetic counterpoint having no reference to actuality objectively recorded. In all Conrad's work every incident, every character, every sentence almost, is made to do at least double duty, and that is the beauty of the fugue. Nowhere is this faculty of significant compression more finely displayed than in *Chance.* That one trivial incident, that accident of Marlow walking by the quarry at the moment when the girl had determined to end her life there, is made to serve half a dozen purposes. It gives Marlow his false intimacy with the Fynes; it gives him his excuse for being outside the East-end hotel early in the morning; it gives him sufficient acquaintance with Flora to take advantage of that chance meeting; it gives Conrad his opportunity to provide the reader with a sharp impression of Flora as a person; it gives Marlow his opportunity to give you the girl's nature as understood by an intelligent and perceptive outsider; it brings into the book in the most delicate manner imaginable the first hint of the fatality which is later to increase and pervade it; it provides the episode of the dog, so perfectly done, which later, during that street-corner conversation, sends a beam of illumination flashing down into the present from the past, assuring for Conrad his ceaselessly sought closeness of texture and strengthening the ironic mood.

This kind of thing in prose fiction is, with "cutting" in the cinema, the only thing strictly analogous to musical counterpoint in all art. And of all music the contrapuntal is the highest, since it permits of the simultaneous expression of innumerable shades of meaning. To its supremacy Mozart, Schubert, and Beethoven, the world's three greatest composers besides Bach, bear witness; in their maturity they all three resort to the fugue for the expression of the inexpressible, the fugue with its infinite power of suggestion. And the greatness of Conrad as a novelist may be measured by the success of what amounts to a contrapuntal structure in his greatest works.

A brief examination of the elementary difficulties brought on Conrad's head by Marlow in *Chance* has led us straight into a technical consideration of his work as a whole. It is not easy here to keep the various elements of technique neatly pigeon-holed. The first technical problem of the novelist is the establishment and preservation of his illusion, but this problem sooner or later is found to be inseparably bound up with the wider problem of how he is to get the last ounce out of his subject. Marlow himself is a clear-cut enough figure and an obvious enough device, but so inseparable in Conrad (at his best, of course) is technique from content that even the superficial consideration of Marlow has led us into the inexpressible.

*Chance* is that rare thing, a work of fine spiritual significance and a technical *tour de force*. It deserves for itself the epithet "great" unqualified. The book itself is a great book, not merely the product of a great writer. The author has undertaken a spiritual revelation of extreme subtlety. The book is pervaded by the air of fatality, and the significance of the ramified conflict which is the "affair" passes beyond the castrophe of physical death to the horror of spiritual annihilation. The subject, which may be seen as the spiritual rescue of Flora de Barral from the forces of darkness, from simple elimination by the evil in the world (Conrad's sense of evil has never been more intense than in this quiet, unmelodramatic story), which all but suffocates and poisons her consciousness, sprawling over her as a gigantic black slug might slime over a border of flowers, is a solemn one. There can be nothing more solemn in the world than the contemplation of a hair's breadth escape from spiritual obliteration. And yet the book itself is not solemn. The book is not solemn in spite of the fact that every ounce is got out of its extremely solemn subject, *that* subject, which is so presented that all its myriad overtones sound freely, unconstrained. And this blessed lack of solemnity it owes to Conrad's exalted sense of perspective which puts **that** solemn episode, that *little* episode, which is nevertheless microcosmic in its meaning, exquisitely in its place in a world which it is fatal to regard with solemnity. His great achievement in *Chance* (and not in that book alone) is his just relating of a dreadful episode to the world as a whole without in the least robbing it of its own implicit horror.

But we were discussing Marlow in his elementary aspects, not Conrad's sensibility. And the immediate point was to show that Marlow was never the device of a novelist too lazy to work in another convention. In *Chance,* if nowhere else, the difficulties of handling him are plain. They are magnificently vanquished, and the effect is, I believe, unique. To turn again to Henry James, who provides an extremely beautiful image of Marlow's part in the story, we have in him "a prolonged hovering flight of the subjective over the outstretched ground of the case exposed. We make out this ground but through the shadow cast by the flight, clarify it though the real author visibly reminds himself again and again that he must—all the more that, as if by some tremendous forecast of future applied science, the upper aeroplane causes another, as we have said, to depend from it and that one still another; these dropping shadow after shadow, to the no small menace of intrinsic colour and form and whatever, upon the passive expanse."

Yet if Marlow is never elsewhere so hard to handle as he was in *Chance,* in those other stories he is very necessary. From him in *Youth* springs that atmosphere of vital enthusiasm in reminiscence which is lacking in *The Shadow Line.* In "Heart of Darkness" he is truly indispensable. For here, through his sensibility, we have the gradual revelation of a character whom we hardly meet and whose death-bed taciturnity would have rendered the use of the third person impossible. The warped character of Kurtz, moreover, would, even had Conrad been able to manage it (which he would not have been), have turned a revelation of character by any interior method into grotesque fantasy; for the whole world viewed through his eyes would have been a place of fantastic abomination, and also, written from his standpoint, there would be no contrast between actuality as perceived by normal eyes and the eyes of insanity. It would have been something like *The Cabinet of Dr. Caligari,* only unbearably hideous and of a limited pathological interest. And, in any case, Conrad was not intent on describing Kurtz nor in revealing his precise mentality, but in rendering the sinister fatality of his environment; and this is an aspect of life which interested him a great deal, which is never absent from his studies of Almayer, Willems, and other white men living in the East. The environment is made to work on Marlow himself until his flesh begins to creep. We remember his atavistic shudders at the sound of the reverberating drums, preparing us insidiously and with great subtlety for the dreadful revelation that is to come. In that way, and in that way only (remembering Conrad's limitations), can he give us the horror—the contrast between the man as he was and the man as he is—in a single sickening glimpse of truth. The method of interior revelation cannot give you the past and the present in a single phrase, for a man in his own consciousness is only what he is at the moment of being, at every moment of being; and even the most poignant retrospective glance will be coloured by the subjective eye of his present state.                                                    (1936)

# DOUGLAS HEWITT

## Conrad, A Reassessment: *Chance**

*Chance* was published in 1913, but Conrad had been long writing it. Begun towards the end of 1906, it was laid aside (because it did not develop as he wished) while he wrote *Under Western Eyes, A Personal Record*, "The Secret Sharer" and a number of less important short stories; and it was then taken up again in the summer of 1910 and finished in March, 1912. It belongs, that is, to the period of crisis and change in Conrad's writing life which I have seen as epitomized in "The Secret Sharer."[1]

It was with this novel that Conrad first achieved popular success, and it always remained one of his own favourites, but it bears, more clearly than *Under Western Eyes,* the marks of the decline in his art, the disappearance of those qualities which give such power to "Heart of Darkness" and *Nostromo.*

It may be objected that in formulating this judgment I am laying *Chance* on a Procrustean bed or blaming Conrad for not rewriting the early books again and again. But it seems plain that the later works, in general, show a retreat from the degree of awareness of the complexity of human emotion found in the early ones. The division of mankind into the camp of the good and the camp of the bad, for instance, is clearly a sign of a restriction rather than a change of interest.

The obvious flaws of *Chance*—its clichés, its defensive irony, its imprecise rhetoric—can be seen to come, I believe, from this evasion of the painful awareness of the darker side of even our good feelings. His theme here is, ostensibly, very much like those of the works we have already examined, the study of "the utter falseness of his [Anthony's], I may say, aspirations, the vanity of grasping the empty air." But in fact the investigation is never undertaken. Too much is exempted from the scrutiny.

The two parts of the novel are entitled "The Damsel" and "The Knight." No better example could be found for the statement at the end

* From Douglas Hewitt's *Joseph Conrad: A Reassessment* (Bowes & Bowes, 1952), VIII, pp. 89-102.

of my last chapter, that in his later works Conrad's irony is normally defensive.[2] These are, fairly obviously, ironic titles; this, we are to infer, is how Anthony sees the situation; we have been told that he inherited an excessive tendency towards the conception of chivalry from his father. But it is also, at bottom, how Conrad sees it, and the irony is intended to defend him against the suspicion of not having realized how oversimplified and falsely romantic is his treatment of the plight of his characters.

The deep misunderstanding between Anthony and his wife is symbolized in previously unheard-of cabin arrangements. The projection of inner states in outer phenomena is affected with all Conrad's usual consistency. One example alone is enough to show his thoroughness: when the ship is in danger young Powell stamps on the deck to summon the captain, but Anthony and his wife do not share a cabin and so he is not warned in time of the danger to his command. There is, indeed, a great deal of emphasis throughout the scenes on board the *Ferndale* on the potential danger to the whole ship's company until the false situation is resolved. In this there is a distinct resemblance to "The Secret Sharer". But the situation of the main characters—of Anthony and Flora—is far different from that of the narrator of the short story. Here we find no haunting feeling of guilt, but a misunderstanding caused by Anthony's excess of chivalrous delicacy acting upon that morbid sensitiveness with which Flora has been affected as the result of horrible experiences in her childhood and youth.

She, the damsel, is one of Conrad's repeated characters. He continually recurs in his later works to the figure of the woman of superlative purity and beauty, smirched by a world which is too gross or evil for her: Rita de Lastaola in *The Arrow of Gold,* Adèle de Montevesso in *Suspense,* Arlette Réal in *The Rover.* We may reasonably suppose that the original of Rita de Lastaola—the woman with whom he was in love in his early gun-running days in Marseilles and for whom he fought a duel—is the original of them all.[3]

The experiences which have scarred Flora's mind are entirely the fault of people depicted either—like the Fynes—as unable to understand her needs because of theoretical preconceptions, or—like the governess and the uncle—as totally evil or despicable. It should be noted that the governess is not described merely as an ordinarily selfish and vindictive woman. Conrad's preoccupation with evil is in evidence here, as in "Heart of Darkness", but the evil is restricted to some characters; Flora bears none of it within herself.

> The girl was astounded and alarmed [he says] by the altogether unknown expression in the woman's face. The stress of passion often discloses an aspect of the personality completely ignored till then by its closer intimates. There was something like an emanation of evil from her eyes and from the face of the other, who, exactly behind her and overstopping her by half a head, kept his eyelids lowered in a sinister fashion . . .

Flora has been hurt by the world before she is old enough to have developed weapons against it. It has taught her fear, humiliation, despair, a "poisoned sleep", until she has "a spirit neither made cringing nor yet dulled but as if bewildered in quivering hopelessness by gratuitous cruelty ... The passive anguish of the luckless!" But it has taught her neither calculation nor evil.

Anthony, the knight, is presented chiefly through the adoring eyes of Powell or through the medium of Marlow's reminiscences, and he, too, is something of a stock character. Clearly he is far too good for this world and he is described continually in the most romantic terms. He paces the deck with his eyes averted with "the tenderness of silent solitary men", at sea, where "you hear no tormenting echoes of your own littleness ... where either a great elemental voice roars defiantly under the sky or else an elemental silence seems to be part of the infinite stillness of the universe". He has "native rectitude, sea-salted, hardened in the winds of wide horizons, open as the day". He is summed up thus:

> Solitude had been his best friend. He wanted some place where he could sit down and be alone. And in his need his thoughts turned to the sea which had given him so much of that congenial solitude. There, if always with his ship (but that was an integral part of him) he could always be as solitary as he chose. Yes. Get out to sea!

What there is in this book of that profound and searching investigation of human nature and beliefs which we find in Conrad's best early work is vague and offset at once by rhetoric. From time to time Marlow throws out dark hints of qualities in Anthony to which he cannot give his unstinted and rapturous admiration, but the hints are always couched in terms which lead us rather to admire than to explore.

> I am convinced [he says] that he used reading as an opiate against the pain of his magnanimity which, like all abnormal growths, was gnawing at his healthy substance with cruel presistence.

He discusses how far the element of vanity entered into Anthony's motives:

> The inarticulate son had set up a standard for himself with that need for embodying in his conduct the dreams, the passion, the impulses the poet puts into arrangements of verses, which are dearer to him than his own self—and may make his own self appear sublime in the eyes of other people, and even in his own eyes.
> Did Anthony wish to appear sublime in his own eyes? I should not like to make that charge . . . I do not even think that there was in what he did a conscious and lofty confidence in himself, a particularly pronounced sense of power which leads men so often into impossible or equivocal situations.

This, coming after the comment that his father's standards of delicacy had worn out two women, might suggest closer investigation of all Anthony's motives, were it not that the passage closes with yet another gesture of adoration before the idealized figure:

> . . . this eager appropriation was truly the act of a man of solitude and desire; a man also, who, unless a complete imbecile, must have been a man of long and ardent reveries wherein the faculty of sincere passion matures slowly in the unexplored recesses of the heart.

There is one section of the book where it seems that we are moving towards that kind of criticism, that ruthless investigation of the sources and nature of our feelings, which is Conrad's special power. Marlow, describing his talk with Flora outside the East End pub, has remarked of Flora's letter to Mrs. Fyne:

> What a sell these confessions are! What a horrible sell! You seek sympathy, and all you get is the most evanescent sense of relief—if you get that much. For a confession, whatever it may be, stirs the secret depths of the hearer's character. Often depths that he himself is but dimly aware of.

He goes on to recount Flora's story of how Anthony declared his love. She says that, walking with her, he was "following her with an air of extreme interest. Interest or eagerness? At any rate she caught an expression on his face which frightened her". A little later, after he has seen how miserable she is, we are told that:

> What seemed most awful to her was the elated light in his eyes, the rapacious smile that would come and go as if he were gloating over her misery. But her misery was his opportunity and he rejoiced while the tenderest pity seemed to flood his whole being . . . the very marks and stamp of this ill-usage of which he was so certain seemed to add to the inexplicable attraction he felt for her person . . . It gave him the feeling that if only he could get hold of her, no woman would belong to him so completely as this woman.

He asks her to come down to him in the garden, and the thought comes to her "that should he get into ungovernable fury from disappointment and perchance strangle her, it would be as good a way to be done with it as any".
Marlow comments:

> This makes one shudder at the mysterious way girls acquire knowledge. For this was a thought, wild enough, I admit, but which could only have come from the depths of that sort of experience which she had not had, and went far beyond a young girl's possible conception of the strongest and most veiled of human emotions.

But, she says, "He was gentleness itself", and the edge of this perception of a possible darker side to Anthony's passion is blunted; the criticism is directed away from him and left as a general reflection on human nature from which the tone of the prose seems to except him, and before long we find such passages, typical of Marlow's descriptions of Anthony, as:

> . . . the desire of that man to whom the sea and sky of his solitary life had appeared suddenly incomplete without that glance which seemed to belong to them both—

the glance, that is, of Flora's eyes—and he is telling her "that to be fair you must trust a man altogether—or not at all", and summing up Anthony as *"un galant homme"*. The section ends with Anthony as

> the son of the poet, the rescuer of the most forlorn damsel of modern times, the man of violence, gentleness and generosity.

The same hint of criticism is seen in Marlow's perception at the climax of the events on board the *Ferndale*:

> . . . if two beings thrown together, mutually attracted, resist the necessity, fail in understanding and voluntarily stop short of the—the embrace, in the noblest meaning of the word, then they are committing a sin against life, the call of which is simple. Perhaps sacred. And the punishment of it is an invasion of complexity, a tormenting, forcibly tortuous involution of feelings.

But there is no attempt to show any inherent inadequacy in Anthony; there is no suggestion of any deep inhibition of feeling in him. The "involution" is entirely a temporary matter—a matter of this particular situation. As soon as Anthony and Flora realize that they are in a false position, all can be well.

Despite these few hints of Marlow, then, a highly romanticized figure is presented to us, a man with no flaw but his overdeveloped delicacy; and from this flaw proceeds, for Flora "this new perfidy of life taking upon itself the form of magnanimity". The situation is summed up in a comment on Marlow:

> In the full light of the room I saw in his eyes that slightly mocking expression with which he habitually covers up his sympathetic impulses of mirth and pity before *the unreasonable complications the idealism of mankind puts into the simple but poignant problem of conduct on this earth.*

We are required to believe in an unbelievably fine man so as to be shown the harm that comes from the overdevelopment of one virtue. But we are not convinced of the reality of the man, nor, therefore, of the significance of the central situation. In place of the interaction of a complexity of motives in which what seems good is ironically linked with bad, such as we find in *Nostromo* or *The Secret Agent* or "The End of the Tether", we are presented with a misunderstanding—a "false situation", in Marlow's words, arising from an excess of a virtue. The effect can, perhaps, be summed up by saying that we are sure that at a number of points in the story the most natural remark (the most natural remark, that is, even of these two inhibited characters) would end the whole misunderstanding. We do not feel it to be "chance", and the previous histories of Conrad's personages which prolong the intolerably false position, but the guiding hand of the story-teller. By contrast with *Nostromo,* where the progress of "material interests" and the idealism and fidelity of Charles Gould lead inevitably to every disaster and every apparent triumph, the issues in *Chance* stand out as contrived.

De Barral ("Mr. Smith") finally resolves the situation by trying to poison Anthony. Throughout the greater part of the book de Barral is treated as one of the "apes of a sinister jungle". In the earlier sections, however, where Marlow reminisces on his financial schemes and his trial, there is some description of his "air of placid sufficiency which was the first hint to the world of the man's overweening, unmeasurable conceit, hidden hitherto under a diffident manner". But Conrad appears to be little interested in creating the man himself—only in showing the dirtiness of finance which is contrasted throughout the book with the cleanness of the sea—and this perfunctoriness seems to be admitted in the description of Flora and her father walking hand in hand: "Figures from Dickens—pregnant with pathos". Once brought to the heart of the story, he is a man apart. Marlow, speaking of his release from prison, says:

> And the release! . . . How do they do it? Pull the string, door flies open, man flies through: Out you go! Adios! And in the space where a second before you were not, in the silent space there is a figure going away, limping. Why limping? I don't know. That's how I see it. One has a notion of a maiming, crippling process; of the individual coming back damaged in some subtle way.

He is maimed, he is the *diabolus ex machina,* and there is no possible contact between him and Anthony. We remember the connection in the earlier works between the man who is supposedly above reproach and the "bad" man whom he cannot disown: Lord Jim and Gentleman Brown, from the realization of similarities between men apparently dissimilar and of the complexity of human character, of the "unforeseen partnership". But here de Barral leads to no further knowledge of Anthony, who could never understand his father-in-law because he is himself presented as immune from all evil but his one excess of chivalry, as "the man . . . of silence made only more impressive by the inarticulate thunders and mutters of the great seas, an utter stranger to the clatter of tongues."

Once the misunderstanding is removed, therefore, there is nothing left to prevent Anthony and Flora living together in perfect happiness and goodness—save that (presumably for the sake of the "shape" of the story) Anthony has to be perfunctorily drowned and Flora given to Powell.

Conrad's tone is especially idealizing and romantic in the scene where Anthony and Flora, for the first time, understand one another's love. Clichés abound. Anthony has "a glance full of unwonted fire", he clasps

Powell's shoulder "as if in a vice", Flora is "whiter than the lilies". Irony, serving no such purpose as the irony of *The Secret Agent,* is there in:

> She looked as if she would let go and sink to the floor if the captain were to withhold his sustaining arm. But the captain obviously had no such intention.

Evil is something external which can be removed and Conrad's tone of surrender to his idealized creations is complete.

But the "shape" of the book demands that Anthony shall die and that Powell shall be sent at the end to claim his widow. The obvious concern for structure is probably the most immediately striking thing about the novel. It drew from Henry James the praise:

> It places Mr. Conrad absolutely alone as a votary of the way to do a thing that shall make it undergo most doing . . . What concerns us is that the general effect of *Chance* is arrived at by a pursuance of means to the end in view contrasted with every other current form of the chase can only affect us as cheap and futile.

It would seem that *Chance* shows the influence of James' own work more than any other of Conrad's books and this is most obvious in the manipulation of the plot. The bringing together of Flora and Anthony and their presentation through the Fynes reminds us at once of James' beloved indirect method, and it is excellently done. But this technique does seem at times to be there for its own sake. We may sympathize, I feel, with those critics, against whom Conrad defended himself in the "Author's Note", who asked whether it could not all have been done more simply.

Why, we have a right to ask, do we have the long—and (in itself) excellent—opening section, the loving reconstruction of a sailor's feelings when he gets his first post as an officer? Our need to understand Powell, who will be our chief source of information about life on the *Ferndale,* hardly demands as much as this.

I have already emphasized* that in *Nostromo,* where shifts in time and viewpoint are also common, they enforce criticisms and judgments. But in *Chance* they rarely serve such a function and there is no such sustained investigation of human motives and actions depending on them. Most clearly of all, we cannot see the casual killing of Anthony—almost an afterthought from Powell—as anything but arbitrary and wanton. The love of a good "shape" is the only possible reason and this "shape" is external; it arises from no inner organization or necessity; it is in no way connected with the spiritual and psychological issues involved.

It is interesting to note that James' praise, part of which I have quoted, is very qualified. One of his conclusions is:

> It literally strikes us that his volume sets in motion more than anything else a drama in which his own system and his combined eccentricities of recital represent the protagonist in face of powers leagued against it, and of which the dénouement gives us the system fighting in

* See pp. 66-69 of Hewitt's *Joseph Conrad: a Reassessment.* [Editor's note.]

triumph, though with its back desperately to the wall, and laying the powers piled up at its feet. This frankly has been *our* spectacle, our suspense and our thrill; with the one flaw on the roundness of it all the fact that the predicament was not imposed rather than invoked, was not the effect of a challenge from without, but that of a mystic impulse from within.

The chief means by which the story is presented to us, however, and that which gives it the "richness" which has so often been found in it, is the commentary of Marlow. Throughout the work he compares, philosophizes, muses. He is not, as in "Heart of Darkness", fundamentally affected by what happens. He is the commentator and his comments are clearly intended to be those of the reader. But what are they?

We find such reflections as:

> You expect a cogency of conduct not usual in women . . . the subterfuges of a menaced passion are not to be fathomed,

or:

> You say I don't know women. Maybe. It's just as well not to come too close to the shrine. But I have a clear notion of *woman*. In all of them, termagant, flirt, crank, washerwoman, bluestocking, outcast and even in the ordinary fool of the ordinary commerce there is something left, if only a spark. And when there is a spark there can always be a flame . . .

[the aposiopesis is Marlow's] or:

> And even in the best armour of steel there are joints a treacherous stroke can always find if chance gives the opportunity.

It seems unlikely that such a commentator will reveal to us much of significance. The large generalizations, the clichés, the vague rhetorical outbursts which we found from time to time in *Lord Jim* are normal here.

It is often difficult to see the relevance of his comments either to the facts of the story he tells or to any deeper logic of mood. We find in close succession in Part I, Chapter II:

> It was one of those dewy, clear, starry nights, oppressing our spirit, crushing our pride, by the brilliant evidence of the awful loneliness, of the hopeless obscure insignificance of our globe lost in the splendid revelation of a glittering soulless universe. I hate such skies.

and

> I . . . went out of the cottage to be confronted outside its door by the bespangled, cruel revelation of the Immensity of the Universe.

and

> . . . it was a fine day; a delicious day, with the horror of the Infinite veiled by the splendid tent of blue.

A passage right at the end of the book stands in striking contrast to these:

> The amenity of a fine day in its decline surrounded me with a
> beneficent, a calming influence; I felt it in the silence of the shady lane,
> in the pure air, in the blue sky. It is difficult to retain the memory of
> the conflicts, miseries, temptations and crimes of men's self-seeking
> existence when one is alone with the charming serenity of the uncon-
> scious nature. Breathing the dreamless peace around the picturesque
> cottage I was approaching, it seemed to me that it must reign every-
> where, over all the globe of water and land in the hearts of all the
> dwellers on this earth.

It would, no doubt, be too naïve to ask that Marlow should have either one
view of Nature or the other. What I am suggesting is that he can move
from one to the other so easily because neither is very real. The "Immensity of the Universe", the "charming serenity", "the dreamless peace
around the picturesque cottage"—these are no more than rhetoricians'
properties and Marlow expresses himself in the most hackneyed clichés
because it is at that level that he is thinking.

But Marlow reserves most of his vague generalizations and purple
patches for the subject of women. He frequently combines a rather obvious irony—"The pluck of women! The optimism of the dear creatures"
—with a tone of rapt adoration:

> Man, we know, cannot live by bread alone, but hang me if I don't
> believe that some women could live by love alone. If there be a flame
> in human beings fed by varied ingredients earthly and spiritual which
> tinge it in different hues, then I seem to see the colour of theirs.

Again and again he emphasizes in general terms the mysteriousness
of women.

> A young girl [he says] is something like a temple. You pass by and
> wonder what mysterious rites are going on in there, what prayers, what
> visions? The privileged men, the lover, the husband, who are given of
> the sanctuary do not always know how to use it.

Again:

> Flora de Barral was not exceptionally intelligent but she was
> thoroughly feminine. She would be passive (and that does not mean
> inanimate) in the *circumstances, where the mere fact of being a woman
> was enough to give her an occult and supreme significance.*

From time to time he defends himself from being an unreliable judge
of women with a heavy irony, as in such a passage as:

> For myself it's towards women that I feel vindictive mostly, in my
> small way . . . Mainly I resent that pretence of winding us round their
> dear little fingers, as of right . . . It is the assumption that each of us
> is a combination of a kid and an imbecile which I find provoking—in
> a small way; in a very small way. You needn't stare as though I were

breathing fire and smoke out of my nostrils. I am not a woman-devour-
ing monster. I am not even what is technically called "a brute". I hope
there's enough of a kid and an imbecile in me to answer the requirements of some really good woman eventually—some day . . . Some day.

But there is no irony directed against him. There can be no doubt that
his comments are supposed to have our approval. Yet they are not ones
which can lay bare any profound moral or psychological or spiritual
issues; they exist rather to cast a haze of romance and mystery over
certain aspects of his theme.

The sea and the sea-captain, too, are continually looked at through this
mist of rhetoric. The two are linked:

> It's true the sea is an uncertain element, but no sailor remembers this
> in the presence of its bewitching power any more than a lover ever
> thinks of the proverbial inconstancy of women . . . the captain of a
> ship at sea is a remote, inaccessible creature, something like a prince
> of a fairy-tale, alone of his kind . . .

Conrad reflects, on the link established between Marlow and Powell,

> . . . the service of the sea and the service of a temple are both detached
> from the vanities and errors of a world which follows no severe rule.

We remember the irony of the narrator's reflections in "The Secret
Sharer" on the simplicity of life at sea, or the voyage of Nostromo and
Decoud in the lighter, or even such passages from *The Mirror of the
Sea*: ". . . the sea that plays with men till their hearts are broken, and
wears stout ships to death". But here, once the intruder—"Mr. Smith"—
who hates the sea is removed, then indeed "The sea was there to give
them the shelter of its solitude free from the earth's petty suggestions".

More and more, as Conrad goes on writing, shall we find rhetoric used
to make us accept valuations and judgments which have not been as
deeply considered as those of his best early work, and already in *Chance*
the process is far developed.[4] We find it—even down to a care for sentence inversion—in such a passage as:

> Captain Anthony had not moved away from the taffrail. He remained
> in the very position he took up to watch the other ship go by rolling
> and swinging all shadowy in the uproar of the following seas. He stirred
> not; and Powell keeping near-by did not dare speak to him, so enigmati-
> cal in its contemplation of the night did his figure appear to his young
> eyes: indistinct—and its immobility staring into gloom, the prey of
> some incomprehensible grief, longing or regret.                    (1952)

## NOTES

1. Hewitt sees "The Secret Sharer" as marking the end of one phase of
Conrad's works; finding the presence of a crisis within the works of this period,
tensions removed from the later works. In the later works there is no longer
the emphasis on the sense of guilt, and his central figures tend more and more

to fall into two groups—the good and the bad. He is no longer preoccupied with the darker "other self." Cf. *Joseph Conrad: A Reassessment*, pp. 77-79. [Editor's note]

2. Whereas in *The Secret Agent* and other early works the irony "is *offensive;* it is a weapon to undermine comfortable assumptions and to make us scrutinize more deeply our beliefs and values. In the later works it is normally *defensive*. . . ." *Joseph Conrad: A Reassessment*, p. 88. [Editor's note]

3. See, however, Jocelyn Baine's "The Affair in Marseilles," *London Magazine*, IV (November 1957), 41-46, reprinted in Appendix II, pp. 347-354. [Editor's note]

4. [Editor's note: Hewitt's judgment here implies a criticism of Virginia Woolf's on *Chance*, in "Mr. Conrad: A Conversation," in her *The Captain's Death Bed, and Other Essays* (1950), originally published in *Nation and Athenaeum* (1923). See also Virginia Woolf's *The Common Reader* (1925), pp. 309-18: "Joseph Conrad."]


# M. C. BRADBROOK


## The Hollow Men: *Victory*\*


*Victory* is the last novel of this period, and if not the greatest, it is the most firmly modelled, the most boldly wrought. The characters are drastically simplified, and take on something of the quality of figures in a morality play; each represents a facet of experience, or a type of mind, and with statuesque impressiveness they remain fixed in that representative pose throughout the simple narrative of few, violent and sudden events. Conrad himself: "It is a book in which I have tried to grasp at more life stuff than perhaps in any other of my works" (*Life and Letters*, vol. II, p. 342). On the only occasion when he gave a public reading from his works, he chose to read the death of Lena.

Baron Heyst, the last of the "Hollow Men", is also the most completely disillusioned. Generous, chivalrous, tender-hearted as he is, he is hopelessly crippled by his nihilistic view of life, inherited and imposed on him by his father the philosopher, of whom he says:

> Suppose the world were a factory and all mankind workmen in it. Well, he discovered that the wages were not good enough. That they were paid in counterfeit money.
>
> (*Victory*, Dent Uniform Edition, pp. 195-6)

In his scepticism, Heyst denies not only the justice of the world but even the validity of human relationships. The earlier figures, the Goulds, Razumov and Natalie, Flora and Anthony, suffered from incomplete and

---

\* From M. C. Bradbrook's *Joseph Conrad: Poland's English Genius* (Cambridge University Press, 1941), pp. 62-67.

frustrated relationships; but Heyst entirely repudiates them. "We perish'd, each alone."

> One gets attached in a way to people one has done something for. But is that friendship? I am not sure what it was. I only know that he who forms a tie is lost. The germ of corruption has entered into his soul.
>
> (*Victory*, pp. 199-200)

> The world went by appearance and called us friends, as far as I can remember. Appearance—what more, what better can you ask for? In fact, you can't have better. You can't have anything else.
>
> (*Victory*, p. 204)

Consequently, paralysed by his stoic creed and his reflective habits—"the most pernicious of all habits found in civilised man"—Heyst strives to become the man of universal detachment, detached, like Hamlet, from even life itself.

> I may truly say, too, that I never did care, I won't say for life—I had scorned what people call by that name from the first—but for being alive. I don't know if that is what men call courage, but I doubt it very much.
>
> (*Victory*, p. 212)

Yet it is Heyst who carries off to his solitary island station Lena, the poor cockney girl from Zangiacomo's Ladies Orchestra, an outcast like Flora, but a child of the people, unselfconscious, illiterate, and downtrodden. He does this out of necessity, for Lena is being persecuted by Schomberg, aided by Zangiacomo, but by the act his "heart is broken into, all sorts of weaknesses are free to enter". Even for Lena, he cannot conquer his "infernal mistrust of all life".

Heyst, with his irony, his stoicism, is plainly very close to part of Conrad himself. His irony has the accent of Conrad: his protective humour is of the same kind too, and has often the same uneasy air of patronage. Heyst might have written some of Conrad's stories—"The End of the Tether," "Freya of the Seven Isles," "The Partner," "Amy Foster". But here Heyst is projected, exorcised, as perhaps Lord Jim exorcised an earlier Conrad.[1] Also by his relation to the other characters, Heyst is "placed" and valued.

Against the nihilism of Heyst is set the nihilism of "Mr. Jones". Mr. Jones is a gentleman without a history. His appearance is spectral (Davy Jones is the sailor's name for death) and he says to Heyst "I am he who is". He had had other formulas: Milton's was "Myself am hell", and Shelley's "He who reigns". He is the Living Skeleton, the Heart of Darkness.

Mr. Jones is attended by Ricardo, the ordinary criminal, and by Pedro, the ordinary savage; "A spectre, a cat, and an ape", as Schomberg sees them (p. 148). The central situation places these three upon Heyst's island, prepared to rob and if necessary kill him for a hypothetical hoard of wealth, which in fact does not exist. Heyst is slowly coming to feel in the company of Lena, with her simple common speech and her lovely voice, "a greater sense of his own reality than he had ever known in his life" (p. 200). But the arrival of the nightmarish trio paralyses him, as the nightmarish Gentleman Brown had paralysed Lord Jim, and perhaps for the same reason—because of the common element of disbelief and scepticism which is mutual to Heyst and Mr. Jones.[2] At all events, he is disarmed and at their mercy, and yet in his trapped helplessness he is responsible for the safety of Lena. But Lena, whose devotion and strength are quite unsuspected by Heyst, is perfectly prepared to sacrifice her life for him, and by deliberately enticing the amorous Ricardo, she gains possession of his weapon—at the cost of suggesting to Heyst that she is faithless and of being shot by Mr. Jones. But she has saved Heyst. Unconscious alike of his suspicions and his remorse, she dies in complete and innocent triumph.

Such is the story, and its bare outline may overstress the intellectual structure, what might be loosely called the "problem" of the book. The tale is simply told; there is no narrator's perspective, there is neither irony, humor nor comment in the telling; the irony, the humor and the comments, such as they are, belong to Heyst.[3] Yet the book is the completest vindication of the values represented by Lena, the vitality, trust and energy springing from the very depths of degradation. The reader is not allowed to forget Lena's origins: her accent betrays them in every sentence. Together, Heyst and Lena symbolise all that Conrad approved of—the power of rectitude and the power of love. They stand for humanity at large, betrayed to evil, but uncorrupted, and in pathos and dignity their fate cannot be matched in all Conrad's work.                    (1941)

## NOTES

1. In *The Polish Heritage of Joseph Conrad* (Sampson Low, 1930) Dr. Gustav Morf attempts an elucidation of Conrad's novels in terms of his psychology. He classes Conrad as belonging to Jung's "intuitive" type and sees in many of the novels a projection of Conrad's personal conflicts. Thus he believes Conrad was haunted by a fear of having betrayed the patriotic traditions of his family by leaving Poland, although he left on the advice of his elders; and this, he thinks, is symbolized in Jim's desertion of the *Patna,* while physically Jim is a compensatory figure. Dr. Morf sees also a projection of Conrad in the figure of Martin Decoud, and his fate symbolises what Conrad fears for himself—an end of lonliness and despair. The captains in "The Secret Sharer" and *The Shadow Line* dramatise Conrad's fears about his ability to live up to the exaggerated personal standard he set up: whilst the Polish hero of "Amy Foster" stands quite unambiguously for Conrad's hidden fears about himself, which are more indirectly expressed in "An Outpost of Progress" and "The Heart of Darkness". [Editor's note: See Morf's text, pp. 140-141, 198-209.]

2. Gentleman Brown represents the profession Jim has disgraced, though he is more of a disgrace to it than Jim. Heyst has never betrayed a trust—he is scrupulously faithful to all his obligations: but he has betrayed humanity by his sceptical pessimism, his denial of man's virtue and heroism.

3. It is noticeable that after this, the playful detachment, the indulgent irony disappears from Conrad's writing altogether.

PAUL L. WILEY

# The Knight: Man in Eden: *The Arrow of Gold**

IN ITS QUALITY of bravura, in its specialized atmosphere of the 1870's
in France, and in its partly autobiographical foundation, *The Arrow of
Gold* (1919) may at first appear somewhat isolated from the main body
of Conrad's work. He himself attributed the note of disappointment in
the reviews to the fact that he had produced something unexpected and
had essayed a method of presentation which was a new departure in his
art.[1] Even today the novel is too frequently set aside by critics as one of
the least successful of the later stories,[2] when it is actually one of the most
interesting when seen in relation to the main tendencies of his writing at
this time. Under the surface glitter achieved by technical craft alone, the
solid lines of the thematic substructure common to all of the work of
Conrad's last phase can be discerned—just as, near the close of the book,
one seems to have heard from the beginning the approaching footsteps of
the crazed Ortega running amok along the back of a forestage shimmering in the light off marble, brocade, and Venetian glass. The action begins
with the first encounter of a man accustomed to an isolated life with the
suddenly unveiled powers of sense, a formula applied at the opening
of "A Smile of Fortune" and afterwards repeated in the varied settings
of *Chance, Victory,* and "The Planter of Malata." The lady in distress
appears again, moreover, in Rita, who bears under her disguise of a modern Gioconda the same psychic wound of fear as Alice Jacobus or Flora
de Barral. Her spirit too has been lamed for her first experience with
mankind by the scorn poured into her ear as a child still too young to
die of fright (1, 96).

Conrad, however, places his familiar theme of damsel and rescuer
against a background which he introduces here for the first and last time.
The novel is his one attempt to deal with the world of art, or at least with
a level of society governed solely by aesthetic standards; and even though
the conspiracy to place a Bourbon pretender on the throne of Spain gives
an air of adventure to the narrative, the political events take place mainly
off stage. In no other book does Conrad work quite so steadily as a painter
in prose; and one remembers *The Arrow* as in many respects a gallery of
portraits and statues: Rita standing in a blue dress on the crimson carpet
of a staircase (1, 66), Therese a figure out of a cracked and smoky painting (1, 138-39), Mrs. Blunt a picture in silver and grey with touches of
black (1, 180), and Blunt a marble monument of funereal grace (1, 212).
The actors move through a succession of rooms as cluttered with bric-a-
brac as those of an antique shop, and the splendor of all these furnishings
seems slightly tarnished and artificial. The Pompeiian panels, the Argand
lamps, the silver statuettes belong to a world as much sealed off from the

* From Paul L. Wiley's *Conrad's Measure of Man* (University of Wisconsin Press, 1954), pp. 162-172.

stir of life as the tomblike chambers of Hervey's mansion in "The Return."

The creator of this world, as dominant a figure in the novel after his death as in his life, is the artist-connoisseur, Henry Allègre, who has the Goncourts' passion for collecting "brocades, pictures, bronzes, chinoiseries, japoneries" (1, 45). He is the high priest of a cult of aesthetic impressions (1, 186, 211) with its doctrine that the soul lives exclusively in sensation; and the supreme achievement of his contemptuous sacrifice of life to art is his transformation of Rita from her childhood state of a wild peasant girl of the hills to her mature position as one of the handsomest and most desirable of the objects in his house in Paris. As a model for his painting, a dummy serves him as well as a human figure (1, 22); for what matters to him is the Byzantine robe to stimulate vision and to clothe his image of the woman of all time (1, 28). After his death, however, both the dummy and the living art object that he has created remain as two awkwardly opposed consequences of his aesthetic belief and practice; for Rita, left with his fortune but deprived of his protection, ceases to be the artist's masterpiece and has to defend herself against a rapacious world. From the contrast between the mutilated dummy and the perfect harmony of Rita's appearance proceeds that note of moral irony which makes *The Arrow* as much a satire on a rigidly aesthetic philosophy as a brilliant portrayal of the milieu of the artist and his circle.

In capturing Rita as a child and placing a wall between her and mankind, Allègre performs an act similar to that of Jacobus in confining Alice to the garden in "A Smile of Fortune." But Allègre's motives are calculated to produce more ambitious results than those of the ship chandler whose imagination is limited to baiting a commercial hook for chance comers. To lift a girl out of the tide of common things at a moment when she has awakened to caprice and passion and to convert physical enchantment into a semblance of plastic art with the power to arouse and then to repel desire is Allègre's expression of the aesthete's scorn for the natural, and *épater le bourgeois* joke. In its ultimate intention, however, the deed transcends sheer mockery. To work this change, Allègre exercises a creative function in which there is something godlike in its "defiance of unexpressed things" for the "unheard-of satisfaction of an inconceivable pride" (1, 108). His whole design is characterized by "something lofty and sinister like an Olympian's caprice" (1, 108). He intends to destroy her past and to raise her by degrees to the position of a goddess of the religion of aesthetic impressions, the only faith that reigns in his studio after every other belief has been "worried into shreds" (1, 56). He attains success when he presents his idol to the world as a modern incarnation of Aphrodite with a dart, the arrow of gold in Rita's hair, a symbol of faith in the artificial and the sterile. The Olympianism of Allègre thus defies the principle of human limitation to the same extent as that of Lingard in *An Outcast,* and its failure to reckon with the problem of evil proves its insufficiency.

The perils of an aesthetic creed become evident from the moment when, after Allègre's death, Rita must descend with her treasure into the open market of the world—"a naked temperament for any wind to blow upon" (1, 84), like the stringed lute of Wilde. Through all of her commerce with the fortune hunters, blackmailers, and adventurers who cross her path in the enterprise to restore the Bourbon pretender, she retains the divinity of the charming animated statue. But a goddess or an art work, being out of time, has no past, whereas Rita's past is all too substantial. The symbol of that history, and of the fear and guilt that bind her to common humanity, is Ortega, the jealous Spaniard from her peasant childhood, who overtakes her at last as Jones overtakes Heyst in *Victory*. Her frigidity is a product of the terror inspired in her as a child by Ortega's sexual wrath (1, 112) and later by the view of mankind stripped of its clothes opened to her by Allègre (1, 96). Against this dread, felt constantly by the woman as opposed to the Mona Lisa illusion of the painter, her hysterical gesture of transfixing her hair with the golden arrow— an attempt to take cover behind the aesthetic mask—provides a simulated defense (1, 307). As if further to illuminate the contrast in Rita between the divinity and the limited human being, Conrad gives her a shadow in her sister, Therese, a peasant whose narrow and morbid mind (1, 138) and predatory instincts (1, 40) mark her as a vessel of roughest clay. Therese with the passion of greed and Ortega with that of lust are the accomplices who threaten Rita at the end as Jones and Ricardo join against Heyst.

Monsieur George, the hero who comes to defend Rita when fear compels her to drop her inscrutable smile, does not present the chivalric front of Anthony, Heyst, or Renouard but something nearer that of a guileless fool whose heart the golden arrow never pierces (1, 332). The comrade and admirer of the Ulyssean Dominic Cervoni, who scorns upper-class people but serves Rita in running guns for the Carlists, George, like Powell in *Chance*, is a member of the seaman's order and thus a believer in that common bond between men which makes him appear a "simple, innocent child of nature" (1, 70) by contrast to the corrupt society into which he is suddenly thrown. Unlike Renouard in "The Planter," George ultimately withstands the enchantment of a "mirage of desire" (1, 268) but not until he has undergone a full initiation into the life of passion and become healed of that "incurable wound" caused by his first encounter with erotic experience (1, viii, ix).

George's approach to the world ruled by a law of aesthetic impressions —his entry into the overlighted café and the bedlam of the Marseilles carnival upon his return from a long West Indian voyage—resembles the beginning of Heyst's contest with the powers of evil in the strident atmosphere of Schomberg's concert hall:

> The carnival time was drawing to an end. Everybody, high and
> low, was anxious to have the last fling. Companies of masks with
> linked arms and whooping like red Indians swept the streets in crazy

rushes while gusts of cold mistral swayed the gas lights as far as the eye could reach. There was a touch of bedlam in all this.

(1, 7)

In both scenes men accustomed to sobriety are caught by a storm of violent sensations; and Blunt and Mills, Rita's lieutenants in the Carlist plot who are attempting to enlist George's aid, complete the mischief for him by their cunning evocation of Rita as a phantom of desire in the superb Part I of *The Arrow*. The potion of exotic impressions administered to George in his ignorance of life by the two conspirators acts with the same effect that a similar drug has upon Anthony and Renouard, although here the subtler ingredients of art spice the draught. When he sees Rita for the first time on the staircase of her villa, George has been made receptive to the intense visual impression that she offers him (1, 66); and from this point he exhausts himself in the effort to penetrate beyond this illusion to the living woman with whom he feels a sense of solidarity (1, 70).

In his account of George's suffering under the spell of this wraith, Conrad not only takes every advantage of the strain of delayed consummation but also presents one of his most complete studies in the morbid psychology of passion. The process of inner destruction goes almost as far in George as in Renouard (1, 229). He falls into a "purgatory of hopeless longing" where he is tormented by exalting and cruel visions (1, 248). He reflects that his love may be a disease:

> Love for Rita . . . if it was love, I asked myself despairingly, while I brushed my hair before a glass. It did not seem to have any sort of beginning as far as I could remember. A thing the origin of which you cannot trace cannot be seriously considered. It is an illusion. Or perhaps mine was a physical state, some sort of disease akin to melancholia which is a form of insanity?

(1, 163)

Conrad employs the pathological, however, to further his larger purpose of completing a satire on aestheticism as a doctrine at variance with normal human feeling and experience.

George breaks this spell, however, in the bizarre and melodramatic scene in the locked room in the street of the Consuls, which is both the climax of the novel and its moral denouement. Conrad wrote to Mrs. Thorne in 1919 that "the inner truth of the scene in the locked room is only hinted at,"[3] thus making it clear that his intentions in this episode went beyond a winding up of the action in a spectacular way. Whatever this inner truth may have meant to Conrad, the dramatic basis of the scene viewed apart from its special atmosphere of gilt and crystal corresponds very closely to that in the cabin of the *Ferndale* in *Chance* or on Heyst's island in *Victory* in that a solitary and not wholly united man and woman are left open to the attack of an embodied force of evil. As in the earlier novels, furthermore, the preparation for this concluding act consists not so much in a knitting up of the lines of conflict between characters as in the filling out of the moral atmosphere, or the "moral topography," of the setting. Early in the story Conrad refers to the run-down and sinister appearance of the house (1, 21); and by repeated emphasis upon such interior details as the silver statuette and the black and white marble hall (1, 136), he establishes firmly both the location and the peculiar atmospheric quality of the scene. The dazzling effect of the illuminated drawing room (1, 286), the main stage for the drama, is as surprising as the revelation of its proximity to the fencing chamber with its rack of weapons. This juxtaposing of the ultrarefined and the barbaric agrees, of course, with the fantastic tone of the novel; but it is also perhaps in keeping with a book which Conrad associated with "the darkest hour of the war" (1, viii) that the rattle of steel shaken by the hand of a homicidal madman can be heard outside the door of a room designed to represent the highest flowering of art and luxury. It is unnecessary, however, to attach secondary meanings to a situation overtly symbolic with reference to the central import of the novel. At the conclusion Conrad's satire on aestheticism attains its greatest concentration as it broadens into allegory.

The movement toward the climax begins with the meeting between George and Ortega during the bedlam of the second carnival. The appearance of the Spaniard with his fixed idea of a violent assault on Rita (1, 319) and his look of a grotesque puppet (1, 267) is timed to coincide with the ebb of George's fortunes after the loss of his ship (1, 257) and with the hour of his blackest despair in his frustrated passion for Rita, very much as the ominous figure of De Barral enters the forestage in *Chance* only after Anthony has taken his vow of renunciation. Just as De Barral stands, moreover, for Anthony's double, so also Ortega seems to have a curious affinity with George. George reflects, for example, that Ortega isn't such a stranger as he had assumed he was (1, 270). He thinks suddenly that Rita's image penetrates both himself and his companion so as to constitute a strange bond between them:

> Yes. There was between us a most horrible fellowship; the association of his crazy torture with the sublime suffering of my passion. We hadn't been a quarter of an hour together when that woman had surged up fatally between us; between this miserable wretch and myself. We were haunted by the same image. But I was sane! I was sane!
>
> (1, 274)

Rita's mockery of Ortega has turned him mad enough for passional crime; and George, though he thinks himself sane, has been brought close to the same state through her resistance to his love. While meditating upon the chance that has thrown him into association with Ortega, George concludes that "a dreadful order seemed to lurk in the darkest shadows of life" (1, 283). He appears, therefore, to catch a glimpse of a fatal train of circumstance that has brought Ortega back to confront Rita with the human passions disregarded or flouted by the doctrine taught her by

Allègre. As a symbol of the evil which springs to life when the claims of normal feeling are denied, Ortega thus manifests himself to George at the moment when he has completed his initiation into the experience of passion and has seen there the face of death disclosed likewise to Anthony and Heyst in their contempt for the principle of human limits.

In terms of allegory the final scene dramatizes again the process of redemption and, as in *Chance* and *Victory,* the triumph of the normal over the abnormal. When Ortega, armed with a weapon from the fencing chamber, rattles at the doors of the locked room where Rita listens in terror, Rita's charmed cloak drops from her; and she is left a mortal woman "naked and afraid," like Hervey in "The Return," in the midst of the artificial paradise of her ornate surroundings. Observing her, George recovers from the illness of the senses in abandoning the illusion that the aesthetic image of Rita suffices for contemplation to infinity (1, 288), that it offers an escape from time and exists apart from the finite human being (1, 296). His worship of the "sublimely aesthetic impression" (1, 304) ends abruptly when Rita, at the mere whisper of Ortega's presence, springs from the couch an all too human bundle of fears with everything gone "except her strong sense of life with all its implied menaces" (1, 308). Her salvation comes through the fidelity of George in the face of danger, a safeguard which quenches her fear and rekindles a flame within her frozen body (1, 331). Drawn together by the human bond, they become once again Conrad's symbolic pair united against the evil of the world that has invaded another false Eden, the palace of art built by Allègre; and Ortega lies self-wounded at the foot of the silver statuette (1, 325).

(1954)

## NOTES

1. G. Jean-Aubry, *Joseph Conrad: Life and Letters,* II, 213, 227.

2. See F. R. Leavis, *The Great Tradition,* p. 182. [Editor's note: Whereas Wiley finds that the "main thematic structure of Conrad's works (is) completed in his last phase" and denies any decline in his artistic powers, Moser in his chapter on the Exhaustion of Creative Energy argues that the productions of Conrad's last years "are virtually without a redeeming feature. They reveal that Conrad has exhausted his creative energy." He finds in *The Arrow of Gold* a "radical lack of form. It has virtually no center of interest, no basic conflict to be resolved, no climax toward which to move. Rather it has a series of possible narrative strands, each of which Conrad picks up, examines, speculates on, and drops." Imperfect as it is, *The Arrow of Gold* remains the best executed of the last three novels. Moser in *Joseph Conrad: Achievement and Decline,* (1957), pp. 180, 185, 198.]

3. Aubry, *Conrad: Life and Letters,* II, 232.

# THOMAS MOSER

## On *The Rescue**

CLEARLY THEN, the later Conrad has a new attitude toward the world, though hardly an affirmative one; he now considers evil to be external to his heroes and heroines and sees man's greatest good as complete repose, usually achieved through love. Such an extreme shift in attitude almost necessarily results in a drastic reorientation of Conrad's artistry. Perhaps the best way to see the effect of the later Conrad's attitude upon his early moral hierarchy of characters and upon his complex handling of structure and language is to compare *The Rescue* of 1920 with those portions of its first version, "The Rescuer," which were written in the nineties.[1]

"The Rescuer" displays all of the important, early types of character that he defines in the first chapter, except one; it contains no perceptive hero like Marlow. We have already noted that the Tom Lingard of "The Rescuer" seems to be a first attempt at Lord Jim, the simple vulnerable hero. Linares prefigures Decoud, the complex vulnerable hero. Carter belongs among the ranks of simple, faithful seamen like Singleton and MacWhirr. While Mr. Travers and Jörgenson do not precisely fit any of our categories, they resemble certain characters of the early period. Mr. Travers has much in common with Alvan Hervey of "The Return," and Jörgenson belongs in the gallery of caricatures who serve as doubles for Lord Jim.

The most significant alteration of "The Rescuer" is the simplification and emasculation of Lingard. Through certain crucial cuts from the original manuscript, the later Conrad obscures the most important and interesting facts of Lingard's psychology: the subtle difference between himself and other seamen, his egoistic longings for power, his lack of self-knowledge, his moral isolation. As a result, he has none of the vitality and intensity of Conrad's great self-destructive heroes.

In revising the manuscript, Conrad cut out two passages that tend to cast doubt upon Lingard's qualifications for membership in the fraternity of loyal seamen. As originally described, Lingard does not quite *look* like a seaman, and his motivation is *not* a perfect love of the work itself. "The Rescuer" portrays him as a man who holds "himself very straight in a most unseamanlike manner." He has "also—for a seaman—the disadvantage of being tall above the average of men of that calling." Moreover,

* From Thomas Moser's *Joseph Conrad: Achievement and Decline* (Harvard University Press, 1957), pp. 145-156. A more complete treatment is given in Moser's " 'The Rescuer' Manuscript: A Key to Conrad's Development—and Decline," *Harvard Library Bulletin*, X (Autumn 1956), 325-355. Another study, appearing after Moser's book was published, is " 'The Rescuer' Manuscript," by Barbara Gaździkówna, in *The Living Conrad,* edited by Wit Tarnawski. *Conrad Zywy* was published in London by B. Swiderski, 1957. [Editor's note]

although the Lingard of "The Rescuer" is passionately devoted to his ship, as any good sea captain ought to be, his devotion seems to be the expression of something different from a perfect love of his calling. The later Conrad obscures Lingard's questionable attitude towards his craft by cutting out the following description of Lingard bringing his brig to anchor:

> A sudden listlessness seemed to come over him. It was one of his peculiarities that whenever he had to call upon his unerring knowledge of his craft, upon his skill and readiness in matters of his calling that big body of his lost its alertness, seemed to sink as if some inward prop had been suddenly withdrawn.

"The Rescuer" tells us further that Lingard expects his brig to answer "without hesitation to every perverse demand of his desire."

That the later Conrad is acting to distort his original conception of Lingard as motivated not by love of the craft but rather by love of self becomes more evident in the account of Lingard's motives for interfering in the political affairs of the native state of Wajo. *The Rescue* follows "The Rescuer" here:

> There was something to be done, and he felt he would have to do it. It was expected of him. The sea expected it; the land expected it. Men also. The story of war and of suffering; Jaffir's display of fidelity, the sight of Hassim and his sister, the night, the tempest, the coast under streams of fire—all this made one inspiring manifestation of a life calling to him distinctly for interference.

*The Rescue* omits, however, the most important of Lingard's motives— his egoism. "The Rescuer" continues the passage thus:

> But above all it was himself, it was his longing, his obscure longing to mould his own fate in accordance with the whispers of his imagination awakened by the sights and the sounds, by the loud appeal of that night.

As originally conceived, Lingard's apparently charitable assistance to his native friends was to have been motivated by unlawful desires for personal power and even violence. The later Conrad cannot tolerate the implication that his hero contains any of the old Adam, and so he eliminates this very damning passage about Lingard's response to the opportunity to make war and history:

> the islands, the shallow sea, the men of the islands and the sea seemed to press on him from all sides with subtle and irresistible solicitation, they surrounded him with a murmur of mysterious possibilities, with an atmosphere lawless and exciting, with a suggestion of power to be picked up by a strong hand. They enveloped him, they penetrated him, as does the significant silence of the forests and the bitter vastness of the sea. They possessed themselves of his thoughts, of his ac-

tivity, of his hopes—in an inevitable and obscure way even of his affections.

But if Lingard obeyed the complex motives of an impulse stealthy as a whisper and masterful as an inspiration, without reflecting on its origins, he knew well enough what he wanted even if he did not know exactly why . . .

The absence of this passage from *The Rescue* deprives the reader of several of the early Conrad's most profound perceptions. The passage reminds us that the romantic's seemingly free act of will, his act of interference, immediately costs him his freedom and brings about slavery to the dark powers. (We recall how Kurtz belongs to the jungle and how Jim is possessed by Patusan.) This remnant of "The Rescuer" also reveals Lingard's lack of self-knowledge. He does not reflect upon the origins of his inspiration and does not know "exactly why" he is doing what he does.

A final, important insight into Lingard that the later Conrad finds of no use is the increasing isolation that results from his egoistic involvement in an unlawful adventure. In revising "The Rescuer," Conrad cut out the account of the change that takes place in the once hearty, bluff, and friendly Lingard, the change to a man isolated and guilt-ridden. Some of his friends try to draw him out by chaffing him but he repulses them:

they grew distant and Lingard had a subtle sense of solitude, the inward loneliness of a man who is conscious of having a dark side to his life. It hurt him. He needed the good fellowship of men who understood his work, his feelings and his cares . . . Before he had been many months engaged in his secret enterprise he began to feel unreasonably like an outcast . . . he imagined himself, at times, to be the object of universal detestation.

Lingard's sense of isolation parallels Jim's in Patusan and, like Jim's, becomes even more intense when white visitors from the West appear to break into his adventurous Eastern dream.

For the later Conrad, Lingard has little in common with the romantic egoists of the early period. The second half of *The Rescue,* wholly written during 1918-19, carries the emasculation of Lingard further by absolving him of responsibility for the deaths of his best friends and by sanctioning his passive acceptance of repose as his greatest good.

In this later portion of *The Rescue* Conrad raises a clear-cut moral issue, presumably to make Lingard decide whether to follow his duty to his native friends or his sudden love for Mrs. Travers. By an unfortunate chance, however, Lingard is unaware that Hassim and Immada have been seized as hostages, and thus he never has a real choice. Moral responsibility for the disastrous outcome of *The Rescue* would seem to lie with Mrs. Travers, who conceals Jörgenson's message to Lingard, and perhaps more seriously with Lingard himself, for loving and trusting such an unworthy person. In fact, critics who admire *The Rescue* tend to interpret it this way.[2] The truth is, however, that although the later Conrad sets up a clear moral problem, no one is really to blame for the evil outcome. Instead, Conrad excuses Mrs. Travers' actions and makes her a victim of chance, unaware of the content of the message, suspicious of Jörgenson's intentions toward Lingard, and convinced by d'Alcacer, the voice of reason, that for Lingard's own good this obscure message must be concealed. Mrs. Travers' dilemma reminds us of similar situations in the later novels, especially in *Victory*. Like Lena, Mrs. Travers deliberately deceives her lover, but with the best intentions in the world. Disaster comes through the agency of an external, implausible, evil figure resembling Mr. Jones: "By the mad scorn of Jörgenson flaming up against the life of men . . ."

If Mrs. Travers is not guilty, then Lingard is utterly blameless. Bad luck, coincidence, the misunderstanding of good intentions, someone else's madness—all these are to blame, not the impeccable hero. Yet like the zealous young captain of *The Shadow Line,* Lingard nobly asserts his guilt. He says that even if Mrs. Travers had given him the message "it would have been to one that was dumb, deaf, and robbed of all courage." Later Mrs. Travers protests: ". . . why don't you throw me into the sea? . . . Am I to live on hating myself? . . . No, no! You are too generous . . ." The reader surely understands the moral of *The Rescue:* responsibility lies not with hero and heroine, but somewhere else.

The later Conrad perverts his original characterization of Lingard in another way, by sapping him of his powerful, if unacknowledged, longings for self-destruction. Although the Lingard of the nineties is a worthy forerunner of the intense, guilt-haunted Jim and Razumov, the Lingard of the second half of *The Rescue* is utterly debilitated. The highest point of his experience seems to be sitting at his beloved's feet, his head upon her knee, telling her, "I care for nothing in the world but you. Let me be. Give me the rest that is in you." He looks upon her as a

> waking dream of rest without end, in an infinity of happiness without sound and movement, without thought, without joy; but with an infinite ease of content, like a world-embracing reverie breathing the air of sadness and scented with love.

It must be emphasized that the later Conrad presents all this absolutely without irony. There is not a hint of judgment against Lingard's lapse into passivity.

The later Conrad's handling of the early Lingard shows simply that Conrad either no longer understands his original creation or chooses to ignore it. What had begun as a most promising portrait of a romantic, egoistic, meddlesome figure becomes in the published book the characterization of a conventional hero of popular fiction, a generous, brave, inherently good man brought low by bad luck, human misunderstanding, and the machinations of fate.

Conrad makes fewer interesting revisions in the other important male characters of "The Rescuer." Yet it is clear from the changes he does make and from the essentially new roles these men assume in the last half of *The Rescue* that he views them in a new light. Linares, converted into d'Alcacer, loses his ironic perceptiveness, Carter his stern, unsentimental rectitude; Jörgenson and Travers become less complicated and more villainous.

Because the early Conrad sketched in Linares much less fully than Lingard, the later Conrad could leave him much as he found him although he saw fit to change his name to d'Alcacer. As originally conceived, Linares prefigures Decoud: a cosmopolitan Spaniard, he is an ironic and skeptical observer of the human comedy. He is immediately attracted to the "picturesque" Lingard, just as Decoud responds to the incorruptible Nostromo. But unhappily, in the second half of the novel, d'Alcacer becomes more of a Heyst than a Decoud, with his "cultivated voice" speaking "playfully." Although he seems to be the *raisonneur,* his analysis of Lingard is actually inept, stuffy, and pretentious:

> More of a European than of a Spaniard he had that truly aristocratic nature which is inclined to credit every honest man with something of its own nobility and in its judgment is altogether independent of class feeling. He believed Lingard to be an honest man and he never troubled his head to classify him, except in the sense that he found him an interesting character . . . He was a specimen to be judged only by its own worth. With his natural gift of insight d'Alcacer told himself that many overseas adventurers of history were probably less worthy because obviously they must have been less simple. He didn't, however, impart those thoughts formally to Mrs. Travers. In fact he avoided discussing Lingard with Mrs. Travers who, he thought, was quite intelligent enough to appreciate the exact shade of his attitude. If that shade was fine, Mrs. Travers was fine, too . . .

D'Alcacer's imperception results naturally from his creator's loss of understanding of Lingard. The early Conrad would never have seen Lingard as "simple" unless, like Jim, he was simple in a complicated way.

Carter suffers even more seriously from Lingard's emasculation. As originally conceived in "The Rescuer," he belongs in the company of Singleton and MacWhirr. He is the calmest person aboard Travers' yacht, but also the one most aware of its dangerous position. He approaches all problems practically and unemotionally. Although he is as young as Jukes and Jim, he differs from them in his readiness to meet unexpected disasters. As "The Rescuer" makes clear, Carter always maintains "the professionally wide-awake state of a man confronted by rapid changes of circumstance." In the later half of *The Rescue,* Conrad does not bother to make Carter's actions plausible; he does not tell us how Carter can accomplish the ten-day job of rehabilitating the yacht in sixty-six hours. More important, the able and experienced ship's officer of "The Rescuer" has regressed and must go through a maturing experience. "His personality was being developed by new experience, and as he was very simple he received the initiation with shyness and self-mistrust." Although Conrad asserts that Carter has not yet matured, he makes him sound like an old retainer in his solicitous conversation with Lingard after the catastrophe: "Why not lie down a bit, sir? I can attend to anything that may turn up. You seem done up, sir."

A long expository passage on Travers in "The Rescuer" (cut completely from *The Rescue*) shows clearly that Conrad intends him to be of the type of Alvan Hervey, in "The Return." Travers is described as a too wealthy, egotistical bourgeois; unimaginative and conventional, he despises other men yet longs for reputation. Conrad's failure with Alvan Hervey makes it unlikely that Travers could ever have become a successful creation. Yet the early Conrad at least makes an effort to understand him and permits him to have a little human inconsistency and to be a somewhat sympathetic figure. For example, in "The Rescuer," Travers seems honestly suspicious of Lingard's motives; he believes that Lingard is lying about the danger from natives in order to trick Travers into letting him seize the yacht for salvage. In revising "The Rescuer," Conrad eliminates any explanation of why Travers is hostile to Lingard. He also makes him completely unsympathetic by deleting passages that show Travers hearing out Lingard and restraining his indignation against Carter, and by removing indications that Carter and Mrs. Travers have some respect for him. Although Travers appears frequently in the later half of the novel, he can hardly be said to exist. He spends almost all of the time in bed, occasionally making some petulant remark from between the sheets.[3]

Jörgenson becomes rather a bore in the second half of *The Rescue*. Yet as originally conceived, he holds much interest. He is, perhaps, the first true double, prefiguring the gallery of caricatures in *Lord Jim*, all of whom, from the "old stager" to Gentleman Brown, serve to illuminate Jim's romantic psychology. As Jörgenson appears in "The Rescuer," he is obviously meant to foreshadow by his past the inevitable destruction of Lingard's hopes: "He demonstrated one way . . . in which prosaic fate deals with men who dream quickly and want to handle their dreams in broad daylight." Even though Jörgenson has been virtually destroyed by his early adventure into native politics, nevertheless, by his act of joining with Lingard in a new adventure, he reveals the power of those illusions that lure the ego into action and self-destruction: "at times the invincible belief in old illusions would come back, insidious and inspiring." In *The Rescue*, "old illusions" become "the reality of existence." To the later Conrad, the adventures in which Jörgenson and Lingard engage are the essence of existence; he finds it difficult to distinguish between illusion and reality.

The early Conrad emphasizes the physical closeness of Jörgenson and Lingard. As soon as Lingard begins to collect supplies for his adventure, Jörgenson starts to shadow him, finally lengthening his stride to come abreast and engage Lingard in conversation. They become partners, and their doubleness is apparent to the other characters. So Belarab, recalling to Lingard Jörgenson's help in former days, says abruptly, "He resembled you." Even Lingard recognizes the equation, in a conversation with Edith. She asks,

> "And this—this—Jörgenson, you said? Who is he?"
> "A man," he answered, "a man like myself."
> "Like yourself?"
> "Just like myself," he said with strange reluctance, as if admitting a painful truth. "More sense, perhaps, but less luck."

This technique of employing a subordinate character to illuminate the psychology of the main character culminates in "The Secret Sharer." In the later half of *The Rescue,* however, it is lost entirely.

The Jörgenson of "The Rescuer" combines with his symbolic function a persuasively human quality. He may be a skeleton, but he is a "powerful skeleton"; he is a drifter who cadges drinks from the traders, but he can also pilot a ship through the Straits of Rhio. Jörgenson is enough of a human being to have inspired the devotion of a native "girl," with a "wrinkled brown face, a lot of tangled grey hair, a few black stumps of teeth." Jörgenson returns her affection, and even though he cannot resist Lingard's enterprise, he still demands that the girl be looked after, indicating a greater sense of responsibility than Lingard has. Jörgenson's past is as if it had never been, in the second half of *The Rescue.* The later Conrad easily convinces us of Jörgenson's "other-world aspect," but this is all that Conrad has to say about him, and he says it many times. The later Jörgenson, with a rather ungrateful disregard for the years he has spent with his "girl," has now become an unassailable misogynist who expresses his opinions in a childish vocabulary and manner:

> "Woman! That's what I say. That's just about the last touch—that you, Tom Lingard, red-eyed Tom, King Tom, and all those fine names, that you should . . . come along here with your mouth full of fight, bare-handed and with a woman in tow.—Well—well!"

We must agree with Mrs. Travers' analysis of the later Jörgenson: "He was invulnerable, unapproachable . . . He was dead." Jörgenson and Travers take their places among the tedious and unbelievable caricature-villains of the later novels. Although they occupy far more space than do the caricatures of the earlier novels, they are greatly inferior to them. The reader longs nostalgically for Jim's many doubles, or for the fine gallery of republicans, revolutionists, and counter-revolutionists in *Nostromo.*

The later Conrad's oversimplification of potentially interesting characters comes as no surprise. A view of the world which finds men not responsible for their actions will hardly reveal great complexity. The emasculation of Lingard is representative of the fate of other similar heroes. Only Captain Anthony of *Chance* can be said to partake at all of the qualities of the simple, excessively romantic, exaltedly egoistic Lord Jim.

Yet Anthony has none of the intensity and vigor of Jim. Moreover, one does not feel that Conrad really senses any plague spots in him.

Again, Conrad's handling of d'Alcacer in the second half of *The Rescue* is of a piece with his treatment of the ironic, skeptical, vulnerable hero in the later period. Only Heyst seems even superficially to partake of this type. He is somewhat skeptical, somewhat ironic; he is detached from society, although he has in the past been twice tempted into action, first exploring in New Guinea, next managing a coal company in the tropics. The second venture comes about, like Decoud's intervention in Costaguana politics, through a personal involvement rather than through commitment to an ideal. Yet Heyst is really much less like Decoud than critics have suggested.[4] In fact, Heyst partly resembles a character completely different from Decoud, Charles Gould. Heyst recalls Gould not only because of his mustache and the ironic equation with "portraits of Charles XII of adventurous memory," but also because he is called a "utopist." It would be an interesting departure, an exciting development, if the later Conrad were trying to combine the character of the skeptic with that of the man of action, if Conrad were revealing that the utopian and the unbeliever share an "infernal mistrust of all life," that romanticism and skepticism are sometimes two sides of the same coin. Yet the feeling persists that Conrad simply does not know what he wants to make of Heyst. This is amply borne out by the conclusion in which, as we have seen, Heyst emerges as neither a romantic nor a skeptic, but as a good man brought down by chance and "other people."

Conrad's revisions of Carter in *The Rescue* are of interest because they signify not only the end of the type of the simple, faithful seaman, but the emergence of a new type. (For the faithful seaman does disappear; Conrad may have intended Peyrol to be a descendant of Singleton but he is not, as we shall see in the next chapter when we turn to *The Rover*.) Carter's altered role as immature hero has several counter parts in the later period.                                                           (1957)

## NOTES

1. We must be cautious in handling "The Rescuer." Its pt. IV seems to belong almost wholly to 1916, when Conrad made an abortive attempt to finish the novel. Therefore only pts. I to III can be considered as authentic early work (1896-1898). We should be a little skeptical about minor differences between "The Rescuer" and *The Rescue* since these revisions could conceivably belong to the early period. When in 1918 Conrad sold "The Rescuer" to collector T. J. Wise, he told him that "several typed copies" had been made from it, "each introducing changes and alterations" (*Life and Letters,* II, 209). We do not know when these copies were made or how much they differ from "The Rescuer." Jean-Aubry indicates that one revision dates from early 1916 (*Life and Letters,* II, 165). In any case, the serial version, which appeared in *Land and Water* from January to July, 1919, retains essentially the language of the original although cuts have been made; only the new, second half represents the language of the later Conrad. The final revision was made between

December 8, 1919, and January 24, 1920 (Gordan, p. 218); *The Rescue* appeared in book form a few months later.

2. See Wiley, pp. 173-187.

3. There are two sides to every question, including that of revision. Our bias has been that most revisions in "The Rescuer" are changes for the worse. Walter F. Wright holds a different view in "Conrad's *The Rescue* from Serial to Book," *Research Studies of the State College of Washington* 13:208 (1945). He has studied the changes that the later Conrad made when he prepared the serialized version of *The Rescue* for book publication. Mr. Wright apparently did not look at "The Rescuer," so his discussion of revisions does not take into account the question of which prose in the serial belongs to 1896, which to 1919. In any case, Mr. Wright sees the changes in Travers and in all the characters as an improvement in the "emotional tone." For Mr. Wright, as for most students of revisions, every alteration is admirable. This is not necessarily a safe assumption; other writers, as well as Conrad—Pope and Wordsworth, for example—have been compulsive revisers, constantly tampering with manuscript, first edition, and collected edition, sometimes to revise brilliantly, sometimes to weaken a satisfactory passage. [Editor's note: Relating to the above matter, Moser adds, p. 220: "Vernon Young, although he has apparently not looked at 'The Rescuer' manuscript, believes that Conrad does a good job of matching the old and new prose in *The Rescue*. Mr. Young, moreover, clearly disapproves of both the early and the late, preferring some middle prose; he writes of *The Rescue*: 'The prose is a piece with the unchecked illusionism of approach; it recovers the will to the mysterious which Conrad, between 1911 and 1917, had brought under control.' Mr. Young goes on to quote two passages from *The Rescue* to demonstrate Conrad's recovery of the 'will to the mysterious.' He grants, however, that the new 'illusionism' shown in his quotes is somewhat inferior to the old: 'In these, and many other passages . . . the symbolic chiaroscure which Conrad had used so deliberately in *The Nigger of the "Naricissus"* has become a formula which confuses thought and observation alike.' The two examples Mr. Young gives do seem to be a startling 1919 recovery of the style of the nineties, but unfortunately they were written in the nineties. Both quotations come from pt. III of 'The Rescuer' and hence, on the basis of the available evidence, must have been written no later than a year after the publication of *The Nigger of the 'Narcissus.'* (See Young, pp. 537-538.)" See pp. 96-108 for the text of Young's essay.]

4. See Leavis, pp. 201-209.

## THOMAS MOSER

## On *The Rover* and *Suspense**

LIKE *The Arrow of Gold, The Rover* focuses briefly on several possible centers of interest but settles on none. In the first pages of the novel, Conrad draws our attention frequently to Peyrol's clumsiness and we shortly discover the cause: a money-belt full of gold. We then learn how Peyrol had got such loot, and we see him carefully hide it at the bottom

* From Thomas Moser's *Joseph Conrad: Achievement and Decline* (Harvard University Press, 1957), pp. 198-203.

of his sea chest at his new home, Escampobar Farm. The later Conrad then characteristically abandons the gold for 246 pages. (At the end of the book the Réals find the money in a well and turn it over to the French government.) In the early pages interest focuses, too, on Peyrol's strong feeling of communion with this portion of the south of France where he had been born but which he had left nearly fifty years before. Again the idea, which has real possibilities, remains undeveloped. Between Chapters Three and Four eight years pass and a nocturnal prowler becomes the new interest. We soon discover that he is a spy from an English corvette lying offshore, and that he has been captured by Peyrol. The Englishman proves to be an old acquaintance of Peyrol's piratical days, whom Peyrol recognizes. This encounter arouses in Peyrol deep feelings of nostalgia for his old life as one of the "Brothers of the Coast." Yet he does not reveal his identity to the Englishman; he allows him to escape and never thinks of him again.

In addition to these three undeveloped fictional ideas, there are two more obvious subjects in *The Rover;* the rivalry between Peyrol and Réal over Arlette, and Réal's mission to trick the English navy by putting into their possession false French documents. The love story, like the George and Rita affair, does not inspire belief. Conrad, in fact, hardly attempts to dramatize the relationship between Arlette and Peyrol; he simply asserts at frequent intervals that violent and incomprehensible passions are engulfing one or all of the trio. Perhaps because of our recollections of the fine sea stories of the early period, we may respond more favorably to the account of Peyrol fulfilling Réal's mission by sailing his tartane, with the documents aboard, in such a way as to be caught by the English corvette. This story of three strangely assorted men in a small boat on a dangerous mission of political intrigue is, however, rather an old one. Twenty years before *The Rover,* Conrad told the story in *Nostromo,* about Nostromo, Decoud, and Hirsch. At about the same time, he described its autobiographical source in *The Mirror of the Sea,* where he tells of Dominic Cervoni, his traitorous, evil cousin, and himself aboard the *Tremolino* on an unsuccessful mission on behalf of the Carlists. In *The Arrow of Gold,* he mentions the story again and also, incidentally, "a money-belt full of gold." The version in *The Rover* probably depends heavily for its effectiveness upon the nostalgia of faithful Conradians. The account conveys little sense of action and conspicuously lacks the details of seamanship which so enrich the sea stories through "The Secret Sharer."

*The Rover* must stand or fall upon the credibility of its central character, old Peyrol. Conrad tries very hard to make him into a dignified and admirable figure. In fact, he uses some of the techniques that he had first employed with Singleton a quarter of a century before. He calls our attention frequently to Peyrol's "Roman" profile, and attempts to make him into something of a mythic figure with a face "like a carving of stone." His profile preserves the "immobility of a head struck on a medal." Yet Peyrol is *not* Singleton. Even though Singleton comes to understand that he is old and will die, the thought of retiring never enters his mind. It is unthinkable that a true Conradian seaman would spend eight years idling in a farmyard. Peyrol may have a Roman profile, he may look longingly at the sea, he may sneer at landsmen, yet the question remains: why did he give up? Why must he wait eight years before he suddenly feels the "longing for a great sea victory for [his] people"? The voyage on the tartane is, after all, a rather easy way out of a tedious and perplexing existence. The seamen of *The Nigger of the "Narcissus,"* *Youth,* and *Typhoon* do not perform their heroic actions in a brief voyage on a lovely afternoon. And only such dubious heroes as Willems and Jim find their solution to life's problems in a quick and painless death by gunshot.

The prose of *The Rover* partakes of all the faults we have noticed in *The Arrow of Gold.*\* Since there are fewer and shorter love scenes, there are (happily) fewer and shorter passages of rhetoric about love. Yet we can easily find enough to know that Conrad has not really made any recovery:

> She dazzled him. Vitality streamed out of her eyes, her lips, her whole person, enveloped her like a halo and . . . yes, truly, the faintest possible flush had appeared on her cheeks, played on them faintly rosy like the light of a distant flame on the snow.

If the instances of love rhetoric diminish, the mechanical faultiness becomes, if anything, more conspicious in *The Rover* than in *The Arrow of Gold.* We find the same difficulty with "as to," the same broken sentences:

> But *as* to that, old Peyrol had made up his mind from the first to blow up his valuable charge—unemotionally, for such was his character, formed under the sun of the Indian Seas in lawless contests with his kind for a little loot that vanished as soon as grasped, but mainly for bare life almost as precarious to hold through its ups and downs, and which now had lasted for fifty-eight years.
>
> *As* to what the farmer man had come for on board the tartane he had not the slightest doubt about it.
>
> The possession of a common and momentous secret drawing men together, Peyrol condescended to explain.

Finally we find in *The Rover,* as in *The Arrow of Gold,* a pervading sense of weariness which infects all of the characters. It has perhaps a certain appropriateness in *The Rover* since the central figure and one of the important minor characters, Catherine, are both old. Nevertheless, their weariness results not only from age but also from despair. As in *The Arrow of Gold,* the most characteristic pose of the characters is seated, head in hand. At various points in the book we find Peyrol,

---

\* See pp. 180 ff of Moser's *Joseph Conrad.* [Editor's note]

Catherine, and Arlette in that position. More often, Peyrol and Réal sit facing each other with their arms folded on their chests. Young Réal habitually sits on a bench "with hardly a movement, for hours." When Peyrol and Réal are not sitting, they can be found leaning against a mast or a wall. The thirty-eight-year-old Scevola appears to be perpetually tired: "the patriot dragged his dirty clogs low-spiritedly" in time "lying open-eyed on his tumbled pallet in raging sulks about something." Sooner or later virtually every character despairs. The young lieutenant feels sick of life, "the desperation of a man under torture." Peyrol reaches "that depth of despondency" in which there is "nothing more before him but a black gulf into which his consciousness sank like a stone." Scevola resembles a "sick child," while Catherine, who tells Peyrol she is "tired of life," staggers under "the weight of her accumulated years." In short, *The Rover* hardly conveys the sense of serenity which its admirers have attributed to it.

*Suspense,* Conrad's unfinished last novel, represents that venture into historical fiction which he had contemplated since 1907. It is curious that Conrad had for so long aspired to write an historical novel, for his talent does not seem to point in that direction. The early Conrad deals with setting, costumes, manners, and public events not so much for their own sake as for their capacity to reveal what happens inside his characters. Even *The Nigger of the "Narcissus,"* which explicitly memorializes a passing phase of life, dramatizes the *spirit* of that life more than its outward manifestations.

The early Conrad, nevertheless, does use history for his psychological purposes. We think, for example, of *Lord Jim.* John D. Gordan shows clearly that the Patusan portions of that book owe much to Conrad's reading in histories of Rajah Brooke of Sarawak. But Conrad there completely assimilated his sources. Mr. Gordan, in the light of his own painstaking study of all the books about Brooke available to Conrad, says that "it is impossible to tell exactly which he knew. He may have known them all equally well."[1]

Finding the source of *Suspense* has proved no such problem. Less than a year after its publication, Miss Mildred Atkinson, in a letter to the *Times Literary Supplement,*[2] showed that the source of *Suspense* is the *Memoirs of the Countess de Boigne.* Conrad does not, however, use the *Memoirs* as he does the history of Rajah Brooke, simply for hints about characters and events. Rather, the *Memoirs* furnish character relationships and even actual wording. Miss Miriam H. Woods quotes six passages from *Suspense,* some of paragraph length, one of almost a page, which follow the *Memoirs* virtually word for word.[3] The *Memoirs,* in fact, supply practically all that is new in *Suspense.* We have already seen that *Suspense* tends to move in the same weary circle as the later love stories, complete with hero, heroine, and voyeur-villain. Some of the scenes appear to be faint echoes of Conrad's previous work: the salon scene, for example, seems to arise from a forty-five-year-old memory of the Carlist intrigue, filtered twice, through *Nostromo* and *The Arrow of Gold*. As history, *Suspense* gives us little sense of the past, and, except for the *Memoirs* material, it contains none but the most obvious historical details. In other words, Conrad, at the end of his career, was using history, not as an adventure into a new kind of writing, but as a crutch for exhausted creativity.

If we are not conscious of the marked decline in the quality of his art after 1912, we may tend to mix indiscriminately in our minds early and late ideas and characters simply because of superficial resemblances. Explicit statements about self-recognition and initiation in *The Shadow Line* and *The Arrow of Gold,* about skepticism and romanticism in *Victory* and *Chance,* may lead us to believe that these novels embody the same profound perceptions as the great early works. Apparent resemblances between Anthony and Jim, Heyst and Decoud, Peyrol and Singleton, between the two young captains in *The Shadow Line* and "The Secret Sharer," may cause us to respond in much the same way to all of them. If this happens, it means that through insensitive reading we have deprived ourselves of the enjoyment and understanding which Jim, Decoud, and the other fine early characters can afford us. In the same way, imprecise attention to technique may lead us, as it has led a number of others, to think *Chance* the most complex of Conrad's novels, rather than the most cumbersome, and to read the opening pages of *The Arrow of Gold* as ingenious plotting rather than confused narration.

It is indeed difficult to conquer the impulse to find greatness in all the works of a man we sense to be great. Yet this impulse is pernicious. It has brought forth complicated mythical and allegorical interpretations of novels that probably ought not even to have been published. Such lack of discrimination is perhaps less reprehensible, however, than the approach that insists that literary greatness lies only in explicitly, unequivocally affirmative works. This approach has led to gross overrating of inferior Conrad and to dismissal of some of his best works as "minor." To fail to perceive the vast differences in his quality or to hunt for the quality in the wrong places means that one listens not to Conrad's voice but to one's own. And to be deaf to the true Conrad is to be deprived of one of the finest voices in our literature: pessimistic, skeptical, ironic— but also courageous, sympathetic, profoundly human.          (1957)

## NOTES

1. Gordan, p. 65. The text of Gordan's "The Four Sources" is given pp. 61-96.

2. Mildred Atkinson, *Times Literary Supplement,* no. 1,258 (Feb. 25, 1926), p. 142.

3. Miriam H. Woods, "A Source of Conrad's *Suspense,*" *Modern Language Notes* 50:390-394 (1935).

# APPENDIX I

# (1) JOSEPH CONRAD:

## A Biographical Note[1]

JOSEPH CONRAD was born on 3rd December 1857, at Berdiczew in Podolia, one of the Ukranian provinces of Poland long under Russian Tsarist rule. He was the only child of Apollo Naleçz Korzeniowski and his wife Evelina Bobrowska, and he was christened Józef Teodor Konrad Naleçz Korzeniowski. His parents were of the landowner class, and his father was deeply involved in the secret national Polish movement. Apollo had literary interests too, wrote poetry and criticism and translated from the French and German.

When Conrad was three his father was arrested by the Russian authorities and exiled to Northern Russia, his wife and child being allowed to go with him under the same conditions of banishment. Evelina's health broke down and she died in exile in 1865. Two years later Apollo was given conditional parole, but seven years of privation had also told on him physically, and he died in Cracow in 1867, leaving the orphaned Conrad in the care of his maternal uncle, Tadeusz Brobowski.

Between the ages of fifteen and seventeen Conrad astonished his uncle and tutor by expressing from time to time a determination to go to sea, a strange calling to people belonging to an inland country and traditionally devoted to agricultural pursuits. Conrad persisted and in September 1874 he travelled to Marseilles to become a seaman. He spoke French fluently and had one or two introductions to people in the port. After some experience on two sailing ships, he became one of a syndicate of four young men who bought the sixty-ton *Tremolino* and sailed her on contraband activities until she was deliberately wrecked as described in a chapter in *The Mirror of the Sea*. More of this phase of Conrad's life is told in the story *The Arrow of Gold*.

Conrad's first English ship was the *Mavis*, which he joined at Marseilles in April 1878, and it was aboard that vessel that he arrived at Lowestoft two months later and saw England for the first time. After some coastal trips in another ship, he joined as ordinary seaman a 'wool-clipper' sailing to Australia. Returning to London at the end of 1880 he passed examination as third mate in June of that year.

From then on he served as officer on several ships, voyaging to many parts of the world, particularly across the Indian Ocean, and in and around the Malay Archipelago and the Gulf of Siam. These are the scenes of some of his best-known stories, *Youth, Almayer's Folly, An Outcast of the Islands, The Nigger of the "Narcissus," "The Secret Sharer," Typhoon, Lord Jim, "Falk," The Rescue, The Shadow Line*, and others. He passed his mate's examination in July 1883, and on 11th November 1886 he succeeded in the final seamanship test and obtained his Master Mariner's Certificate. Conrad's accounts of these examinations are in *A Personal Record*. He became a naturalized British subject on 19th August 1886.

In 1890 he went to the Belgian Congo to command a river steamer—realization of a hope expressed as a child when he put his finger on a map of Central Africa and said he would go there one day. From his experiences in the Congo Conrad was physically weakened but psychologically awakened, and his writing career dates from this period, for he was then writing his first book, *Almayer's Folly*. Years later he gave his Congo story in one of his finest books, "Heart of Darkness."

His last ship was the *Torrens,* a renowned sailing vessel, which he left in October 1893. It happened that John Galsworthy (not then a writer) was a passenger on part of this last voyage, joining the ship at Adelaide; years later he gave a picture of Conrad at the first meeting: "He was superintending the stowage of cargo. Very dark he looked in the burning sunlight—tanned, with a peaked brown beard, almost black hair, and dark brown eyes, over which the lids were deeply folded. He was thin, not tall, his arms very long, his shoulders broad, his head set rather forward. He spoke to me with a strong, foreign accent. He seemed to me strange on an English ship. For fifty-six days I sailed in his company. . . . Many evening watches in fine weather we spent on the poop. Ever the great teller of a tale, he had already nearly twenty years of tales to tell. . . . At Cape Town, on my last evening he asked me to his cabin, and I remember feeling that he outweighed for me all the other experiences of that voyage. . . ."

Conrad took about five years to write *Almayer's Folly,* which, having been read and recommended by Edward Garnett, was published in April 1895. Encouraged by Garnett and other editors to continue writing, he settled down to a shore life, marrying Miss Jessie George of London on 24th March 1896. His early books were appreciated by a discriminating public and praised by eminent writers such as H. G. Wells, John Galsworthy, Henry James, and R. B. Cunninghame Graham; but none of his books attracted a wide circle of readers until *Chance,* 1913. Thereafter his reputation grew considerably, and his books were issued in many forms, both here and in America, from editions de luxe to omnibus volumes, culminating in the Uniform Edition, which the present set supersedes. Critics and authors in general wrote increasingly about Conrad, as the brief appended list of the more important of such writings shows.

During most of his married and writing life Conrad lived in various houses in Kent, occasionally making visits lasting some months to the Continent, usually France or Poland. He had two sons, Borys, born in January 1899, and John Alexander, born in August 1906. He and his family were on a visit to Austrian Poland when war broke out in 1914, and they went through some excitement and hardship in getting out of enemy territory via Italy and the Mediterranean.

His last two novels (*The Rover* and *Suspense,* the latter unfinished) were of the Napoleonic period and set in the Mediterranean, the first sea he had known, and some of the characters had their prototypes in friends of his youthful days there. *The Rover,* probably the best of his later books, has something of both of his adopted countries in it, France, the Rover's native land, and England, in her sailors at war with France. Poland is in it also in spirit, because the author was himself a Rover from that native land of his. Mrs. Conrad has said that a sort of homing instinct was on Conrad towards the end of his life. But he remained in Kent, in his English home, Oswalds, in the village of Bishopsbourne, with his English family, writing until the end. Although he had been ailing for some years his death came suddenly, after a heart attack, on the morning of 3rd August 1924. He is buried in Canterbury, and the stone on his grave bears his full Polish name.   A. J. Hoppé.

## NOTES

1. Reprinted from the COLLECTED EDITION published by J. M. Dent and Sons Ltd., London, by their kind permission. The same for reprint of the list of The Works of Joseph Conrad.

# (2) THE WORKS OF JOSEPH CONRAD:

### A Chronological List

*(Names of the original publishers, or their
present successors, are given in parentheses)*

1. *Almayer's Folly—A Story of an Eastern River.* 1895. (Benn.)
2. *An Outcast of the Islands.* 1896. (Benn.)
3. *The Nigger of the "Narcissus"—A Tale of the Sea.* 1897. (Heinemann.)
4. *Tales of Unrest.* (Contents: "Karain, a Memory," "The Idiots," "An Outpost of Progress," "The Return," The Lagoon.") 1898. (Benn.)
5. *Lord Jim—A Tale.* 1900. (Blackwood.)
6. *The Inheritors—An Extravagant Story.* (In collaboration with Ford Madox Hueffer.) 1901. (Heinemann.)
7. *Youth—A Narrative; and Two Other Stories.* (Contents: "Youth," "Heart of Darkness," "The End of the Tether.") 1902. (Blackwood.)
8. *Typhoon, and Other Stories.* (Contents: "Typhoon," "Amy Foster," "Falk," "To-morrow.") 1903. (Heinemann.)
9. *Romance—A Novel.* (In collaboration with Ford Madox Hueffer.) 1903. (Smith Elder.)
10. *Nostromo—A Tale of the Seaboard.* 1904. (Dent.)
11. *The Mirror of the Sea—Memories and Impressions.* 1906. (Methuen.)
12. *The Secret Agent—A Simple Tale.* 1907. (Methuen.)
13. *A Set of Six.* (Contents: "Gaspar Ruiz," "The Informer," "The Brute," "An Anarchist," "The Duel," "Il Conde.") 1908. (Methuen.)
14. *Under Western Eyes.* 1911. (Methuen.)
15. *A Personal Record.* 1912. (Dent.)
16. *'Twixt Land and Sea—Tales.* (Contents: "A Smile of Fortune," "The Secret Sharer," "Freya of the Seven Isles.") 1912. (Dent.)
17. *Chance—A Tale in Two Parts.* 1913. (Methuen.)
18. *Victory—An Island Tale.* 1915. (Methuen.)
19. *Within the Tides—Tales.* (Contents: "The Planter of Malata," "The Partner," "The Inn of the Two Witches," "Because of the Dollars.") 1915. (Dent.)
20. *The Shadow Line—A Confession.* 1917. (Dent.)
21. *The Arrow of Gold—A Story between Two Notes.* 1919. (Benn.)
22. *The Rescue—A Romance of the Shallows.* 1920. (Dent.)
23. *Notes on Life and Letters.* 1921. (Dent.)
24. *The Rover.* 1923. (Benn.)
25. *The Secret Agent—A Drama in Four Acts.* 1923. (Werner Laurie.)
26. *Laughing Anne* and *One Day More.* (One-act plays, the first from the story "Because of the Dollars," and the second from "To-morrow.") 1924. (John Castle.)

27. *Suspense—A Napoleonic Novel.* 1925. (Dent.)
28. *Tales of Hearsay.* (Contents: "The Warrior's Soul," "Prince Roman," "The Tale," The Black Mate.") 1925. (Dent.)
29. *Last Essays.* 1926. (Dent.)

Uniform Edition of the Works of Joseph Conrad, 1923–8 (22 volumes, including all the above except the plays, Nos. 25 and 26). (Dent.)

> THE DENT COLLECTED EDITION is reprinted from the Uniform Edition and includes the Prefatory Notes written by the Author for the latter. (Two books are contained in one volume, as follows: Nos. 2 and 4, Nos. 3 and 8, Nos. 11 and 15, Nos. 19 and 20, and Nos. 28 and 29.)[1]

## NOTES

1. The COLLECTED EDITION published by J. M. Dent and Sons Ltd., London, is identical with the Doubleday, Page and Company CANTERBURY EDITION, New York (1924-1926). *The Sisters,* not included in either of these editions, was published 1928 by Crosby Gaige, New York.

## (3) BIBLIOGRAPHIES ON CONRAD

"A Selected Bibliography of Criticism of Modern Fiction," compiled by R. W. Stallman, *Critiques and Essays on Modern Fiction,* edited by John Aldridge (Ronald Press, 1952), Joseph Conrad, pp. 574–576.

"Criticism of Joseph Conrad: A Selected Checklist with an Index to Studies of Separate Works," compiled by Maurice Beebe, *Modern Fiction Studies,* I, No. 1 (February 1955), 30–44.

*Joseph Conrad at Mid-Century: Editions and Studies, 1895–1955,* edited by Kenneth A. Lohf and Eugene P. Sheehy (University of Minnesota Press, 1957).

*Publications of Modern Language Association:* Annual Bibliography Supplement.

## (4) CHRONOLOGY OF COMPOSITION

DRAWN FROM similar lists given in Douglas Hewitt's *Conrad: A Reassessment* (Bowes & Bowes, 1952) and Thomas Moser's *Joseph Conrad: Achievement and Decline* (Harvard University Press, 1957), this list presents the probable dates of completion of Conrad's works. The titles of short stories are in roman type.

| | | |
|---|---|---|
| "The Black Mate" | 1886 | ? |
| *Almayer's Folly* | 1894 | May |
| *An Outcast of the Islands* | 1895 | September |
| "The Idiots" | 1896 | May |
| "The Outpost of Progress" | 1896 | July |
| "The Lagoon" | 1896 | August |
| "The Return" | 1896 | Summer (?)* |

  * Moser dates this for September 1897.

| | | |
|---|---|---|
| *The Nigger of the "Narcissus"* | 1897 | February |
| "Karain" | 1897 | February |
| "Youth" | 1898 | May–June |
| ["The Rescuer," Parts I–III] | 1898 | December |
| "Heart of Darkness" | 1899 | Jan.–February |
| | | |
| *Lord Jim* | 1900 | July |
| "Typhoon" | 1901 | January |
| "Falk" | 1901 | May |
| "Amy Foster" | 1901 | June |
| *Romance* (with Ford Madox Ford) | 1902 | March |
| "The End of the Tether" | 1902 | October |
| "To-morrow" | ? | |
| *Nostromo* | 1904 | September |
| "The Brute" | 1905 | Summer |
| "Gaspar Ruiz" | 1905 | November |
| "An Anarchist" | 1905 | November |
| "The Informer" | 1905 | December |
| *The Mirror of the Sea* | 1906 | April (?)** |
| | | |
| *The Secret Agent* | 1906 | September |
| "The Duel" | 1907 | January |
| "Il Conde" | 1907 | late |
| *A Personal Record* | 1908 | Autumn (?)*** |
| | | |
| "The Secret Sharer" | 1909 | November |
| *Under Western Eyes* | 1910 | January |
| "A Smile of Fortune" | 1910 | August |
| "The Partner" | 1910 | Summer |
| "Freya of the Seven Isles" | 1910 | Summer |
| "Prince Roman" | 1911 | ? |
| *Chance* | 1912 | March |
| "The Inn of the Two Witches" | 1912 | early |
| "Because of the Dollars" | 1912 | early |
| "The Planter of Malata" | 1913 | Autumn |
| *Victory* | 1914 | June |
| *The Shadow Line* | 1915 | March |
| "The Warrior's Soul" | 1916 | early |
| "The Tale" | 1916 | early |
| *The Arrow of Gold* | 1918 | June |
| *The Rescue* | 1919 | May |
| *The Rover* | 1922 | July |
| *Suspense* (unfinished; published posthumously) | | |

** Or October 1905, according to Moser.

*** Moser dates this for June 1909.

*APPENDIX II*

# JOCELYN BAINES

## (1) The Affair in Marseilles*

THE FOUR years during which Conrad was based on Marseilles set a biographer his most knotty problem. The facts of the rest of Conrad's life seemed at least to be clear, if not always illuminated by significant detail, but this important and eventful period has so far remained largely impervious to the most probing research.

Until recently a few bare facts were known. Conrad, aged seventeen, arrived alone in Marseilles from Poland in October 1874. Two months later he sailed to the West Indies as a passenger on the *Mont Blanc,* an old ship owned by the firm of Delestang.[1] Two further voyages to the West Indies, one on the *Mont Blanc* and one on another of the firm's sailing ships called the *Saint Antoine,* which was commanded by a Captain Escarras, are also recorded. Then, Conrad's uncle and guardian, Thaddeus Bobrowski, kept notes of the frequent and urgent requests for money from his disturbingly spendthrift nephew. In these notes and in the five surviving letters which Bobrowski wrote to his nephew during this period are also mentioned some of the people with whom Conrad came in contact in Marseilles, among them a genial Frenchman named Baptistin Solary who apparently took Conrad under his wing when he first arrived; two other men who kept a careful, friendly eye on him, Victor Chodzko, a Pole, and Richard Fecht, a German; and M. Delestang himself. Finally, it is known that Bobrowski received a telegram from Fecht in February 1878 telling him that Conrad had been wounded; he immediately went to Marseilles where he stayed for a fortnight setting matters right. On April 14 Conrad sailed from Marseilles on an English ship, the *Mavis,* bound for Constantinople.

This was the factual skeleton. The rest of the body was provided by Conrad's autobiographical and semi-autobiographical writings and by a novel, *The Arrow of Gold.* From these it appears that at the start of his life ashore in Marseilles he divided his time between hobnobbing with the pilots of the port and savouring the fashionable or Bohemian café life. Then at some point he was drawn into the circles which were supporting the attempt of Don Carlos to capture the Spanish throne; the Delestangs themselves held extreme royalist views and their *salon* was a centre of Carlist intrigue. Conrad and three other young men formed a syndicate controlling a *balancelle* called *Tremolino* which was to carry arms for the Carlists from the neighbourhood of Marseilles to the Gulf of Rosas in Spain. Not that Conrad, at least, had any interest in the Carlist cause; he was attracted by the excitement and, moreover, had become involved with a mysterious, fascinating woman, "Rita de Lastaola," who had just been left a fortune by a painter, was reputed to have been the mistress of Don Carlos and was an ardent supporter of the cause. Conrad seems to have been the only active member of the syndicate; and he made a number of successful voyages with Dominic Cervoni, an experienced Corsican seaman who became the *padrone* of the *Tremolino.* But eventually they were betrayed by Dominic's nephew, César Cervoni, and forced to wreck the ship on the Spanish coast to avoid capture by the *garda-*

* From *The London Magazine,* IV (November 1957), 41-46.

*costas.* Back in Marseilles Conrad came increasingly under the spell of "Rita" but found himself the rival of an American soldier of fortune, J. M. K. Blunt, who was being egged on by his unscrupulous mother to make a profitable marriage. Rita decided that she preferred Conrad and they spent several blissful months together in "the region of the Maritime Alps, in a small house built of dry stones and embowered with roses." This idyll ended when, on one of his rare visits to Marseilles, Conrad heard that his rival, Blunt, had been spreading calumnies about him. He fought a duel with Blunt and received a bullet wound in his left side. Rita whisked him away and nursed him but when he emerged from his fever she had disappeared.

Those who knew Conrad, including Aubry, the compiler of the "official" *Life and Letters,* have accepted this version of the events; and Conrad's own comments seemed to justify the otherwise dangerous practice of drawing on a writer's work to fill in the gaps in his biography. Conrad told Sidney Colvin in 1919:

> The Rita of "The Tremolino" is by no means true, except as to her actual existence. I mention her lightly, the subject of the paper [in *The Mirror of the Sea: Memories and Impressions*] being the *Tremolino* and her fate. *That* is literally true, just as the Rita of the *Arrow* is true fundamentally to the shore connections of the time.

Furthermore, there was proof of the existence of Dominic Cervoni who was the leading figure in "The Tremolino" and also came into *The Arrow of Gold;* he had been mate on the *Saint Antoine* when Conrad had sailed on her, and a César Cervoni was listed as an apprentice on this voyage. Then Conrad told Aubry that Blunt's mother was mentioned in a volume of Judith Gautier's memoirs; a Madame Key Blunt does indeed crop up there and, as in *The Arrow of Gold,* she is impecunious, unscrupulous and ruthlessly persistent. Blunt himself is also mentioned, in a book by Sir John Furley describing his experiences among the Carlists where he is referred to as "an American gentleman, who holds a commission in the army of Don Carlos, and whom I constantly met at St. Jean de Luz."

Nonetheless research into these years came up against a number of blank walls. Firstly, the identity of Rita remained a mystery; then no record of the *Tremolino* could be discovered and as Conrad particularly emphasized the *balancelle's* name it was unlikely that he had invented it; and, although he had set his gunrunning at the height of the Carlist war the record of Dominic Cervoni shows that he was employed without interval from June 14, 1875, to October 14, 1877, as mate on the *Saint Antoine.* Now the Carlist war was over by the end of February 1876; Don Carlos had led the remnants of his defeated troops across the Spanish border into France on February 28 and had declared in a proclamation: "Being desirous of preventing further bloodshed I have given up the glorious struggle which at the moment is obviously futile." Then, as if to underline this, he departed for London and in the following year went on a long trip to the New World. Therefore either Cervoni did not take part in the *Tremolino* episode, which would make nonsense of Conrad's assertion to Colvin, or the episode occurred more than a year after the end of the Carlist war.

Moreover there are two sentences in the Bobrowski material which indicate that the facts were not as Conrad had allowed them to appear. In a letter dated July 8, 1878, cataloguing Conrad's misdeeds Bobrowski wrote somewhat incoherently:

You were idle for nearly a whole year—fell into debt, purposely shot yourself—at the worst time of the year, tired out and with the most terrible rate of exchange—I hasten to you, pay, spend about 2,000 roubles—to cover your needs I increase your allowance! . . .

And in his notes Bobrowski again alludes to Conrad having wounded himself (Aubry, who until recently was apparently the only person to have had the Bobrowski material examined at all thoroughly, seems either to have overlooked these passages or failed to realize their significance).

These mysterious references are explained by an exceptionally important letter which Bobrowski wrote to Stefan Buszczynski, a close friend of Conrad's father, on his return from Marseilles.[2] This letter was summarized by Maria Dynowska in an article in the *Kurjer Warszawski* twenty years ago but seems to have passed unnoticed by students of Conrad. Bobrowski gave Buszczynski a resumé of Conrad's recent exploits, but asked him to be discreet. Conrad, he said, had at one point taken all his allowance out of the bank and lent it to his friends; but an illness prevented him from embarking on a proposed voyage and he was thus left destitute in Marseilles. Bobrowski mentions that he set this right and was not particularly worried. Then during the Contract Fair at Kiev he received the laconic telegram: "Conrad blessé. Arrivez." He immediately left for Marseilles on February 24 and arrived three days later. Apparently, he continued, Conrad had finally arranged to embark again under Captain Escarras, but at the last moment the Inscription Maritime forbade him to do so because he was of conscript age and had no proof that the Russian Government had freed him from military service. He was thus forced to stay in Marseilles and again spent all his money. Then a certain Duteil, probably the same Duteil who had commanded the *Mont Blanc* during Conrad's second voyage on her, persuaded Conrad to engage in some form of contraband traffic on the Spanish coast without divulging what it was intended to smuggle. Bobrowski comments that as he was living in a foreign country the boy felt no scruples about breaking the law, while the unusual occupation attracted him from the first. All went well for a time and the earnings were considerable but the outcome was that Conrad lost all that he had, whereupon Duteil "gave him the boot" and sailed for Buenos Aires.

Fecht then lent Conrad 800 francs and with this money he set out for Villefranche with the object of embarking with an American squadron to seek his fortune in the New World. But unhappily Monte Carlo was nearby. The boy who had never gambled before was tempted by roulette, lost all his money and put a bullet through himself which went "*durch und durch* near the heart"[3] without, however, doing him serious harm.

Fecht, said Bobrowski, again promptly came to the rescue and summoned him from the Ukraine. After closely crossquestioning the delinquent and his friends Bobrowski concluded that Conrad had a morally sound character, did not drink or lead a dissipated life, and was universally liked. He tried to persuade Conrad to return to Poland but he refused. Conrad was popular among the sailors and was known as M. Georges, the name which he gave to the hero of *The Arrow of Gold*. Despite his popularity he had no liking for the French and so Fecht persuaded him to enter the British Merchant Navy which moreover had fewer scruples about Russian conscription than the French.

Although this letter still leaves much obscure it does establish one startling fact: Conrad's attempted suicide. It might be suggested that Conrad had been afraid to tell his uncle the truth about a duel, but Conrad was a Roman

Catholic and attempted suicide is a mortal sin to Roman Catholics, whereas no Pole would have seen anything dishonourable in the fighting of a duel. Even if this were not conclusive, further evidence is provided by another letter to Stefan Buszczynski, from Conrad's former tutor Adam Pulman. He is writing a year after these events and mentions having heard in Lwow about Conrad's duel, which indicates that the duel was invented as a cover for attempted suicide and not the reverse.

As to the rest of Bobrowski's letter, his account of the smuggling fits the established facts well. It seems that the episode took place during the last part of 1877 and the beginning of 1878 and had little to do with the Carlist venture; the reference to Conrad losing all that he had could easily apply to the wrecking of the *Tremolino*. Nothing else is known of Conrad's supposed intention of going to America but it is by no means improbable, especially as, two years later, he told his uncle of a scheme to go to the New World as secretary to a businessman.

Finally there is the question of why Conrad tried to kill himself. The main reason may have been his loss of the money lent to him by Fecht. He had run through a lot of money and piled up some serious debts (one man named Bonnard, whom he described as an "acquaintance" but was probably a money-lender, had even written to Bobrowski in the Ukraine demanding payment of a promissory note from Conrad for 1,000 francs); and he probably dared not ask his uncle to help him yet again. On the other hand it does not seem that this final loss would have made much difference to him if he intended to join a ship; no money was needed for that. It is here that "Rita" may come in. If the facts of Conrad's relationship with "Rita" were not precisely as described in *The Arrow of Gold* there is no reason to doubt that he had a love-affair with a "Rita"; everything that he has said suggests that he did. And indeed an expensive woman is the most plausible explanation for the facility with which his money disappeared; far more plausible than a series of loans to his friends.

Perhaps the love-affair had come to a painful end at the same time as he had come to the end of his resources; then he had set off to heal his wounds and make his fortune in the New World but had not been able to resist a last opportunity of making it in the Old and so returning triumphant to his love; and when he failed he decided in despair to kill himself.

But this is all the merest guesswork and the truth will probably never be known. The important fact, however, is that Conrad did try to kill himself, and it is hard to think of any action which would have had a more profound effect on his emotional development. And it is worth recalling that no less than eight characters who play the leading or important roles in Conrad's fiction kill themselves and three more—Jim, Razumov and Peyrol—sacrifice themselves in a manner that is tantamount to an exalted form of suicide.[4]

(1957)

## NOTES

1. This voyage was not unearthed by Jean-Aubry, Conrad's "official" biographer.

2. In a note in *Joseph Conrad: the Making of a Novelist* John Gordan refers to a news item in the *New York Times* of 15 August, 1937, which reported the article in the *Kurjer Warszawski* without giving details or quoting the issue in which it had appeared. As this matter had no relevance to his subject he did not follow it up but it was thanks to his note that I was put on the track

of the article. I am forced to rely on the article because I have so far been unable to trace the original letter; there is apparently no record of it in Polish libraries and surviving members of the Buszczynski family have been unable to help. [Editor's note; The letter subsequently came to light and is here after reproduced.]

3. Mr. John Conrad has confirmed that his father had a scar here. It is worth mentioning that, although Conrad states in *The Arrow of Gold* that M. George was wounded in his left breast, this would have been a most unusual place to receive a bullet wound in a duel. Being right-handed he would have stood with only his right side exposed to his opponent.

4. I must add that neither Mr. Borys nor Mr. John Conrad accept the version of the facts set out in this article.


# (2) LETTER OF THADDEUS BOBROWSKI


ON MARCH 24 (New Style) 1879 Thaddeus Bobrowski, Conrad's uncle and guardian, wrote Stefen Buszczynski, a close friend of Conrad's father, recounting Conrad's activities in Marseilles since his departure from Poland in October 1874. The *Kurjer Warszawski* of June 13, 1937, in an article by Maria Dynowska, summarized this letter, and the New York *Times* of August 15, 1937 reported the article. John D. Gordan in a note to his *Joseph Conrad: The Making of a Novelist* (1941) made reference to the *Times* article. Bobrowski's letter received first publication in English in the London *Times Literary Supplement* of December 6, 1957, p. 748, in an article by Jocelyn Baines (a portion of which is quoted above): "The Young Conrad in Marseilles."

Bobrowski was a shrewd but kindly man, with a touch of complacency and self-righteousness; he seems to have approached life with the mentality of a genial family lawyer. His comments, complimentary and uncomplimentary, on Conrad's character are particularly valuable for their frankness. Then the account of the circumstances which led Conrad to join the British Merchant Navy is interesting because it shows that deliberate choice did not play as large a part as Conrad liked in later life to suppose.

But by far the most important information that the letter contains is the account of Conrad's attempted suicide. There are, in fact, two other mentions of this act, but they are so brief and uninformative that they have been overlooked; it had been assumed, with the tacit encouragement of Conrad himself, that the account of M. George's [*sic*] duel in *The Arrow of Gold* was, broadly speaking, autobiographical. [Editor's note]

Dear Sir,—I am inexpressibly grateful for your concern as to Conrad's whereabouts, particularly as I am acquiring the conviction that he has absolutely no thought of gratitude for all your kindnesses to him. In this matter, I find myself blameless for, as often as I called on him to maintain correspondence at least with his paternal and his maternal uncle, I invariably put your respected person on an equal footing with them—and, giving Conrad their addresses, have also added yours. He has always explained to me that he does not write to his uncles because, not knowing them, he has nothing to say. He informed me, however, that he writes to you. It follows, hence, that he has honoured only me with his correspondence—which can be construed as feeding the hen [*sic*] that lays the golden eggs, as the fable goes. Impatient with this negligence, I even wrote to him some time ago asking how I am to understand this "favour" of his—but it did not help; for, his paternal uncle died [at Tomsk, in January, 1878] without having received the long-awaited letter from him. My brother has always deplored this, and now you are beginning to complain of this indifference. My conscience is clear—for, not only have I made no effort to monopolize Conrad's feelings (as guardians often do) but, on the contrary, have constantly reminded him of his duties towards those who were closest to his father and among whom you occupy a prominent place.

What you have heard of my journey to Marseilles, and perhaps even of its causes, is unfortunately true! But, as you have lost touch with Conrad's activities, I must briefly outline everything. During 1875/76 and 1877, Conrad made four voyages on French merchant vessels belonging to one and the same shipowner though under various captains: to Guadeloupe, Martinique, the St. Thomas Islands, Haiti and New Orleans, in each case sailing from Marseilles and in consideration of an annual premium of 2,000–24,000 francs. It came as a great shock to me when, in 1876, he committed an escapade; he collected his half-yearly allowance in a lump sum from the Bank, and, he said, lent the money to acquaintances in which young Chodzko, his co-protector, participated. I had no reason to doubt that this is what happened, and to this day do not doubt it; I patched up the gap, gave him a good scolding—and he sailed off again. I may add that his employer and the captain wrote to me reporting most favourably on his application to work and his conduct.

At the beginning of 1877, just before embarking on a fresh voyage, he was laid up with an anal abscess for four weeks. The ship left port and, to the great regret of Captain Escarras (who even wrote to me about this), Conrad was left behind. Not wishing to sail under another captain, he remained in Marseilles to pursue theoretical studies while awaiting the return of his captain, with whom he hoped to circumnavigate the globe. In October, 1877, on his urgent demand and as he was to be away between eighteen months and two years, I sent him over and above his allowance an extra 2,000 francs, together with my blessing. I was quite sure he was somewhere in the Antipodes when, suddenly, while engaged in business at the Kieff Fair in 1878, I received a telegram reading: "Conrad blessé envoyez argent—arrivez." Naturally, I could not fly off at once like a bird, so, after concluding my business and having received a reply that Conrad was recovering, I left Kieff on 24th February [Old Style] and arrived in Marseilles on the 27th. On arrival I found that Conrad was already able to walk, and, after a previous talk with his friend Mr. Richard Fecht (a very prudent and decent young man), I visited the delinquent. This is what had happened. When Captain Escarras returned, Conrad was quite certain he would sail under him; but the Bureau de l'Inscription forbade this as he was an alien, aged twenty-one, and liable to military service in his country. Moreover, it was discovered that Conrad had never received permission from his Consul, so the former Inspector of the Port of Marseilles was summoned to explain why he had noted on the lists that such permission had been granted. He was reprimanded and very nearly lost his post. As could be expected, this was very painful for Conrad. The whole affair became too widely known—all the efforts of the Captain and the shipowner were in vain (Monsieur Delestang, the shipowner, told me all this), and Conrad had to stay ashore, without any hope of serving as a seaman in French vessels. Before all this happened, however, another catastrophe, a financial one, had overtaken him. Having the 3,000 francs I sent him for the voyage, he met a former captain of his, a Monsieur Duteil, who persuaded him to participate in some affair on the coast of Spain—simply, some kind of smuggling. He invested 1,000 francs and made a profit of over 400 francs; this pleased them greatly, so he thereupon engaged all he had in a second venture —and lost all. This Monsieur Duteil consoled him with a kiss, and departed for Buenos Aires, while Conrad remained, unable to sign up as a sailor, penniless [literally, "naked as a Turkish saint"] and moreover in debt. For, while speculating, he had lived on credit, had ordered things necessary for the voyage, and so on. Faced by such a situation, he borrowed 800 francs from his friend, Mr. Fecht, and set off for Villa-Franca [Villefranche], where an American squadron was anchored, with the intention of entering American naval service. Nothing came of this, and, wishing to repair his finances, he tried his luck in Monte Carlo, where he lost the borrowed 800 francs at the gaming tables. Having so excellently managed his affairs, he returned to Marseilles, and one fine evening he invited the aforesaid friend to tea; but, before the time fixed, he attempted to kill himself with a revolver shot. (Let this detail remain between us; for I have told everyone that he was wounded in a duel. In this matter I do not want and should not want to keep this a secret from you.) The bullet went *durch und durch* near the heart, not injuring any important organ. Luckily he had left all his addresses on top—so that good Mr. Fecht could immediately notify me and even my brother who, again, bombarded me in turn. That is the whole story.

I spent a fortnight in Marseilles, first studying the whole affair and then the Individual. Apart from those lost 3,000 francs, I had to pay off debts for a like sum. I would not have done this for a son of mine, but, for the son of my dear Sister, I confess, I was weak enough to act contrary to my principles. Nevertheless, I took an oath that even if I knew he should shoot himself again, he could not count on a repetition of this weakness. I was concerned, too, with national honour to some extent: so that there should be no talk of one of us Poles exploiting people's liking for himself—and undoubtedly Conrad was liked by all who had relations with him. He is lucky with people.

My studies of the Individual have convinced me that he is not a bad boy—only exceedingly sensitive, conceited—reserved, yet excitable. In short, I found in him all the defects of the House of Nalecz. He is able and eloquent; he has forgotten nothing of his Polish, though since leaving Cracow he spoke Polish for the first time with me. He seems to know his job well and likes it very much. I suggested that he return to his country—he flatly refused; I suggested that he return to Galicia, get naturalized and seek a career there— he refused this, too, stating that he loves his profession, does not want to change it, and will not do so. I noticed none of the vices common to seamen, though I observed him closely: he drinks virtually nothing, apart from red wine; does not gamble (he told me so himself, and Mr. Fecht also testified that he had never seen him gambling, and that unfortunate trial in Monte Carlo was based merely on a belief in beginner's luck). His manners are very good—as if he spends all his time in drawing-rooms; he is very much liked by his captains and by the seamen—I have more than once seen what cordial greetings were exchanged between him and sailors, who call him Monsieur Georges. During my stay in Marseilles, he was twice summoned to bring ships into harbour, for which service he received 100 francs in each case. I must therefore accept that he knows his profession. After a careful study of the Individual, I have not lost hope that something may yet come of him—as we used to say; it is certain that the Nalecz temperament, unfortunately not of the Father but of his Uncle [Robert], preponderates—I should like to be mistaken in this judgment.

In appearance, his face is more like that of his Mother—quite handsome— while in build he resembles his Father and is quite well-built. In his conceptions and discussions he is ardent, and original. We Poles, the young ones particularly, have an inborn liking for the French and the Republic; but he does not like them at all, and is for the Emperor. *De gustibus non est disputandum*—but I couldn't stand it on several occasions, and scolded him roundly.

It was finally decided he would enter the English merchant marine, which does not apply all those formalities required in France—and thus it was that, after my departure from Marseilles, Conrad's friend, Fecht (a Würtemberger) sent him off to England, to Lowestoft, at the beginning of May last year. . . .